FOURTH EDITION

LABOUR RELATIONS

LARRY SUFFIELD
LAMBTON COLLEGE

GARY L. GANNON
DURHAM COLLEGE

Toronto

Editor-in-Chief: Claudine O'Donnell
Acquisitions Editor: Carolin Sweig
Marketing Manager: Jessica Saso
Program Manager: Karen Townsend
Project Managers: Madhu Ranadive and
  Jessica Hellen
Developmental Editor: Rachel Stuckey

Production Services: Aptara®, Inc.
Permissions Project Manager: Joanne Tang
Text Permissions Research: Phyllis Padula,
  Aptara®, Inc.
Interior and Cover Designer: Aptara®, Inc.
Cover Image: © Nicolesa / Shutterstock

Credits and acknowledgments for material borrowed from other sources and reproduced, with permission, in this textbook appear on the appropriate page within the text.

If you purchased this book outside the United States or Canada, you should be aware that it has been imported without the approval of the publisher or the author.

4 17

Library and Archives Canada Cataloguing in Publication

Suffield, Larry, 1949-, author
  Labour relations / Larry Suffield, Lambton College, Gary L. Gannon,
  Durham College.—Fourth edition.

Includes bibliographical references and index.
ISBN 978-0-13-359367-9

  1. Industrial relations—Textbooks.   2. Industrial relations—Canada—Textbooks.
I. Gannon, Gary L. (Gary Lawrence), 1951-, author   II. Title.

HD8106.5.S83 2014   331   C2014-906100-5

ISBN   978-0-13-359367-9

Contents

Preface

Labour Relations, Fourth Edition, is intended to provide a practical text for labour relations, industrial relations, and collective bargaining courses. The book is based on the premise that employers, unions, and governments are all key players in labour relations and are affected by a challenging environment. Globalization, demographics, technological innovation, societal views, and other environmental factors pose threats and opportunities for the parties in the labour relations system. To deal with this challenging environment, a book on labour relations should be practical and applied, and should not lose sight of the context.

To meet the need for the practical, this book contains more of the "day-to-day" material required to: understand sources of employee discontent in union work settings; correctly respond to events in a union organizing campaign; grasp the nuances seen in collective bargaining behaviours; negotiate new or renewed collective agreements; and provide leadership in the day-to-day administration of a union contract. Common and unique terms seen in a collective agreement are outlined. The factors affecting the critical union–management relationship are also reviewed.

It is known that there are differences between the Canadian and American labour relations systems; however, the differences between Canadian jurisdictions may not have received the attention they deserve. Significant differences in labour relations policy have developed among Canadian provinces. In some jurisdictions, a union can be certified on the basis of membership cards; in others, a representation vote is mandatory. In some jurisdictions, the labour relations board has the authority to certify a union without a vote as a remedy for employer unfair labour practices. Most jurisdictions allow employers to use replacement workers during a strike; however, some restrict the use of replacement workers. Some jurisdictions prevent a union from terminating an employee's union membership for any reason other than failure to pay dues. Students do not need to know what the rules are for all jurisdictions, but it will help them to understand and appreciate the policy options that have been adopted in their jurisdiction if they are aware of the alternatives. Policy options are referred to throughout the text. In the final chapter, there is a new emphasis paid to employee relations. It must be remembered that one in three employees in Canadian work settings are union members. Human resources professionals in such work environments must also provide advice and counsel to line managers in areas related to the needs and demands of both management and non-unionized employees.

CHANGES TO THE FOURTH EDITION

A number of changes have been made to this edition to provide key concepts to human resources professionals and better prepare students for the National Knowledge Exam (Comprehensive Knowledge Exam in Ontario). The following are some of the more noteworthy updates and revisions:

- *Opening vignettes.* Several new vignettes have been written to introduce the reader to the topical content in each chapter. These short accounts draw on recent topical items that reflect the interplay between unions, employers, workers and society.

- *Review and discussion questions.* Based on user feedback, these end-of-chapter activities have been revised and updated to facilitate student understanding and application of key concepts and principles related to labour relations.

- *Collective bargaining rights.* Chapter 6 has been slightly revised to update and clarify external factors affecting unionization and the reasons why individuals consider seeking union representation. Content related to certification has been updated to take advantage of student access to online information.

- *Collective agreements.* In addition to a new opening vignette, Chapter 7's comprehensive outline of collective agreement structure and language has been enhanced with clarifications of topics related to union membership and union security.

- *Contract negotiation.* Chapter 9 has been updated in its perspectives on external factors that may influence union–management relationships as well as management bargaining team composition. Discussion questions have been reframed to facilitate more in-depth exploration of key topics and concepts.

- *Contract administration.* In Chapter 9, the section dealing with grievance procedures has been revised and updated. Enhancements to the Web-research section at the end of the chapter will facilitate further exploration of grievance-related resources available on union websites.

- *Public sector labour relations.* Chapter 11 has been revised to reflect developments in key external forces challenging unions in this sector.

- *Employee relations focus.* In keeping with the HR credentialling body's interest in balancing knowledge resources toward both labour relations and employee relations, Chapter 12 reflects an introduction to key aspects of employee relations that most HR practitioners in a unionized work setting face in their professional lives.

FOR THE STUDENT

This book was written to help you understand an interesting and dynamic aspect of human resources management. Even if you do not intend to work as a HR professional in a unionized setting, an understanding of the labour relations process will increase your awareness of how companies that do not have good HR programs and practices may suddenly find themselves in the midst of union certification drives, collective bargaining, and contract administration. The following features are intended to make learning about labour relations easier and more interesting:

- *Required Professional Capabilities (RPCs) and the HR Professional Competency Framework (Ontario).* Updated lists of specific competencies from both the Canadian Council of Human Resources Associations (CCHRA) and the HRPA in Ontario have been provided in Appendix D. Specific competency references from each source are seen in the table at the beginning of each chapter.

- *Learning objectives* clarify the outcomes expected.

- *Contemporary labour relations vignettes,* which illustrate labour relations issues and processes, are provided at the beginning of each chapter.

- *Key terms* are bolded and defined in margin notes. A list of these terms with page references is provided at the end of each chapter.

- *Numerous examples* are used to illustrate important concepts.

- Numbered *"Key Considerations"* boxes summarize essential points.

- Numbered *"Labour Relations Issue"* boxes highlight questions of interest and importance

- *Websites* listed in the margins and in research activities at the end of chapters refer you to illustrations and sources of information. Labour relations is a changing field, and these sites will help you monitor developments.

- *Case incidents, review questions, and discussion questions* at the end of each chapter help you put the chapter material into practice.

FOR THE INSTRUCTOR

In Chapter 3, which discusses unions, the topics are presented in an order that may be unique: the structure and functions of union bodies are presented before their history. This is because the history of unions and the development of labour relations refer to structural concepts such as the local union, national unions, and international unions. Problems have been encountered when the history has been considered before the student understands the concept of union locals and the distinction between national and international unions. Instructors who wish to follow a more traditional order might refer to the history component of Chapter 3 first.

Appendix A provides cases that could be used in classroom discussion or assignments. A grievance and arbitration exercise is provided in Appendix B, and a contract negotiation simulation is provided in Appendix C. Appendix C could be used to analyze a collective agreement and engage in a negotiation simulation. Additional instructions, which can be provided to union and management teams, are provided in the Instructor's Resource Manual that accompanies this text. The collective agreement in Appendix C is for a casino, and it is based on actual contract language and pricing in the industry. New contract terms have been added to the collective agreement, and new union and management bargaining team instructions are provided in the instructor's manual. The material is set up in a modular fashion so that instructors may choose which issues to cover, and whether to include the financial information provided.

Supplements

The following instructor supplements are available for downloading from a password-protected section of Pearson Education Canada's online catalogue. Navigate to your book's catalogue page to view a list of those supplements that are available. See your local sales representative for details and access.

Instructor's Resource Manual with Test Item File Questions. The Instructor's Resource Manual contains a summary of key points; answers to in-text questions; commentary on questions and cases; and a test item file containing short-answer, true-false, and multiple-choice questions.

PowerPoint Slides. The PowerPoint Slides include over 20 slides per chapter with tables and figures used in the text. This supplement provides a comprehensive selection of slides highlighting key concepts featured in the text to assist instructors.

CourseSmart for Instructors

CourseSmart goes beyond traditional expectations—providing instructors with instant, online access to the textbooks and course materials they need, at a lower cost for students. And even as students save money, instructors save time and hassle with a digital eTextbook that allows them to search for the most relevant content just when they need it. Whether it's evaluating textbooks or creating lecture notes to help students with difficult concepts, CourseSmart can make life a little easier. See how at **www.coursesmart.com/instructors**.

CourseSmart for Students

As mentioned above, CourseSmart gives the student instant, online access to the textbooks and course materials they need at significant savings over the price of the printed text. With instant access from any computer and the ability to search the text, students will find the content they need quickly, no matter where they are. And with online tools such as highlighting and note-taking, they can save time and study efficiently. See all the benefits at **www.coursesmart.com/students**.

Learning Solutions Managers

Pearson's Learning Solutions Managers work with faculty and campus course designers to ensure that Pearson technology products, assessment tools, and online course materials are tailored to meet your specific needs. This highly qualified team is dedicated to helping schools take full advantage of a wide range of educational resources, by assisting in the integration of a variety of instructional materials and media formats. Your local Pearson Education sales representative can provide with more details on this service program.

Pearson Custom Library

For enrollments of at least 25 students, you can create your own textbook by choosing the chapters that best suit your own course needs. To begin building your custom text, visit **www.pearsoncustomlibrary.com**. You may also work with a dedicated Pearson Custom editor to create your ideal text—publishing your own original content or mixing and matching Pearson content. Contact your local Pearson Representative to get started.

Acknowledgements

We wish to acknowledge those who helped make this book possible. We thank the reviewers who offered constructive and valuable suggestions for the book. The book is stronger because of their comments:

Stan Arnold, *Humber College*
Bob Barnetson, *Athabasca University*
Richard P. Chaykowski, *Queen's University*
Leanne Floden, *NAIT*
William Mathieson, *BCIT*
Basu Sharma, *UNB*

Thanks to Claudine O'Donnell at Pearson Canada who piqued my interest in becoming involved in this project, and Rachel Stuckey, developmental editor for this edition, whose patience and guidance was greatly appreciated in steering this edition to its completion.

To the memory of my father, Len

—LS

To my wife, Deborah, who is an endless source of encouragement

—GLG

ABOUT THE AUTHORS

Larry Suffield received his B.A. (Economics) and LL.B. from the University of Western Ontario. After practising law for five years, he received an M.B.A. from the University of Windsor.

Larry is a professor at Lambton College in Sarnia, Ontario, where he teaches in the Business Administration and postgraduate Human Resources Management programs, and where he has served as the coordinator of the Marketing and Management department. His areas of special interest are employment law and labour relations. Larry has also taught human resources management and labour relations at the University of Windsor.

Larry has served as the vice-president and chief steward of the union local representing faculty and counsellors at Lambton College, and he is a member of the Human Resources Professionals Association, where he serves on the Educational Standards Committee. Larry enjoys hiking and you may see him on a trail—he will be the one carrying a recent labour arbitration decision.

Gary Gannon received his B.A. (Social Sciences) from York University. He also holds a Master in Health Sciences (Health Administration) and a Master of Arts (Higher Education) from the University of Toronto. In 2013, he completed his Ph.D. at the University of Toronto/OISE (Leadership, Adult and Higher Education).

Gary is currently the program coordinator and full-time professor in the Human Resources Management programs at Durham College in Oshawa, Ontario. Prior to coming to Durham College in 2001, he worked for 18 years in progressive HR management roles in the health care and higher education sectors. He is recognized as an expert in building and revitalizing HRM services in medium and large organizations in order to fulfill strategic business objectives.

Dr. Gannon is a certified member of the Human Resources Professional Association (HRPA) and is currently active in the Association's local chapter in Durham Region. He has also advised several not-for-profit organizations on HRM-related matters as part of his involvement in the local community.

Chapter 1

Introduction to Labour Relations

Chapter Objectives

1. Define labour relations and industrial relations
2. Explain the importance of labour relations
3. Describe key differences between union and non-union workplaces
4. Outline alternative approaches to labour relations
5. Identify environmental factors affecting labour relations
6. Identify the parties, processes, and results involved in the labour relations system
7. Outline a framework for labour relations
8. Describe alternative positions in the debate regarding union-management collaboration

Required Professional Capabilities (CCHRA)	HRPA Human Resources Professionals Competency Framework
10303, 20103, 20110, 50101, 50104, 50109	C001, C003, C010, C018, C030, C035, C111, C112

Employees in a workplace may experience unfair treatment at the hands of management. If this continues for a prolonged period, and if the unfairness affects a large enough group of workers at the company, one or more individuals may think about seeking outside assistance to restore a balance of interests between the business owner and her employees. Up to the point when a union organizer enters this picture, each person working for the company has an individual contract of employment with the organization. Perceptions of unfairness often stem from the perceived differences in employment terms among individuals in similar types of jobs in the company. The "whys" for these differences can range from a unique or rare skill set that makes one person "indispensable" to petty opinions held by the supervisor regarding the worker's personality or habits. The organizational climate in such circumstances is often characterized by a feeling of powerless for many serving in frontline, non-supervisory positions.

When a non-union work setting transitions to a unionized place of employment, one of the difficulties is that past practices and understandings can be difficult to shed from the organization's culture. Managers still feel that they are empowered to make "one-to-one" decisions with their now "unionized" employees. Conversely, workers who may have been swept into a new bargaining unit, despite their public displays of displeasure at such an option, cannot understand why they can no longer ask their supervisor for approval of a scheduling request that is now covered by the new collective agreement.

Inexperienced human resources practitioners who transition from a non-union to a unionized workplace must also make a mental adjustment to the new rules in what is often a new terrain of hybrid policies, procedures, and a new union contract.

The advice and counsel they offer to their management peers must be clear on the range of choices available to supervisors in their day-to-day handling of staff now governed by a collective agreement. Similarly, the human resources professional's preference for an "open door" policy will be tested when a new union enters the picture—many new union members will need to ask, and more importantly understand, why they can no longer get simple approvals or considerations from their boss.

Such is the unique nature of workplaces that move from a non-union to a unionized environment—no matter the reason. Organizational culture, management practices, and employee perceptions will require time to settle into the new pace and pathways will need to be built in the relationship with a new partner: the bargaining agent now on the scene. Students in this course may already have experienced such work situations but may not have understood the dynamics they witnessed. Others may be intrigued by the overt aspects and subtleties of union management interactions. Those who have not had a great range of work experiences should be prepared to perform with confidence based on the acquired knowledge and discussions generated in the following chapters.

One of the purposes of this chapter is to indicate the importance of labour relations. Approximately 30 percent of the Canadian workforce is unionized; however, labour relations affect all Canadians. Labour relations affect the costs, productivity, and profitability of employers. They impact the wages and working conditions of both union and non-union employees. Union–management relations affect the public through occasional strikes and lockouts, and affect prices in the marketplace. In this chapter, we will define labour relations and outline its significance. Alternative approaches to labour relations will be identified, and a framework for labour relations will be provided.

DEFINING LABOUR RELATIONS AND INDUSTRIAL RELATIONS

Industrial relations is the study of employment in union and non-union organizations.

The term **industrial relations** does not have the same meaning for everyone. Some academics and practitioners define industrial relations broadly to include both union and non-union issues and workplaces. A commonly used definition of industrial relations states that it is "a broad interdisciplinary field of study and practice that encompasses all aspects of the employment relationship."[1] This definition includes both union and non-union workplaces, and means that questions relating to the pay of CEOs (chief executive officers) and to the negotiation of collective agreements would both be industrial relations issues. Others define industrial relations narrowly, contending that the scope of industrial relations is limited to unionized workplaces only.

Labour relations is all aspects of the union–management relationship, including the establishment of union bargaining rights, the negotiation process, and the administration of a collective agreement.

This book adopts the broader definition of industrial relations, and views labour relations as part of industrial relations. **Labour relations** is defined as the study of all aspects of the union–management relationship, including the establishment of union bargaining rights, the negotiation process, and the administration of a collective agreement. As the terms are used here, questions and issues that fall under the heading of labour relations would by definition also be industrial relations issues. However, some industrial relations issues that do not involve union–management relations, for example the question of CEO compensation, are not included as part of labour relations. Because labour relations could be viewed as part of the broader field of industrial relations, some references provided in this text refer to industrial relations instead of labour relations. This explains why the present book may be used in a course in industrial relations.

It would not serve any useful purpose to engage in a debate about the meaning of the two terms. *Labour relations* is used in this book for several reasons. The Canadian Council of Human Resources Associations has identified the competencies required to be a human resources practitioner; one of them is labour relations. Law regulating union–management relations is most commonly called *labour relations legislation*. Although readers of the New Brunswick and federal legislation will see references to industrial relations, this is equivalent to labour relations legislation in other provinces. Contrasts to non-union workplaces will be made to emphasize the importance of labour relations. The effects of unions on non-union employees will also be considered.

The boxes titled "Labour Relations Issue" in each chapter of this book are intended to highlight issues of special importance and interest, and generate discussion. In this chapter, Labour Relations Issue 1-1 provides 12 questions, each relating to its correspondingly numbered chapter. The questions are intended to illustrate the nature of the issues that labour relations is concerned with, and you should consider all of them now.

It will be useful to clarify the meaning of other terms that will be used. **Collective bargaining** also has different meanings. Some authorities use the term to refer only to the negotiation of a collective agreement by a union and the employer. Others give it a broader meaning, referring to the entire relationship between a union representing employees and the employer; this is how the term is used here. This broader usage includes both the negotiation and the administration of a collective agreement. Accordingly, some references to collective bargaining here and elsewhere may mean more than just contract negotiation. For example, a statement might be made that collective bargaining affects the ability of employers to terminate employees. This is a reference to collective bargaining in the broader sense; it is not referring to the negotiation process. **Human resources management**

Website for the Canadian Council of Human Resources Associations: www.chrp.ca

Collective bargaining is the entire relationship between a union and the employer, including the administration of a collective agreement.

Human resources management is a set of interrelated activities designed to plans human resources needs and attracts, selects, and maintains an organization's employees.

Labour Relations Issue 1-1

Labour Relations Questions

Which of the following are true?

1. A non-union employee who has been wrongfully dismissed will be reinstated by the court.
2. A collective agreement provides that any work done on a Sunday will be paid at the overtime rate. A union might be required to waive this term of the agreement to meet its obligations under human rights legislation. That is, the union might be required to agree to an employee working on Sunday and not be paid overtime if the employee cannot work on Saturday because of his or her religious belief.
3. Over the past 30 years, the percentage of employees who are represented by unions has dramatically declined in both Canada and the United States.
4. Some employers attempt to avoid unionization by paying non-union employees wages that are equivalent to the wages paid unionized employees.
5. A government might pass special back-to-work legislation ordering an end to a strike in the public sector; however, strikes in the private sector cannot be ended by such legislation.
6. When a union attempts to organize employees, there is always a vote held to determine if the employees wish to be represented by the union.

7. Collective agreements can provide that employees are required to become union members. Accordingly, an employer could be forced to terminate an employee who refused to join the union.
8. In the course of negotiation of a collective agreement, the employer may be required to reveal information to the union even though the union has not requested it.
9. When an employee takes a complaint to his or her union—for example, the employee alleges termination without cause—the union is required to pursue the matter with the employer.
10. When a vote is held to authorize a strike, all employees in the group that would be on strike are entitled to vote. That is, both union members and employees who are not union members are entitled to vote.
11. Some public sector employees have the right to strike provided that essential services are maintained for the public by having some employees continue to work.
12. Unions reduce productivity and profitability.

is defined as a set of interrelated activities that plans human resources needs, and attracts, selects, and maintains an organization's employees. Its scope can be clarified by examining the table of contents of an introductory HR management textbook. Typically such a text includes chapters relating to human resources planning, recruiting, selection, training, compensation, health and safety, and labour relations. Labour relations can be viewed as part of human resources management. In larger workplaces, there might be a separate labour relations department just as there are separate departments dealing with recruiting or training. HR managers and labour relations specialists may have different perspectives on unions.[2] Human resources management tends to view unions as an external factor, which could be avoided through sound practices. Labour relations specialists are more inclined to think that employee interests and management interests are not the same, and that employees may logically seek to protect their interests through a union. **Employee relations** is another term that should be clarified. Employee relations refers to activities and processes aimed at maintaining a productive workplace while meeting the needs of employees. It includes communication, discipline, employee involvement, diversity management and employee rights. Some authorities distinguish between union and non-union employees by using "employee relations" to refer to non-union employees and "labour relations" to refer to unionized employees. Although employee relations activities such as communication and discipline will not cease if an employer is unionized, we will see in a later chapter that some issues such as discipline must be handled differently in unionized workplaces.

> **Employee relations** encompasses activities and processes aimed at maintaining a productive workplace while meeting the needs of employees.

IMPORTANCE OF UNIONIZATION AND LABOUR RELATIONS

Labour relations is important for employers, unionized employees, non-union employees, and society. The effects and full significance of unionization will become apparent in subsequent chapters; here we will briefly summarize why labour relations is important. Before proceeding, it should be noted that collective bargaining and unions do not have the same strength or importance across Canada. A 2003 study, *Beyond the National Divide: Regional Dimensions of Industrial Relations*, considered differences between the provinces[3] and found that in four provinces—British Columbia, Manitoba, Ontario, and Quebec—unions were well established and important actors in the political and economic life of the province. In four other provinces—Alberta, Newfoundland and Labrador, Nova Scotia, and Saskatchewan—unions lacked the strength to counter hostile governments or employers, and are still minor actors. An example of the dependent nature of unions in some provinces is the Michelin Bill, passed in Nova Scotia in 1979. The legislation, which required a union to organize all of an employer's manufacturing locations, was clearly intended to make unionization in manufacturing more difficult. The legislation was passed over the objections of the labour movement, and the government was subsequently re-elected with an increased majority. The 2003 study is recommended to readers interested in the social, political, and economic differences between provinces.

Employment Relationship

Unionization affects key aspects of the employment relationship. Without a union, the common law, employment legislation, and the agreement between the employer and the employee govern the employment relationship. The **common law** refers to rules of law that originate from the decisions of judges. Key Considerations 1-1 summarizes differences in the employment relationship between unionized and non-union workplaces.

> **Common law** refers to the rules of law that originate from the decisions of judges.

Non-union vs. Unionized Workplaces

	Non-union Workplaces	Unionized Workplaces
Legal basis for relationship	Individual contracts of employment	Collective agreement
Terms of employment negotiated	By individual employees	By the union
Nature of employment terms	Possibly unique for each employee	Identical for all employees in the same job class covered by the collective agreement
Dismissal where no cause or allegation of employee misconduct	Employer has obligation to give reasonable notice based on age, length of service, and position held; subject to minimum provisions in employment standards legislation.	Employer must comply with notice and severance provisions of the collective agreement; subject to minimum provisions in employment standards legislation.
Dismissal where cause or employee misconduct is alleged	If employer establishes just cause, reasonable notice does not have to be provided. If employer fails to establish just cause, employer must provide reasonable notice but does not have to reinstate.*	If employer establishes just cause, notice and severance provisions of collective agreement do not apply. If employer fails to establish just cause, reinstatement is possible.
Changes in terms of employment	Law regarding constructive dismissal prevents significant changes without consent.	Constructive dismissal doctrine does not apply.
Process to resolve disputes	Court action	Grievance and arbitration process provided in collective agreement

*There is an exception in the federal and Nova Scotia jurisdictions. Non-managerial employees who are not covered by a collective agreement have recourse to an unfair dismissal procedure that may lead to reinstatement.

In the non-union workplace, the employer negotiates directly with each employee to establish the terms of employment. When a union negotiates a collective agreement with an employer, the individual contracts of employment of employees are superseded by the collective agreement, which is negotiated by the union. In Chapter 8, which deals with the negotiation of the agreement, we will see that employees have input into the terms that the union seeks to include in a collective agreement; however, it is the union that negotiates the contract before approval by employees. Although non-union employers commonly establish uniform policies to standardize terms of employment such as vacation, the terms of individual contracts of employment might be different for employees who do the same job. For example, the employer might agree to provide one employee with additional vacation time. When employees are unionized, the terms of employment are provided in the collective agreement and they will be the same for all employees in a job class.

There is also a major difference between unionized and non-union workplaces when employees are terminated. When an employer terminates non-union employees where there has not been any employee misconduct—for example in the case of a downsizing—the employer has a legal obligation to provide employees with **reasonable notice**. This should not be confused with the notice required by employment standards legislation, which is minimal, based upon the length of service, and in most cases capped at eight weeks. The reasonable notice required by the common law depends primarily upon the age, length of service, and position held by the employee. Some non-managerial employees, especially older employees with extended service, are entitled to reasonable notice that could be approximately 12 months. If the employer dismisses a non-union employee

Reasonable notice is the notice period employers are required to provide to employees on the basis of factors including age, position, and length of service.

without providing the employee with reasonable notice, the employee can sue the employer for wrongful dismissal. This legal action is concerned with the issue of whether the employer provided sufficient notice, and not with the issue of whether the employer had a valid reason to dismiss the person. In a unionized setting, the obligation to provide reasonable notice is eliminated. Instead, the employer must comply with the notice provisions of the collective agreement. Some unions have been able to negotiate collective agreements that provide for significant notice in the event of termination; however, some collective agreements do not provide as much notice to employees as the common law would require pursuant to the reasonable notice requirement. This may be one area where the terms and conditions available to some unionized employees are not as favourable as those available to non-union employees.

Where the employer dismisses an employee alleging there was cause—that is, the employer contends there was employee misconduct—there is a fundamental difference between the union and non-union settings. If the non-union employer establishes that there was serious misconduct, known as just cause, no notice is required. Even if the employer fails to establish just cause, it will not have to reinstate the employee in most jurisdictions, though it will have to give reasonable notice. In a unionized setting, on the other hand, we will see that the union can challenge a dismissal. An arbitrator might review the employer's decision, and it is possible he or she will order the employer to reinstate the employee. This means the employer's ability to terminate unionized employees is significantly reduced. It also provides unionized employees with job security that non-union employees do not have.

A non-union employer considering changes in the terms of employment must be concerned with the doctrine of **constructive dismissal**. This is a rule of employment law that provides that if the employer makes significant changes to the terms of employment, the changes are viewed as equivalent to a dismissal of the employee. The non-union employer who relocates employees, reduces compensation, or demotes an employee could face a claim that there has been a constructive dismissal and be ordered to pay damages. The doctrine of constructive dismissal does not apply to unionized employees. The employer can make changes in the terms of employment that are provided for in the collective agreement. For example, in a downsizing and layoff situation the employer must apply the seniority provisions in the collective agreement and employees who have been demoted cannot claim that there has been a constructive dismissal.

In the event of a dispute between an employer and a non-union employee, the dispute is typically resolved through a court action if the parties cannot settle the matter. This is disadvantageous to individual employees, who are not likely to be able to afford court proceedings. Although there has been some increase in the use of alternative dispute resolution methods such as mediation, these methods cannot be forced upon the parties. In unionized workplaces, disputes are referred to the grievance and arbitration process, a topic elaborated upon in Chapter 9. This is significant for a number of reasons, including the fact that this process does not involve any cost to the employee.

Unionized Employees: Terms and Conditions of Work

Unionization can significantly affect the wages, working conditions, job security, and job satisfaction of employees. Most employees receive improved wages and benefits as a result of unionization. We will see later that collective agreement provisions increase job security for many employees. There are studies indicating that unionized employees have lower job satisfaction than non-union employees. Some employers may contend that this reduced job satisfaction is due to the fact that unions stir up discontent.

Constructive dismissal is a rule of law providing that fundamental changes made by a non-union employer to the terms of employment are equivalent to a dismissal.

An alternative view is that unions provide a collective voice to express concerns that otherwise remain suppressed.

Employers: Costs and Productivity

Unionization can affect an employer's costs, productivity, and profitability, and labour relations can affect investment and employment decisions made by employers. These issues will be explored further after we have had an opportunity to consider the terms and administration of collective agreements.

Non-union Employees

Unions can have an impact on non-union workplaces and employees. In the final chapter, we will return to this issue. We will see that some non-union employees benefit from the efforts of unions to raise wages.

Society

Unions affect society as a whole. Countries with higher rates of unionization tend to have lower economic inequality.[4] This is significant because societies with greater inequality endure more adverse social consequences, including higher rates of mental illness, illiteracy, lower life expectancies, and higher rates of incarceration. Unions become involved in political and social issues that affect all of society. Unions prevented the privatization of hydro in Ontario by taking court action. Labour relations can affect the general public as well, by influencing the prices and availability of goods and services. The prices of cars are affected by the unionization of auto workers. Strikes and lockouts can affect the availability of services, including health care.

FRAMEWORK FOR LABOUR RELATIONS

The core elements of labour relations are the organization of employees by unions, the negotiation of the collective agreement, and the administration of the contract. Before proceeding to these key areas, we need a framework or overview of the labour relations system, which will provide a point of reference and help us understand the big picture. We should also understand that there are numerous approaches to or perspectives on labour relations, which affect the outlook of individuals who comment on them. Two dominant perspectives are the systems approach and the political economy approach.[5] Let us first review the key points in these two perspectives.

Systems Approach

Discussion of a systems theory for labour relations should begin with John Dunlop's outline of industrial relations systems.[6] Dunlop's model had four key elements: a set of actors, a body of rules that governs the actors, a context of the system, and an ideology that binds the system together. The actors in Dunlop's system are management, workers and their agents, and government agencies. He proposed that any industrial relations system will produce a set of procedural and a set of substantive rules. The procedural rules are processes used to determine the substantive rules or outcomes of the system. Examples of procedural rules are those regarding the grievance procedure to resolve disputes between a union and an employer. The terms of a collective agreement specifying wages are examples of substantive rules. At any one time, one of the actors in the system might play the dominant role in setting rules. The rules referred to might be determined by employers taking unilateral action, established by government, or arrived at by negotiations between the parties. For example, the employer might unilaterally establish hours of operation, government legislation might require a minimum strike notice period, and the parties might negotiate wages. The context of the system refers to the environment consisting of three areas: the technology used in the workplace, the product and factor markets that affect the actors, and the distribution of power in society. The technology used affects the power held by the union or the employer. If technology allowed workers to be easily replaced, the employer would be in a stronger position. The product market (i.e., the market in which the employer sells the goods or services produced) might affect the power of the employer and in turn influence wage rates. The power held by an actor in society might affect its ability to influence rules in its favour. Finally, Dunlop observed that a set of ideas and beliefs commonly held by the actors would bind the system together. In Canada and the United States, the values of the parties would include the acceptance of capitalism and of unions as the legitimate representatives of employees.

The model proposed by Dunlop has been criticized. One criticism is that it underestimates the role of conflict in the system. Consequently, we will refer specifically to conflict in a framework provided here. Others have challenged the assumption or premise of a shared ideology. Specifically, they contend that since the 1980s some managers in the United States have not shared an ideology with unions, and in fact have attempted to eliminate them.[7] Nevertheless, Dunlop's model has served as the starting point for other models of labour relations. An understanding of the basics of the model is valuable, because some commentators refer to components such as a "web of rules" without explanation, assuming that the reader is familiar with the model.

The Canadian scholar Alton Craig has expanded upon Dunlop's model, outlining an "open systems" approach that provides for feedback as an essential component of an industrial relations system.[8] The system outlined by Craig is the basis for a framework provided below.

Political Economy Approach

The political economy approach to labour relations emphasizes that labour relations is affected by broader issues in society and the economy, in particular the distribution of power. Adopting a political economy approach, some observers argue that features of the labour relations system maintain the existing social order and distribution of power in society. It is asserted that employers have the upper hand when dealing with employees, and the establishment of small fragmented single-employer bargaining units means that employees do not have sufficient power to deal with employers. Also, the broad definition of a strike in some jurisdictions, which includes any work stoppage whatever the reason, coupled with the prohibition against strikes during the term of the agreement, means that employees and unions cannot use the strike weapon to pursue political or social change.[9]

John Godard views labour relations from a political economy perspective.[10] He argues that conflict is inherent in the employment relationship for a number of reasons, including: (1) There is a fundamental conflict of interest between employers and employees. It is in the employer's best interests to minimize the wages paid to employees, design work so that it requires lower skill levels, and maximize worker effort. (2) The nature of the employment relationship leads to conflict. In society, the values of freedom and democracy are accepted as the norm. In contrast, the relationship between employers and employees is based on the subordination of the employee, and this is a source of conflict. (3) The nature of one's work is a potential source of conflict. Surveys have established that over 80 percent of employees are satisfied with their jobs; however, employees report high levels of concern regarding workload, stress, and fatigue.[11]

A Framework for Labour Relations

Figure 1-1 provides a framework for approaching labour relations, a simplification and modification of Craig's model. The framework has five elements: the environment that may directly or indirectly influence all other aspects of the model, the actors or parties involved in labour relations, the processes or activities in which the parties are engaged, the outputs or results of the parties' activities, and feedback to the first four elements.

The Environment   The environment refers to the economic, technological, social, political, and legal factors that affect the parties and the processes they engage in. Such factors tend to cause the actors in this framework to react to these influences. The components of the environment and the impact on the parties are elaborated on in Chapter 2. Figure 1-1 does not expressly indicate how the components of the environment are inter-related and affect each other. Changes in technology, which allow employers to track more information and monitor employees, can lead to changes in the legal environment such as privacy legislation to protect employees.

Economic Environment.   The **economic environment** refers to the economy of the nation and the competitive position of a firm in a particular industry. If there is an increase in inflation or new competitors in an industry, the union and the employer will be affected.

Economic environment is the economy of the nation and the competitive position of a firm in a particular industry.

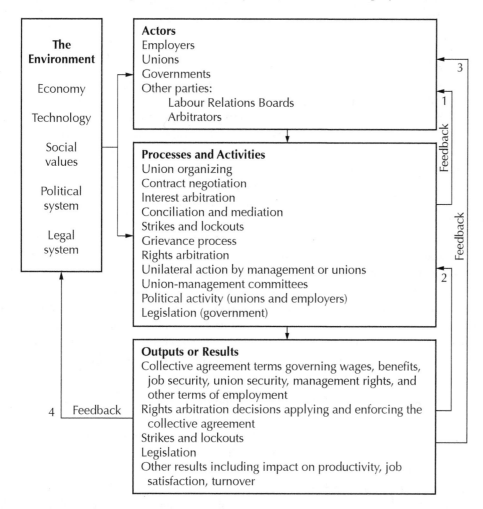

Figure 1-1 Framework for Labour Relations

Technological Environment.   The **technological environment** refers to developments in knowledge that lead to new products and services and changes in methods of production. Technological developments affect union and employer objectives in a number of areas, including job security and health and safety.

Social Environment.   The **social environment** refers to the values and beliefs of Canadians relating to work, unions, and employers. These values and beliefs may make them more or less inclined to join or support unions. Values and beliefs also impact the political environment.

Political Environment.   The **political environment** refers to the Canadian political system and the effect it has on labour relations. The political system directly affects the legislation that regulates unions and employers. The political environment in some jurisdictions such as Alberta appears to be more conservative, and this makes it less likely that legislation favourable to unions will be enacted.

Legal Environment.   The **legal environment** refers to all of the law that affects employees, unions, and employers. In later chapters, we will see that unions and employers are heavily regulated by labour relations legislation, which governs matters such as how a union organizes employees and how employers are allowed to respond. Human rights legislation is playing an important role in the administration of collective agreements. For example, alcoholism is considered to be a disability under human rights legislation and employers have to attempt to accommodate employees who are alcoholics. To this point we have referred to the environment affecting the parties, but it should be noted that the influence can flow the other way: the parties might attempt to influence attitudes in society and legislation through public relations efforts.

Actors or Parties   There are three main parties shown in Figure 1-1: employers, unions, and government. We are concerned with the objectives, power, and values of each, because these variables in turn affect the processes or activities they undertake in the next element of the framework. These variables are referred to in subsequent chapters; only a brief illustration will be given here. If employers perceive that wage increases in recent collective agreements have put them in an unfavourable cost position, their objective will be to hold the line on wage increases in contract negotiations. If unions perceive that job security is threatened, their objective will be to attempt to negotiate provisions such as increased lay-off notice. If governments think that inflation is a problem, they might enact legislation that puts limits on wage increases.

Other parties play a role in addition to the three main actors. We will see later that conciliation officers and mediators are involved in contract negotiations. Arbitrators play a key role in the resolution of disputes relating to the interpretation of collective agreements. Labour relations boards are critical to the system, because they administer legislation that governs unions and employers. It might be argued, too, that organizations such as "think tanks" that comment on public policy and attempt to influence the public and governments are another type of actor. Examples of such organizations include the Conference Board of Canada, the C.D. Howe Institute, and the Fraser Institute.

Processes and Activities of the Parties   The third element of the framework refers to the various activities the parties might engage in. Subsequent chapters elaborate on these activities. It should be noted that the parties do much more than negotiate collective agreements. The list of activities also includes unilateral action by management and unions. This is a reference to the fact that management and unions can both engage in activity independent of the other that affects the working conditions of employees. If an issue is not governed by the collective agreement, the employer might make changes on its own initiative. For example, the employer might establish a "no smoking" policy. The ability of management to enact rules unilaterally is an important point elaborated upon in the chapters relating to the terms of the collective agreement and its administration. The union, for its part, might provide training and education opportunities for employees. Union–management committees are another important process the parties might engage in. Some collective agreements establish various committees relating to job classifications, health and safety, and other issues. In some workplaces, the employer and the union establish numerous union–management committees not referred to in the collective agreement. These committees may deal with issues such as parking and health and wellness. Political activity refers to attempts by unions and employers to influence elections and legislation passed by governments. Employers might attempt to influence legislation regarding the union organizing process. Unions might try to influence government to pass stronger health and safety legislation. Strikes and lockouts are shown in Figure 1-1 as both a process and an output: either as part of the negotiation process that produces collective agreements or as a result of the negotiation process.

Outputs or Results The fourth component of the framework sets out the possible results of the activities of the parties. The primary output or result will either be the achievement of a renewed collective agreement that sets out terms and conditions of employment, or a strike or lockout due to unresolved issues between the parties in collective bargaining. During the term of a collective agreement, unresolved disagreements regarding the interpretation, application, or administration of the terms and conditions set out in the contract will result in a rights arbitration process that will be discussed further in Chapter 9.

Legislation has been included as both a process and an output in the figure—as a process because it is an important activity of government, and as an output to indicate that legislation could be the result of the political activity of unions and employers.

The negotiation process and the collective agreement can affect numerous variables, including productivity and employee job satisfaction. This impact will be considered in the final chapter, after we have studied the terms and administration of collective agreements.

Feedback A final and essential feature of this framework is that its elements are interconnected and affect each other. The feedback loops in Figure 1-1 have been numbered. Each illustrates that an activity or output can in turn affect another element. Loop 1, from processes to actors, indicates that an experience with a particular process can lead to one or both of the parties seeking to change it. We will see later that rights arbitration, which is used to settle disputes relating to the administration of the contract (such as the termination of an employee), can be slow and costly. This might affect the objectives of the parties. They might seek alternative methods to resolve disputes in the future. If the employer takes unilateral action that the union objects to, the union's negotiation objectives will be affected. If the employer introduces a dress code, the union might attempt to deal with this in the next round of negotiations. Loop 2 indicates that an output of the system can affect the processes used by the parties. Legislation, which has been included as an output, might prevent the parties from using a strike or lockout, or provide for regulations such as a strike notice. Loop 3 confirms that outputs from the system can affect the parties, specifically their objectives, power, and values. An extended strike might cause the parties to seek ways to improve their relationship and avoid confrontation in the future. A significant increase in wages might lead the union to focus on alternative objectives in the short term, such as obtaining work sharing or early retirement provisions. Loop 4 indicates that the outputs of the system can affect the environment. Wage increases and work stoppages affect the economy.

Work stoppages can also affect the attitude of the public toward a particular union or unions in general.

In addition to the loops, there might be links within one of the boxes shown. The best illustration of this is that an increase in wages and benefits might affect other outputs such as job satisfaction and turnover.

The framework in Figure 1-1 confirms several key points regarding labour relations. First, it reminds us that labour relations are very much affected by environmental factors such as the economy. Second, it recognizes that there are different actors in the system and these actors might have different objectives, power, and values. Third, it indicates that there are numerous processes involved, which are elaborated on in subsequent chapters. Fourth, it illustrates that there are numerous outputs or results, and that wages and benefits are not the only products of the labour relations system. Fifth, it emphasizes that feedback or the connection between components is an important part of the system. The feedback loops remind us that no one part of the framework can be viewed in isolation.

A change in any of the boxes shown in the figure can lead to changes in one or more other boxes. For example, a change in the economy or government policy in the United States might affect the objectives and power of unions and employers in Canada. The stimulus package adopted in the United States to counter the 2008–09 recession involved a "Buy American" component that affected employers and unions in Canada.

Confrontation or Collaboration

Labour relations in Canada are viewed as being confrontational or adversarial in nature. Although there has been some attempt to move away from confrontation, in many cases—especially in the public sector—distrust and confrontation mark the union–management relationship. Some observers contend that there is a need to move toward more collaboration. They refer to the changing nature of work as one reason why adversarial attitudes cannot continue. It is argued that we now have an information-based economy, which requires all employees to become involved, instead of waiting for instructions from management. This view holds that there is no inherent conflict between labour and management, and the parties need to cooperate in a world of increased competition. Reference is made to the Canadian strike record, which is high compared to that of other countries, as a source of weakness for the Canadian economy. It is also argued that unions and progressive human resources management practices, including increased employee involvement, can coexist. Such collaboration can benefit both employers and employees by increasing efficiency, leading to higher profits, which can be the basis for higher wages and improved job prospects.[12] Others, who adopt a political economy approach, question the extent to which this change is possible. They believe that there is an inherent conflict between labour and management that prevents a full partnership. Some take the view that HR management innovations and strong unions are incompatible.[13] Donald Wells points to a noted experiment in increased collaboration and union involvement at a chemical plant in Sarnia, Ontario. Shell established a new plant that included work teams and extensive employee involvement. The collective agreement was reduced from 70 to 7 pages, and the parties adopted a form of continuous bargaining to deal with issues. The system also involved a pay-for-knowledge feature in which wages depended on the number of jobs employees learned. At another new plant, where the company used the same principles, the union was not able to organize the employees. Wells alleges that the company used the Sarnia experiment to learn how to keep unions out. He argues that instead of being an indicator of successful union–management collaboration, the Shell model is a successful management strategy to avoid unions. He warns against unions becoming involved in such joint efforts.

Perhaps it is not either–or, and some new practices and increased collaboration can coexist with traditional labour relations practices.[14] Can unions and management move toward a more cooperative relationship that includes increased employee involvement? This is a difficult question that cannot be answered here. The reader should keep this question in mind as we proceed to discuss the details of labour relations such as contract negotiation. In 2007, Magna International, an auto parts manufacturer employing more than 18 000 people in 45 Canadian plants, and the Canadian Auto Workers union (now known as Unifor) signed a Framework of Fairness Agreement (FFA), which establishes a new labour relations model. The FFA replaces the traditional confrontational model of labour relations with a collaborative approach. It has implications for several critical labour relations topics, and will be referred to in subsequent chapters as the need arises. For example, in the agreement the union agrees not to strike and this will be covered in Chapter 8, which deals with contract negotiation.

Referring back to Figure 1-1, it is possible that environmental factors, including the economy, may either help or hinder change. We will see later that aspects of the legal environment may hinder labour–management collaboration. Currently, legislation provides for fixed-term contracts, and for the most part does not require negotiation during the term of an agreement. Also, the parties' power and values may be factors. An employer who is in a position of power can implement changes despite union opposition. Employers and union leaders may not believe that collaboration is in their best interest. The processes used by employers and unions—such as traditional confrontational bargaining—may entrench an adversarial relationship.

OVERVIEW OF THIS BOOK

In Chapter 1 we have defined labour relations, referred to its significance, and provided a framework that emphasizes that labour relations issues must be considered in their broader context. The question of the confrontational nature of labour relations and the possibility of increasing collaboration has been left with the reader as we examine labour relations actors, processes, and outcomes.

In Chapter 2 we will explore the environmental factors that affect labour relations actors and processes. The purpose of Chapter 3 is to provide an understanding of unions, so we will review their structures, functions, history, objectives, and methods. The information provided should help employees understand unions and allow employers to have a better understanding of the union they are dealing with. In Chapter 4 we turn to the second actor in the labour relations system—employers—and review their objectives and methods. We will consider alternative employer strategies and approaches to human resources management that will affect labour relations. In Chapter 5 we will review the objectives and methods of governments, the third key actor in the labour relations system; the chapter also briefly refers to labour relations boards, which play a critical role in the system. An employer or employee's first contact with a union may occur when a union attempts to organize a workplace. Chapter 6 reviews the organizing process—a critical time for the employer, employees, and the union—as well as the certification process and the conduct of employers and unions. If a union obtains the right to represent employees, the parties will attempt to negotiate a collective agreement. Chapter 7 considers the possible terms of a collective agreement and reviews the serious implications these terms have for the management of an organization. In Chapter 8 we consider the negotiation of a collective agreement, including the processes the parties engage in prior to and during contract talks. We will also consider interest-based bargaining, an alternative to traditional adversarial bargaining. In Chapter 9 we consider the administration of collective agreements, including the implications of the agreement for matters such as filling job vacancies and discipline, as well as alternatives to traditional grievance arbitration. In Chapter 10 we consider strikes, lockouts, and assistance available to the parties when they negotiate a collective agreement. Labour relations in the public sector have distinctive features that are considered in Chapter 11. In Chapter 12 we review the effects of unionization on productivity and profitability, highlight key aspects of elements of employee relations strategies, and return to the question of increased employee involvement and union–management collaboration that is raised in this chapter.

Implications for Practice

1. Labour relations are an important part of human resources management for employers. The unionization of an organization's employees could affect a number of issues including costs, productivity, recruiting, selection, and profitability.

2. Labour relations are also important for employees. Unionization will affect employees' compensation, job security, and job satisfaction.

3. Labour relations activities such as contract negotiation and strikes should not be viewed in isolation. The activities the parties engage in are affected by the environment and by the parties' objectives, values, and power.

4. There are varying approaches to labour relations that involve different assumptions and values. Alternative labour relations practices should be considered; however, any commentary on labour relations matters should take into account the objectives and values of the observer.

Key Terms

collective bargaining, p. 3
common law, p. 4
constructive dismissal, p. 6
economic environment, p. 9
employee relations, p. 4

human resources
    management, p. 3
industrial relations, p. 2
labour relations, p. 2
legal environment, p. 10

political environment, p. 10
reasonable notice, p. 5
social environment, p. 10
technological environment,
    p. 10

Review Questions

1. Distinguish between labour relations and industrial relations as these terms are defined in this book.

2. Explain why labour relations are significant to all Canadians.

3. The effects of unionization are a matter of ongoing concern in this book. What are two likely consequences of unionization? Explain why these outcomes may be perceived as having a positive or negative impact on those affected by this change.

4. Outline the five key components of the framework for labour relations as presented in this chapter.

5. (a) Explain the meaning of the following statement: "An employer has constructively dismissed a non-union employee."

    (b) Can a unionized employee be constructively dismissed? Explain why or why not.

Discussion Questions

1. Do you agree or disagree with the political economy approach referred to in this chapter? Why?

2. If you have worked in a unionized work setting, to what extent is the relationship between unions and employers collaborative and to what extent is it adversarial?

3. If you have not worked in a unionized environment, to what extent is the relationship between unions and employers collaborative and to what extent is it adversarial? What influences have shaped your opinions?

4. Compare the students' answers to questions 2 and 3 above. Which group perceives the union–management relationship as more cooperative? More adversarial?

5. Find a news item involving a union–management issue, and explain it in terms of the framework for labour relations (see Figure 1-1) provided in this chapter.

Web Research

The Canadian Association of Administrators of Labour Legislation (CAALL) website (www. caall-acalo.org) is one of many providing information relating to employment and labour issues. The association has a resource library containing information relating to all Canadian jurisdictions. Although the information is not standardized, this may be a useful starting point for information searches in your jurisdiction. See what is available for labour relations in your province.

CASE INCIDENT   SAFE WATCH SECURITY

Safe Watch Security sells and services home and commercial security systems. The company employs 15 technicians who do installations and service customers within a 200-kilometre radius of its office and warehouse in Centreville. The technicians are represented by a union; and although the collective agreement did not refer to the issue of company vehicles, Safe Watch supplied each technician with a van, tools, supplies, and equipment. Technicians were allowed to drive their company van home and go directly to a customer's location at the start of each day. An attempt was made to assign technicians to jobs close to their residence. Most technicians were able to carry out their job duties without attending the company's office more than twice a week to pick up supplies.

The company interviewed Judy Thornecrest for a position as a technician. During the interview, it was discovered that Thornecrest resided 70 kilometres away from the company's office in Centreville. Most of the company's technicians reside in Centreville; however, seven technicians lived in other municipalities between 27 and 79 kilometres away from this location. Safe Watch was concerned about the costs of operating the van assigned to Thornecrest if she was allowed to drive her van home. The company made an offer of employment to Thornecrest, which provided that she would have to provide her own transportation to the company's office where her van would be kept. Thornecrest accepted the company's offer and began work, commuting to Centreville. After working for the company for a few weeks and becoming aware that other technicians were allowed to drive their vans home, Thornecrest sought the advice of the union. A union representative took up the matter with the company, and they were told that (1) the company was concerned about the costs of allowing Thornecrest to drive the company van to her home and (2) Thornecrest had agreed to terms of employment that did not provide for her to have use of a van to travel to her job.

Questions

1. Explain the basis upon which the union could pursue a complaint on Thornecrest's behalf.

2. If this dispute goes to a hearing, what arguments will be made by the union and the employer before an arbitrator?

3. If you were the decision maker in this situation, explain what your decision would be. Include any remedies that you would order if you decided in favour of the employee.

Chapter 2
The Environment

Unions in Canada are key advocates for the protection not only of their members but of society as a whole of rights afforded by laws and codes that apply in federal or provincial jurisdictions. Such advocacy is seen in public campaigns aimed at influencing social norms and beliefs. Actions are also carried out by union local representatives in work settings in the day-to-day administration of collective agreements. This wide-ranging involvement can influence change in the broader social and more localized employment environments.

At its 49th convention, the British Columbia Government and Service Employees Union (BCGEU) voted in favour of the constitutional change that read "The equity and human rights committee will consist of two members from each designated equity groups (aboriginal; workers of colour; gay, lesbian, bisexual or transgender; and workers with disabilities) who shall be elected at an Equity & Human Rights Conference." This 2014 conference, called "Rise-up and Reboot," held elections for two members for each of the identified groups to represent their equity network at the BCGEU's executive equity and human rights committee.

BCGEU's Equity and Human Rights Committee works to eliminate all forms of discrimination in the workplace, in the union, and throughout society. It deals with issues ranging from homophobia in the workplace to employment equity strategies and breaking down systemic barriers, and has examined the union's own policies and structures to increase access by members at all levels.

The Equity and Human Rights campaign is one of over a dozen collective actions taken by BCGEU for its members and other British Columbians. At the workplace level, this support is reflected in a comprehensive orientation manual for stewards in its local union structures. Stewards are instructed to understand the diversity of their local's membership, whether it be cultural, racial, gender, or that of sexual orientation or age, and promote solidarity so that management cannot divide workers. The provincial union has also utilized social media to engage the diversity of its membership who are covered by over 500 collective agreements in the province. For the past two years, BCGEU members who identify with one or more of the four equity groups have joined the BCGEU Equity Network. The equity groups include Aboriginal workers with disabilities (this includes any hidden disability), workers of colour, and gay, lesbian, bisexual, and transgender members. Network participants are offered the opportunity to be put on a confidential mailing list to receive information, news stories, and invitations to BCGEU-sponsored cultural events. The union also welcomes any interesting articles or events from your community to distribute to the network.

Website for historical Consumer Price Index information: http://www.statcan. gc.ca/tables-tableaux/sum-som/l01/ cst01/econ46a-eng.htm

Website for current Consumer Price Index information: http://www5. statcan.gc.ca/subject-sujet/result-result at?pid=3956&id=2178&lang=eng&typ e=CST&sortType=1&pageNum=2

The framework provided for labour relations in Chapter 1 referred to the objectives, values, and power of the parties and the numerous activities or processes that the parties engage in. In this chapter, we will consider the environmental factors that affect the parties and the processes of labour relations, especially contract negotiation. The five aspects of the environment that were depicted in Figure 1-1—economic, technological, social, political, and legal—are not separate domains; developments in one may affect others. For example, an economic downturn might affect the political process by leading to the replacement of a fiscally conservative or right-wing government with a more left-leaning government or vice versa. In turn this may affect the legal environment, because the newly elected government may be more or less likely to enact pro-business labour relations legislation. Such political viewpoints may also influence views on demographic factors and related legal entitlements of union members.

ECONOMIC ENVIRONMENT

The economic environment is critical to employers and unions. We will start by considering the overall economic climate and how it affects the parties. If the economy is in a recession, the parties will be adversely affected. Government policy to regulate the economy will also have its effects. For certain industries, such as air travel, economic factors may present unique threats or opportunities. Finally, recent economic trends and issues such as free trade will be considered.

Macroeconomic Environment

The macroeconomic environment is the growth rate, unemployment rate, and the rate of inflation in the economy.

Nominal wages are wages that have not been adjusted for inflation.

Real wages are wages that have been adjusted for inflation.

The **macroeconomic environment** refers to the state of the economy as a whole, including whether it is in a period of recession or growth, what the unemployment rate is, and what the rate of inflation is. The macroeconomic environment impacts the objectives and power of unions and employers, and in turn affects labour relations outcomes. In times of inflation, for example, unions will seek larger wage increases to protect the real incomes of employees. **Nominal wages** are wages that have not been adjusted for inflation. **Real wages** are wages that have been adjusted for inflation. If the inflation rate is 4 percent and employees receive a 2 percent wage increase, real wages have been reduced by 2 percent.

Although inflation has not recently been a problem in Canada, at times in the past it has posed a concern. Increases in the Consumer Price Index exceeded 10 percent in the mid-1970s and early 1980s. In periods of economic growth, many private sector employers may have increased sales, and public sector employers may have additional tax revenue. This raises the wage expectations of employees and prompts unions to pursue increases in compensation. Moreover, in a period of economic growth, the employer may wish to avoid the interruption of production a strike would cause, especially when competitors are continuing to operate. Periods of economic growth have thus been associated with higher rates of union organization and a higher incidence of strikes.

In economic downturns, unions will be concerned with job security. This will lead to union demands such as increased severance payments and notice of layoff. In some cases, where unions have been forced to accept lower wage increases or even make wage concessions, there has been an attempt to make this more palatable by providing increased union access to decision makers. For example, union representatives have been included on boards of directors; however, some Canadian unions reject this role. In a recession there will be increased pressure on some employers to reduce costs, and they will seek to avoid wage increases or even to obtain concessions from the union.

The state of the economy might affect public support for the demands of one of the parties, which in turn might impact its bargaining power. For example, a strike by a teachers' union would more likely be supported by the public in a period of economic prosperity than in a recession; many people might think employees are "lucky to have a job" in a recession and should not be going on strike.

The Canadian economy is open, meaning that we import many goods and are heavily dependent upon exports, especially to the United States. This makes our economy vulnerable to U.S. trade practices and security concerns, and fluctuations in the value of the Canadian dollar. The softwood lumber dispute with the United States in 2002–03 illustrates the significance of U.S. trade practices. The United States claimed that Canadian producers were being unfairly subsidized and imposed tariffs on Canadian lumber. This led to the closure of Canadian lumber operations, especially in western Canada. Increased security concerns could pose an even greater economic threat. Canada's tourism sector has revenue of $55 billion per year, more than five times the value of softwood lumber exports. The United States has adopted a requirement that Americans have a passport to re-enter the country. Most Americans do not have a passport, and the tourism sector, which employs more than half a million Canadians, could be significantly affected. Our dependence on exports to the United States makes the value of the Canadian dollar an important economic variable. For many years, the Canadian dollar traded at less than 70 cents a U.S. dollar, providing Canadian exporters with an advantage. However, in recent years there have been times when the Canadian dollar has approached parity with the U.S. dollar, and jobs have been lost in the manufacturing sector as a result. Because the Canadian economy is open to imports and dependent on exports, there is pressure to keep costs in line with those of foreign producers.

Government Economic Policy

The government may attempt to regulate the economy, specifically unemployment and inflation, through monetary and fiscal policy. **Fiscal policy** refers to changes in government spending and taxation to regulate employment levels and inflation. The government can reduce taxes and increase spending to stimulate the economy and reduce unemployment. To counter the recession of 2008–09, the federal government adopted a stimulus package, spending aimed at increasing economic activity and reducing unemployment. In the process of fighting the recession, governments have added billions of dollars of debt that may constrain policy options in the future. Conversely, taxes could be increased, and government spending could be reduced to control inflation. **Monetary policy** refers to changes in the interest rate to regulate employment levels and inflation. Interest rates can be reduced to stimulate the economy and raised to control inflation. Inflation in Canada remains low. Core inflation was expected to stay well below 2 percent in 2014 due to the effects of economic slack and heightened retail competition, and these effects will persist until early 2016. However, higher consumer energy prices and the lower Canadian dollar will exert temporary upward pressure on total CPI inflation, pushing it closer to the 2 percent. Canada's real GDP growth is expected to average about 2.5 percent in 2014 and 2015 before easing to around the 2 percent growth rate of the economy's potential in 2016. Competitiveness challenges

Website for the Canadian Centre for Policy Alternatives: www. policyalternatives.ca

Fiscal policy consists of changes in government spending and taxation to regulate employment levels and inflation.

Website for the Fraser Institute: www. fraserinstitute.org

Monetary policy consists of changes in the interest rate to regulate employment levels and inflation.

continue to weigh on Canadian exporters' ability to benefit from stronger growth abroad. However, a range of export subsectors have been growing which suggests that as the U.S. recovery gathers momentum and becomes more broadly based, many of our exports will benefit. The lower Canadian dollar should provide additional support. The Bank of Canada continues to believe that rising global demand for Canadian goods and services, combined with the assumed high level of oil prices, will stimulate business investment in Canada and shift the economy to a more sustainable growth track.[1]

The national economic numbers hide regional disparities. There have been times when the unemployment rate in Newfoundland and Labrador was five times the rate in Alberta.[2]

Fighting inflation has not been the only concern of government in recent years. Two other apparently conflicting objectives have been pursued: reduction of government debt and reduction of taxes to be competitive. By the 1990s, government debt had risen to a point where it was a concern to policymakers. To reduce the debt, the federal and provincial governments adopted spending cuts and other policies that affected unions. In the public sector, they imposed wage freezes on employees and in some cases forced the renegotiation of collective agreements. The federal government and some provincial governments pursued a policy of tax cuts in the 1990s. The proponents of these tax cuts have pointed to lower tax rates in other jurisdictions and claimed that taxes in Canada had to be cut to remain competitive and encourage economic growth. Whether such tax cuts are sound public policy is an interesting question, which is left for the reader to consider. The websites cited in the margin here provide information and commentary both in support of and against them. Reduced spending and tax revenue affects labour relations, especially in the public sector. The elimination of some services in the course of spending cuts leads to concerns over job losses. Governments negotiating with their employees may point to reduced revenues and the need to control the debt as reasons why wage increases are not possible.

Government economic policy can also include direct and indirect support for an industry. The Ontario government established an Automotive Investment Strategy that includes three separate funds, totalling $550 million, to support innovation and emerging technologies in the provincial automobile sector.[3] In 2013, the Canadian federal government provided a $50 000 investment to SaskMilk, the provincial milk marketing board, to purchase needed equipment to develop a vaccine to combat a highly infectious condition that occurs in costing the industry roughly $50 million annually.[4]

Industry- and Firm-Level Demand

Economic factors at the level of the firm and of the industry can also have significant consequences for employers and unions. The sensitivity of demand to overall economic changes differs from firm to firm and industry to industry. Shrinking employment in manufacturing has been a common trend in almost all countries in the Organization for Economic Co-operation and Development (OECD) countries. From 1998 to 2008, the United States lost close to one-quarter (4.1 million) of its manufacturing jobs. Elsewhere in the OECD, from 1990 to 2003, manufacturing employment fell by 29 percent in the United Kingdom, 24 percent in Japan, 20 percent in Belgium and Sweden, and 14 percent in France. Canada's manufacturing industry lost 278 000 jobs (1 in 6) from 2000 to 2007, which reduced the sector's share of total employment from 16 percent to 12 percent. That share then declined to 10 percent in 2009 after the 2008–09 recession when manufacturers faced weaker demand and cuts to industrial capacity, resulting in the loss of 188 000 jobs.[5] Producers of major items such as automobiles and appliances generally may be more affected by an economic downturn, which will in turn affect their contract negotiations with unions. Some industries may experience significant changes in a short period of time. In 2005, a news headline proclaimed "Forestry Products Triple."[6] In 2006, a report outlined how the Alberta forest industry had suffered a rapid reversal.[7] It was noted that Alberta's cost advantage had eroded over the previous six months, and record profits from the previous year had turned to losses. The rising Canadian dollar and lower lumber prices because of a decline in U.S. housing starts were cited as factors leading to the closure of mills and job losses. By the time you read this, the situation in the industry may have changed yet again. Some industries are countercyclical—that is, demand for the product will increase in a recession and decrease in a recovery. For example, in the auto repair industry, business may increase in a downturn because people are delaying purchase of a new vehicle. Firms may be competing in either a growing industry or one in which sales are levelling off or declining. The beer industry, for example, may be maturing because of overall aging of the population.

Some industries and firms will be affected to a greater or lesser extent by any given economic variable. Lower interest rates lead to significant increases in demand in the housing industry. Firms may operate in a market that is more or less price-competitive. One aspect of the firm's product that will affect the union and employer is its **price elasticity of demand**—the sensitivity of the demand for the product to a price change. It is a basic principle of economics that there is an inverse relationship between the price of most goods and services and the quantity demanded. If the price is reduced the quantity demanded increases, and if the price is raised the quantity demanded decreases. This is reflected in a downward-sloping demand curve for the good or service. How much a change in price will affect the quantity demanded depends on the nature of the good or service.

> **Price elasticity of demand** refers to how much a change in price affects demand.

A distinction is drawn between an **elastic demand** and an **inelastic demand**. Figure 2-1 illustrates an elastic and an inelastic demand and the effect on the quantity demanded when there is a change in price.

> **Elastic demand** exists when the demand for a product is more price-responsive.

An elastic demand means that the demand for a good or service is more responsive to a change in price. When the price of the good or service changes, the percentage change in the quantity demanded is greater than the percentage change in the price of the good or service. A company producing a product or service for which there are substitutes readily available, such as house insurance, faces an elastic demand. An inelastic demand refers to a situation where the demand is less price-responsive. The percentage change in the quantity demanded is less than the percentage change in the price of the good or service. When the demand is inelastic, for any given change in price the change in the quantity demanded will be less significant. A company producing a product or service that is essential, for which there are few substitutes available, such as a medication, faces an inelastic demand.

> **Inelastic demand** exists when the demand for a product is less price-responsive.

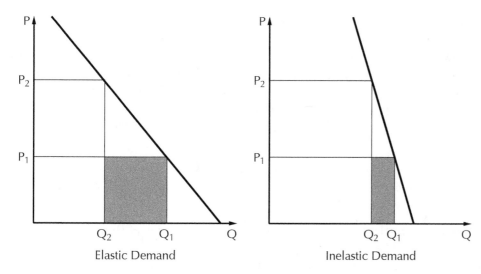

Figure 2-1 Elasticity of Demand

Economic Trends and Issues Affecting Labour Relations

There are several economic trends and issues that may affect labour relations.

Labour Market Changes   In a competitive non-union labour market, the interaction of the demand for labour by firms and the supply of labour by individuals determines the level of employment and wages. The labour market is not perfectly competitive; however, labour economics provides a model that refers to the demand and supply of labour that will help explain changes in wages and levels of employment. A brief review of the effects of a change in the demand for or the supply of labour, holding other factors constant, follows.

Any factor that causes an increase in the demand for labour, such as an economic upturn, should lead to increased levels of employment and higher wages, and any factor that causes a decrease in the demand for labour, such as an economic downturn, should lead to decreased levels of employment and lower wages. On the supply side, any factor that causes an increase in the supply of labour will tend to increase levels of employment and reduce wage levels, and any factor that causes a decrease in the supply of labour will tend to decrease the level of employment and increase wage levels. To illustrate, shortages of employees in some occupational groups, such as computer animators, have led to higher wages and signing bonuses for employees. Governments are also involved in the labour market. Through legislation, the government establishes minimum terms of employment such as vacation and overtime rules, and it affects the supply of labour by providing education and training.

In the absence of unions, individual employees would have to accept the market wage, and it is likely to be low if workers do not have unique skills or abilities. Unions could be viewed as a way to avoid the effects of the labour market that would otherwise be imposed on individual employees. In a labour market without a union, many employees have little or no bargaining power when dealing with their employer. By joining a union, employees may be able to increase their power. Conversely, it is possible that the wage rates in the labour market might be pushed higher than the wages provided for in collective agreements, and this will pose a problem for both parties, especially employers. Recently, private MRI clinics have begun operations, offering wages to technicians higher than those paid by hospitals. Many hospitals have lost technicians to the private clinics, and this has meant that some hospitals are not operating at peak capacity.

Aging Workforce.   The workforce is aging, and this may have significance for unions and employers.[8] As the baby boomers (those born between 1947 and 1966) retire, there may be labour shortages, which will put upward pressure on wages and make it difficult for employers to recruit some types of employees. Older workers have preferences that may affect union demands and negotiations. They may be more concerned with increasing pensions than with current wage increases, and they may also be more concerned with job security as they approach retirement. Some employees, instead of working full-time until retirement, may wish to have the opportunity to work less in the final years of their work life. Others may wish to extend their careers beyond the traditional retirement age.

Younger Employees.   Although the overall trend is toward an older workforce, relative to boomers and Gen X-ers, millennials have a different view of how work should get done and come into the workforce with a different set of expectations.[9] Such differences might affect unions and employers.

Female Participation.   In 1978 approximately 30 percent of the labour force was female, and by 2012 this had increased to 57.9 percent.[10] Men used to be more likely to belong to unions, but that has changed. In 1981, the proportion of men in unionized jobs was 42 percent; by 2012, that had tumbled to 29 percent. By contrast, women's unionization rate has hovered around 30 percent for the past 30 years—leaving them now more apt to be unionized than men.[11] The increased proportion of women in unions means that unions will have to be more concerned with issues, such as flextime, harassment, and daycare. Moreover, unions will have to be concerned with internal policies to ensure that women are adequately represented in union positions.

Diversity.   Canadian society and the labour force are becoming more diverse. **Diversity** refers to a labour force that includes people of different religions, ethnicity, sexual orientations, and disabilities. Unions and employers will have to deal with discrimination, harassment, and accommodation issues, which are discussed below.

Diversity is a characteristic of a labour force that includes people of different religions, ethnicity, sexual orientations, and disabilities.

Non-standard Work.   **Non-standard work** refers to work arrangements other than traditional full-time employment, including part-time and temporary work. Statistics Canada defines part-time employment as a job that involves less than 30 hours per week at their main or only job. There has been a significant increase in the number of employees who hold part-time jobs. In the 1950s, only 4 percent of employees worked part-time, and in 2013, 18.9 percent worked part-time.[12] A significant portion of this part-time work, approximately 25 percent, is involuntary. The vast majority of involuntary part-timers tend to be among youths and women aged 25 to 54. Both of these groups display seasonal patterns: the number of young involuntary part-timers increases during the summer months when full-time hours are preferred, while the number of adult female involuntary part-time workers peaks in the fall, when children return to school. Involuntary part-time work rises and falls with the unemployment rate, an indication that people are forced into part-time work when economic conditions worsen.

Non-standard work is employment in other than traditional full-time work—for example, part-time and temporary work.

Part-time employees pose a challenge for unions. Since they are generally paid lower wages and receive fewer benefits, employers have attempted to use non-union part-time employees to reduce costs. Unions have found it difficult to organize part-time employees for a number of reasons. Many are younger, and they do not have experience with unionization. Many work in industries where unions have not had a presence and unionization is not the norm. Part-time employees who work in smaller organizations may have a stronger connection with the employer than those who work in a larger organization where alienation from the employer develops. Smaller part-time units are more costly for unions to organize. Where worker turnover is higher, there is less commitment to the workplace. Many part-time employees are more likely to quit when they become dissatisfied and move to another job, so unionization is more difficult.

Mergers   There have been periods of significant merger activity in the past, which have affected labour relations. Mergers create the possibility of layoffs. This will affect negotiations between employers and unions, because the union will be concerned with protecting employees from job loss. Mergers in North America in recent years have also led to unique collaborations between unions seeking to secure their membership bases, particularly in the airline industry. These new union partnership arrangements, as seen in the proposed merger of US Airways and American Airlines, are also an attempt to prevent other unions from raiding membership ranks at a time when organized labour in the United States is reeling from membership losses.[13]

Website providing the North American Agreement on Labour Cooperation (NAALC): www.labour.gc.ca/eng/relations/international/agreements/naalc.shtml

Globalization   **Globalization** is the trend toward firms obtaining resources and producing and selling their products anywhere in the world. It means that international boundaries have no significance for commerce: a firm may obtain resources in one country, produce in another country, and sell in many other different countries. Globalization also means that capital will move to wherever the highest return is provided. (Globalization is separate from and predates trade liberalization, discussed next.) This is significant, because it means increased international competition. Firms face pressure to reduce costs and prices, and will locate production where costs are the lowest. Note that when firms consider labour costs,

Globalization is the trend toward firms obtaining resources and producing and selling their products anywhere in the world.

they have to take into account differences in productivity and not just the wage rate. There may be situations in which total labour costs are lower in Canada despite the fact that the Canadian wage rate is higher. One observer has noted that the globalization of goods depends on cheap oil prices and oil prices will rise as the world's supply of oil diminishes. In a world of cheap oil, it is possible to ship iron ore across the Pacific to China to produce steel and subsequently ship the steel back to North America. Higher energy costs in the future may mean that this is no longer economically feasible. Jeff Rubin in *Why Your World is about to Get a Whole Lot Smaller: Oil and the End of Globalization* argues that higher energy costs and concerns over global warming will lead to a rejuvenation of local manufacturing.[14]

Trade Liberalization

Trade liberalization is the trend to international agreements that reduce tariff barriers between countries. The most significant such agreement for Canadian unions and employers is the North American Free Trade Agreement (NAFTA) between Canada, the United States, and Mexico that came into effect in 1992. Unions opposed NAFTA, because they feared Canadian employers could not compete with the lower wages in Mexico and parts of the United States, and would be forced out of business. Unions were also concerned that the agreement would lead to Canadian employers moving to Mexico or the United States. Finally, there were concerns that the other jurisdictions, in particular Mexico, had lower labour standards and that even these were not adequately enforced. This led to fears that there would be a harmonization of standards at a lower level than existing Canadian standards.

Proponents of NAFTA argued that the Canadian economy would benefit from access to markets in Mexico and the United States. The debate about whether NAFTA has been positive or negative for Canada is not resolved. However, a few things seem clear. NAFTA has added to the economic pressure that some employers face and in turn puts pressure on unions. Some firms have used the threat of their relocating to force unions to accept lower wage increases. It has been suggested that NAFTA's effect on labour relations at individual firms will depend on whether it poses a threat or an opportunity to the firm. In firms for which the agreement poses a threat, the union and the employer will be concerned with job loss and possible plant closure. They will have to be more concerned with job security issues, including layoff notices, early retirement options, and work sharing. In firms for which the agreement presents opportunities, there will be concerns relating to possible expansion and change. The union and employer will be concerned with increased adaptability, reclassification, and the use of seniority as a criterion for promotion. It has also been suggested that NAFTA creates an incentive for employers and unions to cooperate on workplace issues because disputes cannot be tolerated in the more competitive environment.[15]

Deindustrialization

Deindustrialization is the shift in the economy from the manufacture of goods to the production of services. This shift has significance for both unions and employers. In manufacturing, forestry, mining, transportation and other sectors, globalization and increased efficiency led to the elimination of hundreds of thousands of high-paying unionized positions in Canada. About 18 percent of private sector jobs are now unionized, compared to 21 percent in 1997, and the proportion was declining even before then.[16] Possibly the loss of manufacturing jobs has been a factor causing some unions to pursue the organization of workers in the service sector, to avoid a decline in total membership. If so, deindustrialization has affected employers in the service sector by indirectly leading to the organization of their employees.

Downsizing

Downsizing refers to the elimination of jobs for the purpose of improving efficiency and improving economic returns. Downsizing has been a frequent strategic move in recent years. A 1992–94 survey covering 336 firms in the private sector, accounting for 42 percent of the private sector labour force, found that there was a major downsizing in 25 percent of the workplaces in the 10-year period preceding the survey.[17] A more recent study found that 56 percent of employers and 57 percent of union local officials surveyed

Trade liberalization is the trend toward international agreements that reduce tariff barriers between countries.

Deindustrialization is the shift from the manufacture of goods to the production of services.

Downsizing is the elimination of jobs for the purpose of improving efficiency and improving economic returns.

reported a permanent reduction of employees within a two-year period.[18] This study found a negative impact on employee satisfaction and the labour relations climate. Specifically, downsizing was associated with higher grievances and increased absenteeism. Downsizing puts unions on the defensive, because they may have to reduce their wage demands in an attempt to save jobs.

Deregulation Deregulation refers to the change from a business regime in which the government regulates market entrants and prices to one in which the market is open to competition. At one time, some industries in Canada, such as airline and phone services, were regulated. There would be one producer, which charged rates approved by a government commission such as the Canadian Radio-television and Telecommunications Commission (CRTC). Deregulation in the phone industry led to the entry of AT&T Canada and Sprint Canada and competition in the market. Deregulation does not mean that all government rules or restrictions on a particular industry are abolished. The airline industry was deregulated in 1988; however, the industry is still subject to various restrictions that will impact employers and unions. For example, the industry has pressed the federal government to change the rules to reduce the number of flight attendants required. Unions have opposed this measure, claiming that safety would be compromised.[19]

Deregulation has put pressure on unions and employers. The employers now have to be more concerned with increasing efficiency and reducing costs; job security can become a more important issue for the unions. For example, after deregulation Bell announced a reduction of 10 000 employees over three years. The company offered a plan to employees to take extended leaves, without which it might have been forced to confront its unions with wage reductions or additional job cuts.[20]

Legacy Costs Legacy costs are the expenses associated with providing pensions and health benefits to retired workers. For some older organizations, these costs are a growing concern. Legacy costs were cited as one of the reasons for the bankruptcy in 2005 of Delphi, the world's largest manufacturer of auto parts. This problem may not be as serious in Canada, because health care is largely funded through taxation. In fact, some auto and auto parts manufacturer may have been shifted to Canada because of lower health care costs.[21] If there is further privatization of the Canadian health care system in the future, these costs may be a growing concern. There are some observers who claim that public sector pensions are a serious problem for Canada.[22] One of the ways to avoid the pension-cost problem is to switch from a defined-benefit to a defined-contribution pension plan, but any proposal to make such a change could be contentious for unions and employers.

TECHNOLOGY

The technological environment refers to developments in knowledge that lead to new products, services, and changes in methods of production. Illustrations of its impact on daily life are easy to find: ultra-thin computer tablets; remote access to home security systems; and automatic parallel parking options on new car models. Technological innovation has important consequences for unions and employers. It will lead to concerns regarding job security because of the possibility of workers being replaced by labour-saving devices or facilitating the transfer of jobs to lower-wage countries. For example, some Canadian call centres have been closed when the work has been moved to India. On the technology issue, unions face a dilemma: technological change may lead to increased productivity that can be the basis for wage increases, but at the same time it may lead to job losses. It might also give rise to concerns regarding ergonomics, health, and safety, such as those surrounding the effects of video display terminals. There is the potential for disagreement between the union and employer over compensation. Where technological change leads to jobs requiring fewer skills, employers will attempt to reclassify the job and reduce compensation.

Where change leads to new jobs, or jobs requiring more skills, unions will seek to increase compensation. Advances in computerization have meant that some employees are now able to work at home, an issue unions and employers will have to address in collective agreements in the future. These advances now allow more employers to monitor employee activity. Some employers are using global positioning systems to track the location of employees.[23] In call centres, a report can be generated that indicates how much time an employee spends with each customer. Technology will also lead to privacy in the workplace becoming an issue. If employers monitor employee email, what should the response be from the union?

The effect of information technology, including the Internet and intranets, will be of interest to unions in the future. Unions can use websites to deliver information to employees they wish to organize, and provide services to members. However, some observers have suggested that information technology may pose a threat to unions.[24] For example, the present model of labour relations is based on employees working at one location for one employer, whereas information technology has allowed more workers to work away from the employer's location or to work for more than one employer. In the United States, there are now more employees working at home than there are union members. This will mean that employees have less connection with their workplace and perhaps with a union. Also, many employers have developed intranets to provide information and communicate with employees. These may pose a threat to unions because they allow employers to develop more direct communication with employees. Intranets might be used to establish discussion groups and other devices to foster closer identification with the company and weaken any link to a union. It is also argued that the Internet and the Web pose a threat to the traditional relationship between the union and its members. In order to survive, unions will have to do more than simply provide services to their members. They will have to "transform themselves into a social movement which pursues social change. . . ."[25] Accordingly, they will have to encourage more member involvement, a purpose not furthered by increased use of websites and online information, as opposed to personal contact with union members at meetings and social activities.

SOCIAL ENVIRONMENT

The social environment refers to the values and beliefs of Canadians relating to unions and employers. Some Canadians may be more supportive of unions and collective bargaining than others. A Harris/Decima survey, carried out for the Canadian Association of University Teachers (CAUT), found 70 percent of Canadians say unions are "still needed," compared to fewer than 30 percent who say they are obsolete.[26] Values and beliefs are important because they might affect the propensity of employees to unionize and the bargaining power of the union and employer. An individual who disapproves of unions is less likely to join one. In some labour disputes, a party that has the support of the public is in a stronger position. The values and beliefs of Canadians in general are important because they will affect employment and labour relations legislation. In the United States, some states have passed right-to-work laws, which prohibit the mandatory deduction of union dues. There is evidence that both the Canadian federal government and some provincial political parties have recently looked at right-to-work legislation options. However, it does not appear likely the Canadian social environment would allow right-to-work legislation to be passed.

Most of the Canadian population approves of unions generally; however, there is a negative relationship between approval of unions and perceived union power. As perceived union power increases, public support for unions declines. Lipset and Meltz explain that this is by noting that people regard unions as self-interested organizations that benefit their members at the expense of society and consumers.[27] Accordingly, people do not want unions to be too strong; and if it is perceived that union power is increasing, union approval goes down.

Labour Relations Issue 2-1 contains some questions, similar to those of a national poll of Canadians, relating to values and beliefs about unions. You should ask yourself these questions, and then revisit them after completing your course to see if your thoughts have changed.

POLITICAL ENVIRONMENT

The political environment refers to the Canadian political system and its effect on labour relations. The political environment in turn has a significant impact on the legislation that regulates unions and employers, which is discussed under "Political Environment" below. A critical feature of the Canadian political environment is the jurisdiction of the federal and provincial governments in employment and labour relations matters.

Divided Jurisdiction

The *Constitution Act* provides a division of powers or authority between the federal and provincial governments. Most issues that could be the subject of legislation are under the authority of either the federal or provincial governments. For example, banking and criminal law are within the jurisdiction of the federal government, and education is a provincial matter. For employment and labour relations issues, there is divided jurisdiction: the federal government has the authority to pass legislation regulating some employers and employees, and the provinces have jurisdiction over other workplaces. The federal government has jurisdiction over approximately 10 percent of the labour force, including interprovincial transport, banking, and broadcasting. The provinces have jurisdiction over 90 percent of the labour force, including the manufacturing, retail, service, and construction sectors. Accordingly, a distinction must be drawn between **federally regulated employers**, who are subject to federal legislation, and **provincially regulated employers**, who are subject to the legislation of each province in which they conduct business. Whenever legislation is referred to, the preliminary question that must be asked is whether it is the federal or the provincial legislation that is relevant. For example, suppose a question arose about how much notice, if any, a union must give before it goes on strike. If the employer is a bank, it is federally regulated and the relevant legislation is the *Canada Labour Code*, which provides for 72-hour notice. If the employer is a retail store, it is provincially regulated, and the answer to the

Federally regulated employers are those subject to federal employment and labour relations legislation.

Provincially regulated employers are those subject to provincial employment and labour relations legislation.

question will depend upon which province the store is located in. If the store is in Nova Scotia, the relevant legislation is the *Trade Union Act*, which requires 48-hour notice to be given to the Minister of Labour. If the store is located in Ontario, the relevant legislation is the *Labour Relations Act*, which does not require notice prior to the commencement of a strike. Similarly, every jurisdiction has its own employment standards legislation, and there might be 11 different rules on the same matter, such as vacation entitlement.

The divided jurisdiction in Canadian employment and labour relations matters has several implications for employers, unions, and the labour relations system. Some of these implications might be viewed as advantages and others as potential disadvantages. Employers who are provincially regulated and carry on business in more than one province will have to deal with different laws in each province. This may cause confusion and increase costs. Depending on the employees they represent, unions may have to know about the federal legislation and the relevant legislation in each province. The divided jurisdiction has allowed provinces to deal with employment and labour issues differently and has provided an opportunity for experimentation. In Chapter 8, we will discuss first-contract arbitration, a remedy that may be available if the parties are unable to negotiate a first collective agreement. It was first adopted in British Columbia in the mid-1970s. Since then, seven more jurisdictions have provided for this remedy in their labour relations legislation.

It has been observed that the Canadian parliamentary system and the presence of a social democratic party supporting labour have led to legislation being passed that is favourable to unions.[28] The Canadian Commonwealth Federation (CCF), a federal political party supporting labour, was established in 1932. The New Democratic Party, successor to the CCF, continues to support labour. In the United States, labour legislation is under the jurisdiction of the federal government, and labour reform legislation has been stalled in the Senate because it is unable to gain the support of a majority. In Canada, on the other hand, labour reforms favourable to unions have been enacted by minority governments under pressure from the NDP at the federal level and in some provinces. It has been noted that the provinces have distinct political cultures. Alberta is the most conservative province, and we will see later that labour relations legislation in that province is generally less favourable to unions. In some other provinces, the NDP has formed a government and enacted legislation more favourable to unions. Although the Canadian parliamentary system and the division of authority between the federal and provincial governments make it easier for reforms to be made, the process can work in reverse. That is, it is possible for a pro-business government to be elected in a province, leading to changes in labour policy that are less favourable to unions. The situation in Ontario in the 1990s illustrates this. In 1990, an NDP government was elected, and it initiated labour reforms favourable to unions, such as providing for the interim reinstatement of employees pending a hearing by the Labour Relations Board. But in the next election, in 1995, a Progressive Conservative government was elected that promptly reversed the previous reforms and made further changes unfavourable to unions, such as a mandatory vote in all applications for union representation.

LEGAL ENVIRONMENT

Employment standards legislation provides for minimum terms of employment.

The legal environment is critical to Canadian labour relations. **Employment standards legislation** mandates minimum terms of employment such as minimum vacations, holidays, and wages. These minimums provide a floor for the negotiation of collective agreements. Any contract terms relating to issues covered by employment standards legislation must provide at least the minimum rights provided in the legislation. If the contract does not refer to an issue covered by employment standards legislation, employees are entitled to the statutory minimum. For example, if the collective agreement did not mention pregnancy leave, employees would still be entitled to the leave provided in the employment standards legislation that covered the workplace. **Human rights legislation** prohibits discrimination and harassment and imposes a "duty to accommodate." We will see below that this duty may require unions and employers to make exceptions in the course of administration of a collective agreement. For example, they may have to agree to a variation on scheduling or overtime rules to meet their human rights obligations. The parties cannot agree on enforceable contract terms that violate human rights legislation. For example, if a union agreed to a contract that discriminated against women, the term is not binding—the union could later challenge the term that it had previously agreed to. **Labour relations legislation** regulates the relationship between the union, employees, and the employer. It dictates who can unionize, the process that must be followed to unionize, rules regarding the negotiation and administration of the collective agreement, and when there can be a strike or lockout. Again, the parties must comply with the relevant labour relations legislation. All labour relations statues provide that a collective agreement must have a term of at least one year. If the union and the employer purported to agree to a shorter agreement, the contract would be deemed to have a one-year term that complied with the legislation. It must be noted that it is not possible to contract out of employment standards, human rights, and labour relations legislation.

In addition to employment standards, human rights, and labour relations legislation, there are statutes that affect the parties in areas such as health and safety, employment equity, pay equity, and workers' compensation. The specific provisions of labour relations legislation and employment standards legislation are described as needed in subsequent chapters relating to collective bargaining rights (Chapter 6), negotiation of the agreement (Chapter 8), and the administration of the contract (Chapter 9). In this chapter, we will refer to human rights legislation that affects the parties and the *Canadian Charter of Rights and Freedoms*.

Human Rights Legislation

All jurisdictions have their own human rights legislation. This legislation and the *Canadian Charter of Rights and Freedoms* are the basis for the law relating to discrimination in each jurisdiction. Human rights law is shaped by the decisions of courts and arbitrators who interpret legislation and the *Charter*. A human rights commission is responsible for the enforcement of the legislation in all jurisdictions except British Columbia and Ontario. The Commission websites are good sources of information relating to human rights, and include guides relating to the application of the legislation. It is highly recommended that you use a preferred search engine to visit the site for your province.

Meaning of Discrimination   Federal and provincial human rights legislation in each jurisdiction in Canada sets out prohibited grounds of discrimination. While there are a number of prohibited grounds that apply to all of these jurisdictions, certain protections are not assured in every part of Canada. For example, discrimination on the basis of age, marital status, physical or mental disability, and sexual orientation are found in federal and human rights laws throughout Canada; demographic factors such as family status, pardoned convictions, and gender identity do not fall within protected grounds in several federal or provincial human rights codes.

An individual or group is discriminated against if they are treated differently on the basis of one of the grounds of discrimination. It is important to note that if an individual is treated differently or even unfairly, but the basis for the differential treatment is not one of the grounds of discrimination provided in the relevant human rights legislation, there has been no discrimination. For example, if an employer does not hire an applicant because the employer perceives that they do not "like" the applicant, and the employer's decision has not been influenced by one of the prohibited grounds of discrimination such as race, gender, or religion, there has been no discrimination. This is subject to the provisions of the *Charter*, which are discussed in this section. The *Charter* might protect an individual or group from differential treatment even if the basis for the treatment is not listed as one of the prohibited grounds of discrimination. The grounds of discrimination can change over time and across jurisdictions, and a detailed review of the grounds of discrimination is beyond the scope of this text. It is suggested that you use a preferred search engine to review the prohibited grounds of discrimination that apply in your jurisdiction(s). Many of the grounds of discrimination such as race are self-explanatory. However, a few require clarification.

Age. Until recently, human rights legislation in some provinces defined age by referring to an upper limit of age 64. When an employee turned 65, he or she lost the protection provided by the legislation relating to age. This was the legal basis for mandatory retirement. The upper limit on age has been removed in all provinces, and mandatory retirement has been eliminated for provincially regulated employers.

Disability. Disability includes both physical and mental impairments and is a significant ground of discrimination in employment. An impairment does not have to be permanent to be a disability. A broken arm or a short-term depression is included within the definition. The condition requires some severity; minor ailments such as a common cold or the flu are not disabilities. Disability includes dependence on alcohol, drugs, or other substances; height; AIDS; alcoholism; drug dependency; depression; fear of flying; dyslexia; and other conditions. It is important to note that if it is perceived that someone has an impairment, even though he or she may not actually have one, there is discrimination if different treatment is accorded the person because of this belief. For example, it would be discriminatory if an employer terminated an employee because it thought the employee was an alcoholic, even though that was not actually the case.

Family Status. Family status refers to being in a parent-and-child relationship. An evolving issue is whether an employee's child or elder care responsibilities could lead to discrimination claims. Is it discriminatory if an employer imposes a change in hours that conflicts with the employee's child care arrangements? The decisions on this issue have gone in two different directions. In the leading case, it was held that there would have to be a serious interference with a substantial parental obligation to establish discrimination—ordinary child care responsibilities would not lead to a finding of discrimination. For example, a claim of discrimination by a single father who could not work overtime because he had to pick up his son at daycare was dismissed. However, in a federal human rights complaint, the proposition that there has to be a serious interference with parental obligations to establish discrimination was rejected. This issue should be monitored for future developments.

Religion. Human rights tribunals and the courts have held that in order for employees to show that there is discrimination on the basis of religion, they only have to show that they have a sincerely held religious belief. The belief does not have to be a tenet of a recognized religion. In one case, an employee adhered to the Wiccan (witchcraft) faith that views Halloween as a holy day. It was held that the employee's beliefs were within the term *religion* as defined by human rights legislation.

Types or Forms of Discrimination Two forms of discrimination require clarification: **direct discrimination** and **indirect discrimination**. Direct discrimination refers to a rule or conduct that is discriminatory on its face; it is intentional. Refusing to promote someone because of their gender or because they were over age 45 would be direct discrimination. Indirect discrimination involves a rule or requirement that does not appear to discriminate; however, the requirement has an adverse impact on an individual or group protected by human rights legislation. It may be unintentional. A height requirement will have an adverse impact on women, and a rule prohibiting beards will have an adverse impact on Sikhs. The absence of malice, or the possible good intentions of the person who imposes

Direct discrimination refers to a rule or conduct that is intentionally discriminatory.

Indirect discrimination refers to a neutral rule that has an adverse impact on an individual because of prohibited grounds of discrimination; it may be unintentional.

the rule or requirement, does not matter. The issue is whether the requirement has an adverse impact. In a leading case, the requirement in question was that all employees were required to work on Saturdays. This rule does not appear to discriminate; it looks like all employees are treated equally. However, it has an adverse impact on members of a religion who have Saturday as a day of religious observance, and therefore it is discriminatory, even though there is no intention to discriminate. There is a possible way to defend against a claim of discrimination; however, in order to understand this defence we must first consider the "duty to accommodate."

Duty to Accommodate   Pursuant to human rights legislation, there is a **duty to accommodate** that requires measures to be adopted preventing people from being adversely affected by workplace requirements or characteristics on the basis of a prohibited ground of discrimination. Requirements or characteristics that might have an adverse impact include rules, work standards, the terms of a collective agreement, or the physical layout of the workplace. For example, a person in a wheelchair has a disability as defined by human rights legislation; prevention of an adverse effect involves accommodation such as installation of a wheelchair ramp or a special desk. It should be noted that the duty to accommodate arises when there is discrimination. If there is no discrimination, there is no duty to accommodate. Some seemingly routine workplace requirements may give rise to a duty to accommodate. Requiring all employees to start work at 7 a.m. could adversely affect pregnant employees with bouts of morning sickness. Here the duty to accommodate might involve a change in hours for such employees. Some measures that might be used in an accommodation are provided in Key Considerations 2-1.

> **The duty to accommodate** requires measures to allow the participation of individuals protected by human rights legislation.

Although the duty to accommodate commonly arises in connection with disability, it might arise in connection with other grounds of discrimination, including religion. There is a limit on the extent of this duty. Measures that would impose an undue hardship for those who would have to carry them out do not have to be undertaken. Determining the point of undue hardship is the critical issue. The factors to be considered are discussed below. A brief example will illustrate the nature of the issues involved. If an employer had a ground-floor office with an entrance that had two steps, the installation of a wheelchair ramp would not involve undue hardship. However, if an employer rented an office on the third floor of an older building that did not have an elevator, it would likely be an undue hardship to require the employer to install an elevator.

Although the primary obligation to accommodate lies with the employer, accommodation is a multi-party responsibility. Unions, other employees, and the employee seeking accommodation all have obligations. Unions and other employees do not have to undertake measures that would impose undue hardship.

Key Considerations 2-1

Possible Measures to Accommodate

1. Allowing a period of absence from work
2. Changes in timekeeping or attendance requirements
3. Changes in shifts or hours of work
4. Reduced hours
5. Modifications of job duties, such as removing some tasks or providing assistance
6. Changes in the design of the workplace, including equipment and tools
7. Training to facilitate a move to another job
8. Training of other employees to allow them to work with the employee
9. Transfer to an alternative job
10. Demotion to a lower job level
11. Transfer of the employee out of the bargaining unit

Factors Determining Undue Hardship. The law does not require an employer, union, or other employees to undertake, as part of an accommodation, measures that would cause them undue hardship. The law regarding what is undue hardship is still evolving. At one time, it was thought that the duty did not require employers to create a position for an employee. However, in some cases accommodation could now involve creating a job that did not previously exist. The factors considered in determining if this would involve an undue hardship have not been authoritatively established. Some human rights statutes refer to only three factors: cost, availability of outside sources of funding, and safety. Courts and arbitrators have referred to a broader list. A leading Supreme Court of Canada decision has indicated that the factors listed in Key Considerations 2-2 might be referred to in determining undue hardship.

Although the cost of accommodation is a factor, an employer attempting to establish cost as the basis of undue hardship must present real financial evidence, not just vague references to increased costs. Moreover, employers are expected to assume significant costs; to constitute undue hardship, the costs involved would have to threaten the viability of the organization. Thus, the size and financial health of the organization would be factors. A small organization or a firm that was in financial crisis might be able to establish undue hardship where other organizations could not. The size of the employer is also a factor, because larger employers have a larger pool of replacement workers. The interchangeability of the workforce and facilities relates to the flexibility in the operations of the employer. Where there are more employees who have the ability to do various jobs, it will be easier to accommodate through measures such as rescheduling, lighter workloads, or the modification of job duties.

The extent to which an accommodation poses a safety risk to the employee seeking accommodation or other employees is a factor. Although employers have an obligation to provide a safe workplace, they cannot rely on that obligation to avoid accommodation. In the course of accommodation, employers are expected to tolerate some risk in the workplace and allow the employee seeking accommodation to assume some risk as well. In one case, an applicant for a firefighter position was denied a job because of a heart condition that posed a very small risk of stroke. A human rights complaint was upheld, and the employer was ordered to hire the applicant. The extent to which a safety risk will be tolerated as part of an accommodation is not yet clear. It is possible that the provisions of a collective agreement such as seniority or scheduling might pose a problem when accommodating employees. The collective agreement might provide that employees be given a preference in shifts on the basis of seniority; however, an employee with less seniority might require a particular shift as part of an accommodation. The extent to which the provisions of the collective agreement may have to be varied in the course of accommodation is discussed in Chapter 9. It is noted that other measures that would not require a variation from a collective agreement must be exhausted before a variation can legally be contemplated. Although employee morale has been cited as a factor in a leading case, and appears on the list in Key Considerations 2-2, it has been given very little emphasis. Other employees are expected to bear some hardship in the course of an accommodation. The objections of employees would have to relate to real hardship such as job loss, or excessively

---

Key Considerations 2-2

Factors Determining Undue Hardship

1. Financial cost	**4.** Safety
2. Size of the employer's operations	**5.** Provisions of any collective agreement
3. Interchangeability of the workforce and facilities	**6.** Effect on employee morale

onerous duties, before they would be viewed as an undue hardship. An employer will not be allowed to claim that complaints from other employees impose an undue hardship unless the complaints are substantial and real. This means that employers should educate employees with regard to the duty to accommodate.

Defence: Bona Fide Occupational Qualification or Requirement When it appears that there is discrimination, there may be defence available to the employer. If it is established that the rule, practice, or policy in question is a **bona fide occupational qualification or requirement (BFOQ or BFOR)**, it is permissible even if it is discriminatory. Simply put, a BFOR is a rule or requirement that the employer can show is essential to the job and cannot be avoided. If an employer required that employees be at least 5 feet 10 inches tall for a job, this would be indirect discrimination because it has an adverse impact on women; however, it would be permissible if the employer could show it was essential. A Supreme Court of Canada decision in September 1999 (*British Columbia* [*Public Service Employee Relations Commission*] *v. BCGSEU*) laid out a revised approach to determining if a BFOR has been established. Note that prior decisions and commentary will have to be read subject to this case. The decision provided as follows:

An employer may justify the impugned standard by establishing on the balance of probabilities:

1. that the employer adopted the standard for a purpose rationally connected to the performance of the job;

2. that the employer adopted the particular standard in an honest and good-faith belief that it was necessary to the fulfillment of that legitimate work-related purpose; and

3. that the standard is reasonably necessary to the accomplishment of that legitimate work-related purpose. To show that the standard is reasonably necessary, it must be demonstrated that it is impossible to accommodate individual employees sharing the characteristics of the claimant without imposing undue hardship upon the employer.[29]

The principle that a rule or requirement is a BFOR only if the employee cannot be accommodated is illustrated by the following two scenarios. Situation 1: A large employer has a rule that employees must work on Saturdays. Situation 2: An employer establishes a rule that all drivers must have a valid licence. Both of these rules are discriminatory. In Situation 1, there might be indirect discrimination on the basis of religion; some individuals cannot work on Saturdays because of their religion. In Situation 2, there might be indirect discrimination on the basis of disability; some individuals may not have a licence because they do not have the eyesight required. In both situations, the rule could be a BFOR if it is established that the rule is essential and the employee cannot be accommodated. Assuming for the moment that the rule can be shown to be essential in both situations, the key question is: Can the employee be accommodated? It would appear that in Situation 1 the employee might be accommodated. Saturday work might be assigned to other employees; therefore, the rule cannot be a BFOR. In Situation 2, if there are no other jobs the person can be moved to, it does not appear that the person can be accommodated. It is not possible to avoid the eyesight requirement. Therefore, in Situation 2 the rule might be a BFOR.

Whenever the question of whether a BFOR has been established arises, the situation should be dealt with in two separate steps. First, consider whether the requirement is discriminatory; ask whether there is direct or indirect discrimination involved. Second, consider whether the employer can establish the requirement as a BFOR. The duty to accommodate might give rise to claims of reverse discrimination—that is, it may be claimed that accommodating some individuals is providing them with preferential treatment. This is an interesting issue that will not be referred to further, other than to point out that unions and employers may need to address the issue of a possible backlash from some employees who do not understand or agree with the accommodation process.

A **bona fide occupational qualification or requirement (BFOQ or BFOR)** is a job requirement that the employer can establish is essential, so that the requirement is allowed although it is discriminatory.

When Is a Discriminatory Requirement a BFOR?

Tawney Meiorin was a forest firefighter working for the province of British Columbia. She had been working for three years and had a good performance record when the province established new fitness tests for her job. Meiorin passed three of the four tests adopted by the employer. However, she failed to meet the final requirement that she be able to run two-and-a-half kilometres in 11 minutes—her best time was 11 minutes 49.4 seconds—and was dismissed. Meiorin's union filed a grievance challenging her dismissal. At the arbitration hearing, it was established that because of physiological differences women have a lower aerobic capacity than men. Although most men could meet the employer's requirements with training, most women would not be able to do so. The arbitrator found that the aerobic standard had a disproportionately negative effect on women and accordingly was discriminatory. Furthermore, the arbitrator found that the employer had not established that Meiorin's inability to

meet the standard constituted a safety risk to herself, her co-workers, or the public. The arbitrator ordered Meiorin to be reinstated.

The employer went to the British Columbia Court of Appeal, and an appeal was granted. Meiorin's case was appealed to the Supreme Court of Canada, which, in a groundbreaking decision, revised the law regarding discrimination and established a three-step test to determine if a rule or requirement was acceptable despite adverse impact. One of the requirements established by the Court was that the rule or standard must be necessary for the safe and efficient performance of the work. The employer in this particular case had failed to meet that requirement. The Court ordered that the arbitrator's decision reinstating Meiorin be restored.*

*British Columbia (Public Service Employee Relations Commission) v. B.C.G.S.E.U. 176 D.L.R. (4th) 1.

Website providing the *Canadian Charter of Rights and Freedoms*: http://www.pch.gc.ca/eng/1356631760121/1356631904950

The *Canadian Charter of Rights and Freedoms*

The *Canadian Charter of Rights and Freedoms* has been part of the Constitution since 1982. The law relating to the *Charter* is complex and evolving, so we will refer to essential points regarding the *Charter*'s effect on labour relations. The *Charter* guarantees specified rights and freedoms. The *Charter* rights that will be significant to labour relations are found in the *Charter*'s Section 2, which includes freedom of expression and association, and section 15, which provides for equality rights and prohibits discrimination as follows:

2. Everyone has the following fundamental freedoms:
    (a) freedom of conscience and religion;
    (b) freedom of thought, belief, opinion and expression, including freedom of the press and other media of communication;
    (c) freedom of peaceful assembly; and
    (d) freedom of association.

15. (1) Every individual is equal before and under the law and has the right to the equal protection and equal benefit of the law without discrimination and, in particular, without discrimination based on race, national or ethnic origin, colour, religion, sex, age, or mental or physical disability.

Application of the *Charter*   Section 32 of the *Charter* limits its application to legislation and government action. The *Charter* does not apply to private activity. This means that the *Charter* is relevant if legislation is being applied or if the government is involved as a party. In a situation where an employer sought an injunction to prevent picketing by a union, the union argued that an injunction would violate the freedom of expression provided in the *Charter*. The Supreme Court of Canada ruled that the *Charter* did not apply to this situation, because it was a private dispute between the employer and the union, and the *Charter* only applies to government action. The problem will be what "government" means. In one case, it was held that the *Charter* did not apply to a university even though it received government funding, because the university established policy independent of government. In contrast, community colleges have been held to be part of government and subject to the *Charter* because they are subject to government control.

Limitations on *Charter* Rights   Any provincial or federal legislation that violates a *Charter* right is invalid, subject to two limitations or exceptions. Section 1 of the *Charter* states that the rights it provides are "subject only to such reasonable limits prescribed by law as can be demonstrably justified in a free and democratic society." This means that a right provided in the *Charter* may be violated if it is established that it is essential to do so for the benefit of society. The classic illustration of this is that a law that prohibits shouting "Fire!" in a crowded theatre violates freedom of expression; however, it is recognized that this limit is necessary. When the Supreme Court of Canada considered legislation that allowed mandatory retirement, it found that although requiring individuals to retire at age 65 is discriminatory, there might be valid reasons for allowing the rule to stand. Mandatory retirement was viewed as creating opportunities for younger employees and as a way to deal with the potential problem of aging employees. The second limit on *Charter* rights is a "notwithstanding" clause provided in Section 33. The clause allows a government to pass a law that would violate the *Charter* if it expressly declares that the legislation is being passed despite the provisions of the *Charter*. The declaration that legislation operates notwithstanding the *Charter* expires after five years; however, it could be renewed. For example, although to this point it has been held that the right to strike is not protected by the *Charter*, a government could pass legislation ending a strike in any event by invoking the notwithstanding clause.

Implications of the *Charter*   The implications of the *Charter* are still evolving. As this is written, there are several cases in the legal system that could affect the law relating to the *Charter*. Some of the impacts of the *Charter* established to date will be reviewed.

Expansion of Human Rights Protection.   The previous section dealing with human rights noted that in order to find discrimination contrary to human rights legislation, it must be established that a prohibited grounds of discrimination is the basis of the differential treatment. It was noted that this was subject to the application of the *Charter*. In a few cases, the *Charter* has been used to expand the protection against discrimination provided in human rights legislation. For example, it has been successfully relied upon to extend benefits to same-sex couples. Prior to 1996, the *Canadian Human Rights Act* did not include sexual orientation as a prohibited ground of discrimination. A collective agreement at Bell Canada provided that the employer would not unlawfully discriminate. Bell Canada refused to provide benefits to same-sex couples. Although the *Canadian Human Rights Act* did not protect the employees, an arbitrator ruled that the legislation had to be applied in view of the *Charter*. The legislation that allowed discrimination on the basis of sexual orientation violated the *Charter*, and to remedy this sexual orientation was to be "read in" to the *Canadian Human Rights Act*. Accordingly, the employer's refusal to provide benefits to same-sex couples was deemed unlawful discrimination. In another important case, an individual in Alberta was terminated because of his sexual orientation. He could not bring a complaint under Alberta human rights legislation because at the time sexual orientation was not included as one of the prohibited grounds of discrimination. The employee challenged the dismissal, and the Supreme Court of Canada found that the failure to include protection against discrimination on the basis of sexual orientation was contrary to the *Charter* and ordered that the grounds of sexual orientation be read into the Alberta legislation.[30] These cases illustrates that the *Charter* has been used to expand the protection provided by human rights legislation.

Collective Bargaining.   In the first cases considering the *Charter*, known as the Labour Trilogy, the Supreme Court of Canada held that the freedom of association provided in Section 2(d) did not include collective bargaining. This meant that the *Charter* did not prevent governments from passing legislation that nullified previously negotiated collective agreements, or impose new collective agreement terms without consulting unions. In June 2007, in *Health Services and Support—Facilities Subsector Bargaining Association v. British Columbia*, the Supreme Court overruled some of its previous decisions and held that collective bargaining rights were protected by Section 2(d). Facing a crisis in health care in 2002, British Columbia passed the *Health and Social Services Delivery Improvement Act (Bill 29)*. The legislation made changes to the health system, including the nullification of previously negotiated collective agreements that provided employees protection against contracting out, layoffs, and bumping rights. The legislation was passed without any consultation with unions. This led to the layoff of hospital support staff who were subsequently hired by independent service providers and paid less money to do the same work they had previously been doing. The trial court and the British Columbia Court of Appeal rejected the union's claim that the legislation violated the *Charter* on the basis that the *Charter* did not protect collective bargaining. On a further appeal to the Supreme Court, the court reversed itself and held that the *Charter* protected collective bargaining when there was "substantial interference" by government. The court found that the provisions relating to contracting out, layoffs, and bumping rights did interfere substantially with the union's bargaining rights and were therefore unconstitutional, while minor parts of the legislation such as changes to schemes for transferring and reassigning employees did not. Having determined that there was a violation of a *Charter* right, the court then considered the issue of whether the infringement was justified by Section 1 of the *Charter* and found that it was not. The court held that provisions of the legislation that violated the *Charter* were unconstitutional and therefore invalid; however, it suspended its declaration for 12 months to allow the government to deal with the situation. The constitutional right to collective bargaining is a procedural one, guaranteeing employees the rights to present demands to government employers and engage in discussion. It does not guarantee that unions will be able to achieve their objectives. It protects against "substantial interference," and it remains to be seen how this will be interpreted in the future. The extension of *Charter* protection to collective bargaining is a dramatic development in the legal environment. In one case, the Ontario Labour Relations Board applied the *Health Services* case and held that sections of the Ontario *Labour Relations Act* were unconstitutional because they amounted to a substantial interference with the freedom of association.[31] The Ontario legislation provides for a system of province wide bargaining in the construction industry. When a construction union is certified to represent an employer's workers, the provincial agreement applies to those employees. The *Act* further provided that a "non-construction" employer such as a school board could apply to the Board to seek a declaration that a trade union no longer represents its employees and that the collective agreement ceased to apply to the non-construction employer. The Board held that the provisions of the *Act* that allowed an employer to obtain an order providing that the employer was no longer bound by a collective agreement with a construction union were unconstitutional. The *Health Services* case will be revisited in Chapter 11 when we consider the public sector.

The Right to Strike.   Unions have unsuccessfully challenged legislation that restricts or denies the right to strike. The Supreme Court of Canada has held that the freedom of association provided in the *Charter* does not include the right to strike.[32]

Union Dues.   In a case that is critical to unions, an employee claimed that legislation providing for the mandatory payment of union dues that were used to support causes—such as the New Democratic Party—that he did not support violated the *Charter*'s provision for freedom of association. The Supreme Court of Canada held in the *Lavigne* case that the mandatory deduction of union dues did not violate the freedom of association provisions in the *Charter*.[33] The court also indicated that even if a *Charter* right had been violated, this would have been a situation where Section 1 of the *Charter* would have been relied upon to allow the legislation to stand.

Right to Organize.   Some labour relations statutes prohibit specified workers from unionizing. For example, the Ontario *Labour Relations Act* prohibits agricultural workers from organizing. This legislation was challenged pursuant to the freedom of association provisions of the *Charter*. The Ontario government was ordered to enact legislation that allowed agricultural workers to organize.[34] It should be noted that the court did not order the province to extend full collective bargaining rights, including the right to strike, to agricultural workers. Ontario subsequently passed legislation that gave agricultural workers limited rights to organize and make representations to employers. A subsequent Charter challenge eventually saw the Supreme Court of Canada uphold the constitutionality of that Ontario legislation (*Ontario Attorney General v. Fraser*, 2011 SCC 20). Legislation that prohibited members of the RCMP from unionizing has been found to be a violation of the *Charter*.[35] The extent to which unions will be able to use the Charter to expand the right to organize is an issue that will continue to evolve.

Leafleting and Other Forms of Expression.   The freedom of expression provided in the *Charter* has labour relations implications. In the course of contract negotiations, employees at two Kmart stores in British Columbia were locked out. The union engaged in leafleting at Kmart stores other than the ones involved in the labour dispute. The leaflets informed customers about the dispute with Kmart and asked them to shop elsewhere. The union leafleting ran afoul of the British Columbia *Labour Relations Code*, which prohibited **secondary picketing**—picketing at a place other than the location of the labour dispute. The union challenged the ban on leafleting as a violation of the freedom of expression. The Supreme Court of Canada distinguished between leafleting and picketing, and said that the prohibition of leafleting was a violation of the *Charter*'s freedom of expression provisions.[36] This case illustrates that legislation that attempts to regulate union activity must not encroach upon the freedoms (such as freedom of expression) guaranteed by the *Charter*. The *Charter* has also been relied upon to protect freedom of expression during the term of a collective agreement. In 2001, negotiations were underway for the renewal of a provincial collective agreement covering public school teachers in British Columbia. The union representing the teachers, the British Columbia Teachers Federation (BCTF), announced that if no agreement was reached by the end of January 2002 it would strike. The provincial government headed off a strike just before the deadline by passing legislation that imposed a new collective agreement. The government also passed legislation that removed class size from the issues that the employer and the union could negotiate. As part of a campaign to pressure the government to change its policy, the union provided information kits to teachers that included cards referring to the increase in class size that could be distributed to parents during parent-teacher interviews. Subsequently, school boards issued directives to teachers stating that teachers were not to post certain material on teacher bulletin boards in areas in schools where students and their parents could see them, and parent–teacher interviews could not be used to discuss class size issues or to distribute certain documents produced by teachers or the BCTF relating to class size or collective bargaining issues. The union successfully challenged the employer's directive on the basis that it violated Section 2(b) of the *Charter*, which guarantees freedom of expression. In Chapter 6, we will see that labour relations legislation imposes restrictions on what employers are allowed to say to employees during the course of a union organizing campaign. It is possible that employers could argue that such restrictions violate the freedom of expression provided for in the *Charter*. In the event of such a challenge, the key issue will be whether any restrictions on the employer's freedom of expression can be justified pursuant to Section 1 of the *Charter*.

> **Secondary picketing** is picketing at a place other than the location of the labour dispute.

In summary, the first cases decided under the *Charter* did not change labour relations. Union attempts to rely on the freedom of association provisions in the *Charter* to challenge legislation restricting the right to strike and federal government wage controls were not successful. An employee challenge of mandatory deduction of union dues also failed.

However, subsequent cases have established that the *Charter* can affect labour relations by extending the protection against discrimination in human rights legislation, protecting freedom of expression, and perhaps extending the right to organize. The extension of *Charter* protection to collective bargaining, seen in the Supreme Court of Canada's 2007 *Health Services* decision is a significant development. Future developments relating to *Charter* cases dealing with the freedom of association must be monitored.

Implications for Practice

1. Several aspects of the environment will affect the desire and ability of employees to join unions. The economic environment will affect the employees' perceived need for a union. The social environment will affect employees' views regarding whether unionization will be beneficial, and will affect the employer's response to unionization. The political and legal environment may make it more or less difficult for employees to join a union.

2. Employers and unions must consider the economic environment when negotiating collective agreements. Economic developments may force unions and employers to modify their relationship from an adversarial contest of wills to a more cooperative relationship.

3. Environmental factors will affect the parties' negotiating objectives and the content of collective agreements. As much as possible, the parties should forecast future environmental developments, such as technological change, so that collective agreements will adequately protect their respective interests.

4. Unions and employers must keep up with legal developments that affect labour relations. In particular, they must be aware of and educate their constituents about the *Charter*, human rights legislation and the duty to accommodate.

Key Terms

bona fide occupational qualification or requirement (BFOQ or BFOR), p. 33

deindustrialization, p. 24

deregulation, p. 25

direct discrimination, p. 30

diversity, p. 23

downsizing, p. 24

duty to accommodate, p. 31

elastic demand, p. 21

employment standards legislation, p. 28

federally regulated employers, p. 27

fiscal policy, p. 19

globalization, p. 23

human rights legislation, p. 29

indirect discrimination, p. 30

inelastic demand, p. 21

labour relations legislation, p. 29

legacy costs, p. 25

macroeconomic environment, p. 18

monetary policy, p. 19

nominal wages, p. 18

non-standard work, p. 23

price elasticity of demand, p. 21

provincially regulated employers, p. 27

real wages, p. 18

secondary picketing, p. 37

trade liberalization, p. 24

Review Questions

1. Discuss two ways in which the macroeconomic environment affects unions and employers.
2. How does the dependence of the Canadian economy on exports affect labour relations?
3. Distinguish between a good or service with an elastic demand and one with an inelastic demand.
4. Explain how possible bargaining priorities may differ for the following employee groups: younger employees, older employees, and female employees.

5. Outline important features of the labour market that could affect labour relations.

6. Why has it been more difficult for unions to organize part-time employees?

7. Describe five economic trends or issues that might affect labour relations.

8. What are the implications of NAFTA for unions and employers?

9. Explain how government economic policy might affect unions and employers.

10. Discuss a current example of technological innovation that unions and employers must resolve.

11. What is the "social environment," and why is it important to labour relations?

12. Provide relevant examples that distinguish among labour relations legislation, human rights codes, and employment standards laws in Canada.

13. What do the phrases "federally regulated employer" and "provincially regulated employer" mean, and why is the distinction important?

14. Distinguish between direct and indirect discrimination in terms of human rights, and provide an example of each that may occur in a unionized work setting.

15. Explain and provide an example of the concept of a bona fide occupational requirement (BFOR).

16. Explain what "the duty to accommodate" means, and provide an example of an employer meeting this duty.

17. Identify a labour relations issue that has been or might be affected by the *Charter of Rights and Freedoms*.

Discussion Questions

1. As a union official would you prefer that the product the employer produces have an elastic or an inelastic demand? Explain.

2. Explain a difference between the work preferences of younger (age 20–30) and older (age 55–65) employees.

3. To what degree does information technology poses a threat to unions? Explain.

4. Do you think that your family and friends have a generally positive or negative view of unions? What is the basis for your opinion?

5. A collective agreement confirmed that there would be no discrimination and the union and the employer would comply with human rights legislation. Some employees covered by the collective agreement were provided with paid parking on a random basis and others were not. The cost of parking at the workplace or nearby was $50 per month. A group of employees who were not provided with parking, all of whom were women, filed a grievance alleging that the employer had discriminated against them. If you were a labour relations officer for the employer, how would you respond to this grievance?

6. A collective agreement provided that if an employee was away from work because of a physical disability the employer would continue to pay his or her salary for one year, and if the employee was away from work because of a mental disability the employer would continue his or her salary for six months. Are there any problems with this agreement?

7. Hodges worked as a child and youth support worker for an association that operated a shelter for women and children. At one time, Hodges worked from 8 a.m. to 2:30 p.m. Hodges' son required special attention because he had a major psychiatric disorder, and this work schedule allowed her to care for him after school. More children were at the shelter after school; and in order to service them, the employer changed Hodges' hours of work, requiring her to start at 11:30 a.m. and work until 6 p.m. This meant that she could no longer care for her son. Is there any basis on which the union can challenge the employer's change in work hours? What is the legal obligation of the employer, and what outcome would you expect in this situation?

8. A collective agreement provided that if employees were unable to carry out their regular duties because of illness or injury, they were given access to a rehabilitation committee. The committee searched for alternative employment for the employees for a six-month period. When an employee with a disability was granted access to the committee, the union filed a grievance alleging that the collective agreement provision regarding the six-month limitation on the committee's assistance contravened the employer's duty to accommodate. The union claimed that because the employer had a duty to accommodate, there could not be a six-month limit imposed. Does the employer have a duty to accommodate? Explain the outcome you expect in this situation.

9. How may certain specific measures to accommodate be an undue hardship for one employer and not for another? Explain.

10. The environment, both external to the work setting and within it, affects many aspects of labour relations, including the items referred to below. For each of the items listed, consider what factors discussed in this chapter could be an influence and what their impact could be.
    (a) willingness or desire of employees to join a union
    (b) overall rate of union membership
    (c) ability or opportunity of employees to join a union
    (d) attitude or approach of employer to a union
    (e) demands made by unions and employers in negotiations
    (f) bargaining power of the union and the employer
    (g) likelihood of a strike or lockout
    (h) content of the collective agreement

Web Research

1. Visit the website for the Canadian Human Rights Commission or for the human rights commission in your province. Most sites have a publications area where you can obtain a guide to the legislation, information on how to file a complaint, and relevant policy statements. Find and briefly explain any policy statement on alcohol and drug testing and explain the employer's obligations related to the duty to accommodate.

2. Locate the website for a national or provincial union in Canada and look for an initiative this union is taking regarding female, ethnic minorities or aging members. Discuss why such an initiative is in the union's interests.

CASE INCIDENT   SAFE PASSAGE TOLL

Armand, Bob, and Courtney worked as customer service representatives at a company that managed a toll road. Employees at the company are represented by a union. All three employees worked at the front counter, and their duties included issuing transponders, receiving payments, receiving faxes to provide service to customers, and assisting in the company's call center when call volumes were high. In order to do their jobs, the customer service representatives on the front counter were required to go to a fax machine in another area of the building and also to escort customers to other areas of the complex several times a day. Security was a concern at the company because of expensive equipment on the premises, client information that was held, and possible hostile customers. The company had a security system in place that required employees to use a swipe card and enter a password to gain entry at various points in the building. The company encountered problems with the misuse and loss of swipe cards. The employer proposed a new biometric scanning system that relied upon the measurement of the right hand when it was placed on a screen.

The system would also work with employees swiping a card and entering a password instead of a hand measurement; however, the employer wanted to incorporate the hand scanning as part of the system to facilitate its attendance management program. Scanning devices would be placed at numerous locations in the complex to control and monitor access to various departments. Eight employees who were members of the Pentecostal faith objected to the proposed scanning system because of their religious beliefs. Although the Pentecostal church is not specifically opposed to biometric scanning, the employees felt that the system was counter to their religious beliefs because it would impose "the mark of the beast" upon them as prophesied in the Book of Revelation. The religious objection related to using measurements of portions of the body for the purposes of identification where such measurements have a number associated with them, the number becomes part of a system of numbers, and that system is involved in the ability to earn a living. The concerns are heightened for some individuals when the measurements are derived from the right hand. When the employees objected to the new system, the employer proposed that they use their left hands and also proposed the employees be allowed to wear a glove over their hand. (The system relied upon a hand measurement, not fingerprints.) Five employees were satisfied with the changes proposed by the employer and dropped their objection to the scanning devices. When Armand, Bob, and Courtney continued to refuse to use the new system, the employer proceeded to apply its progressive discipline policy. The employer did not meet with the union or the employees other than through the disciplinary process. The employees were given warnings, formal letters, and subsequently terminated when they refused to take part in the new system.

Questions

1. Is there any discrimination in this situation? If so, what type of discrimination is involved?
2. What is the obligation of the employer?
3. If this case proceeded to a hearing, explain the outcome you expect.

CASE INCIDENT   DYER'S BAY SCHOOL BOARD

The Dyer's Bay school board employs 90 cleaners. The cleaners are responsible for school classrooms, hallways, offices, and some exterior maintenance work, such as snow shovelling. The cleaners' job duties include lifting 22-kilogram pails that contain five gallons of cleaner and to stack them three pails high in the supply room. The job also includes lifting 21-kilogram boxes of paper, which are stacked five boxes high. It was estimated that the lifting was an occasional demand that accounted for about 13 percent of each shift. The school board established a job specification that cleaners must be able to lift 23 kilograms from floor to shoulder height. The board established a lifting test to determine if candidates could meet the required standard. Three individuals—Sharon, Lucy, and Colleen—were offered jobs as cleaners. The employment offers were conditional upon the candidates passing a physical-demands assessment, which included the lifting test. When it was established that the three candidates could not pass the test because they were only able to lift 16 kilograms, their offers of employment were withdrawn. The union representing the cleaners filed a grievance challenging the 23-kilogram lifting job qualification. At a grievance meeting, it was established that 9 of 68 women and 2 of 245 men who had previously taken the test had failed. It was also found that four of the nine women who initially failed the test passed after being provided training and an opportunity to retake the test. At the arbitration hearing, the union provided evidence establishing that some cleaners took bundles of paper out of the boxes in the stacking process. Also, the cleaning supplies could be ordered in cases containing 4 one-gallon containers, which weighed 4.5 kilograms each. Buying the cleaning supplies in the smaller containers increased the cost by 10 percent. The employer argued that the 23-kilogram lifting requirement was a safety issue, and it was the same for all candidates. The employer provided evidence that it was in financial difficulty and had to cut costs wherever possible.

Questions

1. Is there discrimination in this situation?
2. Assume that you are the decision maker in this situation. Outline what your decision would be and provide reasons for your decision.

Chapter 3

Unions: Objectives, Processes, Structure, and History

Chapter Objectives

1. Outline the nature and extent of unionization
2. Describe the structure of the labour movement
3. Explain the functions of union bodies
4. Describe the nature and significance of present-day union membership
5. Outline the development of unions and the implications of union history for labour relations

---

Required Professional Capabilities (CCHRA)	HRPA Human Resources Professionals Competency Framework
50106, 50108, 50112, 50115, 50402	**C010, C028, C117, C125**

Unifor is Canada's largest private sector union, formed in August 2013 as a result of a merger between the Canadian Auto Workers (CAW) and Communications, Energy and Paperworkers Union of Canada (CEP). It has more than 300 000 members across the country, working in every major sector of the Canadian economy.

Unifor's 77-page constitution outlines its objectives and provides guidelines for the operation of its national, regional, and industry councils. The constitution also details the purpose and operations of over 750 union locals that span the country, from coast to coast to coast, or are firmly established in single-industry communities. Unifor affords each member the opportunity to participate in democratic structures within the union, where every member has an equal vote at membership meetings and in local union elections.

Like most major unions in Canada, Unifor addresses workplace issues such as organizing and representing employees, negotiating collective agreements with employers and protecting the rights of their members on the job. It also uses its website to raise awareness on key political, social, and environmental issues important not only to their members but also to the local and wider communities. A visit to the site (**www.unifor.org**) reveals many topics relevant to those living in its four administrative regions (Western, Atlantic, Ontario, and Quebec). There is also a section that illustrates Unifor's expertise in such areas as health and safety, human rights, political mobilization, research, education, and services of interest to women and pensioners.

The website has a page titled "Briefs and Statements," whose topics might include celebrating Nurses' Week, an open letter to a provincial political leader, or an article about Unifor's collaboration with the Canadian Labour Congress and the University of Western Ontario to launch the first nationwide survey on the impact of domestic violence affecting workers and workplaces.

Unions are key actors in the labour relations system. This chapter considers the extent of unionization, union structure, the functions of various union bodies, and the development of unions and labour relations. A **union** or trade union is an organization of employees that has the primary objective of improving the compensation and working conditions of the employees it represents. These organizations have four main objectives:

- Improving terms and conditions of work for their members
- Protecting employees against arbitrary management actions
- Providing a process for conflict resolution and employee input
- Pursuing economic and social change

Unionization is based on the principle that individual employees have little or no power when dealing with their employer, but as a group they can increase their power and improve their terms of employment.

UNIONS IN CANADA

There are 4.6 million union members in Canada. In this section, the extent of unionization and the characteristics of union members will be explored.

Extent of Unionization

Union density is the percentage of nonagricultural workers who are union members. It indicates the percentage of potential union members who have actually joined a union. As of January 2012, 4,663,736 workers were covered by collective agreements, an increase of 37,595 from January 2011. This corresponds to a coverage rate (covered workers as a percentage of nonagricultural paid workers) of 29.9 percent, slightly below last year's rate of 30.2 percent. This is the first time since 1965 that union coverage has fallen below 30 percent, based on Labour Program records. The coverage rate is slightly lower than Statistics Canada's 31.6 percent.[1] Union density is not the same as the percentage of employees covered by a collective agreement. There are situations where more workers are covered by a collective agreement, because some employees covered by a collective agreement do not become union members. Although in some situations employees are required to become union members, this is not always the case.

Union density can be determined for an entire country, a province, or a sector of the economy such as manufacturing. Figure 3-1 shows union membership and density information for the period 1996–2012.

Union density varies significantly across industries and provinces. It is highest in Newfoundland and Labrador, and lowest in Alberta. Figure 3-2 shows provincial union density rates as of 2012.

As can be seen in Figure 3-3, union density is high in utilities, public administration, education, and health care, and low in banking/finance and accommodation/food. The numbers indicate there is room for growth in some sectors.

Union Density: Canada vs. the United States   Although Canadian union membership has continued to grow, union density has been slowly declining since 1984 because nonagricultural paid employment is increasing faster than unions are recruiting new members. In some countries, notably the United States, the decline in union density has been drastic in recent years. In 1960, in both Canada and the United States, total union density was approximately 30 percent. Now in both the public and private sectors, union density is significantly higher in Canada. Now in both the public and private sectors, union density is higher in Canada than in the US. In the United States, total union density was 11.3 percent in 2013. The number of U.S. wage and salary workers belonging to unions was 14.5 million.

		As a Percentage Of:	
Year	**Workers (000s)**	**Labour Force**	**Nonagricultural Paid Workers**
1996	4,033	27.5	34.4
1997	4,074	27.4	34.6
1998	3,938	26.1	32.9
1999	4,010	26.2	32.8
2000	4,058	26.0	32.2
2001	4,111	26.0	31.6
2002	4,174	25.9	31.4
2003	4,178	25.2	30.7
2004	4,261	25.1	30.5
2005	4,381	25.5	30.8
2006	4,441	25.7	30.8
2007	4,480	25.6	30.5
2008	4,592	25.7	30.5
2009	4,605	25.3	30.0
2010	4,645	25.3	30.9
2011	4,626	25.0	30.2
2012	4,664	24.9	29.9

Figure 3-1 Union Membership and Density in Canada, 1996–2012

Source: Based on Statistics Canada, Labour Force Survey, Labour Statistics Division, CANSIM Tables 282-0002 and 282-0011, http://www.labour.gc.ca/eng/resources/info/publications/union_coverage/unionmembership.pdf.

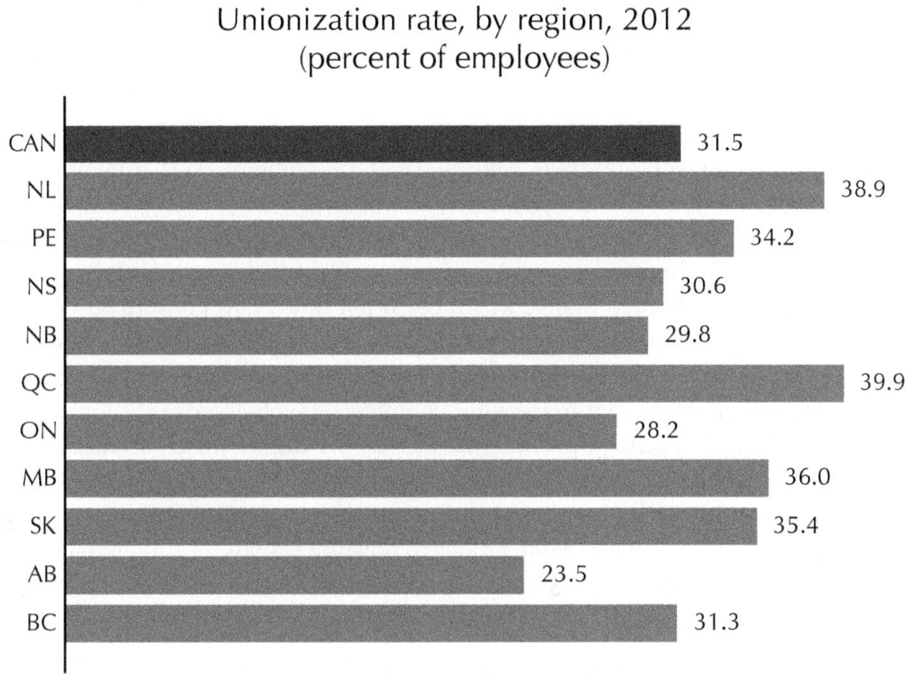
Unionization rate, by region, 2012
(percent of employees)
CAN 31.5
NL 38.9
PE 34.2
NS 30.6
NB 29.8
QC 39.9
ON 28.2
MB 36.0
SK 35.4
AB 23.5
BC 31.3

Figure 3-2 Unionization Rate by Region, 2012 (percent of employees)

Source: Based on HRSDC calculations based of Statistics Canada, "Work—Unionization Rates, by Region, 2012," Table 282-0078, Labour Force Survey Estimates (LFS), Employees by Union Coverage, North American Industry Classification System (NAICS), Sex and Age Group, Annual (Persons), CANSIM database, http://www4.hrsdc.gc.ca/.3ndic.1t.4r@-eng.jsp?iid=17.

Industry	Union Density (%)	
	1999	2012
Goods-Producing		
Utilities	67.8	62.5
Construction	30.2	31.5
Manufacturing	31.2	24.4
Natural resources	26.9	21.8
Agriculture	3.9	3.6
Total Goods-Producing	**31.3**	**27.0**
Service-Producing		
Education	69.3	68.0
Public administration	65.3	67.5
Health care and social assistance	53.0	53.6
Transportation and warehousing	42.7	40.5
Information cultural and recreation	27.6	25.0
Management, administration and support	10.5	15.3
Trade	12.6	12.8
Other	8.7	8.9
Finance, insurance, real estate, and leasing	7.9	8.9
Accommodation and food	6.6	6.7
Professional, scientific, and technical	4.1	4.4
Total Service-Producing	**30.1**	**30.7**

Figure 3-3 Union Density: Rank by Industry, 2009 and 2012

Source: Adapted from Statistics Canada, "Long-Term Trends in Unionization," by Diane Galarneau and Thao Sohn (November 2013). Also available at Statistics Canada, http://www.statcan.gc.ca/pub/75-006-x/2013001/article/11878-eng.pdf.

In 1983, the first year for which comparable union data are available, the union membership rate was 20.1 percent, and there were 17.7 million union workers. American public sector workers had a union membership rate (35.3 percent), more than five times higher than that of private sector workers (6.7 percent).[2] A weaker union movement in the United States could be significant for unions and employers in Canada. It might lead to lower compensation levels in the United States, which could put downward pressure on compensation in Canada. The presence of non-union regions in the United States may induce Canadian employers to relocate to avoid unions. Will the Canadian labour movement be able to avoid a decline similar to that in the United States? One observer in the United States has put forward a convergence thesis that holds that the decline in union density in the United States is based on market forces that will inevitably lead to the same decline in Canada.[3] Canadian studies have questioned the convergence thesis, suggesting that factors such as the superior ability of Canadian unions to organize employees and more favourable political and legal environments in Canada do not make a decline in Canadian union density inevitable.[4]

Political Environment.   Some observers have noted that unions in Canada have benefited from a different political environment than that of the United States. Canada has had a social democratic party, which has promoted labour's interests in provincial legislatures and Parliament, since 1932. Although the New Democratic Party (NDP) has not formed a government at the federal level, it has been able to influence legislation, especially when it has held the balance of power in a minority government. Legislation granting collective bargaining rights to federal public sector employees was enacted by a minority government supported by the NDP. At the provincial level, the NDP has formed governments that have passed legislation favourable to unions, including provisions that made certification of unions easier. The different political environment is one of the reasons why the legal environment is more favourable to unions in Canada.

Legal Environment.   Canadian legislation provides for a certification process that is more favourable to unions. In the United States, representation votes are required for certification under the *National Labor Relations Act*. Reports from the National Labor Relations Board indicate that unions in the United States have recently been winning 65 percent of representation votes.[5] The certification process in Canada is considered in Chapter 6. In several Canadian jurisdictions, a union can be certified without a vote on the basis of signed membership cards. This is favourable to unions, because it reduces the employer's opportunity to campaign against the union or intimidate employees. In Canadian jurisdictions that require a vote as part of the certification process, the vote is held shortly after the application for certification is filed. In the United States, there is a longer delay between the application for certification and the vote, which allows the employer to campaign against the union or intimidate employees.

Union security provisions, discussed further in Chapter 7, are more favourable to unions in Canada. In most jurisdictions, the law allows for union dues to be deducted from the pay of all bargaining unit employees at the request of the union and also provides for compulsory union membership in a collective agreement. In the United States, there are 24 states that have **right-to-work legislation** prohibiting the compulsory deduction of union dues. The more favourable union security provisions in Canada may assist unions by providing a secure financial base and by eliminating the contentious issue of the deduction of dues from the negotiation of first collective agreements. Labour relations legislation is more quickly and strictly enforced in Canada than the United States, and this poses a deterrent to employers who might consider prohibited conduct to oppose a union.[6] In Canada, legislation granting bargaining rights to public sector employees is more favourable to unions than in the United States. The right to strike has also been less restricted in this country, and there are fewer limits on the issues that can be the subject of negotiations. This difference may make unionization more attractive to Canadian public sector employees.

Right-to-work legislation in certain states of the United States prohibits the compulsory deduction of union dues.

Union Organizing Efforts.   Canadian unions have made greater efforts to organize workers than U.S. unions. In some years in the 1990s, Canadian unions organized as many new members as American unions, despite the population difference.

Employer Opposition.   There is evidence that employers in the United States actively oppose unionization more than Canadian employers. A former chair of the National Labor Relations Board in the United States has stated, "The American legal system has clearly permitted employers to vigorously oppose unions, and they have done this with devastating effects upon the labor movement."[7] Although political, legal, and other factors may have allowed unions in Canada to maintain a higher union density than the United States to date, some observers are pessimistic about the future.[8]

Characteristics of Union Members

Employment Status, Full vs. Part Time.   Union density for part-time Canadian employees is 23.3 percent.[9] The organization of part-time employees continues to be a challenge for unions. Many part-time workers are employed in the private service sector, where unions have had difficulty organizing in the past. The use of part-time employees has been a source of conflict between unions and employers. Unions have sought to establish or continue contract provisions that restrict the use of non-union part-time employees.

Increase in Female Membership.   Female union membership relative to male membership has been rising. In 1977 only 12 percent of union members were female. Since 2006 female union membership density has surpassed male membership.[10] This increase in female union membership has practical significance for both unions and employers. Unions have found that they must deal with the issue of female representation in union positions. The presence of female bargaining unit members has led to unions dealing with issues, such as child care, sexual harassment, flexible hours, and pay equity.

Age.   The union density rate for youth (persons between 15 and 24) was only 16 percent in 2012.[11] One study has found that this is not because younger workers desire a union less than older employees; it is bcause they have less opportunity to unionize.[12]

Education.   Union members may have higher levels of education than is commonly perceived. More than 35 percent of union members have a postsecondary certificate or diploma, and 35 percent have a university degree.[13]

Types of Unions

Craft unions organize members of a trade or occupation.

Industrial unions organize workers in different occupations in a firm.

Historically a distinction has been drawn between **craft unions** and **industrial unions**. A craft union limits its membership to a particular trade or occupation such as electricians or airline pilots. The International Brotherhood of Electrical Workers is an example. Such unions have been referred to as *horizontal unions*, because they organize employees across different firms. An industrial union, on the other hand, organizes different types of workers in a company, including skilled and unskilled workers. Unifor is an example of an industrial union.

The distinction between craft and industrial unions is not as important as it was in the early years of the labour movement. Then, it was one of the factors dividing the movement: craft unions, the first to develop, did not support the development of industrial unions. However, in recent times, some craft unions have organized industrial workers, and industrial unions have organized skilled employees.

In the past, there has also been a distinction between public sector and private sector unions. This distinction, too, is breaking down, as public sector unions are organizing employees in the private sector and vice versa. The Canadian Union of Public Employees (CUPE) has organized employees in the airline industry, Unifor has organized employees in the federal public service, and the United Steelworkers Union (USW) has organized taxi drivers and grocery store employees. In short, the name of a union no longer indicates the type of employees represented. It is possible that several unions could organize workers in the same industry. For example, Unifor, CUPE, and other unions have organized workers in casinos.

UNION OBJECTIVES AND PROCESSES

The framework outlined in Chapter 1 provides that union objectives and processes are a key part of labour relations. Processes refer to union activities and methods, such as contract negotiation, which are used to achieve union objectives. This section broadly outlines the objectives and activities of unions; subsequent chapters will elaborate on activities such as contract negotiation. There is significant variation in the extent to which unions pursue the objectives outlined here. For example, some unions do not engage in political activity. John Godard has written about union roles and objectives; and although this section uses different terminology, the objectives referred to here are based upon his analysis.[14] Union objectives and activities are summarized in Figure 3-4.

Objectives	Processes or Methods
1. Improving terms and conditions of work	1. Organizing employees
2. Protecting against arbitrary management action	2. Contract negotiation
3. Providing conflict resolution and employee input	3. Strikes and boycotts
4. Pursuing social and economic change	4. Grievances and arbitration
	5. Court (legal) action
	6. Political activity
	7. Public relations
	8. Union–management collaboration
	9. Other unilateral action

Figure 3-4 Union Objectives and Processes

Improving Terms and Conditions of Work

Unions seek to improve wages, benefits, and other terms of work for employees they represent. Although this is largely an economic role, this objective also includes noneconomic issues such as health and safety, work hours, and job security. Some of the improvements in working terms that unions are able to achieve will be adopted in the non-union sector. Although organizing employees, contract negotiations, strikes and walkouts, and the grievance and arbitration process are the most familiar methods unions use to improve terms or conditions of work, the remainder of the methods listed in Figure 3-4 could be utilized. The *Meiorin* case referred to in Chapter 2 illustrates how a union can use the courts to appeal an arbitration decision and obtain the reinstatement of an employee. Political activity could also include lobbying for changes in legislation that will facilitate the organization of employees. For example, the United Food and Commercial Workers union (UFCW) has lobbied to change legislation that prohibits agricultural workers from organizing in some provinces. Political activity could also include working to elect a government that will enact legislation that could help a union negotiate more favourable terms of employment, such as a ban on replacement workers during a strike. Some public relations efforts are aimed at convincing the public to support unions when they are engaged in negotiations with employers. This is especially significant in the public sector where unions have used full-page newspaper ads and television commercials to try to obtain public support. However, this is an area where a mistake could cause a public relations problem. Unions participate with employers in joint committees like health and wellness that will benefit employees. Some unions engage in unilateral action, such as providing training relating to harassment, which will improve the employee's terms and conditions of work.

Protecting Employees Against Arbitrary Management Action

Godard has referred to a workplace democratization role for unions. Unions can protect employees from arbitrary management decisions through terms that are negotiated in the collective agreement. We will later see collective agreements providing that employees cannot be disciplined unless management provides reasons for the discipline. The grievance and arbitration process, which is elaborated upon in Chapter 9, can be used to challenge rules established by management. A union may be able to protect freedom of speech through the collective agreement and the grievance process. In one case, a hospital employer attempted to prohibit the posting of a legal opinion relating to the issue of mandatory vaccinations. The union successfully challenged the employer directive.[15]

Providing a Process for Conflict Resolution and Employee Input

By providing a process for the resolution of conflict and employee input, unions may assist employers and increase productivity. Briefly, unions provide a voice to employees that provide an alternative to exiting or quitting. Unions can play a problem-solving role with employers, which may increase efficiency. The grievance and arbitration process and union–management committees are the key methods used here.

Pursuing Economic and Social Change

Unions also have objectives for society as a whole outside of the workplace. The United Food and Commercial Workers (UFCW) union developed a national campaign to make child care services a priority for government. The union seeks to build a strong and effective grassroots movement to elect a family-friendly federal government in 2015 that is committed to a national day care program. The union's website (**www.ufcw.ca**) provides a range of resources to its members along with other community groups to support this campaign for social change.

To understand unions, it is necessary to know about their components or structure, the functions of various union bodies, and key developments in the history of unions. We will first look at the present-day structure and functions of unions, and then look back to see how they got to where they are today.

UNION STRUCTURE AND FUNCTIONS

In all unions the *local* is the key unit of organization.

Union Local

A **union local** is an administrative unit of an international, national or provincial parent union.

The **union local**, or simply the *local*, is the fundamental unit of union structure. A local is an organization that has its own officers, constitution, and bylaws. All union members belong to a local, and most locals in turn belong to a parent national or international union. There are over 14 000 locals in Canada. Figure 3-5 illustrates the structure of the Canadian labour movement.

Organization and Governance   Many locals have a membership consisting of those who work for an employer in a municipality. Others have members who work for different employers in a municipality. The latter may be referred to as *amalgamated* or *composite* locals; an example is a local of Unifor (formerly the CAW) in Oshawa, Ontario that represents 21 000 at 27 different employers in the greater Durham Region. In some unions, large locals are organized on a province-wide basis. Many locals in the UFCW cover an entire province.

An employer might deal with one or more locals that belong to one or more unions. In the simplest case, an employer might deal with one local of a union. An example would be the production workers in an auto parts plant who are represented by a local of Unifor. A college could have employees that belong to two locals of the same union, one for faculty and one for support staff. Each local would have its own collective agreement with the employer. In a more complex situation, an employer might deal with several locals, each of which belongs to a different union. For example, a hospital might deal with several locals belonging to different unions who represent nursing staff, clerical staff, maintenance employees, and kitchen staff.

Union local members will elect the officers, usually a president, secretary, treasurer, and stewards. Some locals may have executive members holding various titles such as chairpersons or committee persons. In larger locals, some officers may hold their union positions full-time, but in many locals the officers serve on a part-time basis. Larger locals may also have paid administrative staff.

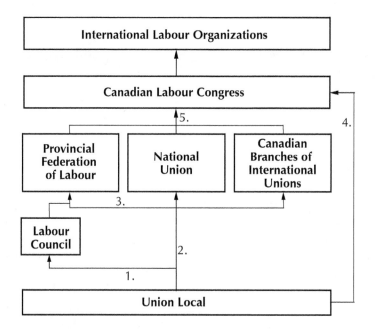

Figure 3-5 Structure of the Canadian Labour Movement

1. A local union may belong to a Labour Council for a municipality or region.
2. Most locals belong to a parent national or international union; a few are independent local unions.
3. Most locals are affiliated with a provincial federation of labour.
4. A small number of local unions are directly chartered by a labour congress.
5. Most national and international unions are affiliated with a labour congress. The CLC is the largest labour congress.

A local has its own bylaws and constitution; however, these must comply with any constitutional provisions of the national, provincial, or international union the local belongs to. The bylaws set out matters relating to the governance of the local, including officers, duties of officers, and regulations regarding meetings. The executive of the local usually has the authority to deal with day-to-day issues. Some matters will be dealt with at general membership meetings. The authority of the executive and the matters that must be referred to the general membership will vary between locals. Some unions require a general membership meeting to be held within specified times, while others allow for general membership meetings to be held when needed.

Some unions, especially craft unions, may make use of a **business agent**—a paid staff person who works for one or more locals handling grievances, assisting with negotiations, and providing other services. Most locals make extensive use of committees. The website for a local will typically indicate that the local has committees for health and safety, education, environmental issues, community affairs, social events, and other matters. Locals obtain the funds required to carry on operations from union dues. Dues are a specified percentage of an employee's earnings, typically 1 to 2 percent, or, less commonly, a flat amount. Unions prefer to base dues on a percentage of earnings so that they can avoid having to go to the membership to have dues increased as earnings rise. A portion of the dues will be remitted to the parent union a local belongs to. A percentage of dues may be allocated to specific areas, such as a strike fund.

Functions of the Local   The local might be involved with one or more of the functions listed in Key Considerations 3-1, depending on its size, the parent union, and the industry.

Most locals have a key role to play in contract negotiation with the employer, which is frequently done at the local level. The details of this activity, including how a local prepares for negotiations, are considered in Chapter 8. Although there is some variation between unions, the local usually plays a key role in the administration of the collective

Website for the largest local union in Canada, UFCW Locals 175 and 633: www.ufcw175.com

A **business agent** is a staff person who works for one or more locals providing expertise and support.

Functions of a Local Union

1. Negotiation of collective agreements
2. Administration of the collective agreement
3. Collection and processing of union dues
4. Education of members

5. Community service
6. Political action
7. Operation of a hiring hall
8. Organizing workers

agreement. If an employee thinks the collective agreement has been violated, he or she contacts a local union officer to file a grievance.

Locals may also become involved with the education of their members, often with the assistance of a national or international union. For example, a local could provide training relating to the filing of grievances. Some locals engage in charitable work such as the United Way campaign or other community affairs. Some locals get involved in political issues. Although national unions and other union bodies described below deal with political questions at the provincial and national level, a large local may also get involved in broader political issues.

The employer should note that locals are democratic organizations, and it is possible that a union local executive body that negotiates an unsatisfactory collective agreement, or does not adequately handle the administration of the agreement, may be replaced.

Independent Local Unions

Independent local unions are not affiliated with a parent national, provincial or international union.

Unions that do not belong to a national or international union, such as faculty associations at some universities, are known as **independent local unions**. Such unions make up only 3.9 percent of union membership. They do not have access to the support or services that national, provincial, and international unions provide to their locals.

National and International Unions

A **national union** is a union whose membership is situated only in Canada.

An **international union** has members in two or more countries (e.g., Canada and the United States) with the parent union headquarters located in one country.

The term **national union** is a bit misleading; it refers to a union whose membership is confined to Canada, although it may not have members in all provinces. Thus, not only the CUPE and the CAW but also the British Columbia Nurses Union and the Ontario Secondary School Teachers' Federation are national unions. An **international union** has members in both Canada and the United States, with headquarters typically located in the United States. The United Food and Commercial Workers International Union and the United Steelworkers of America are examples of international unions. In 2009, there were 173 national and 37 international unions in Canada. Figure 3-6 lists the 10 largest unions in Canada and their websites. It is recommended that you visit some of the sites to see illustrations of the union functions, constitutions, and activities discussed below.

Organization and Governance   Although every national and international union has a unique organizational structure, there are common features and patterns. The union will have a constitution that regulates issues such as officers and elections, the conduct of negotiations and the authorization of strikes, and local officers and their duties. The union constitution may set out the penalties—fines, suspension, or termination of membership—for certain member conduct or actions. Section B.11 of the constitution for the Canadian Union of Public Employees outlines trial procedures for a list of offences, including wrongfully interfering with an officer's or employee's performance of union duties, disseminating information that harms or weakens the union, not respecting a local's picket line, and acting in a way that

Name	Website	Membership
Canadian Union of Public Employees	www.cupe.ca	630,050
National Union of Public and General Employees	www.nupge.ca	340,000
Unifor	www.unifor.org	308,000
United Food and Commercial Workers Canada	www.ufcw.com	245,327
United Steel Workers	www.usw.ca	230,700
Public Service Alliance of Canada	www.psacunion.ca	187,587
Fédération de la santé et des services sociaux	www.csn.qc.ca	129,032
Teamsters Canada	www.teamster.ca	93,351
Laborers' International Union of North America	www.liuna.ca	80,000
Service Employees International Union	www.seiu.org	118,991
Alberta Union of Provincial Employees	www.aupe.org	80,107

Figure 3-6 Largest Unions in Canada, 2013

Source: "Union Coverage in Canada, 2012," Labour Program, Government of Canada, Workplace Information Division, Strategic Policy, Analysis, and Workplace Information Directorate, April 2013.

constitues sex harassment. Labour relations legislation may regulate the disciplinary process. For example, Section 26 of the Alberta *Labour Relations Code* provides that a union member cannot be disciplined unless he or she is served with specific charges in writing, given a reasonable time to prepare a defence, and afforded a full and fair hearing, including the right to be represented by counsel. Recent court decisions have confirmed that unions cannot enforce the payment of fines in the courts. Refer to Labour Relations Issue 3-1 on this issue.

In five jurisdictions (Canada, Alberta, Manitoba, Nova Scotia, and Saskatchewan), labour relations legislation provides that an employee cannot be expelled for any reason other than the failure to pay union dues. The application of the union's constitution may be constrained by the obligations that the union has agreed to under a collective agreement.

Labour Relations Issue 3-1

Should Unions Be Able to Impose Fines?

Employees of the Canada Revenue Agency are represented by the Public Service Alliance of Canada ("PSAC"). During a legal strike, two employees crossed the picket line and worked three days. The union's constitution provides that it is an offence to work during a strike and requires the imposition of a fine equal to the amount earned by the employee during the strike. The union fined both employees $476.75, the total of each employee's gross salary for the three days they crossed the picket line. When the employees refused to pay the fine, the union started a legal action to recover the fines. The case eventually went to the Ontario Court of Appeal where it was confirmed that the union could not use the court system to enforce the payment of fines. The decision sets out the law on the issue of union fines that applies in all provinces except Saskatchewan, where legislation permits the collection of union fines. Should unions have the authority to impose fines? Is there any reason why employers might want unions to have the authority to impose fines?

The union may be prevented from exercising a provision of its constitution because it has agreed not to do so. For example, at the conclusion of a strike the union and the employer may agree that there will be no reprisals against any employees for their conduct during the strike or their failure to support the strike. This agreement would prevent the union from disciplining employees who continued to work during a strike. Although the composition of the executive will vary from union to union, there will typically be a president, secretary, treasurer, and several vice-presidents. The union's executive and administrative staff look after day-to-day operations. National and international unions are typically organized into functional departments and might have experts in economics, health and safety, ergonomics, pensions, and other matters of concern to staff.

Website for the constitution for Unifor: www.unifor.org

The supreme governing mechanism of the union is the *convention*, a general meeting typically held every one or two years to which locals are entitled to send member delegates. In most cases, the number of delegates sent by a local is based upon its size; however, in a few exceptional cases, all locals are entitled to the same representation. At the convention, officers are elected, policy matters are discussed, and resolutions voted upon.

Functions of National and International Unions   National and international unions have several key functions, most of which relate to providing assistance to locals. Their functions are listed in Key Considerations 3-2.

The union may assist locals with contract negotiations by providing research information on collective agreements in the industry and by sending a representative to be part of the bargaining team negotiating with the employer. It may assist locals with the grievance process by providing one or more of the following: advice on the interpretation of the collective agreement, a database of previous arbitration decisions interpreting the collective agreement, research on related arbitration decisions, and a grievance officer or lawyer to appear for the local at an arbitration hearing. It may provide training in various subjects, including the negotiation of collective agreements, grievance handling, human rights, and media relations.

Unions have attempted to influence government policies through lobbying, advertising, and appearances before parliamentary and legislative committees. Unions are also turning to the courts to achieve their objectives. In 2014, the Public Service Alliance of Canada filed a constitutional challenge to Bill C-4 in the Ontario Court of Justice. The challenge focuses on several key areas, including: the definition of essential services and which workers perform them; amendments to dispute resolution mechanisms; and limitations on the fundamental rights of federal public service employees as guaranteed under Canada's *Charter of Rights and Freedoms*.

Unions also provide financial assistance and expertise to locals on strike, and attempt to organize non-unionized workers. The process through which a union obtains the right to represent a new bargaining unit is considered in Chapter 6.

Relationship Between a Local and the National or International Union   The relationship between the local union and the parent national or international union

---

Key Considerations 3-2

Functions of National and International Unions

1. Assisting locals with contract negotiation

2. Assisting locals with grievances

3. Providing education and training for union members

4. Providing strike assistance to locals

5. Engaging in political activity

6. Organizing workers

The Relationship Between a National Union, Local Union, and Union Members

In May 1992 a local of the Canadian Association of Smelters and Allied Workers (CASAW) began a strike at the Giant Mine, a gold-producing facility near Yellowknife owned by Royal Oak Mines Inc. Royal Oak continued operations using replacement workers. The strike became violent and the employer hired Pinkerton's of Canada Ltd. to provide security.

Explosives were set in the mine, apparently by striking workers, and security guards were injured in altercations with strikers. Several strikers, including Roger Warren, were fired after damaging company property. In September 1992 Warren planted an explosive device in the mine. When the device was tripped, nine workers were killed. Warren was later convicted of second-degree murder.

The victims' families sued, and at trial were awarded $10.7 million apportioned between the defendants as follows: Warren, 26 percent; CAW national, 22 percent; Royal Oak, 23 percent; Pinkerton's 15 percent; the Northwest Territories government, 9 percent; and local union

strike leaders, 5 percent. The damages would be paid to the NWT Workers Compensation Board, which had previously compensated the families. On an appeal the decision of the trial judge was overturned. A further appeal by the families to the Supreme Court of Canada was dismissed. (The legal action by the families was a *subrogation claim*—which means the compensation board was attempting to recover monies previously paid to the families by pursuing a legal action in the name of the families.) In its decision, the court made several findings that are significant to national and local unions. It confirmed that the national union and the local union are separate entities, and unless there was wrongful conduct such as incitement by the national union it was not liable for a local's actions. Furthermore, the national union was not liable for the acts committed by union members during a strike.

Should the national union have legal responsibility for the actions of a local union?

may affect an employer. The union constitution may provide that the local cannot go on strike unless the national executive approves the action. The national or international union also also affect the demands negotiated by the local. It may have bargaining objectives of its own to bring to the negotiations through its representative. The constitution of a provincial union may prevent or limit the authority of union local officers in dealings with an employer. For example, a national representative's signature may be required on all grievance settlements. Other unions may accord more discretion to their local executive leaders in these and other matters. Although it rarely occurs, the constitution of a union will provide for the possible **trusteeship** of a local—that is, the national or international union may take control of the local's affairs if it fails to comply with the union's constitution.

Website for the Canadian Labour Congress: www.canadianlabour.ca

Trusteeship refers to a parent union temporarily taking control of a local's management.

Labour Congresses and Federations

Unions have found that they have common concerns and there are benefits to having unions come together in associations at the provincial and the national level. A **labour federation or labour congress** is an association of unions that promotes union interests, coordinates union business, and provides services to its members.

A **labour federation** or **labour congress** is an association of unions.

National Labour Congresses The largest national labour congress is the Canadian Labour Congress (CLC), which represents 3.2 million Canadian workers across national, international, and directly chartered unions in the country.[16] A **directly chartered union** is a local union that has received a charter directly from a labour congress and is not part of a national or international union. There are only a few such unions, and their membership amounts to only about 1.6 percent of total Canadian union membership, mostly chartered by a Quebec labour congress.

A **directly chartered union** receives a charter from a labour congress and is not affiliated with a national or international union.

Organization and Governance of the CLC The constitution of the CLC, which sets out how the CLC is organized and governed, is available at the organization's website (**www.canadianlabour.ca**). Unions that belong to the CLC send delegates to a convention that is held every two years. The conventions elect officers who are responsible for the operations of the CLC between conventions.

Functions of the CLC The functions of the CLC are listed in Key Considerations 3-3. It is recommended that you visit the Congress's website, which illustrates its functions and current activities.

One of the key functions of the CLC is pursuing changes that are favourable to workers and unions in federal employment and labour relations legislation. For example, the Congress advocates for the federal government to be tougher on corporations that fail in their responsibilities for worker health and safety. The CLC wants to avoid what might be seen as a "two-tiered" application of the law. If a corporation fails to meet its obligations to assure the health and safety of its employees, it should be subject to criminal penalties associated with such harm—just as someone would be charged under the law if they assaulted an individual ourside of the work setting. The CLC also comments on numerous social and economic issues.

The CLC has a code of ethical practices in its constitution, which provides for adequate membership meetings in local unions, democratic elections, and honest financial management. A union that fails to adhere to the code can be suspended. The CLC has a disputes protocol, the purpose of which is to prevent raiding between affiliated unions and establish a procedure for employees to change unions. **Raiding** refers to one union persuading members of another union to change unions. The practice is generally discouraged in the labour movement, but if the raiding union successfully applies to represent the employees, a situation that is elaborated upon in Chapter 6, it replaces the first union and becomes the bargaining agent for the employees.

> **Raiding** refers to one union persuading members of another union to change unions.

It should be noted that the CLC does not become directly involved in contract negotiation or the grievance process. Although employers may have contact with national or international union representatives, they are unlikely to have any dealings with CLC officials.

The CLC represents Canadian unions in international labour organizations and provides educational assistance for its own members. It holds workshops and provides materials relating to topics such as union organization, legislation, and contract negotiation.

> A **provincial labour federation** is an organization composed of unions in a province that belong to the CLC.

Provincial Labour Federations Every province has a **provincial labour federation**, an organization composed of unions in a province that belong to the CLC. Figure 3-7 lists the websites for the provincial federations, and the CLC website has a link to them as well.

Provincial labour federations become involved in the following activities: lobbying the provincial governments regarding employment and labour relations legislation, pursuing provincial economic and social policy favourable to workers, educating members, and supporting unions on strike. It is recommended that you go to the website for the federation in your province to learn about its functions and activities.

Key Considerations 3-3

Functions of the Canadian Labour Congress

1. Lobbying the federal government regarding employment and labour relations legislation
2. Pursuing economic and social policy favourable to workers at the federal level
3. Managing jurisdictional disputes between unions
4. Enforcing the CLC code of ethics
5. Education
6. Maintaining links with labour movements in other countries

Name of Federation	Website
Alberta Federation of Labour (AFL)	www.afl.org
British Columbia Federation of Labour (BCFL)	www.bcfed.ca
Manitoba Federation of Labour (MFL)	www.mfl.ca
New Brunswick Federation of Labour (NBFL)	www.nbfl-fttnb.ca
Newfoundland and Labrador Federation of Labour (NLFL)	www.nlfl.nf.ca
Nova Scotia Federation of Labour (NSFL)	www.nsfl.ns.ca
Ontario Federation of Labour (OFL)	www.ofl.ca
Prince Edward Island Federation of Labour	www.peifl.ca
Quebec Federation of Labour (FTQ)	www.ftq.qc.ca
Saskatchewan Federation of Labour (SFL)	www.sfl.sk.ca

Figure 3-7 Provincial Labour Federations

Provinces enact changes to legislation affecting the workplace from time to time. When a province is considering amendments to workplace legislation, the Federation of Labour will put forward a union position. For example, the federations in British Columbia and Ontario have recently made presentations relating to changes to employment standards legislation. The provincial federations also become involved in broader economic and social issues in a province. The website for the British Columbia Federation of Labour has commentary calling the for the B.C. provincial government to reverse its policy on non-involvement in apprenticeship training, which has resulted in a significant drop in completion rates.[17]

A provincial federation's educational efforts are sometimes made in partnership with the CLC. The federations may support striking workers by encouraging a boycott of the employer.

Website for the British Columbia Federation of Labour: www.bcfed.ca

The provincial federations of labour do not become directly involved with the negotiation or administration of collective agreements. Locals handle the negotiation and administration of collective agreements with the assistance of the national or international union.

Labour Councils

A **Labour Council** is an association of unions in a municipality or region, such as the Vancouver and District Labour Council. There are links to Labour Councils at the CLC website.

A **Labour Council** is an association of unions in a municipality or region.

Organization and Governance Local unions that belong to a Labour Council pay a levy based on the size of their memberships, and are represented by delegates who elect officers to do most of the Council's work. The Council will have bylaws and a constitution. The constitution of the CLC requires its affiliated unions to join the Labour Council in their region; however, some CLC-affiliated locals do not join the Council. Locals of unions not affiliated with the CLC may choose to join a Labour Council.

Website for the Vancouver and District Labour Council: www.vdlc.ca

Functions of a Labour Council Labour Councils work to advance the interests of unions at the regional or municipal level. Their functions include political activity, training and education, community and charity work, and assisting locals on strike. An example of a Labour Council's political activity can be found at the website for the Winnipeg Labour Council (**www.winnipeglabour.ca**). You should visit a Labour Council's website to see examples of typical activities. Education and training provided by a Labour Council, often undertaken in conjunction with the CLC, might relate to topics such as union stewardship or legislation. Labour Councils are often active in United Way campaigns. When a local belonging to a Labour Council is on strike, the Council may provide assistance by soliciting financial support from other locals.

Labour Councils do not become directly involved with employers in the negotiation or administration of collective agreements.

Key Features of Union Structure

This section will consider significant aspects of union structure, including the fragmentation of the labour movement.

Union Fragmentation   By international standards, Canada has a large number of small unions, even though the trend has been toward unions with a membership of 50 000 or more. In 2012, 46.6 percent of workers in national and international unions belonged to just eight unions, each covering at least 100 000 employees. At the other end of the spectrum, 167 unions covering fewer than 10 000 workers represent only 8.0 percent of unionized workers, with an average size of 2166 workers.[18] Smaller unions may not have a membership base sufficient to support organizational efforts, or provide adequate support to locals for contract negotiation and the administration of a collective agreement.

Canadianization of Unions   In the early 1900s, 95 percent of Canadian union members belonged to U.S.-based international unions. As of 2009, only 25.3 percent of union members belonged to international unions.[19] There are several reasons for this increase in national union membership relative to international union membership. Some Canadian union branches broke away from their international unions after disagreeing on policy matters. In 1984, the international United Automobile Workers (UAW) in the United States agreed to lump-sum payments linked to the employer's profitability instead of a traditional up-front wage increase. The U.S. headquarters of the international union pressured the Canadian branch to agree to this type of provision in a contract being negotiated with GM Canada. The branch refused to follow the international's lead and negotiated a contract with a standard wage increase instead of payments linked to profitability. Subsequently, most of the Canadian locals of the UAW broke away and formed a new national union, the CAW (now Unifor). When public sector employees were allowed to organize after 1965, they joined Canadian national unions. The establishment of unionization in the public sector increased national union membership relative to international membership. The increase in representation by Canadian national unions may be significant for a number of reasons. Some employers have dealt with national unions that may be more militant than international unions. The CAW gained a reputation for more militancy, fighting against concessions and compensation contingent upon employer profitability. It was noted above that Canadian unions have been more active in organizing employees than American unions. There does not appear to be any research examining whether national unions have made greater efforts to organize than the Canadian branches of international unions. However, there is evidence that international unions are not as effective in organizing campaigns as Canadian national unions. A study of factors affecting the success rate of organizing drives in Nova Scotia over a 10-year period found that national unions had a higher rate of success than international unions.[20]

THE DEVELOPMENT OF UNIONS AND LABOUR RELATIONS

Canada's labour relations system has been evolving since the days of the first unions in the early 1800s. Present-day attitudes and objectives of unions and employers, negotiation practices, and labour relations legislation have been shaped by years of history, which we will summarize here, emphasizing issues and events that have an impact on unions and employers today. Key Considerations 3-4 lists key dates and events. Readers who wish to explore the history of the labour movement further should refer to more detailed accounts.[21]

Events in the Development of Labour Relations

1812	First union locals of skilled craft workers established	1940	Canadian Congress of Labour (CCL) formed to pursue unionization of industrial employees
1860s	U.S.-based unions begin organizing in Canada	1944	*Privy Council Order 1003* establishes collective bargaining rights in Canada
1872	Unions press for nine-hour work day		
1875	Knights of Labour begin organizing Canadian employees	1947–	Federal *Industrial Relations and Disputes Investigation Act* (now the Canada Labour Code) and provincial early 1950s labour relations statutes passed
1886	American Federation of Labour (AFL) established in the United States and Trades and Labour Congress (TLC) established in Canada		
		1956	TLC and CCL merge to establish the Canadian Labour Congress
1900	Federal *Conciliation Act* provides for voluntary conciliation	1961	New Democratic Party established to succeed CCF
1902	Knights of Labour expelled from TLC	1967	*Public Service Staff Relations Act* establishes collective bargaining rights in federal public service; similar provincial legislation subsequently enacted
1907	Federal *Industrial Disputes Investigation Act* passed requiring conciliation in specified industries		
1918	Western unionists expelled from TLC, establish the One Big Union	1975	Federal wage and price controls program
		1982	Federal public sector wage constraint program imposed
1919	Winnipeg general strike		
1920s	Communist Party of Canada active in union organizing	1985	Canadian division of United Automobile Workers breaks away from international and establishes Canadian Auto Workers
1925	*Toronto Electric Commissioners v. Snyder*: federal *Industrial Disputes Investigation Act* found to be beyond federal jurisdiction	1991	Federal government freezes public sector wages; subsequently some provincial governments adopt restraint legislation
1929	Start of Great Depression		
1932	Co-operative Commonwealth Federation (CCF) established	1994	Federal government extends collective agreements with public service employees and suspends salary increments
1935	*Wagner Act* establishing collective bargaining rights passed in United States		
		2007	Supreme Court of Canada holds that the freedom of association provided in the *Charter* includes a procedural right to collective bargaining in the *Health Services* case
1939	Industrial unions affiliated with Congress of Industrial Organization (CIO) expelled from TLC		

We will see that the development of the labour relations system has been affected by economic, political, legal, and social factors.[22] As this history is reviewed, keep the following questions in mind:

1. How have employers reacted to unions, and how does their response affect union-management relations?

2. How has government acted as the regulator of the labour relations system and as an employer?

3. As unions have developed, how unified have unions and workers been, and how does this affect the position of unions today?

4. There are calls for a more cooperative relationship between government, employers, and unions. Does the past help or hinder such cooperation?

Early Unions

The first labour organizations, formed in Canada in the early 1800s, were independent local unions in Halifax, Montreal, and other centres, made up of skilled craft workers such as printers and shoemakers. They were concerned with protecting their craft status from unskilled workers and providing assistance to individuals who were sick or unemployed. We will see that the division between craft unions and industrial unions was an issue that divided the labour movement and delayed its development for many years. Craft unions and the labour congress they belonged to did not encourage the organization of unskilled workers in industrial unions. In the 1860s and 1870s, there were attempts to form a national congress made up of local unions, and the Canadian Labour Union was the first of these to be established. However, an economic downturn in the 1870s led to the demise of this organization—an early indicator of how the economic environment could affect unions.

The legal environment was hostile to the organization of unions until changes in legislation in 1944, referred to below. The basic rights of employees and unions that are part of today's labour relations system, including the right to organize, the obligation to bargain with the union, and prohibitions against discrimination for union activity, did not exist. Prior to 1872, the laws preventing the restraint of trade were applied to union organizing activity. Organizing a union was an illegal conspiracy in restraint of trade and union supporters could be arrested and jailed. Employers engaged in practices to avoid unions, including **yellow dog contracts**—agreements with employees that they would not join a union. Employers also dismissed union supporters and used blacklists to identify and avoid hiring union supporters. As the law did not require employers to recognize or bargain with them, unions used recognition strikes to force employers to deal with them. Until the law was changed in 1944, some recognition strikes escalated into violent conflicts. A strike in Estevan, Saskatchewan, in 1931 led to violence and the deaths of three workers; unfortunately, this was not the only incident in which workers were killed or injured.

<aside>**Yellow dog contracts** are agreements that prohibit unionization.</aside>

In the 1870s, hours of work were an issue. There was no employment standards legislation regulating hours, and workdays could be 10 or more hours a day for six days a week. Unions sought a reduction to a 9-hour day and a 54-hour week. The working conditions of many employees in the late 1800s and early 1900s may be the basis for the claim by some that while unions were necessary at one time, they are no longer necessary because working conditions have improved. Unions would contend that there is still a need for unions, because poor working conditions still exist in some workplaces. The UFCW has referred to employees working at a mushroom factory under conditions the union described as appalling: nonstop 12-hour shifts with little or no time off to eat, rest, or take care of bodily functions; piecework wage rates that varied from worker to worker according to management whim; extremely hazardous working conditions, including unguarded machinery that could amputate limbs; and noxious air quality.[23] In summary, the first unions were local craft organizations, established in a hostile legal environment, that sometimes faced heavy employer opposition. The development of the labour relations system might be viewed in the context of how unions, employers, and legislation have changed since these early years.

Entry of International Unions and Development of Labour Federations

In the 1860s, unions based in the United States started to organize workers in Canada. By 1902, 95 percent of Canadian union members belonged to international unions based in the United States. This American influence, which has since diminished, had both positive and negative effects on the development of the Canadian labour movement.

In the late 1800s and early 1900s, organizing drives initiated by U.S. unions led to the organization of thousands of Canadian workers. The U.S.-based unions sought to organize Canadian workers to avoid the possibility of U.S. employers moving work to non-union workers in Canada. International unions dominated the Canadian labour movement for a number of reasons. Canadian workers were drawn to U.S. unions because they were larger and stronger, and had more resources available, including larger strike funds. This was also a time when some Canadians worked in the United States for part of the year and membership in an American union could be an advantage when seeking employment.

The American Federation of Labour (AFL), a federation of national and international craft unions, was formed in the United States in 1886. In the same year, the first central labour federation to succeed in Canada, the Trades and Labour Congress (TLC), was established, and was heavily influenced by the AFL. For example, the TLC followed the AFL practice of not affiliating itself with any political party.

The influence of the U.S. international unions and the AFL affected the philosophy and scope of the Canadian labour movement. The philosophy of the U.S. unions was what has come to be known as a **business unionism**, which is focused on improving the compensation and working conditions of bargaining unit members, as opposed to seeking broader economic and social reform that might benefit all workers. The primary tool of business unionism is negotiation with the employer; political activity is secondary. Business unionism has taken a more conservative approach to public issues in the past.

Business unionism focuses on the improvement of the terms of employment through negotiation with the employer.

Social unionism is concerned with improving the compensation and working conditions of bargaining unit members, but it also seeks broader economic and social change. Unifor has proclaimed itself to be committed to social unionism, which it describes as follows:

Social unionism is concerned with broad economic and social change that benefits all of society.

> Our goal is transformative. To reassert common interest over private interest. Our goal is to change our workplaces and our world. Our vision is compelling. It is to fundamentally change the economy, with equality and social justice, restore and strengthen our democracy and achieve an environmentally sustainable future. This is the basis of social unionism—a strong and progressive union culture and a commitment to work in common cause with other progressives in Canada and around the world.[24]

Although some Canadian unions became more involved in politics than their U.S. counterparts, business unionism was the dominant philosophy of Canadian unions until the 1970s. Some Canadian unions still maintain a more conservative business unionism philosophy.

The U.S.-based craft unions organized skilled workers and did not pursue the organization of semiskilled and unskilled industrial workers. Subsequently, Canadian unions affiliated with the TLC emphasized the organization of craft—as opposed to industrial workers. Although there were some early efforts to organize industrial workers, it was not until the 1930s that a significant effort was made to organize them in Canada on a widespread basis.

The legal environment continued to be unfavourable to unions. In 1900, the federal government passed the *Conciliation Act*, which was a response to strikes and provided for voluntary conciliation of contract disputes. Following a strike in the coal industry, which caused hardship to the public, the federal government passed the *Industrial Disputes Investigation Act* in 1907. This legislation required employers and unions in affected industries to submit contract disputes to a tripartite conciliation board before a strike or lockout could legally take place. This legislation was the foundation for the compulsory conciliation provisions now found in most jurisdictions. It should be noted that this legislation was aimed at preventing strikes and lockouts, and the law still did not require employers to recognize or bargain with unions.

In 1925, there was a court decision that significantly affected the labour relations system. In the case of *Toronto Electric Power Commission v. Snyder*, the federal government's authority to enact the *Industrial Disputes Investigation Act* was challenged. The employer involved contended that the federal government did not have the authority to pass legislation regulating its business, because labour relations were a provincial matter. Although the Supreme Court of Canada upheld the legislation, the British Privy Council, which heard appeals from the Supreme Court of Canada at that time, ruled that the federal legislation could not be applied to the employer. *Snyder* is significant because it established a divided jurisdiction for Canadian labour relations, the federal government having jurisdiction over only about 10 percent of the workforce, including employees in industries such as banking and interprovincial transport.

Industrial Unions

The first attempts to organize workers were also influenced by U.S. unions. The Knights of Labour, a union originating in the United States, came to Canada in 1875. The Knights sought to improve all of society through education and political efforts and did not seek improvements just in the workplace through collective bargaining. The Knights could be viewed as a forerunner of social unionism that was to develop in Canada many years later. At the TLC convention in 1902, the Knights of Labour was expelled from the TLC under pressure from the AFL. At a TLC convention in 1918, western unionists who held socialist beliefs and sought to organize on an industrial basis were defeated. In 1919, they started a new industrial union in western Canada, the One Big Union.

Some observers view the 1919 Winnipeg general strike as a turning point in the history of labour. It started when metal trades workers walked off their jobs to support demands for union recognition and wage increases. The Winnipeg Labour Council supported the workers' demands, and over 30 000 other employees walked off their jobs in a general strike. The strike ended after strikers clashed with the RCMP and two workers were killed. This episode was significant because it may have ended any further attempts to establish a more radical labour movement in Canada. It also illustrates that the legal environment continued to be hostile to unions. Because there was still not any legal requirement that employers recognize a union, the union had to resort to a recognition strike.

In the 1930s, the conflict between U.S. unionists who wanted to pursue the organization of industrial workers and those who did not continued, and eventually spilled over into Canada. A Committee of Industrial Organization (CIO) was formed in the AFL in 1935 to pursue the organization of manufacturing workers. Some Canadian organizers used the CIO name to organize employees in Canada. The craft unions in the United States opposed the effort to organize industrial workers, and the AFL expelled the CIO in 1937. The CIO became the Congress of Industrial Organization, whose objective was the organization of manufacturing workers. The CIO subsequently had success organizing industrial workers in the auto, rubber, and other manufacturing industries in the United States. CIO affiliates in Canada also organized on an industrial basis; and in 1939 the TLC, again influenced by the AFL, expelled them. In 1940, the affiliates joined the Canadian Congress of Labour (CCL), which pursued organizing by industry and was more active in politics than the TLC. The drive to organize industrial workers in Canada did not have the same success as it did in the United States, largely due to changes in U.S. legislation. In 1935, as part of the U.S. government's effort to rebuild the economy after the Great Depression, the *National Labour Relations Act* (*Wagner Act*) was passed. The **Wagner Act** established a new regime for employers and unions, by providing for the following:

The **Wagner Act** established the right to organize, compulusory bargaining, and prohibition of unfair labour practices in the United Stated.

- The recognition of employees' right to join a union
- The establishment of a National Labour Relations Board
- A certification process through which unions could obtain the right to represent employees by application to the Board

- Prohibition of unfair labour practices by employers, including interfering with employees' right to organize, domination of a union, and discrimination against employees for union activity
- The requirement that employers bargain in good faith with a union certified by the Board

This U.S. legislation was a major public policy development. The law no longer allowed employers to use many of their previous tactics to defeat unions, such as threatening employees with dismissal or relocation, using yellow dog contracts, and refusing to deal with a union.

Similar legislation was not passed in Canada until 1944. World War II led to a period of economic growth and increased union membership—doubled from 1939 to 1944—as unemployment fell and the cost of living increased. The early 1940s was a period of labour unrest with a large number of strikes. Labour leaders called for legislation equivalent to the *Wagner Act*. At this time, the Co-operative Commonwealth Federation, a socialist party, was enjoying political success and attracting support from union members. In 1943, a Gallup poll showed the CCF ahead of both the Liberals and the Conservatives.[25] The demands of labour and the political threat of the CCF led to the enactment of **Privy Council Order 1003** (PC 1003) in 1944. PC 1003 was a wartime labour regulation that brought to Canada the principles established by the *Wagner Act*. The foundation of modern labour relations legislation, it established:

Privy Council Order 1003 established the rights and obligations fundamental to labour relations in Canada.

- The right to join a union
- A Labour Relations Board
- A certification process by way of an application to the Board
- The prohibition of unfair labour practices by unions and employers
- Compulsory bargaining when a union has been certified
- A compulsory conciliation procedure before a strike or lockout
- A provision that no strike or lockout can occur during the life of the collective agreement
- A provision that all collective agreements were deemed to contain an arbitration procedure for the resolution of disputes

PC 1003 prohibited many of the practices employers had previously used to avoid unions, such as threatening, intimidating or discriminating against employees, and for the first time requiring employers to recognize and bargain with certified unions. The law now made it illegal for unions to strike to obtain recognition. After the war, the federal government enacted the *Industrial Relations and Disputes Investigation Act*, which incorporated the principles established in PC 1003. The legislation covered only industries within the federal jurisdiction. The federal legislation is now Part 1 of the Canada Labour Code. Using PC 1003 as a model, the provinces subsequently enacted their own labour relations statutes, which covered provincially regulated employers.

After the formation of the CCL, there were two rival labour congresses in Canada. There was raiding by unions associated with the TLC and the CCL until 1956 when the two congresses merged to form the Canadian Labour Congress.

The key points that should be noted in the development of labour relations are the division between craft and industrial unions, the influence of the U.S.-based AFL, and the 1944 change in the legal environment with the passage of legislation supporting collective bargaining.

Public Sector Unionization

Until the mid-1960s, most public sector workers still did not have the right to unionize. The federal government enacted the *Public Service Staff Relations Act* in 1965, providing federal employees with the right to organize for the first time. By the early 1970s, the provinces had enacted public sector collective bargaining legislation as well, with some provinces providing for arbitration instead of the right to strike. Collective bargaining rights for public service employees indirectly led to the unionization of white-collar and professional employees in the private sector. Some private sector professional employees who had not previously organized pursued unionization after they witnessed the gains made by public sector employees. The granting of bargaining rights to public sector employees had a major effect on total union membership and the composition of the labour movement. From 1964 to 1969, union membership almost doubled, climbing from 1.5 to almost 3 million members. Union membership has experienced spurts of growth caused by the economy and changes in labour relations legislation. Union density increased from 16.3 percent in 1940 to 30.3 percent in 1948, because of the improvement in the economy caused by World War II and the enactment of PC 1003, which facilitated union organizing. Union density started a decline in 1959, which was reversed in 1965 when public sector employees were given the right to organize. From 1965 to 1984, union density increased until it peaked in 1984 at 37.2 percent. Between 1997 and 2011, union density in Canada fell approximately 1.7 percentage points, from 30.9 percent of the labour force to about 29.2 percent. And union density in the private sector now sits at an all-time low of 15.9 percent.[26]

Unions and Politics

Unions become involved in political activity for a number of reasons. One is to influence labour relations legislation, which extensively regulates union–management relations and can make it more or less difficult for a union to obtain the right to represent employees. We will see in Chapter 6 that in some jurisdictions a union can obtain the right to represent employees on the basis of signed membership cards without a vote of employees. In others, a vote is mandatory before a union can obtain bargaining rights. Events in British Columbia and other provinces illustrate how the labour movement's fortunes can change according to who holds power in the province. In British Columbia, legislation at one time provided for a mandatory certification vote. It was later amended by an NDP government to dispense with a vote, and has recently been amended again by a Liberal government to require a vote. Surveys of unions to determine their goals, strategies, policies, and practices have found that the majority of unions engage in political action to change public policy and bring about social and economic change.[27]

Unions are also interested in issues that affect workers away from their jobs, such as the privatization of health care, the environment, and access to education. They can involve themselves in a number of ways: electing independent labour representatives, supporting a political party that adopts favourable policies, working within and supporting one political party such as the NDP, or using more radical methods such as a general strike. However, they have at times disagreed over what political objectives to pursue, and how to pursue them.

Political activity by unions is not a new development. After 1875, the Knights of Labour engaged in political activity in Canada, and was able to make some gains at the municipal level, including earlier closing hours and improved public transit.[28] The federal and provincial governments also implemented some of the Knights' recommendations, including factory legislation, women's right to vote, and the Labour Day holiday. The Communist Party of Canada, established in 1921, worked to organize industrial unions and was connected with much of the organizing activity of the early 1930s. The connection of some unions with the Communist party was the basis for some employers to attack all unions.

In the early 1920s, some labour candidates were elected to municipal, provincial, and federal office. In 1932 the Co-operative Commonwealth Federation (CCF), a socialist party that included labour, farmers, and others, was established. From the creation of the

CCF to the late 1940s, there was an ongoing battle between the CCF and the Communist Party of Canada over who would play the leading role within the union movement. Although at one time the Communist Party of Canada had more connections with unions than the CCF, the CCF eventually prevailed. In 1943, the CCL passed a resolution recognizing the CCF as the political arm of labour.[29] From 1941 to 1943, the CCF had some political success at the provincial level, forming a government in Saskatchewan. This translated into gains for unions in labour relations legislation and social policy. Saskatchewan was the first province to grant collective bargaining rights to public sector employees and establish a public health care system. At the federal level, the CCF was a factor causing the Liberal government to shift to the left and enact social legislation, including the family allowance and PC 1003 in 1944. After that, the CCF went into decline. In 1961, the NDP was established to succeed the CCF, the labour movement playing a central role in the establishment of the party.

With the assistance of unions, the NDP enjoyed some success at the federal level into the 1970s. Although the party never formed a government, it was able to influence policy, especially in years when it was part of a minority government. Despite the fact that union leaders have encouraged union members to vote for the NDP, they have not done so in significant numbers. At the provincial level, the NDP has been able to form governments in several provinces. NDP provincial governments have amended labour relations legislation to make it more favourable to unions. In Ontario, in 1993 an NDP government enacted what is commonly known as Bill 40, which made the union certification process easier and provided for other changes, including a mandatory just cause provision in collective agreements. A Progressive Conservative government elected in 1995 reversed most of these amendments.

The relationship between the NDP and unions poses problems for both sides. In recent elections, some union leaders such as Buzz Hargrove, former national president of the CAW (now Unifor), have advocated strategic voting to attempt to avoid a Conservative government. In the future, unions will have to determine if they should maintain formal ties to the NDP or support whichever party will produce the best results for labour.

Recent Developments   Developments since 1975 have not been favourable to unions. Legislative changes, the economy, and employer policies and practices have all posed challenges. Governments have restricted bargaining outcomes and weakened the position of unions. The economic environment has included periods of recession and the threats posed by free trade. Some employers have fought union certification, and others have engaged in hard bargaining. Recent developments in these three interrelated areas will be briefly considered here.

Legislation   In 1975, in response to high inflation the federal government imposed a program of wage and price controls on both the public and the private sector that prohibited wage increases above specified levels. This meant that restrictions were placed on the results unions could achieve through contract negotiation. Subsequently, in 1982, again in response to inflation, the federal government established in the public sector a wage control program that limited increases to 6 percent in the first year and 5 percent in the second year. The "6 and 5" program resulted in almost one-third of organized workers losing the right to strike for up to three years. The provinces enacted similar public sector wage controls. This legislation did not affect the right to bargain or the form of bargaining; however, it limited the outcomes unions could achieve.

In 1991 the federal government froze public sector wages and imposed back-to-work legislation. Provincial governments followed suit. For example, in 1993 Ontario established **social contract legislation** that rolled back wage increases in collective agreements previously negotiated and effectively displaced free collective bargaining for public sector workers for three years.

Social contract legislation rolled back wage increases in collective agreements.

Economic Developments In the period since 1975, the economy has been less favourable to unions. The high rates of inflation in the mid-1970s reduced the real income of many workers. A recession in 1981 caused the loss of thousands of jobs, especially in the manufacturing sector, and resulted in an unemployment rate of 12 percent. There was another economic downturn in the early 1990s. By 1993, the unemployment rate was 11.5 percent. In the first quarter of 1993, wage increases negotiated under major collective agreements averaged 1.3 percent, the lowest increase level recorded in 15 years, and 41 percent of private sector employees covered by a "major collective agreement" were subject to a wage freeze or a rollback.[30] ("Major collective agreements" covered bargaining units with 500 or more employees, and represented 55 percent of unionized workers at that time.)

The recession of 2008–09 referred to in Chapter 2 has been a challenge for unions and employers. Although there was an economic recovery in early 2010, the unemployment rate remained significantly higher than it was at the start of the recession.

The economic effects of the 1994 North America Free Trade Agreement (NAFTA) are controversial. Unions predicted that the agreement would lead to the loss of jobs and lower wages in Canada. Some studies show that the overall effects of NAFTA have not been as negative as unions predicted.[31] However, NAFTA created both winners and losers, and studies do not likely reassure individual employees who have lost their jobs. Some employers have clearly used the threat of relocation to the United States or Mexico to force unions to agree to lower wage increases or wage rollbacks. Employers have been able to obtain wage concessions as high as 40 percent.[32]

Employer Opposition and Hard Bargaining It may be difficult to determine whether there has been an increase or a decrease in employer opposition to unions. Most employers would not likely admit they oppose their employees unionizing. But clearly some employers still fight unionization by means both lawful and unlawful. In the 1980s, attempts to unionize Eaton's were unsuccessful when the employer stalled negotiations and refused to make any significant concessions in a collective agreement. There was a six-month strike, and the union subsequently lost its bargaining rights. This type of employer opposition was one of the reasons why Ontario adopted *first contract arbitration*, which is discussed in Chapter 8.

Attempts to organize the banking industry have been unsuccessful, largely because of employer opposition that has included harassment and transfer of union supporters.[33] Walmart is another employer that has made headlines with its opposition to unions. The company has closed one store after the employees voted to unionize. Situations involving employer opposition to unions should be put in their historical context. Today Chrysler, Ford, and General Motors accept unions. However, in the 1930s the automakers were "bitterly anti-union."[34] It took a sit-down strike that resulted in workers being attacked by police before General Motors recognized the United Automobile Workers in 1937.

Implications for Present-Day Labour Relations

When we began considering the development of unions and labour relations, four questions were posed. To summarize the developments and capture their significance, let us now return to those questions.

1. How have employers reacted to unions, and how does their response affect union–management relations?

    Some employers have opposed unions using both legal and illegal methods. This opposition will be discussed further in the next chapter, which deals with employer objectives and methods. At this point, we will note that employer opposition to unions relates to the fourth question regarding cooperation. A more cooperative relationship cannot be established where employers continue to oppose unions.

2. How has the government acted as the regulator of the labour relations system and as an employer?

Some governments have formally proclaimed that they support collective bargaining. However, some observers point out that governments have not always been supportive of collective bargaining. Early legislation such as the *Conciliation Act* and the *Industrial Dispute Investigation Act* was aimed at controlling strikes and did not establish collective bargaining rights. Canada did not enact private sector bargaining legislation until a decade after the United States did. Some would argue that the move was forced on government as opposed to its being a policy choice. Governments have ended numerous strikes with back-to-work legislation. We have seen that governments have imposed wage freezes and occasionally rolled back wage increases provided for in collective agreements with their employees. Although some governments have occasionally made amendments to labour relations legislation that are favourable to unions, recent legislation in some jurisdictions, notably British Columbia and Ontario, has been unfavourable. In summary, it does not appear that governments have taken action that would encourage a more cooperative relationship between the three main actors in the labour relations system.

3. As unions have developed, how unified have unions and workers been, and how does this affect the position of unions today?

The history of unions has involved division between craft and industrial unions, differences in philosophy, and different approaches to political involvement. Unions have failed to develop a unified working class culture, where workers support other workers. In the course of researching this book, the author asked a representative of one of the unions that have attempted to organize Walmart if the union had considered a boycott to force the employer to deal with the union. The response was yes, but it was decided this was not a viable option because the action would not likely find support. Apparently the absence of a working class culture leaves some unions in a weak position.

4. There are calls for a more cooperative relationship between government, employers, and unions. Does the past help or hinder such cooperation?

It was noted in Chapter 2 that there might be reasons why conflict between unions and employers is the natural order. Some employers and unions have attempted to move away from an adversarial relationship. We will refer to alternative problem-solving approaches to bargaining when we consider the negotiation of a collective agreement. It does not appear that our past, which includes government and employer opposition to unions, encourages a transition to more cooperation.

Implications for Practice

1. Although Canadian union density has fallen slightly in recent years, unions in Canada have not suffered the decline in membership that U.S. unions have experienced. Canadian unions are still key actors in the labour relations system.

2. Most union locals are part of a parent national or international union that provides support to the local in contract negotiation and administration. Employers should clarify the

relationship between the local union that represents their employees and the parent union, including matters such as the authority to call a strike.

3. Unions have different philosophies, which affect their relationship with employers and the activities they engage in. Some unions have adopted a social unionism philosophy.

4. The labour relations system has been developing since the first unions were established in the early 1800s. Prior to collective bargaining rights being established in legislation, many employers opposed unionization by their employees, and unions relied on recognition strikes to force employers to negotiate. Some employers continue to oppose unionization, and this opposition reduces the likelihood of union–management cooperation.

5. Labour relations legislation that governs the right to organize, contract negotiation, and administration is important to unions. Social issues such as the health care system are also important to unions. Accordingly, unions will continue to attempt to influence governments.

Key Terms

business agent, p. 51

business unionism, p. 61

craft unions, p. 48

directly chartered union, p. 55

independent local unions, p.52

industrial unions, p. 48

international union, p. 52

Labour Council, p. 57

labour federation or labour congress, p. 55

national union, p. 52

Privy Council Order 1003, p. 63

provincial labour federation, p. 56

raiding, p. 56

right-to-work legislation, p. 47

social contract legislation, p. 65

social unionism, p. 61

trusteeship, p. 55

union, p. 44

union density, p. 44

union local, p. 50

Wagner Act, p. 62

yellow dog contracts, p. 60

Review Questions

1. What is union density, and why is this measure important?
2. Why is union density higher in Canada than in the United States?
3. What are some of the characteristics of Canadian union membership, and what is the significance of these features?
4. What are the objectives of unions, and what methods do they use to achieve them?
5. Why is the local union the fundamental feature of union structure?
6. Distinguish between national and international unions.
7. What are the functions of national and international unions?
8. In a conversation, someone has referred to "my union." What are the possible meanings of this phrase?
9. Are there any advantages to belonging to an independent local union?
10. How is the Canadian Labour Congress different from a national or international union?
11. What is a Labour Council, and what are its functions?
12. What are the key features of Canadian union structure?
13. Describe how unions in the United States have influenced the union movement in Canada.
14. How did the *Wagner Act* influence labour relations in Canada?
15. Outline the significance of *Privy Council Order 1003*.
16. Why do many observers say that recent developments have not been favourable to unions?

Discussion Questions

1. Monitor the news media for references to unions. Determine if any news items illustrate the functions of unions referred to in this chapter.

2. Do you think that union density in Canada will decline to the level in the United States? Explain.

3. If you were a union member, would you want the union to have a philosophy of social unionism or business unionism? Explain.

4. A Canada Post employee was charged with theft after he left mail in his garage instead of delivering it. The Canadian Union of Postal Workers referred to the incident as a sign of increasing workloads. Do you think that this was a good approach for the union to take?

Web Research

1. Go to the website of the Laborers' International Union of North America at **www.liuna.org**. Determine the occupation of the workers the union represents, scan the union's constitution, and determine what the stated objectives of the union are, and outline two campaigns or issues the union is involved with.

2. Go to the website of a provincial federation of labour. Identify two issues that are addressed, and briefly describe the federation's position on each.

CASE INCIDENT   HOSPITAL EMPLOYEES' UNION vs. BRITISH COLUMBIA NURSES UNION

Licensed practical nurses (LPNs) in British Columbia hospitals are represented by the Hospital Employees' Union (HEU). There were approximately 5000 LPNs in British Columbia in 2009. LPNs take a one-year course and receive an average starting salary of just under $25 an hour. The British Colombia Nurses Union (BCNU) represents registered nurses in the province. Registered nurses have a four-year degree, and their starting wage is approximately $29 an hour.

In 2009, the BCNU started a raid of the LPNs. A *raid* is an attempt by one union to take away members from another. Such an action is generally frowned upon in the labour movement. To justify the raid, the BCNU claimed that the LPNs would receive higher wages, pay lower union dues, and obtain more competent leadership who did not engage in radical conflict with the government. The HEU had been in a bitter confrontation with the provincial government in 2002 that was only resolved when back-to-work legislation was enacted.

To defend against the raid, the HEU launched an outreach campaign to convince its members to stay. A business manager for the HEU said, "BCNU has been unsuccessful in restricting what the LPNs are able to do, and we believe this is about BCNU trying to control and restrict by other means." One HEU official stated, "The BCNU ought to be quite disappointed with the raid campaign. They have spent a lot of money and used up a lot of people's time and it looks as though they may not have much to show for their efforts."

On November 30, 2009, the BCNU filed an application for certification for the LPNs in the province with the Labour Relations Board. But on January 18, 2010, it applied to withdraw the application when it became apparent that it would not have enough of the LPNs signed up as members to succeed. The BCNU claimed it had not been possible to accurately determine the number of LPNs in the province because of their different locations. An unsuccessful application would mean that a 22-month time bar on a second application would be imposed.

Questions

1. What concerns, if any, would hospital employers have in this situation?
2. What arguments can be made in criticism or in defence of raiding?

CASE INCIDENT   LITTLE EAGLE SCHOOL BOARD

The Little Eagle School Board employs 1300 full-time and 200 occasional elementary school teachers. Occasional teachers fill in for full-time teachers who are sick or on leave. Both groups are represented by the Elementary Teachers Union; however, they have separate collective agreements. The collective agreements covering both teacher groups expired in August 2005.

When contract negotiations did not produce an agreement, the union started a work-to-rule campaign in January 2006. That is, teachers did only their required classroom work and additional duties that the collective agreement required, and declined to volunteer for extracurricular activities such as school theatre presentations.

In February 2006, the union imposed what is known as a "pink listing," advising teachers across the country that there is a labour dispute with a particular school board and they should not apply for or accept a teaching position with the board. The notice also advised teachers that individuals who accepted positions with the board would be disciplined by the union. A second "pink letter" relating to the occasional teachers' bargaining was issued in April of 2006. Both notices advised teachers to boycott teaching positions in the two bargaining units. The union also placed ads in area newspapers, attacking the school board for failing to provide teachers with adequate resources to provide a quality education.

On previous occasions, the board had not hired teachers while a pink listing was in place; however, the board proceeded to hire teachers in 2006. On May 10, 2006, the union and the board reached an agreement for the full-time teachers. A Memorandum of Settlement signed by the parties provided that the pink listing would be rescinded and there would be no reprisals, discipline, or harassment of any bargaining unit member as a result of the member's participation or nonparticipation in the union's job action. The collective agreement provided in Article 3 that there would be no discrimination against a teacher because of the teacher's participation or nonparticipation in the lawful activities of the union.

The union stopped the work-to-rule campaign immediately. However, it advised the board on May 20 that the second pink listing would continue until a new agreement was reached for the occasional teachers. The board advised the union that the pink listing should end immediately, but the union continued it until November 2006 when a new agreement was reached for the occasional teachers.

The union's constitution provided that it was an offence to ignore a pink listing and offenders could be disciplined. In September 2006, the union determined the names of teachers the board had hired and disciplined those involved in accordance with its constitution.

The discipline included publishing in a union publication the names of individuals who had violated the pink listing, denying them services from the union for three years and disqualifying them from holding union office for three years.

This had significant consequences for some of the new teachers. They were not able to access a union program that provided assistance to teachers who were having difficulty and a few had to resign. Morale at several schools suffered because of conflicts between teachers relating to the pink listing.

Questions

1. Discuss the methods used by the union in this situation.
2. What arguments could the employer make, and what counterarguments could the union make?

Chapter 4

Employers: Objectives, Processes, and Strategy

Chapter Objectives

1. Explain the objectives of management and the processes or methods used to achieve those objectives
2. Outline alternative labour relations strategies
3. Identify factors affecting an employer's labour relations strategy
4. Describe the features of high-performance work systems, and explain their implications for labour relations

Required Professional Capabilities (CCHRA)	HRPA Human Resources Professionals Competency Framework
10301, 10310, 10504, 40403, 50401	**C101, C114, C123, C194**

While a majority of public libraries in Ontario are unionized, a few have a special relationship with their employees that may appear to be "union-like" but is a unique and open working environment that permits input on workplace changes, open communication, and a dispute resolution process.

The Whitby Public Library, located in Whitby, Ontario, is a medium-sized library that employs 96 staff, 5 of whom are managers. Mr. Ian Ross, CEO and Chief Librarian, noted that their staff association, which includes front line supervisors. He described the formal and informal interactions between association members and his management team. "There are formal 'touch-base' meetings three times a year, in which managers and the Staff Association Executive members share information and concerns and then address them together. There are also informal meetings to discuss procedural and service changes. For example, when the library went to an online time and attendance program in which every staff member was to be responsible for logging in and reporting hours worked, management discussed with the Staff Association implementation, training, and other issues to gain buy-in and reinforce the collaboration that is a key part of the Library's culture."

The Staff Association at the Whitby Public Library is a committee, elected or appointed on an annual basis by non-management library employees to "represent" their interests and concerns to management. The Association has terms of reference and negotiates every three years a "Personnel Policy," which serves in a manner similar to a collective agreement, with ratification by its membership and passed by the Library's board of directors. There is no negotiation of salaries and benefits, which in practice have been pegged to adjustments seen with the local municipality. Library employees can request a Staff Association member to join in meetings with their managers when there are performance issues. Mr. Ross notes, "Our library's work culture is relatively relaxed and flexible. It is easy to 'pilot' or introduce new services and approaches without the bureaucracy. We work collaboratively to introduce change and thus gain staff support. There is a sense of team—not 'them and us,' but rather an 'us.'"[1]

The above description gives one example of various employer labour relations strategies that will be discussed in this chapter. Keeping in mind that roughly one in three Canadian employers are unionized, this account gives a strategic perspective of what non-union company settings may do to meet the expectations of 21st-century employees.

After World War II, there was a period of economic growth in Canada with low unemployment, which strengthened the position of unions. Unions held the initiative in negotiations with employers, and they were able to negotiate collective agreements that provided for increased wages, breakthroughs in benefits including pensions, reduced work hours, and seniority provisions. Non-union employers adopted some of the developments provided in collective agreements. Most employers initially resisted union certification; however, after the union was certified the employer concentrated on negotiating the best possible collective agreement. The environment changed in the 1980s. Employers had to deal with the competitive pressures caused by environmental factors referred to in Chapter 2. A recession in the early 1980s marked the start of a shift in power from unions to employers. Prior to the 1980s, some employers had been able to buy labour peace by granting concessions to unions. In the new environment, particularly since the 2008 recession, employers have turned increasingly to new technologies, exited some lines of business, downsized their workforces, and, where possible, entered global markets.

MANAGEMENT OBJECTIVES AND PROCESSES

To understand the policies and practices that employers adopt, it is necessary to consider the objectives those policies and practices are trying to achieve. Figure 4-1 summarizes employer objectives and processes or methods. We will review employer objectives here and consider processes below. In the private sector, the conventional wisdom is that management has two core objectives: the maximization of profit and maintaining control over the business. In the public and nonprofit sectors, employers seek to balance operating budgets, comply with government policy initiatives and meet demands for public services at reasonable costs.

Efficiency or Productivity

To maximize profits, private sector employers will seek to increase efficiency or productivity. Efficiency means that goods and services are produced with the lowest possible amount

Objectives	Processes or Methods
1. Efficiency or productivity	1. Union avoidance and opposition measures
2. Control	2. Contract negotiation
	3. Lockouts
	4. Grievances and arbitration
	5. Court (legal) action
	6. Political activity
	7. Public relations
	8. Collaboration with union
	9. Unilateral action

Figure 4-1 Employer Objectives and Processes

of capital, labour, energy, and material resources. Productivity is a measure of how efficiently goods and services are produced. Productivity growth and productivity levels are both important. While the focus in the media is most often on productivity growth rates, the actual level of productivity (i.e., the dollar value of output per hour worked) is equally of interest. Low productivity levels present an enormous challenge for Canada's future economic prosperity. In 2012, Canada's level of labour productivity was US$42, much lower than that of the United States, at US$52. This earned Canada a disappointing 13th place among its 16 peer countries on the level of labour productivity. Worse still, Canada's labour productivity level has fallen to 80 percent of the U.S. level from a high of 91 percent in the mid-1980s. Despite a broad and growing consensus that Canadian productivity needs to be improved, the gap with the United States is widening, not narrowing.[2]

There is disagreement over the measures that should be adopted to improve productivity. Some observers have cited the following as possible reasons for the decline in Canadian labour productivity: insufficient investment in higher education, inadequate quality of math and science education in secondary schools, insufficient employer training, excessive business regulation, and inadequate investment in capital goods.[3] Employers tend to favour measures such as tax cuts and deregulation. Unions prescribe measures such as additional investment in infrastructure and training and development of employees.

Productivity is an important issue facing private sector employers that could affect employees' desire to unionize and union–management relations. Although in the public sector the provision of services is the primary objective rather than the pursuit of profit, there should be the same concern for efficiency or productivity. Governments are facing increased demands for services such as health care, and there is the need to do more with less. Some observers are using the language of the private sector to describe objectives and processes in the public sector. There are references to improving the "business" of government, and viewing the public as "customers."

The nonprofit sector, which may be referred to as the "third sector," provides services in sports and recreation, housing, education, the arts, and social services. Examples include the Canadian Cancer Society, the Vancouver Art Gallery, and Nova Scotia Community Services. The size and importance of the nonprofit sector has been increasing. One of the reasons for this is that some nonprofits are now providing services previously provided by government. There may be some confusion over the size of the nonprofit sector. Some references to the sector include hospitals, colleges, and universities that are also sometimes included in the public sector. In the pursuit of efficiency, employers in all sectors will pursue measures such as outsourcing, making use of temporary workers, and adopting changes in technology, which will have implications for union contract negotiation and administration. The competitive pressures that employers face were referred to in Chapter 2. In some situations where employers have suffered financial reversals, they have made demands for unions to agree to demands for reductions in wages and benefits, referred to as **concession bargaining**. Employer demands may include wage cuts or freezes, lump-sum payments instead of wage increases, loss of holidays, the suspension of cost-of-living wage increases, or the creation of two-tiered wage and benefits systems providing that newly hired workers receive lower compensation than current workers.[4]

Concession bargaining is negotiation over employer demands for reductions in wages and benefits.

Concession bargaining may take place under the threat of business closure. But even where there is no such threat, employers are always concerned with keeping wage increases in line and increasing productivity. Many of the alternatives in this area will lead to confrontations with unions. Union inflexibility is a sore point in employers' eyes. Employers may pursue changes in such rules in the future so that they can increase flexibility and lower costs. They may also press for ability to be given more weight than seniority when filling job vacancies.

When pushing for concessions, employers must be careful that wages stay at a level sufficient to recruit and retain the quality of workers needed to carry out the firm's strategy.

If unskilled labour is all that is needed, employers may be able to limit wage increases or even press for reductions. But if they need a more skilled workforce, firms cannot press for the lowest possible wages without considering the consequences for employee recruiting and retention. Negotiating wage reductions or freezes could backfire and lead to excessive turnover. For the same reason, employers must ensure that benefits such as vacations, health services and pensions are adequate.

Recent environmental developments, including globalization, international trade agreements, and changing workforce demographics, appear to have reduced the power of some unions. It is also possible that a more hostile environment has influenced the attitude of some employers. Employers who once accepted unions, now faced with a competitive environment that threatens their ability to stay in business, might reconsider this position.

Control

Control of the workplace has been cited as a management objective that is as important as efficiency.[5] Managers need control to reduce uncertainty or risk. Additionally, for some managers maintaining control or the right to manage may be based upon personal belief or ideology. They may think that if they are not in control the organization will suffer. For example, if the employer decides to terminate an employee or install video monitoring equipment, there will be an issue with the union. Employers could use all of the measures or processes referred to in Figure 4-1 to achieve the objectives of efficiency and maintaining control. Subsequent chapters will elaborate on most of these processes; an overview is presented here.

Many employers perceive that a union will prevent them from achieving either or both of their objectives of productivity and maintaining control. Accordingly, some employers will take steps, frequently referred to as a *union substitution strategy*, to prevent a union organizing their employees. These measures will include practices such as paying higher wages and providing forms of employee representation. If employees pursue a union, some employers will actively oppose the unionization of their employees by campaigning against the union, or in some cases resorting to legal action to oppose the union. Walmart is one employer that has used various methods, including the courts, to oppose the unionization of its stores. If employers are not successful in avoiding unionization, they can attempt to achieve their objectives when they negotiate a collective agreement with the union. In some cases, employers will be able to avoid a collective agreement entirely, although this is subject to the employer's duty to *bargain in good faith*, a topic discussed in Chapter 8. Alternatively, the employer can pursue terms in the contract that protect its interests, such as avoiding restrictions on outsourcing and technological change. If the employer has difficulty negotiating an agreement with acceptable terms, it may be able to lock out employees to force the union to change its position. An illustration of this was the 2004–05 NHL lockout. When the players' union refused to agree to a salary cap, the league imposed a lockout, and eventually the union backed down, agreeing to the salary cap and salary rollbacks. The employer can use the grievance and arbitration process, which is elaborated upon in Chapter 9, to achieve its objectives. Although unions file most grievances, employers can also use the process to protect their interests. For example, in one case where a union had instructed employees not to participate in an employee suggestion program, an employer filed a grievance and an arbitrator found in favour of the employer. Although very few arbitration decisions are overturned in the courts through the process of judicial review, employers have this available as an option.

In the previous chapter, it was noted that unions engage in political activity. Employers also support political parties and lobby governments for changes in policy, and might also pursue public relations efforts to convince the public to support their cause. An incident in 2004 in Saskatchewan illustrates how employers can use political and public relations activity to achieve their objectives. The Saskatchewan government announced it was going to amend the province's employment standards legislation to require employers with more than 50 workers to allocate additional hours to part-time employees on the basis of their length of service. Employers strongly opposed the proposed legislation, and they organized a campaign to oppose it. Employers formed an association, the Saskatchewan Business Council, which campaigned against the proposal. The council organized a rally, provided a message that employers could transmit to employees, and provided a draft letter opposing the legislation that could be sent to members of the provincial legislature. The message to employees indicated that the legislation would lead to job losses. Letters to newspapers denounced the legislation, calling it a "job killer." The employer's campaign was a success—the government dropped the legislation. Employers can also achieve their objectives by working collaboratively with a union to improve quality and reduce workplace accidents.

Finally, even though a union represents employees, it is still possible for the employer to take unilateral action in areas not covered by the collective agreement. Although such action is subject to constraints, which are referred to when management rights are discussed in Chapter 7, it should be noted that the presence of a union does not eliminate management's residual right to manage. For example, an employer could change the timekeeping system to make it more efficient without consulting the union.

The methods an employer uses to achieve its objectives will be heavily influenced by its labour relations strategy, which we will consider next.

EMPLOYER LABOUR RELATIONS STRATEGY

A labour relations strategy is how an employer deals with the unionization of its employees.

An organization's **labour relations strategy** refers to how the employer chooses to deal with the unionization of its employees. There are several possible broad choices or strategies employers can adopt, ranging from acceptance to extreme opposition. Walmart is known as an employer that vigorously opposes unions and has used various methods to prevent its employees from unionizing. When the United Food and Commercial Workers' union filed an application to represent employees at the store in Weyburn, Saskatchewan, in 2004, Walmart launched a legal challenge that continued for several years. The union was certified in December 2008, but since then the case has been back before the Saskatchewan Labour Relations Board and the courts numerous times. The provincial labour laws changed during this period and a decertification drive was launched at the store. In December 2012, the Saskatchewan Court of Appeal issued a new ruling that sided with Walmart. The union sought to take that decision to the Supreme Court, but its application to appeal was dismissed in August, 2013.

We will first consider the factors that may affect the employer's approach to unions and then consider alternative strategies.

Factors Affecting an Employer's Labour Relations Strategy

Competitive strategy refers to the basis on which a firm competes.

Cost leadership is a competitive strategy based on having the lowest price.

Differentiation is a competitive strategy based on having a distinctive or unique product.

Competitive Strategy of the Employer A firm's **competitive strategy** refers to how it tries to compete in the marketplace over the long term—how it attracts buyers and improves its market share. There are several frameworks that classify strategies by referring to different variables; we will refer to the relevant types of strategy described by Michael Porter in *Competitive Advantage*.[6] **Cost leadership** is a strategy in which the firm competes on the basis of price. It requires cutting costs so that products or services can be sold at a lower price. A discount retail store that carries the same products as other stores, but sells them at a lower price, is using this strategy. In contrast to a cost leadership strategy, a firm might adopt a **differentiation** strategy—one that involves the firm competing on the basis of having a distinctive or unique product. A firm that manufactures appliances that have better design features and dependability is using a differentiation strategy. A successful differentiation strategy allows the firm to charge higher prices because the product is perceived as being worth more.

When a firm's strategy is based on cost leadership, it is more likely to be opposed to unionization, since it would wish to avoid the higher compensation costs that could result. On the other hand, a differentiation strategy may be compatible with the higher costs associated with unionization. Also, unions provide a voice to employees, which may suit a differentiation strategy by encouraging worker input on matters related to quality and customer service.

Union or Non-union Status of Competitors   A firm that competes in an industry that is heavily unionized may be less likely to oppose unionization than a firm whose competitors are all non-union. If the firm were the only unionized competitor, it would have to be concerned about its compensation costs exceeding that of its competitors.

Experience with Unionization   If a firm has several operations, some which have been unionized, its experience with collective bargaining may affect the employer's approach to unions at locations that are not yet unionized. If the experience has been negative, perhaps because of a strike, the employer would more likely oppose unionization at its non-union locations.

Management Values or Ideology   The values or outlook of key managers toward unions could affect the employer's labour relations strategy. If managers oppose unions on a personal level, they may be more inclined to oppose or try to eliminate the union even if the rational choice would be to pursue collaboration. The values and beliefs of the original owner of a company could affect the firm's approach to unions.

Union Philosophy or Policy   The approach or philosophy of the union the employer is dealing with may affect the choices and actions available to it. An employer might wish to pursue a more cooperative approach; however, the success of this will depend on the union's reaction. Some unions have been more receptive to employer efforts to make changes and include the union in the change process.

Union Power and Ability to Oppose Employer   If a firm is already unionized, the union's strength or power may influence how the employer approaches it. If an employer is considering a strategy that involves confronting or challenging the union, it may be more likely to adopt this strategy if the union is in a weaker position. It is reasonable to assume that an employer with only one unionized location among several would oppose the union because it is vulnerable. In the banking industry, if only one branch is unionized, it would be relatively easy for the employer to take a hard-line approach.

Types of Employees   Certain types of employees, such as those who are part-time, younger, or have a higher turnover rate, may make it easier for employers to be more union-hostile. Younger employees may be less familiar with unionization and their rights, and more likely to quit in the face of employer opposition. In contrast, employees who are highly skilled and full-time have more invested in the workplace, may be less likely to quit, and more likely to support the union in a confrontation.

Legal Environment   The legal environment can affect the employer's ability to oppose unionization and the approach taken by the employer. Generally the legal environment in Canada makes it more difficult for employers to oppose unionization here than in the United States. In Canada, some jurisdictions allow a union to obtain the right to represent employees on the basis of signed membership cards without a vote of employees. In the United States, a vote is mandatory in all applications for bargaining rights, and there is a delay between the union application and the vote, which may permit employers to mount a campaign opposing the union. Even after a union obtains bargaining rights, employers in both countries have a second opportunity to defeat the union in negotiations. However, in most Canadian jurisdictions, there is a provision for the arbitration of first contract disputes if an employer takes an unreasonable position in bargaining: a reluctant employer may have a first contract imposed. There is no equivalent provision in the United States. In the United States, there are 24 right-to-work states. The "right to work" principle affirms the right of every American in such states to work without being compelled to belong to a union. Key elements of such state laws are the prohibition of mandatory union membership and dues deduction. This has led to the establishment of a largely union-free region, which employers may relocate to. Moreover, U.S. employers are allowed to hire permanent replacements for striking workers. In several Canadian jurisdictions, employees who have gone on strike have the right to reclaim their jobs at the conclusion of the strike.

Possible Employer Strategies

We will consider five possible labour relations strategies an employer might adopt when dealing with unions.

Union opposition is an employer strategy of attempting to remain union-free.

Union Opposition   **Union opposition** is the strategy used when the employer has no unionized employees and wants it to stay that way. Employers adopting this strategy are likely hostile to unions and may be willing to use both legal and illegal methods to avoid unionization. Some have used tactics such as avoiding the selection of union supporters, transferring union supporters, and dismissing employees. It is reported that the banking and fast food industries have actively opposed unions in the past.

Union avoidance is a strategy aimed at preventing unionization using legal means to convince employees they do not need a union.

Union Avoidance or Substitution   **Union avoidance** is another strategy used to prevent unionization, where the employer uses legal means to convince employees they do not need a union. It might involve matching the union rate of pay in an industry. The steel industry is often cited to illustrate this tactic. Dofasco was a non-union producer that historically had matched union compensation existing at Stelco, a unionized producer of steel, to avoid unionization. The Hamilton, Ontario–based company, an anti-union stronghold in the industry since 1912, merged in 2006 with ArcelorMittal, the world's largest steelmaker, which has both union and non-union plants. In March 2008, the new company announced an opportunity allowing the United Steel Workers' union to approach its employees to test the suitability of a union in its unique working culture. Later that month, the union indicated that it would not pursue an organizing drive at the Hamilton plant.

Union acceptance is a strategy in which the employer remains neutral in an organizing attempt, and if the attempt is successful tries to negotiate the best deal with the union.

Union Acceptance   **Union acceptance** refers to a strategy in which the employer may not want to have a union but remains neutral in an organization attempt. If the drive succeeds, the employer tries to negotiate the best collective agreement possible. The adoption of a union acceptance strategy means that the employer will pursue processes that involve the union, such as joint union–management committees.

Union resistance is a strategy in which the employer attempts to limit the further spread of unionization in the organization.

Union Resistance   A **union resistance** strategy might arise in a firm that is partially unionized. The firm attempts to limit the further spread of unionization. This strategy may involve aspects of the union avoidance strategy, such as extending wage improvements negotiated with unionized employees to non-union employees.

Union removal is a strategy in which the employer attempts to rid itself of any unions.

Union Removal   A **union removal** strategy involves the employer attempting to rid itself of any unions. The tactics used might include stalling in negotiations in the hope employees will become frustrated with the union, enduring a strike in the hope employees will become disenchanted with the union, or attempting to use the legal process to challenge the union. After a union organized employees at a McDonald's in Canada for the first time, the company unsuccessfully attempted to challenge the certification of the union in the courts.[7] Subsequently, the union was not able to negotiate a collective agreement, and employees voted to terminate its bargaining rights.

Strategies of Canadian Employers

It has been commonly thought that Canadian employers do not oppose unions as much as employers in the United States. However, a distinction should be drawn between employer actions before a union obtains the right to represent employees and after the union has obtained bargaining rights. A study examining employer opposition to unions at the organizing stage suggests that employers commonly oppose a union attempting to gain bargaining rights. The study considered employer reaction to organizing attempts in eight Canadian jurisdictions. Opposition to the union was found to be the norm; only 20 percent of employers did not oppose the attempt in some manner. Sixty percent of employers admitted to engaging in active resistance to the union, and 12 percent admitted to committing unfair labour practices during the organizing drive.[8] This study suggests that employer opposition to union certification is more frequent and persistent than has been assumed in the past. Once a union has obtained bargaining rights, there is evidence that the predominant approach in Canada is union acceptance. A survey of unionized private sector firms in the early 1990s found that many firms engaged in hard bargaining and some had obtained concessions on wages and benefits; however, the majority still followed an acceptance strategy. Only 9 percent had the objective of reducing or eliminating union influence, and only 17 percent followed the policy of actively avoiding further unionization.[9]

Importance of Labour Relations Strategy

The labour relations strategy adopted by management, for example union acceptance versus union removal, will affect the processes and policies of the employer and its human resources function. The organization's basic outlook toward unions will affect the extent to which the employer is willing to adopt less confrontational processes such as mutual gains bargaining, referred to in Chapter 8.

ALTERNATIVE HR STRATEGIES OR APPROACHES TO HR MANAGEMENT

When dealing with the new economic realities, employers must consider two alterative human resource management strategies or approaches to human resource management: a **high commitment HR strategy** or a **low commitment HR strategy**. The high commitment strategy may be referred to by alternative names, including a high road approach to HRM. The low commitment strategy may be referred to as a low-road or low-cost approach to HRM.[10] The low commitment approach involves the continued use of traditional production methods, a low emphasis on technological innovation, little concern for the development of workforce skills, and attempts to cut labour costs to compete with low-wage producers. The low-road approach is linked to a cost leadership competitive strategy.

The high commitment approach involves seeking a competitive advantage by pursuing product and service differentiation instead of competing on the basis of price, using labour with more skills and perhaps providing higher compensation, adopting better technology

A low commitment HR strategy involves traditional production methods, and a low emphasis on development of workforce skills.

A high commitment HR strategy involves the adoption of better technology and requires investment in training and development of human resources.

and production systems, investing more in training, using labour with more skills, and perhaps providing higher compensation. As part of this approach, employers might move toward a "high-performance work system," discussed next.

High-Performance Work Systems

High-performance work systems (HPWS) may be referred to by alternative names, including high commitment, high involvement, the mutual gains enterprise, and new human resources management.[11] Some observers have noted that the qualifier "high performance" assumes that the systems actually increase performance and may not yet have been established.

Features of High-Performance Systems   An HPWS assumes that human resources are the key to competitive advantage for firms in an uncertain and changing environment. In order to compete using improved technology and organizational innovations, highly skilled, trained, and motivated employees are required. Just as there is no consensus on the name that should be applied to these systems, there is no definitive set of features or components of an HPWS. Key Considerations 4-1 outlines policies and practices that are frequently associated with a HPWS.[12]

Some of the features of a HPWS, such as employment security, job redesign, higher compensation, and grievance systems, are not new; they are traditional human resource management practices. Many of the features or components listed in Key Considerations 4-1 are self-explanatory; however, a few will be elaborated upon here.

Job redesign could involve job enrichment, increasing the skills and responsibility involved in the work. It frequently involves moving to work teams that have various levels of authority. Some teams may be given authority to make decisions formerly made by managers. Contingent or incentive compensation refers to pay for knowledge systems as opposed to job-based pay to encourage learning. It can also include profit- or gain-sharing programs aimed at encouraging participation. Group bonuses are another possibility. Information sharing includes providing employees with feedback on unit and company performance. Minimizing status differences refers to eliminating practices, such as separate washrooms, eating areas, and preferential parking for managers. Employee involvement is a key component of an HPWS. It includes practices aimed at increasing employee participation, such as quality circles, which may make recommendations to management, advisory committees, and problem-solving groups.

Some forms of participation may be direct, referring to the fact that employees deal directly with management, while others are indirect, meaning that employee representatives deal with management. "Dispute resolution processes" refers to measures to protect

---

Key Considerations 4-1

Policies and Practices for a High-Performance Work System

1. High standards in recruiting and selection
2. Job redesign
3. Comparatively high compensation contingent on organizational performance
4. Employment security
5. Sharing of financial and performance information with employees
6. Minimum status differences
7. Employee involvement
8. Dispute resolution systems
9. Training and skill development
10. Performance expectations emphasizing continuous quality improvement

employee interests, including formal committees with employee and management representatives. Some employers have gone as far as allowing these committees to make binding decisions. The training and skill development required does not refer just to technical skills. In order for employees to be able to work in teams and become more involved, they will need training in areas such as communication, conflict resolution, and decision making. Some of the proponents of HPWS note that in order for a system to be successful, it cannot be adopted in piecemeal fashion because some of the components support each other. For example, if an organization invested additional resources in training and skill development, but did not provide for increased compensation, it is possible that employees would quit and take their additional skills to a new employer.

Adoption of High-Performance Systems in Canada The evidence indicates that high-performance work systems have not yet been widely adopted in Canada. It appears that a majority of Canadian employers have adopted some high-performance workplace features and practices, but only a few have adopted a complete package.[13] The majority maintain a traditional system in which little strategic priority is placed on human resources.[14] The high-performance model seems to have been more widely adopted in the United States.

Effectiveness of High-Performance Practices Whether high-performance practices have been effective is a matter of some debate. A HPWS could entail additional costs, especially in the areas of training and development, and compensation. Some observers point to U.S. and Canadian research that shows high-performance systems produce positive financial results.[15] However, others say that "it would appear that, on average, the full adoption of this paradigm may not yield outcomes that are appreciably more positive than those yielded by practices that have long been associated with good management, including professional personnel practices (e.g., job ladders, employment security, grievance systems, formal training, above-market pay), group work organization, information sharing and accommodative union relation policies."[16] One study indicates that in-depth industry studies show that there are specific industry contexts in which there is a distinct possibility that firms will benefit from the high-involvement route to high performance. The most conclusive evidence comes from the work on automobile manufacturing and from the studies of steel production. In these cases, there is good evidence that willing worker engagement in problem solving in a technologically sensitive production process enhances machine uptime, quality, and on-time delivery. However, the authors of the study also noted that there is clearly a need for caution with overgeneralized claims of economic benefits, and that the path ahead is very much one of studying production processes in specific worksites and industries.[17]

Significance for Labour Relations The adoption of high-performance practices by some employers has implications for labour relations. Some have questioned whether high-performance practices have had negative effects for employees, including increased workload, more stress, longer hours, and a faster pace of work.[18] Unionized employers seeking to adopt features of HPWS will likely encounter union resistance to some components of an HPWS. To improve product quality and productivity, firms must pursue technological innovation. Unions will seek protection in collective agreements from technological change leading to job losses. Employers may seek contingent or variable pay plans for the purposes of increasing productivity that might include gain sharing and profit sharing. Where the employer seeks to implement changes such as variable pay that are different from established collective agreement terms, the likelihood of union resistance appears to be high. Although employers may be able to implement some changes without the consent of the union where the changes are not prohibited by the collective agreement, the effectiveness of this approach is questionable.

There is evidence that union participation and support of innovation programs can improve the chances of their success. In the United States, increased employee involvement has been part of employer attempts to avoid unionization. Canadian unions fear employee involvement as a tactic employers might use to influence employees and weaken the union. Employers who wish to increase employee and union involvement will have to address these concerns.

Implications for Practice

1. The firm's competitive strategy has implications for its labour relations strategy; the reverse is also true. The firm's labour relations strategy should fit its competitive business model. Where the firm's competitive strategy puts a premium on employee involvement and union cooperation, a strategy of union removal may not be advisable.

2. Canadian employers should be wary of copying strategies adopted by some U.S. firms, including union removal, without first considering the social, political, and legal environment in Canada, which may not be suitable for some of these strategies.

3. Employers who wish to pursue high-performance work practices should consider the extent to which the current collective agreement prevents their adoption. The employer should address any such problems in contract negotiations.

4. Employers who wish to pursue high-performance work practices that do not require union approval because they are not covered by the collective agreement should consider the extent to which the union should be involved in designing such practices. Although union involvement may not be required, it may increase the likelihood of acceptance and success.

Key Terms

competitive strategy, p. 76

concession bargaining, p. 74

cost leadership, p. 76

differentiation, p. 76

high commitment HR strategy, p. 79

labour relations strategy, p. 76

low commitment HR strategy, p. 79

union acceptance, p. 78

union avoidance, p. 78

union opposition, p. 78

union removal, p. 78

union resistance, p. 78

Review Questions

1. What are two key objectives of employers? In the light of each of these objectives, explain at least one process or method a company could use to achieve each objective.
2. Identify three different factors affecting an employer's labour relations strategy.
3. Distinguish between a cost leadership and a differentiation strategy for a business.
4. Outline the difference between a union substitution strategy and one other possible employer labour relations approach.
5. Describe the implications of a cost leadership or differentiation strategy for labour relations.
6. Explain the significance of a high-performance work system for labour relations.

Discussion Questions

1. Walmart is one firm that seems opposed to its employees joining a union. What are the possible reasons for this organization's approach toward unions?
2. Generally, Canadian employers have not adopted a strategy to eliminate unions. What are the possible reasons for this?

3. Contrast the likely desire and ability of the following two employers to oppose unionization:
   (a) A fast-food outlet
   (b) A publicly owned nuclear power facility

4. Why will it be difficult for some employers to adopt what is known as a low commitment approach to human resources?

5. Review the policies and practices associated with a high-performance work system in Key Considerations 4-1. Explain which of these items could lead to disagreement between a union and an employer.

Web Research

LabourWatch (**www.labourwatch.com**) has a public website operated by the Canadian LabourWatch Association. Members of the association include the Canadian Federation of Independent Business, the Canadian Restaurant and Foodservices Association, and the Retail Council of Canada. The site provides information for employers who want to avoid or eliminate a union. Here are some suggested activities:

1. Go to the Resource Centre tab on the site's homepage. In the drop-down menu, select Decisions and Legislation to choose an example of a federal or provincial court decision that may have an impact on Canadian employers.

2. Under the tab Special Topics, select Union Fines and read a Related Press story that may be of interest to a Canadian company.

CASE INCIDENT   WALMART AND THE UFCW

In November 2003 Walmart opened a new store in Weyburn, Saskatchewan. Soon afterwards, employees contacted the United Food and Commercial Workers Union (UFCW) seeking representation. In April 2004 the union filed an application with the Saskatchewan Labour Relations Board to represent these employees. The application to represent is an application for certification, the details of which are referred to in Chapter 6. This filing was the start of a legal battle that lasted until 2013.

The union sought an order from the Board to require Walmart to produce documents. It was alleged that Walmart had provided managers with materials that showed Walmart was guilty of illegal practices, including a document titled "A Manager's Toolbox to Remain Union Free." The Board ordered Walmart to produce records and Walmart appealed this decision. On the appeal a lower court judge quashed the subpoena and in his decision appeared to suggest that the Board was biased in favour of unions.

Subsequently there were numerous comments on the situation in the media, some of which were critical of the Labour Relations Board and the provisions of the *Trade Union Act* that allowed a union to be certified without an employee vote. There were calls for amendments to the legislation and changes at the Board. Some critics alleged that union contributions to the NDP party which was in power at the time made change unlikely.

The Court of Appeal overturned the lower court decision and ordered Walmart to produce the documentation. The Court of Appeal also indicated that the lower court's concerns regarding a possible bias in favour of unions by the Labour Relations Board were unfounded. Walmart attempted to appeal this decision to the Supreme Court of Canada, and this further delayed the certification application.

While the Weyburn battle raged, there was a related development in Quebec. In February 2005, Walmart announced that it would close a store in Jonquière, Quebec, which had been unionized for four months. Labour activists claimed that this closing was intended to send a message to employees in Weyburn and elsewhere in North America about the negative consequences of seeking unionization. The president of the Saskatchewan Federation of Labour referred to "economic terrorism" against Canadian workers.

In April 2005, one full year after the original application for certification, the Supreme Court of Canada refused to grant Walmart leave to appeal, and the certification process continued. Walmart filed an application to block the Labour Relations Board from hearing the application, alleging the Board was biased; however, a court decision rejected that application.

Through this process, a Walmart website stated that the company respects "the individual rights of our associates and encourage them to express their ideas, comments and concerns. Because we believe in maintaining an open environment of open communications, we do not believe there is a need for third-party representation." Walmart had some supporters in the ongoing battle. One newspaper commentary provided as follows: "This province's unions are aggressive by nature, helped along by labour laws that favour unions far more than business, something that has been used by businesses as a clear illustration as to why companies avoid coming to Saskatchewan. . . . Presumably the union has jobs for the approximately 3500 to 4000 employees who would be put out of work if Wal-Mart . . . walked. Wal-Mart is a huge player in Saskatchewan. It provides hundreds of employees with jobs. It pays taxes. It is possibly the most popular retail outfit in the province. To lose something like that would be a major blow to the province's economy and employment levels not to mention the government's open for business slogan it shops around the country."

In a 2007 provincial election, the NDP government was defeated by the Saskatchewan Party. In March 2008 the new government ended the term of the chair of the Saskatchewan Labour Relations Board who had been dealing with the UFCW certification application, and in May 2008 amendments to the *Trade Union Act* that required a vote on certification applications came into effect. The chair of the Board continued to deal with the Weyburn application, asserting he had the authority to finish applications started before his term was ended on the basis of the law as it was at the time. In December 2008 a certification order was granted. In 2009 Walmart challenged the certification in court on the basis that the chair did not have jurisdiction and that the amendments to the *Trade Union Act* required a vote. In June 2009 a lower court overturned the certification. Subsequently the union indicated that it would be appealing the decision.

In July 2009 Walmart filed an application for a court injunction to restrict the activity of a union website critical of the company. UFCW Canada National President Wayne Hanley responded, "This injunction request is an over the top assault on effective freedom of speech. . . . It's a kneejerk response by Walmart to the idea of its employees trying to understand their options as workers, and trying to share experiences with other 'associates'. Walmart's response to the success of **www.walmartworkerscanada.ca** is just another outrageous example of how the largest retailer in the history of the world will use its bottomless legal budget to manipulate the collective bargaining process and do just about anything to discourage its 'associates' from joining the union."

In August 2013, the Saskatchewan Labour Relations Board made the decision to decertify the United Food and Commercial Workers union which had been unsuccessful in its attempts to negotiate a collective agreement with the retail giant. Employees at the Weyburn store had voted to remove the union by a margin of 51–5.

Questions

1. Identify the employer's labour relations strategy, and explain possible reasons for this strategy.

2. Outline the environmental factors referred to in Chapter 2 affecting this situation.

3. In the light of the Supreme Court of Canada decision (June 2014) involving Walmart and a Quebec store closure in 2005, how might the company's labour relations strategies be modified?

Chapter 5

Governments, Labour Relations Boards, and Other Parties

Chapter Objectives

1. Explain the objectives of governments and the processes or methods used to achieve those objectives
2. Explain the composition, roles, and importance of Labour Relations Boards

Required Professional Capabilities (CCHRA)	HRPA Human Resources Professionals Competency Framework
10101, 10102, 10303, 10405, 10509, 20301, 20302, 20307, 50304, 50305, 50402, 50405	C035, C036, C037, C038, C112, C116, C117, C119, C120, C122, C125

Federal and provincial governments in Canada are frequently challenged by overseeing the economic well-being of citizens in their jurisdiction as well as creating structures and systems to enable various groups within our society to interact in a manner that reflects the principles of our political, social and economic beliefs and values. Sometimes the notion of a "free market" economy and the impact it may have on the lives of average Canadians creates a policy dilemma for politicians. Should the government look the other way when a corporation decides to close a plant or relocate it to another country leaving area residents without jobs? Political leaders are then suddenly thrust into the spotlight being asked if they will offer any form of incentives, via cash inflows or tax breaks to help persuade the company to stay in a large urban industrial centre or a smaller, rural outpost. Since the depths of the recession in June 2009, 830 000 new jobs were created in Canada. At that time, government bailouts to both General Motors ($10.9m) and Chrysler ($2.9m) had some questioning whether such financial aid was justified for a combined workforce of some 22 000 auto industry employees. Others argued that the loss of key manufacturing plants in affected cities, particularly in Ontario, would cause insurmountable hardship not only from immediate job loss at either auto company but also on Tier 2 supporting industries as well as the local economies in affected communities. A completely different challenge for government is ensuring that a legal framework is created and maintained to oversee relationships in the workplace. Labour boards and related agencies at the federal, provincial, and territorial levels are products of such government responsibility. This framework provides protection against employer excesses and assures individual workers of a means to claim that their rights as protected by the *Charter of Rights and Freedoms*, other legislation, and the common law. These legal frameworks are continuously tested by new situations and the resulting decisions made by the judicial system, third-party interveners, and parties to the collective bargaining.

In Chapter 3, we considered unions as actors in the labour relations system, and outlined their objectives and methods. In Chapter 4, we looked at employers and their objectives and methods. In this chapter, we will consider the third main actor, government. This will include government objectives—the reasons for government involvement in labour relations—and methods available to governments to achieve their objectives. We will briefly refer to other parties involved in labour relations, paying special attention to labour relations boards.

GOVERNMENT OBJECTIVES AND PROCESSES

Figure 5-1 summarizes government objectives relating to labour relations, and the methods governments use to achieve their objectives.

Some of the objectives and processes we will explore, including the regulation of labour relations outcomes through labour relations legislation, have a direct impact on unions and employers. Other objectives, such as regulating the economy through monetary and fiscal policy, have an indirect effect on employers and unions. Monetary policy that provides for higher interest rates to control inflation is not directly aimed at employers and unions; however, it will affect them. Some of the objectives overlap: for example, government attempts to regulate labour relations outcomes also protect the public interest. Government efforts to regulate the economy also affect the distribution of rewards that may be a government concern. Fiscal policy that reduces taxes to stimulate the economy should increase employment and thus affects the distribution of rewards. There may be conflict between some of the objectives and processes. Some observers argue that efforts to pursue equal opportunity and regulate employment conditions through employment equity and employment standards legislation deter business, and negatively impact the economy. One process could help achieve several different objectives. For example, providing financial assistance to a particular industry serves the government objectives of regulating the economy and maintaining office.

Regulation of Labour Relations Processes

The key processes in labour relations are union organizing, contract negotiation, and the administration of collective agreements. The need for government regulation in this area was illustrated in the history of labour relations in Chapter 3. Prior to government regulation of

Objectives	Processes or Methods
1. Regulation of labour relations processes	1. Legislation relating to labour relations, employment standards, human rights, health and safety, pay equity, and employment equity
2. Regulation of labour relations outcomes	
3. Protection of the public interest	
4. Regulation of the economy: employment and inflation	2. Specific dispute resolution (back-to-work) legislation
5. Aid to particular industries	3. Contract negotiation
6. Regulation of the results of a market economy: monitoring equitable opportunity, rewards, and minimum employment conditions	4. Grievances and arbitration
	5. Public relations initiatives
	6. Providing assistance and information to employers and unions regarding labour relations issues
7. Government employers: efficiency and control	7. Monetary and fiscal policy
8. Maintenance of political office	8. Ownership of some enterprises
	9. Legal action

Figure 5-1 Government Objectives and Processes

Jurisdiction	Statute	Website
Federal	*Canada Labour Code,* Part I: Industrial Relations	www.canlii.org/en/ca/laws/stat/rsc-1985-c-l-2/latest/rsc-1985-c-l-2.html *Note: Federal legislation also applies to Northwest Territories, Nunavut and the Yukon*
Alberta	*Labour Relations Code*	www.canlii.org/en/ab/laws/stat/rsa-2000-c-l-1/latest/rsa-2000-c-l-1.html
British Columbia	*Labour Relations Code*	www.canlii.org/en/bc/laws/stat/rsbc-1996-c-244/latest/rsbc-1996-c-244.html
Manitoba	*Labour Relations Act*	www.canlii.org/en/mb/laws/stat/ccsm-c-l10/latest/ccsm-c-l10.html
New Brunswick	*Industrial Relations Act*	www.canlii.org/en/nb/laws/stat/rsnb-1973-c-i-4/latest/rsnb-1973-c-i-4.html www.gnb.ca/0062/acts/acts/i-04.htm
Newfoundland and Labrador	*Labour Relations Act*	http://www.assembly.nl.ca/legislation/sr/statutes/l01.htm
Nova Scotia	*Trade Union Act*	www.canlii.org/en/ns/laws/stat/rsns-1989-c-475/latest/rsns-1989-c-475.html
Ontario	*Labour Relations Act*	www.canlii.org/en/on/laws/stat/rso-1990-c-l2/latest/rso-1990-c-l2.html
Prince Edward Island	*Labour Act*	www.canlii.org/en/pe/laws/stat/rspei-1988-c-l-1/latest/rspei-1988-c-l-1.html
Quebec	*Labour Code*	www.canlii.org/en/qc/laws/stat/rsq-c-c-27/latest/rsq-c-c-27.html
Saskatchewan	*Trade Union Act*	www.canlii.org/en/sk/laws/stat/rss-1978-c-t-17/latest/rss-1978-c-t-17.html
Northwest Territories	*Canada Labour Code,* Part 1: Industrial Relations	www.canlii.org/en/ca/laws/stat/rsc-1985-c-l-2/latest/rsc-1985-c-l-2.html
Nunavut	*Canada Labour Code,* Part 1: Industrial Relations	www.canlii.org/en/ca/laws/stat/rsc-1985-c-l-2/latest/rsc-1985-c-l-2.html
Yukon	*Canada Labour Code,* Part 1: Industrial Relations	www.canlii.org/en/ca/laws/stat/rsc-1985-c-l-2/latest/rsc-1985-c-l-2.html

Figure 5-2 Private Sector Labour Relations Legislation

the organizing process, strikes—sometimes violent—were used to force employers to recognize and negotiate with unions. Prior to government regulation, employers discriminated against union supporters. The primary method governments use to regulate labour relations processes is labour relations legislation. Figure 5-2 provides online sourcing of labour laws affecting private sector employers in federal, provincial, and territorial jurisdictions.

This legislation sets out rules regulating how a union obtains the right to represent employees, listing the rights of employers during an organizing campaign, imposing a duty to bargain in good faith on both the parties, and requiring disputes during the term of a collective agreement to be resolved through arbitration.

Regulation of Labour Relations Outcomes

Collective agreements, strikes, and lockouts are key outcomes in the labour relations system, while strikes and lockouts are viewed as both processes and outputs of the system. Collective agreement terms could affect the economy by causing inflationary pressure, and some strikes and lockouts could harm the public. Some unionized employees may still need protection regarding the terms and conditions of their work, because being in a union does not guarantee adequate rewards or safe working conditions. Governments use several methods to regulate labour relations outcomes. Labour relations legislation in all jurisdictions requires a strike to be approved by an employee vote, and a strike notice is required in some jurisdictions. As noted earlier in this chapter, governments can pass back-to-work legislation to end a particular strike. Employment standards legislation sets out minimum terms of employment such as maximum hours that can be worked, minimum wages, vacations, and pregnancy and parental leave.

Protection of the Public Interest

There is a broader public interest that needs protection. It is possible that a strike might not seriously harm the employer because it can carry on business using an inventory of finished product. It is possible that a strike might not seriously harm the union because of strike pay, financial assistance from other unions, and the attainment of alternative work by striking employees alternative work during a work stoppage. However, a strike could inconvenience or harm the public interest by eliminating an important service such as public transit. To limit the impact of such labour disruptions to the public, governments may seek to avoid strikes and lockouts through one or more of the following: labour relations legislation that places restrictions on strikes and lockouts, assistance during negotiation in the form of conciliation and mediation, and back-to-work legislation. Figure 5-3 lists websites for the government ministries responsible for labour issues. It is recommended that you review the site for your jurisdiction. A government may also use legal action to achieve its objectives. For example, in 2009 the federal government started legal proceedings against U.S. Steel to enforce commitments the company had made to Ottawa when it was allowed to take over Stelco.

	Website
Federal: Ministry of Labour	www.labour.gc.ca/eng/home.shtml
Alberta: Employment and Immigration	http://work.alberta.ca/index.html
British Columbia: Ministry of Labour	www.lrb.bc.ca
Manitoba: Labour and Immigration	www.gov.mb.ca/labour
New Brunswick: Post-Secondary Education, Training and Labour	http://laws.gnb.ca/en/deplinks?subjectnumber=32
Newfoundland and Labrador: Labour Relations Agency	www.gov.nl.ca/lra
Northwest Territories: Labour Relations	www.hr.gov.nt.ca/about/labour-relations
Nova Scotia: Labour and Workforce Development	www.gov.ns.ca/lwd
Nunavut: Labour Standards	www.nucj.ca/lso/#en
Ontario: Ministry of Labour	www.labour.gov.on.ca
Prince Edward Island: Community Services, Seniors and Labour	www.gov.pe.ca/jps/index.php3
Quebec: Les services en relations du travail	www.cnt.gouv.qc.ca/en
Saskatchewan: Advanced Education, Employment and Labour	www.labour.gov.sk.ca
Yukon	www.psc.gov.yk.ca/staffrelations/staffrelations.html

Figure 5-3 Ministries Responsible for Labour Issues

Regulation of the Economy

The regulation and improvement of the economy is a key government objective that will affect employers and unions. Governments may wish to control inflation and unemployment through monetary and fiscal policy. They may also seek to establish a positive climate for investment through measures such as tax cuts and aid for industry. Concern about government debt levels could lead to reductions in government spending and employment. The federal government may pursue trade deals, such as NAFTA, that will impact employers and unions.

Assistance to Industry

All levels of government may engage in efforts to provide assistance to an industry. In 2009, the federal and Ontario governments decided to use massive amounts of taxpayer cash to rescue two corporations deemed too big to fail, General Motors and Chrysler. The cost to Canadians was nearly US$14 billion in total. In early 2013, the Government of Newfoundland and Labrador announced a $3.6 million loan to be provided to Carino Company Ltd. to bail out the declining sealing industry.[1] The previous year, the provincial government provided a $2 million dollar subsidy to the company. At the time, Carino pledged to repay the entire loan, but then repaid only half of the debt. Despite this, the Newfoundland government announced even more subsidies to Carino.

Regulating Market Practices and Results

There are concerns about the practices and results in an unregulated market economy. It is possible that without regulation, safety in the workplace would be diminished and undesirable practices such as discrimination could increase. There may also be concerns about the equitable distribution of job opportunities and rewards. This is a controversial area, because there are those who think there is no need for government intervention, or that such intervention does not work. There has been a long-standing debate about whether minimum wage laws protect employees or cause unemployment. Government methods in this area include employment standards legislation that sets out minimum terms of employment, including wages, vacations, leaves of absence, and work hours. Employment standards legislation will affect the negotiation and administration of collective agreements referred to in later chapters. The collective agreement must provide employees with at least the minimum provided in the legislation. If the relevant legislation provides for a minimum bereavement leave, a collective agreement cannot provide less time off. This is sometimes referred to as not being able to "contract out" of such employment standards obligations. In the course of the administration of the agreement, employers and unions will have to ensure that employment terms minimum wage not expressly referred to in the collective agreement at least meet the minimum provided in employment standards legislation. If the agreement did not include leave for parents adopting children, the leave provided for in the legislation would have to be granted. The employer and the union will also have to ensure that changes in employment standards legislation, which may provide new or additional protection to employees that is not provided in the agreement, have been complied with. Recently, employment standards legislation in most jurisdictions has been amended to provide for compassionate care leave. This development allows employees to take unpaid time off to attend to seriously ill family members. Employment standards are continually amended and updated, so reference should be made to the legislation and government ministry for current information. For information relating to employment standards, refer to the websites listed in Figures 5-4 and 5-5.

Employment Standard	Labour Canada Website
Minimum wage	www.labour.gc.ca/eng/standards_equity/st/pubs_st/minimum_wages.shtml
Hours of work, overtime, breaks	http://www.labour.gc.ca/eng/standards_equity/st/pubs_st/hours.shtml?
Days of rest, Sunday work	www.labour.gc.ca/eng/standards_equity/st/pubs_st/hours.shtml
Holidays	http://www.labour.gc.ca/eng/standards_equity/st/pubs_st/general_holidays.shtml
Vacations	www.labour.gc.ca/eng/standards_equity/st/pubs_st/annual_vacations.shtml
Maternity and parental leave	www.labour.gc.ca/eng/standards_equity/st/pubs_st/maternity.shtml
Compassionate care leave	www.labour.gc.ca/eng/standards_equity/st/pubs_st/compassionate.shtml
Notice of termination—individual employee or groups of employees	www.labour.gc.ca/eng/standards_equity/st/pubs_st/terminations.shtml

Figure 5-4 Employment Standards Information: Labour Canada

Alberta	www.employment.alberta.ca/SFW/1224.html
British Columbia	www.labour.gov.bc.ca/esb/
Manitoba	www.gov.mb.ca/labour/standards/index.html
New Brunswick	www.gnb.ca/0308/index-e.asp
Newfoundland and Labrador	www.gov.nl.ca/lra/faq/labourstandards.html
Nova Scotia	www.gov.ns.ca/lwd/employmentrights
Ontario	www.labour.gov.on.ca/english/es
Prince Edward Island	www.gov.pe.ca/sss/index.php3?number=1002354&lang=E
Saskatchewan	www.labour.gov.sk.ca/standards/index.htm

Figure 5-5 Employment Standards Information: Provinces

There are important considerations associated with employment standards legislation. First, many of the standards are set at a low level. Although some standards appear to provide a reasonable level of protection and have been adopted by some employers as established policy, others offer minimal protection, and many employers provide more than the legislation requires. For example, the provided vacation entitlement is minimal and the minimum wage could not be considered a living wage. Second, certain categories of employees are exempted from some employment standards provisions. Third, there are problems with the enforcement of the legislation. In 2013, the Ministry of Labour in Ontario announced actions to protect retail workers' rights and promote fairness in the workplace by launching a province-wide employment standards retail inspection blitz. Government inspectors visited retailers—such as grocery stores, gas stations and shopping malls—between October and December that year to make sure workplace rights were being protected in areas including public holiday pay, overtime pay, hours of work, and vacation pay. Since 2004, Ontario's Employment Standards Program recovered more than $100 million in wages and other monies owed to employees.[2]

Human rights legislation protects employees from discrimination and harassment. Health and safety legislation provides protection against accidents, industrial diseases and in some jurisdictions harassment. This legislation sets out minimum terms for the workplace, such as a health and safety committee, which may be exceeded in a collective agreement. All jurisdictions have equal pay for equal work legislation, usually provided for in employment standards legislation. Some jurisdictions have gone further and enacted pay equity laws to achieve equal pay for work of equal value to female predominant job classifications. Unions have a role in the administration and enforcement of such legislation via applicable collective agreement language. Employment equity legislation in some jurisdictions attempts to address historical discriminatory staffing practices on the part of employers by removing barriers and taking proactive measures to ensure that four designated groups—women, visible minorities, individuals with disabilities, and Aboriginal people—are adequately represented in the workplace. Unions may have a role in the preparation of required plans and the enforcement of this legislation through grievance and arbitration processes.

Government Employers: Objectives

In 2011, there were 3.6 million Canadian public sector employees. Ninety-three percent were employed directly in federal, provincial, and local government offices or publicly funded organizations such as schools and hospitals. Special provisions regarding labour relations in the public sector are described in Chapter 11. Government employers will have the objectives of efficiency and control referred to in the previous chapter.

The manner in which governments deal with their own employees and unions may have an effect on employers in the private sector. If governments take a leading role by providing innovative terms of employment, such as daycare, private sector employers and unions will likely negotiate the same issues. On the other hand, governments have recently taken a harder line with unions representing public sector employees, and this too may influence private sector labour relations. Although public sector employees in some jurisdictions are regulated by the legislation governing the private sector, some governments enact special public sector labour relations legislation. For example, in Saskatchewan government employees are regulated by the same *Trade Union Act* that regulates the private sector, whereas in Ontario there is a *Crown Employees Collective Bargaining Act*, which covers government employees. The public sector legislation regulates who can unionize, the issues that can be bargained, and the employee's right to strike. Governments have from time to time made use of back-to-work legislation. They also have the same labour relations processes as private sector employers, including contract negotiation, lockouts in some cases, grievances and arbitration, and public relations campaigning.

Maintaining Office

Cynics may claim that all of the objectives previously referred to really come down to the objective of a government maintaining office. A government's desire to maintain office may make it susceptible to political and public relations activities of unions and employers referred to in previous chapters. For example, in 2004 the Saskatchewan government announced it was going to change the province's employment standards legislation to require employers with more than 50 workers to allocate additional hours to part-time employees on the basis of their length of service; employers strongly opposed the change. Some employers and the chambers of commerce in several cities formed an association, the Saskatchewan Business Council, that campaigned against the proposal. Eventually the government dropped the idea. It has also been alleged that some contract negotiations between governments and public sector employees just prior to an election have been influenced by the government's desire to win votes.

Finally, it must be noted that government plays other roles and engages in other activities not referred to here that affect employers and unions. For example, governments provide secondary and post-secondary education, which affects the supply of labour available to employers.

LABOUR RELATIONS BOARDS

The framework for labour relations provided in Chapter 1 indicated that in addition to the three main actors—unions, employers, and governments—there are other parties involved. A separate fourth category was established to emphasize that it is independent of the three main actors: labour relations legislation establishes a **Labour Relations Board** in each jurisdiction, which is responsible for administration of the legislation.

A **Labour Relations Board** is an independent body responsible for the administration of labour relations legislation affecting employers, employees and unions in each jurisdiciton.

Composition of Labour Relations Boards

Most Labour Relations Boards in Canada are tripartite representational bodies consisting of a neutral chairperson and vice-chairs, and representatives from employers and unions. Although in some jurisdictions there is a provision for hearings to be conducted by a neutral chair or vice-chairperson, some hearings are conducted by a three-person panel including one labour representative, one employer representative, and a neutral chair or vice-chair. While the government appoints Board members and the Board must apply the relevant legislation, the Board is independent from government.

Board Responsibilities

Labour Relations Boards have responsibility for the matters listed in Key Considerations 5-1.

The roles and responsibilities of the Boards will be developed in subsequent chapters as the need arises. At this point, it will merely be noted that the Boards play a central role in the labour relations system. They have the authority to grant bargaining rights to unions and to terminate those rights. When it is alleged that an employer or a union has violated labour relations legislation, a complaint is filed with the appropriate Board.

The jurisdiction of Labour Relations Boards has been increasing in recent years. Some have a broader jurisdiction than others; for example, in British Columbia the Board has responsibility in areas that other Boards do not, including the mediation of disputes through a mediation division. In some jurisdictions, there is special legislation and a separate Board that deals with the public sector. This topic is discussed in Chapter 11.

Procedure and Remedies

On an application to a Board, a settlement officer attempts to resolve disputes so that a formal hearing is not required. Very often a hearing is avoided. The Boards have extensive remedial powers, including ordering the reinstatement of employees and the payment of damages.

Key Considerations 5-1

Labour Relations Board Responsibilities

1. Processing union applications to represent employees
2. Processing applications to terminate union bargaining rights
3. Hearing unfair labour practice complaints by unions, employers, and employees
4. Hearing complaints and issuing declarations regarding unlawful strikes, lockouts, and picketing
5. Resolving disputes arising under a collective agreement in some jurisdictions
6. Dealing with arbitration of first and subsequent contract disputes in some jurisdictions

---

Although Board decisions cannot be appealed, two courses of action are open to a party not satisfied with a decision. An application can be made either for the Board to reconsider or for judicial review of the decision. An examination of Board annual reports shows that although the Boards make thousands of decisions every year, very few undergo judicial review.

Referring disputes under labour relations legislation to a Board instead of the court system has a few advantages. Individuals with expertise in labour relations make the decisions, and they are made faster, with less expense. One of the reasons Canadian labour relations legislation is viewed as being more strictly enforced than the U.S. legislation is the reliance on Labour Relations Boards. In the United States, some disputes are referred to the court system, and this entails additional expense and delay.

OTHER PARTIES

The framework for labour relations in Chapter 1 referred to other parties such as arbitrators. We previously referred to the courts and human rights tribunals in Chapter 2. Arbitrators will be discussed as necessary in subsequent chapters.

Arbitrators

Arbitrators hear disputes between unions and employers and render final and binding decisions.

Arbitrators play an important role in the labour relations system. When a union and an employer have a dispute about the meaning or application of a collective agreement, it is referred to *rights arbitration*. Arbitrators hear evidence presented by the parties and render decisions that are binding upon them. The termination of an employee is one important issue we will see referred to arbitration in Chapter 9. In Chapter 10, we will see that in parts of the public sector, arbitrators settle the terms of the collective agreement when the parties are not able to negotiate a contract. This is known as *interest arbitration*. The point emphasized here is that arbitrators are independent from government.

Courts

The courts play a role in labour relations. Although it is seldom done, it is possible to have an arbitrator's decision reviewed in the courts. The *Meiorin* case (*British Columbia (Public Service Employee Relations Commission) v. B.C.G.S.E.U.* 176 D.L.R. (4th) 1), referred to in Chapter 2, which established the requirements for a bona fide occupational requirement, illustrates the role of the courts.

Implications for Practice

1. Government plays a key role in labour relations as a regulator, facilitator, and protector of the public interest. Employers and unions need to monitor proposed changes in government policy and should become involved in activities to attempt to influence government policy.

2. Labour Relations Boards also play a vital role. Unions and employers should be familiar with Board rules, policies, and practices. Where necessary, employers and unions should consult lawyers or consultants.

3. Other parties in the labour relations system include the courts, arbitrators, and human rights tribunals.

Key Terms

Review Questions

1. Why does government become involved in labour relations?
2. What methods do governments use to regulate and influence the labour relations system?
3. What is the composition of a labour relations board?
4. How do Labour Relations Boards serve as key actors in the labour relations system?

Discussion Questions

1. Give two examples of how employment standards legislation protects the terms and conditions of work for employees. Are these examples of "minimum" terms? Could each standard be exceeded in a collective agreement? Explain.

Web Research

Visit the website of the Labour Relations Board in your province or the Canada Industrial Relations Board. Find out information about the Board's composition and a key process that is carried out for employers, employees or a union.

CASE INCIDENT   QUALITY INN & SUITES BRANTFORD v. UFCW LOCAL 175

In January 2012 the Ontario Labour Relations Board was asked to consider an application for the termination of bargaining rights filed under the *Labour Relations Act*, 1995, S.O. 1995, c.1, as amended (the "Act"). When the representation vote was taken, as directed by the Board, more than 50 percent of the ballots cast by employees of the Quality Suites and Inns located in Brantford, Ontario, who were also members of the United Food and Commercial Workers (UFCW), Local 175, opposed continuing to be represented by the union.

The Board's rules of procedure regarding the taking of the representative vote by hotel employees had been followed. No statement of desire to make representations by the parties concerning an outstanding issue in dispute had been filed with the Labour Relations Board following the vote.

The Board declared that the UFCW no longer represented the hotel employees. It ordered the ballots cast in the representation vote to be destroyed following the expiration of 30 days from the date of the decision unless a statement requesting that the ballots should not be destroyed was received by the Board from one of the parties before then. Additional meetings and hearing dates were cancelled. The hotel's management was also directed to post copies of the Board's decision within the employment setting.

Questions

1. Which role of government referred to in this chapter is illustrated in this case?
2. How might this situation be explained in terms of the "Framework for Labour Relations" seen in Chapter 1?

Chapter 6
Collective Bargaining Rights

Chapter Objectives

1. Explain reasons why employees may, or may not, want to join a union
2. Outline how a union could obtain bargaining rights
3. Describe the significance of a union obtaining bargaining rights
4. Outline the steps in a union organizing campaign and application for certification
5. Outline the factors determining and the significance of the bargaining unit
6. Explain limits on employer and union conduct during the organizing process
7. Outline the process to deal with unfair labour practices at certification and the remedies available
8. Explain the grounds and procedure to terminate a union's bargaining rights
9. Outline the effect of a sale of a business on the union's bargaining rights

Required Professional Capabilities (CCHRA)	HRPA Human Resources Professionals Competency Framework
10101, 10102, 10211, 10304, 50101, 50102, 50104, 50201, 50202, 50203, 50205, 50301, 50302	C010, C012, C013, C014, C016, C021, C024, C029, C031, C112, C113, C114, C115, C117, C119, C120, C121, C122, C123, C124, C125, C128, C133, C134

In the midst of a union certification drive at a tier-two automotive manufacturing company, employees were gathered in the company lunchroom. There was even more energy and lively conversation these days during breaks at the plant. So far, the organizing committee had done a good job, convincing more than the required number of employees, according to provincial law, to sign membership cards. The company's general manager, as expected, was not pleased when he received official notice that his factory employees were seeking union representation. That morning, the GM called in his production supervisor and wanted an update on how "this union thing" was likely to play out by the end of the week. "Don't worry Mr. Spencer, I have a plan to speak to the employees during their lunch break." said Steve.

Just after 12 p.m., Steve strolled into the lunchroom and closed the door behind him. He asked for everyone to be quiet as he stood by the door. Steve started to talk about how Mr. Spencer was very disappointed with recent talk about unionizing the plant. He also mentioned that if everyone thought long and hard, they would realize that joining a union was not a very wise idea. "Union dues, complex collective agreements, lack of flexibility; is that what you really want?" bellowed Steve above the noise from the shop floor. "We won't be able to compete if we pay union wages and that is not good for our future!" The supervisor noted that almost every face in the lunch room focused on his words. "Just remember, it's an important decision you will make at the time of the vote on Friday. It will be important for you and important for this company!" Steve turned and opened to door and left a rather silent group of employees.

Labour relations legislation regulates the conduct of employers and unions during the organizing and certification process. It is at this time, when a union is attempting to enter into a representative role on behalf of unhappy company employees that the classic display of power between an organization and its workers is displayed. The law protects unions from significant interference by the employer when forming a bargaining unit. The account at the start of this chapter provides a subtle example of what may be considered an unfair labour practice on the part of the company's production supervisor. The rules related to how union support is measured will be explored in this chapter. The legal framework regarding unfair labour practices and remedies will also be reviewed in this chapter. Finally, we will consider how a union can lose the right to represent employees and what happens if the employer sells the business.

THE UNIONIZATION DECISION

The reasons why employees join unions and maintain union membership are important to both unions and employers. The factors affecting an individual employee's decision whether to support a union are important to the union when it determines how to persuade employees to join. If the union addresses issues of greater interest to employees, and is able to set aside employee concerns about unionization, it is more likely to be successful in an organizing campaign.

One study in the United States suggests that unions have misunderstood the reasons for employees failing to support the union. Many union supporters have assumed that it was fear of strikes, job loss, or management retaliation. However, the study found that a significant bloc of employees were concerned about possible conflict in the workplace.[1] For those employees, the union's campaign, aimed at countering the assumed fears relating to job security, was misdirected.

Why Employees Unionize

An individual's decision to join a union is affected by factors internal and external to the workplace. Employers may have some ability to affect internal factors such as compensation; however, external factors are beyond the employer's control.

Workplace Factors Affecting Unionization   There are numerous studies examining why employees decide to join unions. One group of studies is based upon the premise that employee dissatisfaction leads to a consideration of whether a union would improve the employee's situation. According to this approach, dissatisfaction with pay or other working conditions by itself will not be enough to lead to unionization; employees also have to perceive that a union will be able to help them improve things. Other studies indicate employee dissatisfaction is not a requirement for employees to unionize.[2] Employees may choose a union as a rational decision to improve their situation even if there is no dissatisfaction. These areas of potential dissatisfaction and improvement are considered next.

Compensation.   Many employees join a union to obtain improved wages and benefits. Although the compensation advantage for unionized employees has diminished in recent years, they have on average earned 10 to 25 percent more than non-union employees. The details of the effects of unions on wages and benefits are reviewed in Chapter 12. At this point, it is sufficient to note that some employees may perceive that unionization is a method to improve compensation.

Fairness, Equity.   In addition to the amount of their compensation, some employees may be concerned with their relative compensation when they compare themselves to other employees or managers. If employees perceive that there is an inequity, they may think that unionization is a way to achieve fairness.

Job Security.   Some employees may be concerned that termination, layoff, outsourcing, or technological change threatens their job, and believe that a union may provide increased job security.

If employees are not unionized, the employer can terminate employees even though there is no employee misconduct, as long as reasonable notice is given. If a non-union employee is not provided with sufficient notice, they can sue and the courts will award damages, but not reinstatement. A non-union employee could be dismissed for a frivolous reason, and the only remedy available is compensation for the reasonable notice period—the employee will not be reinstated. There is an exception in three jurisdictions, Canada, Nova Scotia, and Quebec, where employment standards legislation protects qualifying non-managerial employees from unjust dismissal. Reinstatement is a possible remedy in those jurisdictions if the employee files a complaint and it is found that there was an unjust dismissal. However, in most jurisdictions when non-union employees have been dismissed, the only remedy available is damages to compensate them for inadequate notice of termination. On the other hand, in a unionized workplace the collective agreement will provide that employees can only be terminated if there is just cause. A termination may be the subject of a grievance, and an arbitrator might eventually hear the matter and order reinstatement. Approximately 50 percent of unionized employees who are terminated are reinstated through this process. The grievance and arbitration process relating to the termination of employees is considered in Chapter 9. The requirement for just cause to terminate a unionized employee and the possibility of reinstatement provides unionized employees with additional job security.

In the event of a loss of business, organizations may be forced to lay off employees. Without a union, the employer may lay off whomever it wishes. Although some non-union employers apply seniority rules, so that those with the longest service record are last to be laid off, there is no legal requirement that they do so. In a unionized workplace, although seniority is not the only consideration governing layoffs, employees who have more time on the job have more job security.

Technological changes and contracting out (outsourcing) also pose a threat to employees' job security. Contracting out refers to the employer arranging for work to be done by the employees of another firm or independent contractors. For example, an employer operating a hotel might eliminate the jobs of some of its housekeeping staff if it contracted out the cleaning of the common areas of the building. Although unions cannot guarantee that technological change or contracting out will not affect employees, we will see later in Chapter 7 that collective agreements may contain terms that provide some protection against job loss.

Working Conditions.   There are numerous working conditions that employees may perceive would be improved if a union represented them. Employees may pursue unionization to obtain greater notice for scheduled hours, to obtain a fairer distribution of shifts, or because of concerns with health and safety. Health and safety legislation provides that employees have the right to refuse unsafe work; however, it appears that non-union employees may not be willing to exercise this right. A study reviewing work refusals in Ontario found that over 90 percent of work refusals occurred in unionized workplaces.[3] This may suggest that the legislation is not protecting non-union employees and that employees may perceive they need to pursue unionization to deal with health and safety concerns.

Workload.   Economic pressures have forced employers in both the public and private sectors to try to "do more with less." Many employees have likely encountered increased workloads including assembly line speedups and increased workloads after a downsizing. In the public sector, health care workers have been required to look after more patients, and teachers may have encountered larger class sizes. Employees may perceive that joining or maintaining their membership in a union will help them counter attempts by employers to increase their workload.

Voice in Policymaking.   Some employees may want input into policy decisions made by their employer. Teachers may want a voice in decisions made by school boards affecting students. Employees may find that their concerns are not addressed. Some workers may pursue or maintain unionization for the purpose of establishing a collective voice, which the employer is more likely to listen to.

Inadequate Managers.   Some employees may perceive that they are being harassed or intimidated by their manager. Their experience with their manager, who may not have been adequately trained, may lead them to believe that a union will help them resolve this issue.

Complaint Mechanism.   Although some non-union employers establish complaint mechanisms for employees to resolve workplace issues, there is no legal requirement that they do so. Non-union employees may hear about unionized employees grieving and winning disputes with employers, and they may be attracted to unionization because they desire a complaint resolution process too. In the non-union workplace, there is no way to challenge legal management directives. In Chapter 9, dealing with the administration of the collective agreement, we will see that unions have sometimes been able to challenge management directives such as the installation of video cameras. Employees may perceive that the grievance and arbitration process found in collective agreements will provide them with a means to challenge some management decisions.

Employer Policies.   Some employers have adopted union substitution and avoidance strategies referred to in Chapter 4, which reduce employees' desire to unionize. By establishing practices such as complaint mechanisms and providing compensation equivalent to unionized employers, the employer may be able to reduce the likelihood of employees seeking unionization.

External Factors Affecting Unionization   Chapter 2 referred to environmental factors such as the economy affecting overall union density. External factors may affect an individual employee's decision regarding unionization.

Attitudes Toward Unions.   Some employees have attitudes shaped by external factors that make them more or less likely to support unionization. Individuals who have been raised in households where parents have experience with unions and have positive attitudes toward unions are more likely to support unionization. The influence of family, the news media, and others can affect an individual's decision to vote for or against a union.[4] In Chapter 2, it was indicated that a significant number of Canadians do not have positive attitudes toward unions. However, public opinion varies with the political and economic situation over time.

Economic Factors.   During periods of inflation, employees may perceive that a union may help them protect their real incomes. Employees may observe cost-of-living provisions that unions have been able to negotiate in some collective agreements during periods of inflation. In a recession, higher unemployment rates might prompt concerns regarding job security, causing employees to seek unionization. In a study examining the attitudes of Edmonton and Winnipeg residents, the authors found an increased willingness to join a union in Edmonton during a period of economic downturn. After considering possible factors that might explain this trend, the authors concluded, "the evidence points back to a changing economic climate as the key causal agent."[5]

The decision to join a union or to maintain membership is complex and involves more than financial issues. In any particular setting, there might be reasons other than those mentioned here. In some cases, one critical incident, such as a dismissal, accident, or wage freeze, may be the catalyst. Employers who wish to avoid unionization should ensure that their compensation system is competitive and fairly structured. Some have established a policy of matching the wages paid by similar unionized firms. Companies have also established complaint mechanisms or grievance procedures to avoid employees perceiving that they need a union.

Why Employees Do Not Join a Union

In view of the fact that only 29.9 percent of employees are union members, and not all union members have chosen union membership voluntarily, there must be reasons why employees do not unionize. The following outlines some of the possible reasons why employees may not pursue unionization.

Union Dues   Some employees may object to joining a union because they do not want to pay union dues. They may think that they will not receive service from the union that is worth the dues they will have to pay.

Political and Social Activities of Unions   Unions have supported political parties and social causes that some employees do not agree with. Many unions have supported specific political parties at the federal and provincial levels. Unions have also taken up social causes such as affordable housing, anti-bullying programs and protection of minority rights, Some individuals may not be willing to support or be associated with these political and social movements.

Strikes   Some employees may associate unions with strikes. Although a strike is actually an exceptional event because most collective agreements are negotiated without a strike, employees may fear the economic hardship that they have seen a few long strikes cause.

Loyalty to the Employer   Some employees may feel an obligation to the employer and view joining a union as being disloyal. Similarly, some employees may wish to move into management, and they perceive that if they support a union they may be harming their careers.

Conflict   Many employees prefer to work in a cooperative setting. They may have observed or heard of the adversarial nature of some unionized workplaces, and they do not think that they would be comfortable in that type of setting.

Merit   Some employees may perceive that if compensation and promotion decisions are made on the basis of merit, they will succeed. They may fear that a uniform compensation system, which most collective agreements provide for, and the application of seniority rules in a unionized workplace, will not be to their advantage.

Belief That Unions Protect Lazy and Incompetent Employees   A discussion of the advantages and disadvantages of unions in the classroom or elsewhere often leads to someone claiming that unions protect lazy and incompetent employees. It is apparent that some employees think that this is the case and accordingly oppose unionization.

Flexibility   Many employees perceive that a collective agreement involves an inflexible set of rules and terms of work including set hours, start times, and vacations. They may think that without a union they may be more likely to establish individual variations that they desire in their work arrangements.

Employer Retaliation   Some employees may wish to pursue unionization, but they fear that their employer may retaliate. When a union is attempting to organize a work setting, workers may shy away from becoming directly involved in the organizing campaign fearing if their involvement is discovered they may experience less preferred shifts, job reassignments or loss of privileges due to their pro-union support.

Job Loss   Industry and labour experts in 2012 were convinced that the Big Three automakers would move some production out of Canada if this country's plants did not reduce costs and increase their competitive position in the North American marketplace. Canada's unionized autoworkers, perhaps the best rewarded in the world, faced the possibility of making concessions in talks regarding renewed labour contracts or risk watching their jobs head to the United States or Mexico.

Lack of Opportunity to Unionize   Some employees do not have an opportunity to pursue unionization even though they would like to do so. Some industries, such as banking, have lower levels of unionization because of employer opposition, legal rules, or other factors. Whatever the reason, the lower rate establishes a barrier to the development of unions because unionization is not a norm for employees in the industry.

HOW BARGAINING RIGHTS ARE OBTAINED AND THEIR SIGNIFICANCE

The acquisition and retention of bargaining rights by a union is critical to the labour relations system. A union can obtain bargaining rights in two ways: by being voluntarily recognized by the employer or by applying to the Labour Relations Board and obtaining a certificate providing that the union is the bargaining agent for employees. A **voluntary recognition agreement** is an agreement between a union and an employer providing that the employer recognizes the union as the bargaining agent for a group of employees. As the name suggests, the employer cannot be forced to recognize the union. Voluntary recognition agreements are not common. Employees do not have to consent to the recognition, and there is a procedure available to employees to terminate the union's bargaining rights if they object to the recognition, which is considered in the discussion of decertification below.

A **voluntary recognition agreement** is an agreement between a union and an employer providing that the employer recognizes the union as the bargaining agent for employees.

Most unions gain bargaining rights by certification. Labour relations legislation provides a **certification process** whereby a union may obtain the right to represent a group of employees by applying to the Labour Relations Board. If the union is successful, the Board issues a certificate that affirms the union as the exclusive bargaining agent for the employees holding the jobs specified in the certificate. The term *certification* refers not only to the process through which a union applies to the Board but also to the end result of the process; for example, there may be reference to the fact that there has been "certification" of a union. Once a union has been certified, it has the right to represent employees until the Board terminates that right, as outlined later in this chapter.

The **certification process** is a way for a union to obtain bargaining rights for employees by applying to the Labour Relations Board.

When a union is certified, there are significant consequences for the employees and the employer. The union becomes the exclusive bargaining agent for the employees, who are no longer able to enter into individual contracts of employment with the employer. The employer could not make an agreement with the employee that he or she can take a longer vacation in exchange for working extra hours. When a union has been certified, there is a duty to bargain in good faith—to honestly attempt to reach a collective agreement. The duty to bargain in good faith and the negotiation of a collective agreement will be considered in Chapter 8.

Labour relations legislation in each jurisdiction governs the certification process, the conduct of the parties, and how bargaining rights can be lost. Employers and unions should be familiar with the legislation that governs them. Figure 5-2 in the previous chapter listed the private sector labour relations statutes for each jurisdiction in Canada. Although the basic principles relating to the establishment and termination of bargaining rights are the same across jurisdictions, there are some differences between jurisdictions that will be referred to in this chapter.

CERTIFICATION OF A UNION

To be certified the union must conduct an organizing campaign to have employees join the union and then make an application for certification to the labour relations board. Figure 6-1 provides an overview of the certification process.

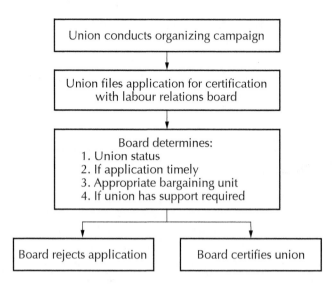

Figure 6-1 Certification Process

Organizing Campaign

An **organizing campaign** consists of union activities to convince employees to become union members.

A **union organizer** is a member of union staff who direct an organizing campaign.

An **organizing committee** is a group of employees who work on the campaign to sign up union members.

An **organizing campaign** refers to the union's attempt to convince employees that they should become union members. Often a campaign will start after employees contact the union and request its assistance. The union will assign a **union organizer** to the campaign, a person on the staff of the union who attempts to sign enough employees as members for an application for certification. Some unions attempt to use union organizers for the campaign who speak the language of the workplace and have similar work experiences and background. Unions have moved away from relying exclusively on full-time staff organizers towards using some organizers who are workers from another workplace on a temporary assignment. The union trains workers who take time off from their jobs to work as union organizers. It has been established that when the first contact between the union and the workplace being organized is made by a person from another workplace, the success rate of organizing drives is increased. An **organizing committee** will likely be established—a group of employees who support the union and work with the organizer. Members of the organizing committee attempt to have their co-workers sign on as union members. The use of an organizing committee increases the chances of success in an organizing campaign. Organizing committees are more effective when they include workers from the different departments in the workplace and represent the gender/racial/ethnic groupings in the workplace.[6]

Some campaigns are conducted openly. The union may advise the employer about the upcoming organizing campaign and the right of employees to join a union without interference from the employer. In other cases, the union may attempt to keep the campaign secret for as long as possible to avoid a response by the employer. The organizing campaign might involve distribution of leaflets to employees outlining the advantages of unionization, newspaper advertisements, and information meetings held away from the workplace. The union may attempt to generate support by giving employees articles of clothing, hats, or buttons to wear. Unions are using websites and social media to provide information to employees and convince them to become members. Members of the organizing committee will speak to employees and try to get them to sign membership cards. Organizers or organizing committee members may visit employees at their homes. The union attempts to get as many employees as possible in the proposed bargaining unit to sign cards. Employees may have to make a small payment to become a member, depending on the jurisdiction. In five jurisdictions—British Columbia, Manitoba, Newfoundland and Labrador, Ontario, and

Saskatchewan—no fee or payment to join a union is required; in other jurisdictions, there is a nominal membership fee ranging from one to five dollars. In most jurisdictions, the membership evidence must have been signed within a prescribed time prior to being submitted to the Board in the application for certification. This period ranges from 90 days to 12 months.

Application for Certification to Labour Relations Board

If the union signs up a sufficient percentage of employees as members, it will make an application for certification to the Labour Relations Board at the federal or provincial jurisdiction. Some Boards provide guides or other useful information regarding certification, and it is recommended that you check the Board in your jurisdiction for information. When the union applies to the Board, it will have to establish that: (1) it is a trade union as defined in labour relations legislation, (2) the application is timely, (3) the group of employees specified in the application is an appropriate bargaining unit, and (4) the union has adequate support of employees in the proposed unit. An overview of the certification process is provided here. Additional details are provided in the following subsections, and provincial variations are covered in Appendix 6.4, referred to below.

1. The union files an application for certification for a unit of employees that it considers appropriate for collective bargaining with the Labour Relations Board. The membership evidence gathered in the organizing campaign is submitted with the application.

2. The employer is notified about the application and the Board requires the employer to post a notice to employees. The employer is not advised of the names of employees who have supported the union.

3. The employer is required or allowed to reply to the application. In some jurisdictions, the reply must include the names of employees in the bargaining unit. In the reply, the employer could challenge the status of the applicant as a union, the timeliness of the application, and the appropriateness of the bargaining unit proposed by the union.

4. If the applicant qualifies as a union, and the application is timely, the Board determines an appropriate bargaining unit. The Board can add or remove positions from the unit proposed by the union.

5. Depending upon the jurisdiction, the board determines if the applicant has sufficient support for certification on the basis of the membership cards filed or by holding a representation vote.

6. If there are any issues in dispute that cannot be settled, a hearing will be held by the Board. In most jurisdictions, the hearing is held after any vote. This is done by sealing the ballot box and segregating any disputed ballots in a manner that protects the identity of the voter.

We will now consider the key issues in the application for certification, the status of the applicant, employee status, timeliness of the application, the appropriate bargaining unit, and the determination of union support, in further detail.

Who Can Apply for Certification: Trade Union Status Labour relations legislation provides that to apply for certification, an organization must be a *trade union*—an organization that has as one of its purposes the regulation of relations between employees and employers. The organization must not be dominated by, or influenced by, the employer. A union will not have to re-establish itself as a union every time it makes an application for certification. Once it has established its union status, it will be deemed to be a union in subsequent applications unless it is proved otherwise.

Employees or a second union might oppose an application for certification on the grounds that the applicant is not a trade union because it is dominated by the employer, or it does not have the regulation of relations between employees and employers as its purpose. All jurisdictions provide that an organization that discriminates on the basis of human rights cannot be certified.

Who Can a Union Represent? Employee Status and Exclusions

Employee Status. To be eligible for unionization, a person must be an employee, not an **independent contractor**—someone engaged in his or her own business. In some cases, this may be difficult to determine. Some examples may help.

An **independent contractor** is someone engaged in his or her own business.

Someone who uses his or her own equipment to remove snow from residential driveways and charges each household an amount based on the size of the driveway is clearly an independent contractor. Someone who works for a company and uses the company's equipment to remove the snow from its parking lot as one of his or her duties is an employee. There will be situations where the status of an individual doing work is not as certain. For example, in one case there was a dispute relating to an individual who was responsible for cleaning a library. The individual charged a monthly fee, anyone could do the work, there were no directions given regarding the work, and she was free to work for others. The union contended that the worker was an employee and the employer submitted that she was an independent contractor. Ultimately the Labour Relations Board found that the individual was an independent contractor.[7] If an employer challenges the employee status of an individual, the issue will be determined by the Labour Relations Board. The courts have developed tests to determine if an individual is an employee or an independent contractor that have been applied by labour relations boards. One important test is the **fourfold test**, which involves consideration of: (1) the degree of control over the worker, (2) the ownership of the tools and equipment used to complete the work, (3) whether the worker has a chance to make a profit, and (4) whether the worker may suffer a loss. None of the four factors are conclusive or binding by itself.

The **fourfold test** determines if an individual is an employee by considering control, ownership of tools, opportunity for profit, and risk of loss.

The more control the person having the work done exercises over the worker, the more likely the worker is an employee. Any requirements relating to when, where, and how the work must be done are indicators of control. If the worker uses his or her own tools and equipment to complete the work, he or she is more likely an independent contractor; if he or she uses the tools and equipment of the person having the work done, he or she is more likely an employee. If the worker has an opportunity to make a profit, he or she is more likely an independent contractor; if he or she is earning a specified rate of pay so that there is no opportunity to earn additional profit, he or she is more likely an employee. If the arrangement is structured so that it is possible that the individual might suffer a loss, it is more likely he or she is an independent contractor and not an employee.

Labour Relations Boards have applied and expanded the factors in the fourfold test to include the following:

- If the worker can use other individuals or substitutes to complete the work, it is more likely he or she is an independent contractor.

- If the work arrangement is structured so that the individual must personally complete the work, it is more likely he or she is an employee.

- If the person works for several persons or firms, the provision of services to the market is an indicator that he or she is an independent contractor and not an employee.

- If the worker has the freedom to reject work opportunities and may complete the work when he or she wishes, it is more likely the worker is an independent contractor.

- If the worker has duties that are the same as other persons doing work who are employees, it is more likely that he or she is an employee.

Dependent Contractors. It has been recognized that if Labour Relations Boards only applied the common law tests to determine if an individual was an employee, some workers would be found to be independent contractors, when in fact they are just as dependent upon a particular organization as an employee would be. This would mean that these individuals would not have access to unionization. For example, persons who own and drive their own taxis or delivery vehicles might be viewed as independent contractors. In five jurisdictions (Canada, British Columbia, Newfoundland and Labrador, Ontario, and Prince Edward Island), labour relations legislation provides for the concept of a **dependent contractor**.[8] The definition of a dependent contractor is similar across these jurisdictions; an example from the British Columbia *Labour Relations Code* is as follows:

> [A] person, whether or not employed by a contract of employment or furnishing his or her own tools, vehicles, equipment, machinery, material or any other thing, who performs work or services for another person for compensation or reward on such terms and conditions that he or she is in relation to that person in a position of economic dependence on, and under an obligation to perform duties for, that person more closely resembling the relationship of an employee than that of an independent contractor.[9]

A **dependent contractor** is someone who appears to be an independent contractor, but is economically dependent on a single organization.

The definition of "employee" in the legislation provides that individuals who are dependent contractors are employees. This should be viewed as a statutory extension of the definition of employee for the purposes of labour relations. The result is that some workers who would otherwise be found to be independent contractors fall within the definition of an employee, and they can join or form a union.

Even in jurisdictions without a dependent contractor provision in the legislation, someone economically dependent upon a single organization might be found to be an employee. For example, although the Alberta legislation does not provide for dependent contractors, taxi drivers in that province who are dependent upon a single organization have been found to be employees.

Each case dealing with the issue of employee versus independent contractor status must be considered on its own merits. This is illustrated by considering three cases involving applications for certification by unions seeking to represent drivers delivering newspapers to retail outlets.[10] Although the drivers in all three cases owned their own vehicles, there were other differences among the cases that led to different results. In one of the cases, *Journal Le Droit*, the drivers were found to be dependent contractors and therefore could unionize. In the other two cases, the drivers were found to be independent contractors and the applications were dismissed. In the one case where the drivers were found to be dependent contractors, the newspaper exercised some control over the use of substitute drivers, drivers worked longer hours so that they were more dependent upon the newspaper, and there was no negotiation of the fees paid to the drivers.

Labour relations legislation prevents some employees from joining or forming a union. The legislation may exclude employees from unionization because of their level of responsibility, job duties, or occupation.

Managerial Exclusion. All jurisdictions provide that managerial employees are excluded from unionization in order to avoid a conflict of interest. Managerial employees may be involved in the determination of how the employer will negotiate with the union or the settlement of disputes regarding the interpretation of the collective agreement. Accordingly, they should not be part of the union to avoid a conflict of interest. The application of the managerial exclusion varies between jurisdictions and in some jurisdictions more employees are classified as managers. Appendix 6.1, "Managerial Exclusions," at the end of this chapter provides additional information relating to the managerial exclusion in each jurisdiction.

The legislation does not define "manager" or "managerial functions." When a Labour Relations Board determines whether someone is a manager, the person's real job or actual duties are examined. A job title that refers to someone as a manager does not decide the question.

Similarly, a Board will consider the job description to determine if it accurately reflects the authority an individual exercises. If it refers to duties including hiring and the discipline of employees, but in reality the individual does not become involved in these tasks, he or she will not be found to be a manager. An individual will be found to be a manager if he or she has a direct impact on the terms of employment of others. If someone has the authority to hire, discipline, terminate, or determine the compensation of other employees, he or she will be considered managerial. The person will also be viewed as a manager if he or she makes effective recommendations regarding the terms of employment of other employees. In some jurisdictions, employees may be classified as managers even though they do not have anyone reporting to them if they are involved in independent decision making and have authority over matters of policy or the direction of the organization. A distinction must be drawn between supervisory personnel and managerial personnel. If the supervisor does not exercise managerial functions, he or she is eligible for unionization. Any potential conflict between supervisory and non-supervisory employees can be alleviated by putting the supervisory employees in a separate bargaining unit. The appropriate bargaining unit is referred to below.

Employees Engaged in a Confidential Capacity Regarding Labour Relations. All jurisdictions except Quebec exclude persons working in a confidential capacity relating to labour relations. This exclusion applies when individuals have more than just access to information. They must actually be involved in the use of the information for the exclusion to apply. This exclusion is aimed at avoiding a conflict of interest. It would not be practical to have the assistant to the director of labour relations, who prepares alternative contract proposals that will be presented to the union during collective bargaining, to be part of the union.

Occupational Exclusions. In some jurisdictions, individuals are excluded from unionization on the basis of their occupation. Appendix 6.2, "Occupational Exclusions," at the end of this chapter provides additional information relating to the occupational exclusion in each jurisdiction. In Alberta, New Brunswick, Nova Scotia, Ontario, and Prince Edward Island, specified professional employees such as members of the architectural and medical professions employed in their professional capacity are prevented from joining or forming a union. The policy reasons for these exclusions are not clear. For example, why should members of the engineering profession be allowed to unionize in most jurisdictions, but not in Alberta, Nova Scotia, or Prince Edward Island? The legislation in Alberta and Ontario prevents agricultural employees from unionizing. There have been cases where unions have attempted to organize individuals who work on mushroom farms, and it has been held that they cannot unionize. The legality of the agricultural exemption has been challenged pursuant to the *Charter of Rights and Freedoms*. After the Supreme Court of Canada held that the Ontario exception of agricultural employees was a violation of the *Charter*, the province enacted legislation granting them limited collective bargaining rights. That legislation was subsequently the subject of another *Charter* challenge. In April 2011, the Supreme Court of Canada issued its long-awaited judgment in the case of *Ontario (Attorney General) v. Fraser*, 2011 SCC 20 ("Fraser"). For employers in the agricultural industry in Ontario, the most immediate result was that agricultural workers remained excluded from the LRA and its detailed obligations relating to collective bargaining. However, these workers were now able to organize under the Ontario law and also to make representations to their employers regarding terms and conditions of work. The employer in such instances is expected to consider such representations in good faith.[11] Some provinces have special legislation relating to police, firefighters, and teachers, which is discussed in Chapter 11, where we consider public sector employees.

The Employer When a union applies to be certified as the bargaining agent for a group of employees, it must name the employer. In some cases, a question might arise as to whether the company named is in fact the employer, for example when a temporary help agency provides workers to a unionized employer. Are they employees of the agency or of the agency's client?

1. The party exercising direction and control over the employees performing
2. The party bearing the burden of remuneration
3. The party imposing any discipline
4. The party hiring the employees
5. The party with the authority to dismiss the employees
6. The party perceived to be the employer by the employee
7. The existence of an intention to create the relationship of employer and employee

Figure 6-2 Factors Determining the Identity of the Employer

The Ontario Labour Relations Board has set out seven factors that may be referred to when determining which of two organizations is the true employer. These factors, which have been referred to and applied in other jurisdictions, are provided in Figure 6-2.

Board decisions have confirmed that where one organization is responsible for the compensation of the worker and another organization has the day-to-day control over the worker's activities, the organization exercising control will be found to be the true employer. Workers who have been engaged and paid by an employment agency and who are working under the control of a client of the agency have been found to be employees of the client for labour relations purposes.

Timelines: When an Application for Certification Can Be Made   There are restrictions on when an application for certification can be filed that depend on whether employees are currently represented by a union.

Where Employees Are Not Represented by a Union.   If no union currently represents employees, the general rule is that an application for certification can be filed at any time. However, there are restrictions in various jurisdictions that could prevent an application for certification until a later time where there has been a recent withdrawal or refusal of an application, or a previously certified union has lost the right to represent employees.

In some jurisdictions, the withdrawal of a previous application for certification might mean that an application is not timely. The policy alternatives are no restrictions at all, a discretionary period against another application by the same union, or a mandatory time bar. In all jurisdictions, the refusal of a previous application could affect the time when an application can be made. The policy alternatives relate to the length of the time bar to another application, and whether such a bar affects only the unsuccessful union or prevents any union from applying. Ontario and Saskatchewan illustrate the most restrictive policy alternatives. In Saskatchewan, the Board may impose a bar that prevents an unsuccessful applicant or any other union from applying for one year. In Ontario, the Board must generally impose a mandatory bar that prevents any union from applying for one year.

Later in this chapter, we will refer to a union losing its bargaining rights through a **decertification** process that involves an application to the Labour Relations Board. Another policy alternative is to prevent an application for certification for a period of time after a decertification. This alternative is the policy in two jurisdictions in Canada.

Decertification is the process through which a union's right to represent employees is terminated by the Labour Relations Board.

Where Employees Are Represented by a Union.   There is a different set of restrictions that could affect the timing of an application for certification when employees are currently represented by a union. The purpose of these restrictions is to give the first union an opportunity to establish a collective agreement with the employer, and to avoid the disruption that repeated organizing drives could cause. The restrictions on an application by a second union depend on whether the first union certified was able to negotiate a collective agreement with the employer.

In all jurisdictions, while the first union certified is negotiating a collective agreement with the employer, there is a minimum time before another union can file an application for certification. This bar to an application ranges from six to twelve months after the first union was certified, depending on the jurisdiction.

If the first union negotiates a collective agreement with the employer, a second union can apply only after the expiration of a specified time. The span of time within which a second union can make an application for certification is referred to as the **open period**. The open period is commonly the last two or three months of the collective agreement. In the case of collective agreements that have a longer term, there is an additional open period during the last two or three months of each year of the agreement, depending upon the jurisdiction.

An **open period** is the time span within which a second union can apply for certification.

The effect of the certification of a second or *raiding* union on any collective agreement that has not yet expired varies across jurisdictions. The policy alternatives are as follows: (1) the collective agreement ceases to operate, or (2) the collective agreement continues to operate with the replacement union being substituted for the first union, or (3) the collective agreement continues to operate with the replacement union being substituted for the first union, and allow the replacement union to give notice to terminate the existing collective agreement, or (4) the collective agreement continues to operate with the replacement union being substituted for the first union, and allow the replacement union to terminate the existing collective agreement with the approval of the Board.

There are significant consequences for the employer, union, and employees involved. Employers in some jurisdictions should note that a long-term collective agreement might only be valid until the open period in which the union can be replaced by another union. An employer might enter into a collective agreement with a union that provided for a six-year term; however, the collective agreement could cease to operate if a second union was certified in any of the open periods that arise before the collective agreement expires. On the other hand, employees will be able to replace one union with another; however, whether they will be able to renegotiate the collective agreement depends on which jurisdiction they are in.

The conciliation or mediation processes in contract negotiation, which are elaborated upon in Chapter 10, might delay an application for certification depending upon the jurisdiction. Also, a strike or lockout could delay an application for certification in some jurisdictions.

Appropriate Bargaining Unit   A union cannot submit an application for certification for just any group of employees. The legislation requires that the application must relate to a group that is "appropriate" for collective bargaining. In the case of a hotel, the union could not submit an application for only some of the kitchen staff. Bargaining units are often described by exception; that is, the description refers to a group of employees and then lists jobs that are not included in the unit. A bargaining unit composed of production workers might be described as follows: "All employees of [employer] save and except forepersons, persons above the rank of foreperson, office staff, security guards, and technical employees." It is important to note that the bargaining unit is described in terms of jobs, not individuals, meaning that the death, termination, or retirement of individual employees does not affect the scope or composition of the bargaining unit. Labour relations legislation provides some rules regarding the appropriate bargaining unit; however, each Labour Relations Board has developed its own guidelines. Standard approaches to the determination of the appropriate bargaining unit in particular industries have developed in each jurisdiction, with significant variations across jurisdictions. Managerial employees and employees engaged in a confidential capacity regarding labour relations matters cannot be included in a bargaining unit, and in some jurisdictions there are additional restrictions on combining specified occupational groups, such as security guards, with other employees in one bargaining unit. Appendix 6.3, "Appropriate Bargaining Unit," at the end of this chapter provides additional information about the requirements relating to the appropriate bargaining unit in various jurisdictions.

If some employees who should be included in the bargaining unit do not support unionization, the union cannot just omit them. The appropriate bargaining unit is determined by the Board after allowing the employer and any interested employee(s) an opportunity to make representations to the Board regarding the appropriateness of the proposed unit.

Significance of Bargaining Unit. The determination of the appropriate bargaining unit is important to the union, the employer, and the employees. The nature and size of the unit deemed appropriate can affect whether the union is certified and the negotiation of the collective agreement if the union is certified. At the time of the application, it may be easier for the union to apply to represent a smaller unit; however, when the union negotiates with the employer, it will be in a stronger position if the bargaining unit is larger. The banking industry illustrates this situation. Prior to 1977, the Canada Labour Relations Board refused to recognize the employees at a single bank branch as an appropriate bargaining unit, agreeing with the employer that the minimum size should be at least all the branches in a particular geographic area, such as a city. As a result, there were very few successful organizing drives. The Board realized that this policy was a barrier to establishing collective bargaining in the banking industry, and changed the policy to allow a single branch to be an appropriate unit. This new policy made it easier for unions to be certified; however, it led to the establishment of small bargaining units that had to bargain with the employer on their own, and in some cases the units were not large enough to successfully negotiate a collective agreement. Also, if employees who have more skills and expertise are not included, the union's bargaining power is reduced because a unit composed of a small number of unskilled employees who could be easily replaced if there is a strike puts the union in a weaker position. The fact that there are still very few unionized bank employees demonstrates how setting an appropriate bargaining unit that is too large can prevent unionization, while setting an appropriate bargaining unit that is too small can result in an inability to conclude a successful collective agreement because the employer is able to resist the economic power of the union. As is the case with many labour relations issues, determining the appropriate bargaining unit is a question of balancing competing concerns and issues.

Variables Affecting Determination of the Bargaining Unit. In some situations, there may be several possible bargaining units, some of which may be more appropriate than others. The union does not generally have to establish that the unit it proposes is the most appropriate one. The Board will certify a bargaining unit as long as it is appropriate for collective bargaining even though there could be other, more appropriate ones.

The key determinant of whether jobs or classifications should be included is the "community of interest" of the employees in the proposed unit. This concept is not exact. The British Columbia Labour Relations Board has referred to **community of interest** and the determination of the appropriate bargaining unit as follows: "community of interest is capable of spanning, at a single workplace, several different appropriate bargaining units,... there is an obvious inherent flexibility or elasticity to the concept."[12]

Community of interest is determined by the following factors:

Community of interest refers to the common characteristics regarding terms and conditions of work and the relationship to the employer for those in a proposed bargaining unit.

- The similarity in skills, duties, and working conditions of employees
- The structure of the employer
- The integration of the employees involved
- The location or proximity of employees

A key determination that will have to be made is whether part-time and full-time employees have a sufficient community of interest to put them in the same bargaining unit.

Although there may be separate bargaining units certified for full-time and part-time employees, the units might negotiate collective agreements at the same time. This possibility is considered in Chapter 8.

Generally the union cannot carve out a particular department or a job classification as an appropriate bargaining unit. In a case where a union applied to be certified to represent registered nursing assistants at a hospital, and did not include other service employees such as ward clerks and housekeeping aides, the Board found that the bargaining unit proposed was not appropriate.[13] An exception to this general rule is found in the historical trades—millwrights, electricians, and other trades that have traditionally been represented by a craft union are usually permitted to be in a separate bargaining unit.

If the employer has more than one location in a municipality or province, it must be determined if the bargaining unit should include multiple locations. If the Board determines that the bargaining unit will include all locations in a municipality or province and the employer moves within the municipality or province, the union continues to hold the right to represent employees. It also means that if the employer establishes a second location in the same municipality or province, the second location will be covered by the certification, and the union will represent the employees there.

Avoiding fragmentation is a major factor in the determination of the appropriate bargaining unit. If the Board allowed several smaller bargaining units to be established, there might be conflict between different unions, and several negotiations and possible strikes. One of the goals of the Labour Relations Board will be to prevent the situation of an employer having multiple unions and bargaining units to deal with—a situation that could cause major instability in the workplace as unions contested with other unions for jurisdiction and the employer might be in constant negotiations with one or another of the unions.

Some Boards have considered the effect the size of the bargaining unit will have on the likelihood of establishing collective bargaining in an industry. If a Board's policy is that the appropriate bargaining unit should be larger in terms of job classes or locations, it will be more difficult for a union to organize employees, as previously illustrated in the example of the banking industry. It is noteworthy that establishing smaller bargaining units to facilitate unionization may lead to the creation of units that are not large enough to bargain effectively with the employer.

Although the preferences of the union and the employer are a factor they do not determine the appropriate bargaining unit. Some Boards have established a unit different from the one agreed upon by the union and the employer. The preference of the union has more significance because the union will set out a proposed bargaining unit in the application for certification and the unit only has to be appropriate for bargaining, not the perfect unit. One consideration that the Board may apply is the number and status of those employees who are not included in the certification. Generally speaking, the Board will not want to set up a situation where there is a small "rump" group who would be denied the opportunity of entering into collective bargaining because they were left out of a larger unit.

Boards are concerned with the possibility that the determination of the bargaining unit could cause labour relations problems for the employer. Boards do not want to establish bargaining units that would result in employees moving back and forth between two different bargaining units or between a bargaining unit and a group of unorganized employees.

Determination of Union Support   In order for a union to be certified, it must show that it has the support of a majority of employees. There is an important policy issue on the question of how support of employees is determined. In some jurisdictions legislation provides that employee support must be determined by a representation vote. A **representation vote** is a secret ballot vote conducted by the Labour Relations Board to determine if employees want a union to represent them. In other jurisdictions, the legislation provides that employee support can be evidenced without a vote if it is established that a specified percentage of

A **representation vote** is a secret ballot vote to determine if employees want a union to represent them.

employees have signed membership cards. In the jurisdictions that allow certification on the basis of membership cards without a vote, it is also provided that a representation vote will be held if the union establishes through membership cards that it has the support of a lower minimum level of employees. Accordingly, it is possible that in the jurisdictions that permit certification on the basis of membership cards alone, a representation vote will be directed when the union has sufficient support for a vote but does not have enough membership cards signed to be certified on the basis of the cards alone. Figure 6-3 lists the jurisdictions in which certification can be obtained without a vote and the support required.

The question of whether support for the union should be determined on the basis of membership cards or a representation vote is a critical issue that has been extensively debated. Employers favour a system in which a vote is required; unions prefer reliance on membership cards without a vote. A mandatory vote is a feature of the labour relations system in the United States and is viewed as favouring the employer. The requirement for a representation vote is based on the premise that the true wishes of employees cannot be determined unless there is an opportunity for employees to express their preference secretly. Proponents of a mandatory vote argue that membership cards may be signed under pressure, or employees may not appreciate the consequences of signing. They suggest that since we use the secret ballot in a democratic society to choose political representatives and determine some issues, we should use the same method to resolve the question of union representation in the workplace. Proponents of a card system argue that the workplace is different from society as a whole because of the authority and power held by the employer. They maintain that if there is a vote, employees may be threatened or unduly influenced by the employer.

The vote is held shortly after the application for certification is filed in order to minimize the opportunity for employers to interfere. In some jurisdictions, the vote is held within five days of the application for certification being filed and the ballot box is sealed

Figure 6-3 Certification Without a Vote: Availability and Support Required

Federal	Yes, if more than 50% of employees in proposed bargaining unit support union
Alberta	No, representation vote is mandatory
British Columbia	No, representation vote is mandatory
Manitoba	Yes, if 65% or more of employees in proposed bargaining unit support union
New Brunswick	Yes. If Board is satisfied that more than 50% of employees in proposed bargaining unit are members it may certify without a vote. If Board is satisfied that more than 60% of employees in proposed bargaining unit are members it shall certify without a vote.
Newfoundland and Labrador	Yes, when 65% of employees in proposed bargaining unit sign union cards. If support is between 40 and 64%, then a vote is required.
Nova Scotia	No, representation vote is mandatory
Ontario	No, representation vote is mandatory
Prince Edward Island	Yes, if more than 50% of employees in proposed bargaining unit support union
Quebec	Yes, if more than 50% of employees in proposed bargaining unit support union
Saskatchewan	No, representation vote is mandatory

pending the resolution of issues such as the eligibility to vote. It has been shown that requiring a representation vote reduces the success rate of union organizing efforts. A study that reviewed the effect of mandatory votes as opposed to relying on membership cards found that votes reduced certification by approximately 9 percent.[14]

Certification on the Basis of Membership Cards.   In six jurisdictions—Canada, Manitoba, New Brunswick, Newfoundland and Labrador, Prince Edward Island, and Quebec—a union can be certified without a representation vote if the membership cards filed with the application establish that the union has the support of a specified percentage of employees in the bargaining unit. The Board will grant a certification if the union has obtained the required level of support listed in Figure 6-3. If the union does not have the level of support required for certification based on membership cards, but shows it has the minimum support required for a vote, the Board will order a representation vote. For example, in Manitoba the Board will certify the union without a vote if it establishes that it has the support of 65 percent or more employees, and will order a vote if the union has the support of less than 65, but more than 40 percent of employees.

Certification on the Basis of a Representation Vote.   All jurisdictions provide that a representation vote will be held if the union establishes a minimum level of support on the basis of signed membership cards. The minimum level of support required is shown in Figure 6-4.

	Minimum Level of Support Required for Representation Vote	Minimum Percentage of Voters Required	Required Level of Support for Union to Win Vote
Federal	35%; 50% +1 when union applies to displace another union	Vote is void if less than 35% vote	Majority of votes cast
Alberta	40%; vote is mandatory	None specified	Majority of votes cast
British Columbia	45%; 50% +1 when union applies to displace another union; vote is mandatory	Board may order another vote if less than 55% vote	Majority of votes cast
Manitoba	40%; 45% when union applies to displace another union	None specified	Majority of votes cast
New Brunswick	40%	None specified	Majority of those who are in attendance on day of vote
Newfoundland and Labrador	40%	None specified	If at least 70% vote, majority of votes cast; if less than 70% vote, majority of employees who could vote
Nova Scotia	40%; vote is mandatory	None specified	Majority of votes cast
Ontario	40%; vote is mandatory	None specified	Majority of votes cast
Prince Edward Island	50% +1	None specified	Majority of votes cast
Quebec	35%	None specified	Majority of those eligible to vote
Saskatchewan	45%	Majority of eligible voters	Majority of votes cast

Figure 6-4 Rules Relating to Representation Votes

In five jurisdictions—Alberta, British Columbia, Ontario, Nova Scotia, and Saskatchewan—a representation vote is mandatory, regardless of the level of support for the union shown in the application. In a few jurisdictions, a minimum percentage of employees must vote for the election to be valid. In most jurisdictions, the results of the representation vote are determined by a majority of those who actually do vote; the union does not have to obtain the support of the majority of those eligible to vote. If 100 employees in the bargaining unit are eligible to vote and 80 employees actually vote, the union would have to obtain 41 votes to be certified in most jurisdictions. Accordingly, employees who do not want to see the union certified must actually vote against the union. Appendix 6.4, "Certification Procedure," at the end of this chapter provides additional information on the certification process in various jurisdictions.

FRAMEWORK OF FAIRNESS: AN ALTERNATIVE APPROACH TO OBTAINING BARGAINING RIGHTS

Most unions gain the right to represent employees by making an application for certification to the Labour Relations Board after conducting an organizing campaign to obtain employee support. During the organizing campaign, employers are allowed to campaign against the union provided that they do not commit unfair labour practices such as threatening, coercing, or intimidating employees discussed in the next section. If the union is certified, the employer and the union then attempt to negotiate a collective agreement.

In October 2007, Magna announced that it had entered into the Framework of Fairness Agreement (FFA) with the Canadian Auto Workers union (CAW) (now Unifor). This was seen at the time as a radical departure from traditional industrial relations practices between a major industrial company and a large private sector union. The FFA is a set of principles which balance the needs of employees and the needs of business to be competitive. If a majority of workers in a facility vote in favour, then that plant will be covered by a new Magna-Unifor national collective agreement.

The key terms and conditions of the FFA include:

- preservation of Magna's Fair Enterprise culture and operating principles, including the sharing of our financial success through equity ownership, as set out in our Corporate Constitution and Employee's Charter;

- comprehensive no strike, no lock-out provisions with unresolved collective bargaining issues being settled through final offer selection arbitration;

- progressive concern resolution and plant representation mechanisms that preserve Magna's Open Door Process, Fairness Committees, Employee Advocates and the Employee Hotline;

- competitive wage and benefit principles consistent with the company's Employee's Charter;

- tying of annual wage adjustments to a manufacturing inflationary index, plant specific performance measures and competitive considerations;

- secret ballot voting on workplace issues; and

- generally, depoliticization of the workplace and labour-management relations.[15]

As of March 2014, employees at three Canadian Divisions of the company were covered by the Magna-Unifor national collective agreement under the FFA. These agreements were extended for an additional four years in November 2013.

Employees at one Magna facility in Canada are covered by a collective agreement with Unifor that does not fall under the FFA. This agreement was extended by three years in November 2013.[16]

CONDUCT DURING ORGANIZING AND CERTIFICATION PROCESS

An **unfair labour practice** is a contravention of labour relations legislation by an employer, union, or employee.

It is a basic principle of our labour relations system that employees have the right to join or decline to join a union free of any intimidation or coercion by either the union or the employer. To protect this basic right, labour relations legislation prohibits certain employer and union conduct. An **unfair labour practice** is a contravention of the relevant labour relations legislation by an employer, union, or employee.

Note that the term "unfair" is not a reference to a subjective opinion about whether certain conduct is fair. The issue is whether the conduct is prohibited by legislation. An employer might have a practice of providing wage increases to its non-union employees when a unionized competitor agrees to wage increases with its union. The purpose of this practice may be to avoid unionization. This conduct is not an unfair labour practice, because it is not prohibited by labour relations legislation. Even though the employer's practice is aimed at preventing unionization and may appear to be "unfair" to union sup-porters, it is not deemed an unfair labour practice because the legislation has not been vio-lated. However, an employer who provides an out-of-the-ordinary wage increase at the time of a union organizing campaign is committing an unfair labour practice, because this con-duct is prohibited by labour relations legislation.

Although Canadian labour relations statutes are similar, it is possible that conduct that is an unfair labour practice in one jurisdiction may not be an unfair labour practice in another jurisdiction. For example, soliciting union members during working hours is an unfair labour practice in most, but not all jurisdictions. Conduct that is an unfair labour practice at one point in time may not be an unfair labour practice at another point in time because of changes in the legislation. In most jurisdictions, there is a provision that the employer has the right to express an opinion or exercise "free speech," provided it does not threaten or coerce employees. At one time, there was no free-speech provision in the *Canada Labour Code*. The Canada Industrial Relations Board held that this meant that employers were required to remain neutral during an organizing campaign. The employer was allowed to respond to union campaigning that was defamatory, but the reply could not go further and include statements that might be viewed as campaigning for a vote against the union.[17] This was changed when the *Code* was amended to add a provision that employ-ers could express their views.

Although most unfair labour practices arise during the organizing campaign and certi-fication process, the term has broad meaning. An unfair labour practice might also occur during the negotiation of the collective agreement, or during the administration of the agreement, because one of the parties contravenes labour relations legislation. The legisla-tion includes the duty to bargain in good faith, as well as the union's duty of fair representa-tion in the course of administration of the contract; unfair labour practices relating to those areas are discussed in subsequent chapters.

We will now consider employer and union unfair labour practices during the organiza-tion campaign and the certification process, the remedies available, and permissible employer and union conduct.

Employer Unfair Labour Practices

Employer conduct that labour relations legislation prohibits during the organizing cam-paign and certification process is noted in Key Considerations 6-1. The legislation prevents two broad categories of employer behaviour: (1) threats, intimidation, and coercion and (2) interference or influence by the employer. Most observers would agree that threats, intimidation, and coercion by employers should not be allowed, actions such as firing union supporters, interrogating employees regarding their possible support for a union, transferring

Employer Unfair Labour Practices

Labour relations legislation in most jurisdictions provides that employers cannot:

1. Participate in or interfere with the formation, selection, or administration of a trade union or contribute financial or other support to a union

2. Refuse to employ or discriminate regarding the terms of employment because of union membership

3. Impose a condition in a contract of employment that restrains an employee from becoming a member of a union

4. Threaten, intimidate, or coerce an employee to compel him or her to become or refrain from becoming a member or officer of a union

5. Change the terms and conditions of employment during the certification process

6. Take any action against an employee because the employee has exercised any of his or her rights under labour relations legislation

union supporters, and threatening to move or shut down operations if the employees unionize. It may be more difficult to understand why some employer conduct, such as a change in working conditions in the face of an organizing campaign, is an unfair labour practice.

Changes in Working Conditions   Boards have held that employers who have changed working conditions in response to a union organizing campaign have committed an unfair labour practice. The basis for this is that the legislation prohibits employers from interfering with the employees' decision regarding unionization. This prohibition is not limited to changes in compensation, but includes any changes made for purposes of influencing the employees' decision.

In one case, an employer had not taken action on employee complaints relating to working conditions. After a union organizing campaign started, the employer solicited employee concerns and attempted to address the problems raised, including hiring additional employees so that excessive hours would be avoided. The Board found that this was an unfair labour practice because it was interfering with the employees' decision regarding unionization. The Board summarized the situation as follows:

> There is nothing in the Act which prohibits an employer whose employees are unorganized and who are not the subject of a union organizing campaign, from providing terms and conditions of employment which are designed to, and may have the effect of causing employees to turn their back on the option of collective bargaining. However, once a trade union begins to organize, it is protected by... the Act and the employer is prohibited from acting with an intention to interfere with the selection of a trade union.... The granting of benefits or the solicitation of employee grievances during the course of the union organizing campaign if motivated even in part by a desire to undermine a trade union breaches these prohibitions.[18]

Changes made by an employer in response to a union organizing campaign might be viewed as threatening because of the possible inference that future benefits or improvements depend upon the employees not supporting a union. Employers are not allowed to make promises tied to the defeat of the union. A promise to provide longer vacations if the union is defeated would be an unfair labour practice.

Statutory Freeze   The legislation in all jurisdictions specifically prohibits the employer from making any changes in the terms of employment when an application for certification is filed with the Board or the employer is notified of the application. This prohibition on changes is known as a **statutory freeze**. There is also a freeze imposed during the negotiation process, which is reviewed in Chapter 8. The freeze does not prevent the employer from making any changes; it prevents changes that are not "business as usual." For example, if the employer has an established practice of providing wage increases at a particular time of the year, it would be required to provide the wage increase during the freeze. However, it

The **statutory freeze** is a period when the employer is prohibited from making changes in the terms of employment, unless the change is carrying on business as usual.

would be a violation of the freeze to provide the wage increase earlier. Employers who have changed the method of payment from cash to cheque, failed to schedule overtime in accordance with past practice, and altered rules regarding access to and use of phones have been found guilty of violating the freeze provision.

The knowledge or expectations of employees are a factor affecting whether the employer has violated the freeze. Where the employer has made a decision to implement a change, but has not communicated the change to employees before the freeze begins, that change would be a violation. In one case, the employer informed employees of a benefit plan that had been in existence but employees had been unaware of. The Board found that this was a violation of the freeze.[19] The reason for this was that in the eyes of employees, the plan was a change. When the employer brought the plan to the attention of employees during the freeze, the employer had in effect changed their terms of employment. The employer had claimed that advising the employees about the benefit plan was exercising free speech, which the legislation allows. This case illustrates that the free speech provisions of the statute are subject to the restrictions against changing the terms of employment. Furthermore, it illustrates that employers should ensure that all employees are fully aware of all of the rights, privileges, and benefits they are entitled to.

In Alberta, New Brunswick, Ontario, Quebec, and Saskatchewan, the employer is allowed to make changes in the terms of employment during the freeze if it obtains the consent of the union. The federal, British Columbia, Manitoba, Newfoundland and Labrador, Nova Scotia, and Prince Edward Island legislation provides that the employer is allowed to make changes if the consent of the Board is obtained. The freeze imposed during negotiation, referred to in Chapter 8, is subject to the same exception. Whether the consent must be obtained from the Board or the union might be significant to the employer. In one case where the legislation required the consent of the union, the employer, a retailer, wanted to implement Sunday shopping hours in response to competition. When it requested the union's consent, the union refused. The employer sought volunteers to work the Sunday hours. Even though the employer had a valid business reason to open Sunday, the Board found that the change was a breach of the statutory freeze because the Sunday opening was not business as usual and the union had not consented to the change. In a jurisdiction where the employer can make changes with the approval of the Board, instead of obtaining permission from the union, the business case for the change could have led to the Board granting its approval.

Permissible Employer Conduct

It will be helpful to summarize what the employer is allowed to do during a union organizing campaign. Key Considerations 6-2 summarizes conduct that the law permits.

Key Considerations 6-2

Permitted Employer Conduct During an Organizing Campaign

1. Prohibiting entry into the workplace by persons who are not employees

2. Prohibiting entry into the workplace by employees during their off hours

3. Establishing rules that prevent solicitation of union membership during working hours

4. Communicating with employees regarding unionization and employer practices, provided that such communication does not:
   (a) Threaten, intimidate, or coerce employees; or
   (b) Involve promises or benefits linked to the defeat of the union

5. Changing working conditions and practices prior to the start of the statutory freeze, provided that such changes are not an attempt to influence employees

6. Changing working conditions and practices during the statutory freeze, provided that any such changes are part of business as usual, or have the required approval

7. Responding to union claims, provided that the response does not:
   (a) Threaten, intimidate, or coerce employees; or
   (b) Involve promises or benefits linked to the defeat of the union

Communicating with Employees Employers are allowed to communicate with employees and express an opinion regarding unionization of their employees provided they do not coerce or intimidate. In most jurisdictions, there is provision similar to the one in the Canada Labour Code, which provides as follows: "An employer is deemed not to contravene [the Code] by reason only that they express a personal point of view, so long as the employer does not use coercion, intimidation, threats, promises or undue influence."[20] There are some differences between jurisdictions regarding limits on employer communication with employees.

Labour Relations Issue 6-1 illustrates actual statements that have been made by employers.

Prohibiting Entry Employers can prohibit individuals who are not employees, including union organizers, from coming into the workplace. It is also possible for employers to prohibit employees who are part of a union organizing committee from coming into the workplace during their non-working hours. However, if the employer has not previously had a rule preventing employees from returning to the workplace during their non-working hours and such a rule was introduced in response to a union organizing campaign, this might be viewed as interference with the organizing process.

Prohibiting Solicitation Although employers in most jurisdictions cannot establish rules that prohibit the solicitation of union membership during non-working hours such as breaks and meal times, the employer could establish rules that prevent such solicitation during working hours. The situation appears to be different in Nova Scotia. A court decision in that province indicates that an employer may be able to establish a blanket rule against solicitation of union membership on employer property covering both working and non-working hours.[21] Enforcing such a rule would be difficult and establishing the rule might backfire because the union could use it as an illustration of the employer being unfair.

Labour Relations Issue 6-1

What Employers Have Said in Response to a Union Organizing Campaign

The following are excerpts from employer letters and pamphlets in response to union organizing campaigns.

> We feel that nobody will ever represent you better than yourself. Every one of our employees has been treated as an important contributor.... [W]e have had an open door policy. If an employee had a concern or if there was something that rightfully should have been looked at, re-examined in light of the employee's needs, we have been ready, willing and able to deal with it right away.
>
> .... the Steelworkers tried to unionize . . ., but not enough employees were interested. Is this union really any different?
>
> Will the union involve you in strikes or picket lines? If there is a strike, will the union pay you if you are on a strike? If so, how much?
>
> It is difficult to think of trying out a union. Once a union is certified, it is very difficult for employees to undo that decision. Check with the Labour Board or check out the law for yourself and you'll find out how difficult it is.

> Ask yourself why the union is interested in you: is it because the union needs the money that it will receive from union dues deducted from your cheque? How much are these union dues and what would you get in return for these dues?
>
> [U]nions can make promises just like a politician trying to get elected[;] however, ... law prevents the company from making any such promises to you. It is important to remember that in this election, only one candidate—the union—can make promises.
>
> How well do you really know the union leaders, including those union representatives in the workplace? Ask yourself, what voice will they let you have in running the union's affairs?
>
> [In a jurisdiction where the legislation provides that the results of a representation vote are determined by a majority of those who vote.] It [is] essential that you vote, because the results will be decided by those who vote. This means that the union will be certified if more than 50 percent of those who vote, vote yes.... Don't let the union get in by default.

Rules imposing restrictions against union activity may be subject to the condition that the employer has not allowed other non-work-related communication between employees in the past. In one case, the employer had allowed members of a staff association to use the employer's internal mail system to communicate with each other. Subsequently, after a union organizing campaign started, the employer prohibited use of the system for union-related communication. The Board held that the employer had committed an unfair labour practice by interfering with the organizing of the union.[22]

Employers should not think that a union organizing campaign prevents them from making changes in compensation, working conditions, or policy prior to the start of the statutory freeze period. They can make changes, provided the changes are not made for the purpose of discouraging unionization. Employers should document the business reasons for changes during an organizing campaign. After the statutory freeze has started, the employer must be careful to continue with business as usual. The employer can depart from business as usual if it obtains the consent of the union or the Board, depending upon the jurisdiction.

Union Unfair Labour Practices

There are two possible unfair labour practices unions must avoid at certification: (1) intimidation, threats, or coercion to compel a person to become or cease to be a member of a trade union and (2) solicitation of union support during working hours. All jurisdictions prohibit the union from using threats, intimidation, or coercion to sign members. Statements made by individual employees during the course of an organizing campaign may not be violations of the legislation even though similar statements would be an unfair labour practice if made by union officials. For example, if individual employees make statements to their co-workers that their jobs could be at risk if they do not join the union, the statements are not unfair labour practices even though they would be if made by union officials. Boards have received complaints of false or misleading statements made by unions during organizing campaigns. The Boards do not view such statements as equivalent to coercion or intimidation and will not interfere with a vote preceded by misleading or false information provided by the union. There is nothing to prevent the union from making promises to employees during an organizing campaign. It may be frustrating for employers to know that during the course of an organizing campaign they cannot make promises to employees because they would be viewed as interfering with employees' choice as discussed above, while there is no equivalent restriction on the union.

All jurisdictions except Manitoba and Ontario expressly prohibit attempting to persuade an employee to become or refrain from becoming a union member during working hours. Accordingly, solicitation of membership during working hours is an unfair labour practice; however, solicitation during non-working hours is permitted. It has been established that working hours do not include breaks and lunch periods even if they are paid.

The provisions in Manitoba and Ontario regarding workplace solicitation are unique and may be widely misunderstood. Instead of prohibiting solicitation during work hours, the legislation provides that nothing in the *Labour Relations Act* authorizes any person to persuade an employee during working hours to become or refrain from becoming a union member.[23] Accordingly, in Manitoba and Ontario, solicitation during working hours is not automatically an unfair labour practice, and the solicitation would only be prohibited if it disrupted the workplace.[24]

Remedies for Unfair Labour Practices

The rights and obligations provided in labour relations legislation, including the right to join a union, would be meaningless without an effective enforcement mechanism. We will now examine the procedure followed and remedies available in the event of unfair labour practices by employers or unions during the organizing campaign and certification process.

Procedure   If either the union or the employer thinks that an unfair labour practice has been committed, they may file a complaint with the Labour Relations Board. Referring unfair labour practice complaints to Boards instead of dealing with them in the court system has at least two advantages. Individuals with expertise in labour relations will consider the complaints, and they may be dealt with faster. In the federal jurisdiction, New Brunswick, and Nova Scotia, a complaint must be filed within 90 days. In other jurisdictions, the Board may exercise its discretion to refuse to deal with the complaint when there has been an undue delay.

In most jurisdictions, there is a provision for a labour relations officer, who is a Board employee, to attempt to settle the complaint so that a Board hearing is not required. Most unfair labour practice complaints are settled, and many are withdrawn. If a complaint is not settled or withdrawn, the Board will hold a hearing to determine whether there was a violation of the legislation and the remedy that should be provided. A hearing might take a few hours or a few weeks, depending on the number and complexity of the issues. Each side has an opportunity to present witnesses and documents as evidence to determine whether the legislation was contravened, and, if so, to propose an appropriate remedy.

Burden of Proof   Labour relations legislation in most jurisdictions (Canada, British Columbia, Nova Scotia, Ontario, Prince Edward Island, Quebec, and Saskatchewan) provides that where a complaint alleges an employee has been threatened, coerced, or dismissed because of union activity, the onus of proof is reversed and placed on the employer. The employer must establish there was no violation of the legislation. In the case of a dismissal, the employer will have to show there was a reason for the dismissal other than union activity. When a union supporter has been dismissed, the Board will carefully determine if the explanation provided by the employer is credible.

Remedies   If the Labour Relations Board determines that unfair labour practices have been committed during the organizing campaign, it might order one or more of the remedies listed in Figure 6-5 depending upon the nature of the unfair labour practice.

Most unfair labour practice complaints during the organizing campaign are allegations of employer misconduct such as threatening employees, interference with the union, and the discharge of employees involved in union activity. The purpose of the remedy a Board grants is to compensate the victim and deter future misconduct, not to punish the party who has violated the legislation.

Reinstatement of Discharged Employees.   Where it is found that employees have been terminated because of their union activity, the Board will order them reinstated.

Figure 6-5 Remedies for Unfair Labour Practices

1. Reinstatement of discharged employees
2. Compensation for financial losses
3. Interest on monies awarded
4. Posting or mailing of a notice to employees
5. Access order
6. Freeze on working conditions
7. Cease and desist order
8. Order prohibiting future unlawful conduct
9. New representation vote
10. Certification without a vote or remedial certification (not available in all jurisdictions)
11. Prosecution

Making whole attempts to put the innocent party in the position they would have been in if the legislation had not been violated.

Compensation or Damages. The Board will order the innocent party to be compensated for any financial losses flowing from the unfair labour practice. This action, often referred to as **making whole**, attempts to put the innocent party in the position they would have been in if the legislation had not been violated. Employees who have been discharged for union activity will be awarded compensation equivalent to their lost earnings, in addition to reinstatement. However, discharged employees have a duty to mitigate or take reasonable steps to reduce their loss. Any monies an employee earned or could have earned after they were dismissed will be deducted from any damages awarded. Boards have also awarded compensation to unions when they have incurred additional costs in countering unfair labour practices of the employer. For example, unions have been awarded the costs of printing additional materials to respond to employer threats of moving the business in the face of an organizing campaign. If the Board orders the employer to pay compensation for lost earnings for an earlier period, the Board will order that interest be paid on the amount owing.

Notice to Employees. Some Boards have ordered employers to post or mail a notice to employees that admits they have violated the legislation and promises that they will not violate the *Act* again. The purpose of this order is to allay employee fears of retaliation by the employer for future union activity.

Access. Where employers have threatened employees or provided false information, Boards have ordered that the union have an opportunity to meet with employees on employer property during working hours. The purpose of this order is to allow the union to respond to employer claims and alleviate employee concerns about unionization. Boards have also ordered employers to provide unions with the names and addresses of employees, and to allow the union to use bulletin boards and other communication tools in the workplace. Some Boards have ordered the employer to provide the union with notice of any meetings of employees and an opportunity to attend and respond.

Freeze on Working Conditions. Where employers have changed working conditions in violation of the legislation, Boards have ordered a freeze on working conditions.

Cease and Desist Order. One of the most common Board orders is a cease and desist order, which directs the employer to stop violating the legislation. For example, employers have been ordered to cease and desist from questioning employees about union involvement. Similarly, a Board could make an order that prohibits future unlawful conduct.

New Representation Vote. When either the union or the employer has been guilty of intimidation or coercion so that employees would be afraid to vote as they wish, the Board may order a new vote.

Certification Without a Vote. In the federal jurisdiction, British Columbia, Manitoba, New Brunswick, Nova Scotia, and Ontario, the Board has the authority to certify the union without a vote or despite the fact that the union has lost the vote. The certification of the union without a vote (remedial certification) is one of the most contentious remedies a Board may grant, and it is invoked only in exceptional circumstances where the employer has been guilty of serious misconduct. Labour Relations Issue 6-2 addresses this critical issue.

Prosecution. A contravention of the legislation or a Board order is an offence for which the guilty party can be prosecuted. In most jurisdictions, prosecution is not allowed unless the consent of the Board or the Minister of Labour is obtained. The consent to prosecute will only be granted in exceptional cases. The relationship between the union and the employer is ongoing, and a prosecution might harm the relationship.

Should Certification Without a Vote Be Available as a Remedy for Unfair Labour Practices?

The United Steelworkers of America launched an organizing campaign at a Walmart store in Windsor, Ontario in 1996. Subsequently the union filed an unfair labour practice complaint because of several events during the organizing campaign. Walmart had adopted practices that were intended to establish open communication with employees. One practice was an open-door policy; another was a "sundown rule." Employees were supposed to get answers to questions before the end of the business day on which the questions were raised. Walmart held meetings with employees at the beginning and end of each day. At one meeting, an anti-union employee spoke out against the union and said that the employer would not put up with a union. The managers present did not distance the company from the employee's remarks. Pro-union employees were not given an opportunity to respond, because the store was about to open.

Prior to the representation vote, four senior managers from outside the store circulated among employees. When employees asked if the store might close if the union won, the managers replied that it would not be appropriate to answer the question. Management continued with this approach after being advised by the union that the refusal to answer the question was causing employees

concern. The union lost the representation vote by a vote of 151–43.

The Board found that there were three violations of the *Act* by the employer. The most serious was the refusal to answer the question about the possibility of the store closing, in light of the employer's previous commitment to respond to questions. The Board concluded that the employer had led employees to believe that if they supported the union they would lose their jobs. At the time of the hearing, the Ontario *Labour Relations Act* provided that the Board had the authority to certify a union without a vote when the employer had violated the *Act* and the true wishes of the employees would not be revealed by a vote. The Board certified the union despite the results of the vote. Subsequently, a Conservative government amended the *Act* and removed the Board's authority to certify a union without a representation vote. Later still, a Liberal government was elected, and they restored the Board's authority to certify a union without a representation vote.

Should a Labour Relations Board be allowed to certify a union without a vote? If the Board does not have this authority, what is to prevent employers from flagrantly violating the legislation in order to avoid unionization?

DECERTIFICATION

Decertification is the process by which a Labour Relations Board revokes the right granted to a union to represent employees and bargain on their behalf. Depending on the jurisdiction, the legislation will refer to decertification, termination, rescission, or revocation of bargaining rights. Previously it was noted that the term *certification* might refer to either the process by which a union obtains bargaining rights or the end result of the application for such rights. Similarly, decertification or rescission may refer to either the process followed to revoke the union's bargaining rights or the Board's order terminating the rights.

Decertification allows employees to rid themselves of an ineffective union or change unions. The possibility of decertification helps ensure union democracy and fair representation because of the threat of the union losing its bargaining rights if it fails to maintain the support of the majority. However, the process poses a policy dilemma. If decertification is too difficult to obtain, employees will lose protection against union inefficiency and freedom of choice regarding their bargaining representative. If decertification is available without any restrictions, unions may be subject to attack by employers and anti-union employees. Accordingly, there are restrictions on the decertification process, including who can apply, the basis for the application, and when the application can be made.

A union's bargaining rights can be terminated on different grounds, depending upon the jurisdiction. We will first consider the most common ways a union loses bargaining rights that apply in all jurisdictions—a decertification application by employees or the certification of a different union—and then consider additional grounds for decertification that vary across jurisdictions. Appendix 6.5, "Decertification Procedure," at the end of this chapter provides information relating to unique features of the decertification process in some jurisdictions.

Decertification Application by Employees

All jurisdictions provide that employees can apply to decertify the union on the basis that they no longer support or wish to be represented by the union.

Procedure The process for decertification is similar to that for certification. Employees in the bargaining unit sign a statement confirming that they do not want the union to represent them, and this evidence is filed with the Board, together with an application to decertify the union. The key policy issues here are the minimum level of support required for an application, whether a vote is required, and how the results of any vote are determined. The minimum level of support that is required for the application in each jurisdiction is shown in Figure 6-6.

Three jurisdictions—federal, Manitoba, and Quebec—require a higher level of support for a decertification application than is the case for a certification application. Seven jurisdictions (Alberta, British Columbia, New Brunswick, Newfoundland and Labrador,

	Minimum Support Required on Application	Vote Required
Federal	50% + 1	No. Where vote held majority of ballots cast required.
Alberta	40%	Yes. Majority of ballots cast required.
British Columbia	45%	Yes. Majority of ballots cast required.
Manitoba	50% + 1	Yes, unless union does not oppose application. Majority of ballots cast required.
New Brunswick	40%	Yes. A vote of 50% of employees eligible is required. Absent employees are not counted as eligible.
Newfoundland and Labrador	40%	Yes. If more than 70% of employees vote the union is decertified if 50% + 1 casting ballots vote against the union. If less than 70% of employees vote 50% + 1 of employees eligible to vote must vote against union.
Nova Scotia	50% + 1 of employees or, "significant number" of union members	Yes. Majority of ballots cast required.
Ontario	40%	Yes. Majority of ballots cast required.
Prince Edward Island	50% + 1	No. Where vote held majority of ballots cast required.
Quebec	50% + 1	No. Where vote held majority of ballots cast required.
Saskatchewan	45% + 1	Yes. Majority of ballots cast required.

Figure 6-6 Decertification Application by Employees: Support and Vote Requirements

Ontario, Prince Edward Island, and Saskatchewan) require the same minimum level of support for a decertification application as a certification application. Nova Scotia is a special case that is dealt with in Appendix 6.5. The employer and the union are not given the names of the employees who apply. Figure 6-6 also shows whether a vote is required. Most jurisdictions provide that a representation vote must be held if a specified minimum percentage of employees indicate that they no longer want the union to represent them. In the jurisdictions where a vote is not required, the Board may still direct a vote to satisfy itself that the majority no longer wish to be represented by the union. The federal Board's policy is to require a vote if the union challenges the application.[25] When a vote is held, there is variation across jurisdictions on how the results are determined, as shown in Figure 6-6. The vote is held within the same time frame as a representation vote on a certification application.

Timelines: When an Application for Decertification Can Be Made
There are restrictions on when employees are allowed to make an application. As in the case of an application for certification, the restrictions depend on whether a collective agreement has been negotiated. If no agreement has been negotiated, in all jurisdictions with one exception, the decertification application cannot be made until the time an application for certification by a second union is allowed. In British Columbia, the policy is to prohibit an application for decertification for a longer time. When there is no collective agreement in place, a second union can apply to be certified after six months in British Columbia, but an application for decertification cannot be made until 10 months after the union was certified.

When a collective agreement has been negotiated, generally an application for decertification can only be made during one of the open periods for a certification application. Three jurisdictions provide an exception where the union was voluntarily recognized instead of being certified. All jurisdictions except Quebec allow a union to obtain bargaining rights through voluntary recognition by the employer instead of certification by the Board. In the federal jurisdiction, New Brunswick, and Ontario, there are special provisions allowing for the decertification of a union that has been voluntarily recognized. In these jurisdictions, an application for decertification can be made at any time in the first year of a collective agreement. The purpose of this provision is to protect against an employer entering into a voluntary recognition agreement and a collective agreement with a union that does not have the support of employees. An employer and a union in these jurisdictions who have concluded a collective agreement after entering into a voluntary recognition agreement face uncertainty in the first year of the agreement's operation that would not exist if the Board had certified the union. In Ontario and New Brunswick, the legislation also allows for the termination of the union's bargaining rights during the first year of a voluntary recognition agreement where no collective agreement is reached.

In summary, there are significant periods of time when employees cannot make an application for decertification. If there is no collective agreement negotiated, employees must wait 10 months to a year after certification to make an application to decertify, depending on the jurisdiction. If there is a collective agreement with the employer, the open period in which a decertification application can be made could be delayed even longer. In some jurisdictions, the first time an application could be made will be the open period that arises just prior to the expiration of the third year of an agreement.

In most jurisdictions, there is a provision to protect the union against repeated decertification applications. These provisions protect the union for 90 days to a year depending on the jurisdiction. Figure 6-7 provides the relevant bars.

Federal	No application by any employee for six months unless the Board bridges this time. (Regulations Section 39, 46)
Alberta	If Board refuses a decertification application, the applicant cannot reapply for 90 days. (s. 57)
British Columbia	Board can bar another application if the union wins vote; 90-day minimum bar if imposed. (s. 30, 33)
New Brunswick	Board may refuse another application from unsuccessful applicant for up to 10 months. (s. 126 (2))
Newfoundland and Labrador	A six-month bar is imposed after any decertification application is dismissed. (s. 52)
Ontario	An application by any employees affected by an unsuccessful application can be barred for one year. (s. 112 (2)(k))

Figure 6-7 Bars to Repeated Decertification Applications

Restrictions   An application for decertification must be a voluntary act by employees. If the employer provides assistance to the employees making the application, or encourages it, it will be rejected. Applications have been rejected when employers have allowed employees to collect signatures during working hours or paid the legal expenses of the employees making the application.

In Manitoba and the federal jurisdiction, there are some additional restrictions relating to whether the employer has failed to bargain in good faith or the union has made reasonable efforts to reach an agreement. These restrictions are provided in Appendix 6.5.

Significance   To put decertification in perspective, we might observe how many decertification votes unions lose and compare the number of losses to the number of certifications for the same time period. The annual report from the Ontario Labour Relations Board for 2011–12 indicated that there were 215 applications for certification granted and 30 declarations of termination made. The terminations were 12 percent of the certifications granted.[26] In 2012, British Columbia's Labour Relations Board granted, there were 67 applications for certification and 21 declarations of termination made. Certification applications covered 8769 employees in that province, while 416 employees removed themselves from a union.[27]

Certification of a Different Union

Employees who wish to change unions do not have to apply to decertify their current union before a second, or replacement, union is certified to represent them. A second union can apply to represent employees in the open period for a certification application. If the second union is certified, the first union loses its bargaining rights.

Additional Grounds for Decertification

Some jurisdictions provide additional grounds to decertify the union that will be briefly referred to here. Decertifications on the basis of these additional grounds, which are listed by jurisdiction in Figure 6-8, are not common.

Failure to Give Notice to Bargain, or to Bargain   Labour relations legislation provides that after a union is certified, it must give the employer notice that it wishes to bargain to reach a collective agreement. Prior to the expiry of a collective agreement, either the union or the employer can give notice to the other to negotiate its renewal. Legislation in Ontario and New Brunswick provides that if a union fails to give notice to bargain, or

Federal	Fraud (s. 40)
Alberta	No collective agreement: employer can apply where no agreement reached in 3 years after certification or 3 years pass after an agreement expires (s. 51(1), 52(5))
Manitoba	Fraud (s. 52)
	Failure to exercise bargaining rights within 12 months of certification (s. 53)
New Brunswick	Fraud (s. 25)
	No employees in bargaining unit for 2 years (s. 25)
	Failure to give notice to bargain or bargain (s. 24(1)(2))
Ontario	Fraud (s. 64(1))
	Failure to give notice to bargain or bargain (s. 65)
Prince Edward Island	Employer can bring application on ground that majority of employees no longer wish union to act on their behalf (s. 20(1))
Saskatchewan	Fraud (s. 5(k), 16)

Figure 6-8 Additional Grounds for Decertification

fails to bargain, the union may be decertified. The purpose of this provision is to prevent the union from "sleeping on its rights." An application to decertify the union because of its failure to bargain can be made by either the employer or the employees.

The Board does not automatically decertify the union when it has failed to bargain. It will direct a representation vote, unless the union indicates that it no longer wishes to represent the employees.

Termination Where Certificate Obtained by Fraud   The federal jurisdiction, Manitoba, New Brunswick, Ontario, and Saskatchewan provide for termination of the union's bargaining rights if the certification was obtained by fraud. Fraud refers to making false statements to the Board, and does not include false statements made to other parties. Fraud would include such actions as forging signatures on union membership cards or deliberately misstating the number of employees in the application for certification. A letter containing false information circulated among employees would not be covered by these provisions.

An application for termination for fraud can be made at any time. There is variation across jurisdictions regarding who can make the application.

Failure to Reach Agreement   In most jurisdictions, the failure to reach a collective agreement does not provide a basis for decertification; the union continues to hold bargaining rights for the employees. However, in Alberta there is a provision for decertification of the union when there is a failure to reach a collective agreement after three years.

SUCCESSOR RIGHTS

When a union is certified, the certificate issued by the Board provides that the union represents a bargaining unit of employees working for the employer named in the certificate. Similarly, any collective agreement negotiated will provide that the agreement is between the union and the employer named in the agreement. If the employer sold the business, the union's bargaining rights and any collective agreement with the first owner could be nullified unless labour relations legislation provided for the possibility of a sale of the business. **Successor rights** provisions in labour relations legislation deal with these issues.

The purpose of successor rights is to protect the bargaining rights of the union and any collective agreement in the event that the business is sold. Generally the successor rights

Successor rights protect the rights of the union and any collective agreement if a business is sold.

provisions confirm that, subject to some exceptions, any previous certification and collective agreement bind the purchaser of the business. There is some variation in the provisions across jurisdictions, including how it is determined whether there has in fact been a sale of a business. Readers should refer to the legislation in their jurisdiction for further information and possible variations.[28]

In all jurisdictions, a critical question will be whether there has been a sale of the business as defined in the legislation. *Sale* has been broadly interpreted and will likely include a business transfer that may not normally be viewed as a sale. The definition in the *Canada Labour Code* provides that a sale "includes the transfer or other disposition of the business. . . ."[29] In one case, a municipality had a contract with a company to provide drivers, mechanics, and other staff to the municipality for the operation of the municipality's transit system. A union represented the employees of the company. The municipality terminated the contract and hired its own drivers, mechanics, and other staff. Many of the employees the municipality hired were former employees of the firm the municipality had previously contracted with. The union that held the bargaining rights for the company's employees sought a declaration that there had been a sale as defined by the legislation. This would mean that the municipality was a successor employer and was bound by the terms of the collective agreement. The Board found that there had been a sale of the business as defined by the *Act*—even though no money had changed hands—and the municipality was bound by the collective agreement.[30]

When an application for certification is pending at the time of the sale, the purchaser is treated as the employer for purposes of the application. Accordingly, the purchaser will be bound by any certification order made after the purchase is finalized. In cases in which the union has been certified and negotiations with the employer are under way when the sale of the business occurs, the union may give a notice to bargain to the successor employer. Any previous negotiations with the seller of the business do not carry forward to the buyer. When we review the negotiation process in Chapter 8, we will see that in most jurisdictions there cannot be a strike or lockout until the union and the employer have completed a conciliation or mediation process. When there is a sale during the negotiation of a collective agreement, the successor employer (purchaser) and the union must go through this process even if there has already been conciliation between the business seller and the union. If a strike or lockout is under way at the time of the sale, it must cease until the successor employer and the union have gone through the conciliation process. If there is a collective agreement between the union and the seller of the business, it is binding upon the successor employer.

Additional issues will arise when the buyer of a business combines employees of the business purchased with employees of another business. If a union already represents the buyer's employees, the Board may direct a representation vote to determine which of the two unions will represent the employees.

Implications for Practice

1. Employees join unions for a number of reasons, many of which relate to matters other than compensation. Employers who wish to avoid unionization should review the factors discussed in this chapter, including compensation, management training, and complaint mechanisms. Unions seeking to organize a workplace should determine the issues that employees are concerned with.

2. The certification of a union has important consequences for employers and employees. When a union is certified, the employer has an obligation to negotiate with the union to attempt to reach a collective agreement. Certification establishes the union as the exclusive

bargaining agent for all employees in the bargaining unit, and changes in the terms of employment must be negotiated with the union.

3. The certification process, including a possible requirement for a vote of employees, varies across jurisdictions. Employers and unions should refer to the legislation and information available from the ministry responsible for labour issues in their jurisdiction.

4. The conduct of employers and unions during the organizing campaign and certification process is regulated by labour relations legislation. Employers and unions should familiarize themselves with and avoid unfair labour practices. In some jurisdictions, serious unfair labour practices by the employer could lead to the certification of the union without a vote.

5. Employees have the right to terminate the bargaining rights of their union or replace the union that represents them with another. Employers must not influence any decertification application made by employees.

6. Generally a union does not lose its bargaining rights because the employer sells the business. The purchaser is bound by any collective agreement.

Key Terms

certification process, p. 101

community of interest, p. 109

decertification, p. 107

dependent contractor, p. 105

fourfold test, p. 104

independent contractor, p. 104

making whole, p. 120

open period, p. 108

organizing campaign, p. 102

organizing committee, p. 102

representation vote, p. 110

statutory freeze, p. 115

successor rights, p. 125

unfair labour practice, p. 114

union organizer, p. 102

voluntary recognition agreement, p. 101

Review Questions

1. Why do some employees want to have a union represent them?

2. Outline the factors external to the workplace that could affect employees' desire to unionize.

3. Why do some employees oppose unionization of their workplace?

4. How can the union obtain the right to be the bargaining agent for a group of employees?

5. What are the four things that a union will have to establish when it applies to a labour relations board to be certified?

6. Identify employees who are prevented from unionizing and the reasons for their exclusion.

7. Who decides what the appropriate bargaining unit is when a union applies for certification and what is the significance of this determination?

8. What are the factors considered when the appropriate bargaining unit is determined?

9. Why do unions prefer a process that allows for certification on the basis of membership cards without a representation vote being held?

10. Outline four employer and two union unfair labour practices during the organizing campaign and certification process.

11. What is the meaning and significance of the phrase of "business as usual" at the time of a certification application?

12. Are employees allowed to sign up their co-workers as union members on the employer's property?

13. What are the remedies for unfair labour practices during an organizing campaign and certification application?

14. Why is decertification an important part of labour relations legislation?

15. What does the phrase "successor rights" refer to and why are successor rights a necessary part of labour relations legislation?

Discussion Questions

1. Consider a non-union organization that you have worked for in the past or are familiar with. Which of the reasons for employees seeking unionization referred to in this chapter might have led employees in that organization to seek union representation? Were there any other reasons why employees might have tried to unionize?

2. Consider a non-union organization that you have worked for in the past or are familiar with. This chapter provided reasons why some employees may not support unionization. Would any of these reasons apply to you or your co-workers? Are there any other reasons why you or your co-workers might oppose unionization?

3. What is the significance of the group of employees found to be the appropriate bargaining unit at certification?

4. An automotive dealership has four departments: service, sales, office, and a body repair shop. There is a supervisor for each of the departments. The mechanics and mechanics' helpers in the service department have a separate incentive compensation system. The employees in the service department and body repair department have the same benefits package, and they work in the same building that is separate from the auto showroom. There is no interchange of employees between departments. A union has applied for certification seeking to represent the mechanics and mechanics' helpers in the service department. What, if anything, should the employer's response be?

5. Confirm whether the labour relations legislation in your province provides for the possibility of certification of a union based on membership cards or requires a representation vote. If the legislature was considering changes to the legislation, what arguments would you make in favour of relying on membership cards instead of requiring a vote? Conversely, what arguments would you make in favour of requiring a vote in all applications for certification?

6. An employer has been notified that a union has filed an application for certification for a group of its employees. The employer is considering implementing the changes or taking the steps referred to below. In each case, explain whether the employer should take the action referred to.
   (a) The employer is considering the amount that will be paid to employees who use their vehicles in the course of their employment. For five years, the employer has increased the mileage allowance on an annual basis after reviewing the costs of gas and other factors affecting the cost of operating a vehicle. No announcements relating to an increase have been made.
   (b) The employer is considering a new incentive pay system. The system has been designed by a consultant, the consultant has been paid, and the senior management team has approved the system; however, employees have not yet been informed about the system.
   (c) Same situation as in (b), except that the system was announced to employees two weeks before the application for certification was filed by the union.

7. Confirm whether the Labour Relations Board in your province can certify a union without a vote as a remedy for employer unfair labour practices. What are the arguments for and against the Board having this authority?

8. Confirm when labour relations legislation in your province allows employees to make an application for decertification. Do you think that the restrictions on a decertification application are appropriate? That is, explain the labour relations policy behind the restrictions on an application for decertification, and whether the restrictions are too broad or too narrow.

Web Research

Use your favourite Web browser to locate a news source that covered a decertification of a union.

CASE INCIDENT   GROS MORNE ELECTRIC

Gros Morne Electric is an electrical contractor that does work in the residential construction industry. All of the company's work comes from non-union general contractors. The company pays wages that are approximately 20 percent lower than the union rate of pay. The International Brotherhood of Electrical Workers (IBEW) started an organizing campaign at Gros Morne. Shortly after the organizing campaign became public knowledge, the president of the company said at a meeting of employees that he could not compete in a union market, and stated that the company would have to close its doors if the union was certified. When individual employees approached the president and asked him about his thoughts on the situation, he said that he did not like the IBEW. In response to the organizing campaign, the company president sent a letter to all employees, making the following points:

- Employees and management were part of a team, and the company had been successful with people working together.
- The president was pleased that the company was able to report to inquiring banks and mortgage companies that employment was full-time and permanent.
- Certification of the union would mean that employees would have to pay union dues.
- Certification would mean that the company would be on shaky ground because it would now be competing in a new unionized market.
- The company had never laid people off for more than a few weeks in the past.
- Certification would mean that the company would lose a few good people.

Questions

1. Has the employer committed any unfair labour practices?
2. If any unfair labour practices have been committed, what remedies could the union pursue and how would it do so?

CASE INCIDENT   TOWNSHIP OF RAIN LAKE

The Township of Rain Lake has a population of 20 000. The municipality has a public works department with five full-time employees, and additional seasonal employees are hired when required. Three of the employees, including John Mills, are equipment operators who do road-grading work in the summer and snow removal in the winter months.

The Township has employed John Mills for eight years. The other two equipment operators have 10 and 3 years of experience. Mills has no disciplinary record; however, he is the only equipment operator with two accidents noted in his file. Neither of these accidents involved traffic charges. The council for the municipality meets every January to determine the wages of employees for the year. Mills and the other two equipment operators met with council in January, requesting a guarantee of 130 hours per month in the January–March period. The employees did not request a wage increase. Council agreed to increase the guaranteed hours to 115 per month.

The three employees were very disappointed with council's decision, and they approached a union about the possibility of organizing. A meeting with a union representative was held at the home of John Mills a few days later, and all five full-time employees were present. The union representative outlined the advantages of unionization and presented membership cards for signature. Mills and two others were in favour, one was opposed, and one was undecided.

When the employees' supervisor heard about the meeting, he convened a meeting of employees at his home. He suggested that the employees allow him to approach council members before they proceeded with unionization. The supervisor spoke to several members of council and advised them that the employees were likely going to join the union. Arrangements were made for the supervisor to attend the next council meeting in February to address the issue of working conditions for employees. At the February meeting, the supervisor proposed that the Township agree to the guaranteed hours requested by the employees, and provide a one-dollar-per-hour wage increase and an improvement in benefits. After the supervisor left the meeting, the council agreed to change the hours guaranteed; however, no further changes were made. At the same council meeting a resolution was passed to eliminate one of the equipment operator positions. Council directed that John Mills be the operator terminated.

When the supervisor asked why council had done this, he was told there were several reasons. The Township was facing a deficit, and costs would have to be cut to avoid a tax increase. Councillors also noted that the municipality had purchased a new, more efficient snow plough two years ago. Mills had been chosen for termination because of his accident record. Finally, council did not agree to the wage increase because they thought they knew the views of operators other than Mills on unionization. They believed the others would not join a union, and that the threat to join was a bluff. The town clerk said that prior to the February meeting she had checked with the provincial Ministry of Labour and confirmed that there was no requirement that employees be laid off in order of seniority.

Questions

1. Outline the basis, if any, for Mills to file a complaint with the Labour Relations Board in your jurisdiction.

2. Assuming the Mills files a complaint with the Labour Relations Board, how would the employer likely respond to the claim(s) made in any filing with the Board?

3. Explain the outcome you expect in this case in light of your understanding of theories and concepts discussed in the course.

CASE INCIDENT   SAFE ENVIRONMENT SERVICES

Safe Environmental Services resolves environmental problems in buildings including asbestos and mould removal. The company is a privately held corporation owned by Rob Canting. The company employs 30 technicians who do the day-to-day work required. There is one supervisor, Janice Smith, whose main responsibilities are scheduling and on-site inspections; and three lead hands who direct the technicians and complete any paperwork required.

The Safety Technicians Union was certified as the bargaining agent for the technicians and lead hands in 1998. Subsequently there has been a series of collective agreements between the union and the employer, the most recent of which ran from 2007 through 2010. The collective agreement provides a wage schedule for the technicians and lead hands. The top hourly rate for technicians is $20 per hour and the hourly rate for lead hands is $23 per hour. The agreement also contains a closed shop provision requiring the employer to hire new technicians who are union members through the union's office. If the union is not able to respond to a request for a technician within 48 hours the agreement allows the employer to proceed to hire someone who is not a union member, however, the individual hired must join the union. The collective agreement requires technicians to have at least 6000 hours of work experience before they are eligible to move to the lead hand position.

The company hired John Parker as a technician in 2005 without contacting the union. Parker had no previous training or experience with hazardous materials and he was not a union member. Parker had a social connection with Janice Smith—his daughter took music lessons from Smith's spouse. After he worked for the company for eight months Parker was promoted to a lead hand position. When Parker was made a lead hand his hourly rate was increased to $25 per hour. The company paid several employees more money than the collective agreement required. At the time of Parker's appointment there was another technician with over 20 years' experience whom the employer passed over. Parker operated with more freedom and authority than the other lead hands, for example, he was the only lead hand to choose the technicians who worked on his projects. There was no formal announcement of Parker's appointment as a lead hand and some employees thought that he was a supervisor. The business agent for the union held bimonthly union meetings; however, Parker only attended one meeting to become a union member after he was told union membership was required.

The union had a benefit plan that was financed by employer contributions. The collective agreement required the employer to remit to the union 3 percent of gross wages to finance the plan. In 2010 a few employees had problems with their benefits because the employer did not remit all of the money it should have to the union and also failed to report the names of employees to the union. There was extensive discussion in the workplace about the union and employees discontent on some issues. Employees were particularly concerned over (1) the fact that the business agent had resigned and was not replaced for four months, (2) the fact that other firms in the industry were not unionized, and (3) the problems with benefits. In December 2010, Parker moved to try to get rid of the union. After some discussion with employees Parker raised the issue of decertification at two employee meetings. The first meeting was held on December 10, when Parker raised the issue at the end of a meeting that had been set up by Smith to discuss safety issues. Smith remained in the room while the discussion relating to the union took place. On the issue of benefits Parker told employees he would investigate an alternative plan with an independent firm. When some employees referred to the possibility of a pension or retirement savings plan if the union was decertified, Parker said that he would check with Mr. Canting to see what contributions he was willing to make to a pension plan. After the December 10 meeting, Parker obtained the forms necessary to apply for decertification. He completed the forms with a technician who also opposed the union, using a computer in Canting's office. Parker and his colleague arranged an employee meeting on December 20 at a restaurant to discuss the decertification and get employees to sign the application. They encouraged employees to attend the meeting by indicating they would pay for their lunch. The employees' normal lunch break was 30 minutes long; however, on December 20 the meeting at the restaurant went on for two hours. Prior to the employees signing the application, Parker told the group that no one should feel that they were being forced to sign the application. The majority of the employees present signed the application for decertification and Parker filed it with the Labour Relations Board one day later.

Questions

1. Assume that you are an official in the union and you have an opportunity to respond to the decertification application. What would your response be?

2. Explain how you think the Labour Relations Board would dispose of the application for decertification.

APPENDIX TO CHAPTER 6 Collective Bargaining Rights Appendices

6.1 MANAGERIAL EXCLUSIONS

Employees who exercise management functions in their jobs are excluded from membership in a bargaining unit in Alberta, New Brunswick, Newfoundland and Labrador, Nova Scotia, and Prince Edward Island. Other Canadian jurisdictions include some provisos related to this limitation.

Canada

See http://laws-lois.justice.gc.ca/eng/acts/L-2/index.html.
Section 3(1) excludes individuals who perform management functions. However, the *Code* specifically refers to the possibility of the certification of supervisory employees in Section 27(5).

British Columbia

See www.lrb.bc.ca/codeguide, Chapter 1.
Section 1(1) of the British Columbia *Labour Relations Code* provides that a person who performs the functions of a manager or superintendent is not an employee for the purposes of the *Code*. The British Columbia Labour Relations Board applies an "effective determination" test to decide if an individual is performing the functions of a manager. The BCLRB applies a fairly narrow definition to "manager," generally excluding only employees who are involved in making decisions concerning discipline and discharge. For example, an employee who, as part of his or her job, reported on the attendance or activities of other employees would not be considered a manager unless he or she also decided what the employer's response to misconduct would be. Those with authority over rates of pay, often used as a determining factor in other jurisdictions, are not considered managers unless they have additional responsibilities.

Manitoba

See http://web2.gov.mb.ca/laws/statutes/ccsm/l010e.php.
Sections 1 and 142 (5) provide that the employee must "primarily" perform management functions to be excluded. The Board also has the authority to classify individuals as employees, and as a result persons who would be excluded in other jurisdictions, including persons who hire and fire, have been allowed to organize and bargain collectively, albeit not necessarily within the same bargaining unit[1] as their staff.

Ontario

See http://www.e-laws.gov.on.ca/html/statutes/english/elaws_statutes_95l01_e.htm.
The definition of employee in Section 1(3)(b) of the *Labour Relations Act* excludes an employee who "exercises managerial functions." The phrase "managerial functions" is not defined. Employees will be found to be exercising managerial functions in two situations: (1) where they are involved in independent decision-making responsibilities in matters of policy or the running of the organization and (2) where they have the authority to make effective recommendations relating to conditions of employment.[2]

The Board has also had to consider the status of persons who, due to their skill, education, training or experience, are asked to act in a supervisory role towards others. This could include situations as varied as a research scientist's relationship to a technician or a master craftsperson dealing with an apprentice. In *Oakwood Park Lodge*, the Board determined that the factor to consider was "those functions which have a direct and provable impact . . . upon the terms and conditions of employment"[3] of those other employees. The Board has excluded those who act in a managerial capacity on a seasonal basis,[4] but has not excluded those who have an ownership stake in the enterprise.[5]

Saskatchewan

Section 2(f)(i)(A) excludes individuals whose primary responsibility is to actually exercise authority and actually perform management functions.

In 2013 the *Saskatchewan Employment Act* passed third and final reading in the Legislative Assembly. The *Act* consolidates 12 pieces of labour legislation into one updated and comprehensive act. Part VI of the *Act* deals with labour relations matters. At the time of this writing, the Supreme Court of Canada is hearing a *Charter* challenge of provincial Bills 5 and 6. The Saskatchewan Federation of Labour is arguing that so-called "essential services" elements of the new legislation, and other changes made to the former *Trade Union Act*, are not consistent with the *Canadian Charter of Rights and Freedoms*.

6.2 OCCUPATIONAL EXCLUSIONS

There are no occupational exclusions from bargaining unit membership in the Canada Labour Code or in provincial labour statutes in British Columbia, Manitoba, Newfoundland and Labrador, and Saskatchewan.

Alberta

See www.qp.alberta.ca/1266.cfm?page=L01.cfm&leg_type=Acts&isbncln=9780779753635. Professionals in the architectural, dental, engineering, legal, and medical fields employed in their professional capacity; agricultural employees; and domestics employed in a private home are excluded.

New Brunswick

See http://laws.gnb.ca/en/ShowTdm/cs/I-4. Professionals in the architectural, dental, engineering, legal, and medical fields employed in their professional capacity; and domestics employed in a private home are excluded.

Nova Scotia

Professionals in the architectural, dental, engineering, legal, and medical fields employed in their professional capacity are excluded.

Ontario

See http://www.e-laws.gov.on.ca/html/statutes/english/elaws_statutes_95l01_e.htm. Professionals in architectural, dental, legal, land surveying, and medical fields employed in their professional capacity; and domestics employed in a private home are excluded.

Prince Edward Island

See www.gov.pe.ca/law/statutes/pdf/l-01.pdf. Professionals in the architectural, dental, engineering, legal, and medical fields employed in their professional capacity are excluded.

Saskatchewan

The *Act* does not contain any occupational exclusions. In 2013 the *Saskatchewan Employment Act* passed third and final reading in the Legislative Assembly. The *Act* consolidates 12 pieces of labour legislation into one updated and comprehensive act. Part VI of the *Act* deals with labour relations matters. At the time of this writing, the Supreme Court of Canada is hearing a *Charter* challenge of provincial Bills 5 and 6. The Saskatchewan Federation of Labour is arguing that so-called "essential services" elements of the new legislation, and other changes made to the former *Trade Union Act*, are not consistent with the *Canadian Charter of Rights and Freedoms*.

6.3 APPROPRIATE BARGAINING UNIT

Canada

See www.cirb-ccri.gc.ca/eic/site/047.nsf/eng/00105.html.
A bargaining unit must have at least two employees. Professional employees, supervisors, and dependent contractors can be included in units with other employees, or a separate bargaining unit can be established. The Board's normal practice is to have separate bargaining units for production and office employees; however, there have been exceptions. The Board does not generally establish separate bargaining units for full-time and part-time employees.

Alberta

See http://www.alrb.gov.ab.ca/alrb_code.htm#s32.
A bargaining unit must have at least two employees. All firefighters of an employer must be included in one bargaining unit.

British Columbia

See www.lrb.bc.ca/codeguide, Chapter 4.
The *Code* contains few provisions that restrict the Board's determination of the appropriate bargaining unit. The *Code* allows for a bargaining unit to have only one employee. The *Code* specifically refers to supervisors, providing that supervisors who do not perform as managers may form their own bargaining unit or may be included in another unit (s. 29). The Board's approach to standard bargaining units has been different from that in other jurisdictions. The Board has not assumed that production and white-collar employees should be in separate bargaining units and has established more "all-employee" bargaining units. The Board has not established separate bargaining units for part-time and full-time employees. The Board has indicated that it will vary from its general practice of certifying all employee units and certify smaller units in sectors of the economy that have been hard to organize in the past. Although the *Code* provides for the establishment of separate craft units in section 21, this is subject to the requirement that the unit "is otherwise appropriate for collective bargaining." This has meant that the Board must find that there are exceptional circumstances in order to determine that it should establish a separate craft unit instead of following its general policy favouring all-employee units. The *Code*'s provisions relating to dependent contractors also favour the inclusion of dependent contractors in a bargaining unit with other employees instead of establishing a separate unit. Section 28 requires the Board to consider whether the inclusion of dependent contractors with other employees would be more appropriate for collective bargaining and, if so, vary the existing certification to include the dependent contractors.

Manitoba

See http://web2.gov.mb.ca/laws/statutes/ccsm/l010e.php.
The *Act* allows for a bargaining unit to have only one employee.

The Board cannot include professional employees practicing a profession with employees in another unit unless it is satisfied that a majority of the professional employees wish to be included in the unit.

New Brunswick

See http://laws.gnb.ca/en/ShowTdm/cs/I-4.
A bargaining unit must have at least two employees. In the agricultural industry, a unit must have at least five employees. A bargaining unit consisting solely of professionals is appropriate for collective bargaining, but the Board may include members of a profession in a unit with other employees only if it is satisfied that is the wish of the majority of the professional employees.

Newfoundland and Labrador

See www.hrle.gov.nl.ca/lrb.
A bargaining unit must have at least two employees. Dependent contractors can be included in a unit with other employees. The Board may find a unit of professional employees of one or more professions appropriate, and may include in the unit employees who do work that in the opinion of the Board is closely related to the work of the professional employees in the unit. Where the Board considers it desirable to do so, professional employees may, on the request of the majority of them, be formed into a unit restricted to members of one profession and employees who do work closely related to the work of those professional employees. Where the application for certification relates to an offshore petroleum production platform, the unit must comprise all the employees employed on the platform except those employees the Board determines are employed in construction and start-up on the platform.

Nova Scotia

See http://www.canlii.org/en/ns/laws/stat/rsns-1989-c-246/latest/part-1/rsns-1989-c-246-part-1.pdf
A bargaining unit must have at least two employees. The *Act* specifically refers to the community of interest of employees as follows in Section 25(14): "The Board in determining the appropriate unit shall have regard to the community of interest among the employees in the proposed unit in such matters as work location, hours of work, working conditions and methods of remuneration." Section 24(1) provides that "where a group of employees of an employer belong to a craft or group exercising technical skills by reason of which they are distinguishable from the employees as a whole and the majority of the group are members of one trade union pertaining to that craft or other skills, the trade union may apply to the Board and… may be certified as the bargaining agent of the employees in the group, if the group is otherwise appropriate as a unit for collective bargaining." The *Act* has special provisions relating to employers engaged in manufacturing at two or more interdependent locations. An employer can apply to the Board for an order that the appropriate bargaining unit consists of all employees at such locations. The employer must apply within one year of the start of production at the second location, and cannot apply if there was a previous certification order or voluntary recognition at one of the locations.

Ontario

See http://www.e-laws.gov.on.ca/html/statutes/english/elaws_statutes_95l01_e.htm.
The *Act* contains specific provisions that affect the determination of an appropriate bargaining unit. A bargaining unit must have more than one employee. Section 9(3) requires the Board to establish a separate craft bargaining unit where a group of employees and the union

applying for certification meet specified criteria. This allows for the continuation of previously established craft units, but makes it difficult to carve out a new one. Professional engineers and dependant contractors are allowed to form their own bargaining units, unless the Board finds that a majority of them wish to be included in a bargaining unit with other employees. The issue of security guards has received special attention because of concern about a conflict of interest if security guards are included in a bargaining unit with other employees. At one time, security guards had to be in a separate bargaining unit and represented by a different union than other employees. Currently the *Act* provides that any union can apply to represent security guards and the guards can be in a unit with other employees; however, the employer is given an opportunity to object that there is a conflict of interest. If the employer objects the onus is on the union to establish that there is no conflict of interest. Generally, if the guards are present to protect the employer's property from the public, there is no conflict of interest, but if the guards perform a security function in regards to the other employees, the Board will find that a conflict exists and can require a separate bargaining unit.

The Board generally establishes a separate bargaining unit for blue- and white-collar employees: office, clerical, and technical employees are put in bargaining units separate from production employees. If the employer has only one location in a municipality, the Board's practice is to establish the bargaining unit as the employer's operations within the municipality meaning that if the employer moves within the municipality, the union continues to hold the right to represent employees. This also means that if the employer establishes a second location in the same municipality, the second location will automatically be covered by the certification, and the employees there will not have an opportunity to choose the union they wish. Where the employer has two or more locations within a municipality, the Board generally views each location as an appropriate bargaining unit unless there is an interchange of employees between the locations. At one time, separate bargaining units were established for part-time and full-time employees. Part-time employees are defined by the OLRB as persons not working more than 24 hours per week. The Board now finds that a unit including both full- and part-time employees is appropriate in most cases.

Prince Edward Island

See www.gov.pe.ca/law/statutes/pdf/l-01.pdf.
A bargaining unit must have more than one employee.

Saskatchewan

In 2013 the *Saskatchewan Employment Act* passed third and final reading in the Legislative Assembly. The *Act* consolidates 12 pieces of labour legislation into one updated and comprehensive act. Part VI of the *Act* deals with labour relations matters. At the time of this writing, the Supreme Court of Canada is hearing a *Charter* challenge of provincial Bills 5 and 6. The Saskatchewan Federation of Labour is arguing that so-called "essential services" elements of the new legislation, and other changes made to the former *Trade Union Act* are not consistent with the *Canadian Charter of Rights and Freedoms*.

6.4 CERTIFICATION PROCEDURE

Canada

See www.cirb-ccri.gc.ca/eic/site/047.nsf/eng/00105.html.
Sections 24-36 of the *Canada Labour Code, Part I* set out provisions relating to the certification of unions in federally regulated workplaces. The Canada Industrial Relations Board

regulations made pursuant to the *Code* provide rules relating to applications to the Board. The Canada Industrial Relations Board has published information circulars that outline Board activities, including the certification of unions. The information circular relating to applications for certification provides a summary of the process and it is recommended.

1. The union files an application for certification with the Canada Labour Relations Board for a unit it considers appropriate for collective bargaining. Support for the union is determined as of the date of the application.

2. The Board gives notice to the employer and requires the employer to post a notice of the application to employees.

3. The employer must file a response to the application within 10 days after it receives a copy. The employer must include a list of names of employees in the bargaining unit in its response.

4. A Board officer attempts to resolve any outstanding issues, including the appropriate bargaining unit.

5. A pre-hearing conference to settle any outstanding issues may be conducted by conference call.

6. In most cases, the board can determine the issues of the appropriate bargaining unit and support for the union on the basis of the officer's report and submissions of the parties. If a hearing is required, it may be conducted by video or teleconference.

Alberta

See www.qp.alberta.ca/1266.cfm?page=L01.cfm&leg_type=Acts&isbncln=9780779753635. Sections 32–41 of the *Labour Relations Code* set out provisions relating to the certification of unions. The Board has published a general *Guide to Alberta's Labour Laws*. The Board has also provided information bulletins that contain commentary on processing applications, board hearings, the role of settlement officers, and other issues. The information bulletin regarding certification provides a summary of the process, and it is recommended. Rules of procedure and voting rules are also available.

1. The union files a certification application with the Labour Relations Board. A complete application for certification includes: a completed application form signed on behalf of the union, a declaration by a union organizer, and evidence of 40 percent support in the unit applied for. The evidence can be in the form of membership evidence or a petition supporting the application. Membership evidence can be copies of completed membership cards along with proof of payment of a sum of not less than $2, and/or copies of documents usually kept by the union showing membership in good standing. Membership applications must be no more than 90 days old when the certification application is filed. Petition evidence and membership evidence cannot be combined. Signatures collected more than 90 days before the date of the certification application will not be counted.

2. The Board notifies the employer, employees, and other affected persons of the application, and schedules a hearing. A Board officer notifies the employer by phone and in writing. Employees are notified by a "Notice to Employers and Employees" posted at the worksite. The notice tells employees about the procedures and time limits for filing objections and the possibility of cancelling the hearing if no one objects to the application.

3. The Board officer investigates to ensure that the group of employees is a unit that is appropriate for collective bargaining, and that the application is timely and has the necessary level of employee support. During the investigation, an officer will determine who can provide the necessary information for the report and will usually attempt to speak to

one person on behalf of each party. The officer reviews the employer's records. The officer obtains a complete list of employees for the Board to use later when determining how many employees are in the appropriate unit and who should be on any voters' list. The officer, employer, and union discuss the persons they believe are included in, or excluded from, the unit. At the end of the investigation, the officer completes a report and gives it to all the parties. The employee list in the report will include persons employed in the bargaining unit applied for, but will not show if they supported the application.

4. Any parties may object to some or all of the contents of the report. An employee or group of employees objecting to the application must file their objections at least one full business day before the hearing.

5. If objections are filed, on the hearing date the Board will usually rely on the facts set out in the officer's report unless a party objecting to the report presents additional evidence. The Board normally orders the vote once it is satisfied that the union has 40 percent support in the unit applied for.

6. If no objections are received one full business day before the hearing, the officer notifies the employer and the trade union(s). The officer discusses the voting arrangements with the parties. The officer prepares a "Notice of Vote" and arranges for its posting at the worksite.

7. A vote is conducted at the workplace. The act provides that the vote is to be held as soon as possible after the application. If there are no disputed ballots, the Returning Officer counts the ballots and advises the employees of the results.

8. If a majority of employees voting choose the union, the Board then issues a certificate that includes the proper name of the trade union and employer, the bargaining unit description, and the date of certification.

The certification procedure in Alberta has distinctive features:

- No application may be made until 60 days after the union has filed its constitution and bylaws with the Board unless the Board gives its consent.

- Support for the union may be established by a petition instead of membership evidence.

British Columbia

See www.lrb.bc.ca/codeguide, Chapter 4.

Sections 18–32 of the *Labour Relations Code* set out provisions relating to the certification of unions. The regulations and the Board's rules provide details relating to an application for certification.

1. A union that claims to have as members in good standing not less than 45 percent of the employees in a unit considered appropriate for collective bargaining may apply to the Labour Relations Board for certification.

2. The Board must determine if the unit is appropriate for collective bargaining and may, before certification, include additional employees or exclude employees from the unit.

3. The Board must make the examination of records and other inquiries including the holding of hearings it considers necessary to determine the merits of an application for certification. Evidence of union membership occurring in the three-month period prior to the date of the application for certification will be accepted by the LRB. The minimum criteria for establishing membership in good standing in a union are a membership card signed and dated at the time of signature, or active membership that has been maintained by dues payments within 90 days prior to the application for certification.

4. If the Board is satisfied that on the date it receives the application, at least 45 percent of the employees in the unit are members in good standing of the trade union, the

Board must order that a representation vote be taken among the employees in that unit. A mandatory representation vote must be conducted within 10 days from the date the Board receives the application for certification, or, if the vote is to be conducted by mail, within a longer period the Board orders. The Board may direct that another representation vote be conducted if less than 55 percent of the employees in the unit cast ballots.

5. After a representation vote is taken, if the Board is satisfied that the majority of votes favour representation by the trade union, and the unit is appropriate for collective bargaining, the Board must certify the trade union as the bargaining agent for the unit.

Manitoba

See http://web2.gov.mb.ca/laws/statutes/ccsm/l010e.php.
Sections 34–48.1 of the *Labour Relations Act* set out provisions relating to the certification of unions. The Board's rules of procedure include requirements relating to applications for certification. The Board has also published information bulletins and a *Guide to the Labour Relations Act*.

1. A union seeking to be certified as the bargaining agent for employees in a unit appropriate for collective bargaining may apply to the Board for certification. If no collective agreement exists and no bargaining agent has been certified to represent the employees in the unit, an application may be brought at any time.

2. Where a union applies for certification to represent employees in a proposed unit and the Board is satisfied upon a preliminary examination of the material filed that the matters stated in support of the application are substantially true, the Board determines whether the proposed unit is appropriate for collective bargaining. In deciding if a unit is appropriate for collective bargaining, the Board may alter the description of the unit, add additional classes of employees, exclude classes of employees, separate the unit into two or more units, or take whatever steps it deems appropriate to determine the wishes of the employees. However, the Board shall not include professional employees practicing a profession in a unit with other employees unless it is satisfied that a majority of professional employees wish to be included in the unit.

3. Following the determination of the appropriate unit for collective bargaining, the Board determines the wishes of the employees in the unit. Evidence that an employee is a member of a union at the date of filing of the application for certification is conclusive evidence of the employee's wish to have the union represent him or her.

4. The Board must be satisfied that the employees were not subject to intimidation, fraud, coercion, or threat, and that their wishes for union representation were freely expressed. If it is shown that at least 40 percent but fewer than 65 percent of the employees in the proposed unit wish to have the union represent them as their bargaining agent, the Board conducts a representation vote among the employees in the proposed unit. Where fewer than 40 percent of the employees in the proposed unit wish to have the union represent them as their bargaining agent, the Board dismisses the application. In any certification application, the Board may, in order to satisfy itself as to the wishes of the employees, order that a representation vote be taken. The vote must be held within seven days after the application for certification is filed with the Board.

5. If it is demonstrated that 65 percent or more of the employees in the proposed unit wish to have the union represent them as their bargaining agent, the Board certifies the union without a vote.

6. If a vote is held and the result indicates that the majority of employees in the unit who voted wish the applicant union to represent them as their bargaining agent, the Board certifies the union.

New Brunswick

See http://laws.gnb.ca/en/showdoc/cs/I-4/ga:s_10#anchorga:s_10.
Sections 10–22 of the *Industrial Relations Act* set out provisions relating to the certification of unions. The Board's Rules of Procedure provide detailed information relating to an application for certification.

1. The union files an application for certification with the Industrial Relations Board for a unit it considers appropriate for collective bargaining.

2. The Board fixes a terminal date for the application that is 5 to 12 days after notification of the application is sent to the employer. The terminal date is the deadline for the filing of all relevant documentation, including reply documents and all membership evidence.

3. The Board determines the appropriate bargaining unit and the number of employees in the unit who are members of the union. The Board directs a vote if 40 to 60 percent of employees in the bargaining unit are members of the union. If the Board is satisfied that more than 60 percent of the employees in the bargaining unit are members of the union, or more than 50 percent of those eligible to vote cast ballots in favour of the union, the union is certified. Employees who are in attendance on the day of the vote are eligible to vote. Accordingly, the union must obtain the support of a majority of employees who are in attendance on the day of the vote. This is different from many jurisdictions in which the union must obtain only a majority of the votes actually cast.

4. On an application for certification, the union may request a pre-hearing vote. The Board determines a voting constituency from the records of the union and the employer. If it appears that at least 40 percent of employees in the voting constituency were members of the trade union, the Board may direct a representation vote among employees in the voting constituency. The ballots cast in the pre-hearing vote will be sealed and will be counted after the parties have been heard by the Board. The pre-hearing vote is a way to determine the wishes of employees before they can be influenced by the employer. The ballots are counted after the parties have been given an opportunity to present evidence and make representations to the Board.

Newfoundland and Labrador

See www.hrle.gov.nl.ca/lrb.
Amendments to the *Labour Relations Act* in 2012 brought changes to the certification process in the province. Certification of a union is now automatic when 65 percent of employees sign union cards. If at least 40 percent, but less than 65 percent, of employees sign union cards, a certification vote by secret ballot is still required.

Nova Scotia

See http://nslegislature.ca/legc/statutes/trade%20union.pdf.
Sections 23–27 of the *Trade Union Act* set out provisions relating to the certification of unions. The regulations made pursuant to the *Trade Union Act* provide more detailed rules relating to applications for certification and other applications to the Board. The Board has published procedural and policy statements that include information relating to certification, including time bars and secret ballot votes. The key feature of the process is that a vote is held within five days of the application and any outstanding issues are resolved after the vote is taken.

1. The union files an application for certification with the Labour Relations Board for a unit it considers appropriate for collective bargaining. The application must include a copy of the constitution, rules and bylaws of the union, and a list of employees applied for who are members in good standing of the union, supported by their membership cards and dues receipts.

2. The Board notifies the employer, and a notice to employees is posted in the workplace. The employer is required to provide a list of employees to the Board.

3. If the Board determines that a unit of employees is appropriate for collective bargaining, and the Board is satisfied that at the date of the filing of the application for certification the applicant trade union had as members 40 percent or more of the employees in the unit, the Board directs a vote. Normally, the vote is conducted no more than five working days after the Board receives the application and three working days after the Board's notices are received by the employer. The Board may delay the vote if it decides that further investigation is required.

4. A secret ballot vote is conducted by a Board officer. Any ballots not in dispute are folded and placed in the ballot box. If any are in dispute, they are folded and placed in an unmarked envelope, which is placed in a second envelope marked with the name of the individual. The ballot box is sealed and returned to the Labour Relations Board. Subsequently, only the votes of employees determined by the Board to be properly in the unit will be counted. When the ballot box is opened, the envelope for any employee excluded by the Board's decision is immediately destroyed and not opened. The remaining ballots then have the outside envelope containing the name removed and the inner plain, unmarked envelope put back into the box. The box is again opened and the folded ballots removed from the envelope and returned to the box. The ballot box is opened once again and the ballots counted.

Ontario

See www.e-laws.gov.on.ca/html/statutes/english/elaws_statutes_95l01_e.htm.

Sections 7–15 of the *Labour Relations Act* set out provisions relating to the certification of unions. Information bulletins and the Board's rules of procedure that provide details regarding the certification process including the application, the employer's reply, and votes are available at the Board's website. The certification process is illustrated in Figure A.

1. With the exception of the construction industry (which has its own rules), the certification process in Ontario begins with the union sending both the employer and any current union(s) notification of the application. The Certification Package that the union sends out is described in the Ontario Labour Relations Board's (OLRB) *Information Bulletin #1*, which also contains the information needed for the other parties to prepare their responses to the application.

2. The union then makes its application to the OLRB, which includes membership evidence (usually membership cards that have been signed by the employees and dated) and an estimate of the number of employees in the bargaining unit being applied for.

3. The OLRB contacts all the parties to ensure that the notification has occurred, and direct the employer to post a notice to employees in the workplace informing them that a vote will likely be held and that they are invited to make submissions to the Board.

4. The employer and any other union that may be representing some or all of the affected workers make their response to the OLRB within two days of the application being filed. The employer's response normally includes information on the actual number of employees in the bargaining unit proposed by the union and any alternative bargaining unit being proposed, and list(s) of the employees who would be included in the possible bargaining unit(s). The employer will also have to decide if it is challenging the union's application under Section 8.1 of the Ontario *Labour Relations Act, 1995*, the implications of which are discussed below.

5. Based only on the information provided to it by the union, the OLRB determines if it appears the union has the support of at least 40 percent of the employees in the

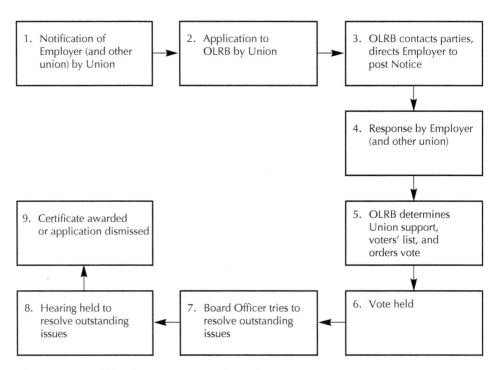

Figure A Certification Process in Ontario

bargaining unit being proposed. If that condition is met, the Board normally orders that a secret ballot vote be held at the workplace within five days of the filing of the application. A challenge under Section 8.1 may change this, and the Board has the discretion to change this timeline as necessary. The Board sets the voting list that includes all persons who might be entitled to vote. Voters whose status as members of the bargaining unit is in doubt, including those not appearing on the list, have their votes segregated by being placed in double envelopes with their names on the outside. If they are later determined to be entitled to vote, the outer envelope is opened and the sealed, unmarked envelope inside is added to the ballot box.

6. The OLRB appoints a Board Officer to oversee the voting process. The officer will attempt to resolve any outstanding issues (which may include unfair labour practice complaints) with the parties both before and after the vote. Depending on the success of this process, the votes may or may not be counted without a hearing. All parties, including individual employees, are entitled to make representations to the OLRB following the vote.

7. If agreement cannot be reached, a hearing before the OLRB will be scheduled for four weeks after the vote. It is possible that the votes will not be counted until after the Board issues its decision. If more than 50 percent of the ballots are in favour of the union, the OLRB will grant a certificate to the union.

Section 8.1   The determination of the union's support is based only on evidence provided by the union, and this could lead to a situation where the union applies for certification underestimating the number of employees in the bargaining unit or proposing a bargaining unit that is inappropriate. As a response to these concerns, Section 8.1 was added to the legislation in 1998, allowing an employer the opportunity to object to the union's estimate of the number of employees and provide the Board with evidence as to the actual numbers, and remove the possibility of a union being certified without having met the requirement of demonstrating 40 percent support in the proposed bargaining unit. When an objection under this section is filed, the OLRB will normally allow the vote to proceed, but will order that the ballot boxes be sealed (unless the employer and the union agree to have the votes counted) until after a hearing. If the OLRB determines that the union did not demonstrate 40 percent support in a unit that could be appropriate for bargaining, the application is dismissed, but the dismissal is not a bar to the union making another application. There have been cases in which the votes have been counted, and the union has garnered over 50 percent support in the bargaining unit, but the OLRB has dismissed the application because the union did not demonstrate it had the necessary 40 percent support of the employees in the bargaining unit for which it applied.

The key features of the Ontario process are:

- A mandatory vote as opposed to certification by membership cards—the cards are used to qualify for a representation vote, but certification requires a vote (except in the construction industry)

- A fast-track process (vote usually held within five days of the application) in which issues such as the status of employees are resolved after the vote is held

- Requirement of 40 percent of unit support to obtain a vote proposed by union

- Requirement of a majority of the votes cast by the employees in the bargaining unit to win vote

Prince Edward Island

See www.gov.pe.ca/law/statutes/pdf/l-01.pdf.

Sections 12–18 of the *Labour Act* set out provisions relating to the certification of unions. The regulations provide detailed requirements for an application and any reply from the employer. Information relating to the certification of unions is available on the Web.

1. The union files an application for certification with the Labour Relations Board for a unit it considers appropriate for collective bargaining.

2. A terminal date is set and the employer is notified about the application. The terminal date is the deadline for the filing of all relevant documentation, including reply documents, all membership evidence, petitions/statements of desire, and counterpetitions. The terminal date is usually 21 days after notice of the application is mailed to the employer for posting in the workplace.

3. The employer is required to post a notice about the application and must reply before the terminal date. The reply must include a proposed bargaining unit description, if different from the union's, and a complete list of all employees in the bargaining unit as proposed by the applicant, as well as their classification. If in the reply document the employer proposes a bargaining unit different than the one proposed by the applicant, the employer must show the name and classification of any person he or she proposes to exclude from the bargaining unit, as well as the name and classification of any person he or she proposes should be added.

4. Employees may withdraw their previous support for the union by filing a statement of desire or petition before the terminal date.

5. After reviewing the reply, and on the basis of the level of membership support for the trade union among employees in the bargaining unit, the Board will make a determination on whether to dismiss the application, certify the trade union, or order a representation vote to determine the wishes of the employees in the bargaining unit. The Board determines the level of support by comparing the number of employees in the bargaining unit on the date of application with the number of employees who were members in good standing in the trade union on the terminal date. If necessary, the Board holds a hearing.

6. On an application for certification, the union may request a pre-hearing vote. The Board determines a voting constituency from the records of the union and the employer.

The ballots cast in the pre-hearing vote will be sealed and will be counted after the Board has heard from the parties. The pre-hearing vote is a way to determine the wishes of employees before they can be influenced by the employer. The ballots are counted after the parties have been given an opportunity to present evidence and make representations to the Board.

There are distinctive features of the certification procedure in Prince Edward Island:

- Support for the union is determined as of the terminal date as opposed to the date of application
- A pre-hearing vote is available as an alternative

Saskatchewan

In 2013 the *Saskatchewan Employment Act* passed third and final reading in the Legislative Assembly. The *Act* consolidates 12 pieces of labour legislation into one updated and comprehensive act. Part VI of the *Act* deals with labour relations matters. At the time of this writing, the Supreme Court of Canada is hearing a *Charter* challenge of provincial Bills 5 and 6. The Saskatchewan Federation of Labour is arguing that so-called "essential services" elements of the new legislation, and other changes made to the former *Trade Union Act* are not consistent with the *Canadian Charter of Rights and Freedoms*.

6.5 DECERTIFICATION PROCEDURE

Canada

See www.cirb-ccri.gc.ca/eic/site/047.nsf/eng/00108.html.
In the federal jurisdiction, there is a unique restriction on an application for decertification where a collective agreement has not been negotiated. Section 39(2) of the *Code* provides that a decertification order cannot be made unless the Board is satisfied that the union has failed to make reasonable efforts to reach an agreement. Accordingly, even though a majority of employees may have supported the application for decertification, it may not be granted if the union can establish that it has made reasonable efforts to reach an agreement.

Manitoba

See http://web2.gov.mb.ca/laws/statutes/ccsm/l010e.php.
In Manitoba, there is a restriction on the decertification process that is not found in any other jurisdiction. Section 50(4) of the *Act* provides that even if 50 percent or more of the employees in the unit support a decertification application, the Board may dismiss the application without a vote if it is satisfied that the union made reasonable efforts to reach an agreement, but no agreement was reached because the employer failed to do so. This provision appears to be aimed at ensuring that the employer does not encourage an application for decertification by failing to negotiate.

Nova Scotia

See http://nslegislature.ca/legc/statutes/trade%20union.pdf.
In Nova Scotia, there is an additional basis—unique to that province—upon which the Board may order a decertification vote. In addition to ordering a vote if it appears that the union no longer has the support of a majority of employees, the *Act* provides in Section 29(a) that the Board may order a decertification vote if a "significant number" of union members allege that the union is not adequately fulfilling its responsibilities. It is not clear what a significant number is. However, this provision appears to allow for a decertification vote on an application supported by something less than a majority of employees.

Chapter 7

The Collective Agreement

Chapter Objectives

1. Summarize the importance of collective agreements
2. Identify the collective agreement terms that labour relations legislation requires
3. Describe the significance of terms commonly found in a collective agreement
4. List the preferences of unions and employers for various collective agreement terms
5. Explain the effect a collective agreement could have on human resource management

Required Professional Capabilities (CCHRA)	HRPA Human Resources Professionals Competency Framework
10303, 10405, 10601, 50101, 50107, 50204, 50205	C016, C019, C021, C036, C037, C038, C116

Can management in a unionized work setting assign work to employees not in a bargaining unit that has a collective agreement with that employer? The following situation illustrates that the freedom to do so depends not only on the language in the agreement but also on the circumstances of the situation at the time.

In the case *Hydro Electric Commission of the City of Ottawa v. IBEW*, the dispute was over a foreman performing tasks normally done by bargaining unit members though not specifically identified in the collective agreement as bargaining unit work. The work in question was part of a special hydro pole replacement project, for which the union had agreed to a more flexible arrangement on work hours to ensure the employer's success in bidding on the project. As a remedy, the union demanded that the employer remit union dues for the foreman.

Union members testified that the foreman would, on a daily basis, perform site cleanup and materials transport duties, which were normally performed by linemen in the bargaining unit. One union member testified that the foreman had told him that he spent 50 percent of his time doing this work, though conceding that, while the bargaining unit had lost some 25 members over a period of five to six years, this had been achieved through attrition, and no losses had occurred since the pole replacement project had started. More to the point, he confirmed that no bargaining unit members were on layoff during the relevant period, and none had been denied work on the project.

The union argued that, on the evidence, the foreman was making substantial inroads on bargaining unit work over a four-month period, to the extent that the "implied restriction" rule was triggered. This concept refers to whether the collective agreement allows the assignment of bargaining unit work to non-union employees. In cases where there is no outright ban on such assignments but there are related provisions dealing with issues such as seniority, layoff, and union recognition, some arbitrators have held that such provisions serve as a limitation on a management rights clause when the assignment of work threatens the integrity of the bargaining unit.

Employer counsel responded that, at most, the evidence showed that the foreman spent 50 percent of his time on some days on bargaining unit work, not enough to bring him within the unit. Further, the duties in question did not form anyone's exclusive job function; no one was on layoff; and no one had been denied work on the project because of the foreman's work. The arbitrator agreed with the employer, holding that the foreman's activities had posed no threat to the security of the bargaining unit. The restriction on management's right to assign bargaining unit work, he stated, "is implied in order to remedy a real infringement on the collective agreement job security protection of an employee on layoff or subject to layoff."

While it is not easy to know at what point the implied restriction is triggered, the arbitrator noted, one must look at the evidence, in light of the collective agreement's definitions of jobs in terms of classifications and hours, and ask whether the assignment of work to the foreman is depriving a unit member of a job. The arbitrator concluded this was not the case in this situation. There were no layoffs, nor did there appear to be any intent to layoff an employee as a result of the foreman doing the work. The arbitrator also noted that the bargaining unit had shrunk by attrition but there was no basis for finding that the assignment of this work to the foreman facilitated the decrease. As a result, the grievance was dismissed.

Websites for collective agreements: British Columbia Labour Relations Board: www.lrb.bc.ca/cas; Alberta Union of Provincial Employees: www.aupe.org/member-resources

Website for Negotech: http://negotech.labour.gc.ca

This chapter reviews the terms commonly found in a collective agreement and discusses employer and union preferences for the agreement. There are thousands of Canadian collective agreements, and they vary in their terms, length, and complexity, based on a number of factors including the industry and the employees covered. Collective agreements are not confidential documents: most jurisdictions require a copy to be filed with the government ministry responsible for labour issues. Some government ministries and unions are making collective agreements available on the Web. HRSDC provides collective agreements in a database called Negotech that is accessible on the Web. Refer to one of the websites mentioned in the margin for an example of a collective agreement.

IMPORTANCE OF COLLECTIVE AGREEMENTS

The collective agreement is critically important to the employer, the union, employees, and the public. The employer's control over the workplace and profitability will be affected by its contents. Wage and benefit provisions affect the employer's compensation costs. Seniority provisions may impose constraints on layoffs and promotions. The grievance and arbitration process could lead to the review and reversal of management decisions such as the termination of an employee. The union's rights to continue to represent employees and its influence are affected by the contents of the agreement. The union is protected from a raid by another union or a decertification application by employees for most of the term of a collective agreement. Union security provisions in the contract, which may require membership and the payment of dues by employees, are vital. For employees, the collective agreement deals with the crucial matter of wages and benefits. In addition, provisions that might limit contracting out or technological change can affect the employees' job security. A collective agreement might also impact the public by affecting the cost and availability of services. For example, collective agreements in education might contain restrictions on student–teacher ratios, affecting the quality of education.

LEGAL REQUIREMENTS FOR COLLECTIVE AGREEMENTS

Collective agreements must comply with employment standards, human rights, and labour relations legislation in the employer's jurisdiction(s). Labour relations legislation provides that a few terms must be included in collective agreements.

Mandatory and Voluntary Terms

A distinction can be drawn between mandatory and voluntary terms in a collective agreement. **Mandatory terms** are provisions that must be included because they are required by law. **Voluntary terms** are provisions that the parties agree to include but are not required by legislation. Labour relations legislation requires the contract to include the following mandatory terms, which are discussed below:

Mandatory terms are provisions that must be included in collective agreements because they are required by legislation.

Voluntary terms are provisions that the parties agree to include in the collective agreement; however, they are not required by legislation.

- A prohibition against strikes and lockouts during the term of the agreement
- A provision for the arbitration of disputes relating to the administration of the agreement
- A minimum term of one year

In some jurisdictions, the parties must include a term that provides that the employer recognizes the union as the bargaining agent for employees specified in the bargaining unit. In the private sector, the parties can include any additional voluntary terms in a collective agreement that do not violate the law. In the public sector, the governing legislation may provide that there are some issues or terms of employment that cannot be included in collective agreements, and these are discussed in Chapter 11. The terms or clauses in a collective agreement are referred to as **articles**. The articles most commonly found in collective agreements are listed in Figure 7-1, and discussed in the next section.

Articles are the terms or clauses in a collective agreement.

1. Recognition	11. Seniority
2. Grievance and arbitration process	12. Health and safety
	13. Wages
3. Bargaining unit work	14. Holidays
4. Strikes and lockouts	15. Vacations
5. Duration or term of agreement	16. Benefits
6. Union security	17. Hours of work and scheduling
7. Management rights	18. Overtime
8. Contracting out	19. Technological change
9. Discipline and discharge procedure	20. Leave
10. Discrimination	21. Union business

Figure 7-1 Collective Agreement Terms

COLLECTIVE AGREEMENT TERMS

A collective agreement will have major implications for human resources management in an organization. As each of the terms most commonly found in collective agreements is considered here, we should be thinking about the possible consequences for recruiting, selection, training, compensation, and other human resource management activities.

Recognition

A **recognition article** is a term in a collective agreement providing that the employer recognizes the union as the bargaining agent for a specified group of employees.

The **recognition article**, which may be referred to as the *scope clause*, is usually found at the beginning of the collective agreement. It provides that the employer recognizes the union as the bargaining agent for a specified group of employees that make up the bargaining unit. The recognition article will usually describe or limit the bargaining unit in terms of location and jobs. This is important because it will identify the jobs which are in the bargaining unit and covered by the collective agreement, and by implication will indicate which employees are not in the bargaining unit. Key Considerations 7-1 lists some of the issues relating to recognition and provides examples of recognition articles.

When the union is certified, the Labour Relations Board issues a certificate that confirms the jobs included in the bargaining unit. The recognition clause might simply refer to the certificate as in Sample Article 1 in Key Considerations 7-1. In Sample Article 2, the bargaining unit described refers to the entire municipality. Accordingly, if the employer moved or established another plant within the municipality, it would be covered by the collective agreement. In Sample Article 3, the bargaining unit includes employees located anywhere in the province; however, there are a number of exceptions, including nurses. The employees in the jobs excepted might be included in a separate bargaining unit, represented by the same or a different union, or might not be unionized.

Sample Article 2 illustrates a bargaining unit that includes part-time employees. In Sample Article 3, part-time employees are not included. Generally employers would prefer to have part-time employees and students excluded, so that individual contracts of employment can be established with them. Unions would prefer to have part-time employees included in the bargaining unit or organized in a separate bargaining unit, because they are concerned that work might be shifted to these non-union employees. If part-time employees are not unionized, the union would like to see the agreement contain restrictions on work

---

Recognition Article

Issues

- Will the bargaining unit be described by referring to the Labour Relations Board certificate or by describing the jobs included?
- Will the bargaining unit include employees such as part-time staff and students?
- What are the geographical limits on the bargaining unit: a specific location, a municipality, or some broader limit?

Sample Articles

- The employer recognizes the union as the exclusive bargaining agent for employees in the bargaining unit described in the Certificate of the Manitoba Labour Relations Board dated January 14, 2000.
- The company recognizes the union as the exclusive bargaining agent for all employees working in the municipality of _____, save and except foremen, persons above the rank of foreman, and office employees.
- The company recognizes the union as the exclusive bargaining agent for all employees in its nursing homes in the Province of British Columbia, save and except registered nurses, physiotherapists, foremen, persons above the rank of foreman, office staff, persons employed for not more than 24 hours per week, and students employed during the school vacation period.

being done by those employees. The employer might also prefer to have each location in a separate bargaining unit so that negotiation for each location could be conducted separately. The advantages and disadvantages of this are referred to in the chapter on negotiation. The point to be emphasized is that it is the recognition article that sets out the parameters of the bargaining unit.

When the parties attempt to negotiate their first agreement after the union is certified, they might ask whether the recognition clause can be varied from the bargaining unit set out in the certificate issued by the Labour Relations Board, and whether the parties can agree to change the bargaining unit or amend the recognition clause when they negotiate a renewal of the collective agreement. The short answer to both of these questions is yes. The employer might wish to amend the recognition article so that it excludes a new job classification, or the union might wish to expand the bargaining unit to include employees presently excluded, such as part-time workers. However, there is a restriction on the negotiation of changes to the recognition clause. Neither side can press this issue to an impasse that would cause a strike or lockout. The parties can discuss the recognition clause and agree to a change; however, insisting on a change and taking the issue to a strike or lockout would be a breach of the duty to bargain in good faith discussed in Chapter 8.

Grievance and Arbitration Procedure

This subsection will consider the collective agreement terms that establish the grievance and arbitration process. Chapter 9, which deals with the administration of the collective agreement, will review the application of the grievance and arbitration process in particular areas, such as terminations and disputes regarding the application of seniority to job vacancies and layoffs. We cover this topic here only because the discussion of other contract terms requires an understanding of the grievance and arbitration procedure—in most collective agreements, it would not follow the recognition clause. For additional information on the legal aspects of grievance and arbitration, readers may wish to refer to specialized sources.[1]

Grievance Defined   At one time, a "grievance" simply referred to a claim that the collective agreement had been violated. Some arbitrators held that because their jurisdiction flowed from the agreement, they did not have jurisdiction in a dispute that involved legislation unless the agreement provided a connection to the legislation. However, the Supreme Court of Canada has recently held that all employment and human rights statutes are incorporated into collective agreements.[2] Accordingly, a grievance can be filed whenever it is claimed that such legislation has been violated. In view of this development, a **grievance** should now be defined as an allegation that the collective agreement or an employment statute, including human rights legislation, has been violated, together with the remedy that is claimed to rectify the situation. A sample grievance is provided in Figure 7-2. Similar examples may also be located at some unions' websites.

> A **grievance** is an allegation that the collective agreement or an employment statute has been violated, together with the remedy that is claimed to rectify the situation.
>
> The **grievance procedure** is a series of steps in which union and employer representatives at progressively higher levels meet to try to resolve the dispute.

Grievance Procedure   The **grievance procedure** includes a series of steps, usually three or four, in which union and employer representatives at progressively higher levels meet to

Grievance: I grieve that I have been laid off contrary to the terms of the collective agreement.

Settlement desired: Compliance with the collective agreement, including compensation, interest, reinstatement in [position], and any other appropriate remedies.

Date: _____

Signature of grievor(s): _____

Figure 7-2 Sample Grievance

try to resolve the dispute. The collective agreement will set out the number of steps in the process and time limits for each. An example of a grievance procedure is provided in Figure 7-3. The procedure article will refer to union stewards and other union officials who represent the union. A **steward** is an elected local union official who assists employees with issues, including grievances, that arise in the course of administration of the collective agreement. His or her duties include explaining collective agreement terms to employees, preparing grievances, attending grievance meetings, and attempting to settle grievances. Labour relations legislation requires collective agreements to contain a term providing that any disputes regarding the administration of the agreement that the parties cannot resolve be referred to arbitration. **Arbitration** is a dispute resolution method in which the parties present evidence and arguments to a third party who makes a final, binding decision. The details of the arbitration process are covered in Chapter 9.

Types of Grievances   A grievance might be filed by an individual employee, a group of employees, the union, or the employer. There is no requirement that the grievance specify the articles of the collective agreement that have been violated unless the collective agreement says they must be provided. An employer might prefer that the grievance identify the articles, but unions generally prefer to avoid this. As is noted below, there might be rules in the collective agreement that affect who can file a grievance in a given situation.

There are several types of grievances. An **individual grievance** is an allegation by an employee that the employer has violated the collective agreement or statute and it includes

1.1 It is understood that an employee has no grievance until they first give their immediate supervisor an opportunity to deal with their complaint. If an employee has a complaint they shall discuss it with their supervisor. In order to be considered a grievance, such discussion must take place within five working days after the circumstances giving rise to the complaint first occurred. The supervisor shall communicate a reply to the complaint within five working days.

1.2 If the complaint of an employee is not settled to the satisfaction of the employee then the following steps of the grievance procedure may be invoked.

Step 1

The grievance shall be reduced to writing and shall be presented to the supervisor, with the assistance of a union steward, within five working days from the reply of the supervisor. After such discussion as is necessary, the supervisor shall deliver a decision in writing within five working days following the day on which the grievance was presented.

Step 2

If the decision of the supervisor is not satisfactory, the chief steward shall within eight working days present the grievance to the department manager. The department manager will meet with the chief steward and the department steward within eight working days to discuss the grievance and will give a decision in writing to the chief steward within four working days after the meeting has been held.

Step 3

Failing satisfactory settlement of the grievance at Step 2 the union president shall within five working days of receipt of the department manager's decision present the grievance to the manager of labour relations or their designate. A meeting between the union president and the manager of labour relations will be held within a further four working days. The written decision of the labour relations manager shall be rendered within five working days following the date of such meeting.

1.3 Failing a satisfactory settlement being reached in Step 3, then the grievance may be referred by either party to arbitration as provided in Article _____, at any time within 14 working days after the decision is given in Step 3.

Figure 7-3 Grievance Procedure

a statement of the remedy sought by the employee. For example, if an employee was unsuccessful in a bid for a job vacancy, he or she might think the employer did not properly take seniority into account. An individual grievance might be filed that alleged the employer had violated the seniority provisions of the agreement and state that the remedy sought is the placement of the grievor in the job. A **group grievance** is a claim by a number of employees that the employer has violated the collective agreement in the same manner for all the employees affected. For example, a group may claim that the employer incorrectly calculated their holiday pay and claim compensation. A **policy grievance** is an allegation by either the union or the employer that the other has violated the collective agreement. An example of a policy grievance is a claim that the employer has violated the collective agreement by banning the use of personal cell phones on company property, in violation of the management rights article, with a request for an order that the rule be rescinded. The grievance procedure article will set out the process to be followed for any grievances. Employers would prefer that the procedure provide for an employee to first make a complaint before filing a grievance as in Article 1.1 in Figure 7-3. At each step in the process the grievance could be settled, withdrawn, or denied by the employer. If the employer denies the grievance the union will have to decide whether to withdraw it or proceed to the next step. If the grievance is not resolved it might be referred to arbitration. The collective agreement usually provides that some types of grievances are started at a higher step in the process or have different time limits. For example, the agreement may provide that a policy grievance starts at Step 2 and a discharge grievance starts at Step 3. Unless the collective agreement prevents it, the union may file a grievance even if an individual employee does not.

Time Limits   The time limits in the grievance process may be either mandatory or directory. A **mandatory time limit** is one that must be met, and the grievance might be dismissed if a step is not taken within the time allowed. **Directory time limits** are viewed as a guide, and the grievance may be allowed to proceed even if they are not met. If the agreement provides that a step "may" be taken within a specified number of days, it is directory only and failure to meet it does not prevent the grievance from going to arbitration. The grievance is still arbitrable. If the time limits are mandatory and a step is not taken within the time specified, the grievance cannot proceed to arbitration unless there is an extension granted by the arbitrator, as explained below. Many arbitrators are of the opinion that the word "shall" in a time limit is not enough to make the time limit mandatory. They have held that unless the agreement also provides specific consequences for failing to meet the time limit, such as "the grievance shall be deemed to have been abandoned," the time limit is not mandatory. Employers usually prefer to have mandatory time limits and may seek language in the agreement that will meet this objective. Unions usually prefer that time limits be directory.

The issue of time limits is further complicated by labour relations legislation in six jurisdictions—Canada, British Columbia, Manitoba, New Brunswick, Ontario, and Saskatchewan—that gives an arbitrator authority to extend a time limit in the grievance process.[3] This means that even if the time limits are mandatory, an arbitrator could allow a grievance to go to arbitration. Employers may wish to attempt to have the agreement provide that the arbitrator does not have the authority to extend time limits, but the union would likely resist this.

When a party, usually the employer, fails to reply within the time specified it does not mean that the grievance is decided in the other party's favour. But it permits the other party to proceed to the next step in the process.

Probationary Employees   Employers may wish to know if the agreement can prevent probationary employees from grieving a dismissal. Labour Relations Issue 7-1 illustrates that the agreement should not directly prohibit the probationary employee from filing a grievance. However, with the proper wording, the agreement could provide that the employer has the sole discretion to hire and will be able to avoid grievances relating to the dismissal of probationary employees.

Can the Collective Agreement Prevent Probationary Employees from Challenging Dismissal?

The question of whether a collective agreement can prevent probationary employees from filing a grievance if they are dismissed has been the subject of several arbitration and court cases. Consider the following:

1. A collective agreement provided that "No employees shall be discharged without just cause" and further provided that "The grievance procedure in respect of dismissal is not applicable to new employees during the first three months." This provision, which barred probationary employees from accessing the arbitration process, was held to be void because it contravened labour relations legislation that provides that any differences between the parties must be resolved by way of arbitration. A collective agreement provision that directly states probationary employees cannot grieve dismissal is invalid.

2. In another case, the collective agreement provided that "Employees will be regarded as probationary employees for the first sixty working days. . . . During this period the employer will be the sole judge of their ability and suitability for employment, and termination will be at the employer's discretion."

When probationary employees were terminated, grievances were filed, but were dismissed as not arbitrable.

The arbitrator found that because the collective agreement stated that the employer would be the sole judge of an employee's suitability, the decision could not be reviewed.

The difference between these two cases is that in number 2 the agreement did not expressly deny probationary employees the right to grieve. The agreement in number 2 did provide that the employer had the sole discretion to decide whether to employ. It might very well be asked if this is not just a technical word game, especially when another arbitrator summed up the situation as follows: "What the above cases . . . appear in their totality to be saying then is the following: parties can write a collective agreement specifying the employer's right to discharge that, by converse inference, clearly takes away the right of a probationary employee to grieve a discharge for cause, and that is lawful; however, the parties cannot write a collective agreement whose only bar to the right of a probationary employee to grieve (and arbitrate) a discharge for cause is expressed as just that."

Forms of Arbitration   Alternative forms of grievance arbitration are summarized in Figure 7-4. The agreement will specify the form of arbitration, and the parties should consider this issue, especially before the negotiation of the first collective agreement. A single or *ad hoc arbitrator* is an individual appointed to hear and decide a grievance. An arbitration board is

Type of Arbitration	Potential Advantages	Potential Disadvantages
Single arbitrator	Faster and less expensive than an arbitration board.	Arbitrator may be less familiar with the collective agreement and the technical issues in the industry.
Arbitrator board: employer nominee, union nominee, and neutral chairperson	Union and employer nominees are able to advise chair and may ensure that each side's view is fully heard.	Delay and higher cost
Single arbitrator—list of arbitrators set out in collective agreement	Faster and less expensive than an arbitration board. Arbitrators may become familiar with collective agreement and parties.	Parties are limited to using arbitrators named.
Single arbitrator (permanent umpire) appointed to hear all grievances for a specified period of time	Faster and less expensive than an arbitration board. Arbitrator is familiar with collective agreement and parties.	Possibility of too much work causing a delay. May not be able to avoid an arbitrator whose decisions are viewed as adverse.

Figure 7-4 Alternative Forms of Arbitration

a three-person panel and at one time was the most common form of arbitration. Each of the parties nominates its representative to the board, who in turn select a neutral chairperson. A board is more costly because each side has to pay for its own representative on the board in addition to half the fees of the chairperson. Because more people are involved, an arbitration board also requires more time to establish and function. The costs and delay associated with arbitration boards have led to the increased use of single (sole) arbitrators. Some agreements specify a list of arbitrators, and the dispute is referred to the next available one on the list. It is also possible for the parties to appoint one person to hear all disputes for a period of time. This person is sometimes referred to as a *permanent umpire*.

Problems with Arbitration   One of the criticisms of the arbitration process is that it is too slow; delays of a year or more from the filing of a grievance to the completion of the arbitration are possible. To deal with this problem, the agreement can provide for an **expedited arbitration** process, which might include a single arbitrator, and shorter time limits for his or her appointment, the hearing, and a decision. The agreement may provide that the expedited procedure is available only for certain issues or requires the consent of both parties.

> **Expedited arbitration** is an alternative arbitration process that provides for a faster result.

Each of the parties will be responsible for their own legal and other expenses associated with arbitration. Most collective agreements provide that the parties will split the common expenses such as the arbitrator's fees and the cost of a meeting location. A few agreements have provided that the losing side will pay these expenses, but a union would likely oppose such a term. A few unions have been able to negotiate a "justice and dignity" provision in the process that provides that, subject to some restrictions, an employee who has been suspended or discharged will be allowed to retain his or her job while the process is going on. An employer would likely oppose such a term.

Key Considerations 7-2 lists some of the key questions that must be addressed when the grievance and arbitration procedure is considered.

Bargaining Unit Work

The phrase **bargaining unit work** refers to the work normally done by employees in the bargaining unit. If there is no provision in the collective agreement preventing the employer from assigning work to employees who are not in the bargaining unit, the employer is free

> **Bargaining unit work** is the work normally done by employees in the bargaining unit.

Protection of Bargaining Unit Work

Issues

- Will the agreement include a provision preventing non–bargaining unit employees from doing bargaining unit work?

- How extensive is any restriction on non–bargaining unit employees doing bargaining unit work? Does it allow for a supervisor or others outside the bargaining unit to train employees, and is it allowed in the case of emergencies? Does it impose a complete ban on others doing bargaining unit work or only protect against a reduction of hours or a layoff?

Sample Articles

- The employer agrees that only employees in the bargaining unit shall perform the work normally performed by employees in the bargaining unit provided that there are bargaining unit employees qualified to do the work available.

- Persons not in the bargaining unit shall not perform work that is normally done by employees in the bargaining unit, except in cases of emergency or for job training.

- Employees who are not in the bargaining unit shall not do work normally performed by employees in the bargaining unit if the performance of such work causes a reduction of working hours for bargaining unit employees or the layoff of bargaining unit employees.

to do so. Arbitrators have held that if an individual not in the bargaining unit does a certain level of bargaining unit work, he or she will be included in the unit. Unfortunately, arbitration decisions vary on how much work must be done to make someone part of the bargaining unit. Unions would prefer an article that prevents non–bargaining unit employees from doing the work of employees in the bargaining unit, and employers would prefer to avoid this type of restriction.

Key Considerations 7-3 refers to issues relating to protecting bargaining unit work and illustrates a range of restrictions that are possible. Sample Article 1 provides a complete ban on work being done by employees outside of the bargaining unit. The union would prefer this type of protection. Sample Article 2 is a prohibition with exceptions for training and emergencies. Sample Article 3 prohibits supervisors and others outside the bargaining unit from doing bargaining unit work if that would cause a layoff or reduction of hours for bargaining unit employees.

Strikes and Lockouts

A **strike** is the refusal to work or the restriction of output by employees.

A **lockout** is an employer's refusal to allow employees to work in order to force the union to agree to certain terms of employment.

A **strike** is the refusal to work or the restriction of output by bargaining unit members. A **lockout** refers to an employer's refusal to allow employees to work, in order to force the union to agree to terms of employment proposed by the employer. A lockout should be viewed as the employer's weapon equivalent to the union's strike threat. One of the basic principles of Canadian labour relations is that strikes or lockouts are prohibited during the term of the collective agreement, and most collective agreements include an article to this effect. However, in most jurisdictions labour relations legislation provides that the collective agreement shall be deemed to include a term that there will be no strikes or lockouts during the term of the agreement, if it does not include such a term.

Duration or Term of the Agreement

In all jurisdictions, the collective agreement must have a term of at least one year. If the term is not specified, or is stated to be less than a year, it will be deemed to be one year. Many collective agreements have a term of two to three years; some have a duration of six years or more. It was noted in Chapter 6 that there are open periods in the term of a collective agreement during which employees can apply to decertify the union or another union can apply for certification. If a union is decertified, the collective agreement is terminated. Accordingly, it is possible that a collective agreement will not continue to operate for the term specified.

The average duration of the 238 agreements signed in 2012 was 36.8 months; almost 40 percent of all agreements had durations falling in the 36-to-47-months range. This was a slight decline compared to the average of 40.2 months in 2011, when the largest proportion of collective agreements concluded (29.9 percent) had durations falling between 48 and 59 months. Despite a slight recent decrease in duration, the trend toward longer-term settlements continued in the private sector. In 2012, the average duration of agreements in the private sector (46.3 months) was much longer than in the public sector (34.7 months). The longest agreements were signed in Quebec, where the average duration was 64.5 months, in line with the trend witnessed in the past five years. On the other hand, Prince Edward Island (one agreement, 12 months) and British Columbia (27 months) registered the shortest average durations.[4]

Employers have usually sought longer terms, to avoid having to renegotiate and to have certainty for planning purposes. Unions have generally sought shorter terms, because a collective agreement with a longer term delays the opportunity to improve the terms of the agreement, and exposes employees to the risk of future inflation.

Union Security

Union security may be understood as measures taken by the union in collective bargaining to help "secure" the ongoing presence and influence of the bargaining agent in a unionized work setting.

Key issues related to union security include:

- The deduction of union dues from employees' pay
- Whether employees in the bargaining unit are required to become union members as a condition of employment
- Performance of employees in union representative roles in the bargaining unit
- Access to company premise by external union officials

Check-off refers to the deduction of union dues from employees' pay by the employer and their remittance to the union. A **Rand formula**, or **agency shop**, is a provision in a collective agreement that does not require employees to become union members, but requires the employer to deduct union dues from the pay of all employees in the bargaining unit.

Figure 7-5 summarizes the legislative provisions relating to the deduction of union dues from employees' pay and union membership requirements.

Union Dues In most jurisdictions, legislation provides for the compulsory check-off of union dues upon the request of the union. This could be viewed as legislative imposition of the Rand formula. In jurisdictions with this type of provision, all employees in the bargaining unit, not just union members, will have union dues deducted from their pay, and the consent of employees is not required. In a few jurisdictions, listed in Figure 7-5, the deduction of union dues is not mandatory. However, in 2009 the Alberta Labour Relations Board, applying the *Health Services* case, referred to in Chapter 2, held that the failure to require the deduction of union dues from the pay of all employees in the bargaining unit was a substantial interference with collective bargaining and a violation of the *Charter*. The Board ordered an employer to agree to the union's proposal requiring the deduction of union dues and allowed the government 12 months to amend the Alberta *Labour Relations Code*. This decision is not binding in the other jurisdictions that do not require the deduction of union

Union security may be understood as measures taken by the union in collective bargaining to help "secure" the ongoing presence and influence of the bargaining agent in a unionized work setting.

Check-off is the deduction of union dues from employees' pay by the employer and remittance of the dues to the union.

A **Rand formula** or **agency shop** is a collective agreement term requiring the deduction of union dues from all employees in the bargaining unit, even for those employees who decide not to formally join the union.

	Dues Check-off	Union Membership	Religious Exemption
Canada	Compulsory upon request of union	Collective agreement may require	Yes
Alberta	Employee authorization required*	Collective agreement may require	Yes
British Columbia	Compulsory upon request of union in first agreement; employee authorization required in subsequent agreements	Collective agreement may require	Yes
Manitoba	Compulsory	Collective agreement may require	Yes
New Brunswick	Employee authorization required	Collective agreement may require	No
Newfoundland and Labrador	Compulsory upon request of union, except in construction industry	Collective agreement may require	No
Nova Scotia	Employee authorization required	Collective agreement may require	No
Ontario	Compulsory upon request of union, except in construction industry	Collective agreement may require	Yes
Prince Edward Island	Collective agreement may require; otherwise employees must approve by vote and individual employees must authorize	Collective agreement may require	No
Quebec	Compulsory	Collective agreement may require	No
Saskatchewan	Compulsory upon request of union	Compulsory upon request of union	Yes

Figure 7-5 Legislative Provisions Relating to Union Dues and Membership

* In 2009 the Alberta Labour Relations Board ruled that the failure to provide for the mandatory deduction of dues was a violation of the *Charter* and gave the province 12 months to revise the *Code*.

Sources: Canada, *Canada Labour Code*, ss. 68, 70; Alberta, *Labour Relations Code*, ss. 27, 29; British Columbia, *Labour Relations Code*, ss. 6, 15, 16, 17; Manitoba, *Labour Relations Act*, ss. 23, 76, 77; New Brunswick, *Industrial Relations Act*, ss. 8, 9; Newfound and Labrador, *Labour Relations Act*, ss. 31, 83.1; Nova Scotia, *Trade Union Act*, ss. 59, 60; Ontario, *Labour Relations Act*, ss. 47, 51, 52; Prince Edward Island, *Labour Act*, ss. 9, 45; Quebec, *Labour Code*, ss. 47, 62, 63; Saskatchewan, *Trade Union Act*, ss. 5(1), 32, 36.

dues; however, if the same argument succeeds elsewhere, it will mean that the mandatory deduction of union dues will be required in all jurisdictions. This development illustrates the significance of the *Charter* and the Supreme Court of Canada decision in the *Health Services* case. Most agreements that contain a dues check-off provide that the dues will be remitted to the union on a monthly basis.

Union Membership   Saskatchewan is the only jurisdiction where the legislation provides that a provision in the collective agreement requiring union membership will be included if the union requests. In other jurisdictions, the collective agreement will only provide that union membership is a condition of employment if the parties agree to such a requirement, and this could be an important issue in the negotiation of a first contract. Unions want union membership to be mandatory; employers prefer to avoid this requirement. Whether or not they become union members, all employees in the bargaining unit are covered by the terms of the agreement. It is important to note that the union security provisions do not affect the union's obligations to represent all employees in the bargaining unit fairly. In the United States, some states have adopted "right-to-work" laws, which prohibit mandatory union membership. There is no equivalent legislation in Canada, and this is one of the ways the Canadian legal environment is friendlier to unions.

In six Canadian jurisdictions, listed in Figure 7-5, legislation allows employees to be exempted from union membership and dues requirements on religious grounds. The requirements for the exemption vary between jurisdictions and reference should be made to the legislation for details. Variations of the union membership requirement that may be contained in a collective agreement are listed in Figure 7-6. The **closed shop** is generally limited to the construction industry.

A **closed shop** is a place of work in which an individual must be a union member before being hired; new employees are hired through the union.

Type of Union Security	Collective Agreement Term
Closed shop	An individual must be a union member before being hired; new employees are hired through the union.
Union shop	New employees do not have to be union members to be hired, but must become union members within a specified number of days.
Modified union	remain in the union.
Maintenance of membership	Employees are not required to join the union as a condition of employment, but all workers who voluntarily join must maintain their membership for the duration of the agreement as a condition of employment.
Open shop	Union membership is not required to obtain a job or to continue employment.

Figure 7-6 Possible Union Membership Requirements

In most industries, the union will want the agreement to provide for a **union shop**. If employees must be union members to retain their job, it will be easier for the union to maintain solidarity in the event of a strike. Employees who do not honour the strike face the possibility of losing their union membership, and as a result losing their job. However, in five jurisdictions—Canada, Alberta, Manitoba, Nova Scotia, and Saskatchewan—legislation provides that the union cannot terminate an employee's membership for any reason other than the failure to pay union dues. In those jurisdictions, the union will have less control over its membership. Employers would generally prefer that employees not be required to become union members. The **modified union shop**, in which union membership is required only for employees hired after the agreement is in force, is a possible compromise. In certain situations, a form of union security known as **maintenance of membership** does not require an employee to join a union as a condition of employment, but those who voluntarily join the union must maintain their membership for the duration of the collective agreement. An **open shop** does not require the employee to be a union member at time of hire or as a condition of continued employment.

When the collective agreement is negotiated, the union and the employer will have to deal with the union security issues listed in Key Considerations 7-4.

Unions are external organizations whose "line of business" is to represent the interest of workers who believe that their collective needs are best served by seeking a bargaining agent to serve as an spokesperson and advocate for bargaining unit members with the employer. Union security is aided by allowing company employees to adopt internal representative roles to conduct bargaining unit work through leadership roles within the union local (e.g. president, treasurer, chief steward), negotiating collective agreements and filing and processes grievances. Having individuals who are "inside" the work place assists the union in these monitoring and advocacy functions. At certain stages of some of these processes, external staff experts from the parent union are needed to access the employer's premises to participate in various types of meetings. Without such access to this form of expertise, the employer may have the advantage in such interactions. Access to internal and external union representatives affords the union a more secured position in supporting members of the bargaining unit in their interactions with various levels of management in an organization.

A **union shop** is a place of work in which new employees do not have to be union members to be hired, but must become union members within a specified number of days.

A **modified union shop** is a place of work in which non-union employees already employed do not have to join the union, but all new employees must join, and those already members must remain in the union.

Maintenance of membership is a type of union security in which employees are not required to join the union as a condition of employment, but all workers who voluntarily join must maintain their membership for the duration of the agreement as a condition of employment.

An **open shop** is a place of work in which union membership is not required for an individual to obtain a job or continue employment.

Union Security

1. Will the agreement require union membership prior to being hired (closed shop)?

2. Will the agreement require union membership after being hired (union shop)?

3. If union membership is required, will employees who already work for the employer be excepted (modified union shop)?

4. Will the agreement require the check-off of dues? If so, is the authorization of employees required?

5. When are dues to be remitted to the union?

6. For employees serving in bargaining unit roles, what permission is required to attend to union duties that may occur during scheduled work periods, and will such time be paid by the employer or the union?

7. Will there be restrictions in how many employees may be absent at one time in order to attend external union meetings or conferences?

8. What notification to the employer is expected regarding the attendance of external union officials on company premises?

Management Rights

Management rights is an article providing that management retains the authority to manage the organization, except as otherwise provided in the collective agreement.

Reserved or residual rights is a theory that the employer has all rights to manage the organization except as expressly restricted by the collective agreement.

Most of the provisions of a collective agreement, such as the seniority and job posting articles, restrict management's rights and flexibility. The **management rights** article may be the only term protecting or benefiting the employer. Most arbitrators apply the **reserved or residual rights** theory that provides that the employer has all rights to manage the organization except as expressly restricted by the collective agreement. For example, if the collective agreement did not refer to the issue of uniforms, management would have the right to introduce a uniforms policy. The management rights article expressly sets out that management retains the authority to manage the organization, except as otherwise provided in the collective agreement. The management rights article has been relied on to make numerous management decisions such as changing the method of payment, eliminating smoking facilities, and establishing a rule to search toolboxes. The two types of management rights clause are a general (short) form and a detailed (long) form. Figure 7-7 provides an illustration of both.

Sample Articles

General (short) form:

1. It is recognized that the employer exercises rights and responsibilities as management, which are subject to the terms of this collective agreement.

Detailed (long) form:

2.1 It is recognized that the Management of the Company, the control of its properties and the maintenance of order on its premises is solely the responsibility of Management.

2.2 Other rights and responsibilities belonging to the Management of the Company and are hereby recognized, include: the right to decide the number and location of plants; the amount and type of machinery and technical equipment required; the amount and type of supervision necessary; methods, procedures and standards of operation; judgment and final evaluation of personnel qualifications; operating schedules and the selection, procurement, designing and engineering of equipment which may be incorporated into the Company's plant. It is further recognized that the responsibility of management of the Company for the selection, direction, and determination of the size of work forces, including the right to hire, suspend or discharge for just cause, transfer, promote or relive employees from duty because of lack of work is vested exclusively in the Company.

2.3 The management rights of the Company as above set forth shall be exercised in all respects in accordance with the terms of this agreement.

Figure 7-7 Management Rights

The short form, which is preferred by unions, is a simple statement confirming that the employer has the right to manage the organization. The long form, which is preferred by employers, is a general statement regarding the employer retaining the right to manage, to which are added specific provisions such as the right to change methods of operation. Although the employer may not have to refer to a specific item in a long form to justify a management decision, the long form makes it more likely that management will be able to refer an arbitrator to a specific right provided in the agreement. Accordingly, the long form may increase the likelihood of an arbitrator making a decision favourable to the employer.

Possible restrictions on the application of the management rights article will be explained in Chapter 9, which deals with the administration of the collective agreement. The law relating to the obligation of management to be fair and reasonable in the administration of the agreement is unclear. One school holds that management has a duty to act reasonably only in connection with matters specifically set out in the agreement. According to this approach, if the agreement provides for the assignment of overtime, management would have to do so fairly and reasonably. Another interpretation holds that there is an overriding duty to act fairly and reasonably with regard to any issue, whether or not it is specifically set out in the agreement. In Manitoba, this issue has been clarified by legislation that requires management to act reasonably in the administration of the collective agreement. The cases referred to in Labour Relations Issue 7-2 illustrate situations where the question of management's duty to act fairly has arisen.

In view of this uncertainty in the law, the wording of the article could be important. If it does not provide that the employer must act reasonably, management may be able to argue that there is no such requirement, as illustrated in the cases in Labour Relations Issue 7-2. The article might specifically state that management has the right to make "reasonable" rules. Unions prefer a provision that clarifies that management rights must be exercised reasonably. Employers prefer a provision that does not put constraints on management.

Labour Relations Issue 7-2

Does Management Have to Act Reasonably?

Some court and arbitration decisions have considered the question of whether management must act reasonably in the exercise of management rights. For example, in one case the management rights article provided as follows:

> The Union recognizes and acknowledges that the management of the plant and its facilities and direction of the employees are fixed exclusively in the Employer. . . . The Employer agrees that it will not exercise its functions in a manner inconsistent with the provisions of this Agreement and the express provisions of this Agreement constitute the only limitations upon the Employer's rights.

The employer introduced security cameras into the workplace and the union filed a grievance alleging that the installation of the cameras was unreasonable. The arbitrator found that there was no express limitation in the management rights article requiring the exercise of management rights to be reasonable and accordingly refused to consider the issue of reasonableness and dismissed the grievance.

In another case the employer established a rule that employees could not bring personal cell phones into the workplace. The union filed a grievance challenging the rule. After referring to other cases, the arbitrator noted:

> Taking all of those cases together, what they appear to say is that an arbitrator may take jurisdiction to review an exercise of discretion if it is based on some provision of the collective agreement, either express or implied, but if it involves the promulgation of a rule through an exercise of management rights in an area that is not touched upon by the agreement, an arbitrator may not review it, except in its application, where the employer purports to discipline an employee who is alleged to have breached the rule.

Should labour law require management to have to act reasonably?

Contracting Out

Contracting out occurs when an employer arranges for another firm to do work that could be done by the employer's own employees.

Contracting out refers to an employer arranging for another firm to do work that could be done by the employer's own employees. Employers will want to maintain the capability to contract out to provide flexibility and reduce costs For example, if a hospital had its own laundry staffed by hospital employees, it could contract out this work to a laundry service provider. This will mean that the employees who formerly did the work will not be needed and layoffs could result. Unions will seek to have language in the agreement that prevents or restricts contracting out to protect existing jobs in the bargaining unit. Their motivation is to protect the size and influence of the bargaining unit in the work setting. A reduction of jobs also means a loss of revenue by the union caused by less union dues being collected. Arbitrators have held that if there is no collective agreement term preventing contracting out, an employer is free to contract out provided it is done in good faith, for a sound business reason It should be noted that contract provisions relating to contracting out are separate from any restrictions relating to previously referred to restrictions on bargaining unit work. A contract term relating to bargaining unit work only prevents other employees from doing work; it does not prevent contracting out. Key Considerations 7-5 refers to key issues the parties will have to consider and provides sample articles on contracting out.

A complete ban on contracting out as in Sample Article 1 is unusual. If a collective agreement contains any restrictions on contracting out, it is more likely to be a limited ban on contracting out as in Sample Article 2, which prohibits contracting out if it would cause a layoff. Sample Article 3 provides in part that the employer shall not contract out unless a certain level of savings can be realized. Sample Article 4 is the least restrictive for the employer because it only requires notice to be given.

Discipline and Discharge

Most collective agreements provide in the management rights article or elsewhere that the employer has the authority to discipline or discharge employees for misconduct that amounts to just cause. Some jurisdictions have provided that the collective agreement must contain a just cause article, but currently only British Columbia and Manitoba require this.

Key Considerations 7-5
Contracting Out

Issues

- Is there to be any type of restriction on contracting out in the collective agreement?
- If there is a restriction on contracting out, how extensive will it be? Will it be a complete ban, a ban for a certain period of time, a provision requiring notice to the union and consultation, a prohibition on contracting out that will result in layoffs, or a provision that prohibits contracting out unless a certain level of cost savings is realized?

Sample Articles

- The employer shall not contract out work normally performed by employees in the bargaining unit.
- The employer agrees not to contract out any work presently performed by employees covered by this agreement that would result in the laying off of regular employees.
- The employer may contract work out only if the contracting out meets the requirements of this article. There shall be no contracting out unless no bargaining unit employee is available and capable of doing the work and no bargaining unit employee may be hired to do the work; or the contracting out will result in cost savings to the employer of at least $_____.
- Except in the case of emergency, the employer agrees to give the union at least 90 days' notice prior to contracting out any work that may result in the layoff of any employees in the bargaining unit. Within two weeks of such notice the parties will meet and make every reasonable effort to provide alternative employment for employees affected.

Discipline and Discharge

Will the collective agreement contain any of the following terms?

1. Employees must be allowed to have union representation in any disciplinary meetings.

2. Notice and written reasons for any discipline must be provided.

3. Disciplinary action must be taken within specified time limits.

4. Sunset clauses that require any previous adverse reports or incidents to be removed from the employee's file after a specified time without any issues arising.

5. Specific penalties are provided for misconduct.

Even if the agreement does not contain such an article, most arbitrators will require that the employer establish just cause to discipline or discharge. Key Considerations 7-6 refers to issues that the parties may refer to in the agreement.

There may be articles in the collective agreement that lay down procedures that must be followed when the employer imposes discipline, or impose limitations on the employer's right to discipline or discharge. Unions generally prefer to have contract language related to employee discipline or discharge that addresses union representation, notice and reasons, time limits, and what is referred to as a **sunset clause**.

To maintain flexibility, and avoid having disciplinary decisions reversed by arbitrators, employers would prefer to avoid this type of procedural requirement. If the disciplinary procedures provided in the collective agreement are not followed, an arbitrator might order that the discipline or discharge be reversed. This would mean that a suspended employee would be entitled to reimbursement for any lost wages, or a discharged employee would have to be reinstated. In one case, the collective agreement at Canada Post required the employer to take disciplinary action within 10 days of any misconduct. Canada Post conducted an investigation into employee theft that included hidden video cameras. Although some employees were caught on tape stealing from the mail, Canada Post was ordered to reinstate them because it had failed to take disciplinary action within the time limit required.[5] Labour relations legislation in all jurisdictions except British Columbia provides that unless the agreement provides for a specific penalty for the misconduct, the arbitrator has the authority to reduce the penalty imposed by the employer. The factors arbitrators consider when determining whether to do so are reviewed in Chapter 9. This also means that, in all jurisdictions except British Columbia, an arbitrator's authority to reduce the penalty could be eliminated by providing for a specific penalty in the collective agreement. If the collective agreement provided that the penalty for having alcohol at the workplace was a suspension for a specified time or discharge, the arbitrator would not have the authority to reduce the penalty. Although it is not commonly done, employers outside of British Columbia may wish to have the agreement provide for specific penalties for certain misconduct so that the arbitrator's authority to reduce the penalty is eliminated. Some collective agreements provide for a demerit point system that provides that acts of misconduct, such as being late, result in a certain number of demerit points and provide that if the employee accumulates a specified level of demerit points over a time period they are terminated. Unions would prefer the agreement not to provide for specific penalties so that an arbitrator could reduce the discipline imposed.

A **sunset clause** is language in a collective agreement that effectively removes from the employee's record previous discipline after a certain period of time or a length of time in which the employee has been "discipline-free."

Discrimination

Chapter 2 referred to human rights legislation, which prohibits discrimination, and Chapter 6 referred to labour relations legislation, which protects employees from retaliation for union activity. Most collective agreements contain articles that expressly provide that the parties will not discriminate against employees and prohibit retaliation against employees for union activity.

Two types of discrimination articles are illustrated in Figure 7-8. The first refers to the relevant legislation and confirms that the parties will comply. The second lists the grounds of discrimination prohibited without referring to the legislation. Articles that set out specific grounds of discrimination, as in number 2 in Figure 7-8, might mean that the parties have provided for greater protection than human rights legislation contains. This might be done by providing a broader definition for a prohibited ground of discrimination, or eliminating the BFOR (bona fide occupational qualification or requirement) defence referred to in Chapter 2, that the employer would otherwise have available. The parties cannot contract out of human rights legislation. Here the commonly understood interpretation of "contracting out" does not refer to seeking external providers to perform the work of company workers at a reduced price. Rather, it means terms in a collective agreement cannot provide less protection than is provided by legislation. In one case, a collective agreement prohibited discrimination on the basis of sex. The employer posted a job for a personal care attendant, specifying that candidates must be male because the work involved health care for male clients. A female employee filed a grievance claiming there was discrimination in violation of the collective agreement. In response, the employer put forward the defence that gender was a bona fide occupational requirement. The union argued that the agreement did not provide for the BFOR defence and accordingly it was not available because the parties had agreed to a higher standard. The Supreme Court observed that the parties may negotiate a non-discrimination clause that does not provide for a BFOR defence.[6]

In another case where the agreement prohibited discrimination on the basis of sex and did not define discrimination or refer to the BFOR defence, the arbitrator ruled that the collective agreement should be interpreted as meaning discrimination as defined in the relevant human rights legislation, thus incorporating the BFOR defence.[7] The uncertainty in this area could be avoided by providing specifically for the BFOR defence in the agreement, or providing that the agreement will be interpreted in accordance with human rights legislation.

Seniority: Establishment and Termination

Seniority is an employee's length of service with the employer.

Seniority Defined   **Seniority** is an employee's length of service with the employer. Most collective agreements contain seniority provisions that give a job preference or benefits to employees on the basis of seniority. A distinction should be made between two different uses of seniority: (1) *competitive* status issues or job rights, in which seniority is being used as a factor in determining promotion, layoff, or recall and (2) *benefit* status, in which seniority determines an entitlement such as the amount of vacation. In the case of competitive status, seniority is being used as a factor to determine which of two competing employees will be assigned to or allowed to keep a job. In the case of benefit status, there is no competition between employees; a gain by one employee does not come at the expense of another.

Seniority provisions and their application can be quite complex. Key Considerations 7-7 refers to some key issues relating to the definition, establishment, and termination of seniority.

1. In accordance with the Ontario *Human Rights Code* and *Labour Relations Act*, the parties agree that there will be no discrimination against any employee covered by this agreement.

2. The Company and the Union agree that they will not discriminate against any employee on the grounds of age, marital status, sex, race, citizenship, creed, colour, national origin, political or religious affiliation, disability, record of offences, sexual orientation, or union membership or status.

Figure 7-8 Sample Discrimination Articles

Seniority Definition, Establishment, and Termination

1. For what issues will seniority be considered a factor? Consider job vacancies, layoffs, recalls, vacation scheduling, overtime distribution, etc.

2. How is seniority defined or calculated for each application? Consider the length of service with the employer, or referring to some other period such as time in a particular classification or department.

3. How much weight is seniority given as opposed to skill and ability? Consider sufficient ability versus relatively equal, or some other provision.

4. What is done when two employees have the same seniority date?

5. How long is any probationary period?

6. When the probationary period is completed, is seniority backdated to the start of employment or does it begin with the completion of the probationary period?

7. What are the details of any seniority list, including how often and where it must be posted?

8. Is there a provision for super-seniority, and if so which union officers does it apply to?

9. What happens to seniority if employees move to jobs outside of the bargaining unit?

10. When will seniority be lost? Consider when an employee quits, retires, is absent for a specified number of days, fails to return to work after a recall, or is laid off for a specified time.

Application of Seniority   Seniority applies only to the terms of employment specified in the collective agreement. If the agreement provides that seniority is a factor in determining layoffs and promotions, it will not be a factor regarding other issues such as shift assignments. Unions prefer seniority to apply to more workplace issues and for seniority to be given more emphasis, because this provides increased job security for longer-term employees and avoids favouritism by management. Employers generally prefer seniority to apply to fewer workplace issues and to have less emphasis so that they have more flexibility and are able to make job decisions on the basis of ability.

A collective agreement may provide for different ways to calculate seniority for different applications. For benefit status issues such as vacation, seniority may be defined as the entire period of employment or service in the bargaining unit. For competitive status issues such as promotions, seniority may be defined as the time spent in a department or job classification. The agreement may include a provision to deal with the possibility that two employees have the same seniority. The parties might specify a tie-breaking formula such as the alphabetical order of the employees' names or a random draw.

Collective agreements may contain a provision that employees are on probation for a specified length of time. There is no probationary period unless the collective agreement provides for one. If there is no probationary period, employees are entitled to all rights provided in the collective agreement from the time they start their job. A distinction is made between probationary periods that provide that an employee is on probation for a certain period of employment such as three months, and periods that refer to a specified number of working days. Employers would prefer the reference to be to working days so that the employee must actually have worked a day for it to count. The collective agreement will usually provide that the employer will periodically prepare and post a seniority list and provide a copy to the union.

The agreement may also provide for **super-seniority** for specified union positions, which means that the individuals who hold the union office referred to will be the last to be laid off. The purpose of super-seniority is to ensure union representation for employees when layoffs occur. The application of such a provision will mean that bargaining unit members who have more seniority than union officers will be laid off before the union officers.

Super-seniority is a provision that specified union officers will be the last to be laid off.

Termination of Seniority   The agreement should specify what happens to an employee's seniority if the employee leaves the bargaining unit. The general rule is that employees who are transferred or promoted out of the bargaining unit no longer have any rights under the collective agreement. They lose their seniority and do not have the right to return to the unit unless the agreement provides otherwise. The agreement might specify that time outside of the bargaining unit is included in seniority, and put a time limit on a return to the unit. The agreement might also put conditions on an employee returning, such as prohibiting a return if that would result in the displacement of another employee.

The collective agreement should specify what causes seniority rights to be lost. Seniority might be lost in the event that the employee quits or retires, is discharged and is not reinstated through the grievance and arbitration process, is laid off for a specified length of time, or for other reasons. The period of time that employees can be on layoff without losing their seniority rights, the **recall period**, can be an important issue for the parties. It determines how long an employee has the right to be recalled. The union will seek a longer recall period. The employer may prefer the recall period to be shorter.

Loss of seniority is a separate issue from the termination of employment; termination does not happen unless the agreement provides that is the case. Many collective agreements combine the loss of seniority with the loss of employment; that is, they provide that the same factors that cause loss of seniority also cause termination. A **deemed termination** provision states that if an employee is absent for a specified length of time, he or she is automatically dismissed. Human rights legislation may mean that this type of provision cannot be applied to an employee who is absent because of a condition that is within the definition of a disability. This possibility will be elaborated upon in Chapter 9, which deals with the administration of the collective agreement.

A question that might arise is whether the agreement may provide that seniority does not accumulate for employees who are away from work on leave or because of a disability. The answer depends on whether the seniority is viewed as a benefit all employees are entitled to simply because they are employees or categorized as part of compensation. Labour Relations Issue 7-3 illustrates a collective agreement that contained restrictions on seniority

The **recall period** is the length of time an employee on layoff is entitled to reclaim their job.

Deemed termination is a contract term providing that an employee is dismissed if he or she is absent for a specified time.

Labour Relations Issue 7-3

Can the Collective Agreement Deny Seniority and Benefits to Disabled Employees?

A collective agreement between a hospital and a union representing nurses provided for the following:

1. *Seniority.* For layoffs, recalls, and promotions, seniority governed when qualifications were otherwise equal.
2. *Service accrual.* Accumulated service affected vacation pay and placement on a salary grid, with longer-service employees being entitled to more vacation and higher pay.
3. *Benefits.* The employer paid premiums for benefits.

The agreement further provided that if employees were on unpaid leave for more than 30 days, the seniority and service accrual stopped and the hospital stopped paying benefit premiums. Employees who were away from work because of a disability were caught by these provisions, and accordingly would stop accumulating seniority and service accrual, and would have to pay for the continuation of their benefits. The union claimed that this was discrimination in that disabled employees were being treated differently because of disability, which was a violation of human rights legislation.

The Court of Appeal made an important distinction between:

1. Benefits or other contract terms that are part of compensation in return for work
2. Benefits that flow from the employment relationship, which are not part of the compensation-work bargain

Benefits and other elements of compensation do not have to be provided to employees who are unable to provide work in return. Accordingly, because benefits and the service accrual were found to be part of the compensation scheme for work done, they did not have to be provided to disabled employees. Items that were not part of compensation had to be provided to all employees in the same manner to avoid discrimination. Because the seniority provisions relating to layoffs, recall, and promotions were not part of the compensation scheme, and were based solely on employee status, seniority had to be credited to disabled employees.

This case establishes that if benefits and seniority are a form of compensation, the agreement may state that they are only provided to employees providing service. However, benefits and seniority that flow from employee status and are not part of compensation for work done must be provided to disabled employees.

accumulation and the payment of benefits to employees who were not working. It appears that a collective agreement term providing that seniority for the purposes of job competition does not accumulate during a leave is discriminatory if it has the effect of denying seniority to employees who are disabled. However, it is permissible to provide that employees who are not working do not accumulate seniority for purposes of pay or vacation increases.

Seniority: Application to Layoffs, Recalls, and Job Vacancies

Key Considerations 7-8 outlines key issues in the application of seniority to layoffs, recalls, and job vacancies.

Layoffs   The definition of a layoff in the collective agreement is important, because if a layoff occurs a number of collective agreement rights and obligations might be triggered. In addition to determining who should be laid off after taking into account seniority, skill, and ability, the employer may also be required to provide early retirement or severance options to employees who have been laid off. The assessment of skill and ability is reviewed in Chapter 9. Some collective agreements have defined a layoff in a manner that means more than the displacement from work will be caught. In one hospital collective agreement, a layoff was defined as: "a reduction in a nurse's hours of work and cancellation of all or part of the nurse's scheduled shift . . . a partial or single shift reassignment of a nurse from her or his area of assignment will not be considered a layoff." When the hospital reassigned nurses from one unit to another, the union contended that there had been a layoff as defined in the collective agreement. An arbitrator upheld the grievance noting that by stating that a partial or single shift reassignment would not be considered a layoff, the implication was that the alternative, a longer reassignment, did constitute a layoff.[8] Accordingly, all of the agreement's provisions relating to layoffs, including notice, early retirement, and severance offers were engaged. It is beneficial to the employer if a layoff is defined in a manner that would exempt short interruptions. If a layoff is defined as a period of at least five working days, the layoff provisions including notice are not an issue for a shorter period. **Bumping** or **bumping rights** refer to an employee who would otherwise be laid off displacing another employee with less seniority. Bumping articles can come in three different forms depending upon the relative importance of seniority versus skill and ability.[9] One type of provision

Bumping or **bumping rights** is the displacement of an employee by another who has more seniority and would otherwise be laid off.

Seniority Application to Layoffs, Recalls, and Job Vacancies

Layoffs and Recalls

1. What is the definition of layoff? That is, how long does the interruption of work have to be caught by the layoff provisions?

2. What notice of layoff is required?

3. What benefits, if any, do laid-off employees receive?

4. What bumping rights do employees have, and what if any are the restrictions on bumping?

5. If a layoff becomes permanent, what termination and severance pay are employees entitled to?

6. What are the details of the recall process, including how much notice is required, how the recall notice is given, and how long employees have to respond?

Job Vacancies

1. What is the definition of a vacancy? For example, how long does a job have to last in order for it to be a vacancy, which must be posted?

2. What are the details of the job posting process, including the method, duration, and time to respond?

3. What, if any, are the restrictions on who can bid for a job?

4. How much weight is seniority given as opposed to skill and ability: sufficient ability versus relatively equal, or some other provision?

refs to seniority as the only factor to be considered. As long as the employees have more seniority, they can bump a more junior employee. In the second type of provision employees with more seniority can bump more junior employees provided that they have the minimum job requirements for the position. In the third type of bumping, the employee with the most seniority can only bump a more junior employee if they have equal or better skills than the junior employee. Employers would prefer to have restrictions on bumping in order to avoid having employees move or bump into positions they are not qualified for, and to reduce the number of bumps. The contract might provide that employees can only move into certain job classifications, and must have the required ability to do the work. It might also provide that the employee exercising bumping rights must move into the job held by the lowest seniority employee in the bargaining unit. If there is no requirement that an employee must bump the lowest-seniority employee, there might be a series of bumps (referred to as "chain" bumping) when an employee with five years' seniority bumps one with four years' seniority, who in turn bumps one with one year's service. Unions would prefer that there be fewer restrictions on bumping, possibly combined with training periods for employees who wish to move to another position.

Recalls   The agreement will usually provide that employees who have been laid off will be recalled to work in order of seniority.

Job Vacancies   The collective agreement may define job vacancies and require the employer to post them. When the employer is filling short-term openings, it would be beneficial if vacancies were defined to exclude shorter-term jobs. For example, if the agreement defined a vacancy as a job that was going to last more than 90 days, it would be possible to avoid posting and seniority requirements for shorter assignments. The agreement might place restrictions on bidding or applications for a job. The employer might wish to avoid having someone successfully bid for and move into one job and then bid for and move to another. The employee might be required to remain in a job for a certain length of time before bidding on another.

A **sufficient ability clause** is a provision that the employee with the most seniority is awarded a job provided he or she has enough ability.

A **relative or competitive ability clause** is a provision that seniority will only be referred to if the skill and ability of two employees competing for a job are relatively equal.

A **hybrid seniority** provision combines sufficient and relative ability.

Most collective agreements do not provide that seniority is the only factor referred to when a decision is made regarding which employee is entitled to a particular job. The parties can agree that skill and ability will also be a factor, and the agreement can specify how much weight will be given to skill and ability as opposed to seniority. There are two primary ways that skill and ability can be combined with seniority: a sufficient ability clause or a relative ability clause. A **sufficient ability clause**, also known as a *threshold ability clause*, provides that the employee with the most seniority is awarded the job if he or she has enough ability, even if another employee has more skill and ability. A **relative or competitive ability clause**, on the other hand, provides that seniority will only be referred to if the skills and abilities of two employees competing for a job are relatively equal. The employee with the most seniority will be awarded the job only if he or she has skill and ability equal to or greater than that of other employees. Because the sufficient ability type of provision gives more weight to seniority, unions favour it; whereas employers favour the relative ability provision, because it gives more weight to skill and ability. Alternatively, the parties could agree on a **hybrid seniority** provision that falls between a sufficient ability and a relative ability term. In this approach, seniority is included along with skill and ability when the determination is made. Arbitrators have held that the employer must demonstrate that the decision was made by considering the factors listed, including seniority, in a reasonable manner giving each the appropriate weight.

It has been established that unless the collective agreement provides for a training period, employees are not entitled to one. An employee must have the skill and ability to do a job at the time he or she applies for it. The agreement might provide for a training period of a specified number of days. The union would prefer that the agreement provide for a longer training period, and allow the employee to return to a previous job if he or she is not successful in the new one. The employer would likely prefer to avoid a required training period, so that an employee who has the ability to do the job without any additional training can immediately move into the job.

The exact wording of the agreement regarding skill and ability might be significant. The phrase "capable of" doing certain work is not the same as having the "skill and ability required." A reference to capability is less demanding than a requirement that the employee have the skill and ability necessary. It has been held that when the contract refers to capability, an employee is entitled to a period of familiarization with the job even though the agreement did not specifically allow for one. Accordingly, employers would prefer the contract to require that employees have the skill and ability required.

Health and Safety

All jurisdictions in Canada have health and safety legislation that sets out rights and obligations for employers and employees. Pursuant to the legislation, employers have a duty to establish and maintain a safe workplace. Employees must follow safe work practices and use protective equipment. Joint health and safety committees or representatives must be appointed, and employees have the right to refuse unsafe work. The legislation is enforced by inspections and provides for the prosecution of employers and employees who do not comply. A reference to health and safety legislation across Canadian jurisdictions is found at the Canadian Centre for Occupational Health and Safety (CCOHS) at Joint Health and Safety Committee www.ccohs.ca/oshanswers/hsprograms/hscommittees/whatisa.html.

Key Considerations 7-9 refers to issues that the parties will have to address regarding health and safety.

The union may prefer that the agreement contain specific health and safety provisions. The agreement might provide for requirements over and above those legislated—for example, it may require a larger health and safety committee or more frequent meetings of the committee.

Wages

The agreement will set out the wages that are to be paid to various job classifications, including any increases that will be made over the term of the agreement. The pay rate and procedure stated in the agreement will have to comply with employment standards and human rights legislation. Employment standards legislation establishes rules including a minimum wage and the form of payment (cash, cheque, or direct deposit). Figures 5-4 and 5-5 in Chapter 5 provided sources of information regarding minimum wages and other terms of employment.

Unless the agreement provides otherwise, management can change the job classifications referred to in the agreement, provided the change is prompted by a valid business

---

Key Considerations 7-9
Health and Safety

1. Will the agreement refer to compliance with legislation, or will it set out specific terms for the workplace?

2. If the agreement establishes a health and safety committee, who are on the committee and how are they selected? How often does the committee meet? What are the functions of the committee?

3. Is the right to refuse unsafe work included in the agreement?

4. Does the agreement require the employer to provide and pay for protective equipment?

reason. Consequently, the union may seek to have the agreement provide that job classifications will not be changed for the term of the agreement, or that the union will be consulted if there are any such changes. The union would prefer that if the parties cannot agree on a classification the matter be referred to arbitration. In addition to the basic wages, the agreement might provide for numerous additional allowances and payments including shift premiums, mileage allowances, pay for meals, additional pay for hazardous work, and clothing allowances. Employment standards legislation provides a minimum amount that employees who report for or are called in to work must be paid. The union may seek to have the agreement provide for call-in pay that is greater than the minimum set out in the legislation.

Although inflation has been reduced in recent years, at times it has been a serious concern for employers and unions. In the years 1975–76 and 1980–82, inflation exceeded 10 percent per year. Unions have sought **cost-of-living allowances (COLA)** in collective agreements to protect against the risk of inflation. COLA provisions require that an increase in pay will be provided to employees on the basis of a formula linked to the rate of inflation.

Cost-of-living allowances (COLA) are provisions that provide an increase in pay for employees based on a formula linked to the rate of inflation.

Holidays and Holiday Pay

Statutory holidays such as Thanksgiving are paid days off, and should not be confused with vacations, which are discussed below. The agreement must provide for at least the minimum holidays required by employment standards legislation, but the union may seek to have the agreement provide for additional holidays. The parties should clarify the issue of a holiday falling on a day an employee is absent because of a leave or vacation. Key Considerations 7-10 provides issues the parties will have to address regarding holidays.

Vacations

Employment standards legislation provides for a minimum amount of vacation time and pay for employees. The vacation entitlement in the legislation is not very generous, and it is common for the collective agreement to provide for greater vacation time than the legislation requires. Key Considerations 7-11 lists issues relating to vacations.

Benefits

In addition to the legally required benefits such as the Canada Pension Plan to which employers must contribute, there are many additional benefits that collective agreements may provide, including dental care, drug expenses, eye care, life insurance, semiprivate hospital care, disability protection, and pension plans. Key Considerations 7-12 lists issues relating to benefits.

Key Considerations 7-10

Holidays and Holiday Pay

1. How many holidays are provided for in the agreement?
2. Who is entitled to a holiday? Are probationary employees excluded?
3. What restrictions are there on receipt of holiday pay, such as working the scheduled day before and the scheduled day after the holiday?
4. What is the amount of the holiday pay?
5. What is the compensation for work done on a holiday?
6. What happens when a shift starts on a day before a holiday and extends into a holiday?
7. What happens when a holiday falls on a vacation day or on a day of leave?
8. What happens when a holiday falls on a scheduled day off?

Vacations

1. What is the amount of vacation time?

2. How is vacation pay calculated? What formula will be used? Will the formula refer to a number of regular weeks' pay or to a percentage of earnings?

3. How is vacation time scheduled? Does the agreement provide for a defined vacation period? Are employees

allowed to choose vacation times? Are vacation times allocated on the basis of seniority?

4. What happens if another leave, for example sickness or bereavement, is taken during a vacation? Does the agreement provide for employees to obtain both the leave and the vacation time?

The employer might provide benefits in alternative ways such as paying any amounts owing directly to employees (self-insurance), arranging coverage through an insurance carrier, or using some combination of self-insurance and insurance coverage. How benefits are referred to in the agreement will determine whether any disputes regarding benefits are dealt with by making a claim against the employer, through the grievance and arbitration process, or against the insurance carrier, through the courts. Arbitrators have identified four possible scenarios:

1. Benefits are not referred to in the collective agreement, but the employer provides benefits through an insurance carrier. In this situation, any claims must be made against the insurer; a grievance cannot be filed.

2. The collective agreement outlines benefits employees are entitled to and the employer arranges insurance coverage. Sample Article 1 in Key Considerations 7-12 illustrates this possibility. In this situation, the employee can file a grievance and an arbitrator determines the issue. The risk to employers with this type of provision is that if the insurer denies a claim, an arbitrator might order the employer to pay.

3. The employer is obligated by the collective agreement to pay premiums for a plan. Sample Article 2 in Key Considerations 7-12 illustrates this possibility. In this situation, any claims must be made against the insurer; a grievance cannot be filed.

Benefits

1. What benefits will be provided?

2. Will benefits be included in the collective agreement or will benefit provisions be left outside the agreement?

3. If benefits are included in the agreement, will benefits provisions be set out in detail in the agreement or will the agreement simply require the employer to pay insurance premiums that provide specified benefits?

4. If benefits are provided outside the agreement, does the agreement refer to or incorporate the benefits documentation?

5. If a benefit issue would not be otherwise arbitrable, because the agreement does not incorporate the benefit provisions, or only refers to the payment of

premiums by the employer, will there be an additional provision that provides that arbitration will be the mechanism used to resolve disputes?

6. How much will employees contribute to the cost of benefits?

Sample Articles

- The employer shall provide the following benefits:
  (a) $75 000 life insurance
  (b) dental benefits in accordance with the 2010 Ontario Dental Association (ODA) schedule

- The employer shall pay the premiums for insurance plans that provide the following benefits:
  (a) $75 000 life insurance
  (b) dental benefits in accordance with the 2010 ODA schedule

4. A benefit plan or policy exists, and it is incorporated by reference into the collective agreement. If the agreement refers to a benefit handbook or other document that describes benefits, it could be deemed that the benefit provisions have been made part of the agreement. The employee can file a grievance, and an arbitrator determines the issue.

Employers want to avoid grievances and arbitration relating to benefits. They would prefer that the employee make any claims against an insurer instead of the employer. Accordingly, the employer might attempt to leave benefits outside of the collective agreement or only agree to pay premiums in the agreement. Employers should avoid references to a benefit handbook, manual, plan, etc. in the agreement to ensure that the plan is not incorporated into the agreement. If there are current references to benefit handbooks or manuals, the employer might attempt to negotiate their removal. If benefits are included in the agreement, the employer might try to obtain agreement on a clause to provide that disputes will be resolved through the appeal process in the insurance carrier's policy, not through arbitration.

A question that might arise is whether the agreement may provide that benefits do not have to be provided to employees who are away from work on leave or because of a disability. The answer depends on whether the item in question is viewed as a benefit that all employees are entitled to simply because they are employees, or whether it is categorized as part of compensation. This issue was considered in the court decision referred to in Labour Relations Issue 7-3. If benefits are provided as part of compensation, as opposed to being provided to all employees on the basis of employment, the agreement can stipulate that benefits are not paid to employees who are not working. Employers may wish to structure benefits as part of compensation and avoid benefits being categorized as an employment entitlement. To do this, the employer should ensure that all employees on leave are treated in the same manner. If benefits are paid to some employees who are not working, such as employees on educational leave, it will be difficult to argue that benefits are part of compensation and do not have to be paid to other employees who are away because of a disability.

Some collective agreements have provided for innovative benefits such as daycare and prepaid legal plans.

Hours of Work and Scheduling

Employment standards legislation provides for maximum hours of work, minimum lunch or break periods, and minimum rest or time away from work. The rules relating to maximum hours should not be confused with the separate requirements regarding overtime. The terms relating to hours, which are referred to here, focus on the issue of when and how many hours the employee works. The overtime provisions, referred to in the next subsection, deal with the separate issue of how much additional pay employees are entitled to if they exceed a specified number of hours.

Unless the collective agreement provides otherwise, the employer has the authority to establish schedules, start times, and shift changes. The agreement may provide for a guaranteed number of hours. This would be a provision the union would want and the employer would prefer to avoid. The agreement might specify the work days, hours of work, and details regarding shifts. If the agreement specifically sets out such items, the employer would have to get the consent of the union to make any changes. The employer would prefer to avoid having work days, hours of work, and details regarding shifts in the contract. Instead, it might be provided that notice will be given for shift and other scheduling changes. The union would prefer longer notice and a provision that there will be compensation provided if the required notice is not given. Conversely, the employer would prefer to maintain as much flexibility as possible, have notice periods be shorter, and avoid any compensation if adequate notice is not given. The agreement might also provide that a premium be paid for certain shifts, such as nights. Key Considerations 7-13 lists some of the issues relating to hours of work and scheduling that will have to be addressed.

Hours of Work and Scheduling

1. Will the agreement specify hours of work and shift schedules?

2. Will the agreement guarantee a minimum number of hours that will be available for employees?

3. What lunch or break periods will be provided?

4. What notice is required for a shift change?

5. Will there be provisions for any additional pay for particular shifts?

Overtime

Key Considerations 7-14 lists some of the issues relating to overtime that will have to be addressed.

Employment standards legislation provides for minimum rules regarding overtime, which vary between jurisdictions. Typically unions will seek to improve upon the legislated minimums in collective agreements. Overtime legislation and collective agreement terms should be kept separate from hours of work terms and legislation. Overtime deals with the issue of when an employee is entitled to additional pay for working extra hours and the amount of the additional compensation. The employer can impose overtime unless the agreement provides otherwise. It could require employees to work overtime as long as the employment standards legislation and collective agreement provisions relating to the hours of work are complied with. Hours-of-work provisions in employment standards legislation usually provide an exception for emergencies. Unions will seek to have agreement terms that require notice to employees or their consent for overtime. Employees do not have a right to overtime unless the agreement provides for it. Unions may push for terms that require an equal distribution of overtime or alternatively give priority to employees with more seniority. Some arbitrators may award cash to an employee who has not been correctly allotted overtime, instead of ordering the employee be given the next opportunity to work overtime. Employers would prefer that the agreement clarify that the remedy is the next opportunity to work.

Technological Change

Labour relations legislation in some jurisdictions regulates the introduction of technological change into the workplace. The legislative provisions range from requiring the parties to submit any disputes relating to technological change to arbitration (New Brunswick) to requiring notice from the employer and mid-term bargaining in four jurisdictions (Canada, Manitoba, Saskatchewan, and British Columbia). In other jurisdictions, including Ontario,

Overtime

1. What restrictions, if any, will be placed on the employer imposing overtime: notice to employees, consent of employees, caps on the amount of overtime, etc.?

2. How is overtime defined? Does overtime begin after a specified number of hours per day or per week?

3. What is the rate of overtime pay, and will it vary with the number of hours or the day worked?

4. What rules, if any, will be provided for regarding the distribution of overtime?

5. Will there be any additional overtime compensation such as a meal or transportation allowance?

6. If an error is made in the distribution of overtime, will the agreement specify if the remedy is an opportunity to work or cash?

Technological Change

1. Will the agreement contain any provisions regarding technological change?

2. What is the definition of technological change?

3. What limitations are placed on the introduction of technological change: notice, negotiation and arbitration, job guarantees, income protection, retraining, severance payments?

the legislation does not deal with the issue. In jurisdictions without technological change legislation, the employer will be able to introduce technological change relying on the management rights article, unless the collective agreement imposes limitations. Unions will likely seek collective agreement terms to protect against technological change causing job losses, and employers would prefer to avoid such provisions to be able to maintain flexibility and reduce costs.

In any article dealing with technological change, a critical issue will be its definition. It might be defined narrowly to include only new equipment that causes job loss, or more broadly to include additional matters such as changes in methods of operations and techniques to complete the work. The definition can be extremely important because it will determine whether the notice and other protective measures referred to below are available. In one case, the agreement defined technological change as involving equipment of a different kind or nature, and it was held that a change made to an existing computer system did not fall within the definition.

There is a broad range of protection that might be provided for employees if there is a technological change. The agreement might simply require the employer to give a specified period of notice to the union. The agreement might require the parties to negotiate the implementation and effects of the change and refer the matter to arbitration if they cannot agree. The most restrictive type of provision might provide job guarantees for employees. Articles might provide for income protection in the event that an employee's job is reclassified as a result of the change, or if the employee is transferred to a lower-paying job. Another possibility is a provision for retraining and preference in future job openings. If the employee's job cannot be saved, the agreement might provide for a severance payment.

Key Considerations 7-15 lists some of the issues relating to technological change that must be addressed.

Leave

The collective agreement might provide employees with numerous types of leave, some of which have legislated minimums. The employer and the union will have to negotiate what leaves are to be provided and the extent to which any leaves will exceed the minimum the law provides. Key Considerations 7-16 summarizes the key issues relating to leave that have to be addressed.

Jury Duty Legislation provides that the employer must grant leave for jury duty and protect the job, seniority, and benefits of employees. However, the compensation paid to individuals by the court system for jury duty is minimal. Unions may seek to have terms added to the agreement to provide that the employer will pay any difference between the allowance paid to jurors and the employee's pay.

Bereavement Leave Employees are entitled to bereavement leave as provided in the employment standards legislation governing their workplace. The legislation usually provides for leave in the event of the death of specified relatives, most commonly the employee's spouse, child, parent or guardian, sibling, grandchild, or grandparent. The length of the

Leave

1. What leave will be provided for in the agreement?

2. Will leave exceed any minimum provided for in legislation?

3. *Jury duty leave.* What amounts, if any, will the employer be required to pay employees?

4. *Bereavement leave.* How long is the leave? Is the leave paid or unpaid? Whose death will entitle the employee to leave? What happens if a death occurs while the employee is on vacation or some other leave?

5. *Maternity leave.* How long is the leave? What notice is required to commence the leave? What notice is required to return from the leave? What payments is the employee entitled to during the leave; for example, to what extent will the employer have to "top up" benefits provided by employment insurance?

6. *Parental leave.* How long is the leave? What notice is required to commence the leave? What notice is

required to return from the leave? What payments is the employee entitled to during the leave? For example, to what extent will the employer have to "top up" benefits provided by employment insurance?

7. *Sick leave.* If sick credits are used, how many days per month are allowed? What happens to any remaining credits when employment is terminated? If a leave with pay is provided, how long is the leave and what is the rate of pay?

8. *Union leave.* Will the agreement provide for both short- and long-term leave? What is the length of any leave? How much notice is required? How many employees at one time can be on leave? Is there a right to the leave or does the employer have discretion to deny it?

9. *Personal leave.* Will the agreement provide for personal leave? What limits, if any, will be placed on the employer's discretion to grant the leave? Will there be limits on the length of the leave?

leave varies across jurisdictions from one to five days, and it may depend on the nature of the relationship. Most bereavement leave provided in legislation is unpaid; however, there are exceptions. Federally regulated employees who have been employed for at least three months are entitled to three days paid bereavement leave.

Maternity Leave Employment standards legislation provides for unpaid maternity leave that ranges from 15 to 18 weeks depending on the jurisdiction. Employees entitled to maternity leave may also be entitled to additional unpaid parental leave. The unpaid leave should not be confused with the monetary benefits provided by the federal *Employment Insurance Act*. In some jurisdictions, employees are entitled to maternity leave as soon as they start employment. In other jurisdictions the person must have been employed for a minimum period of time. The legislation also contains rules regarding notice to commence the leave and to return to work, restrictions on when the leave can commence, and provisions regarding extension of the leave. Any collective agreement terms regarding maternity leave must at least meet the standards provided for in the relevant legislation, and the union may seek leave provisions greater than the legislated minimum.

Website for maternity and parental benefits information: www.servicecanada.gc.ca/eng/sc/ei/benefits/maternityparental.shtml

Parental Leave Employment standards legislation provides for parental leave that ranges from 34 to 52 weeks, depending on the jurisdiction, and is available for both birth and adoptive parents. In some jurisdictions, the leave must be split between the parents; in others, including Ontario, both parents are entitled to the leave. There are rules regarding eligibility that vary across jurisdictions. The legislation sets out requirements regarding notice to commence the leave, notice to return to work, and restrictions on when the leave can commence. Any collective agreement terms regarding parental leave will have to at least meet the standards provided for in the relevant legislation and should address the issues referred to in Key Considerations 7-16.

Sick Leave Although a few jurisdictions provide for unpaid sick leave (Canada, New Brunswick, Newfoundland and Labrador), there is no legal requirement for employees to be paid while they are off sick. Employees have entitlement only to sick pay provided in the agreement. The agreement might provide for a system of sick leave credits in which employees will accumulate a certain number of sick days for each week or month worked, and the days can later be used if the employee cannot work. The employee will be entitled only to the sick credits accumulated. Employers may prefer to avoid this type of system so that they do not have to deal with the costs of paying out unused sick credits on termination. Also, some employees might abuse the system if they think they have sick credits accumulated that they should use even though they are not sick. Instead of a credit system, the agreement might provide for leave with pay, specifying the length of the leave and the amount of the pay. It might provide that the length of the leave increases with seniority and the pay diminishes with a longer leave. For example, the pay provided might be 100 percent of regular pay for the first week and 75 percent of pay for an additional 10 weeks.

Union Leave   Collective agreements commonly provide for unpaid leave for union officers (e.g., the president of a union local) to attend to union matters. This type of leave can be either short-term—to allow for attendance at union conventions and other meetings—or long-term— to allow for taking on a union executive position or serving the union in some other manner.

Personal Leave   In addition to the various specified leaves referred to, the agreement may provide for additional personal leave to attend to sick family members, to serve a jail sentence, or for other matters. Personal leave is often stated to be at the employer's discretion— that is, the employer may grant the leave but does not have to. An employer might be surprised to find out that some arbitrators have required employers to act reasonably when they consider whether to grant such leave. This means that even though an agreement states that the employer may or may not grant the leave, it will have to show a valid reason to deny it. In one case, an arbitrator held that an employer who denied a leave to serve a jail sentence had violated the personal leave article in the collective agreement because it had failed to establish it would be harmed if it granted the leave.[10] Unions would prefer that the agreement confirm that the employer may not unreasonably deny a leave. Employers would prefer that the agreement provide that the employer has sole discretion to grant or refuse leave, and the decision cannot be grieved, provided that it is made in good faith.

Union Business

The contract may contain terms relating to the union's representation of employees. Key Considerations 7-17 lists issues in this area.

The agreement may require the employer to provide information about the union to new employees and introduce them to a union officer. Some agreements specify that a minimum amount of paid time be provided for a meeting with union representatives. The employer may be required to make bulletin boards available for the union. Agreements may confirm that the union may hold meetings on the employer's premises. Some agreements, especially in the public sector, require the employer to provide office space to the union. The agreement should deal with the issue of union officers conducting union business during paid working hours. For example, the agreement might specify that union stewards be

---

Key Considerations 7-17

Union Business

1. Will the agreement require that union information be provided to new employees?

2. Will the agreement require the employer to provide bulletin boards, provide office space, or allow union meetings on the employer's premises?

3. Are union officials allowed to conduct union business during work time?

allowed to investigate grievances and attend grievance meetings during working hours. The employer may wish to monitor the amount of time union officials are away from their jobs and attempt to negotiate limits on the amount of working time spent on union business.

Figure 7-9 lists the collective agreement terms we have reviewed so far, and summarizes possible union and employer preferences.

A review of the contents of a collective agreement and the employer concerns listed in Figure 7-9 will draw attention to the human resources management implications, which are explored further in subsequent chapters. The grievance and arbitration process provides unionized employees an avenue to challenge management decisions that most non-union employees do not have. The seniority and layoff provisions put restrictions on the recruiting and selection functions. The wages, benefits, holidays, and vacation provisions limit the employer's ability to use individual incentives to motivate employees. Terms relating to contracting out and technological change might prevent changes to staffing and operations.

Website with information relating to innovations in collective agreements: www.hrsdc.gc.ca

Other Possible Terms

There are countless other possibilities for collective agreement terms. We will briefly review some of them here.

Protection Against Liability   In some occupations, employees face the risk that legal action may be taken against them. For example, a police officer could be sued for action taken while carrying out their duties. Collective agreements may provide that employees will be compensated for any legal expenses or damages they are ordered to pay as a result of their lawful work.

Joint or Union–Management Committees   Collective agreements may provide for union–management committees to deal with specific issues such as job security and attendance. Alternatively, an agreement might, at either party's request, provide for the establishment of a joint committee to deal with matters that arise during the operation of the agreement.

Retirement   With an aging population, many firms are concerned about issues relating to retiring employees and are establishing appropriate human resources policies. To deal with retirement issues, some unions have sought collective agreement provisions for reduced workload prior to retirement (phased retirement), post-retirement part-time work, pre-retirement leaves and vacations, and retirement preparation programs including counselling.

Compensation   Some collective agreements have provided for gainsharing plans, which typically set performance objectives in areas such as financial return, customer satisfaction, quality improvement, or health and safety, and provide for a payment to employees if targets are met. Some agreements also have profit-sharing provisions that specify the amount to be paid to employees if a defined profit measure exceeds a specified level. Unions generally prefer increases in wages or benefits instead of provisions for profit sharing, because the factors that determine the profit levels are beyond the control of employees. Some agreements have share purchase plans that allow employees to buy shares and may provide for the employer to contribute shares on a specified ratio.

Telework   Telework refers to employees working at their homes instead of the employer's premises. Telework is often dealt with outside of the collective agreement in employer policies. Provisions relating to telework might deal with issues such as providing equipment and reimbursement for expenses incurred in the home.

Training and Education   Collective agreements may provide for on-the-job training to upgrade the skills of employees for future job openings. Some agreements have established a fund to pay for the education of employees, and require the employer to pay a specified amount into it for each hour worked. Agreements have included provisions for lending money to employees to buy personal computers and reimbursement for courses taken.

Contract topic	Union	Employer
Recognition	• Broader description of bargaining unit so that part-time employees and others are included	• Narrower description, exclusion of part-time employees, students and others
	• Bargaining unit description that includes all of a municipality so that employees are covered by the collective agreement if the employer moves	• Bargaining units that are described by reference to location
Grievance and arbitration process	• Longer time period for each union step	• Shorter time period for each union step
	• Directory time limits	• Mandatory time limits
	• Avoid requirement to specify collective agreement articles breached	• Specify that arbitrator does not have authority to extend time limits
		• Require sections of collective agreement breached to be identified
	• Avoid complaint procedure prior to grievance	• Require complaint prior to grievance
	• Union representation at all steps including any complaint meeting	• Avoid union representation at complaint stage
	• Provision for expedited arbitration	• Require that expedited arbitration be agreed upon by both parties
Protection of bargaining unit work	• Prohibition against supervisors and others doing bargaining unit work; alternatively a prohibition that prevents others from doing work that would cause a reduction in hours or a layoff	• Avoid restrictions on bargaining unit work; ensure that agreement provides for work to be done in emergencies and for training
Term of agreements	• Union may wish to avoid a longer term unless a cost of living allowance is provided	• Longer term
Union security: dues	• Mandatory check-off of dues for all employees in the bargaining unit	• Avoid dues check-off if legislation does not require
Union security: membership	• Mandatory union membership for all employees in the barganing unit	• Avoid mandatory union membership; allow employees choice
Management rights	• Short form that is specified to be subject to remainder of collective agreement	• Long or detailed form
	• Requirement that management rights be exercised reasonably	• Avoid requirement regarding reasonable exercise of rights
Contracting out	• A complete ban on Contracting out; alternatively provide for restrictions on contracting out	• Avoid any provisions so that right to contract out is maintained
Discipline and discharge procedure	• Restrictions on the imposition of discipline such as notice, written reasons, and union representation	• Avoid restrictions so that discipline cannot by overturned on a procedural technicality
		• Specific penalty provisions to eliminate arbitrator's authority to reduce discipline imposed

Figure 7-9 Employer and Union Preferences for the Collective Agreement

Contract topic	Union	Employer
Discrimination	• Broad definition of discrimination	• Ensure that BFOR defense is maintained
Seniority	• Shorter probationary period	• Longer probationary period
	• Probationary period specified in calendar days	• Probationary period specified in working days
	• Provisions for super-seniority	
	• Seniority to be given more weight: sufficient ability clause	• Seniority given less weight: relative ability clause
	• Longer period for employment to be maintained while on layoff	• Shorter period for employment to be maintained while on layoff
Health and safety	• Specific provisions in collective agreement over and above legislated minimum	• Rely on provisions in health and safety legislation
	• Employer obligation to pay for clothing and other protective equipment	
Wages	• Call-in pay: payment for a greater number of hours and higher rate of play than provided in legislation	• Call-in pay: Exemptions from call in pay for emergencies
	• COLA protection	• Avoid COLA
Holidays	• Additional holidays over and above employment standards legislatio	• Avoid additional holidays
Vacations	• Vacation periods longer than employment standards legislation minimum	• Limit vacation
	• Choice in scheduling	• Allow for scheduling of vacations during periods of employer shut down
Benefits	• Additional benefits such as daycare, etc.	• Benefit disputes not subject to grievance
	• Benefit disputes subject to grievance	
Hours of work and scheduling	• Guarantees for hours of work	• Avoid guarantees
	• Hours or schedule specified in agreement	• Leave scheduling out of agreement
Overtime	• Broad definition of overtime	• Narrow definition of overtime
	• Overtime voluntary	• Assignment of overtime
	• Rules regulating distribution	• Limit restrictions on distribution of overtime
	• Cash remedy for error in distribution of overtime	• Opportunity to work as remedy for error in distribution
Technological change	• Include in agreement, avoid reliance on legislation	• Avoid contract provision, rely on legislation
	• Broad definition of technological change	• Narrow definition of technological change
	• Extensive protection such as job guarantees	• Less extensive protection such as notice requirement
Leave	• Leave over and above legislated minimum	• Leave as required by legislation
	• Broader definition of leave terms such as "family members" in bereavement leave	• Qualifying provisions for leave eligibility

Figure 7-9 (*Continued*)

Contract topic	Union	Employer
Union business	• Time allocated for union orientation of new employees • Bulletin boards, office space, use of employer premises for meetings • Provision allowing union officers to conduct business on paid time	• Limits on amount of time spent on union business

Figure 7-9 (*Continued*)

Implications for Practice

1. A collective agreement affects numerous human resources functions, particularly recruiting, selection, compensation, and employee relations. Measures should be taken to ensure compliance with the agreement and avoid unnecessary disputes with the union. Managers who are involved in human resources functions that might be affected by a collective agreement should receive training relating to the impact of the agreement.

2. Although there are some terms a collective agreement must contain, nothing prevents employers and unions from attempting to incorporate innovative terms.

3. Human rights, employment standards, and labour relations legislation affect the content of collective agreements. Organizations may need labour relations specialists, or access to outside experts, who are familiar with the legislation that applies to their workplace.

4. Although collective agreements in different industries have common features, some terms may be unique to a firm or industry. Organizations should not attempt to copy the terms found in other collective agreements unless they determine how those terms have been interpreted and ensure that the terms will assist them to achieve their objectives.

5. Collective agreements and arbitration decisions interpreting agreements are ever-evolving. Employers should monitor developments so that they are prepared to deal with union proposals and make proposals of their own regarding the content of an agreement.

Key Terms

arbitration, p. 150
articles, p. 147
bargaining unit work, p. 153
bumping or bumping rights, p. 165
check-off, p. 155
closed shop, p. 156
contracting out, p. 160
cost-of-living allowances (COLA), p. 168
deemed termination, p. 164
directory time limit, p. 151
expedited arbitration, p. 153
grievance, p. 149
grievance procedure, p. 149

group grievance, p. 151
hybrid seniority, p. 166
individual grievance, p. 150
lockout, p. 154
management rights, p. 158
mandatory terms, p. 147
mandatory time limit, p. 151
maintenance of membership, p. 157
modified union shop, p. 157
open shop, p. 157
policy grievance, p. 151
Rand formula or agency shop, p. 155
recall period, p. 164

recognition article, p. 148
relative or competitive ability clause, p. 166
reserved or residual rights, p. 158
seniority, p. 162
steward, p. 150
strike, p. 154
sufficient ability clause, p. 166
sunset clause, p. 161
super-seniority, p. 163
union security, p. 155
union shop, p. 157
voluntary terms, p. 147

Review Questions

1. Identify the terms that must be included in a collective agreement.

2. Discuss a situation in which an employer may assign work normally done by bargaining unit employees to employees outside of the unit, including supervisors.

3. Explain the meaning of the term "contract out," and provide reasons why unions seek restrictions on contracting out.

4. Why would an employer seek to have a specific penalty for misconduct included in the collective agreement?

5. Explain why a union would seek to have provisions regarding technological change included in the collective agreement.

6. Describe the preferences of the union and the employer regarding any personal leave provisions in the collective agreement.

Discussion Questions

1. A collective agreement provided that the union represented "all employees of the university for whom the Association is the certified bargaining [agent]." The union certification provided that the union was certified as the bargaining agent for "all employees of the university . . . except . . ." (the exceptions are not relevant; student employees of the university were included in the bargaining unit). Pursuant to a special federal program designed to provide work for handicapped students, the university allowed a student to work in the library cleaning books and shelves. This person did work that was the same as that of some bargaining unit employees. The university did not pay the person; the federal government did. The union filed a grievance that claimed the person was covered by the collective agreement, should be paid the wages mandated there, and should pay union dues. The university's response was that the person was not covered by the collective agreement because the university did not pay them. Also, the university relied on the fact that no bargaining unit employees were displaced. Should the grievance be upheld?

2. How can an employer ensure that the time limits provided in the grievance processes will be enforceable?

3. The grievance procedure in a collective agreement provides that a union grievance "shall not include any matter upon which an individual employee would be personally entitled to grieve. . . . " Why would a union want to negotiate the removal of this provision from the collective agreement?

4. Explain the importance to the union of union security provisions in a collective agreement and the implications of these provisions to the employer.

5. In some jurisdictions, legislation provides that an employee's union membership cannot be terminated for any reason other than the failure to pay union dues. Do you agree or disagree with this policy?

6. A unionized employer is hiring students to work in its office and production departments for the months of May through August, on both a full-time and a part-time basis. How would the employer determine whether union dues should be deducted from the students' pay?

7. Why do unions want specific provisions relating to issues such as discrimination and health and safety included in collective agreements even though there is legislation covering these issues?

8. A discrimination article in a collective agreement provided that there would be no discrimination on the basis of sex, age, religion, etc. When employees turned 65, they were told they would have to retire, but they did not want to retire. Is there a basis for the union to file a grievance? If this matter goes to arbitration, what result do you expect? Explain your reasons.

9. An employer and a union have been discussing what will happen if two employees are hired on the same day. The concern is how to determine who has the most seniority. The employer has proposed that the tie be broken on the basis of the employees' birthdays—the employee

with the earliest birth date would be deemed to have the most seniority. Explain any problems that could arise if this tie-breaking formula is adopted.

10. Distinguish between sufficient ability, relative ability, and hybrid seniority provisions. For each one, what is the critical initial question or issue?

11. Why would an employer want restrictions on bumping in the collective agreement?

12. An employer is negotiating a first contract with a union. It has found two alternative provisions regarding job vacancies that could be included in the agreement:
    (a) One provides that seniority will be the determining factor if the skill and ability of two contending employees is equal.
    (b) One provides that the employee with the most seniority will be awarded the job provided he or she has sufficient ability to do the job.

    Decide which of the two provisions the employer should seek to have included in the collective agreement and explain why.

13. You are part of a management team that is preparing to negotiate a renewal of a collective agreement. The agreement contains the article set out below. Explain how the present wording of the agreement may be unfavourable to management, and how the provision should be changed from management's perspective.

    All job vacancies shall be posted for three days. If there is more than one applicant for a job posting plant, seniority shall prevail.

14. An employer is negotiating a first contract with a union. It has found two alternative provisions regarding benefits that could be included in the agreement:
    (a) One provides that the employer is obligated to pay insurance premiums to provide certain levels of dental, eye care, and other benefits.
    (b) One provides that the employer will make available specified dental, eye care, and other benefits.

    Assuming that benefits will be provided, explain which of the two provisions the employer should seek to have included in the collective agreement.

15. Describe the preferences of the union and the employer regarding any overtime provisions in the collective agreement.

16. A collective agreement provided for the following definition of technological change:

    Technological change, . . . shall include automation, mechanization, and process change, and means the introduction of equipment or material of a different nature or kind than that previously utilized. . . .

    The employer had an existing computer system in its two locations, connected in a network via modem. Changes were made to the computer system that resulted in layoffs. The union claimed that there had been a technological change, and accordingly certain protection in the collective agreement was available to employees. What could the employer's response be?

17. A collective agreement provided that an employee would be entitled to five days' leave with pay upon the death of a parent. Gwen worked Monday through Friday. Her stepfather died on a Saturday. If you represented the union, what leave would you claim Gwen is entitled to? If you were the employer's human resources manager, and you wanted to reduce the leave as much as possible, what would your position be? If you were an arbitrator, what leave would you order be provided to Gwen?

18. Obtain a copy of a collective agreement. If you cannot, refer to one of the websites at the beginning of this chapter.
    i. Find the union security article in the agreement, and identify what type it is.
    ii. Find the seniority article, and identify what type it is.
    iii. Find the grievance and arbitration procedure, and identify how it is different from the one provided in this chapter.

19. One of the union's concerns is job security. Which articles in the collective agreement will directly or indirectly affect job security?

Web Research

Negotech is a repository of collective agreements made available as a courtesy by the Human Resources and Skills Development Canada's (HRSDC) website (http://negotech.labour.gc.ca/cgi-bin/search/negotech/search-eng.aspx). Use the search framework on the site to locate a current collective agreement related to a particular union or company in a national or provincial jurisdiction. Once a current collective agreement is found, look for three examples of contract language headings that are similar to those found in Figure 7-9. Explain whether these collective agreement terms in your chosen example more closely resemble the preferences of the union or those of the employer.

CASE INCIDENT   GRANT OFFICE LTD.

Grant Office Ltd. manufactures office equipment including filing cabinets, desks, and cabinets. The production employees at the company are represented by a union. The only terms of the collective agreement that are relevant to the situation below are as follows:

Article 1 The Company agrees that work normally performed by employees within the bargaining unit shall continue to be so performed by bargain unit employees. However, the union recognizes that the flexibility necessary to the Company's operations requires that such work be carried out from time to time, for varying periods of time, by employees not within the bargaining unit. This will not be exercised in such a way as to cause the layoff or permanent replacement or reduction in the regular earnings of any bargaining unit member.

Article 2.01 Seniority with the Company shall continue to accrue during an employee's period of layoff, as long as the employee remains eligible for recall. An employee on layoff shall not be entitled to any benefit conferred by this Agreement on regular employees, except as specifically provided for in this Agreement.

Article 2.02 When work again becomes available in a classification, the laid-off and displaced employees shall be recalled in accordance with their bargaining unit seniority provided the employee is able to do the work available.

A letter of understanding between the parties provided as follows:

RE: TEMPORARY RECALL/TRANSFER

Further to discussions held on November 5, 2009, between management and union representatives, the company and the union agree to the following, which hereby forms part of the collective agreement:

1. For the purpose of this agreement, "temporary work" shall mean work normally performed by employees within the bargaining unit.

2. A Temporary Work List will be created on a classification-by-classification basis. An employee will be placed on the list if he or she has previously held the classification and is out of plant on layoff unless he or she has expressly and in writing indicated his or her wish not to be on the list.

3. Where the employer determines that temporary work is available, the employer will by telephone begin contacting employees with the requisite classification background in order of seniority to offer that temporary work, and the first employee to accept the offer will receive it.

After a decline in sales, the company laid off eight maintenance employees on January 4, 2010. The employees work included installation and repair of equipment, and maintenance of facilities including painting. In April 2010, the company decided to paint the production area of the plant. To complete this project, the company entered into a contract with the General Maintenance Company. The union filed a grievance claiming that the work being completed by General Maintenance should have been done by recalling employees on layoff.

Questions

1. i. What is meant by the term "bargaining unit work"?
   ii. In Article 1, how would this term apply?

2. i. What is meant by seniority and why do unions prefer it to be included in a collective agreement?
   ii. What is the significance of seniority in this case?

3. What is the "value" of paragraphs (1) and (2) in the letter of understanding to both the union and the employer in this case?

4. Do you think management representatives could successfully use Article 1 in the agreement to defend their decision to contract with General Maintenance Company? Why?

CASE INCIDENT   MERCY HOSPITAL

Christine Lane worked as a nurse at Mercy Hospital Monday through Friday. Lane's son, who lived 800 kilometres away in a city of 75 000 people, was suffering from diabetes. On a Sunday morning, Lane received word that her son was very ill and had been taken to hospital by ambulance, apparently suffering from pancreatitis. Lane contacted her supervisor and advised him that she wished to take time off to be with her son. The supervisor advised Lane to go ahead and they would "work it out later." The collective agreement covering nurses at the hospital provided that employees were entitled to up to four days of special leave each calendar year without loss of pay. The special leave related to family leave or a pressing necessity. The contract provided that the family leave was "for use when the employee's attendance is necessary and they are unable, through other means, to change the time when they need to be in attendance, or to arrange in advance time off work when needed through other means such as shift trades, time off in lieu, or vacation." The pressing necessity referred to a situation where there was "a sudden or unusual circumstance that could not, by the exercise of reasonable judgment, have been perceived by the employee and requires the employee's immediate attention or makes the employee's attendance at work impossible."

Lane went to her son and remained with him for one week. Lane helped care for her son in hospital for two days and subsequently provided care for him in his residence after he was discharged. When Lane returned to work, she was advised that only the first day she was absent would be viewed as being eligible for special leave. Lane's supervisor told her that for the remaining days, she could have made other arrangements and accordingly they would be treated as vacation days.

Questions

1. What argument can be made by the employer to justify its decision?

2. If this issue proceeded to an arbitration hearing and you were the arbitrator, explain what your decision would be.

Chapter 8
Negotiation of the Collective Agreement

Chapter Objectives

1. Identify the determinants and significance of the bargaining structure
2. Outline the sub-processes of negotiation
3. Describe the importance of the union–management relationship
4. Explain practices and procedures in traditional adversarial bargaining
5. Outline the implications of labour relations legislation for negotiation
6. Identify strategy and tactics used in positional or distributive bargaining
7. Describe the principles of interest-based bargaining

Required Professional Capabilities (CCHRA)	HRPA Human Resources Professionals Competency Framework
10101, 10102, 10504, 20105, 20106, 20107, 20110, 20206, 20611, 50102, 20103, 50107, 50114, 50117, 50404, 50411	C013, C018, C022, C114, C116, C117, C120, C121, C122, C123, C124, C125, C126

About 1600 Region of Durham employees, including paramedics, daycare staff, court services workers, public health inspectors, and administrative workers in several different departments, went on strike in June 2014. According to CUPE Ontario, a key cause of this work stoppage was the regional government's attempt to change the sick leave benefit plan for emergency service workers. Specifically, management negotiators were proposing a change to current practices that would now see EMS workers not paid for the first three days of a sick leave. The union characterized this as "divide and conquer" strategy against one important group or employees within the union local. CUPE has proposed that the matter of EMS sick pay be referred to interest arbitration; however, management negotiators showed no interest in that proposal as the strike dragged on. Spokespersons for both sides in bargaining claimed that their team was prepared to continue discussions on a new contract, but looked to the other side to make a move that indicated a willingness to continue negotiations. The strike caused service interruptions at six daycare centres serving community residents.

Every year, thousands of collective agreements are negotiated in Canada. The negotiation process is critical for employers, unions, employees, and the public. The process and the resulting collective agreements determine employer costs, employee compensation, and job security. Strikes and lockouts, which are occasionally a part of the process, might affect the availability of goods and services for the public.

Although labour negotiations share some features with commercial negotiations, other features make them unique.[1] Labour negotiations take place between parties who are in an ongoing relationship. The union and the employer will have to work with each other after the negotiation is completed, and they will likely be negotiating in the future. Labour negotiations are often much more complex than other types of negotiations, because they cover many different issues: wages, benefits, health and safety, union security, vacations, and more. Labour negotiations are subject to unique legislative requirements as well. The parties have a duty to bargain in good faith and cannot engage in a strike or lockout in most jurisdictions until they have completed a conciliation or mediation process, referred to in Chapter 10. Finally, labour negotiators are representing either senior management or bargaining unit employees. They must reach a settlement that their respective constituents will approve.

This chapter will examine the practices, procedures, and tactics of traditional, adversarial collective bargaining. At the end of the chapter, an alternative, interest-based approach will be considered.

BARGAINING STRUCTURE

The certification process results in a union representing a specified group of employees working for an employer at one or more locations. At minimum, contract negotiations must involve at least one employer and one union representing employees working at one location. That is, negotiations must cover at least one certified bargaining unit. However, an employer might be dealing with one or more unions at one or more locations, or several certified bargaining units. There may be more than one employer in a province or region with the same type of employees. For example, there may be several colleges in a province employing teachers at different locations. Labour relations legislation may require, or the parties might agree, that contract negotiations cover several locations, or include different unions, or even more than one employer. To relate this to certification, the parties can agree to have contract negotiations cover more than one certified bargaining unit. **Bargaining structure** refers to the number of unions, employers, and locations or establishments involved in contract negotiations. It has been referred to as dealing with the issue of "who bargains with whom."[2]

> **Bargaining structure** refers to the number of unions, employers, and establishments involved in contract negotiations.

Possible Bargaining Structures

There are numerous possible bargaining structures, depending on the number of employers, unions, and locations involved in contract negotiations. Let us look at the most commonly used structures.

- *Single employer, single establishment, single union.* This structure is common in Canada. The employer may have more than one location or more than one union at a location; however, negotiations are conducted between the employer and a union representing one group of employees at one location. For example, at a hospital there might be separate bargaining units for nurses, kitchen staff, and maintenance employees, each of which is represented by a different union. The contract negotiations for the three bargaining units are conducted separately, and there are three separate collective agreements.

- *Single employer, multiple establishments, single union.* The auto industry is an example of this type of structure, which involves the negotiation of one collective agreement that will affect the various workplaces operated by the employer. There may be a master agreement between the employer and the union and secondary agreements that involve only the locals at each workplace.

Other bargaining structures include combinations such as a single employer with a single establishment, negotiating with multiple unions; however, they are rarely found in Canada.

Centralized vs. Decentralized Bargaining

An important feature of possible bargaining structures is the degree of centralization involved. **Centralized bargaining** refers to contract negotiations that involve one or more of the following: multiple employers instead of a single employer, multiple establishments instead of a single establishment, and multiple unions instead of a single union. Centralization reduces the number of rounds of contract negotiations. Centralization is not a yes-or-no issue; rather, we should view negotiations as being more centralized or less centralized. **Industry bargaining** is a structure in which multiple employers, with multiple locations, bargain with a single union. This type of structure might be found in hospitals where the hospitals in a province negotiate with a provincial nurses' union and the agreement covers all locations in the province. This bargaining structure is not common in Canada, where there is generally **decentralized bargaining** between a union and the employer. Such negotiations commonly involve one union representing employees at one location dealing with one employer.

Centralized bargaining refers to negotiations that cover more than one location, bargaining unit, or employer.

Industry bargaining is a centralized bargaining structure in which one negotiation covers all employees in an industry.

Decentralized bargaining refers to negotiations between one employer and one union for one location.

Factors Affecting Bargaining Structure   Bargaining structure in Canada is decentralized for a number of reasons. The division of authority to legislate and administer labour relations between the provinces and the federal government is a factor. If an employer had one location in Ottawa and another a few kilometres away in Hull, Quebec, the two establishments would be organized in separate bargaining units in each province, and would be subject to different labour relations legislation governing contract negotiation. The existence of 11 separate labour relations jurisdictions makes negotiation for a group of employees that are in different provinces difficult.

Another factor leading to decentralization is the bargaining unit that Labour Relations Boards have deemed to be appropriate and certified. In the past, some Boards have established separate bargaining units for full-time and part-time employees, and separate bargaining units for employees at different locations in some provinces. To facilitate organization, some Boards have certified establishments in a municipality separately when there is no interchange of employees. Once a certified bargaining unit has been established, the bargaining for that unit will occur separately from other units unless the employer and the union agree otherwise.

There may also be economic factors leading to decentralization. Some employers have recently attempted to move to decentralized bargaining so that they can deal with each establishment separately and perhaps gain concessions that they would not be able to obtain if they were negotiating with multiple establishments.

Significance of Bargaining Structure   Bargaining structure is significant because it can affect the negotiation process, the contract terms agreed upon, the incidence of strikes and lockouts, and the relationship between the management and the union. Centralized bargaining might reduce the costs of contract negotiation because fewer negotiations are involved. However, it might make reaching an agreement more difficult. If there are different workgroups or different locations included in the same set of negotiations, these groups may have different priorities or interests. A group of workers in one part of a province might be more concerned with job security, and employees in other regions might not have the same concern.

Centralized bargaining may help the employer avoid the union practice of **whipsawing**. In this tactic, a union negotiating with several employers might reach a settlement with one of them—likely the one it can get the best deal from—and then use this as leverage to get the others to agree to similar terms. Employers might also use whipsawing against unions. If employers negotiate as a group, the union cannot strike one employer and force it to grant concessions to avoid losing business to the others. In some countries, centralized bargaining has led to a reduction in inflation. This may be because in negotiations involving

Whipsawing involves establishing an agreement with one party and then using the agreement to pressure others.

larger units, or all of the industry, the parties recognize the inflationary effects of wage increases. Conversely, where bargaining is decentralized, there is a free-rider effect, meaning that a contract negotiation affecting a relatively small number of employees is not perceived to lead to inflation.[3]

Centralized bargaining in some countries has led to fewer work stoppages and less time lost to strikes. However, in Canada this has not happened. More centralized bargaining can affect the relationship between the management and the union and alienate employees. Some employee groups may perceive that their interests have not been adequately met in negotiations and they may be frustrated. This in turn may affect their relationship with the employer. The bargaining structure might affect the relative bargaining power of the union and the employer. In the banking industry, a decentralized bargaining structure—bargaining on a branch-by-branch basis—would likely leave each bargaining unit of employees with very little bargaining power.

There is variation in bargaining structures across industries and provinces. In one province, contract negotiations for school teachers may be decentralized, with separate negotiations between numerous school boards and the teachers' union. In the same province, the negotiation for college teachers may be centralized, with one set of negotiations between a body representing all colleges and the teachers' union.

Informal Bargaining Structure

There is an informal element in bargaining structure. Even in cases where the formal structure is less centralized, there may be factors in the bargaining situation that produce results or behaviours associated with more centralized bargaining. Although an employer might bargain separately with different employee groups, it might be difficult to grant wage increases to one group and not provide them to other groups. Another aspect of informal bargaining structure is **pattern bargaining**, where a union negotiates an agreement with one employer and then attempts to have it copied with other employers. Pattern bargaining has been common in the auto industry. The Canadian Auto Workers union selects one of the three North American auto manufacturers—likely the one it thinks it will be able to obtain the best contract from—as a target, negotiates a collective agreement with it, and then attempts to negotiate similar agreements with the other two manufacturers.

In some situations, pattern bargaining does not mean the first or lead contract negotiated and subsequent agreements are the same. Instead there may be a standard prorated relationship between the lead and subsequent contracts. For example, in some provinces the union representing firefighters in smaller cities waits until the contract in a large urban centre has been negotiated and then negotiates a similar contract providing for slightly lower compensation.

SUB-PROCESSES IN NEGOTIATION

"Negotiation" conjures up thoughts of individuals confronting each other across a table. Meetings between the parties are an important part of negotiation, but there is much more involved. In *A Behavioral Theory of Labor Negotiations: An Analysis of a Social Interaction System*, Richard Walton and Robert McKersie describe four sub-processes that might be involved in any bargaining situation: distributive bargaining, integrative bargaining, attitudinal structuring, and intraorganizational bargaining.[4] We will briefly describe these elements and their implications.

Distributive Bargaining

Distributive bargaining refers to activities and behaviours that are commonly associated with negotiation. It is used where resources are limited and there is a conflict between the

In **pattern bargaining** a union negotiates an agreement with one employer and then attempts to have it copied with other employers.

Distributive bargaining is a negotiation activity whereby limited resources are divided between the parties.

parties. A good example is the determination of wages: a gain for one party involves a loss for the other. Because distributive bargaining is based upon demands made by the parties or positions taken, it may be referred to as *positional bargaining*. The strategy and tactics of distributive bargaining are discussed below.

Integrative Bargaining

Integrative bargaining refers to a form of negotiation or activities in which the parties' objectives are not in fundamental conflict and there is a possibility of a win-win situation. For example, both the union and the employer would like to see workplace accidents reduced. In addition to being concerned with employee safety, employers have a financial interest in reducing workers' compensation costs.

> **Integrative bargaining** is negotiation in which the parties' objectives are not in conflict and joint gain is possible.

Some observers view integrative bargaining as the basis for an alternative approach to bargaining, one that is considered later in this chapter. This approach is referred to as *interest-based* or *mutual gains bargaining*. In integrative bargaining, the parties focus on problem solving and the interests of the parties as opposed to demands or positions.

The distinction between demands or positions as opposed to interests is critical to an understanding of the distinction between distributive and integrative bargaining. Mary Parker Follett developed the following illustration. Suppose two siblings have one orange that they both want. In a distributive or positional negotiation, each sibling would demand the orange and would try to justify his or her position. Perhaps one would say that the other got a previous orange. The siblings would have to agree that one of the parties got the orange before, or they might compromise and cut the orange in half. In an integrative negotiation, the siblings would determine what their interests were. Each would find out why the other wanted the orange. They might find that one of them wanted the orange to use the peel in a recipe, and the other wanted it for the fruit inside. An integrative approach, focusing on interests, might improve the outcome for both parties.[5]

Attitudinal Structuring: Shaping the Parties' Attitudes and Relationship

There are a number of possible relationships between union and management negotiators, which are discussed in the next section. These parties may have little or no trust, or be more or less cooperative with each other. **Attitudinal structuring** refers to the relationship the parties have and what they do to change their relationship. The relationship between the parties may be a concern for a number of reasons. The relationship could affect the likelihood of reaching an agreement. Where the parties are hostile, they may miss opportunities for settlement. The relationship could also affect future negotiations and the administration of the collective agreement.

> **Attitudinal structuring** refers to the parties' relationship and what they do to change it.

Intraorganizational Bargaining

The first three sub-processes referred to activities between the union and the employer. Each negotiator has to deal with two sets of demands: those made by the other side and those made by the people they represent. The negotiators for the employer and the union must eventually answer to their respective constituencies. Union negotiators in particular must be concerned with obtaining the approval of the bargaining unit for any agreement negotiated. Within either side, there may be differences of opinion regarding the objectives that should be pursued in negotiations and the methods that should be used. Some members of a bargaining unit may be more concerned with job security, while others give

Intraorganizational bargaining
refers to activities within each side to
build a consensus.

priority to a wage increase. Some employees may be more willing than others to strike to obtain a favourable agreement. **Intraorganizational bargaining** refers to activities within the employer or union organizations to build an internal consensus. Union negotiators may face a problem reconciling the expectations of employees with additional information that they are provided during the course of negotiations. Union representatives may go into negotiations demanding a significant wage increase, which bargaining unit members perceive the employer can afford. In negotiations, the union bargaining team may be provided with financial information that shows the employer cannot afford the wage increase expected. This difference in information might lead to problems for union negotiators, because they may know they have negotiated the best deal possible, but it does not meet the expectations of employees. The union negotiators will have to work to convince employees that the contract should be approved despite the initial demand for a large wage hike.

So far, the four sub-processes have been discussed separately. In reality, they are inter-related. A tactic or move aimed at dealing with an issue in one area might affect one or more of the other three. If a negotiator in the process of distributive bargaining makes a concession in order to reach an agreement, this might affect the relationship with the negotiator's constituents. Some employees might be unwilling to approve an agreement if concessions have been made that affect them. The failure to reach a consensus on demands—in other words, to resolve intraorganizational bargaining issues—will make distributive bargaining more difficult.

Implications of Sub-processes in Negotiation

The sub-processes described by Walton and McKersie help us understand the complexity of negotiation and have important implications. Although some issues are distributive in nature—that is, a gain for one party necessarily involves a loss for the other—there may be room for an integrative approach on other issues. The relationship between the parties is important. The relationship could be a factor determining whether an agreement is reached, and the contents of the agreement. Intraorganizational issues affect negotiators. Before negotiations, each side will have to work to obtain a consensus on their demands; and after an agreement is reached, may have to convince their constituents to ratify the agreement. We will now consider the union–management relationship further before proceeding with the negotiation process.

UNION–MANAGEMENT RELATIONSHIP

The relationship between the union and the employer will vary according to each party's views regarding the legitimacy of the other's claims and the level of trust between the parties. The nature of the relationship is important, because it might affect the type of bargaining the parties engage in, and the likelihood of a strike or lockout. The possible relationships between the union and the employer, the factors determining the relationship, and the consequences of the relationship will be considered here.

Types of Union–Management Relationships

The relationship between the union and the employer can be classified into one of five types: conflict, containment-aggression, accommodation, cooperation, and collusion.[6]

Conflict   The conflict relationship is the most hostile. In this relationship, the employer opposes the union's representation of employees and only deals with the union as required by law. The union and the employer compete for the loyalty of the employees. The union views management as the enemy who is exploiting employees. Trust between the union and the employer is extremely low. The parties dislike or hate each other to the point that there may be irrational behaviour to inflict damage upon the other. With this type of relationship, the parties will not be able to move away from distributive bargaining that is not only harsh and critical, but likely increases the chances of a strike or lockout.

Containment-Aggression   In a relationship classified as containment-aggression, the employer grudgingly accepts the union. The union attempts to increase its influence, and the employer attempts to contain or minimize the union's impact in bargaining. The parties view each other with suspicion and are mutually antagonistic. Management may attempt to undermine the union with direct communication to employees such as newsletters and meetings. With this type of relationship, it will be difficult for the parties to move away from distributive bargaining that is adversarial.

Accommodation   In a relationship classified as accommodation, each of the parties recognizes the legitimacy of the other, and there is a moderate amount of respect between them. There is also, however, limited trust between the union and the employer. This type of relationship may allow the parties to move away from traditional adversarial bargaining.

Cooperative   In a cooperative relationship, the parties completely accept each other's legitimacy in the workplace and are willing to collaborate. There is mutual trust between union and management leaders. This type of relationship is the one most likely to be the basis for more integrative bargaining.

Collusion   In a collusive relationship, there is a coalition between the union and the employer to pursue common goals and practices that may be illegal. Management may pursue unfair competition practices or improper payments to themselves. The union goes along with this situation and does not adequately protect the interest of employees. In some cases, the employer may bribe union leaders to avoid labour problems. In a collusive relationship, there is no true bargaining. The relationship between the National Hockey League Players' Association and the National Hockey League during the period 1967–92, while Alan Eagleson was the executive director of the players' union, has been cited as collusive.[7] During this time, hockey players had the lowest average salary in North American professional sports and received the lowest percentage of gross revenues. At the same time, it appears that Eagleson enjoyed personal gain.

Factors Determining the Union–Management Relationship

Some of the factors that affect the union–management relationship are matters the parties have little or no control over. On other issues, the parties do have some control over and might attempt to vary to change their relationship.

External Economic, Technological, and Legal Factors   The competitive environment the employer faces might affect the relationship with the union. If the employer faces an economic downturn or increased competition, it will place increased pressure on unions to maintain the status quo or offer concessions when bargaining the terms and conditions of work for its members. Technological innovation might lead to hostility when the employer seeks to implement changes that threaten job security of union members. The legal environment might also affect the relationship. The issue of the deduction of union dues from the pay of bargaining unit employees has caused conflict between unions and employers. This source of conflict, linked to advocates for "right to work" legislation, has been eliminated in jurisdictions that have passed laws requiring the deduction of dues by employers.

Personalities of Leaders   Union and management leaders may have personalities that make them more or less friendly, trusting, and cooperative. Authoritarian personality types are typically more competitive, have lower levels of trust, and are less tolerant of the views of others.

Beliefs and Values of Leaders   The social beliefs of union and management leaders may also be important. Some employers may be dominated by free-enterprise individualists who do not believe in the legitimacy of unions. Some union leaders may have a basic mistrust of the market system that extends to resentment toward most managers.

Experience with Collective Bargaining   The relationship between union and management negotiators might also be affected by past experiences with collective bargaining. If either of the parties has had a negative experience with previous negotiations or the administration of a collective agreement, it could be more hostile. A manager who has had a decision challenged through the grievance process and experienced cross-examination at an arbitration hearing may be uncomfortable in some collective bargaining situations.

NEGOTIATION PROCESS

Figure 8-1 provides an overview of the negotiation process.

Notice to Bargain

A **statutory freeze** means that the employer cannot change the terms and conditions of employment.

The union or the employer can give a notice to bargain to the other. Labour relations legislation provides that once a notice to bargain has been given, the employer cannot change the terms and conditions of employment. This **statutory freeze** continues until the union has the right to strike or the employer has the right to lock out employees. The prerequisites for a strike or lockout are discussed in Chapter 10.

Figure 8-1 The Negotiation Process

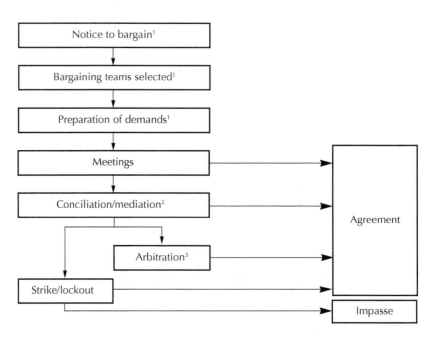

Notes

[1] The notice to bargain, selection of bargaining teams, and preparation of demands might occur in a different order.

[2] Conciliation or mediation, elaborated upon in Chapter 10, is a prerequisite for a strike or lockout in most jurisdictions.

[3] For some public sector employees, arbitration must be used instead of a strike or lockout.

Bargaining Teams

The union and the employer will each assemble a bargaining team. Each side can include whomever it wishes on its team. Both sides have a duty to bargain in good faith, and it is a breach of this duty to object to the presence of an individual on the other side's team. The size and composition of bargaining teams will vary according to the bargaining structure and the number of employees covered by the collective agreement.

Employer Bargaining Team   The employer bargaining team may include a labour relations staff person or consultant, operations managers, a financial resource person, and others. In some cases, the employer's team may include the chief executive officer or president; however, there may be disadvantages to this. A key drawback may occur when the CEO, in such a situation, is "put on the spot" by a member of the union negotiating team regarding a key demand such as wage increases or layoff protocols. Not having the top decision maker present at the time of such demands allows the management bargaining team to say that such union concerns will be reviewed in due course with company executives and responded to in subsequent negotiations. Bargaining teams may also include, or add, as needed, experts in specialized areas such as pensions.

Union Bargaining Team   The union's constitution and bylaws may affect the composition of the union bargaining team. These documents may provide that certain officers, such as the local president, are designated as part of the bargaining team, and outline the process to select other team members. The national or international union may provide a representative to be part of the team and act as a resource person. This representative may be important, because he or she may have more experience than local union officers in some cases. The union team may also include experts in particular areas such as pensions and health and safety.

Both teams require individuals who will maintain solidarity and confidentiality. Team members must not reveal the team's priorities or willingness to make concessions. The spokesperson or chief negotiator must have persistence and outstanding listening skills. He or she may be required to face rejection and sarcasm from the other side, and must be able to explain proposals and pick up on cues from the other side.

Preparations for Negotiation

The union and the employer team must do extensive work before the first meeting of the parties. Each side will have to prepare its own demands and consider what are the likely the demands of the other party.

Union Demands   The union will prepare contract demands after considering the items listed in Figure 8-2.

1. Experience with the collective agreement
2. Grievances and complaints filed by bargaining unit members
3. Arbitration decisions
4. Input from bargaining unit members
5. Input from national or international unions
6. Economic forecasts
7. Contract settlements, industry and local

Figure 8-2 Factors Affecting Union Demands

Where the parties are negotiating a renewal of the collective agreement, the experience with the expiring agreement will be important. For example, if the expiring agreement did not require overtime to be equally distributed among employees and it appeared that the employer favoured some employees, the union would seek contract provisions governing the distribution of overtime. The union might refer to employee complaints that have arisen over the life of the previous agreement. If the union filed grievances that were lost at arbitration because of the wording of the agreement, the union would seek an amendment to the contract. Some unions obtain specific membership input prior to negotiations through surveys and membership meetings. This input may be required by union bylaws.

The national or international union may have recommendations for demands. The union will attempt to obtain information regarding projected increases in the cost of living. Some sources of economic information were referred to in Chapter 2. The Canadian Labour Congress and some larger unions develop economic forecasts. Unions will consider wage increases that have been provided in agreements in the industry and other collective agreements in the region.

Employer Demands   The factors affecting the demands of the employer are listed in Figure 8-3.

The employer will consider its experience with any expiring collective agreement. If the job posting procedure provided for in the agreement has caused delays in filling vacancies, the employer would seek a shorter notice for job postings. The employer would also refer to any grievances and arbitration decisions and attempt to change terms in the collective agreement that have caused problems. It might also get feedback from managers through meetings and surveys. Future business plans should be considered. If the employer is planning on making use of more part-time employees and the agreement restricts the use of part-time employees, it will seek an amendment to the agreement. The employer will also obtain economic information, including the projected rate of inflation and forecasts of sales and revenues, and refer to contract settlements in the industry and regional collective agreements.

Meetings of the Bargaining Teams

Caucuses are separate meetings of members of the union or management bargaining teams used to discuss strategy or decisions related to negotiations.

The meetings between the employer and the union bargaining teams will often occur at a neutral location such as a hotel meeting room. The parties meet in one room to discuss issues and will require additional rooms for separate union and management meetings or **caucuses**.

Stages of Negotiation   Researchers have considered the negotiation process and broken it down into three or four stages using various names for the stages. It might appear that in some negotiations the parties have a good idea of where they are going to end up, and an observer might ask why all the haggling is necessary. The concept of stages in negotiations may help us understand why it is not possible or advisable to short-circuit the process. Three stages of negotiation will be referred to here.

1. Experience with the collective agreement
2. Grievances and arbitration decisions
3. Feedback from managers
4. Business plans
5. Economic forecasts
6. Contract settlements, industry and local

Figure 8-3 Factors Affecting Employer Demands

Stage One: Establishing the Negotiation Range. In this stage, each side explains its concerns and positions on the issues. Often the union will proceed first with the presentation of written demands and an explanation of the demands. Each chief spokesperson will attempt to forcefully present his or her side's position. Both sides recognize that the positions taken are flexible, some much more so than others, and that concessions will have to be made. In this phase, there may be some antagonism as the parties express their concerns and frustrations. This phase may take several meetings. Each side is trying to see how the other reacts and determine what the other side may be willing to agree to.

Stage Two: Search Phase. This is the longest phase, when parties make concessions moving toward agreement, and may take numerous meetings over an extended time. It will involve bluffing and other tactics, as discussed below. **Non-monetary issues**—items that do not involve a direct financial cost, such as the number of days to file a grievance—are usually addressed before monetary issues. **Monetary issues**—relate to wages, benefits, vacations, etc.—are matters that involve a financial cost.

The non-monetary issues are usually considered first, because they may be less contentious, and there may be some momentum built up by settling some of them. There is also a very practical reason for the union to prefer to deal with the critical monetary issues last. If no agreement is reached, the ultimate union weapon is a strike. But this is only an effective threat if employees are willing, and employees would be more likely to support a strike over the core monetary issues.

Stage Three: Crisis Phase. In the third stage, a strike or lockout is a clear possibility. The parties are forced to make decisions and final concessions if they are going to avoid this crisis and reach an agreement. This phase is shorter and might be marked by a series of last-minute proposals, counterproposals, and agreement. In some cases, the crisis phase may involve off-the-record meetings between the chief negotiators. In the crisis phase, the employer may increase a monetary offer or the union could withdraw a demand. This phase may also involve the participation of a mediator to assist the parties to reach an agreement.

> **Non-monetary issues** are issues that do not involve a direct financial cost.
>
> **Monetary issues** are issues that involve a direct financial cost.

Duty to Bargain in Good Faith

Labour relations legislation in all jurisdictions imposes a **duty to bargain in good faith** on both the employer and the union. In most jurisdictions, there is a dual obligation to bargain in good faith and make a "reasonable effort to enter into a collective agreement."[8] The duty to bargain in good faith does not guarantee that a collective agreement will be reached. The legislation does not require any particular concessions be made to reach an agreement. If the reason for the failure to reach an agreement is a conflict over wages, there is no breach of the duty. Generally, if a party has a strong bargaining position that allows it to virtually dictate the terms of the agreement, there is also no breach of the duty. This is subject to the qualification that in some jurisdictions, when the parties are negotiating their first agreement, either of them may apply for the agreement to be determined by arbitration, if the failure to agree is caused by unreasonable demands. First contract arbitration is discussed below.

> The **duty to bargain in good faith** means that both the union and the employer must make reasonable efforts to reach agreement.

Purpose of the Duty to Bargain in Good Faith The purpose of the duty to bargain in good faith is to ensure that the employer recognizes the union and to facilitate an agreement being reached without a strike or lockout. It is recognized that some employers will not stop their opposition to a union after certification. The certification of the union would be meaningless if the employer were allowed to refuse to bargain.

Requirements of the Duty Generally the duty relates to the approach to contract negotiations or the form in reaching an agreement, not the contents of particular proposals. However, a few exceptional contract proposals are a breach of the duty. Although the parties are allowed to negotiate the coverage of the collective agreement so that employees are either added to or removed from the bargaining unit, it is a breach of the duty to insist upon changes in the bargaining unit. The employer or the union cannot take this issue to an impasse that would cause a strike or lockout. Similarly, the bargaining structure and coverage of the collective agreement cannot be pressed to impasse. A union's insistence upon a single set of negotiations and one collective agreement for several bargaining units is also a breach of the duty. Insisting upon any illegal condition in the agreement, such as a discriminatory wage, would also be an example of bad faith bargaining.

Figure 8-4 lists various conduct that has been found to be a breach of the duty.

A distinction has been drawn between **hard bargaining** and **surface bargaining**. Hard bargaining refers to persistent attempts to obtain an agreement on favourable terms and is legitimate. An employer who is willing to sign an agreement, but refuses to agree to any wage increase so that more profits can be provided to owners, is engaging in hard bargaining. Surface bargaining refers to going through the motions of negotiation with no intent to reach an agreement. An employer who knows that the union cannot agree to a wage increase of less than 3 percent, and deliberately offers a wage increase of 1 percent to avoid an agreement, is engaging in surface bargaining.

It may be difficult to tell the difference between an employer who wants a contract on favourable terms and an employer who does not want a contract at all. Refusing to meet will usually be a breach of the duty. A distinction must be drawn between a refusal to meet in the early stages of negotiations and a refusal that occurs later in negotiations after the parties have exhausted an issue. If the parties have met and discussed proposals, it is possible for a party to take the position that it will not meet again unless the other side is willing to change its position. A sudden, unexplained change in position may be a breach of the duty. A Labour Relations Board will consider the evidence and determine whether there was a valid reason for a change in position, or if it appears the change was designed to avoid reaching an agreement. In one case, the parties were divided on the issue of the deduction of union dues from employees' pay. There was an intervening change in legislation that required the employer to deduct and remit union dues. This meant that the dispute over union dues was no longer an issue. The employer then withdrew its previous monetary offer. The Board found that this change in position was designed to avoid a collective agreement and was a breach of the duty.

A party who takes the position that an item will not be discussed or included in the collective agreement will have to proceed carefully. Although the duty to bargain in good faith is an overarching obligation to negotiate an entire collective agreement, not a duty that attaches to each item raised in negotiations, a party who refuses to discuss or include

Hard bargaining is a legitimate attempt to obtain a favourable agreement.

Surface bargaining is bargaining aimed at avoiding an agreement.

1. Surface bargaining
2. Refusal to meet
3. Objections to composition of a bargaining team
4. Unlawful strike or lockout threats
5. Circumventing the union
6. Failing to provide information
7. Failing to explain proposals
8. Changing position without justification
9. Last-minute demands
10. Illegal demands

Figure 8-4 Action Deemed to Indicate Bad Faith

an issue should make it clear that it is willing to sign a collective agreement that does not contain the issue involved. It would appear that multiple refusals to discuss or include terms taken together would be a breach of the duty. Complaints about a breach of the duty will be resolved on a case-by-case basis. In one situation where an employer refused to discuss changes in pension benefits for retired employees, it was found that there was a breach of the duty. However, in another case when a public school employer association refused to discuss or include an issue raised by the union, it was found that there was no breach of the duty because it was established that the employer was willing to enter into an agreement. A refusal to explain one's position is also a breach of the duty. In one case, an employer made a monetary offer and refused to explain or discuss the offer because of anti-inflation guidelines that were in force at the time. It claimed that the guidelines prevented it from providing a greater wage increase. The employer's refusal to discuss and explain the interpretation of the wage guidelines was found to be a breach of the duty to bargain in good faith.

In order to meet the duty, the employer has an obligation to disclose information. Employers who have refused to provide wage and classification information have been found to be in breach. Employers must provide the union with the names and addresses of bargaining unit members. The employer is also obligated to disclose information that the union has not solicited if that information is relevant to the negotiations. In a case where the employer had decided to move some operations and did not reveal this information in the course of negotiations, it was found that there was a breach of the duty, even though the union had not asked about the possibility of a move. It appears that the employer does not have to reveal information when the matter is still under consideration. To avoid problems relating to the revelation of information, the union should make inquiries. It might ask the employer whether there are any plans such as relocation or contracting out that will affect the bargaining unit.

The employer is allowed to communicate with employees and the community during negotiations; however, it is obligated to explain and discuss any proposals with the union prior to any such communication. It is permissible for the employer to send letters to employees, or put notices in newspapers to explain its position, provided the issues have been fully discussed with the union beforehand. These communications must not be misleading or threaten employees. It may be difficult to distinguish between permissible communications in which the employer expresses a view or informs, as opposed to threats or intimidation. Employers have been given more leeway when the bargaining relationship between the parties has been of a long-standing and positive nature.

It is a breach of the duty to bargain in good faith to send representatives to negotiations who do not have adequate information or authority. For example, if the employer is claiming it does not have the ability to pay, the employer bargaining team should have, or be able to obtain, financial information to support this claim. It would be a breach of the duty for an employer to send representatives to negotiations who make commitments, and then attempt to back away from them, claiming they have received new instructions from senior management.

Breach of the Duty to Bargain in Good Faith: Procedure and Remedies
Failure to bargain in good faith is an unfair labour practice, and a union or employer who thinks there has been a breach of the duty may file a complaint with the Labour Relations Board. A Board officer will attempt to settle the matter; however, if there is no settlement, the Board will conduct a hearing. If it is found that there has been a breach of the duty, the Board may issue a cease-and-desist order with a direction to resume bargaining. In a few exceptional cases, damages have been awarded. Boards have ordered damages equal to the amount of compensation employees would have earned if an agreement had been reached earlier without a breach, and unions have been compensated for the additional expenses they incurred because of an employer's breach. First contract arbitration, which is reviewed in the next section, might also be viewed as a remedy for a failure to bargain in good faith following certification.

First Contract Arbitration

At one time, there were a significant number of situations where a union was certified, and there were negotiations with the employer, but the parties could not reach agreement. In response to this, eight jurisdictions have added a provision to their labour relations legislation to provide that either the union or the employer may apply to have a first collective agreement settled by arbitration in some circumstances. **First contract arbitration** is now available in the federal jurisdiction, British Columbia, Manitoba, Newfoundland and Labrador, Ontario, Prince Edward Island, Quebec, and Saskatchewan.[9] This means that a neutral arbitrator or the Labour Relations Board will hear representations from the union and the employer and then determine the contents of the first agreement. There are minor differences between jurisdictions. The key points relating to the availability of this remedy and the contents of the agreement will be reviewed here.

First contract arbitration provides for the imposition of an agreement where efforts to reach a first contract have failed.

Availability of First Contract Arbitration   If the parties are unable to reach an agreement, either the union or the employer can apply for first contract arbitration. The legislation specifies the criteria used to determine whether the remedy will be granted. In most jurisdictions, the legislation provides that failure to bargain in good faith is a factor to be considered; however, a finding of bad faith bargaining is not a prerequisite to the remedy. First contract arbitration has been ordered where employers have taken unreasonable positions without justification. It has been awarded where employers have refused to agree to any seniority provisions and have offered lower compensation to unionized employees than non-union employees doing the same work.

Contents of the Agreement   The Labour Relations Board or an arbitrator determines the content of the collective agreement after hearing representations from union and management bargaining leaders. The compensation and working conditions of similar employees are factors influencing the terms imposed. First contract arbitration cannot be used by either party to obtain exceptional provisions that it could not obtain through negotiations. The union will not be able to obtain benefits not provided in the industry sector. The employer will not be able to obtain a contract that entirely avoids seniority provisions. The statutes require the term of the agreement to be between one and two years depending upon the jurisdiction.

Significance of First Contract Arbitration   First contract arbitration is significant for a number of reasons. This remedy prevents employers from avoiding a union by adopting unreasonable positions in bargaining. In the jurisdictions that do not have first contract arbitration—Alberta, Nova Scotia, and New Brunswick—the employer could avoid the union in this manner. The remedy also illustrates the importance of the divided jurisdiction in Canadian labour relations, which has allowed for experimentation and change. First contract arbitration was first adopted in the 1970s in British Columbia, and it has been added by other jurisdictions since that time. The remedy also illustrates how the legal environment in Canada is generally more favourable to unions than it is in the United States, where first contract arbitration is not available.

Strategies and Tactics in Distributive Bargaining

In distributive bargaining, each side may have three key reference "points" in mind for each issue as it enters negotiations: a resistance point, a target point, and an initial position.

A **resistance point** is a negotiating party's bottom line—the least favourable offer it will accept.

The **resistance point** is the party's "bottom line"—the point it will refuse to go below (or above, as the case may be). If a union's resistance point on wages is a 2 percent increase, the union would go on strike before agreeing to any increase less than 2 percent. If the employer's resistance point is a 2.75 percent wage increase, this means it would endure a strike or impose a lockout rather than go any higher.

The **target point** is the result a party hopes to obtain. Although a union thinks it will not accept anything less than a 2 percent wage increase going into negotiations, the union hopes to achieve a greater increase, for example 3 percent. Similarly, the employer will have a target point it hopes to achieve.

The **target point** is the result a negotiating party hopes to achieve.

Each party will have an **initial position** on each issue at the start of negotiations. If the union hopes to achieve a 3 percent wage increase, it will have to demand more than that initially. Similarly, the employer will have to begin negotiations by providing less in its initial offer than it is willing to pay, so that it has room to increase its offer.

An **initial position** is a party's first offer or demand in negotiations.

In summary, a union might be willing to go as low as a 2 percent wage increase (the resistance point), hopes for a 3 percent increase (the target point), and has an initial position or demand of 4 percent. The employer's points would be in the reverse order. The three points referred to for each party are illustrated in Figure 8-5, based on Walton and McKersie's *A Behavioral Theory of Labor Negotiations*.

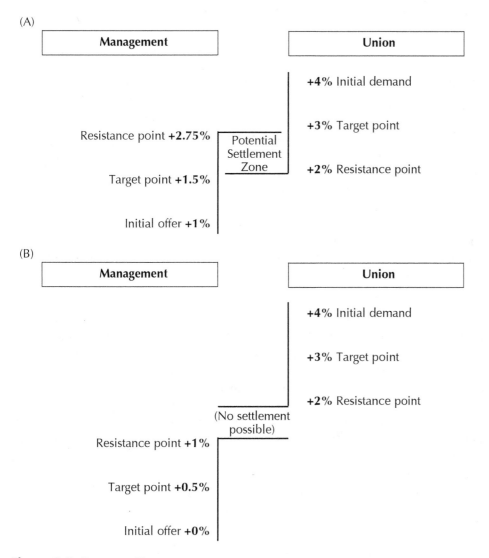

Figure 8-5 Contract Zone

Sources: Based on Richard E. Walton and Robert B. McKersie, *A Behavioral Theory of Labour Negotiations: An Analysis of a Social Interaction System* (New York: McGraw-Hill, 1965); Roy Lewicki, Joseph Litterer, John Minton, and David Saunders, *Negotiation,* 2nd ed. (Homewood, IL: Irwin, 1994).

Where there is an overlap of the resistance points between negotiating teams as in Figure 8-5(A), there is a contract zone or settlement zone, within which the two parties should be able to reach an agreement. Where the parties end up in the contract zone (between 2 percent and 2.75 percent in the illustration provided), depends in part on the negotiation skills of the parties. Where there is no overlap of the parties' resistance points, as in Figure 8-5(B), there is no contract zone. Even if the union lowers its demands to its bottom line or resistance point, it is still demanding more than the employer is willing to pay. There cannot be an agreement unless one or both of the parties changes their resistance point.

Strategy In distributive bargaining, each side will attempt to find out what the other side's resistance point is so that it can push for a settlement as close as possible to it. In the previous example, the employer would like to find out that the union is prepared to settle for as low as a 2 percent wage increase. Conversely, each side will hide its resistance point from the other. The union in the illustration is not going to announce that it would go as low as 2 percent, because that is all it would likely obtain. Each side will attempt to convince the other that its resistance point is higher or lower than it actually is. This approach, used by both parties, may also be referred to as a "reveal and conceal" strategy.

Each side would like to influence the other side's resistance point. In the case of wages, the union would like to see the employer raise its resistance point and the employer would like to see the union lower its resistance point. A party's resistance point is based on the benefits and costs associated with it. For example, a union may initially think that a wage increase of 2 percent can be obtained without a strike. If it finds otherwise, the costs associated with the resistance point have increased and the union may revise the point downward to where an agreement can be achieved without the cost of a strike. Conversely, an employer's resistance point may initially be based on the presumption that an agreement can be achieved without a strike or lockout. If it is determined that the resistance point will involve a costly strike or lockout, the employer may revise it upwards.

Although explicitly threatening a strike or lockout early in negotiations is not acceptable, each side in negotiations may have to convince the other that it is willing to strike or lock out to achieve its objectives. There may be a strange paradox here for some employees. Although most employees may not want to go on strike, they may have to vote for a strike so that the union appears to have the support of employees and an agreement can be reached.

Opening Positions Both parties will begin negotiations with certain positions, demands or offers, on various items. Over the course of negotiations, some or all of these positions are going to have to be changed to reach an agreement. All positions or demands made are not of equal importance to the negotiating team presenting the particular issue at the bargaining table. Each party goes into negotiations knowing that some demands it makes may have to be significantly reduced, or dropped entirely, in order to obtain concessions from the other side. For example, a union might make a demand for a new benefit such as a prepaid legal plan knowing that it is willing to drop the demand later in exchange for a concession from the employer.

The opening positions in negotiations are significant. There is research that shows that commercial negotiators who make more extreme opening offers achieve better results.[10] This may be because the offer causes the other side to rethink its position and there is more room for concessions. In commercial negotiations, the negotiator who makes an extreme opening offer is taking a risk that the other side will reject the offer, and not make any further attempts to negotiate. In labour negotiations, it is not possible for a party receiving an extreme offer to break off negotiations, because the duty to bargain in good faith requires each side to at least explain and discuss proposals. However, a union or employer concerned with public support, for example a teachers' union or a school board, may want to avoid extreme offers that will cause the public to support the other side.

In the past, some employers have thought that they could avoid the haggling involved in negotiations by making their best offer first, in other words making a "take it or leave it" first offer. This approach, known as *Boulwarism*, is not advisable today. An employer who adopted this strategy would have several problems. The belief that the employer will eventually improve on its first offer is entrenched. An employer must allow room to improve an offer later in negotiations. An employer who adopted Boulwarism would likely have to deal at a Labour Relations Board with complaints that it had failed to bargain in good faith. This approach could also harm the relationship between union and management representatives.

Concessions　When a first offer and demands are exchanged, a bargaining range is established. Subsequently there will be numerous concessions and counteroffers. A party who receives an offer may take the position that it will not respond with a counterproposal until the other side makes an improved or more reasonable offer.

The size and pattern of concessions that are made can send a significant message. If concessions are made in successively smaller increments, whether they relate to one issue or cover a package of issues, a message is sent to the other party. If an employer makes an initial offer of a 1 percent wage increase, and subsequently follows this with three successive increases, each of which is 1 percent more, the employer's offer has been increased to 4 percent. However, the union may think that if it delays, it can obtain a further increase. However, if the employer made three successive increases, to 3 percent, then to 3.75 percent, and then to 4 percent, the offer still ends up as 4 percent, but a message has been conveyed that there is no further room for concessions.

Negotiators may not draw attention to concessions they are making. One study that examined the language in contract negotiations found that concessions were made quietly without drawing attention. Concessions may be made by shifting positions from one meeting to the next instead of formally backing down in a negotiation session. Saying something like "We will get back to you" may be a way to signal that a party is willing to make a move at the next meeting.[11]

Hardball tactics　Some negotiators may attempt to use an array of tactics to convince the other side to agree to their terms. Some possible tactics are mentioned here, although they are not recommended. The tactics referred to here are outlined in Lewicki, Litterer, Minton, and Saunders's *Essentials of Negotiation*, cited earlier.[12] Readers wishing further information should refer to a reference on negotiation. Some negotiators may engage in a "good cop/bad cop" routine. As the name suggests, this tactic involves one negotiator playing the role of the bad cop making threats and offering poor terms, and the other negotiator playing the role of the good cop, attempting to reach an agreement. In labour negotiations, this might involve negotiators taking on the role of the good cops and blaming the tough position being taken on people who are higher in the organization who are not at the bargaining table. Another tactic is the "highball or lowball." This involves making an opening offer that is deliberately high or low. It is used to try to convince the other side that they need to revaluate their position. An example in labour negotiations would be an employer making an initial monetary offer that provided for wage concessions or a wage freeze. The tactic involves pretending that an issue of little importance is significant so that it can subsequently be given up to obtain a concession from the other side. The "nibble" approach involves asking for a small concession on an item that has not previously been discussed in order to finalize the agreement. In labour negotiations, an example would be asking for additional vacation at the last minute when vacations had not previously been discussed. This tactic may violate the duty to bargain in good faith. "Playing chicken" refers to threatening the other side to force them to agree on terms that are favourable to the party making the threat. An example would be management advising the union that if its offer is not accepted the employer will shut down operations.

Finally, some negotiators may engage in intimidation and aggressive behaviour such as staged temper tantrums, or attacks on the competence or integrity of the other team.

Bargaining Power

The bargaining power of the union and the employer are important factors that influence the outcome of distributive bargaining. A party with more bargaining power should be able to obtain an agreement that is more favourable. The bargaining power of the union and the employer will be affected by external economic, social, and legal factors and internal factors including the commitment of employees to the demands of the union.

Figure 8-6 lists factors that affect the employer's bargaining power:

■ An employer able to build up sufficient inventory of materials or products for sale at a later date is in a stronger bargaining position because it will be able to withstand a strike. A mining company able to stockpile nickel would be in a stronger bargaining position than one that has to meet just-in-time delivery dates. Companies that supply services that cannot be stockpiled or prepared in advance would be in a weaker position.

■ If the output of the bargaining unit is required by other business units of the employer, a strike will have a greater impact and the employer is in a weaker bargaining position. Conversely, if the bargaining unit is an independent operation and other units can replace its output, the employer is in a stronger bargaining position. In the meatpacking industry, employers who can replace the output of one operating unit with that of another have more bargaining power.

■ The competitive position of the employer refers to the possible loss of customers during a strike and their subsequent recovery. If customers lost during a strike will likely return after the strike ends, the employer is in a stronger bargaining position. The economic environment may also be a factor. If employees are able to find alternative jobs elsewhere if customers do not return to the employer after a strike and jobs are lost, the employer is in a weaker position.

■ The time of bargaining in a seasonal business can affect the employer's bargaining power. A construction employer would be in a weaker bargaining position in the peak season.

■ The ability of the employer to use replacement workers during a strike is a critical factor affecting the employer's bargaining power. This will be determined by the size of the employer's operations, the technology used, and legislation. In some cases, the bargaining unit is so large that it is not practical for the employer to use replacement workers. It would not be practical to replace 2000 workers in an auto plant. Where the technology allows a few supervisors to continue operations, such as in a refinery, the employer is in a stronger bargaining position. Legislation in British Columbia and Quebec prohibits the use of replacement workers during a strike. In the federal jurisdiction, there is a qualified restriction on the use of replacement workers. In all other jurisdictions, employers are allowed to use replacement workers during a strike. The prohibition against the use of replacement workers is a controversial issue, which is referred to in Labour Relations Issue 8-1. In most jurisdictions when the strike ends, the employer is required to reinstate employees who have been on strike.

1. Inventory levels
2. Interdependence of bargaining unit
3. Competitive position of employer
4. Time of negotiations
5. Ability to continue operations
6. Bargaining structure
7. Public opinion

Figure 8-6 Factors Affecting the Employer's Bargaining Power

Should Labour Relations Legislation Prohibit the Use of Replacement Workers During a Strike?

This question obviously has produced different answers from unions and employers. Unions support a general prohibition on the use of replacement workers during a strike. They argue that allowing the use of replacement workers gives employers an unfair advantage in bargaining. Unions also contend that the use of replacement workers leads to prolonged and bitter strikes, and picket-line confrontations and violence. A bomb explosion at the Yellowknife mine in 1992 during a strike where replacement workers were used caused the death of nine workers. Opponents of legislation prohibiting the use of replacement workers contend that the legislation increases unemployment and leads to an imbalance in bargaining power.

Would you support legislation that prohibited the use of replacement workers during a legal strike?

- The bargaining structure, referred to earlier in this chapter, might also affect employers' bargaining power. An employer who operates a chain of Tim Hortons outlets is in a stronger bargaining position when it negotiates with each outlet separately.

- Public opinion might affect the bargaining power of the employer. If the public supports employees on strike and does not deal with the employer, the employer may be forced to reconsider its position. Public opinion is especially important in parts of the public sector where voters may not re-elect political representatives, such as school board trustees.

Figure 8-7 lists factors affecting the bargaining power of the union:

- The key factor determining the bargaining power of the union is whether bargaining unit members are sufficiently committed to go on strike if negotiations on key issues are not achieved. If employees refuse to support a strike, the union's bargaining power is drastically reduced. All jurisdictions provide that a strike vote must be held. In addition, employers in some jurisdictions have another opportunity to test the support of employees for the union. In Alberta, British Columbia, New Brunswick, and Ontario, labour relations legislation provides for the employer to have a vote by employees on the employer's final offer. A slightly different policy option is illustrated in Saskatchewan where the employer may request the appointment of a special mediator who may recommend a vote. The **final offer vote** can be held only once in a round of negotiations. If a majority of the employees who vote support acceptance of the employer's offer, that offer becomes the basis for a collective agreement, and any strike in effect must cease. An employer who thinks employees will accept a proposal the union has refused might use this provision, but it should think about the consequences of losing a final offer

A **final offer vote** is a vote by employees on an offer made by the employer.

1. Support of bargaining unit members
2. Size of strike fund
3. Timing of a strike
4. Effectiveness of a strike
5. Effect of picketing
6. Labour cost/total cost
7. Elasticity of demand for product or service provided by employer
8. Public opinion

Figure 8-7 Factors Affecting the Union's Bargaining Power

vote before taking this step. If the employer loses the vote, it will have to restart negotiations and will likely have to improve its offer to obtain agreement.

- The larger the union strike fund, the more bargaining power the union has.
- If the timing of the strike will cause harm to the employer, the union is in a stronger bargaining position. A strike at a banquet hall during the holiday season could seriously affect the employer.
- If the strike will force the employer to shut down operations, the union has more bargaining power.
- If picketing causes customers and suppliers to avoid the employer, the union is in a stronger bargaining position.
- Where the labour costs being negotiated are a smaller part of the employer's total cost, the union is in a stronger position.
- The price elasticity of demand for the employer's product or service was referred to in Chapter 2. This concept refers to the price-responsiveness of the demand for the product or service provided by the employer. If the demand is less price-responsive (inelastic), the union is in a stronger bargaining position, because the employer has the ability to increase prices without losing as many customers.
- Public opinion may affect the union's bargaining power. Unions have sometimes sought the help of churches and other community organizations to rally public support against the employer.

Conciliation and Mediation

If the parties are not able to reach a collective agreement, they may seek the assistance of a government-appointed conciliator or mediator. In most jurisdictions, conciliation or mediation is required before a strike or lockout is legal. The conciliation and mediation process is discussed in the Chapter 10, which deals with strikes and dispute resolution.

Memorandum of Settlement and Ratification

If the union and the employer reach an agreement, it will typically be documented in a Memorandum of Settlement, illustrated in Figure 8-8.

This memorandum sets out the terms agreed upon and provides for the tentative agreement to be ratified by members of the bargaining unit and the employer. The employer may be particularly interested in having the memorandum of settlement require the parties to use their best efforts to ensure that the agreement is ratified. Unless the memorandum of settlement provides that the union is to use its best efforts to obtain ratification, it is not required to do so. In one case where the memorandum required the union to use its best efforts to obtain ratification and the union executive committee campaigned against the agreement, the employer pursued a complaint against the union for failing to bargain in good faith and obtained an order directing a second ratification vote.[13] The Memorandum in Figure 8-8 refers to a situation in which the parties have negotiated a contract renewal. If the agreement was a first contract, it would set out all of the contract terms instead of referring to changes in the previous agreement. A **ratification vote**, a vote in which employees in the bargaining unit approve or reject a negotiated agreement, is required by legislation in British Columbia, Manitoba, Ontario, and Quebec. In other jurisdictions, ratification votes are normally conducted, and may be required by the union constitution. In the provinces requiring a ratification vote, except Quebec, the legislation provides that it must be conducted by secret ballot and that all employees in the bargaining unit, including those who are not union members, are entitled to vote. If the employees reject the agreement, the union and management bargaining teams will have to resume negotiations.

A **ratification vote** is one in which employees approve or reject an agreement that has been negotiated.

Memorandum of Settlement Between _____ **(the "Employer") and**
_____ **(the "Union")**

The Union and Employer representatives agree, subject to ratification, that the previous collective agreement [which expired on or expires on _____] shall be continued subject to the following amendments:

1. The term of the agreement shall be from _____ to _____.

2. The wages shall be as provided in Schedule A.

3. The Benefit shall be as provided in Schedule B.

4. Other terms of the collective agreement shall be amended as provided in Schedule C.

[_Examples:_ Article 8.1 shall be amended to provide for 35 weeks of maternity leave.

Article 10 shall be amended by adding the following: All employees who are members of the bargaining unit shall, as a condition of employment, become union members not later than 30 calendar days after the start of employment.]

5. The parties agree to use their best efforts to ensure that their principals will ratify this memorandum of settlement.

Dated the _____ day of _____, 20xx

For the Employer: For the Union:

_____   _____

Figure 8-8 Memorandum of Settlement

INTEREST-BASED OR MUTUAL GAINS BARGAINING

Traditional distributive bargaining has been criticized for a number of reasons. The process can be time-consuming and costly. It may result in the perception that there has been a winner and a loser. It may harm the relationship between union and management representatives, with negative consequences for future negotiations and the administration of the agreement. For example, a union might refuse to participate in workplace committees or might file more grievances. Such bargaining may also produce results that are less than optimal if the parties resort to compromise instead of engaging in problem solving. Recall the example of the two siblings with one orange earlier in this chapter; if a positional bargaining approach had been used, they likely would have each ended up with half of the orange.

Interest-based bargaining is an approach to negotiations in which the parties use problem solving and attempt to find a settlement that produces gains for both. It may be referred to as _mutual gains bargaining_ or _principled negotiation_, and is based upon the principles outlined by Roger Fisher, William Ury, and Bruce Patton in _Getting to Yes: Negotiating Agreements Without Giving In._[14] The book is not limited to labour negotiations; it provides principles and tips that can be used in any conflict situation, including domestic relations, and it is recommended to the general reader. We will now review the principles of interest-based bargaining, consider an illustration of it, and refer to the adoption of this approach to union–management relations.

> **Interest-based bargaining** is an approach to negotiations in which the parties use problem solving and attempt to find a settlement that produces gains for both.

Principles for Interest-Based Bargaining from _Getting to Yes_

Interest-based bargaining does not mean being soft; it is based on the four principles discussed below.

Separate the People from the Problem   This point emphasizes that negotiators are people who have emotions, values, and needs. In most negotiations there is an issue of substance in dispute and a relationship to be concerned with. The best illustration of this may come from outside of the area of labour relations. Spouses who are dealing with the question of where to go on a vacation have to be concerned with both their destination and what the discussion does to their relationship. The people or relationship problem is important in most negotiations, and it is especially important in labour negotiations where the parties will have to deal with each other after negotiations have been completed. The other side's ego and feelings must be taken into consideration. As the statement of the principle suggests, the problem should be the focus of attention, not the attitudes or behaviours of the people we are dealing with. To separate the people from the problem, negotiators should avoid placing blame and thinking the worst of the other side. Management should not attack the union because there are attendance, productivity, or quality issues. These items should be viewed as problems the parties have to address together. Union leaders should think in terms of the issues and not assume that management is "out to get them." *Getting to Yes* outlines tactics to pursue the problem, such as having individuals sit on the same side of a table focusing on an issue on a board in front of them.

Focus on Interests, Not Positions   The difference between interests and positions was previously referred to when the distinction between distributive and integrative bargaining was made. This is a critical distinction.

Interests can include needs, desires, concerns, and fears. Interests are the reasons behind demands or positions. A demand or a position will set out a specific solution to an issue instead of leaving the door open to different solutions. It is clear that the parties will have some interests that are different. In fact, agreement is only possible because the parties have different interests. One party may want the orange; the other may want the peel. Asking critical questions such as "Why?" or "Why not?" can identify interests. Interests will also be identified if one of the parties takes the lead and talks about its own interests.

Invent Options for Mutual Gain   This principle is founded on the basic concept that there is often more than one solution to a problem. Steps must be taken to generate alternative solutions and to avoid starting the evaluation or judgment of alternatives too early. Fisher, Ury, and Patton mention various tactics to develop options, such as designating a minimum specified time for the generation of solutions and brainstorming techniques.

Insist on Using Objective Criteria   The fourth principle is that the parties should base their choice or agreement on some objective criteria. They should avoid having one party impose their will or falling back upon a compromise. In *Getting to Yes*, a dispute between a builder and a customer over the depth of a foundation is referred to. If the builder said it was using a two-foot foundation and the customer wanted a six-foot foundation, the parties should not split the difference. They should refer to the objective criteria that establish what is required for the building.

In order to proceed with mutual gains or interest-based bargaining, the parties will take four steps, incorporating the principles noted: (1) identify the issues, (2) explore and clarify interests, (3) generate alternative solutions, and (4) evaluate the solutions and determine agreement.

Interest-Based Bargaining: An Illustration

The following situation illustrates mutual gains or interest-based bargaining and how it is different from the traditional, adversarial approach. It is based upon an example provided in *Beyond the Walls of Conflict: Mutual Gains Negotiating for Unions and Management*.[15]

Suppose that a collective agreement between an employer and a union provides that jobs are awarded to employees with the most seniority who have sufficient ability. However, the agreement also provides that in the event that a new job is created, the employer can fill it by holding an open competition among employees. The employer wants to introduce new technology that requires employees to have exceptional spatial reasoning and visual acuity. The employer views this as a new job and claims that it can conduct an open competition. The union views the job as a modification of a current job and claims that the job should be filled on the basis of seniority. If the parties followed a traditional, positional approach, it is likely that a grievance would be filed, and an arbitrator would determine whether the job was new. Either the employer or the union would win, and the other would lose. If the parties adopted an interest-based approach, they would proceed differently. They would view this situation as a problem to be solved. They would consider their interests instead of positions. The interests the parties might identify would include increasing efficiency and quality, providing higher-paying jobs, and increasing the challenge and satisfaction involved in jobs. The parties would explore or invent options that might include eliminating the seniority provisions for the job in question, providing training for the job, and testing for job candidates. An interest-based solution might involve the following:

- Allowing all interested employees to apply
- Offering training to employees on the basis of seniority
- Testing candidates after completion of the training
- Providing jobs to employees who successfully complete the training.

Both parties gain using this approach. The employer has ensured that employees doing the work have the skills required; the union has been able to protect the interests of employees with more seniority, and has obtained access to training that might not have otherwise been provided.

Adoption of Interest-Based Bargaining

Interest-based bargaining has some proponents who think it is the key to labour peace, employment stability, and other benefits.[16] There are others who view it as simply a reaffirmation of sound bargaining practices; in their opinion, good negotiators have always sought creative solutions to mutual problems and interest-based bargaining is not new.[17] In any case, the employer and the union should engage in joint training before proceeding with interest-based bargaining. The parties could also use a facilitator to guide them in the process. Readers interested in pursuing a mutual gains approach could refer to *In Search of the Eighteenth Camel: Discovering a Mutual Gains Oasis for Unions and Management*.[18]

Some unions and employers have used interest-based bargaining for as many issues as possible, and reverted to traditional positional bargaining on monetary issues. In the United States, a national survey revealed that one-third of management negotiators and one-half of union negotiators reported using interest-based bargaining.[19]

Some unions are suspicious that interest-based bargaining is a device that employers will use to obtain concessions from the union. There may have to be a significant shift in attitudes by Canadian unions and employers before it is widely adopted. The possibility of its further use will be considered again in the final chapter, when we return to the question of the extent to which employers and unions can develop a more cooperative relationship.

Implications for Practice

1. Bargaining structure is a significant variable affecting negotiations. Employers can join associations to bargain as a group and avoid whipsawing by unions. Unions that are involved in centralized bargaining will have to ensure that the interests of all employees are being addressed.

2. The relationship between the employer and the union can affect negotiations. The parties may wish to improve their relationship to facilitate contract negotiations and the administration of the agreement.

3. Union and employer negotiators need to be concerned with the relationship between themselves and their constituents. Union representatives should take steps to ensure that bargaining unit members perceive that the bargaining team has achieved the best deal possible.

4. Unions and employers must ensure that they comply with the legislative obligation to bargain in good faith. Senior management must ensure that the employer bargaining team is provided with the information that it requires.

5. Unions and employers could consider interest-based bargaining as an alternative to traditional adversarial bargaining. To use interest-based bargaining, the parties must invest time and money in training.

Key Terms

attitudinal structuring, p. 187

bargaining structure, p. 184

caucuses, p. 192

centralized bargaining, p. 185

decentralized bargaining, p. 185

distributive bargaining, p. 186

duty to bargain in good faith, p. 193

final offer vote, p. 201

first contract arbitration, p. 196

hard bargaining, p. 194

industry bargaining, p. 185

initial position, p. 197

interest-based bargaining, p. 203

integrative bargaining, p. 187

intraorganizational bargaining, p. 188

monetary issues, p. 193

non-monetary issues, p. 193

pattern bargaining, p. 186

ratification vote, p. 202

resistance point, p. 196

statutory freeze, p. 190

surface bargaining, p. 194

target point, p. 197

whipsawing, p. 185

Review Questions

1. What are the distinctive features of labour negotiations?

2. What is bargaining structure, and how can it affect negotiation?

3. Why is most contract negotiation in Canada decentralized?

4. What is the meaning and significance of each of the following: integrative bargaining, distributive bargaining, attitudinal structuring, and intraorganizational bargaining?

5. What are the factors affecting the union–management relationship?

6. Outline the possible composition of a bargaining team representing the employer and the union.

7. Identify the procedures the union and the employer will likely follow in the course of preparing for negotiations.

8. What are the possible stages of negotiation, and why are they important?

9. Briefly describe four employer or union actions that would be a breach of the duty to bargain in good faith.

10. Explain the significance of the pattern of concession-making in negotiations.

11. Describe hardball tactics that a party could use in negotiations.

12. Identify the principles for interest-based bargaining.

Discussion Questions

1. What is the significance of the union–management relationship for negotiations?

2. Why should a negotiating party not lead with its best possible offer?

3. Why is it important that labour relations legislation provide for a duty to bargain in good faith?

4. What is the significance of first contract arbitration, and why do you think some jurisdictions have not made provision for first contract arbitration in labour relations legislation?

5. Two months prior to the expiry of the current collective agreement, a union gave the employer notice to bargain. The parties could not agree on any meetings dates for negotiation, and the employer sent a note directly to employees that it was not able to negotiate because it had encountered a "major financial problem."
   (a) How can the union proceed?
   (b) Explain the outcome you expect.

6. For the issue of wages, give an example of the union and employer resistance points, target points and initial offers, where there is a contract or settlement zone.

7. Which of the following statements are interests, and which are demands or positions?
   (a) We need to reduce our costs by 5 percent by contracting out the work of Department A.
   (b) We are concerned about the effects of the new machinery on our employees.
   (c) We need a wage freeze to remain competitive.
   (d) Our concern is for the job security of our members.
   (e) We need flexibility to meet family responsibilities.
   (f) We need flextime to meet family responsibilities.

8. Consider a disagreement or dispute you have had with someone at home, school, or the workplace. How would you resolve it using distributive bargaining, and how would you resolve the dispute using integrative bargaining?

9. Why might an employer be opposed to the introduction of interest-based bargaining?

Web Research

The question of whether legislation should prevent the use of replacement workers during a strike is controversial. Unions refer to this as "anti-scab" legislation. Contrast the views of the Canadian Labour Congress (**www.canadianlabour.ca/home**) and unions to the Fraser Institute (**www.fraserinstitute.ca**) on this issue.

CASE INCIDENT   KELOWNA RETREAT

The Hotel Workers Union was certified in 1995 as the bargaining agent for employees at the Kelowna Retreat. Over the years, the union and the employer were able to negotiate a series of collective agreements without any strikes or lockouts. The most recent agreement expired on April 1, 2010. Prior to the expiry of the last contract, the parties had several negotiation meetings; however, they were not able to reach an agreement on several key issues including wages, sick leave, and a uniform allowance. At a bargaining session on March 15, the employer bargaining team advised the union that it was not able to make any further concessions and any agreement had to be based upon the employer's proposals on the outstanding issues including wages and uniforms. The union indicated that it was not willing to agree to the employer's terms and doubted if there was any point to further talks. The union also stated that in view of the employer's position it would be conducting a strike vote. The employer sent a letter to the union setting out the terms of the proposal outlined in the meeting on March 15 and offered to meet again; however, it reiterated that the employer was not able to make any further concessions. On March 18, the union held a meeting with employees to update them on negotiations. The union advised employees that talks had broken off and provided them with a written summary of the union and employer positions. The written material from the union indicated that the employer was proposing to delete the existing uniform allowance and replace it with a 65 percent increase in pay. The employer had actually proposed that the uniform allowance be replaced with a .65 percent increase in pay. The union also indicated that it would be seeking a strike vote and approval for a strike from the national union.

On March 19, the employer provided employees a memo with their paycheques that set out the employer's position. The memo included the following:

> We want all staff to know what the employer has proposed to your union on the remaining issues. This is a summary of our offer to settle the contract, which was discussed with the union on March 15. You can also obtain additional information about this offer from the union. Management is asking for deletion of the current uniform allowance, reduction of sick leave from 12 days to 8 days per year, an amendment to vacation paycheques to comply with employment standards legislation, and a three-year contract. Management is offering to add the value of the uniform allowance (.65 percent) to pay rates (a permanent increase, not one-time money), a 14.65 percent wage increase over three years, and to pay sick leave from day one if an employee is hospitalized. We have offered to continue meeting with the union but no further dates have been agreed to by the union at this time.

After the memo was issued, employees approached the union with questions. Employees asked why the memo had come from the employer instead of the union. There were also questions about the wage increase and uniform policy. The union sent a letter to the employer claiming that the employer had violated the provisions of labour relations legislation, which provided as follows:

> It shall be an unfair labour practice for an employer to, in any manner including by communication, interfere with, restrain intimidate, threaten or coerce an employee in the exercise of any right conferred by this Act to fail or refuse to bargain collectively with [union] representatives. . . .

The union responded to the employer's memo in a letter that stated the employer's claim that the wage increase was 14.65 percent misled employees because the .65 percent component of the wage increase was replacing the uniform allowance and was not actually an increase. Furthermore, the union argued that the .65 percent wage increase could not be viewed as a simple substitution for the uniform allowance, because under the previous agreement all employees received the same uniform allowance, and the employer's proposal based on wages would lead to employees receiving different amounts. When the employer did not reply, the union filed a complaint with the Labour Relations Board alleging that the employer's memo was an unfair labour practice.

Questions

1. In your opinion, is the management team for Kelowna Retreat engaged in hardball tactics as discussed in this chapter? Use an example to support your viewpoint.

2. Do you believe an unfair labour practice complaint by the union would be upheld before the Labour Relations Board? Explain.

CASE INCIDENT   PLAZA FIBERGLAS

Plaza Fiberglas is an auto parts manufacturer situated in Moncton, New Brunswick. The United Steelworkers of America was certified to represent Plaza's production employees, and a first contract was negotiated between the union and the employer. Prior to the expiry of this first agreement, the union and Plaza began negotiations for the renewal of the collective agreement. A bargaining team composed of the employer's solicitor, accountant, and personnel director represented the employer.

The sole owner and general manager of Plaza Fiberglas was Emily Jones, who maintained close control over all aspects of the company's operations. Jones selected the bargaining team and instructed it not to make any concessions before consulting with her. The negotiations between the parties did not produce an agreement. The parties could not agree on wages, rules, seniority, or the provision of names and addresses to the union.

The employer wanted the agreement to be amended to provide that a violation of any company rules would be sufficient reason for discharge. The union objected to this provision because it might prevent an arbitrator from reinstating an employee. With respect to seniority, the expiring agreement provided for seniority on a company-wide basis. The employer proposed that this be changed to a departmental basis. The company rejected a union proposal that the contract require the employer to provide an updated list of employee names and addresses twice a year.

The company moved moulds that were used in the production process to another location outside of the municipality to which the union's certification referred. Subsequently the company approached some employees and offered them higher wages to work at the new location. To avoid a problem if the company moved, the union had proposed in a previous negotiation session that the recognition clause in the agreement be amended so that any move or relocation within 80 kilometres of the existing plant would be covered. This proposal was eventually withdrawn on the basis of assurances from the employer's bargaining team that the company would not be relocating its operations.

It was later determined that the decision to move the moulds had been made previously by Jones; however, she had not told the bargaining team about this decision.

Questions

1. Is there any basis for the union to file a complaint with the Labour Relations Board? Refer specifically to each of the items referred to: rules, seniority, wages, addresses of employees, and the hiring of employees to work at the new location.

2. What remedies could the Board order for any violations of labour relations legislation by the employer?

Chapter 9

Administration of the Collective Agreement

Chapter Objectives

1. Explain the significance and functions of the grievance and arbitration process
2. Outline the formal and informal steps of the grievance procedure
3. Outline the procedural and legal aspects of the arbitration process
4. Identify possible limitations on the exercise of management rights
5. Describe the disciplinary measures that are available to the employer
6. Apply discipline in compliance with the collective agreement and the law
7. Explain how seniority might affect the placement, layoff, and recall of employees
8. Discuss the implications of human rights legislation for the administration of the collective agreement
9. Describe the union's duty of fair representation and indicate how the employer could be affected
10. State problems with grievance arbitration and identify alternatives

Required Professional Capabilities (CCHRA)	HRPA Human Resources Professionals Competency Framework
10101, 10102, 10301, 10503, 20105, 20106, 20107, 20204, 50113, 50404, 50411	C113, C116, C117, C117, C118, C119, C120, C121, C122, C123, C124, C125, C126, C127, C128, C129, C130, C131, C132

A collective agreement establishes the terms and conditions of work for members of a bargaining unit. It acknowledges certain management rights in directing employees and provides protection to union members against abuses of this authority through a grievance and arbitration process. Unionized workers are also protected against harassment by supervisors, peers, and customers in the work setting.

Harassment cases frequently involve unwanted and repeated verbal remarks on the part of another person to the victim. However, human rights investigators and arbitrators also consider a perpetrator's conduct as a source of harassment against another individual. Such a complaint was dealt with by the United Food and Commercial Workers (UFCW) union at a meatpacking plant.

A fellow union member used a hammer to unnecessarily pound on a steel tank for up to two hours whenever a particular employee entered the work area. The loud noise not only affected the person targeted for this form of harassment, but also caused fellow employees to not effectively carry out their duties.

The employer terminated the worker who repeatedly hammered the tank. The UFCW filed a grievance against this level of discipline. The arbitrator dismissed the grievance and upheld the termination of this employee. A key reason for this arbitration decision was that the grievor already had a disciplinary record resulting from a lack of cooperation with other employees and management. This same individual had also been previously suspended from work for three months following the physical assault of the same co-worker who was now harassed by this employee's repeated hammering on the empty tank.

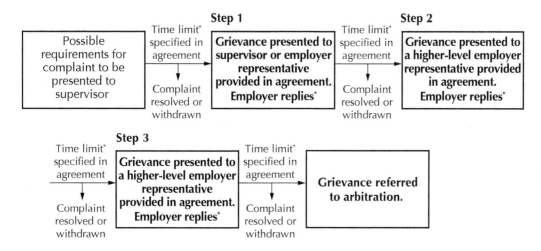

*The collective agreement provides a time limit for each step in the grievance process and replies from the employer.

Figure 9-1 Grievance Procedure

This chapter will consider the nature and significance of the grievance procedure, the application of the arbitration process to some key issues including discipline and seniority, and alternatives to arbitration. The details of the grievance procedure, including the number of steps and time limits, are set out in the collective agreement. Figure 9-1 summarizes a grievance procedure that has three steps. Some have four or more steps.

The grievance and arbitration process, not the court system, must be used to resolve disputes between the management and union parties that flow from the collective agreement. In the leading case on this issue, a unionized employee tried to sue his employer who had investigated him using the services of a private investigator. The Supreme Court of Canada confirmed that a court action was not permissible because the dispute arose from a collective agreement and it should have been dealt through the grievance and arbitration process.[1] Labour Relations Issue 9-1 illustrates that this requirement applies to both employers and employees.

Labour Relations Issue 9-1

Can Unionized Employees and Employers Sue?

Haynes was a school teacher employed by the Vancouver School Board. Teachers are covered by a collective agreement between the Board and the British Columbia Teachers Federation. After a complaint against Haynes, she was eventually examined by a psychiatrist who concluded that she was unemployable. Haynes went on a medical leave; however, her benefits were terminated because she refused psychiatric treatment. Haynes commenced a legal action against the Board, claiming she was the victim of false and misleading statements and asserting that the Board did not have the right to require her to undergo psychiatric assessment as a condition of employment.

The employer raised the defence that the court did not have jurisdiction (authority) to hear the matter because it was a dispute that arose from the collective agreement and therefore any claim had to be made through the grievance and arbitration process, not through the courts. The court agreed with the employer, and the court action was dismissed.

In another case, Bowie, an ambulance driver covered by a collective agreement between OPSEU and the Province of Ontario, was involved in an accident that caused damage to the vehicle. The employer, thinking the damage was either deliberate or caused by negligence, sued the employee, claiming compensation for the damage. The suit was dismissed; the court held that the employer should have used the grievance procedure in the collective agreement to make the claim.

These cases illustrate the principle that if a dispute between the parties arises from the collective agreement, it must be resolved through the grievance and arbitration process, not in the courts. This includes any claims made by the employer against the union or employees.

The law does not provide that all disputes between an employee and the employer must go through the grievance and arbitration process. If the dispute does not arise from the collective agreement, it is possible to sue. In another case, an employer accused an employee of theft and pursued a complaint with the police. Subsequently the criminal charges were withdrawn and the employee sued the employer for malicious prosecution. The employer responded that the employee's court action could not proceed because the employee should have filed a grievance. The court rejected this argument, and said that because the dispute did not arise from the collective agreement a court action was permissible.

In some cases it may not be clear whether a claim should be made through the grievance and arbitration process or the courts, and legal advice should be obtained.

SIGNIFICANCE OF THE GRIEVANCE AND ARBITRATION PROCESS

The grievance procedure has been referred to by some as the heart of the collective agreement.[2] The procedure serves several functions, and has potential benefits for employers, unions, and employees that are summarized in Figure 9-2.

Functions of Grievances and Arbitration

Dispute Settlement   A dispute settlement mechanism is necessary because there are many potential sources of conflict between the parties during the term of the collective agreement. It is likely that there will be disagreements regarding the meaning of contract terms. The parties may not anticipate that a term in the agreement might be ambiguous and they may fail to clearly define it. Contract language may be left vague when it is negotiated because the parties cannot agree on more specific terms.

Functions

1. Provides a dispute settlement mechanism
2. Ensures compliance with the collective agreement
3. Provides a forum for additional bargaining during the term of the collective agreement

Benefits to the Employer, Union, and Employees

1. Settles disputes without interruption of work
2. Settles disputes prior to next round of negotiations

Benefits to Management

1. Provides a communication or consultation mechanism
2. Establishes a check on the quality and consistency of management decisions
3. Provides a voice mechanism that reduces turnover

Benefits to Unions and Union Officials

1. Provides a potential pressure tactic
2. Provides a method to oppose or resist management directives
3. Increases union solidarity
4. Provides political benefits to union leaders

Benefits to Employees

1. Provides a review of workplace decisions by outside party
2. Increases job security

Figure 9-2 Grievance and Arbitration Process: Functions and Benefits

For example, the collective agreement might refer to certain benefits being paid to employees who are hospitalized, without clarifying what the term "hospitalized" means. If an employee received treatment as an outpatient and did not remain in hospital overnight, there might be a dispute about whether the employee was hospitalized. The grievance procedure will provide a mechanism to resolve the meaning of the term and the rights of the employee. The procedure also provides a mechanism to resolve disputes flowing from management decisions made pursuant to the terms of the agreement, which typically gives management the right to discipline and discharge for just cause and determine whether an employee has sufficient ability for a job. It is likely that employees or the union will disagree with some of these decisions. Grievances dealing with discipline, discharge, and seniority are considered later in this chapter. There might be disputes because collective agreement terms appear to be in conflict with each other. The management rights article might appear to allow the employer to install new equipment, but another article dealing with technological change might appear to prohibit such a change.

Canadian labour relations legislation prohibits strikes and lockouts during the term of a collective agreement and complements this with a requirement that disputes relating to the administration of the agreement must be referred to arbitration. This is summarized in the **obey now, grieve later** rule, which means that unless the disputed management directive is illegal or would entail a safety risk, the employee must follow it even if it appears to violate the collective agreement, and pursue a grievance later.

Obey now, grieve later is a rule that summarizes the requirement that employees must obey management instructions and file a grievance at a later time.

Enforcement of the Collective Agreement   The grievance and arbitration process can be used to enforce the collective agreement and remedy any breaches. If an employee was not assigned overtime that he or she was entitled to, the grievance process provides a way to recover the wages lost. If a grievance was filed and the matter was not settled, an arbitrator can order the employer to pay the compensation owing.

Additional Bargaining During the Term of the Agreement   The grievance process may provide a forum for additional bargaining between the parties during the term of the agreement. The agreement may specify general terms relating to work conditions that need to be clarified or expanded upon. For example, if it provided for a workload formula for teachers, there might be a dispute about the application of the formula in a particular case. A settlement of the grievance might include an elaboration on the terms of the collective agreement. These settlements might be incorporated into the collective agreement in subsequent contract negotiations.

Benefits of Grievances and Arbitration

The grievance process has potential benefits for the union, the employer, and employees.

Benefits Common to All the Parties   All parties will benefit if disputes are resolved without a stoppage of work. Employers will not lose production and employees will not lose compensation. Settling disputes during the term of the agreement instead of allowing them to build up until the next contract negotiations may help the parties improve their relationship and make contract negotiations easier.

Benefits to Management   The process could be used as a communication or consultation mechanism through which management may learn of possible problems and take corrective action. The procedure may also improve the quality and consistency of decision making by managers, because they know that employees may turn to the grievance process if decisions are not made fairly and consistently with the collective agreement. It has been suggested that employees who are dissatisfied have two primary methods to deal with their situation: exit or voice.[3] This means that dissatisfied employees can either leave the employer or stay and attempt to resolve problems. It has been argued that unions give employees a voice, and the grievance procedure is one way this voice is exercised. Unionized firms have lower turnover rates, which may benefit employers. Some of the costs of this voice mechanism, especially at the lower levels of the process, are borne by the union.

Benefits to Unions and Union Officials   The union may be able to use the grievance procedure as a pressure tactic by filing a large number of grievances prior to contract negotiations. We will see later that the union could use the grievance procedure to oppose and even overturn some management directives. For example, in one case a municipality employed ambulance drivers and attendants. The employer adopted a policy requiring lights and sirens to be used on all calls that were designated as emergencies. The rule was a change from past practice, which allowed drivers some discretion in the use of lights and sirens. The ambulance drivers and attendants thought that the policy posed a safety risk for themselves and the public. The employees filed grievances claiming that the new rules were unreasonable. An arbitrator found that there was no justification for the rule and that any discipline imposed under the rule would be unjust. It ordered that the policy be suspended.[4] A grievance might increase union solidarity by rallying support against the employer. The procedure might benefit union leaders seeking re-election, because the membership sees them fighting for employee interests.

Benefits to Employees   Employees may benefit from having workplace issues resolved by an impartial third party. If an employee was passed over for a promotion, a grievance might result in the employee being awarded the job. Even if the employee does not win the grievance, the procedure may show that the decision was not arbitrary and he or she may appreciate the opportunity to be heard. The procedure also provides job security; approximately half of terminated employees are reinstated through the grievance process.

Potential Employer Concerns Regarding the Grievance Process

Because the grievance process can be used to challenge management decisions, it has the potential to be a source of problems for the employer. Later in this chapter, we will see that collective agreement terms and the grievance procedure will affect several human resources functions, including recruiting, selection, training, and discipline.

The relationship between the union and the employer will affect the extent to which the grievance process is a problem for the employer. Where it is positive, grievances may be limited to a few legitimate disputes. If the relationship is poor, grievances will more likely be a source of difficulty, and may be used to harass and obstruct management actions. The attitude of the employer toward the collective agreement and the union may be a factor. Some disputes and grievances might be avoided if the employer respects the agreement and consults with the union on planned or unanticipated changes affecting the organization.

GRIEVANCE PROCEDURE

Typically, the union initiates the grievance procedure by preparing a grievance and submitting it to the employer representative specified in the agreement. The union may use pre-printed grievance forms that contain basic information and are completed by a union official, who fills in the particulars. Union stewards play a key role in advising employees about their rights and assisting them with grievances.

Informal Issue Resolution

Conflict is seen in all workplaces for a variety of reasons. However not all problems and complaints become grievances. In many workplaces, there is an attempt to resolve an issue by having a discussion with the line manager or the human resources department prior to filing a grievance. This is frequently identified as a "complaint" which precedes a formal grievance being filed by the union.

The extent and success of attempts to resolve disputes before a grievance is filed, or prior to the arbitration hearing, are likely related to the relationship between the parties. Where the relationship is more cooperative, there will be more attempts to settle prior to arbitration. At least one study has confirmed that there is a relationship between the labour relations climate and grievance outcomes. It found that when the relationship was more cooperative, grievances were dealt with more quickly, and the likelihood of a grievance being granted increased.[5] After a grievance has been filed, informal discussions may take place to try to resolve the issue, in addition to the meetings prescribed in the collective agreement. Typically after the grievance has been submitted to arbitration, there will be further attempts to settle the dispute and avoid arbitration.

The **grievance rate** is the number of grievances filed divided by the number of employees in the bargaining unit. The grievance rate is higher in bargaining units where the labour relations climate is poor.[6] It should be noted that there might not be a causal relationship between the labour–management relationship and the grievance rate. Furthermore, it is not clear whether a more cooperative relationship leads to lower grievance rates or lower grievance rates lead to a more cooperative relationship. In some workplaces where the relationship between the union and the employer is poor, the grievance rate is high and there may be thousands of grievances outstanding at any one time.

> The **grievance rate** is the number of grievances filed divided by the number of employees in the bargaining unit.

Ownership of the Grievance

The **ownership of the grievance** refers to the issue of who decides whether a grievance is filed, settled, withdrawn, or referred to arbitration. In most cases, it is the union and not the employee who has ownership or control of the grievance, subject to the duty of fair representation referred to below. It is up to the union, not the employee, to decide whether a grievance will be filed and how it will be resolved. There may be rare exceptions to this rule in some unions. For example, the constitution of the Ontario Public Service Employees Union (OPSEU) provides that the individual employee has control over a grievance.

> **Ownership of the grievance** refers to the issue of who decides whether a grievance is filed, settled, withdrawn, or referred to arbitration.

Procedural Matters

The discussions between the parties at grievance meetings are **privileged communications**, which means they cannot be referred to at any subsequent arbitration hearing. Any admissions or offers to settle made during the course of grievance meetings cannot be presented as evidence at the arbitration hearing. Documents that are part of the formal grievance procedure, including management's replies at each step of the process, may be introduced as evidence at the hearing. Accordingly, the employer's replies should be clear and concise, and any offers to settle should be in separate documents. Written communication between grievance meetings should be labelled as **without prejudice**, meaning that the documents cannot be referred to at a subsequent arbitration hearing. For example, if the union offered to settle a grievance relating to a dismissal in a letter headed "Without Prejudice," by having a suspension imposed on an employee; this offer could not be referred to at the hearing.

> **Privileged communications** refers to discussions that cannot be referred to at an arbitration hearing.

> **Without prejudice** is a label identifying documents that cannot be referred to at a subsequent arbitration hearing.

Waiver is a legal concept meaning acceptance of the rule that if a party does not object to a procedural error it cannot raise the issue later.

The parties should be aware that a failure to follow the procedural requirements set out in the grievance process by one side may require a response from the other. **Waiver** is a legal concept meaning acceptance of the rule that if a party does not object to a procedural error, for example a missed time limit, it cannot raise the issue later. If the grievance procedure provided that after Step 1 the union had 10 days to refer the grievance to Step 2, and the union did not take action for 20 days, the employer should object in writing before proceeding to the Step 2 meeting. If the employer goes ahead with the meeting, and waits until the arbitration hearing to raise the issue of the failure to meet the time limit, it may be found to have waived the failure to comply. Alternatively, the employer may want to carefully consider whether it wants to rely on the time limits to dismiss a grievance on a technicality. There may be disadvantages to doing so, including harming the relationship between the parties, and leaving an employee with an unresolved issue. The issue may arise in other grievances shortly anyway. If a dispute is not resolved through the grievance process, it may become a point that will have to be dealt with at the next round of contract negotiations.

In six jurisdictions—Canada, British Columbia, Manitoba, New Brunswick, Ontario, and Saskatchewan—legislation provides that arbitrators have the authority to allow an arbitration to proceed even though a time limit in the grievance process was not met.

Settlement Agreements

The **minutes of settlement** is a document that sets out the terms of an agreement to resolve a grievance.

Without precedent is a basis for settlement that means it cannot be referred to in any subsequent proceedings.

If a grievance is settled prior to the conclusion of the arbitration hearing, which is often the case, the settlement should be set out in a written document, which may be referred to as **minutes of settlement** or a *memorandum of settlement*. This document should refer to the grievance, confirm the grievance has been resolved, and set out the terms of the settlement, such as a reinstatement or payments to be made. It should be signed by the employer, the union, and any employees involved. Consideration should be given to providing that the settlement is done on a **without precedent** basis, meaning it cannot be referred to in any subsequent proceedings. Suppose the employer dismissed an employee who was in possession of an illegal substance in the workplace, and a settlement included reinstatement of the employee. If the settlement was on a without precedent basis, it could not be referred to in any subsequent case, and the employer would be free to discharge another employee later for the same offence.

ARBITRATION

Although only a few grievances, approximately 2 to 3 percent of those filed, proceed all the way to arbitration, employers and unions must have an understanding of the arbitration process. The alternative forms of arbitration that the collective agreement might provide for, including a single arbitrator or an arbitration board, were referred to in Chapter 7. Arbitration is an adversarial process in which the parties present evidence to the arbitrator who makes a decision or order on the basis of the evidence.

Rights vs. Interest Arbitration

Rights arbitration refers to the resolution of a dispute relating to the administration of a collective agreement.

Interest arbitration refers to the determination of the terms of a collective agreement.

A distinction must be drawn between grievance, sometimes referred to as **rights arbitration** and **interest arbitration**, which relates to the determination of contract terms. Grievance or rights arbitration resolves disputes relating to the administration of the agreement. If an employee was discharged, he or she could file a grievance alleging that there was a violation of the collective agreement because there was not just cause. If the dispute was not settled, it could be referred to grievance or rights arbitration for final resolution, including possible reinstatement of the employee. Interest arbitration relates to an entirely different type of dispute, where the parties cannot agree on the terms of a collective agreement through negotiation. In interest arbitration, the employer and union present evidence and make submissions regarding what the agreement should contain, and the arbitrator's decision sets out the terms of the contract. Interest arbitration is used primarily in areas of the public sector such as police and fire services, in which strikes are not allowed.

Arbitrators

Most arbitrators have a legal background, but there is no requirement that the arbitrator be a lawyer. Many arbitrators are university professors and lawyers. Although a few do arbitration work full-time, many do arbitrations on a part-time basis. Usually a few experienced arbitrators are handling a disproportionately large number of cases in each province. The parties may be interested in the track record of an arbitrator to see how much experience he or she has and to determine how he or she has decided cases similar to the one at hand. The Ontario Federation of Labour has published a survey with an extensive list of arbitrators who have decided cases in over 50 areas such as discharge and discipline, the duty to accommodate, and job posting, indicating if the decision was in favour of the employer or the union. The Federation cautions that the survey is designed to be only a guide for the selection of arbitrators with experience in a particular subject area.

Website for Ontario Federation of Labour arbitrator survey: http://ofl.ca/index.php/publications

The Arbitration Hearing

The proceedings where unresolved grievances between union and management representatives are commonly referred to as a hearing. At the hearing, these representatives will be allowed to make an opening statement, present evidence through witnesses and documents, cross-examine the other side's witnesses, and make a final argument. Lawyers may represent the parties, but this is not required. If both sides have agreed on some or all of the facts, such as dates of employment or certain events that have occurred, they might prepare and present an **agreed statement of facts** to the arbitrator. The facts set out in the statement will not have to be proven at the hearing, which will shorten the time required to establish the factual issues and allow the parties to move on quickly to the argument stage of the hearing.

An **agreed statement of facts** sets out the matters that the parties have agreed upon.

The hearing is held at a neutral site, typically a meeting room in a hotel. Each side is responsible for ensuring that its witnesses are present, and arrangements can be made to subpoena witnesses to compel them to attend. The arbitrator might render a decision immediately in cases that are clear; however, commonly the arbitrator requires more time to review the evidence resulting in a delay in the decision of several weeks or longer depending on the complexity of the case.

The labour relations legislation of each jurisdiction sets out the authority of arbitrators. Arbitrators have been given the authority to do whatever is necessary to conduct a hearing, including fix the dates for hearings, issue summonses for witnesses, and determine the admissibility of evidence.

Burden of Proof In any arbitration case, either the union or the employer will bear what is known as the **burden of proof**—that is, it will have the job of proving the facts in dispute. The general rule is that the burden of proof is borne by the party filing the grievance, which in the majority of cases is the union. Discipline and discharge cases are an exception. In such cases it is the employer that bears the burden of proof. The burden of proof will be significant if the arbitrator cannot decide whose version of the facts is true, because in that event the party bearing the burden of proof will lose. If a union filed a grievance alleging that an employee had sufficient ability for a job vacancy, and the evidence

The **burden of proof** refers to who must prove the facts in dispute.

was not clear, the burden of proof would not be met and the arbitrator would dismiss the grievance. Another way to state this is that the union had the onus to show that the employee had sufficient ability and it failed to do so.

An **argument in the alternative** refers to a party making an argument it wishes the arbitrator to accept if its primary argument is not accepted.

Argument in the Alternative   Either side can make an **argument in the alternative**. This means that neither the union nor the employer is restricted to putting forward only one claim or defence; they can make secondary or alternative arguments if the arbitrator does not agree with their primary position. In effect, either side can say, "Our position is A; however, if you do not agree with A, we submit that you should find B." An example of a union making an argument in the alternative might arise in a discipline and discharge case as follows. The union's first position might be that there was no misconduct by the employee; however, if the arbitrator finds there was misconduct, the union's alternative position might be that the penalty imposed by the employer should be reduced. The authority of an arbitrator to reduce a penalty is discussed later in this chapter.

Arbitration Decisions

Thousands of arbitration decisions are made every year. Previous decisions on an issue are often influential on later ones; however, they do not establish binding precedents. Because arbitrators may have different views on some matters, it is possible to have conflicting decisions or two schools of thought on some issues. On the issue of the appropriate remedy for an employer's failure to properly distribute overtime, some arbitrators take the approach of providing the employee with the next opportunity to work overtime. Others think the remedy should be an award of cash to compensate the employee for lost earnings.[7]

At the hearing, the union and the employer will both try to refer to previous cases that support their position. In the cases dealing with the dismissal of employees later in this chapter, the arbitrator has to decide whether to uphold the dismissal or substitute a lesser penalty. At the hearing, the employer would refer the arbitrator to previous decisions in which arbitrators upheld the dismissal of employees guilty of similar misconduct. The union would try to present similar cases in which arbitrators ordered reinstatement.

One source of arbitration decisions is Labour Arbitration Cases, a series that reports important decisions.[8] Commentary on arbitration cases useful to both employers and unions can be found in *Canadian Labour Arbitration* (4th ed.)[9] and *Leading Cases on Labour Arbitration*.[10] Some arbitration decisions are also available online at the Canadian Legal Information Institute. Previously decided cases establish points of labour law that can also guide the parties when negotiating the collective agreement. For example, numerous decisions have clearly established that the employer is permitted to contract out work unless the agreement prohibits it. Knowing this, the parties can negotiate accordingly. The union will seek to have the collective agreement limit the employer's right to contract out, perhaps even making a concession in another area to obtain some limitation. Employers will try to avoid limits on the right to contract out, knowing they can contract out unless the agreement provides otherwise. The parties may also use previous decisions to help settle a grievance. In a situation in which an employee has been guilty of minor insubordination, the matter to be resolved is the discipline that should have been imposed. If it were found that previous decisions set the penalty at a one-day-to-one-week suspension, this would guide the settlement negotiations. Arbitrators are bound by the relevant legislation in their jurisdiction and by court decisions interpreting that legislation. The Supreme Court of Canada has confirmed that arbitrators have the authority to enforce the rights and obligations provided in human rights and other employment-related statutes.[11]

Arbitrators must deal with questions of fact and questions of law. In regards to questions of fact an arbitrator would have to determine include whether an employee was guilty

Website for Canadian Legal Information Institute: www.canlii.org/en/index.php

of theft, or whether an employee has sufficient ability for a job. For a question of law, an arbitrator may have to determine whether an employer has met the duty to accommodate. In the course of determining points of law, references will be made at arbitration hearings to legislation and to previous court and arbitration decisions.

Arbitrability

The arbitrator does not have authority to deal with all disputes that might arise between the union and the employer. **Arbitrability** refers to whether an arbitrator has the authority to hear the dispute and render a decision. A dispute is referred to as *arbitrable* if the arbitrator has the authority to hear it, and *inarbitrable* if he or she does not.

Arbitrability refers to whether an arbitrator has authority to hear a dispute.

There are several possible reasons why a dispute is inarbitrable. First, the dispute must relate to a matter covered by the collective agreement. Labour Relations Issue 9-2 refers to a situation in which there was a question of arbitrability. Second, if the agreement has been complied with, a matter is not arbitrable even though the results may seem harsh or unfair. It should be noted that an arbitrator only decides issues relating to the interpretation or alleged violation of the agreement; he or she cannot amend the agreement. In one case, the collective agreement provided that contract employees could be terminated with one week's notice. A grievance was filed when a contract employee was terminated with the required notice. When it was established that the employer had in fact given the notice required, the arbitrator held that the grievance was inarbitrable.[12] Finally, the arbitrator may not have jurisdiction if the procedural requirements of the grievance process have not been followed, for example, when there has been a failure to meet a mandatory time limit. This is subject to the possibility of an arbitrator extending a time limit in some jurisdictions referred to above.

Cost of Arbitration

The employer and the union may have lawyers represent them, and this will be a factor affecting the cost for each side. Most collective agreements provide that the parties will split the arbitrator's fees and expenses regardless of who wins. A few agreements provide that the losing party pays the costs of the arbitration; however, this is unusual. Arbitrator's fees range from $2000 to $3500 per day for the hearing and writing up the award. There will be additional expenses, including the cost of the room for the hearing. If an arbitration board is used instead of a sole arbitrator, the parties will also have to pay the additional fees owing to their representatives on the board. Depending on whether lawyers are used and the length of the hearing, arbitration can be expensive. The costs can be especially significant for a small union or employer, and may be a factor in reaching a settlement prior to the arbitration hearing. One of the parties may back down, or the parties may compromise, to

---

Labour Relations Issue 9-2
When Is a Dispute Arbitrable?

An employer established an early retirement plan that offered financial incentives to employees to participate. The plan provided that the employer could deny an employee's request to participate if the company would have to hire a new person to replace the prospective retiree. On this basis, the employer denied several requests to participate in the plan. The collective agreement did not refer to the issue of early retirement.

When some employees who were denied access to the plan filed grievances, an arbitrator dismissed them. It was held that because the disputes related to a matter not referred to in the collective agreement, the grievances were not arbitrable. In order for a grievance to be arbitrable, it must deal with an alleged breach of a term of the agreement or a violation of employment legislation.

avoid the expense of going to a hearing. The expense of arbitration is one of the factors leading some academics and practitioners to recommend alternatives, such as grievance mediation, which is discussed later in this chapter.

Remedies

Arbitrators have authority to issue orders that will resolve the violation of the collective agreement. Remedies are referred to below in greater detail in subsections relating to discipline, seniority, and other issues. Arbitrators have the authority to: order the reduction of discipline imposed upon employees, including ordering reinstatement; make a declaration that a party has violated the agreement and direct compliance; and order the payment of damages for financial loss. In one case where it was found that a supervisor had been guilty of harassing an employee and the employee had been off work as a result, the arbitrator ordered the employer to restore the employee's sick leave credits, pay the difference between the employee's regular pay and sick leave pay for the time the employee had been away from work, ensure that the employee would not come into contact with the supervisor in the future, establish an anti-harassment training program for managerial staff, and pay the employee $25 000 in general damages.[13] In a recent case, one arbitrator has extended the remedies granted in arbitration.[14] The employer fired an employee claiming that she had been guilty of making a false sick leave claim. The arbitrator found that the employer's investigation was superficial and the employer had failed to comply with the collective agreement when it did not request an independent medical examination as required by the agreement. The arbitrator upheld the grievance and awarded the grievor in excess of $500 000 for a "bad faith" dismissal. It was found that the employer's highhanded conduct had been the cause of the employee's mental condition, and the arbitrator awarded $50 000 for emotional stress, $50 000 in punitive damages, lost salary, and losses for future pay and benefits. This case should be monitored to determine if it is upheld upon judicial review or appeal.

Review of Arbitration Decisions

What can the employer or the union do if it thinks that an arbitrator's decision is wrong? In most jurisdictions, it is possible to make an application for judicial (court) review of an arbitration decision. In British Columbia, decisions can be reviewed by the Labour Relations Board. The Supreme Court of Canada has recently restated the law relating to the judicial review of decisions by tribunals and arbitrators.[15] This is a topic beyond this text; however, one critical point must be noted. When a court reviews an arbitration decision, the standard applied is one of reasonableness as opposed to correctness. The standard of reasonableness has been described in one case as follows: "Reviewing courts cannot substitute their own appreciation of the appropriate solution, but must rather determine if the outcome falls within a range of possible, acceptable outcomes which are defensible in respect of the facts and law. There may be more than one reasonable outcome. However, as long as the process and the outcome fit comfortably with the principles of justification, transparency and intelligibility, it is not open to a reviewing court to substitute its own view of a preferred outcome."[16] Accordingly, it is possible that an arbitration decision could be viewed by some as incorrect; however, a judicial review will not be successful because the decision meets the reasonableness standard.

Although a grievance can arise from any term in the collective agreement, grievances relating to management rights, seniority issues, and discipline and discharge are the most common. Issues relating to grievances in these areas are discussed in the following sections.

MANAGEMENT RIGHTS

In Chapter 7, it was noted that the management rights article is different from most collective agreement terms because its purpose is to benefit management, whereas most of the other terms in a collective agreement benefit employees. Sample contract provisions were provided in Figure 7-7. Relying on this article, management can make decisions relating to methods of operation and levels of production. However, the management rights article does not allow the employer to do anything it wants; there are limitations on the exercise of management rights.

Limitations on the Exercise of Management Rights

Any action taken by the employer relying on management rights is subject to the following limitations: (1) the measures must not contravene other provisions of the collective agreement, (2) the action taken must be legal, (3) there must not have been previous statements or conduct that creates an estoppel, and (4) any rules established must meet the requirements set out in the case *KVP Co. Ltd.*[17]

Provisions of the Collective Agreement   When the employer claims to exercise any management rights, it must comply with other provisions in the agreement. A fundamental principle in labour relations is that the collective agreement must be read as a whole document. If the contract requires the employer to provide clothing, the employer could not rely on the management rights article to adopt a policy on uniforms that requires employees to pay for them.

Compliance with the Law   Any action the employer takes relying on the management rights article must meet the basic requirement of complying with any relevant legislation and the common law. An employer cannot take any action that violates legislation, including human rights, employment standards, or other statues, or the common law. In one case, an employer relied upon the management rights provisions in the collective agreement to attempt to introduce a biometric payroll and time keeping system that used employee fingerprints. Although it should be noted that the law relating to privacy is still evolving, an arbitrator prohibited the establishment of the system on the basis that it was an invasion of the employee's privacy interests.[18] Similarly, arbitrators in some jurisdictions have not allowed employers to require employees to obtain flu vaccinations where there was no legislated basis for the requirement; and in the absence of such legislation, the vaccination was an illegal assault.[19]

Estoppel   The doctrine of **estoppel** may prevent the union or the employer from relying on and enforcing the terms of the collective agreement. Where a party makes a representation to the other, by way of words or conduct, indicating that an issue will be dealt with in a manner different from the provisions of the agreement, the party who made the representation will not be able to later insist upon the collective agreement being enforced.

Statements made by a party to the agreement could be the basis for an estoppel. In one case, a collective agreement provided that layoffs would occur in reverse order of seniority. The employer, a hospital, hired two laboratory technicians. The hiring manager assured both technicians when they were hired that they would not be laid off because of funding cuts or the return of other employees to the department. However, the hospital laid off the technicians 14 months after they were hired when other employees returned to the bargaining unit. When the employees objected, they were told that the collective agreement was clear on the question of seniority on layoffs and there was nothing that could be done because they had the least seniority. A grievance was filed, and the arbitrator held that the doctrine of estoppel applied.[20] Because of the representations made to the technicians before they were hired, the employer could not rely on the collective agreement, and the layoff of the technicians was nullified.

Estoppel is a legal concept providing that if a party makes a representation that an issue will be dealt with in a manner different from the provisions of the collective agreement, it will not be able to later insist upon the collective agreement being enforced as written.

The union and the employer should be alert to the possibility of estoppel based on conduct or past practice. In one case, the collective agreement provided that certain benefits would be paid to employees after a three-day waiting period.[21] Despite the terms of the collective agreement, the employer had a long-established practice of paying employees benefits during the three-day period. When the employer indicated it would enforce the three-day waiting period in the future, the union filed a grievance relying on estoppel. The arbitrator upheld the grievance and ordered the employer to continue to pay the benefits according to its practice for the balance of the term of the agreement.

Similarly, a union might be caught by an estoppel argument based on prior past practice if it failed to enforce all the terms of the agreement. For example, a collective agreement will usually provide for a probationary period. If the employer made a habit of extending the period, in breach of the agreement, and the union took no action, the union may not be allowed to object to an extension of the period on the basis of estoppel.[22]

An estoppel will not be established by a single failure to comply with or enforce the collective agreement; however, employers and unions should be aware of the risk of repeated failures to enforce a term of the agreement. An employer who wanted to vary from the collective agreement to deal with a short-term issue might consider consulting with the union and attempting to reach an agreement that would prevent an estoppel argument being raised when the employer wished to revert to the terms of the agreement. If the agreement provided for a rate of remuneration for employees who drove their own cars, and the price of gas increased significantly, an agreement might allow the employer to increase the mileage allowance for a time and avoid any possible estoppel arguments later.

Estoppel does not mean that a party will be prevented from enforcing the terms of the agreement indefinitely. An estoppel will cease at the next round of contract negotiations if the union or the employer advises the other that it will rely on the strict terms of the agreement in the future. The party that has previously relied on the variation from the collective agreement will have to negotiate a change to the agreement. If it fails to do so, it will be deemed to have agreed to the application of the agreement as written.

Requirements for Rules Established in *KVP Co. Ltd.* Most arbitrators hold that any rules established by management pursuant to the management rights article must comply with the requirements established in the case of *Re Lumber and Sawmill Workers' Union, Local 2537, and KVP Co. Ltd.* An excerpt from the case setting out the requirements for rules is provided in Figure 9-3.

In the *KVP Co. Ltd.* case, the arbitration board's decision provided that:

A rule unilaterally introduced by the company, and not subsequently agreed to by the union, must satisfy the following requisites:

1. It must not be inconsistent with the collective agreement.
2. It must not be unreasonable.
3. It must be clear and unequivocal.
4. It must be brought to the attention of the employee affected before the company can act on it.
5. The employee concerned must have been notified that a breach of such rule could result in his discharge if the rule is used as a foundation for discharge.
6. Such rule should have been consistently enforced by the company from the time it was introduced.

Figure 9-3 Requirements for Employer Rules

One of the requirements that may be of particular interest to employers is that a rule must not be unreasonable. For example, employers who attempt to establish rules relating to personal appearance may encounter difficulty. The employer has the right to establish reasonable rules to protect its image and business interests. However, the employer must show that the rule prevents a threat to its business and is not just imposing the employer's preferences on employees. In cases where employers have established rules prohibiting facial jewellery, the employer has been required to produce evidence of harm or loss through opinion surveys or customer feedback to establish that the rule is reasonable. When determining if a rule is reasonable, some arbitrators have distinguished between rules that affect employees' personal choices outside of the workplace, such as prohibiting beards, as opposed to rules that only affect employees at the workplace, such as prohibitions against jewellery.

The requirement that a rule or policy be reasonable may mean that employers in unionized workplaces cannot use random drug testing because they cannot establish the reasonableness of the testing. Refer to Labour Relations Issue 9-3 on this issue.

If management establishes a rule, the union does not have to wait until management applies it and disciplines someone before filing a grievance. Earlier in this chapter, a case where a union successfully challenged a rule regarding the use of lights and sirens in ambulances was referred to. The union was able to challenge the rule through the grievance process before it was applied.

Labour Relation Issue 9-3

Should Random Drug Testing Be Allowed?

Imperial Oil is concerned about the risk posed by drugs and alcohol in the workplace. In the 1990s, the company established a policy that included random drug and alcohol tests (urinalysis) for employees in safety-sensitive positions. A human rights tribunal in the *Entrop* case found random drug testing to be discriminatory because it did not determine current impairment. It should be noted that this decision relating to random testing did not preclude testing for cause where employees exhibited impairment or had been involved in an incident. In 2003, Imperial Oil started a new random drug testing program in a unionized workplace at its Nanticoke, Ontario, refinery. The test relied upon a mouth swab that would establish whether employees had used marijuana within four hours of taking the test. Imperial claimed that with this test, it could now determine current drug impairment. The union filed a grievance, and the matter went to an arbitration board, which held that the testing was contrary to established labour law. The decision provided that employees in a unionized workplace could not be subjected to a drug test unless there was reasonable cause or an incident to justify the testing. It is important to note that this arbitration decision was based on the basis of the collective agreement and long-standing labour law relating to the reasonableness of the test, and not on the basis of human rights

legislation as was the case in *Entrop*. Subsequently, the arbitration decision was upheld on judicial review and by the Ontario Court of Appeal. With technology that allows drug testing to determine current impairment, it may be possible that in a non-union workplace the employer could argue that the human rights problem with random drug testing in *Entrop* has been resolved and random drug testing could be introduced. This raises the possibility that the new technology may lead to random drug testing being allowed in non-union workplaces under some circumstances, whereas it might not be allowed in unionized workplaces. Unfortunately the many variables involved in the topic of drug and alcohol testing make this topic complex. The employer's authority to use alcohol or drug testing may vary depending on whether the employees are unionized; whether the test is pre-employment, random, or subsequent to an incident; and the jurisdiction. The jurisdiction involved may be a factor because the courts in Alberta have indicated a greater willingness to allow testing in the non-union setting. This is an evolving area that must be monitored for developments. At the time of this writing it appears that unionized employers cannot use random drug testing as opposed to testing for cause, after an incident, or as part of a rehabilitation program, even in safety-sensitive work environments.

DISCIPLINE AND DISCHARGE

Grievances relating to the discipline or discharge of employees account for the largest number of disputes referred to arbitration. The grievance and arbitration process is one of the key features distinguishing union and non-union workplaces. Some non-union employers may adopt a conflict resolution process and refer to it as a grievance procedure, but the arbitration of disputes is mandatory in unionized workplaces. The law does not allow non-union employers to suspend employees unless the employment contract provides for suspension. Most employment contracts do not refer to discipline; accordingly, a non-union employer cannot usually suspend employees who are guilty of misconduct. The law does allow unionized employers to suspend employees who are guilty of misconduct, subject to the possibility that the suspension will be reduced or rescinded by an arbitrator, which is referred to below. The non-union employer may dismiss an employee without giving any notice if the employee is guilty of misconduct that is severe enough to be just cause for dismissal, such as theft. A non-union employee who wishes to challenge a dismissal for just cause will have to sue the employer for wrongful dismissal. If employee misconduct is not proven or the court does not view the conduct as being severe enough to amount to just cause, the employer will have to give reasonable notice to end the employment relationship. Reasonable notice is based on the employee's age, length of service, position held, and other factors. The only remedy available to the non-union employee is an award of damages to compensate the employee for the reasonable notice that he or she should have been provided. The courts will not order the reinstatement of a non-union employee. When a unionized employee has been disciplined or discharged, he or she may file a grievance; and as explained below, an arbitrator may order the penalty imposed by the employer be reduced. This could involve a suspension being reduced or rescinded, or a discharged employee being reinstated. Studies have found that arbitrators have reinstated approximately one-half of employees who have been discharged.[23] The possibility of reinstatement is one of the most significant implications of unionization for employers and employees.

Possible Grounds for Discipline or Discharge

A list of possible grounds for discipline is provided in Figure 9-4. The list is not exhaustive, but it illustrates the broad nature of the grounds for discipline. If an employee is guilty of misconduct away from the job, the employer cannot impose discipline unless the misconduct impacts the employer's business interests. When there is such impact, discipline up to

1. Failure to attend
2. Leaving work without permission
3. Lateness
4. Theft
5. Falsification of employment records or documents such as attendance records or expense statements
6. Misconduct on the job, including damaging property or assaulting co-workers
7. Incompetence
8. Insubordination, including refusal to follow orders
9. Off-duty behaviour that affects the employer's business
10. Breach of company rules

Figure 9-4 Grounds for Discipline

and including discharge is possible. The nature of the misconduct and the business conducted by the employer will be important. The same misconduct may or may not justify dismissal or discipline depending on the nature of the business. In one case, a residential care worker in a facility for mentally challenged individuals pleaded guilty to theft after a shoplifting incident away from the job. The employer dismissed the worker, but an arbitrator ordered her reinstatement because it was not shown that the conviction was related to the nature of the work done by the employee and the employer's reputation was not affected. In another case, the discharge of a municipal electrical inspector who had been convicted of growing marijuana was upheld.

In short, a criminal conviction for conduct away from the job will not in itself justify discipline. The employer will first have to establish a connection with and harm to the employer's business or reputation.

Procedural Matters

Stating the Grounds for Discipline   Arbitrators generally require employers to justify the discipline on the basis of the grounds stated at the time the discipline was imposed. They cannot add to the grounds or reasons for discipline after it has been imposed if the additional misconduct relates to behaviour the employer knew about or could have easily discovered. For example, if an employee was discharged for assaulting a co-worker, the employer could not try to substantiate the discharge at the arbitration hearing by arguing that the employee was also guilty of theft, unless the employer could not have known about the theft at the time of the termination. This is a point on which the union and non-union workplaces are different. If a non-union employer dismisses an employee and is defending against a wrongful dismissal action claiming there was just cause, it is allowed to refer to misconduct that came to the employer's attention after the dismissal without any problem relating to whether the employer should have previously known about and referred to the misconduct. In the previous example of a theft, even if the employer did not know about the theft at the time of the dismissal, it may use the theft as a defence in a subsequent wrongful dismissal action brought by the employee.

Because unionized employers may encounter difficulties when they refer to misconduct not raised at the time of the dismissal, they should carefully investigate before imposing discipline. If the employer discovers additional misconduct after the termination, it should immediately advise the union of the additional grounds that it will be relying upon. In one case, a teacher was terminated on basis of attendance and performance issues. After the termination, the employer discovered that the teacher had apparently downloaded pornographic material to the school's computer system. Although the union objected to the introduction of the evidence relating to the misuse of the computer system, because it was not referred to at the time of the discharge, the arbitrator held that it could be referred to because the employer could not have known about it previously, and the union had been immediately advised about the additional grounds for termination.[24]

Culminating Incident   The unionized employer is allowed to refer to the employee's previous record when determining the penalty to impose. The doctrine of **culminating incident** provides that if an employee has been guilty of a final act of misconduct, the employer is allowed to take into consideration the employee's previous disciplinary record when determining the appropriate penalty for the most recent incident. Applying this doctrine, the employer may be able to discharge an employee after misconduct that by itself would not justify dismissal. If an employee was guilty of making a false claim for sick days, which might not justify dismissal by itself, the employer may discharge the employee if the previous record included numerous other offences for which warnings and suspensions had

Culminating incident is a doctrine providing that if an employee has been guilty of an act of misconduct the employer is allowed to take into consideration the employee's previous record in determining the appropriate penalty.

been applied. When a discharge or other discipline is imposed, the employer should advise the employee of the previous record that has been considered. Failing to specify the past misconduct in reasons for the discipline might mean that the employer will not be allowed to rely on it at an arbitration hearing.

Possible Discipline

An employer may impose the following discipline on an employee guilty of misconduct, depending on its severity: (1) a written warning; (2) suspension (time off without pay); (3) demotion; (4) dismissal. Except for serious misconduct such as attacking a supervisor, employers are expected to apply **progressive discipline**, meaning they should impose a lesser penalty for a first offence and apply more severe penalties if there is further misconduct. Progressive discipline is based on the assumption that the purpose of discipline is to correct misconduct and restore the employment relationship.

Progressive discipline often begins with a verbal warning, followed by a written warning, a suspension, subsequent longer suspensions, and ultimately discharge. The employee would be given a final warning.

Restrictions on possible discipline are as follows:

- Employers cannot impose fines unless the collective agreement provides for them. However, a fine should be distinguished from an order to compensate the employer for damages. If an employee deliberately damaged or destroyed property, an arbitrator might order the employee to compensate the employer.

- Employers cannot penalize employees by reducing or eliminating their seniority.

- Employers cannot impose discipline twice for the same misconduct. For example, the employer could not impose a one-day suspension and then later decide that the penalty was not severe enough and impose a three-day suspension. The employer can suspend an employee while an investigation is being conducted; however, it should be made clear that the matter is still under investigation and a final decision on discipline is forthcoming.

Arbitration Issues and Outcomes

At the arbitration hearing, there are three main areas of potential dispute: (1) the procedural requirements of the agreement; (2) factual issues, that is, establishing whether there was any misconduct; and (3) the severity of the penalty imposed by the employer.

Procedural Requirements in the Agreement   Discipline imposed by the employer can be reversed because the procedural requirements of the collective agreement have not been complied with. Arbitrators have ordered discipline to be reversed in cases where employers have not complied with provisions requiring union representation at disciplinary meetings, written reasons for discipline, and time limits for imposing discipline.

Factual Matters   The employer has the onus of proving that there was misconduct by the employee. If it is alleged that the employee has abused the employer's email system or damaged employer property, the employer must establish this misconduct through witnesses and documentary evidence. If the employer fails to establish the misconduct, the grievance will be upheld and the discipline reversed. An arbitrator would order reinstatement if necessary, payment of any earnings lost because of a suspension, and the removal of any warnings or related material from the employee's record. Accordingly, employers should carefully investigate before proceeding with discipline.

Some employers have attempted to use surreptitious videotape evidence to show that an employee is guilty of misconduct such as making a false injury claim. This involves

Progressive discipline means that the employer imposes a lesser penalty for a first offence and applies more severe penalties if there is further misconduct.

Is Surreptitious Videotape Admissible as Evidence?

An individual employed as a security guard at a mental health institution was off work with pay while the employer investigated a complaint against him. A co-worker advised the employer that she thought the employee was working for another employer while he was on the paid suspension. The employer hired an investigator to determine if the employee was working elsewhere. In the meantime, the employee was transferred to the job of a dietary technician as part of an accommodation. The employee claimed that this accommodation was not sufficient because he had an aversion to water and the dietary technician job involved washing dishes and other cleaning. The investigator videotaped the employee in his driveway washing his car and watering a tree. In a subsequent interview with the employer, the employee denied that he was able to wash a car. The employer dismissed the employee on the basis of the videotape evidence and the interview.

A grievance was filed, and at the arbitration hearing the employer attempted to introduce the videotape as evidence. The union objected to the admissibility of the videotape, and the arbitrator ruled that the evidence was inadmissible. The arbitrator held that the employer did not have a reasonable basis for undertaking the surveillance of the employee to begin with. The employer did not have a policy against moonlighting, and the employee had not been told that he could not work while he was away. There was no evidence that the employee had been called to work and had declined. Because the employer did not have reasonable grounds to engage in the surveillance of the employee, the videotape was not admissible.*

Should the test for the admissibility of video evidence be based on relevancy or reasonableness?

Centre for Addiction and Mental Health and O.P.S.E.U. 131 LAC (4th) 97.

videotaping of the employee away from the workplace without the employee's knowledge. There is no consensus among arbitrators across Canada on the issue of whether such evidence will be admitted. Some arbitrators have applied a relevancy test, and admitted videotape evidence on the basis that it is relevant to the issue at hand. However, many arbitrators are now applying a reasonableness test to protect the privacy rights of employees; and if the employer does not meet the requirements of the test, the videotape evidence will not be admitted. The reasonableness test requires the employer to show that (1) it was reasonable for the employer to have engaged in video surveillance and (2) the surveillance was conducted in a reasonable fashion. To meet the requirements of the test, the employer will have to show that it considered less intrusive steps to determine if the employee was guilty of misconduct. Labour Relations Issue 9-4 illustrates how the reasonableness test could lead to a videotape being excluded. This is an evolving area, and employers may wish to consult with legal counsel in their jurisdiction before proceeding with the videotaping of employees.

Appropriateness of the Penalty Imposed   Labour relations legislation in all jurisdictions except British Columbia provides that unless the agreement provides for a specific penalty for the misconduct, the arbitrator has the authority to reduce the penalty imposed by the employer. British Columbia illustrates an alternative policy option where the arbitrator's authority to reduce the penalty cannot be eliminated by a specific penalty provision in the collective agreement. This means that unless the collective agreement provides for a specific penalty for the misconduct, the arbitrator has the authority to reduce a discharge to a suspension or reduce the number of days of a suspension. In discharge cases where the arbitrator has determined that there has been misconduct, the arbitrator must determine whether the misconduct was serious enough to deserve dismissal. The arbitrator may uphold the discharge, or, where the conduct is not sufficiently serious to warrant dismissal, order that the employee be reinstated with a lesser penalty such as a suspension. The arbitrator cannot order the penalty to be increased.

Factors Arbitrators Consider When Reviewing Discipline Imposed by the Employer

1. The seriousness of the misconduct
2. The length of service of the grievor
3. The previous record of the grievor
4. Provocation by management or other employees
5. Whether the misconduct was premeditated or committed on the spur of the moment
6. Whether the penalty creates special economic hardship

7. The uniformity of enforcement of rules
8. Whether rules were brought to the attention of employees
9. Whether the grievor initially denied or admitted the misconduct
10. Other factors that might be considered—for example, the failure of the grievor to apologize

Key Considerations 9-1 lists the factors that arbitrators have considered when determining whether to uphold or reduce a penalty. In any particular case, one or more of the factors listed may be referred to. The seriousness of the misconduct is an important factor. If an employee is merely guilty of swearing at a supervisor, the penalty of discharge may be too severe. However, if the employee struck the supervisor, a discharge would be more likely to be upheld. If the employee has a long record of service without any previous discipline issues, or was provoked by management or another employee, it is more likely the penalty would be reduced. The penalty may be reduced in cases where the offence was part of an emotional outburst as opposed to being premeditated. Arbitrators have reduced the penalty in cases where it would impose a special economic hardship; for example, where the discharged employee would have special difficulty finding another job.

Employers should ensure that rules are consistently enforced, because failing to do so may lead to a penalty being reduced or reversed. If the employer has established rules relating to parking, but the rules have not been enforced, an arbitrator would not uphold a suspension.

Discipline and discharge cases are decided on a case-by-case basis. Because there are so many different factors that might affect the outcome and possibly lead to a penalty being reduced, there may be different outcomes in cases that look similar. In cases where employees have been found guilty of using an employer credit card to purchase gasoline for personal use, there have been different outcomes. In one case, a long-term employee with a clean record confessed to the theft and made an offer of restitution, and it was established that there were family problems causing stress. The arbitrator ordered that a 13-month suspension be substituted for dismissal. In another case, a long-term employee with a clean record confessed to the police, but subsequently in the employer's investigation claimed that he had the right to take the gasoline. The discharge was upheld.

The following question may arise: Does an arbitrator have to order reinstatement when it is found that the misconduct is not severe enough to merit dismissal? The answer to this question is no. In a few exceptional cases, where employees have not shown a willingness to change their behaviour, arbitrators have awarded compensation instead of reinstatement.[25] When dealing with a problem employee, the employer may wish to pursue a settlement with the union that avoids reinstatement, perhaps including some compensation. If the union and the employee insist upon reinstatement, the employer may wish to get legal advice about the possibility of convincing an arbitrator to award compensation instead of reinstatement.

Last Chance Agreements

A **last chance agreement** (LCA) is an agreement between the employer, the union, and an employee guilty of misconduct that the employee will be retained or reinstated subject to certain conditions being met, such as maintaining a certain level of attendance or obtaining help for a substance abuse problem. The agreement further provides that if the employee fails to meet the conditions, he or she will be terminated and will not have the right to have the dismissal referred to arbitration, except to determine whether the agreement has been breached. If an employee has a poor attendance record, and discipline including warnings and suspensions has not remedied the problem, an LCA might be entered into. In this situation, the agreement could provide that if the employee does not maintain a specified attendance level in the future, he or she will be dismissed. The agreement would further provide that the only point that might be arbitrated is the determination of the attendance level to establish if the agreement had been breached.

An LCA is potentially advantageous to all parties involved. The employee avoids dismissal, and the possibility of discharge may motivate the individual to rehabilitate. The union avoids the trouble and cost of an arbitration hearing. The employer retains an employee who might be valuable if rehabilitated, and avoids the cost and uncertainty of an arbitration hearing. There are potential human rights problems with LCAs, discussed below.

An arbitrator may make an order similar to an LCA with or without a request from one of the parties.[26] The arbitrator has the authority to order an employee to be reinstated subject to certain conditions, such as maintaining a certain level of attendance or obtaining medical treatment. If the employee failed to meet the conditions, he or she would be discharged.

> A **last chance agreement** provides that an employee guilty of misconduct will be retained or reinstated subject to conditions being met and will be discharged if the agreement is breached.

Implications for Employers and Unions

Because a discipline or discharge decision made by management might be reviewed at arbitration, there are guidelines that management should follow, which are listed in Key Considerations 9-2. Key Considerations 9-3 outlines steps the union should take

---

Key Considerations 9-2

Considerations for Employers When Imposing Discipline

1. Ensure that the procedural requirements of the collective agreement, such as union representation at disciplinary meetings and written reasons for discipline, are being met.

2. Ensure that any rules have been communicated to employees and have been consistently enforced.

3. Carefully investigate and document any misconduct through statements from witnesses and written material.

4. Take up the alleged misconduct with the employee and allow the employee an opportunity to respond.

5. Before imposing any discipline, review the factors that an arbitrator would consider when reviewing the severity of the discipline, including the employee's record, length of service, the seriousness of the misconduct, any confession or apology, and whether the misconduct was deliberate.

6. When imposing discipline, refer to all of the misconduct that is the basis for the discipline, including previous misconduct.

7. Where appropriate, consider the option of a last chance agreement.

8. In a disciplinary meeting and letter, review the misconduct for which discipline is being imposed, inform the employee of the discipline being imposed, advise the employee of the future consequences of misconduct, and if necessary clarify expectations for future behaviour.

Considerations for Unions Responding to Discipline

1. Advise the employee about the steps in the grievance and arbitration process.

2. Obtain the assistance of legal counsel or the parent union if necessary.

3. Determine if the procedural requirements of the collective agreement, such as union representation at disciplinary meetings and written reasons for discipline, have been met.

4. Determine if any rules involved have been communicated to employees and consistently enforced.

5. Investigate the incident(s) leading to the discipline, and obtain statements from potential witnesses.

6. Consider the factors that an arbitrator might refer to when determining whether to reduce the penalty, such as the employee's length of service.

7. In the case of a discharge, take up, where appropriate, the possibility of a last chance agreement with management.

to ensure that an employee who has been disciplined or discharged is provided with proper representation.

SENIORITY

Accumulation and Termination of Seniority

Employers must ensure that seniority is recorded in accordance with the collective agreement and the law. Seniority continues to accumulate during periods when employees are not working, including a leave or layoff, unless the agreement provides otherwise. Employment standards legislation may require seniority to continue to accumulate during leaves such as pregnancy and parental leave. Collective agreements that do not permit seniority to accumulate may contravene the legislation. Grievances have been filed in cases where employees have lost jobs because their seniority did not accumulate during absences caused by illness or accident, and arbitrators have found this discriminatory. In Chapter 7, it was noted that the collective agreement could specify whether time spent working outside of the bargaining unit would be counted towards seniority.

The collective agreement may contain a deemed termination provision that states that if the employee is absent for a specified time, he or she is automatically terminated. The administration of this provision may require the employer to notify the employee about the termination and allow him or her to respond. Some arbitrators have held that the employment relationship is not terminated if the employer fails to do so.[27] A human rights issue arises if the deemed termination provision is applied to an employee who was absent because of a disability, as a termination relying on the deemed termination provision could be discriminatory. Accordingly, employers will be able to justify a termination on the basis of a deemed termination article only if it is established that the employer has met its duty to accommodate.

Job Posting and Selection Process

Although an employer might prefer to hire part-time employees to fill an opening instead of posting for a full-time job that is not permitted if the agreement requires vacancies to be posted. In cases where the employer gives additional work to part-time employees instead of posting to fill a full-time vacancy after a full-time employee has resigned, arbitrators have held that there is a breach of the agreement and ordered the employer to post the job.[28]

There are some procedural matters in the job posting and selection process that employers should be aware of. The employer may determine the job specifications for a position; however, those specifications must be reasonable requirements for the job. In one case where an employer provided that the ability to speak a second language was required, when in fact it was not a legitimate job requirement, an arbitrator found that the procedure was flawed and ordered the job to be reposted.[29] The job posting procedure must be applied in a reasonable manner without any discrimination. The employer cannot post a job setting out certain criteria and then make the selection decision on the basis of different criteria. In one case, the posting for the position of a charge nurse referred to clinical skills; however, managerial ability was subsequently an important criterion referred to in the selection process. An arbitration board ordered that the job be posted again and the selection process be repeated.[30]

Layoffs

The employer will have to look at the definition of a layoff provided in the collective agreement to determine whether the layoff provisions of the contract apply. Unless the agreement provides otherwise, the employer can reduce hours of all employees in a bargaining unit, and this will not be viewed as a layoff. In a case where the employer reduced hours for some employees but not others, it was held that there had been a **constructive layoff**. The employer cannot avoid the layoff and seniority provisions of the agreement in this manner.[31] Instead of reducing the hours for some employees in a bargaining unit, the employer will be required to lay off employees, applying the seniority rules in the agreement. The collective agreement in the case referred to did not define layoff. It is possible for the parties to establish a definition of layoff providing that a temporary reduction of hours does not constitute a layoff.

Constructive layoff refers to the reduction of hours for some employees.

Recalls

Individuals who have been laid off are still employees until the collective agreement provides otherwise. As noted in Chapter 7, the agreement will usually provide that employees lose their seniority and employment status after a specified time on layoff. One of the rights of an employee on layoff whose seniority has not yet been terminated is the right to be notified of any job vacancies posted.[32] The employer may encounter a situation where there is a job posting requirement in the collective agreement and there are employees on layoff who have recall rights. If there is a job opening, the question the employer faces is whether the job should be filled by recalling an employee on layoff or by posting the job. Although the terms of a particular collective agreement might affect this situation, it has been held that unless the job that is open is the one an employee on recall was previously laid off from, the job posting requirement must be complied with. The employer must post the job instead of simply recalling employees on layoff.[33] This gives more emphasis to seniority. If the employee on layoff had two years of seniority and another employee in the bargaining unit had three years, granting the job to the employee on layoff without posting would mean that the employee with less seniority was being given priority.

Assessing Skill and Ability

The collective agreement may require the employer to determine the ability of employees when filling job openings, laying off, and recalling employees. Relative ability and sufficient ability provisions were referred to in Chapter 7. When employers are determining the skill and ability of employees competing for a job, they may use a range of tools. Testing can be used; however, tests must be conducted fairly, the same for all employees, and relevant to the job requirements. Interviews can be used; however, they must be conducted fairly, be related to job requirements, and given the appropriate weight. The weight that should be given to the interview will depend on the type of job involved. In one case where the position being filled was in maintenance and involved welding and other manual work, the employer did not consider the application of a candidate who was unresponsive during the interview. An arbitrator found that the employer put too much emphasis on the interview and should have referred to other methods to assess the candidate's ability such as his work record and observation.[34] How valid and fair are interviews conducted by employers? A study that examined labour arbitration cases where the interview was in dispute indicates there is room for improvement.[35] The study examined all reported arbitration cases relating to the employment interview from two sources, *Labour Arbitration Cases* and *Canadian Labour Arbitration Summaries*, from 1987 to 1996. In a majority of the 56 cases (52 percent), it was found that the interview was unfair. Grievances were allowed in 46 percent of the cases. The grievances were not allowed in all cases where the interview was found to be unfair because it was not the only factor in the selection process. There were cases in which the interview was found to be unfair but the grievance was dismissed because the grievor had not been selected for other valid reasons. The main problems found with the interview process were: (1) using interview questions that failed to measure the knowledge, skills, and abilities required for the job and (2) giving the interview results too much emphasis and failing to consider factors such as performance appraisals and work history. It is recommended that employers refer to the literature relating to employment interviews and consider adopting measures listed in Key Considerations 9-4.

The employer may take into consideration an employee's discipline record if it is relevant to the job the employee is being considered for. If the job required tact and diplomacy to deal with customers, a disciplinary record that indicated the employee had difficulty relating to others would be a factor.

Remedies at Arbitration

Arbitrators considering promotion decisions made by management take two different approaches. Some only intervene when it is established that the decision process has been arbitrary, discriminatory, or unreasonable. They think they should defer to management's decision unless evidence shows it to be fundamentally flawed. Others look into whether the management decision was actually correct. In cases relating to job posting and promotions, the most common remedy is an order that the employer post the position again and repeat

---

Key Considerations 9-4

Ways to Increase the Validity and Fairness of Employment Interviews*

1. Ensure that the information relating to job duties and qualifications is current.

2. Restrict the use of the interview to important job-related knowledge, skills, and abilities that the interview can be used to assess.

3. Use a structured interview format.

4. Limit the use of pre-interview data about candidates.

5. Use more than one interview question to assess key attributes.

6. Use a formal scoring system that measures each attribute separately.

7. Train interviewers on the interview process and human rights issues.

*Robert D. Gatewood and Hubert S. Feild, *Human Resource Selection*, 5th ed. (Fort Worth, TX: Harcourt College Publishers, 2001).

the selection process. However, in some circumstances, an arbitrator may simply award the job to the grievor. In layoff cases, the arbitrator has the authority to order an employee to be placed in a particular job and award damages for lost earnings.

HUMAN RIGHTS ISSUES IN THE ADMINISTRATION OF THE AGREEMENT

Human rights issues are critical in the administration of collective agreements. One arbitrator has summed up the importance of human rights legislation as follows: "The growing pre-eminence of human rights laws in Canada has profound implications for both our established labour relations institutions and the administration of the workplace itself."[36]

The principles of human rights legislation were considered in Chapter 2. Here we will look at the implications of human rights legislation for the administration of the collective agreement.

Employer and Union Obligations

Employers and Accommodation   Employers and unions are prohibited from discriminating on the basis of any of the prohibited grounds provided in human rights legislation. The employer has a duty to accommodate provided that the accommodation would not impose an undue hardship. A rule or requirement that is discriminatory is permissible if it is established to be a bona fide occupational qualification (BFOQ) or bona fide occupational requirement (BFOR). The elements required to establish a BFOR were reviewed in Chapter 2. In particular, it was noted that a discriminatory rule or requirement cannot be a BFOR if the employee can be accommodated. For example, a requirement that an employee have a specified level of hearing could not be established as a BFOR if the employee could use a device or equipment that would compensate for a hearing deficiency.

Unions and Accommodation   The union has a duty to accommodate if it is a party to discrimination. A union could become a party to discrimination in two ways: (1) the union may participate in the formation of a rule that has a discriminatory effect, by agreeing to the rule or provision inside or outside of the collective agreement, or (2) where the union did not participate in the formulation of the rule, it may become a party to the discrimination by impeding the employer's reasonable efforts to accommodate. The nature and extent of the union's accommodation obligations will vary depending on how the duty arises. A union that has agreed to a discriminatory term is jointly responsible with the employer to seek accommodation for the employee. Although the employer will normally be in a better position to facilitate an accommodation, the union still has a responsibility to put forward measures to accommodate. In the second situation, where the union has not agreed to the discriminatory measure, the employer must canvass methods that do not involve the union or a disruption of the collective agreement before calling upon the union to participate in the accommodation. The union's duty only arises when its involvement is required to make an accommodation possible because no other reasonable accommodation can be found.

Discipline   Employees cannot be disciplined for behaviour caused by a disability. If it was established that an employee guilty of misconduct had a bipolar disorder that could be controlled with medication, an arbitrator would likely overturn any discipline imposed. The employee would have an obligation to control the situation by taking the necessary medication. If an employee's absence is caused by a disability, the employer cannot impose discipline. However, the employer is allowed to respond; this is discussed in a separate section below.

Last Chance Agreements.   Human rights legislation presents special problems regarding the enforceability of LCAs. Dependency on alcohol or drugs is a disability under human rights legislation, and it is discrimination to withhold employment or treat a person differently because he or she has a disability. An employer cannot terminate an employee with a drug or alcohol dependency unless it has accommodated the employee to the point of undue hardship. If an LCA imposes conditions on the employee with disabilities that are more onerous than those imposed on other employees, it may be found that the agreement violates human rights legislation and is unenforceable. In one case, an employee was discharged because of absenteeism caused by a mental disorder. The employee was reinstated pursuant to an LCA providing that if the employee's attendance fell below the six-month average for the department he would be terminated. Subsequently the employee was absent because of a blood pressure condition and was discharged. It was held that the agreement was discriminatory because it imposed a level of attendance not required of other employees.[37] Establishing an LCA does not by itself mean that the employer has met the duty to accommodate to the point of undue hardship. The terms of the LCA must be considered. When the agreement contains terms that are unreasonable—terms that the employee could not be expected to meet—the agreement may not be enforceable. If it would not have been an undue hardship to impose less stringent conditions, the LCA will not be upheld if the employee breaches the terms. In a case where an employee had attendance and performance problems caused by a mental disability he was reinstated pursuant to an LCA that contained numerous conditions. The arbitrator commented on the conditions as follows: "In my view, the imposition of more reasonable terms such as I have outlined, instead of those stipulated by paragraph 5 of the LCA would not have imposed undue hardship on the employer. I can only conclude that this provision was put in the LCA because that was the bargain that the employer expected in return for Burns' reinstatement."[38] This means that if an employer insists on more onerous conditions in an LCA because it has the upper hand when it is negotiated, the result may be that the agreement is unenforceable. In summary, an LCA involving an employee with a disability cannot (1) impose conditions more onerous than those imposed on other employees or (2) impose excessively stringent conditions if less stringent conditions would not impose an undue hardship on the employer. Because an LCA will have to be carefully prepared, it may be advisable to seek legal counsel.

Job Posting and Selection If any requirement in a job posting is discriminatory, an arbitrator will order that it be eliminated unless the employer can show that it is a BFOQ or BFOR. For example, the job posting may not specify the gender of applicants unless that is a BFOR. In determining an employee's seniority, the employer must ensure that periods of absence caused by disability are not excluded.

Accommodation of Employees and Seniority Although employees may require accommodation because of any protected ground of discrimination, most accommodation issues relate to religion, gender, and disability. Some of the possible measures to accommodate an employee were referred to in Chapter 2. The employer does not have to create a position that is unproductive or serves no useful purpose for the employer, because that would impose an undue hardship. The union has an obligation to cooperate with the employer's attempts to accommodate; however, it does not have to agree to any measures that would impose undue hardship upon other employees in the bargaining unit or the union. If there is no way to accommodate other than an arrangement that involves a variation from the collective agreement, the union must agree to this variation, provided it does not impose an undue hardship. In one case, the collective agreement provided that work done on a Sunday required the payment of overtime. When an employee was not able to work on Saturday because of religious belief, the company proposed that the employee be allowed to work Sundays without the payment of overtime. The union did not agree with this proposal and insisted that any work done on Sunday be paid at the overtime rate as provided in the agreement. In the end, it was held that the union's failure to agree to a variation from the agreement to allow the employee to work Sundays without the payment of overtime was a violation of its human rights obligations. The union does not have to agree to a variation from the agreement unless other measures to accommodate that do not involve a breach of the collective agreement cannot be found.

The employer's duty to accommodate may lead to a conflict with seniority provisions. For example, a possible accommodation might involve moving an employee to a job that is open; however, another employee who has more seniority may want the job. Cases have established that accommodation can override seniority only as a last resort to allow an employee with disabilities to be given preference. Other measures that do not require a variation from the collective agreement must first be considered. A distinction has been drawn between bumping an employee with more seniority from his or her job to accommodate, and allowing an employee in need of accommodation to move into an open job ahead of other employees. Arbitrators have not been willing to require an incumbent employee with seniority to be displaced from a job as part of an accommodation. They may be willing to allow an employee who needs accommodation to move into an open job ahead of employees who have more seniority, if there is no other way to accommodate.

Employee Obligations

Employees have three primary obligations relating to accommodation: (1) they must communicate their need for accommodation, (2) they must cooperate in attempts to provide accommodation, including providing necessary medical information and where necessary seek treatment, and (3) they must accept reasonable attempts to accommodate—they cannot expect a perfect solution. In one case, a nurse was terminated for drug use and theft of drugs from the hospital where he worked. The employee had been given opportunities to overcome his addiction and had signed an LCA. The arbitrator confirmed that the employee had a duty to take some responsibility for his rehabilitation; and when he failed to discharge that duty, the employer's duty to accommodate had been met. If an employer was attempting to accommodate an employee's religious beliefs by rescheduling the employee's work, the employee could not refuse to work evening hours if that was a reasonable accommodation.

NON-DISCIPLINARY MEASURES FOR INNOCENT ABSENTEEISM

Culpable vs. Innocent Absenteeism

A distinction must be drawn between culpable and non-culpable or innocent absenteeism. **Culpable absenteeism** is absenteeism in which the employee is at fault or there is blameworthy conduct. Skipping work to attend a baseball game or repeated absences on Fridays are examples. **Innocent absenteeism** is caused by factors beyond the employee's control, such as absences caused by sickness or injury. This distinction is important because employers cannot impose discipline for innocent absenteeism. Employers should ensure that any attendance management programs or policies distinguish between culpable and innocent absenteeism. Although the law does not allow the employer to discipline employees for innocent absenteeism, it is still possible for the employer to take action to deal with this issue.

Culpable absenteeism is absenteeism in which the employee is at fault or there is blameworthy conduct.

Innocent absenteeism is absenteeism where the employee has no control over the absence from work.

Non-disciplinary Discharge

Employers may terminate employees for innocent absenteeism where: (1) the employee's past absence has been significantly greater than the bargaining unit average, (2) there is no reasonable likelihood of attendance improving in the future, and (3) the employer has accommodated the employee to the point of undue hardship. In one case, an employee had an absenteeism record 10 times worse than the bargaining unit average, largely due to injuries incurred while playing football. The arbitrator ruled that the employer acted improperly when it dismissed him, because it had not taken into consideration the fact that he had undertaken to give up playing football, and it was likely that his attendance would improve.

The employer has an obligation to notify the employee of the standard of attendance required and the consequences of failing to meet it. Where the absence is caused by a disability, the employer cannot discharge the employee if he or she might be accommodated without undue hardship. For example, if the employee could be moved to an alternative position that was within his or her capabilities, the employee could not be discharged. An employee cannot be discharged for innocent absenteeism if the discharge would prevent the employee from receiving benefits payable under the agreement for disability. If the disability payments provided for in the agreement require individuals to be employees to be eligible for payments, the employee cannot be discharged until the disability coverage has lapsed. If the disability benefits vest so that employee status is not required for the continued payment of benefits, the employee may be discharged. Disability payments, which provide employees with income when they are unable to work, must be distinguished from health benefits such as eye and dental protection. A contract provision for health benefits does not prevent a discharge for innocent absenteeism.

Responses Other Than Discharge

There might be circumstances in which a response other than termination for innocent absenteeism would be appropriate. An employer might deal with the issue using alternative measures including transfers, medical leaves, or demotion, subject to any provisions in the collective agreement. If an employee has special skills and training for a particular department, and his or her absence imposes an undue hardship for the employer, it would be possible to transfer or demote the employee to another area.[39]

DUTY OF FAIR REPRESENTATION
Nature of the Union's Duty of Fair Representation

The **duty of fair representation** prohibits the union from acting in a manner that is arbitrary, discriminatory, or in bad faith.

Labour relations legislation in most jurisdictions provides that the union has a **duty of fair representation**—that is, a duty to act fairly in the course of representing employees in the bargaining unit. The *Canada Labour Code* provides that "The trade union . . . shall not act in a manner that is arbitrary, discriminatory or in bad faith in the representation of any of the employees in the unit with respect to their rights under the collective agreement. . . ."[40] All jurisdictions other than New Brunswick and Prince Edward Island have a similar provision.

In all nine jurisdictions, the duty applies to the administration of the agreement; and in some jurisdictions noted in Figure 9-5, the duty also applies to the negotiation of the agreement. In one case, a group of federally regulated employees filed a complaint that a union had failed to negotiate a wage increase for them. The complaint was dismissed because, at the time, the duty of fair representation did not apply to contract negotiation in the federal jurisdiction.[41] The Canada Industrial Relations Board now interprets the *Code* so that the duty applies to contract negotiation, and a complaint relating to a union's conduct during negotiation could be made.

In the jurisdictions in which the duty of fair representation includes the negotiation of the contract, the union does not necessarily have to follow the instructions of employees. In one case, the union negotiated a provision for a pension plan despite the fact that employees indicated they did not want the plan. The employees subsequently filed a complaint that the union had breached its duty of fair representation. The Labour Relations Board held that the union is not limited to following instructions of employees who are

	Extent of Duty	
	Negotiation of Agreement	**Administration of Agreement**
Canada	X	X
Alberta		X
British Columbia	X	X
Manitoba	X	
Newfoundland		X
Nova Scotia		X
Ontario	X	X
Quebec	X	X
Saskatchewan	X	

Figure 9-5 Jurisdictions Providing a Union Duty of Fair Representation

presently in the bargaining unit. The union was allowed to pursue the plan because it had reasonably considered the employees' wishes and determined that the plan would be in the long-run interest of the bargaining unit.[42]

The duty applies to all members of the bargaining unit, whether or not they are union members. In Saskatchewan, the duty does not arise where the union has been voluntarily recognized; in other jurisdictions, the duty applies both to unions that have been certified and to unions that have been voluntarily recognized. It has been held that unintentional errors are not a violation of the duty. However, some cases have held that gross negligence is a violation. The duty could become an issue regarding the filing of grievances and referral of grievances to arbitration. Generally, the union has ownership of the grievance and arbitration process, and it is not a violation of the duty to refuse to refer a dispute to arbitration if the union acts fairly. If the union listens to an employee's complaint and considers the matter, and fairly determines that it would not be of any value to proceed, it is not a breach of the duty if a grievance is not processed or referred to arbitration.

In the jurisdictions without a duty of fair representation provided in labour relations legislation, there may be an implied duty at common law and legislation may prohibit specific union practices.[43]

Implications for Employers and Unions

A breach of the duty of fair representation is an unfair labour practice. An employee who thinks there has been a breach of the duty may file a complaint with the Labour Relations Board. If the Board determines there has been a breach, it has the authority to order remedies as listed in Figure 9-6, some of which might affect the employer.

1. Directing the union a take a grievance to arbitration and require the employer to proceed even though the time limits have not been met
2. Providing the employee with independent legal counsel at the arbitration hearing, at the union's expense
3. Directing the union to pay damages to the employee
4. Directing the union to meet with bargaining unit employees
5. Directing the union to post a notice confirming it will refrain from any future violations

Figure 9-6 Possible Labour Relations Board Orders to Remedy a Breach of the Duty of Fair Representation

Employers should note that even though the time to refer a grievance to arbitration may have expired, a Board could order an employer to proceed to arbitration as part of an order providing a remedy for the union's breach of fair representation. Accordingly, the employer should ensure that any information relating to a grievance is retained for a few years.

PROBLEMS WITH ARBITRATION

The arbitration process has been criticized as being too legalistic, expensive, and slow. Some alternatives that may be less expensive or help the parties improve their relationship are reviewed here.

Expedited Arbitration

Expedited arbitration enables faster resolution of disputes referred to arbitration by providing for shorter time limits in the process.

Expedited arbitration resolves issues more quickly by providing for shorter time limits for arbitration. The possibility of the parties including a voluntary expedited arbitration process in the collective agreement was referred to in Chapter 7. They might also agree on a process that will not allow lawyers, or require evidence to be limited to written statements. The labour relations legislation in seven jurisdictions—Alberta, British Columbia, Manitoba, Newfoundland and Labrador, New Brunswick, Nova Scotia, and Ontario—provides for an expedited procedure that is available upon the request of one of the parties.[44] There is some variation between jurisdictions on the details. Generally the legislation provides that either the union or the employer may request the Minister of Labour to appoint a single arbitrator. The Minister is required to appoint an arbitrator who must commence hearings on the matter within a specified number of days of the request. In some jurisdictions, if the parties agree, the arbitrator is required to deliver an oral decision immediately or as soon as possible.

Grievance Mediation

Grievance mediation is a confidential process in which a mediator helps the parties negotiate a settlement to a grievance.

Grievance mediation is a confidential process in which a mediator helps the parties negotiate a settlement. Instead of hearing evidence and providing a binding decision, the mediator helps the parties reach a voluntary agreement. Grievance mediation has several potential advantages, including (1) the resolution of disputes in less time, (2) a lower cost than arbitration, (3) the potential to develop better solutions, and (4) protection of the relationship between the parties.

When grievances are referred to arbitration, it usually takes six to nine months to move from the request for arbitration to the final award. It takes much less time to start the grievance mediation process. One study indicates that it takes only an average of 15 days to get to a mediation conference.[45] Grievance mediation will not take as long as arbitration because the parties are not delayed by the painstaking examination and cross-examination of witnesses. The costs of grievance mediation are much lower because mediators' fees are significantly less than those of arbitrators, and usually lawyers are not involved. Through grievance mediation, the parties may negotiate a win-win solution that will improve their relationship; in arbitration, there will typically be a winner and a loser, which may harm the relationship.

Mediation may work better with some types of grievances. If the grievance relates to a seniority issue there may be less incentive for the employer to negotiate and make concessions, because arbitrators tend to be more deferential to management decisions in this area. In discipline and discharge cases, where there may be less certainty about the outcome of an arbitration hearing, there may be more incentive to negotiate. It appears that the process works best if the mediator is an experienced arbitrator with mediation skills. If he or she is familiar with the arbitration process and the possible outcomes, he or she may use this information at the appropriate times to pressure the parties to avoid the costs and uncertainty of arbitration if the mediation fails. Some studies have found that grievance mediation has a high success rate, with over 80 percent of cases referred being resolved.[46] These results may be distorted because the parties may have referred cases to grievance mediation that had a high likelihood of success. However, because of the lower costs and other potential advantages, grievance mediation may be worth considering. It will not be suitable for all cases. If one of the parties wishes to establish a precedent, they will want to proceed to arbitration.

Implications for Practice

1. In unionized workplaces, the employer's authority to manage will be affected by the collective agreement. Policies and rules established by the employer may be subject to review at arbitration and may be overturned. The discharge of employees may also be challenged and an arbitrator may reinstate employees. The procedures used to promote, layoff, and recall employees may be reviewed at arbitration, and the employer's decision may be overturned.

2. Employers should ensure that managers who might be affected by the grievance procedure receive the training they need to properly represent the organization. Training should cover the procedural aspects of handling grievances, replying to grievances, and the settlement of disputes.

3. Arbitration is an important process in unionized workplaces. Employers will likely have to engage the services of a law firm to deal with any grievances taken to arbitration. In consultation with legal advisers, the employer should determine whether to proceed with an arbitration that could be costly, or attempt to settle any particular grievance.

4. The management rights article is an important term of the collective agreement that the employer may rely on to hire employees and make other operational decisions. It is important that managers avoid an estoppel argument being raised by the union. Accordingly, managers should be cautious regarding statements or conduct that could establish a practice that is different from the terms of the agreement.

5. The employer can use discipline and discharge to correct behaviour or remove employees who refuse to comply with workplace rules. Employers should take the measures referred to in this chapter, including communication and consistent enforcement of workplace rules, to avoid an arbitrator overturning disciplinary or discharge decisions.

6. The seniority provisions in a collective agreement can have major implications for employers regarding promotions, layoffs, and recall of employees. Employers should confirm that any procedures established comply with the collective agreement and are fairly administered to avoid a possible challenge at arbitration. Employers should ensure that they are properly using instruments such as testing and carefully constructed interviews to select the most qualified individuals and avoid decisions being overturned at arbitration.

7. Human rights legislation affects the administration of the collective agreement and in exceptional cases might even require the employer and union to vary from its terms. In the course of accommodating employees, the employer must examine possibilities that would allow the employee to be accommodated within the terms of the agreement. If an employee cannot be accommodated without a variation from the agreement, a contract provision may have to be suspended or waived, if this would not impose an undue hardship. Employers should consider consulting with the union to establish an accommodation policy and protocol.

8. Employers are not helpless when dealing with innocent absenteeism, including absenteeism caused by a disability. Employers must have records to confirm past absenteeism and must investigate the likelihood of future attendance improving before taking action. The employer must also show that an employee who is not attending because of a disability cannot be accommodated.

9. The union has a duty to fairly represent all employees in the bargaining unit. Employers should be prepared for the possibility that a Labour Relations Board might order an employer to proceed to arbitration even though the union failed to refer a grievance to arbitration within the time limits provided.

10. There are problems associated with grievance arbitration, including delay and expense. Employers and unions should investigate alternatives such as expedited arbitration and grievance mediation to reduce costs and improve the union–management relationship.

Key Terms

agreed statement of facts, p. 217

arbitrability, p. 219

argument in the alternative, p. 218

burden of proof, p. 217

constructive layoff, p. 231

culminating incident, p. 225

culpable absenteeism, p. 235

duty of fair representation, p. 236

estoppel, p. 221

expedited arbitration, p. 238

grievance mediation, p. 238

grievance rate, p. 215

innocent absenteeism, p. 235

interest arbitration, p. 216

last chance agreement, p. 229

minutes of settlement, p. 216

obey now, grieve later, p. 213

ownership of the grievance, p. 215

privileged communications, p. 215

progressive discipline, p. 226

rights arbitration, p. 216

waiver, p. 216

without precedent, p. 216

without prejudice, p. 215

Review Questions

1. What are the primary functions of the grievance process?

2. Explain the possible benefits of the grievance and arbitration process to the employer, unions, and employees.

3. An employee with a poor disciplinary record who was caught stealing the employer's property has been dismissed. The union has filed a grievance. Does the union have to take the grievance to arbitration?

4. Distinguish between rights and interest arbitration.

5. At an arbitration hearing, either of the parties can make arguments "in the alternative." Explain what this means, and give an example of a union argument that illustrates this concept.

6. What is the meaning and significance of the burden of proof in arbitration?

7. Explain the meaning of the terms *arbitrable* and *inarbitrable*. Provide an example for each.

8. An employer wishes to establish rules for the workplace. Explain the criteria that would have to be met to ensure that the rules established are enforceable.

9. Explain why an employer may not be able to implement a measure relying on the management rights article in a collective agreement.

10. What are the factors an arbitrator would consider when reviewing the discipline imposed by an employer?

11. Explain the meaning of a *last chance agreement*.

12. What are the advantages of a last chance agreement to employers, unions, and employees?

13. What are the key points that an employer should be aware of in connection with a job posting?

14. When can an employer discharge an employee for innocent absenteeism?

15. Describe the union's duty of fair representation, and explain how the employer could be affected by this obligation.

16. Explain why an employer may or may not wish to resolve a dispute using grievance mediation.

Discussion Questions

1. A collective agreement contains a grievance procedure providing that if a grievance is not resolved at Step 1 the union has five days to refer the matter to Step 2. If the union fails to refer the dispute to Step 2 until a month after the Step 1 response is received, what should the employer do?

2. A collective agreement included the following articles:
    (a) "If the Union fails to submit a grievance at each level in the grievance procedure within the time limits stipulated in this article, the grievance shall be deemed abandoned. Similarly, if the Corporation fails to reply to a grievance in writing within the time limits stipulated in this article, the grievance may be referred to the next level of the grievance procedure, including arbitration."
    (b) "After exhausting the provisions of the grievance procedure, either of the parties may notify the other party in writing within thirty (30) days of the final level reply, of its intention to submit a grievance to arbitration."

    The employer discharged an employee and a grievance was filed on his behalf by the union. The grievance went through the steps in the grievance procedure and the union received the reply from the employer at the last step in the procedure, denying the grievance, on July 9. The union referred the matter to arbitration on September 20. Subsequently the parties agreed to an arbitration date of July 5 in the next year. One week before the hearing, the lawyer for the employer advised the lawyer for the union that an objection would be made to the arbitrator's jurisdiction. What is the basis of the employer's objection, and will the arbitrator allow the arbitration to proceed?

3. A collective agreement between a hospital and the union contained the following:
    • A management rights article
    • A provision regarding contracting out that provided: "12.01. The Hospital shall not contract out any work usually performed by members of the bargaining unit if, as a result of such contracting out, a layoff of any employees other than casual part-time employees results from such contracting out"
    • A technological change article that provided for notice to the union for technological change plus notice to employees who might be laid off

    The hospital proposed the adoption of a new food preparation system that would involve food being assembled elsewhere by an outside company. The final preparation would be done at the hospital using new equipment that would be installed. The system was similar to one used in the airline industry and involved a $5.5 million investment. If the new system was adopted some hospital employees including cooks would be laid off.
    (a) Assume you are a union official. On what basis might the union challenge this?
    (b) Assume you were an employer representative. On what basis might the employer defend the plan?
    (c) If you were an arbitrator dealing with this situation, what would your decision be?

4. A collective agreement provided that when a disciplinary interview was held a union steward would be present (in an article hereafter referred to as Article 6). An employee left work on a Friday afternoon prior to the end of his shift. The employee's position was that he had permission to leave. The employer's position was that the employee did not have permission to leave early. On the day of the incident a manager called the employee at home and talked with him. In the course of the telephone conversation the employee was advised he would be suspended for one week. The employee asked that the suspension be reduced and it was agreed that there would be a meeting to review the matter on Monday. On Monday there was a meeting at which a union steward was present; however, there was no change in the suspension. A grievance was filed that stated there was an "unjust suspension" and did not refer to Article 6.
    (a) What argument will the union make at the arbitration hearing?
    (b) If you were the arbitrator, what would your decision be?
    (c) If the grievance is allowed, what remedy should be ordered?

5. After an employee left work without permission, a supervisor imposed a two-day suspension after consulting with the human resources department. One week later, a more senior

manager reviewed the situation and found that the employee had previously been suspended for two days for the same misconduct and that the problem of employees leaving work early was increasing. The senior manager ordered that the suspension be increased to one week. Can the union challenge this?

6. Is there a problem if an employer negotiates a last chance agreement that contains conditions that the employee will not likely be able to meet? Explain.

7. An employee was guilty of misconduct, including threatening a supervisor. He was discharged and a grievance was filed. During the grievance procedure it became apparent that the employee had an alcohol problem. The grievance was settled pursuant to an agreement that provided the grievor would be on probation for a year and seek treatment. The agreement also provided that if the employee was absent from work without a reason acceptable to the company he would be discharged without recourse to the grievance and arbitration procedure. Four months after the grievor was reinstated there was another absence for two days. The employer terminated the employee.
   (a) Can a union and the employer agree that the grievance and arbitration procedure will not be used?
   (b) Is there any problem with this agreement? That is, is there any way the union can avoid the termination?

8. The collective agreement for a fire department provided that promotions would be based on skill, ability, and efficiency and that, where candidates were equal, seniority would govern. The employer posted the job of lieutenant, indicating that candidates would be evaluated on their knowledge, abilities, and personal suitability. The employer used written tests and an oral interview to determine qualifications. To assess dependability the employer relied solely on the interview, and the candidates were asked questions such as "What does dependability mean to you?" The employer scored the results of the interviews and tests to two decimal places and insisted that candidates would have to have scores that were absolutely equal before seniority would be considered.
   (a) On what basis, if any, can the union file a grievance?
   (b) What outcome do you expect at an arbitration hearing? Explain.

9. A collective agreement provided that seniority would govern for promotion decisions if skill, ability, and other qualifications were relatively equal. The employer posted a job for a hospital porter and evaluated the candidates on the basis of an interview, written test, and past performance. The results were scored. The second and third candidates were within 5 percent and 10.8 percent of the highest-scoring candidate. The job was given to the highest-scoring candidate. On what basis, if any, can a grievance be filed? What outcome do you expect?

10. Comment on the following statement: "Merit does not matter in a unionized workplace because of the seniority principle."

11. Labour Relations Issue 9-4 referred to a situation where an arbitrator refused to admit a surreptitious videotape as evidence. Do you agree with that decision? Under what circumstances would you allow this type of evidence to be used?

Web Research

1. Some unions provide electronic copies of the grievance form used by local bargaining units for unresolved complaints with employer. Go to the Canadian Union of Public Employee (CUPE) website (http://cupe.ca) and search for the link for the generic grievance form. Note key elements that are required to be completed by the employee, the union and the employer as well as key procedural elements also detailed in the form.

2. Some unions provide arbitration decisions at their websites. Go to the website for the Ontario Public Service Union (www.opseu.org), and then go to "Grievances." Find an arbitration case dealing with discharge and the penalty imposed by the employer by entering the term "discharge" in the search engine. Did the arbitrator uphold the penalty imposed by the employer? What factors did the arbitrator refer to when making the decision?

CASE INCIDENT   ARLINGTON HOME FOR THE AGED

Gordon worked as a food service attendant at Arlington Home for the Aged. His job description included preparing food and assisting residents who could not feed themselves. Gordon had been working for his employer for almost three years when he was involved in an incident that led to his dismissal.

On the day in question Gordon was working in the kitchen with two female co-workers, washing dishes and preparing food. Music was playing on a radio, and one of Gordon's co-workers asked him, "Are you going to do a little dance for us?" The other employee asked, "Are you uncomfortable with your body?" Gordon left the kitchen, went to a nearby storage area, removed all his clothing and went back to the kitchen. He streaked in front of his two co-workers, waving his arms to get their attention. This incident lasted a few seconds. Gordon returned a few minutes later with his clothes on and laughed about what he had done.

The next day Gordon bragged to several co-workers about what he had done and how funny it was. When management questioned Gordon, he admitted that he had streaked his co-workers. The employer investigated the incident and found that Gordon had no explanation for his behaviour other than he was joking with his co-workers. Gordon apologized to his co-workers after management spoke to him.

The employer had a code of conduct and policy on workplace harassment in place, which provided that if the policy was breached the penalties included dismissal. It was confirmed in the investigation that Gordon had attended training on these policies and was aware of their content. The employer terminated Gordon and a letter of termination provided that he had violated the employer's policies, and the employer could not condone sexual harassment in the workplace. The union representing Gordon filed a grievance and eight months after the incident, an arbitration hearing was held.

Questions

1. What arguments will the employer make at the arbitration hearing?

2. What arguments will the union make at the arbitration hearing?

3. Assume that you are the arbitrator hearing this case. Explain what your decision would be, including the reasons for your decision.

CASE INCIDENT   DECORATIVE CONCRETE PRODUCTS

Ross worked as a general labourer for Decorative Concrete Products. The company made precast concrete beams and other products. Ross injured his elbow at work, and was advised by his chiropractor that he should recover in two weeks if he was assigned light duties. The company accommodated Ross's injury, even though Ross continued to have problems with his elbow and required light duties for five months.

Subsequently, Ross injured his back at work. Ross's chiropractor indicated that he should recover within two weeks if he complied with limitations on his activities: standing less than 15 minutes, no lifting, and no ladder climbing. The employer accommodated Ross by assigning him to light duties. Ross's back problems continued and he made repeated trips to his chiropractor. Ross's supervisor became suspicious about the extent of his back injury. The supervisor became more concerned when another employee told her that Ross had been talking about playing hockey. The employer decided to put

Ross under video surveillance to determine if his injuries were as severe as he claimed. Ross was videotaped outside of the workplace and the video showed him walking and bending over to pick up an object, lifting a barbecue off the back of a truck, and playing no-contact ice hockey. Ross was dismissed on the basis that he had been misrepresenting his capabilities. The union filed a grievance and at the arbitration hearing the employer attempted to introduce the videotapes as evidence.

Questions

1. What argument will the union make regarding the videotapes? Explain fully.
2. If you were the arbitrator, how would you proceed?

CASE INCIDENT   BENTLEY SCHOOL BOARD

A collective agreement contained an article that provided as follows:

> In making promotions, demotions, and transfers, the required knowledge, ability, and skills for the position as outlined within the appropriate class specification shall be the primary consideration; and where two or more applicants are capable of filling the position applied for, seniority shall be the determining factor. In all the instances, present qualified employees shall be given preference.

The employer posted a job vacancy for a labourer as follows:

> Performs a variety of unskilled and semi-skilled grounds maintenance tasks, including raking, sweeping, and cleaning grounds; cutting and trimming grass; removing snow; loading/unloading equipment, materials, and tools. Operates and maintains manual and power-operated equipment. Applies fertilizers, pesticides, etc. as directed. Performs other related duties as assigned. *Qualifications:* Several years' grounds-related experience. Ability to perform repetitive manual tasks for an extended period; to lift heavy objects; to work in all weather conditions. Knowledge of and ability to perform minor repairs and maintenance on grounds-related small machinery, tools, and equipment. Possession of or willingness to obtain pesticide applicator ticket within a specified time. Training in practical horticulture is an asset. Knowledge of WHMIS. Safe work practices. Valid driver's licence and safe driving record.

The contract also provided that an employee who moved to a new position would have a trial period of three months to determine his or her suitability. There were two applicants, Franks and Martin. Franks had 10 years of seniority, had worked as a labourer, and had been assigned to grounds duties approximately 40 percent of the time. Martin had five years of seniority, had worked as an assistant to the gardener, and had filled in when the gardener was absent. Martin had also taken courses in horticulture and completed training in pesticide use. The foreman described the work done by grounds labourers as "simple, dirty, . . . shovelling, raking, levelling, . . . loading, moving, and assisting the gardener." It was estimated that each of the tasks involved in the job could be mastered within a day or less of work. Martin was awarded the job.

Questions

1. On what basis can Franks file a grievance?
2. On what basis can the union file a grievance?
3. If Franks and the union file grievances, what outcome do you expect at an arbitration hearing? Explain.

Chapter 10

Contract Dispute Resolution, Strikes, and Lockouts

Chapter Objectives

1. Explain methods to resolve contract disputes
2. Describe the significance of strikes
3. Identify factors affecting strike activity
4. Outline the prerequisites for a strike or lockout
5. Identify the functions of strikes and lockouts

Required Professional Capabilities (CCHRA)	HRPA Human Resources Professionals Competency Framework
10304, 10407, 50113, 50114, 50201, 50203, 50404, 50411	C010, C018, C022, C028, C029, C030, C030, C031, C032, C037, C038, C115, C116, C117, C119, C120, C121, C122, C124, C126, C127, C128

In 2013, Canadians witnessed a public sector strike with international implications. The federal government and the Professional Association of Foreign Service Officers (PAFSO), which represents diplomats and immigration officers abroad, were involved in a six-month legal strike that had begun April 2, 2013. PAFSO represents foreign service workers employed by Citizenship and Immigration Canada (CIC) and the Department of Foreign Affairs, Trade, and Development. These professionals include the employees of Canadian embassies around the world who manage and process visa applications.

As part of the union' s escalating job action, PAFSO members at key centres around the world scaled back some of their services, including processing visas required for international tourists and students studying at Canadian universities and colleges. The Canadian tourism industry claimed that the strike not only would damage the "brand" of the country in the eyes of international tourists, but also would see a real economic loss of several hundred million dollars in tourism. Leaders in Canadian colleges and universities were concerned as well about delays that could cause a drop of up to 40 percent in international student applications. It was estimated that each foreign student individually contributed $10 000, beyond tuition, to the Canadian economy.

Citizenship and Immigration Canada dealt with the pressures of six months of rotating strikes involving foreign service workers by training more staff to assist in processing visa documentation and offering overtime to staff to deal with the backlog of applications.

Three months into the labour disruption, the president of PAFSO president wrote to the government proposing the outstanding bargaining issues be submitted to binding arbitration. Treasury Board President, Tony Clements responded that he would accept arbitration, but only on certain conditions. However, the Public Service Labour Relations Board found that such terms were contrary to what was outlined in the law, and that the federal government knew the union could never accept such terms.

Thus, the Board found the government was guilty of bargaining in bad faith. This ruling hastened the settlement that was finally reached in late September, 2013.

The memorandum of settlement between the parties gave PAFSO members the higher wage scale they were seeking, but gave up severance pay for those who leave voluntarily—a key government demand. Union members received retroactive lump-sum raise payments to 2011. PAFSO leaders acknowledged that the backlog of visa applications would take months to clear but union members were eager to get back to work.

Website providing information regarding third-party assistance in the private sector, Human Resources and Skills. Labour Canada: www.labour. gc.ca/eng/relations/dispute/index.shtml

In this chapter, we will consider the assistance that is made available to the parties so that they can avoid a strike or lockout; issues relating to strikes, including the causes of strikes; and the legal requirements for a strike or lockout.

CONTRACT DISPUTE RESOLUTION

If the parties cannot agree on the terms of a collective agreement, various forms of assistance are available. This is referred to as *third-party assistance*, because it involves an outside party conferring with the union and the employer. The most common forms of assistance— conciliation and mediation—involve a neutral third party attempting to help negotiate an agreement. In most jurisdictions, this assistance is available from the government ministry responsible for labour issues, identified in Chapter 5. In all jurisdictions other than Ontario, the parties can request assistance, or the Minister can initiate the process without a request. In Ontario, the legislation requires a request to the Minister by one of the parties. There are significant differences between jurisdictions regarding the form and significance of assistance to the parties. No two jurisdictions provide for the same procedure. Some of the key policy issues involved are listed in Key Considerations 10-1. The most important of these is whether some form of third-party assistance is required before a strike or lockout is allowed. We will consider these issues, the possible advantages and disadvantages of different forms of third-party assistance, and the extent of their use. Appendix 10.1 at the end of this chapter summarizes the third-party assistance available in each jurisdiction.

Website for federal mediation and conciliation services: www.hrsdc.gc.ca

Types of Third-Party Assistance

Conciliation   In all jurisdictions except British Columbia and Alberta, legislation provides for a conciliation process. There is either a one-stage conciliation process involving either a conciliation officer or a conciliation board, or a two-stage process involving a conciliation officer and then a conciliation board if no settlement is reached with the conciliation officer. **Conciliation officers** are ministry employees who confer with the parties, endeavour to help them reach an agreement, and report to the Minister. Conciliation officers function as facilitators; they do not have any authority over the parties and do not make recommendations regarding the terms of the dispute. In most jurisdictions, the

Conciliation officers are ministry representatives who attempt to assist the parties to reach an agreement.

Minister may appoint a conciliation officer when either or both of the parties make a request to the ministry responsible for labour issues or the Minister may appoint a conciliation officer on his or her own initiative. In Saskatchewan, the legislation provides for the appointment of a conciliation board instead of an officer.

A **conciliation board** consists of a union nominee, an employer nominee, and a neutral chairperson selected by the parties' nominees. The board hears evidence from both sides and makes recommendations to the Minister regarding a settlement. The Minister may make the board's report public. In the normal course of events, the board's recommendations are not binding; however, there is a provision in most jurisdictions that the parties can agree that the recommendations will be binding.

After a conciliation officer or a conciliation board reports to the Minister, there is an additional waiting period that must run before the parties can strike or lockout in all jurisdictions that provide for conciliation except Saskatchewan. This is known as a **cooling-off period**, and it ranges from 7 to 21 days depending on the jurisdiction. In those jurisdictions where the Minister decides whether to appoint a conciliation board, the notification that one will not be appointed may be known as a **no-board report**. In some jurisdictions, including Ontario, the optional conciliation board is not being used, and a no-board report after the conciliation officer completes his or her work is the standard procedure.

The conciliation process is viewed as having advantages and disadvantages. It could help the parties reach an agreement because the third party may bring a new perspective to the negotiations, and the cooling-off period may allow the parties to reconsider their positions. However, there is no empirical evidence that it reduces the overall incidence of strikes. In situations where a strike or lockout is going to be necessary to force the parties to reconsider their positions, conciliation may only delay the process. Some unions have claimed that the process favours the employer because it provides management with time to prepare for a strike. A conciliation board has the same potential advantages as a conciliation officer. In addition, when the board's report is made public, it may lead to public pressure to moderate demands, leading to a settlement. The extent to which conciliation board reports actually have this effect is difficult to determine. Conciliation boards will even further delay a strike or lockout. This is a disadvantage where a work stoppage is necessary to force one or both of the parties to reevaluate their positions.

Mediation   In Alberta and British Columbia, the legislation refers to mediation instead of conciliation. In all other jurisdictions, the legislation allows for the appointment of a mediator instead of, or in addition to, the conciliation process. **Mediators** attempt to assist the parties to reach an agreement. There are numerous policies relating to the role of mediators across Canadian jurisdictions and the main alternatives will be considered here. One alternative is to have the mediator function similar to a conciliation officer. This is the policy in British Columbia. However, there is a provision that either party may request or the Minister may direct the mediation officer to provide a report that may include recommended terms of settlement. Another alternative is to allow the mediator to become much more involved in a contract dispute and possibly make recommendations. This is the policy in Alberta, where one party can accept a mediator's recommendations and require a vote by the other side. A third alternative, adopted in some of the jurisdictions that provide for conciliation, is to allow a mediator to replace a conciliation officer or a conciliation board. In some jurisdictions, the legislation provides that the mediator has the same powers and authority as a conciliation board. A fourth alternative is simply to allow for the Minister to appoint a mediator to assist the parties at any time.

In addition to these policy alternatives provided in the legislation, it is possible that the parties could bring in a private mediator to help them reach agreement. Mediators may

A **conciliation board** is a three-person panel that hears the parties and makes recommendations for a settlement.

A **cooling-off period** is the time the parties must wait after conciliation before they can strike or lockout.

A **no-board report** confirms that a conciliation board will not be appointed and begins the countdown to a strike or lockout.

Mediators attempt to assist the parties to reach an agreement; their role and authority vary across jurisdictions.

play an active role in negotiations. They may suggest compromise terms or even privately voice an opinion to one of the parties on their position. There are a number of ways a mediator might help resolve a dispute. He or she might help each side understand the other's position. Where the parties are hostile, the mediator might encourage them to focus on the issues and separate them if necessary. The mediator could repackage proposals or come up with new compromises the parties have not previously considered. Most importantly, the mediator might make proposals allowing negotiators to back away from a previous position without losing face.

In most jurisdictions, conciliation or mediation and a cooling-off period is required before the parties can strike or lockout. Figure 10-1 summarizes these requirements.

Conciliation or Mediation Requirements and Cooling Off Period Before a Strike or Lockout	
Canada	Conciliation may be required.
	21 days have elapsed from the day on which the Minister either: notified the parties that there will be no conciliation; or notified the parties of the receipt of the report of a conciliation officer; or released the report of a conciliation commissioner or conciliation board to the parties.
Alberta	Mediation is required.
	If the mediator notifies the parties that he or she does not intend to make recommendations: 14 days after the notification.
	If the mediator makes recommendations to the parties: 14 days after the recommendations are rejected by the parties; or where there is a vote on the recommendations of the mediator: 14 days after the date on which the parties are notified of the results.
British Columbia	Not required. However, if a mediation officer has been appointed: 48 hours after the notification that the mediator's report has been received.
Manitoba	Not required.
New Brunswick	Conciliation or mediation may be required.
	A party has requested the appointment of a conciliation officer, and 7 days have elapsed from the day on which the Minister either: notified the parties that a conciliation officer, mediator or conciliation board will not be appointed; or releases the report of a conciliation board to the parties.
Newfoundland and Labrador	In 2012 legislative reform introduced a card-based certification system, granting automatic union certification where 65 percent or more of the employees in the bargaining unit sign a union membership card. The 40 percent threshold to trigger a certification vote was maintained in 2012.
	In 2014 the provincial movement introduced amendments the legislation to: (1) remove the possibility of card-based automatic certification; (2) remove the requirement for the parties to formally request a conciliation board; and (3) rearrange and restate provisions relating to conciliation proceedings, strikes, and lockouts. The reader is advised to check the status of legislative changes regarding reform to the use of third parties when an impasse occurs in collective bargaining.
Nova Scotia	Conciliation or mediation is required.
	If a conciliation officer or mediator is appointed: 14 days after a report is submitted to the Minister.
	If a conciliation board is established: 7 days after the Minister receives the board's report.
Ontario	Conciliation or mediation is required.

Figure 10-1 Third-Party Assistance Before a Strike or Lockout

	Conciliation or Mediation Requirements and Cooling Off Period Before a Strike or Lockout
	After a conciliation officer's report to the Minister:
	1. 14 days after the Minister notifies that a conciliation board will not be established, or
	2. If a conciliation board is established, 7 days after the report is released to the parties
	or
	2. If the minister appoints a mediator instead of a conciliation officer, 7 days after the mediator's report is released to the parties
Prince Edward Island	Conciliation or mediation is required.
	After a conciliation officer's report to the Minister:
	1. If the Minister does not appoint a conciliation board or mediator: 14 days after the conciliation officer's report is received
	2. If the Minister appoints a conciliation board or mediator: 7 days after the Minister receives a report
Saskatchewan	The employer or union shall provide a notice to the Minister that they have reached an impasse in good faith bargaining and as soon as possible after receipt of a notice pursuant to subsection (1), the minister shall appoint a labour relations officer or a special mediator, or establish a conciliation board, to mediate or conciliate the dispute. A 14-day cooling-off period must occur following the report of the Minister's appointee.

Figure.10.1 (*Continued*)

Fact-Finding   **Fact-finding** is a process found in private sector legislation in British Columbia and some public sector labour relations statutes. A fact-finder is an individual who investigates the issues and reports to the Minister. The report may contain non-binding recommendations and is usually made public.

> **Fact-finding** is a process found in some private and public sector labour relations statutes.

Arbitration   **Arbitration** is a completely different form of third-party assistance, because the arbitrator makes a final and binding decision establishing the terms of the collective agreement after hearing the parties. The arbitration of a contract dispute is referred to as *interest arbitration*.

> **Arbitration** involves a third party hearing the parties and then deciding the terms of the agreement.

Interest arbitration should not be confused with grievance or rights arbitration, which deals with a dispute relating to the administration of the collective agreement. For example, if an individual was dismissed, a grievance might be filed; and if the grievance is not settled, the issue could be referred to rights arbitration.

Interest arbitration is used primarily in the public sector where it is provided as an alternative to a strike or lockout for some employees. In the private sector, interest arbitration could be used if the parties agreed to do so. However, it is seldom used in the private sector because at least one of the parties may perceive that it does not want an arbitrator to make an award containing terms that it would not agree to. The arbitrator is a neutral third party who hears evidence from both parties regarding the possible contents of the collective agreement. Both sides will present evidence attempting to convince the arbitrator to make an award favourable to it, including references to comparable collective agreements.

Conventional interest arbitration has been criticized for several reasons. Establishing arbitration as the final dispute resolution mechanism may hinder the parties negotiating a collective agreement on their own. It has been argued that arbitration may have a **chilling effect** on negotiation. That is, the parties may be discouraged from making concessions that might lead to agreement. Considering the issue of wages, suppose the union is demanding a 4 percent increase and the employer is offering a 1 percent increase. Assuming that an arbitrator would order a wage increase somewhere between the parties' positions, a party may

> The **chilling effect** refers to parties' unwillingness to make concessions during negotiation.

A **narcotic effect** refers to the parties losing the capability to negotiate their own agreement.

decide it would end up better off if it made no concessions before arbitration. It has also been suggested that arbitration may have a **narcotic effect**. Negotiators may become dependent on an arbitrator making a decision for them instead of making the tough decisions required to reach an agreement. Another way to view the narcotic effect is that it may be safer for union or employer negotiators to say they did their best and that the agreement was the decision of an arbitrator.

Final Offer Selection.

An alternative form of arbitration may avoid the problems associated with traditional or conventional arbitration. **Final offer selection** is a form of arbitration in which both the union and the employer submit their final offer to the arbitrator, who chooses one of the offers. The terms provided in the offer chosen are incorporated into the collective agreement.

Final offer selection is a type of arbitration in which the arbitrator chooses between the union's and employer's offers.

There are two forms of final offer selection: total-package and item-by-item. In **total-package final offer selection**, each side presents an offer that covers all of the outstanding issues between the parties such as wages, benefits, and vacations. The arbitrator then must choose the entirety of either the union's or the employer's proposal. In **item-by-item final offer selection**, the arbitrator chooses between the union and the employer proposals for each item in dispute separately. The arbitrator might accept the union's proposal on the issue of wages and the employer's proposal on the issue of vacations.

In **total-package final offer selection** the arbitrator selects all of the union's or the employer's offer.

In **item-by-item final offer selection** the arbitrator chooses between the union and the employer offers separately for each contract issue.

The major advantage of final offer selection is that it should encourage the parties to reach their own agreement. This is especially true when total-package final offer selection is used, because both parties face the substantial risk that the arbitrator might choose the offer made by the other side. However, there are potential disadvantages associated with final offer selection. The process creates winners and losers, and this may cause hostility that affects the administration of the agreement and subsequent negotiations. There may be less risk of creating hostility where item-by-item selection is used, because both parties may see parts of their offer incorporated into the agreement.

First Contract Arbitration.

In Chapter 8 first contract arbitration (FCA) was described as a policy alternative that has been adopted in most jurisdictions. FCA can be used to resolve an impasse in the first negotiation between the parties. However, as previously outlined, there are some restrictions on the availability of FCA, and it will not be ordered in all situations when there is a bargaining impasse.

Second or Subsequent Contract Arbitration.

Another policy option, which has been adopted in Manitoba, is to make arbitration available in second and subsequent contract negotiations on the application of one of the parties. The legislation allows either of the parties to apply to the Board for a settlement. The Board inquires into the negotiations to determine if the parties have bargained in good faith and whether they are likely to conclude an agreement within 30 days if they continued to bargain. If the Board finds that the party making the application is negotiating in good faith and the parties are unlikely to conclude an agreement within 30 days, any strike or lockout must be terminated and the terms of an agreement are settled by an arbitrator that the parties agree upon or by the Board. This is a significant policy development. After FCA was introduced by one jurisdiction, it was subsequently adopted by eight other jurisdictions. Second or subsequent contract arbitration could also be adopted by other jurisdictions in the future. However, it appears to be a departure from previous policy, and its widespread adoption appears to be unlikely.

Mediation-Arbitration

Mediation-arbitration is a two-step process, sometimes referred to as *med-arb*. The individual assisting the parties first tries—as a mediator—to help them reach their own agreement. If a settlement is not reached, the same person then acts as an arbitrator and decides the terms of the agreement.

In **mediation-arbitration** the third party first acts as a mediator, and if no agreement is reached they act as an arbitrator and settles the dispute.

Med-arb has not been extensively used in interest arbitration. An advantage of med-arb is that if the mediation attempt is not successful, the parties can get to the arbitration process faster. Also, if the dispute proceeds to arbitration, the arbitrator will have accumulated a large amount of knowledge about the issues. A potential problem is that the parties may not be totally candid with a mediator when they know that the same person may later be acting as an arbitrator. There is also a concern that the person assisting the parties may obtain information in the mediation process that may improperly influence his or her decision as an arbitrator.

Other Dispute Resolution Methods

In addition to the various forms of third-party assistance, a contract dispute could be resolved by a final offer vote in some jurisdictions and by back-to-work legislation in all jurisdictions.

Final Offer Vote   In Chapter 8, it was noted that in some jurisdictions the employer may request a final offer vote or the Minister may direct a vote. These votes should be viewed as an alternative way to resolve a contract dispute.

Back-to-Work Legislation   Back-to-work legislation refers to a special statute passed to end a strike or lockout. It orders the strike or lockout to end, and usually provides for the terms of a new agreement to be determined by arbitration. In some cases, the legislation sets out the terms of work instead of providing for arbitration. Back-to-work legislation has been used in the public sector in cases where employees have the right to strike, but it is deemed that the continuation of a strike will impose excessive hardship on the public; for example, it has been used to end transit and teacher strikes.

> **Back-to-work legislation** ends a strike or lockout and usually imposes arbitration.

There has been a major change in the frequency of back-to-work legislation in Canada in recent years. Since the early 1980s, the number of instances of back-to-work legislation is higher than any other period in the history of labour relations in Canada. In the last three decades, the federal government alone passed 19 pieces of back-to-work legislation while provincial governments across the country have enacted 71 pieces of back-to-work legislation.

Most of this legislation (51 of the 90 pieces of legislation) not only forced workers back to work after taking strike action, but also arbitrarily imposed settlements on the striking workers.[1] Figure 10-2 shows a summary of labour laws restricting collective bargaining and trade union rights, between 1982 and 2014, in federal and provincial jurisdictions.

Back-to-work legislation was first used by the federal government in 1950. Parliament has used this legislative remedy 34 times prior to 2011. As a result of strikes at Canada Post and Air Canada in 2011, the government passed return-to-work legislation in both disputes. It has been suggested that this action established not only a new norm in labour relations but de facto amended the *Canada Labour Code* to prevent strikes in the transportation and communications sectors while leaving the legislation untouched.[2]

Type of Legislation	Jurisdiction											
	Fed	**BC**	**AB**	**SK**	**MB**	**ON**	**QC**	**NB**	**PE**	**NS**	**NL**	**Total**
Back to work: Dispute sent to arbitration	11	4	—	3	—	14	3	2	—	2	—	39
Back to work: Settlement imposed	8	6	4	3	—	5	17	4	—	1	3	51

Figure 10-2 Summary of Labour Laws Restricting Collective Bargaining and Trade Union Rights, 1982–2014 (updated April 2014)

Source: Based on "Summary of Legislation Restricting Collective Bargaining and Trade Union Rights in Canada 1982–2014: Restrictive Labour Laws in Canada," Canadian Foundation of Labour Rights site, http://labourrights.ca/issues/restrictive-labour-laws-canada, accessed September 3, 2014.

STRIKES AND LOCKOUTS

Strikes and Lockouts Defined

Strikes and lockouts are referred to by various names such as economic sanctions, *industrial action*, and *industrial conflict*. The legal definition of a strike is broader than might be expected. Most jurisdictions provide a definition similar to the following from the *Canada Labour Code*:

> [S]trike includes a cessation of work or a refusal to work or to continue to work by employees, in combination, in concert or in accordance with a common understanding, and a slowdown of work or other concerted activity on the part of employees in relation to their work that is designed to restrict or limit output.[3]

According to this definition, a strike is not limited to a situation where employees walk off the job; it also includes situations where employees continue to work but restrict output. It has been held that employees who refuse overtime in collaboration with each other are engaging in a strike. In some cases, unions have used the slowdown tactic of following work procedures exactly, and not engaging in any activity the collective agreement does not require. This is referred to as a **work-to-rule** campaign, and in some situations it could be regarded as a strike action because it is restricting output.

A **work-to-rule** campaign is a work slowdown carried out by strictly adhering to work rules and the collective agreement.

Rotating strikes occur when employees at different locations alternately stop working.

Where employees work at different locations, unions have sometimes used the tactic of **rotating strikes**, in which employees strike at some locations, while at other locations they continue to work. For example, in the postal system the union could have employees strike in different cities on different days. The purpose appears to be to force concessions without completely shutting down the employer, and without employees losing all of their income. In response to a rotating strike the employer might initiate a lockout.

In three jurisdictions—Manitoba, Alberta, and Nova Scotia—the definition of a strike also includes a requirement that the purpose of the refusal to work or the slowdown is to compel the employer to agree to certain terms and conditions of employment. Accordingly, a refusal to work for some other purpose would not be a strike. This difference in definition could mean that the same union action is considered a strike in one province and not in another. When unions held a national day of protest in the 1970s against anti-inflation guidelines, this was found to be a strike in Ontario, but the Board in at least one other province did not find this action to be a strike.

A **wildcat strike** is an illegal strike that has not been authorized by the union.

As explained below, a strike is only legal at certain times and if the prerequisites for a strike including a strike vote have been met. A strike during the term of the collective agreement is illegal. It is an unfair labour practice to threaten an illegal strike. A **wildcat strike** is an illegal strike that has not been authorized by the union—for example, if a group of employees walked off the job to protest the discipline or dismissal of a co-worker.

A **lockout** occurs when the employer closes a portion or all of its premises so that bargaining unit members cannot enter the workplace to perform their jobs.

As is explained in Chapter 7, a lockout is the employer's refusal to allow employees to work in order to force the union to agree to certain terms of employment. In most jurisdictions, labour relations legislation formally defines a lockout similarly to the following from the *Canada Labour Code*:

> **Lockout** includes the closing of a place of employment, a suspension of work by an employer or a refusal by an employer to continue to employ a number of their employees, done to compel their employees or to aid another employer to compel that other employer's employees to agree to terms or conditions of employment.

It is important to note that there are two components to the definition. First, there must be a suspension of work or a refusal to employ, and second, there is a requirement that the purpose of the refusal to employ is to compel employees to agree to terms or conditions of employment. The second requirement refers to the motivation of the employer. If the employer suspends operations for economic reasons and there is no intent to force employees to agree to terms and conditions of employment, there has not been a lockout.

Significance of Strikes

For many people, a reference to unions or labour relations leads to negative thoughts about strikes. Periodically news reports contain references to exceptionally long strikes or clashes between pickets and police. Before examining the significance of strikes, it should be noted that some perceptions about them may be incorrect.

Strikes are the exception, not the rule, in Canadian labour relations. However, the number of work stoppages in Canada increased significantly in 2012. This increase was due primarily to numerous one-day strikes by public elementary school teachers in Ontario in response to Bill-115. Other occurrences of multi-unit collective bargaining, such as the Construction Association of Windsor (17 work stoppages) or the Community Social Services Employers' Association (11 work stoppages), contributed to the high level of stoppage activity. The number of work stoppages stood at 278, up 89.1 percent from the 2011 figure of 147. Complementing the surge in work stoppages, the number of workers involved increased by 49.7 percent to 136 425. This is the highest number of workers involved since 2005. This significant increase can be attributed to the participation of public school teachers in British Columbia (42 450 workers) and in Ontario (56 588 workers). In fact, if we exclude these two work stoppages from the overall figure, the number of workers involved in work stoppages in 2012 was lower than the previous year.[4]

There are still reasons why strikes are significant and could be a cause for concern. Some have led to violence and property damage. Nine replacement workers were killed in a bombing incident at a mine in Yellowknife in 1992. A college professor on strike in Ontario was struck by a car and killed when he was on the picket line in 2006. Strikes may cause employers to lose business, and a few have led to a business being permanently closed. Some strikes cause inconvenience to the public. Transit strikes in large cities have caused traffic gridlock. The possibility of the public being harmed by strikes has led to restrictions on strikes in the public sector, and government action to curtail some strikes.

A strike might have a significant economic impact on a community, especially where the employees involved represent a significant portion of the local workforce. Other businesses and charities in a community might be affected. Strikes might have a significant impact on the income of employees and in some cases lead to the loss of jobs. It has also been suggested that strikes adversely affect the competitive position of the Canadian economy. However, one study which considered the macroeconomic effects of strikes found that "in the long run, strike activities in Canada have an insignificant effect on its trade balance, and, hence, on its economy."[5] Labour Relations Issue 10-1 refers to one specific labour dispute, the NHL lockout in 2004–05, and its effects.

Labour Relations Issue 10-1

What Are the Effects of Strikes and Lockouts?

The lockout of NHL players and the cancellation of the 2004–05 hockey season illustrate some of the potential impacts of a work stoppage. The NHL was the first professional league in North America to lose an entire season because of a strike or lockout. The players lost $1.1 billion in salary, and the owners lost even more in revenue. The CBC lost $20 million in revenue when one of its programs, *Hockey Night in Canada*, was suspended. Thousands of arena and league staff lost income when they were laid off. The lockout led to changes in the collective agreement, including a salary cap that imposes a maximum for individual players and a limit on the total amount paid to the team. Prior to the salary cap, a free-spending team like the Toronto Maple Leafs could possibly buy a championship if it chose to, but the salary cap will prevent this from happening and will require teams to manage their resources more efficiently.

Functions of Strikes

Strikes serve several legitimate purposes in the labour relations system. Although it may sound strange, strikes can be a way to resolve conflict. There is evidence that where strikes are not allowed, conflict emerges in a different form, such as grievances. In one study, it was found that the grievance rate for employees who were not allowed to strike was significantly higher than the rate for employees who could strike.[6] The possibility of a strike may cause negotiators to make concessions that are required to reach an agreement. After a strike starts, the union and the employer will be forced to reevaluate their positions. A strike might also play a part in intraorganizational bargaining, by bringing the expectations of bargaining unit members into line with what the bargaining team can achieve.

Factors Affecting Strikes

There is a large body of research examining the factors affecting the incidence and duration of strikes. This section will review some of the variables that have been considered. Every contract negotiation is unique, because it involves different employees and employers, a unique bargaining history, and unique economic factors. Figure 10-3 lists factors that have been linked to strikes.

Information Differences Between Union and Employer Some observers have contended that strikes are caused because the union and the employer are basing their negotiations on different information. The employer will have access to information, such as sales and revenue forecasts, which the union does not have. This leads to the union and the employer having different expectations. The union may think the future looks bright and the employer has the ability to provide a wage increase; the employer may see tough times ahead and think that granting wage increases is not prudent.

Economic Factors Generally, strike activity increases in periods of higher employment and decreases as unemployment rises. A possible explanation for this is that as the business cycle reaches its peak and unemployment is lower, workers are more willing to strike because it is easier to find an alternative job. Strike activity is lower in bargaining units that have experienced higher increases in their real wage during the previous contract.[7] A distinction can be drawn between different types of strikes on the basis of when the strike occurs. Strikes might occur when the parties negotiate their first collective agreement, on the renewal of an agreement, or during the term of the agreement. Although wildcat strikes during the term of an agreement are illegal, they do occur. Economic factors are more significant for contract renewal strikes. In some first contract situations, a dispute may relate to a non-monetary issue such as the establishment of seniority for the first time or compulsory union membership. A strike during an agreement is likely caused by a non-economic dispute, such as a safety issue.

1. Differences in information between union and employer
2. Economic environment
3. Bargaining unit characteristics
4. Internal conflicts within the union or employer
5. The relationship between the union and the employer
6. Negotiators' skill and experience
7. Bargaining history
8. Legislative environment
9. Worker discontent

Figure 10-3 Factors Affecting Strikes

Bargaining Unit and Community Characteristics   Some researchers have considered employee and community characteristics as factors affecting strikes. Generally it has been found that male-dominated bargaining units and larger bargaining units are more likely to be involved in strikes.[8] It has been suggested that gender is a factor because female employees are more likely to quit to express dissatisfaction than to strike. In larger bargaining units, there may be more alienation toward the employer, which increases the likelihood of a strike.

Conflict Within the Employer or Union   Internal conflict within either the employer or the union could be a factor affecting strike activity. Within the union, there will be various interests and differences along the lines of gender, age, seniority, and other factors. These differences may mean that the union cannot agree on demands or concessions that are necessary to reach an agreement. Similarly, there might be divisions within the management team that contribute to an impasse in negotiations. In some cases, management representatives may lack the authority required to reach an agreement. Where the real decision makers are not involved in the negotiations, they may underestimate the union's commitment to issues. The union may be forced to strike in some cases to get the real decision makers involved.

Relationship Between the Union and the Employer   The relationship between union and employer negotiators may be a factor affecting strike activity. Where there is hostility, the parties may lack the objectivity required to reach agreement.

Negotiator's Skills and Experience   The negotiation skills and experience of the negotiating teams can affect the likelihood of a strike. Inexperienced negotiators are more likely to make errors such as committing themselves to a position they cannot withdraw from without a loss of reputation. Less experienced negotiators may not send out proper signals regarding where they would be willing to settle, or pick up on the cues from the other side about settlement possibilities. Inexperienced negotiators might also think that in order to establish a reputation they must obtain more in negotiations and this leads to a bargaining impasse.

One study in the United States found that the experience of negotiators had an impact on the incidence of strikes. Strikes were found to be less likely to occur when negotiators had more experience. The study also found that strikes were less likely to occur when the chief negotiators for each side had equal levels of experience.[9]

Bargaining History   The previous bargaining between the parties might affect the likelihood of a strike. Previous negotiations and strikes might have caused hostility that in turn leads to an impasse. If a previous strike was brief and did not cause employees to lose a large amount of income, they may be more willing to support a strike. Alternatively, it has been argued that a previous strike may have imposed costs that the parties will want to avoid, thus making a strike less likely.

Legal Environment   The legal environment might affect the frequency and duration of strikes.[10] The allocation of authority in labour relations matters to the provinces has led to differences in policy on issues such as the requirement for conciliation or mediation, and replacement worker legislation. Some jurisdictions have legislation that prohibits the use of replacement workers. It has been found that legislation banning the use of replacement workers increases the incidence and duration of strikes.[11] This particular finding is interesting, because unions have previously contended that a ban on the use of replacement workers would decrease the incidence of strikes. It has been found that while legislation requiring conciliation is largely ineffective in reducing the incidence of strikes, mandatory strike votes have reduced the incidence of strikes. In some jurisdictions, legislation allows for a contract to be reopened during the term of the agreement. It has been found that such reopener provisions lead to a reduction in strikes. A possible explanation for this is that the reopening provision allows the parties to resolve any problems before discontent accumulates and leads to a strike.

Employee Discontent   Worker discontent and frustration may be a factor that affects strike activity. It has been suggested that a "collective voice" approach, which views strikes as an expression of worker discontent, explains strike activity.[12] This approach notes that because strikes involve costs and uncertainties, workers must be convinced to strike on the basis of fairness and legitimacy, not just by appealing to their economic self-interest. It is contended that the employment relationship involves a subordination of employees to management. This is the basis for discontent, which can be expressed in a number of ways, and will more likely be expressed by a strike when alternatives are not available. Research has found that workplaces with more autonomy and progressive human resources management practices have lower strike levels. Strikes are more likely to occur where union leaders are under pressure to be more militant because of employee discontent.[13]

The nature of many of the factors affecting strikes has led some observers to view strikes as mistakes—something that could be avoided if the parties had the same information, avoided negotiation errors, and acted rationally. However, according to the collective voice approach, strikes are an expression of fundamental worker discontent and cannot be viewed as mistakes.

There is disagreement over the factors influencing strikes. Some see union bargaining power as affecting the size of any wage increase; however, it will not necessarily affect the incidence of strikes. It is argued that if the union has more bargaining power, management has an incentive to increase its offer and avoid a strike. Hence, the view that "differential bargaining power is a theory of wages, not of strikes."[14] Alternatively, if strikes are viewed as a consequence of employee discontent, bargaining power plays an indirect role in the determination of whether they will occur. If discontent is high and union strike power is high, union negotiators will be under more pressure to be militant in bargaining, and the likelihood of a strike is increased.

It is apparent that the causes of strikes are complex. Strikes should not be viewed simply as tests of economic strength. Strikes may be affected by numerous factors including negotiator experience, the legal environment, and worker discontent. Because there are so many variables, it is difficult to deal with the question of how strike frequency and duration might be reduced. If strikes are viewed as mistakes such as negotiation errors, they might be avoided by improving the bargaining process. More centralized bargaining would mean that more experienced negotiators with more authority would be involved. Mutual gains bargaining, which focuses on the interests of both parties, might also be beneficial in some situations. Providing conciliation and mediation assistance may also help avoid strikes that are caused by mistakes. If strikes are viewed as being an expression of worker discontent, it will be necessary to take steps to reduce that discontent. It has been suggested that having employers adopt more progressive employment practices and enacting legislation that ensures satisfactory compensation, safe working conditions, and fair treatment may help reduce discontent.[15]

When Can the Parties Strike or Lock Out?

Several restrictions govern when a union may strike or an employer may lockout employees. These are listed in Figure 10-4. A strike or lockout that does not meet the requirements is illegal. Let us expand on these restrictions.

The parties cannot strike or lock out while a collective agreement is in force. This leads to the question of whether employees not on strike, who are covered by a different collective agreement, can refuse to cross the picket line of employees in other bargaining units.

1. No collective agreement in force
2. Parties have bargained in good faith
3. Conciliation or mediation process completed[†]
4. Strike vote
5. Notice of strike or lockout[‡]
6. Essential services agreement in place[§]

Figure 10-4 Requirements for a Strike or Lockout

†Applies to federal jurisdiction, Alberta, New Brunswick, Newfoundland and Labrador, Nova Scotia, Prince Edward Island, and Ontario.
‡Applies to federal jurisdiction, Alberta, British Columbia, New Brunswick, Nova Scotia, and Saskatchewan.
§Applies to parts of the public sector.

The employees involved might work for the same employer—for example, where production workers face a picket line set up by striking office workers. The striking employees might work for another employer, and employees must enter the second employer's place of business to make deliveries or provide services. Generally, a refusal to cross a picket line is an illegal strike, but there are exceptions, and differences between jurisdictions. If an individual refused to cross a picket line, it would not constitute a strike, because a strike is defined as a collective refusal to work. Action taken by one employee cannot be a strike. To further complicate the matter, some collective agreements have a provision that employees will not be required to cross a picket line. Such provisions are in conflict with legislation that prohibits a strike during the term of an agreement, and will not prevent a Labour Relations Board from declaring a strike illegal in most jurisdictions, because the parties are not allowed to contract out of the legislation. Unions and employers in most jurisdictions should be aware that the provisions in collective agreements allowing employees to refuse to cross a picket line will not prevent a Labour Relations Board from declaring a strike illegal. The parties are not allowed to condone activity the legislation makes illegal. However, provisions like this may have significance if the employer disciplines employees who refuse to cross a picket line. An arbitrator might refuse to uphold the discipline because of the contract provision allowing the refusal. In summary, where there is a provision in a collective agreement allowing employees to refuse to cross a picket line, employers can likely still pursue a remedy from the Board for an unlawful strike, but they may not be able to discipline employees.

Some unions have negotiated terms in collective agreements that give employees the right to refuse to work on, handle, or deal with goods coming from or going to an employer involved in a labour dispute. A **hot cargo clause** may be restricted so that the employees can refuse the work only if the dispute involves their union or their employer. In most jurisdictions, this type of clause has been found to be unenforceable, because it is an attempt to contract out of the statutory prohibition against a strike or lockout during the term of the agreement. Labour Relations Issue 10-2 illustrates a situation in which an attempt was made to rely on a hot cargo clause.

A **hot cargo clause** allows employees to refuse to work with goods associated with an employer engaged in a labour dispute.

Before there can be a strike, the parties must have negotiated and complied with the duty to bargain in good faith. If this requirement is not met, a Labour Relations Board might order the parties to resume negotiations, as outlined in Chapter 8.

In six jurisdictions, the parties must have completed a conciliation process before a strike or lockout is permitted. Some jurisdictions have a one-stage process involving a conciliation officer. Other jurisdictions provide for a second stage involving a conciliation board. In all jurisdictions, the process includes a cooling-off period after the conciliation officer or board has reported. The parties cannot strike or lock out until after the cooling-off period, which ranges from 7 to 21 days. The details of the conciliation process are provided in the appendix to this chapter.

Should a "Hot Cargo" Clause Be Enforceable?

A collective agreement between a newspaper and the union representing its composing room employees provided as follows:

Article 16. The union reserves the right to its members to refuse to execute all work received from or destined for struck offices, unfair employers or publications where lockouts or strikes recognized or authorized by the Printing, Publishing and Media workers sector of the Communication Workers of America are in effect.

The employer assigned work to composing room employees that was normally done by employees belonging to the union who were locked out at another newspaper. The union filed a grievance alleging that the employer had violated Article 16 of the agreement. The employer's position was that the employees who refused to do the work were engaging in an illegal strike. The arbitration board that heard the matter held that the refusal to do the work assigned was a strike. Furthermore, the Board held that the article relied upon by the union was in conflict with the provisions of the *Labour Relations Act* providing that there be no strike or lockout during the term of the agreement. Accordingly, the union's grievance was dismissed. This decision illustrates that a provision in a contract relating to "hot cargo" may not be enforceable. Should the parties be allowed to agree that employees are allowed to refuse to do certain work?

All jurisdictions require that a strike vote be held by secret ballot. In all jurisdictions except Nova Scotia, a strike must be approved by a majority of those who vote. In Nova Scotia, the strike must be approved by a majority of employees in the bargaining unit, a more restrictive provision because the union will have to obtain the support of a majority of employees, not just of those employees who actually vote. It has been found that mandatory strike votes reduce the incidence of strikes.[16]

In certain jurisdictions the union must give a strike notice ranging from 24 to 72 hours. In some, notice must be given to the employer; in others, both the employer and the Ministry of Labour must be given notice. In British Columbia, there is a provision for the Labour Relations Board to order a longer strike notice where perishable property is involved.

In the event of a strike or lockout that causes special hardship, governments can pass special legislation ending the labour dispute. In some jurisdictions, instead of relying on special or ad hoc legislation, a special mechanism has been established to deal with labour disputes that may cause hardship. Restrictions on strikes and lockouts in the public sector will be discussed in the next chapter.

In the federal jurisdiction, British Columbia, and Alberta, legislation provides for the designation of essential services or an emergency in a strike or lockout.[17] If a service is declared essential, or an emergency is declared, a strike is prohibited.

Remedies for Illegal Strikes and Lockouts   If there is an illegal strike or lockout, the employer or union may pursue remedies through the grievance and arbitration process, or the Labour Relations Board. The possibility of obtaining a remedy in more than one forum, and the differences between jurisdictions make this a complex area. The union or employer should seek legal counsel in its jurisdiction. The union does not automatically have liability in the event of an illegal strike by employees. It will only be liable if union officers are involved in the illegal activity or the union fails to take action to halt it. It follows that in the event of an illegal strike, the employer should call it to the attention of union officials immediately.

Because an illegal strike or lockout is a breach of the collective agreement, the union or employer might file a grievance, and if the matter is not settled an arbitrator could award damages. The damages would be the amount required to compensate the innocent party for the breach of the agreement. Employers can be ordered to pay lost wages and the union can be ordered to pay the costs and lost profits associated with the strike. An arbitrator cannot order employees involved in an illegal strike to pay damages. In most jurisdictions, the union or the employer might also seek a declaration from the Labour Relations Board that there has been an unlawful strike or lockout. The Board might order damages to be paid.

Strike Activity and the End of a Strike

When employees go on strike, the employer is allowed to continue to operate. In Chapter 8, we referred to legislation prohibiting the use of replacement workers during a strike in the federal jurisdiction, British Columbia, and Quebec. Even where the law allows replacement workers to be used, in some cases the employer will not be able to continue operations because it cannot find a sufficient number of employees with the skills required. While employees are on strike, they will usually receive **strike pay** from the union, usually a relatively small amount of money linked to the number of dependents the striker has. In order to receive strike pay, individuals must usually engage in picketing. If employees cannot engage in picket duty because of a disability, the union will accommodate them by assigning them to alternative duties such as clerical work associated with the strike. The union may arrange with the employer for some benefits to be continued by paying the relevant premiums. Some employees on strike may find other jobs.

Strike pay is money paid by the union to employees on strike.

Picketing   The union will likely establish a picket line at the employer's place of business. Pickets cannot trespass on private property. Accordingly, pickets may be excluded from areas such as shopping malls. There is a difference between what the law allows pickets to do and what some actually do. Legally a picket line can only be established to inform or persuade the public. The law does not allow pickets to obstruct entry or intimidate. Pickets will usually carry signs to advise the public about the strike and may also hand out leaflets. In some strikes, unions have also attempted to inform the community by putting notices in newspapers and distributing leaflets to homes. However, some picket lines are apparently set up and operated to block entry. If pickets engage in such unlawful activity, the employer can apply to the courts in most provinces for an injunction to limit the number of pickets.

In all provinces except British Columbia, labour relations legislation does not extensively regulate picketing, and picketing issues are dealt with in the courts. One court decision deserves mention. Until 2002, the courts had held that **secondary picketing**—picketing at a location other than where striking employees work, for example at a customer of the employer—was automatically illegal. In 2002, the Supreme Court of Canada handed down a decision that secondary picketing only violates the law if it involves "wrongful action."[18] In the future, some jurisdictions could pass legislation to regulate secondary picketing; however, any such regulation must not contravene the freedom of expression provisions of the *Canadian Charter of Rights and Freedoms*. Until the law is clarified by additional court decisions or legislation, it should be noted that some forms of secondary picketing that were formerly illegal are now permissible.

Secondary picketing refers to picketing at a location other than the workplace of striking employees.

End of the Strike   In five jurisdictions—Canada, British Columbia, Manitoba, Newfoundland and Labrador, and Ontario—labour relations legislation provides that the Minister of Labour or cabinet may order a final offer vote by employees where it is in the public interest to do so. For example, if a strike by garbage handlers was causing exceptional difficulties, a vote could be ordered. If employees vote in favour of the offer made by the employer, it will be the basis of an agreement and the strike will end. This is another illustration of government as an actor in the labour relations system.

The parties may enter into a back-to-work protocol that could include terms prohibiting discipline for actions during the strike, providing that there will be no discrimination or retaliation for actions during the strike, and requiring any proceedings such as bad faith bargaining complaints to be withdrawn. These agreements encourage the parties to put the strike behind them and move on.

A strike will usually continue until the parties reach a collective agreement; however, a union may call an end to the strike without a new contract being negotiated. In a few cases, the parties have not reached an agreement and a strike has continued indefinitely. Legislation in the federal jurisdiction, Alberta, Manitoba, Ontario, Prince Edward Island, Quebec, and Saskatchewan provides that when a strike has ended, striking employees must be reinstated and given priority over any employees hired as replacement workers. In other jurisdictions that do not have an express right to reinstatement, the union could file an unfair labour practice complaint if an employee was not reinstated. This should be contrasted to the situation in the United States, where employers are allowed to hire permanent replacement workers and striking employees do not have the right to reclaim their jobs. In Ontario the provisions for the reinstatement of employees have a qualification: an employee may make an unconditional application in writing to return to work within six months of the start of the strike, and the employer must reinstate him or her unless the work the employee normally performs is no longer done. Therefore, unions in Ontario have to be concerned about a strike lasting longer than six months, because the right to reinstatement provided by the act could expire. To avoid problems or disputes regarding the reinstatement of employees, the union will seek an agreement with the employer to deal with the issue.

Extent of Strike Activity. Figure 10-5 shows that unionized employers in Canada experienced a significant increase in the number of work stoppages in 2012 totalling 278 occurrences, up 89.1 percent from 147 incidents in 2011. In the federal jurisdiction, annual stoppages increased from 10 in 2011 to 18 in 2012. The average duration of these strikes also increased, from 32.4 to 67.3 days. The number of work stoppages under provincial jurisdiction increased from 135 in 2011 to 260 in 2012. From this total, Ontario registered 142 work stoppages, 75 of them by the elementary teachers' strikes against Bill-115. The drop in the average duration of work stoppages was particularly sharp, declining by 64.1 percent to 17.9 days in 2012. This is the lowest average duration of work stoppages in the provincial jurisdiction since 1960. The lower average duration was strongly influenced by multiple rotating strikes by Ontario elementary teachers.[19]

International Comparisons When considering the Canadian strike record in comparison to other countries, several measurement problems must be noted. Countries have different definitions of what constitutes a strike. In Canada, all disputes in which 10 or more work days are lost are counted as a strike. In the United States, a strike is only included in the statistics if it is a work stoppage of 1000 or more workers. Accordingly, comparisons between Canada and the United States of the number of strikes are of little value. For example, in 2001 there were 379 strikes and lockouts in Canada and only 29 in the

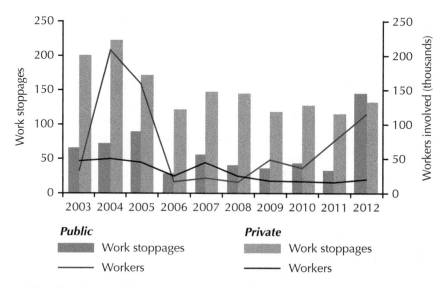

Figure 10-5 Number of Work Stoppages and Workers Involved, by Sector

Source: "Number of Work Stoppages and Workers Involved, by Sectors" from Workplace Information Division, Labour Program in Collective Bargaining in Canada 2012. Copyright © by Employment and Social Development of Canada. Used by permission of Employment and Social Development of Canada.

United States.[20] Unless the reader of these numbers takes into account the definition of a strike used in each country, the wrong conclusion might be reached. In Canada, strike data includes time lost due to lockouts; in some other countries, lockouts are not included. The Canadian strike data do not include employees laid off as a consequence of a strike; they only include those who are on strike. In the United States and some other countries, strike data also include employees laid off as a result of a strike.

However, despite these measurement problems, the time lost because of strikes in Canada is high by international standards. This is largely because Canadian strikes generally last longer than those in other countries.

Implications for Practice

1. Strikes are caused by both economic and non-economic factors. Unions and employers may be able to avoid some work stoppages by exchanging information, reducing conflict within bargaining teams, and ensuring negotiators are experienced.

2. There are legal restrictions on strikes and lockouts, and unions and employers should ensure these are met. Unions must conduct strike votes, and in some jurisdictions provide notice of a strike.

3. Employers in most jurisdictions are required to reinstate workers at the end of a strike. The union and the employer should reach an agreement that provides when workers who have been on strike will return to work.

4. In all jurisdictions, conciliation and/or mediation are available to the parties through the government ministry responsible for labour issues or the Board. The union and the employer should also consider having a private mediator help them reach a collective agreement.

Key Terms

arbitration, 249

back-to-work legislation, 251

chilling effect, 249

conciliation board, 247

conciliation officers, 246

cooling-off period, 247

fact-finding, 249

final offer selection, 250

hot cargo clause, 257

item-by-item final offer selection, 250

Lockout, 252

mediation-arbitration, 250

mediators, 247

narcotic effect, 250

no-board report, 247

rotating strikes, 252

secondary picketing, 259

strike pay, 259

total-package final offer selection, 250

wildcat strike, 252

work-to-rule, 252

Review Questions

1. Identify the key policy variables relating to third-party assistance in contract dispute resolution.

2. Distinguish between conciliation or mediation, and arbitration.

3. Describe the possible problems that are associated with arbitration.

4. Why is arbitration infrequently used in the private sector?

5. What concerns may unions and employers have regarding final offer selection?

6. Describe the functions of strikes.

7. Identify the factors that affect the incidence of strikes.

8. List the legal requirements for a strike or lockout in your jurisdiction.

Discussion Questions

1. Why do some individuals views strikes as harmful?
2. On the basis of your experience and the reading of this chapter, to what extent do you think strikes can be viewed as mistakes?
3. A newspaper report indicates that a union can "legally" go on strike or the employer may lock out employees at midnight on a specified date. What does the reference to legality mean? Why is the strike or lockout legal at midnight as opposed to some other time?
4. Arbitration of second and subsequent contract disputes on the request of one party is provided for in only one jurisdiction. What are the arguments for and against this policy?
5. Is it possible that some employees and unions would not want the right to strike? Explain.

Web Research

1. Go to the website for a union referred to in Chapter 3 or a union you are familiar with. What information is provided regarding any strikes the union is currently involved in?
2. "The Workplace Bulletin," available at www.labour.gc.ca/eng/resources/info/publications/bulletin/bulletin.shtml, provides information on major work stoppages. Determine the issues that have led to a bargaining impasse in a recent listed example.

CASE INCIDENT   DAIRY FRESH

Dairy Fresh distributes milk, ice cream, and related products to grocery and convenience stores across the province. The company employs driver/salespeople who operate out of warehouses in larger municipalities. The company leases its warehouses, and it renewed a lease on its warehouse in Anytown for a five-year term in June of 2013. A union was certified to represent the 10 driver/salespeople working at the company's Anytown location on November 11, 2013. In January 2014, the company sent a memo to employees outlining an incentive bonus that would be available to employees over the next year. The union and the employer began contract negotiations on March 10, 2014; however, they were not able to reach an agreement. The union started a strike on December 4, 2014. A collective agreement was eventually reached after the president of the company intervened and directed the manager of the Anytown location to agree to a contract providing that the Anytown employees would receive the same wages as provided in a collective agreement in the capital city of the province. Employees outside of the capital city, none of whom were unionized, were paid four dollars less per hour. The collective agreement contained a recognition article that provided:

> The company recognizes the union as the sole collective bargaining agent of all employees of the company employed in the city of Anytown, save and except supervisors and persons above the rank of supervisor.

The manager of the Anytown location complained to the company's head office that she could not operate profitably if employees were paid the same wages as employees in the capital. Subsequently, the manager was authorized to investigate cost-cutting measures including moving the warehouse. On April 27, 2015, the company made a formal announcement to employees indicating that it was changing its distribution system. The company would be leaving its warehouse in Anytown and relocating to four smaller warehouses in communities 5 to 10 kilometres from Anytown. Employees who wished to remain with the company would be assigned to one of the new locations and their terms of work would be the same as other driver/salespeople operating outside of the capital city.

Questions

1. Explain the basis for any complaint by the union.
2. Explain the outcome you expect in this situation.

CASE INCIDENT   COASTAL FOREST PRODUCTS

Coastal Forest Products operates a plant that produces plywood. The International Wood-workers Association, Local 423 (IWA), represented Coastal's production workers. In the course of an expansion, the company called for tenders for concrete. The contract was awarded to M & K Ready Mix (M & K), a non-union company. The union claimed that there was an understanding that Coastal would use union suppliers. The collective agreement between Coastal and the IWA contained the following provision:

Section 3: No Strike Pending Grievance and Arbitration Procedure

The Union agrees that it will not cause, promote, sanction, or authorize any strike, sit down, slowdown, sympathetic strike or other interference with work by the employees for any cause whatsoever until all provisions of this agreement relating to the grievance and arbitration procedure have been complied with. . . .

Murray Irving was the local union president at Coastal. When Irving saw an M & K truck arrive to make a delivery, he left his tools at his workplace and went to the lunch-room. Irving told a supervisor that he was engaging in a personal protest. An hour later, Irving was told that a group of 40 employees had stopped working and were gathered in a patio area. Irving went up to the gathering and saw that one of the employees there was a union steward. Irving told the employees that what they were doing was wrong and they should go back to work. He then returned to the lunchroom.

When Wayne Best, a union vice-president, was told about the M & K truck on the property, he advised his supervisor that he would not continue working, and joined the other employees in the patio area. Approximately a half-hour after Best arrived, he spoke to the employees and told them that by law he was required to tell them to go back to work. After making this statement, he remained in the patio area. About two hours after the disruption had started, a district officer for the union, Fern MacGregor, came to the workplace and told employees that they should return to work.

When the M & K truck left Coastal property, approximately three hours after it had arrived, all employees returned to their workplaces.

Questions

1. Is the union's claim regarding the use of union suppliers a valid one? How could it be proved?
2. How does Section 3 of the collective agreement "help" or "hinder" the union in this situation?
3. What action might the employer take in response to the situation? Be specific.
4. What outcome do you expect in this case? Explain.

CASE INCIDENT   SUN POOL ACCESSORIES

Sun Pool Accessories manufactures swimming pool equipment, including pumps, diving boards, slides, and ladders. The company employs 120 people who are represented by a union. The collective agreement between the employer and the union expired on May 30, 2010. After negotiations did not lead to a renewal of the collective agreement, the union started a legal strike on July 30, 2010. The parties signed a protocol that provided that the union could delay management vehicles entering or leaving the company property for up to 30 minutes. The picket line established by the union prevented transport trucks from bringing in supplies and taking away finished products. Non-union employees were delayed by the picket line for hours when they entered or left the premises. Several customers of the company who were advised that there would be a delay in delivery advised the company that they were cancelling their orders.

Questions

1. How can the employer respond?
2. What remedies are available to the employer?

APPENDIX TO CHAPTER 10 Third-Party Assistance in Contract Disputes

This appendix summarizes the key provisions relating to third-party assistance in each jurisdiction.

CANADA

Complete details are set out in Sections 71–79 and 81–87 of the *Canada Labour Code*. http://laws-lois.justice.gc.ca/eng/acts/L-2

Conciliation

1. Either party may send a notice of dispute to the Minister of Labour, advising that negotiations have not started within the time required or the parties have reached an impasse.

2. After receiving the notice of dispute, or on his or her own initiative where it is deemed advisable, the Minister may:

   1. Appoint a conciliation officer, or

   2. Appoint a conciliation commissioner, or

   3. Establish a conciliation board, or

   4. Notify the parties that a conciliation officer, conciliation commissioner, or conciliation board will not be appointed.

3. If the Minister notifies the parties that there will not be conciliation, a strike or lockout can commence 21 days after such notification, and a 72-hour strike or lockout notice is provided.

4. If the Minister appoints a conciliation officer, conciliation commissioner, or conciliation board, there is a report to the Minister and a strike or lockout is possible 21 days after the parties are notified of the receipt of the report and a 72-hour strike or lockout notice has been provided.

5. The parties may agree in advance that a conciliation commissioner's report or a conciliation board's recommendations will be binding.

Mediation

1. The Minister may appoint a mediator to assist the parties at any time on their request, or on his or her own initiative. At the request of the parties or the Minister, a mediator may make recommendations for a settlement.

Distinctive Features

1. The completion of conciliation or mediation is not a prerequisite to a strike or lockout. The parties may strike or lockout 21 days after the Minister directs that there will be no conciliation.

2. When conciliation is directed, it is a one-step process.

ALBERTA

Complete details are set out in Sections 64–70 and 105–111 of the *Labour Relations Code*.
www.alrb.gov.ab.ca/ALRB_Code.htm

Mediation

1. Either or both parties may ask the Director of Mediation Services to appoint a mediator. Alternatively, the Minister may require the Director to appoint a mediator.

2. If there is no settlement, the mediator either makes recommendations to settle the dispute—which the parties are required to respond to within the time specified—or notifies the parties that no recommendations will be made.

3. If the mediator makes recommendations and both parties accept them, they are incorporated into a collective agreement.

4. If one of the parties accepts the recommendations made by the mediator, it may ask the Board to conduct a vote on the acceptance or rejection of the recommendations by the other side.

5. If the mediator does not make any recommendations, or the parties reject the recommendations, or the time allowed to respond to the recommendation expires, or the parties are advised of the results of a vote on the mediator's recommendations, the parties may strike or lockout after a 14-day cooling-off period. A strike or lockout is also subject to a 72-hour notice to the other party, and a strike requires a secret ballot vote.

Disputes Inquiry Board

1. The Minister may establish a disputes inquiry board. The board attempts to reach a settlement; and if no settlement is reached, the board makes recommendations to the Minister. The Minister notifies the parties of the board's recommendations.

2. The parties may accept the recommendations of the disputes inquiry board; and if that is the case, they become the basis for the terms of a collective agreement.

3. Unless a party notifies the Minister that it accepts the board's recommendations within 10 days, the board directs a vote of the members of the party; and if the vote approves the recommendations, they are binding upon that party.

4. If a disputes inquiry board is established before the commencement of a strike or lockout, a strike or lockout cannot begin until 10 days after the parties received a copy of the board's recommendations or until 72 hours after the parties have been notified of the results of a vote on the recommendations. If the disputes inquiry board is established after a strike or lockout has begun, it has no effect on the strike or lockout.

Distinctive Features

1. The legislation provides for mediation instead of conciliation as the primary method of dispute resolution.

2. The provisions to refer a mediator's recommendations to a vote are unique.

3. The mediator's report is a prerequisite to a strike or lockout.

BRITISH COLUMBIA

Complete details are set out in Sections 74–78 of the *Labour Relations Code*. www.bclaws.ca/Recon/document/ID/freeside/00_96244_01

Mediation

1. At the request of either party, the associate chair of the mediation division at the Board may appoint a mediator. Alternatively, the Minister may appoint a mediator who meets with the parties and works on resolving the areas of disagreement for a new collective agreement. The mediator reports to the associate chair on the outcome of the mediation. If requested by the parties, or directed by the minister, the mediator must also give a report to the parties, and the report may include recommended terms of settlement.

2. A strike or a lockout is not legal during the mediation process. The parties must wait until 48 hours after the associate chair has advised them that he or she has received the mediator's report before they can legally engage in a strike or lockout. A strike or lockout is also subject to a 72-hour notice.

Fact-Finding

1. The associate chair of the mediation division at the Board may appoint a fact-finder.

2. When the parties are notified of the appointment, each must provide the fact-finder with a notice setting out the matters agreed upon and all matters remaining in dispute.

3. The fact-finder confers with the parties and makes a report to the associate chair of the mediation division, setting out the matters agreed upon, those matters remaining in dispute, and any findings relevant to the making of a collective agreement.

4. The associate chair of the mediation division provides a copy of the report to the parties and may make it public.

Distinctive Feature

1. Neither mediation nor fact-finding is a prerequisite to a strike or lockout.

MANITOBA

Complete details are set out in Sections 67–68 and 95–118 of the *Labour Relations Act*. http://web2.gov.mb.ca/laws/statutes/ccsm/l010e.php

Conciliation

1. At the request of either party or where the Minister deems it advisable, the Minister appoints a conciliation officer.

2. The conciliation officer meets with the parties and tries to assist them to reach an agreement. Each party is required to advise the conciliation officer which terms and conditions are acceptable to them.

3. The conciliation officer reports to the minister regarding the issues the parties cannot agree upon and any recommendations regarding further proceedings that could facilitate an agreement.

4. If a conciliation officer is not able to help the parties reach an agreement, the Minister may appoint a conciliation board.

5. The conciliation board reports to the Minister, and the Minister may make the report public. The parties may agree that the recommendations of the conciliation board will be binding.

Mediation

1. The parties may jointly request that the Minister appoint a mediator they have agreed upon, and the Minister is required to appoint that person. If one party requests that the Minister appoint a mediator, the Minister may do so and may also appoint a mediator on his or her own initiative.

2. The mediator provides an opportunity to each party to present evidence and also has the power to summon witnesses and take evidence under oath.

3. The mediator reports to the Minister; the report is made available to the parties and may be made public by the Minister.

4. The parties may agree that the recommendations of the mediator will be binding.

Second or Subsequent Contract Arbitration

1. When the parties have bargained with the assistance of a conciliation officer or mediator, and there is a strike or lockout in progress, either party may apply to the Board for the settlement of the contract by arbitration.

2. The Board inquiries into the negotiations and determines if there has been bargaining in good faith and whether or not the parties are likely to conclude an agreement within 30 days if they continue to bargain. If the Board finds that the parties are negotiating in good faith, and it is likely that an agreement will be reached within 30 days, it must allow bargaining to continue and any strike or lockout can continue. If the parties do not conclude an agreement within 30 days, either of them may make a new application for the settlement of the agreement by arbitration.

3. If the Board finds that the party making the application is negotiating in good faith and the parties are unlikely to conclude an agreement within 30 days, it directs that the contract terms be resolved through arbitration. The parties may agree upon an arbitrator. If the parties do not agree on an arbitrator, the Board settles the terms of the agreement.

Distinctive Features

1. Conciliation or mediation is not a prerequisite to a strike or lockout.

2. The provisions for the arbitration of a second or subsequent contract are unique to Manitoba.

NEW BRUNSWICK

Complete details are set out in Sections 36 and 61–80 of the *Industrial Relations Act*. http://laws.gnb.ca/en/ShowPdf/cs/I-4.pdf

Conciliation

1. Either party may request the Minister to appoint a conciliation officer. The Minister determines whether or not to appoint a conciliation officer. Alternatively the Minister may appoint a conciliation officer on his or her own initiative.

2. If the Minister decides not to appoint a conciliation officer, a strike or lockout is possible seven days after the parties are notified, and a 24-hour strike or lockout notice has been provided.

3. When a conciliation officer is appointed, the officer meets with the parties and subsequently reports to the Minister. The report includes the officer's opinion as to the advisability of appointing a conciliation board.

4. Upon receiving a conciliation officer's report, the Minister may appoint a conciliation board or advise the parties that a conciliation board will not be established. If the Minister advises the parties that a conciliation board will not be established, the parties can strike or lockout seven days after the notification, provided that a 24-hour strike or lockout notice is provided.

5. If a conciliation board is established, it hears the parties and tries to bring about an agreement. The parties may agree to be bound by the conciliation board's report. The conciliation board reports to the Minister, and the Minister releases the report to the parties. The parties can strike or lockout seven days after the release of the board's report, provided that a 24-hour notice for a strike or lockout is provided.

Mediation

1. At the request of either party or where the Minister deems advisable, he or she may appoint a mediator. The appointment of a mediator terminates any previous appointment of a conciliation officer.

2. The mediator confers with the parties and attempts to assist them reach an agreement.

3. The mediator reports to the Minister, and the report of the mediator is treated in the same manner as the report of a conciliation officer. The Minister decides whether or not to appoint a conciliation board, and the parties may strike or lockout, as noted above under conciliation.

Distinctive Features

1. There may be no conciliation, a one-step conciliation process, or a two-step conciliation process involving a conciliation board.

2. A strike or lockout cannot be declared unless a party has requested the appointment of a conciliation officer; however, the legislation does not require an appointment to be made.

NEWFOUNDLAND AND LABRADOR

Complete details are set out in Sections 79–80 and 106–121 of the *Labour Relations Act*. http://assembly.nl.ca/Legislation/sr/statutes/l01.htm

Conciliation

1. In 2014 the provincial movement introduced amendments the legislation to: (i) remove the possibility of card-based automatic certification; (ii) remove the requirement for the

parties to formally request a conciliation board; and (iii) rearrange and restate provisions relating to conciliation proceedings, strikes, and lockouts. The reader is advised to check the status of legislative changes regarding reform to the use of third parties when an impasse occurs in collective bargaining.

Mediation

1. When there is a request for a conciliation board—or at any time—the Minister may appoint a mediator. The appointment of a mediator terminates any previous appointment of a conciliation officer.

2. A mediator has the same responsibilities and authority as a conciliation board and reports to the Minister. The parties may agree that the report of a mediator will be binding.

Distinctive feature

1. A strike or lockout cannot be declared unless one of the parties has requested a conciliation board and the conciliation board has reported, or the Minister determines that a conciliation board will not be appointed.

NOVA SCOTIA

Complete details are set out in Sections 37–40, 61–75 of the *Trade Union Act.* http://nslegislature.ca/legc/statutes/trade%20union.pdf

Conciliation

1. At the request of either party, or on his or her own initiative, the Minister may appoint a conciliation officer.

2. The conciliation officer confers with the parties and reports to the Minister regarding the matters that the parties have agreed upon, the matters they have not agreed upon, and any other relevant issues.

3. If no agreement has been reached, and the parties request it, the Minister appoints a conciliation board that attempts to assist the parties to reach an agreement and reports to the Minister. The parties may agree that the report of the conciliation board will be binding. The Minister provides the report to the parties, and it may be made public. Seven days after the Minister receives the conciliation board report and upon giving 48 hours' notice to the Minister, the parties may strike or lockout.

Mediation

1. The Minister may appoint a mediator at any time. The mediator endeavours to assist the parties reach an agreement and reports to the Minister. With the Minister's permission, the mediator's report takes the place of a conciliation officer's report.

2. If the mediation is unsuccessful, the parties may request a conciliation board as noted above. If the parties do not request a conciliation board, there may be a strike or lockout 14 days after the mediator's report has been submitted to the Minister, and a 48-hour notice of the strike or lockout is provided.

Distinctive Features

1. The parties determine whether a conciliation board will be established.

2. A strike or lockout cannot be declared unless a conciliation officer, mediator, or conciliation board has reported to the Minister and the relevant cooling-off period has expired.

ONTARIO

Complete details are set out in Sections 18–40 of the *Labour Relations Act*. www.e-laws. gov.on.ca/html/statutes/english/elaws_statutes_95l01_e.htm

Conciliation

1. Either party may request the Minister to appoint a conciliation officer.

2. The conciliation officer confers with the parties, attempts to assist them to reach an agreement, and reports to the Minister.

3. If no agreement has been reached, the Minister must advise the parties whether or not a conciliation board will be established. If the Minister advises the parties that a conciliation board will not be established, which is the common practice, the parties may strike or lockout 14 days after the notification.

4. If a conciliation board is established, it endeavours to assist the parties to reach an agreement and reports to the Minister. The Minister releases the report to the parties. The parties may strike or lock out seven days after the report has been released.

Mediation

1. At the request of the parties, the Minister may appoint a mediator they have selected. The appointment of a mediator terminates any previous appointment of a conciliation officer.

2. The mediator attempts to assist the parties to reach an agreement and reports to the Minister. The report of a mediator has the same effect as a report of a conciliation board, and the parties may strike or lock out seven days after the mediator's report is released.

3. Any time after the conciliation process has been completed, either of the parties may apply for a mediator to be appointed. The appointment has no effect on a strike or lockout.

Distinctive Features

1. Although the legislation provides for a two-step conciliation process, only the first step, a conciliation officer, is commonly used.

2. The parties cannot strike or lockout until a conciliation officer, conciliation board, or mediator has reported to the Minister and the relevant cooling-off period has expired.

PRINCE EDWARD ISLAND

Complete details are set out in Sections 25–34 of the *Labour Act*.

Conciliation

1. At the request of either party or on his or her own initiative, the Minister may appoint a conciliation officer.

2. The conciliation officer meets with the parties and reports to the Minister on the matters the parties have agreed upon, the matters upon which the parties cannot agree, and the advisability of appointing a conciliation board or a mediator to endeavour to bring about an agreement.

3. The Minister may appoint a conciliation board that attempts to assist the parties to reach an agreement and reports to the Minister. The parties may agree that the conciliation board's recommendations will be binding. The report is provided to the parties and may be made public by the Minister. Seven days after the conciliation board report is filed with the Minister the parties may strike or lockout.

4. If a conciliation board is not established, the parties can strike or lock out 14 days after the conciliation officer's report is filed with the Minister.

Mediation

1. After the conciliation officer submits a report, the Minister may appoint a mediator instead of a conciliation board. The parties may agree to be bound by the mediator's recommendations.

2. The mediator attempts to assist the parties to reach an agreement and files a report with the Minister. The mediator's report is provided to the parties and may be made public by the Minister. Seven days after the report is filed with the Minister, the parties may strike or lock out.

Distinctive Features

1. The appointment and report of a conciliation officer must precede the appointment of a conciliation board or a mediator.

2. The parties cannot strike or lock out until a conciliation officer, conciliation board, or mediator has reported to the Minister and the relevant cooling-off period has expired.

SASKATCHEWAN

On May 13, 2013, the Government of Saskatchewan passed *The Saskatchewan Employment Act*, S.S. 2013, c. S-15.1. The SEA was proclaimed in April 2014. It repealed every significant piece of employment-related legislation currently in effect in Saskatchewan, including the *Occupational Health and Safety Act*, 1993, SS 1993, c O-1.1, the *Labour Standards Act*, RSS 1978, c L-1, and the *Trade Union Act*, RSS 1978, c T-17.

Complete details are set out in Sections 6-29, 6-33, and 6-92–6-116.

Conciliation

1. At the request of either party to a labour–management dispute or on the minister's own initiative, the minister may establish a conciliation board to investigate, conciliate and report to the minister on the dispute.

2. Under the new legislation, the Minister has broad powers with respect to the role and duties of a conciliation board.

Mediation

1. If an employer and a union are unable, after bargaining in good faith, to conclude a collective agreement, the employer or union shall provide a notice to the minister that they have reached an impasse.

2. As soon as possible after receipt of a notice the Minister shall appoint a labour relations officer or a special mediator, or establish a conciliation board, to mediate or conciliate the dispute.

Labour Relations Board

1. The parties may agree to submit a dispute to the Labour Relations Board. The Board hears the parties, and its finding is binding upon them.

Distinctive Features

1. Under the new legislation, a strike or lockout can only occur after 14 days have passed in one of two instances: the Minister's third-party appointee(s) to the dispute states that no recommendation will be advanced to the Minister; or the parties have reviewed the appointee(s) recommendations and decided not to accept those recommendations.

2. Once the labour relations officer, special mediator, or conciliation board has informed the Minister that the dispute has not been settled, a 14-day cooling-off period must occur before any strike or lockout can commence. No strike or lockout can occur before 48 hours' notice is provided to the other party, and promptly served on the Minister, confirming the date and time the strike or lockout will commence.

Chapter 11
Public Sector Labour Relations

Chapter Objectives

1. Identify the size and importance of the public sector
2. Outline the development of labour relations in the public sector
3. Describe the distinctive features of labour relations in the public sector
4. Outline recent trends in public sector labour relations

Required Professional Capabilities (CCHRA)	HRPA Human Resources Professionals Competency Framework
10101, 10211, 10303, 10504, 20111, 20301, 20307, 20406, 50102, 50106, 50113, 50114, 50205, 50206, 50302, 50304, 50402, 50403	C001, C002, C003, C004, C010, C030, C035, C036, C037, C038, C116, C117

The ups and downs of Western economies often result in interesting public policy strategies. Governments grapple particularly with the downs that are tied to recessions, unemployment, and a general public sensitivity to increases in income and property taxes to refill public coffers. In the 1990s, the Ontario government, under Premier Bob Rae, promoted a "Social Contract" policy and invited public sector unions to participate in discussions around cost-cutting measures that would avoid significant layoffs in the public service. The provincial government at that time faced a $12 billion annual deficit. Several key public sector unions boycotted these meetings. Twelve union groups agreed to the imposition of unpaid days. This policy was imposed on non-union civil servants and collective bargaining agreements with public sector unions could be opened under this government policy. Despite their unpopularity with many public sector unions, "Rae Days" saved the province nearly $2 billion dollars and prevented large-scale layoffs among public sector employees.

Fast-forward to 2014, when North American government policymakers again struggled with significant budgetary deficits, this time as a lingering effect of the 2008 economic recession. The economic recovery in both the United States and Canada after the 2008 crisis was fragile and slow, and in 2014 there was again evidence that government officials planned to impose unpaid days off upon public sector employees—this time involving municipal workers in a major Canadian city.

CUPE Local 500 represents about 5000 employees of the City of Winnipeg who deliver frontline services in public works, community services, water and wastewater, recreation, and other service areas. As a cost-savings strategy, Winnipeg's municipal council mandated 3.5 days of unpaid leave per employee. In March 2014, CUPE Local 500 filed a policy grievance against the mandatory unpaid leave, calling on the city to ensure that services remain fully staffed and open to the public. The City denied the grievance, forcing the union local to consider a costly and lengthy arbitration process. CUPE argued that an imposed furlough on municipal employees would directly affect those seeking important services. Subsequently, municipal officials announced that they would suspend the plan for such unpaid leave to be imposed on city staffers later that year.

Public sector unions in Canada are like a resilient old oak tree. They have maintained their presence to this day, and continue to grow despite the buffeting winds of change caused by "boom-to-bust" economic cycles, shifts in government policy, and community backlashes. Many of those inconvenienced by public sector strikes see union members as a drain on the public purse and a scourge whenever transit systems stop, garbage is not picked up, and other government employees "work to rule."

As the economy in many parts of the country continues to suffer through a sluggish North American market recovery, many elected officials believe they must cut government spending, challenge strong unions, and appease their constituents, many of whom have little sympathy for public sector employees, whom they perceive to already have better-than-average pay, benefits, and job security.

In addition to economic and political influences, union leaders are faced with demographic changes due to the retirement of many baby boomers, whose numbers contributed to the growth of the public sector in the 1950s and 1960s. Many of this generation went on to be employed in public sector jobs, in large part tied to the expansion of the union movement in this country. Today's union leaders must appeal to a new generation of workers and seek convincing reasons to rebuild their membership base now that many of the traditional battles over fair wages, safer workplaces, and a reasonable employee benefits safety net have already been won.

THE PUBLIC SECTOR: SIZE AND IMPORTANCE

Definition of the Public Sector

Before discussing the size and importance of the public sector, we should clarify its definition. The **public sector** is defined here as including three components: persons working directly for local, provincial, and federal governments; persons employed in various public sector agencies or services such as health care, social services, or educational institutions funded by government; and persons who work for government business enterprises and Crown corporations such as the Canadian Broadcasting Corporation.

The **public sector** includes all persons employed directly by local, provincial, and federal governments; indirectly in health, social services, and education; and government business enterprises.

Some commentary on the public sector does not include individuals working in government business enterprises. Whenever we are considering reports and commentary on the public sector, we should check to determine how the public sector has been defined.

Scope of the Public Sector

Total employment within various parts of Canada's public sector between 2007 and 2011 is seen in Figure 11-1.[1]

Importance of the Public Sector

The public sector is important for several reasons. The number of people employed makes it an important part of the economy. It provides vital services such as health care, education, police, and fire protection. Unlike the private sector, where if an employer suspends operations customers can obtain services elsewhere, many public sector employers are the only provider of their service.

The public sector is an important component of the labour relations system, and slightly more than half (58 percent) of all union members are public sector employees. Union density is much higher in the public sector than in the private sector. In 2013, Statistics Canada reported that 74 percent of unionized employees worked in the public sector. This represents 2.7 million employees out of a total public sector workforce of 3.6 million. This was in sharp contrast to the private sector, where only 17 percent of 11.4 million persons employed in the private sector belonged to a union.[2]

	2007	2008	2009	2010	2011
	Employment (persons)				
Public sector	**3 383 821**	**3 493 580**	**3 563 406**	**3 609 274**	**3 631 837**
Government	3 090 234	3 183 310	3 248 253	3 294 159	3 313 320
Federal general government*	387 121	400 196	415 397	420 685	427 093
Provincial and territorial general government	352 931	361 988	358 461	358 237	356 709
Health and social service institutions, provincial and territorial	783 142	800 200	822 904	844 762	859 350
Universities, colleges, and vocational and trade institutions, provincial and territorial	358 138	365 137	374 745	387 056	382 245
Local general government	548 298	581 221	596 144	605 562	608 094
Local school boards	660 603	674 568	680 603	677 857	679 828
Government business enterprises	293 587	310 270	315 154	315 114	318 519
Federal government business enterprises	99 121	104 864	104 692	104 042	102 319
Provincial and territorial government business enterprises	135 876	144 779	147 616	145 616	147 914
Local government business enterprises	58 589	60 627	62 845	65 456	68 286

Figure 11-1 Public Sector Employment, Wages, and Salaries (employees)

Notes: As at December 31. Employment data are not in full-time equivalent and do not distinguish between full-time and part-time employees. Includes employees both in and outside of Canada.

*Federal general government data includes reservists and full-time military personnel.

Source: Statistics Canada, CANSIM, "Public Sector Employment (Employees)," Table 183-0002, May 30, 2012, www5.statcan.gc.ca/cansim/search-recherche?lang=eng&searchType ByBalue=1&pattern=183-0002&p2=37.

DEVELOPMENT OF COLLECTIVE BARGAINING IN THE PUBLIC SECTOR

The development of collective bargaining in the public sector is fairly recent. Most public sector employees were not allowed to unionize until the late 1960s and early 1970s. In 1946, only 40 000 public sector employees were unionized; by 2013, that number had increased to 2.7 million Canadians. The federal and provincial legislation that established collective bargaining rights in the 1940s and 1950s, referred to in Chapter 3, generally did not include the public sector. There were some exceptions. Legislation establishing bargaining rights in 1944 in Saskatchewan covered both the public and private sectors. Also, most municipal employees other than police and fire services are covered by private sector labour relations legislation, and they have had the same right to organize as private sector employees.

Why Public Sector Employees Were Not Allowed to Unionize

Several reasons have been cited for the delay in extending the right to unionize to the public sector. The essential nature of some of the services provided was a concern. A strike could mean an interruption of the service. It was also thought that governments should not be forced to give up control of the public sector, in particular control over budgets. There was also a concern that a unionized public sector would have too much power, in view of the services provided, and this would lead to excessive increases in compensation.

Employee Associations

Prior to public sector employees being granted the right to unionize, they formed employee associations to promote their interests. These were different from unions in several respects. Because these associations were not certified by a labour relations board, they did not have the right to strike. They included members of management, and did not join labour federations. The associations consulted with governments to voice employee concerns regarding compensation and working conditions; however, the employer maintained final decision-making authority. Eventually employees perceived that this process did not adequately protect their interests, and they sought the right to unionize. The associations were important, however, because they were the basis for public sector unions that were able to develop rapidly when legislation extended collective bargaining rights to public sector employees.

Collective Bargaining Rights Extended to the Public Sector

In 1967, the federal government enacted the *Public Service Staff Relations Act* (now the *Public Service Labour Relations Act*), which gave federal government employees the right to unionize. A distinctive aspect of this legislation was a provision for a choice of contract dispute resolution mechanisms. Prior to the start of each contract negotiation, the union could choose either interest arbitration or a strike as the final dispute resolution mechanism. Subsequently, the provinces enacted legislation granting collective bargaining rights to their employees. In many jurisdictions, separate statutes covering parts of the public sector such as teachers or health workers were passed. There was a great deal of variation with respect to the right to strike in the provincial legislation. In some provinces, government and other public sector employees were given the right to strike. In other provinces, employees were not allowed to strike, and interest arbitration was established as the contract dispute resolution mechanism. Whether some public sector employees should be allowed to strike is an important question, which is referred to in Labour Relations Issue 11-1.

DISTINCTIVE FEATURES OF PUBLIC SECTOR LABOUR RELATIONS

Labour relations in the public sector have distinctive features from those in the private sector.

Employers

Several unique features of public sector employers affect labour relations.

Dual Role   Some public sector employers have a dual role: they function as both an employer and a regulator of the system. Public sector employers engage in contract negotiation and administration with unions; however, the capacity of some public employers to

Should Teachers Be Allowed to Strike?

In some provinces, teachers are not allowed to strike. The question of whether teachers should be allowed to strike has been an election issue in some provinces. Supporters of a ban on teacher strikes contend that public education is an essential service. Those who say that teachers should be allowed to strike claim that public education is not an essential service. They admit that strikes may be inconvenient, but contend that public education is not in the same category as other essential services, such as medical care. They also argue that the alternative to a strike, arbitration, leads to higher costs.

They point to cases in which arbitrators have ordered higher wage increases than have been budgeted for and claim that this has caused cuts in other areas, which have harmed students. Finally, they claim that a ban on teacher strikes would take away a fundamental freedom.

Should teachers have the right to strike? If "yes" are there any conditions that should be placed on such actions? If "no" why should teachers not be permitted to use a strike to leverage their demands in negotiations?

legislate affects these processes and labour relations outcomes. Governments can pass legislation that grants or takes away the right to strike from specific public sector employees such as teachers. Governments can also pass legislation that imposes wage restraints or freezes, affecting contract outcomes.

Divided Authority   In the private sector, there is one voice for management, and it is usually known where the employer stands. In the public sector, management authority is sometimes divided; meaning that it is possible that authority is divided between administrators the union usually deals with and elected government officials. This may prompt union leaders to attempt to go around administrators and influence elected officials. For example, in the case of a public transit system, the union may determine that it will not be able to obtain a wage increase from the transit administrators negotiating for the employer, and it may attempt to pressure politicians to intervene in contract talks.

Political Bottom Line   In the private sector, employers are profit-seeking organizations, and collective agreement outcomes are largely determined by economic factors. The employer's ability to pay and retain customers is a key factor. Wage increases that go beyond this ability cannot be sustained in the long run. In the public sector, the political factor is crucial. Governments are concerned with public opinion and how it affects re-election, not profits. Strikes in the private sector are aimed at imposing losses on the employer so that it will agree to a wage increase. In the public sector, governments do not always incur losses during a strike; they may actually save money. The purpose of some public sector strikes is to influence public opinion so that government will be pressured to agree to more favourable terms of employment. Some public sector employees such as teachers and nurses attempt to frame any dispute with the employer to maximize a favourable reaction from the public by referring to the quality of patient care or the quality of education. However, it is possible that some public sector strikes will not generate public interest. For example, if the clerks who process payments of water bills at city hall go on strike, it is not likely that this will generate much public concern. In contrast, if college or university professors strike, there will likely be calls for government action after a short time.

Financial Constraints   At one time, it was thought that the public sector was different because governments would have the authority to raise taxes when necessary to provide for wage increases. In view of the present economic and political climate, this does not appear to be possible. The deficit spending undertaken by governments in response to the 2008–09 recession has left governments with increased debt that will make future contract negotiations more difficult.

Employees and Unions

There are more unionized white-collar and professional employees in the public sector than in the private sector. This may result in public sector unions having different priorities and objectives. Teachers in the public sector may be concerned with issues relating to class size and professional development. In the private sector, most bargaining unit members are men. In the public sector, most are women. This leads to increased concerns regarding issues such as pay and employment equity.

The importance of public opinion will affect the methods unions employ. Public sector unions make greater use of media campaigns to achieve their objectives. In 2013, the Public Service Alliance of Canada used a media event to describe how cuts to Veterans Affairs regional offices would affect them.[3]

Legislative Framework

Private sector labour relations in each jurisdiction are regulated by a statute that provides a uniform set of rules covering union certification, contract negotiation, and contract administration. This legislation also applies to municipal employees. All jurisdictions except Saskatchewan also have a general public sector labour relations statute that applies to government employees. For example, in British Columbia there is a *Public Service Labour Relations Act*, and in Nova Scotia a *Civil Service Collective Bargaining Act*. Police, firefighters, health care workers, and teachers are covered by the private sector legislation, the general public sector statute, or special legislation relating to one occupation, such as the *Public Schools Act* covering teachers in Manitoba. There are over 40 federal and provincial statutes across Canada regulating public sector labour relations. Depending on the jurisdiction, there may be only two statutes that possibly affect public sector employees, or there may be seven. To illustrate how varied the legislative framework is, teachers are regulated by the general public sector statute in the federal jurisdiction, by the private sector statute in British Columbia, and by special teacher legislation in Nova Scotia.

The key point is that there is a patchwork of legislation across the country, and groups such as teachers and nurses may or may not have the right to strike depending upon the jurisdiction.

Establishment of Bargaining Rights

In the private sector, Labour Relations Boards determine bargaining units after receiving input from the parties. In the public sector, bargaining units in some cases are set out in legislation. For example, the federal *Public Service Labour Relations Act* establishes bargaining units based on occupation. There is considerable variation across the provinces regarding the number and composition of bargaining units provided for provincial employees. In British Columbia, the legislation has established three bargaining units. In some provinces, one province-wide bargaining unit is established.[4]

Scope of Contract Negotiation

In the private sector, the parties are allowed to negotiate all terms of employment and also the scope of the bargaining unit. In the public sector, legislation often restricts the number of issues that can be the subject of negotiations. With the exception of Saskatchewan, provincial employees have been prohibited from bargaining over pension plans. Most provinces prohibit bargaining over employee training programs and promotion issues. The *Public Service Labour Relations Act* prohibits bargaining over pensions, promotions, and technological change.[5] It is not possible to list all of the restrictions on public sector employees in various jurisdictions here. It should be noted that the scope of bargaining in the public sector is narrower than in the private sector, and reference should be made to the relevant legislation.

Contract Dispute Resolution

If the parties are not able to negotiate an agreement in the private sector, the final dispute resolution mechanism is a strike or lockout. In the public sector, because some services provided are essential, it is not always possible to allow a strike or lockout. Hence, four primary methods of dispute resolution have developed: an unrestricted right-to-strike model, a no-strike model that relies on interest arbitration, a designated or controlled strike model, and legislation.

Strike Model   Parts of the public sector have been allowed to engage in unrestricted strikes in the same manner as the private sector. This model is typically applied to workers, such as municipal clerks, doing work that is not essential. Some public sector employees have been granted the right to strike despite the fact that their work appears to be essential. However, in the event these employees actually exercise their right to strike, they could be legislated back to work very quickly. In May, 2012, federal government legislation received royal assent, ending a strike between the Canadian Pacific Railway and the Teamsters Canada Rail Conference.

The **replication principle** holds that an arbitration award should reflect the agreement that the parties would have reached in negotiations.

No-Strike, Interest Arbitration Model   Conventional interest arbitration as a method to resolve contract disputes was referred to in Chapter 10. Both sides submit evidence to an arbitrator or an arbitration board that decides the terms of the collective agreement. The **replication principle**, a fundamental feature of interest arbitration, holds that an arbitration award should as much as possible reflect the agreement that the parties would have reached had they been able to do so in negotiations. In cases in which the memorandum of settlement has been recommended by a majority of the bargaining team, it has been given significant weight by the arbitrator. In one case in which the memorandum of settlement had only been recommended by half of the union's bargaining team, an arbitrator held that it should be given less weight and proceeded to award an additional increase to some employees. Accordingly, it has been recommended that the employer should attempt to ensure that a memorandum of settlement is unanimously recommended by the union bargaining team so that the chances of a higher award at subsequent interest arbitration are reduced if the agreement is not ratified. The employer could consider making an offer conditional upon unanimous approval of the union bargaining team.

Website providing an interest arbitration decision: www.opseu.org

The compensation and working conditions of employees at other workplaces doing similar work is a critical factor considered by arbitrators. For example, in the case of teachers, the union and the employer would present information regarding the salaries of teachers employed by other school boards. Arbitrators have also taken into account factors such as inflation, productivity increases, and the need to maintain minimum living standards, especially for lower-paid employees. Arbitrators do not believe public sector employees should be required to subsidize taxpayers by being paid lower wages to avoid tax increases.[6] The margin note above refers to a website that provides an interest arbitration decision.

There is evidence that interest arbitration leads to higher increases in compensation than increases obtained pursuant to bargaining where a strike is the final dispute resolution mechanism.[7] In response to the possibility that arbitrators award higher compensation to unions than they would be able to obtain through the strike route, governments have passed legislation requiring arbitrators to consider the ability to pay and other factors. In Ontario, legislation has required arbitrators in education to render decisions that comply with legislation regulating instruction time and class size.[8] The federal government has at times suspended the use of interest arbitration for a period, for example in 1996 and 1999.[9]

Designated or Controlled Strike Model   In the **designated or controlled strike** model, employees are given the right to strike, but an agreed-upon number of employees must continue working to provide essential services to the public. If this model was applied to workers maintaining roads in the winter, some workers would have to remain on the job if there was a strike. This model is used in parts of the public sector in the majority of the jurisdictions in Canada: the federal jurisdiction, British Columbia, Manitoba, New Brunswick, Newfoundland and Labrador, Ontario, Quebec, and Saskatchewan.

In the **designated or controlled strike** model, employees have the right to strike, but a specified number of employees must continue working to provide essential services to the public.

The parties attempt to agree on who will continue to work in the event of a strike. If the union and the employer cannot agree on this, the dispute goes to the Labour Relations Board or a board created by legislation governing the employees involved. A hearing is held, and the Board resolves the issue. Because the parties will have different preferences and objectives regarding who is deemed essential, an agreement may be difficult to reach. Employers prefer that as many workers as possible be designated essential so that the disruption of service is reduced; unions prefer that a smaller number of workers be designated essential so that the strike will be effective and create pressure for a settlement. The number of employees designated as essential varies extensively depending on the work done. Under the *Public Service Labour Relations Act*, 2 percent of librarians and 100 percent of air traffic controllers have been designated as essential.

The history and details of the designation process in various jurisdictions is beyond the scope of this text. The essential services model, including the designation of employees, is described in *Strikes in Essential Services*, which is recommended to the reader who wishes to obtain more information.[10]

Legislation   Governments can also pass back-to-work legislation to end a strike and resolve a contract dispute. In most cases, such legislation provides for the dispute between the union and the employer to be resolved by interest arbitration. However, some statutes have instead set out the terms and conditions of work. Prior to the Supreme Court of Canada's decision in the *Health Services* case, a government could pass legislation nullifying the terms of previously negotiated collective agreements. As noted in Chapter 2, the Supreme Court held in 2007 that legislation that substantially interferes with the union's collective bargaining rights violates the *Charter*. Accordingly, there is now a constraint on legislation that purports to invalidate existing collective agreements or impose restrictions upon contract negotiations.

Comparing Alternative Contract Dispute Resolution Methods

Why don't we simply ban all public sector strikes and provide for interest arbitration in all cases where the parties cannot reach an agreement? To answer this question, we will consider the possible advantages and disadvantages of strikes, arbitration, and designated employees. Four criteria are considered in Key Considerations 11-1: how the method will affect the likelihood of the parties negotiating their own agreement, the acceptability of the outcomes, the efficiency of the process, and the extent to which the method ensures the provision of essential services.

Interest Arbitration.   Interest arbitration should ensure the provision of essential services because strikes are not allowed. Although there have been situations in which employees have gone on strike even though a strike is not legal, these are exceptional. Interest arbitration means that the parties avoid spending time and energy negotiating a designated employee agreement. However, interest arbitration reduces the likelihood that the parties will be able to negotiate their own agreement because of the chilling and narcotic effects referred to in Chapter 10. A study that contrasted interest arbitration and the strike in Ontario found that there was evidence of chilling and narcotic effects when arbitration is used.[11] The study found that bargaining units using arbitration failed to negotiate a settlement 8.7 to 21.7 percent more often than bargaining units that could strike. The failure to

Advantages and Disadvantages of Alternative Contract Dispute Resolution Mechanisms

	Possible Advantages	Possible Disadvantages
No-strike, interest arbitration	Essential services are provided—minimizes disruption to public.	Reduced likelihood of voluntary settlement due to chilling and narcotic effects.
	Avoids negotiation of agreement regarding designated employees.	Outcomes may not be acceptable to the parties.
		May lead to increase in other forms of industrial conflict.
Unrestricted strike	Avoids negotiation of agreement regarding designated employees.	Potential for disruption of service and harm to the public.
	Increased likelihood of voluntary settlement.	Possibility of back-to-work legislation being required to settle strike.
Designated employees, or controlled strike	Avoids complete loss of services caused by an unrestricted strike.	Requires time and energy be spent on negotiation of designated employee agreement.
	Greater likelihood of voluntary settlement than interest arbitration.	Designation levels may be set too high or too low.
		Strikes might last longer.

negotiate a settlement was more pronounced in some sectors. A bargaining impasse was more likely in the health care sector, especially among hospitals. It was also found that a centralized bargaining structure led to higher levels of impasse. This may be due to the fact that in centralized bargaining the parties are seeking a common solution to various localized problems. It was also found that the size of the bargaining unit was a factor. Smaller bargaining units (less than 21 employees) were 9.5 times more likely to reach an impasse using arbitration. This may be caused in part by the fact that smaller bargaining units do not have as much power when the strike is the dispute resolution mechanism. Arbitration would allow these bargaining units to press for demands when they could not do so using a strike. The study made an interesting observation relating to unions that bargain under both strike and arbitration regimes. It was found that unions that went to arbitration more where arbitration was the dispute resolution method had higher strike rates in bargaining elsewhere where a strike was possible. This suggests a narcotic effect—the inability to negotiate settlements that has developed under the arbitration regime has spilled over into negotiations in which a strike is possible. Also, there is a possibility that when an outsider determines the outcomes, they may be less acceptable to the parties. In particular, employers may perceive that arbitration will lead to the union gaining terms it would not be able to obtain by going on strike. It is also noteworthy that strikes are not the only form of industrial conflict. There is evidence that when strikes are banned and replaced with interest arbitration, other forms of conflict such as grievances and slowdowns are increased.

Strikes. The unrestricted strike model is more efficient than the designation model because the parties do not have to negotiate a designated employee agreement. It should encourage a voluntary settlement because it imposes higher costs than the other two methods. But it poses the highest risk of disruption of service to the public, and accordingly should only be used where disruption does not entail a danger to the public. Allowing clerks who process income tax returns to strike makes sense, whereas allowing firefighters to strike does not. There is also the possibility that a strike will not produce a settlement and eventually back-to-work legislation will have to be imposed. For example, where teachers have the right to strike, it has been necessary to end some strikes through legislation.

Designated Employees. The designation model has the advantage of avoiding a complete loss of services. Because some costs are imposed on the parties, a voluntary settlement is encouraged. However, the parties will have to spend time and energy negotiating the designated employees. The first designated employee agreement has posed a problem in a number of cases, and the parties have become involved in proceedings in which the Board was required to resolve the matter. There is also the possibility that the designation levels might be set too high or too low. Because the government is still able to provide some services, there may not be enough pressure to force a settlement and the strike might last longer.

A recent study examined the use of the three methods referred to here in several provinces. It was concluded that the designation model was an improvement over the other two models because it "is the most conducive to adequate provision of essential services, to voluntarily negotiated collective agreements, and to outcomes that all parties can live with."[12] The study noted that the designation model is gaining popularity and has replaced the other two models in several jurisdictions.

RECENT DEVELOPMENTS IN PUBLIC SECTOR LABOUR RELATIONS

Labour relations in the public sector have been affected by environmental variables, in particular by economic, political, and social factors.

Economy

For the period 2012–13 the federal and nearly every provincial government expected to be in deficit; Saskatchewan was the only exception. Partly as a result of ongoing deficits, the direct debt burden in Canada has grown considerably. Consider that the federal government's net debt (gross debt minus financial assets) is expected to reach $676 billion in 2012–13 more than $160 billion from the level in 2007–08. As a percentage of the economy (GDP), the federal debt burden will increase to 36 percent from 34 percent in 2007–08. A similar trend has been seen at the provincial level. Collectively, provincial net debt has grown to $517 billion (28 percent of GDP) from $321 billion (21 per cent of GDP) over the same period. If the $1.2 trillion in combined federal and provincial government direct debt were equally distributed among all Canadians, each person would be on the hook for $34 209.[13] To deal with the debt situation, governments had tended to pursue two broad options: they could either increase revenues by raising taxes or decrease expenditures by cutting costs and services. The former option is usually avoided due to its likelihood to anger the electorate. It has also been argued that globalization made the option of increasing taxes impractical because higher taxes would push investment capital to other jurisdictions.

The recession near the end of the first decade of the 21st century reduced revenues while governments engaged in stimulus spending to rejuvenate the economy, leading to budget deficits. In 2010, Ontario was projecting a $25 billion deficit, and other provinces including Alberta were also facing deficits. In this economic situation, there was talk of wage freezes, unpaid days off, and job cuts across the country. Alberta Health Services announced in October 2009 that it was imposing a two-year freeze on the compensation of management and non-union staff. In February 2010, the NDP government in Manitoba warned public sector unions that they would have to accept a two-year wage freeze. Ontario enacted a *Public Sector Compensation Restraint to Protect Public Services Act*, which froze compensation of non-union employees for two years until March 31, 2012. Although this legislation did not directly affect union employees, the government indicated that when current collective agreements expire it would be seeking renewed agreements that imposed a two-year wage freeze.

Political and Social Environment

The political and social environments are interrelated and will be considered together. Some governments have enacted legislation and policies that are stated to be aimed at reforming or improving the public sector. In 2002, the British Columbia Liberal government passed Bill 29, which affected the health care sector by allowing for the privatization of health services, eliminating no-contracting-out language in collective agreements, and eliminating successor rights. Subsequently, the jobs of 8000 Hospital Employee Union workers were contracted out to multinational service corporations. In 2009, the Ontario government announced that it would "become more efficient by reducing the size of the Ontario Public Service by 5 percent over the next three years." One observer has summed up the political and social situation as follows:

> Governments, faced with declining tax revenue and on the hook for so-called stimulus spending, are already announcing plans to cut back. With few social programs left to slash expect them to directly attack unionized public sector wage bills. It will be mean and bloody minded. Given the fact that almost everyone else in the country has already been whacked, it will also be darkly popular.[14]

However, in the 2014 Ontario provincial election campaign the Conservative leader promised that, if elected, his party would cut 100 000 public servant jobs—which ultimately did not work, resulting in a loss of seats for this party in the legislature.

In summary, environmental factors will likely lead governments to seek reductions in labour costs. To meet this objective, governments have three options:[15]

- They can attempt to reduce labour costs through collective bargaining. This would involve demanding reductions in wages and benefits from the unions that governments negotiate with directly. The demands might be supported by threats of contracting out or privatization. Where employees have the right to strike, governments will have to be willing to bear a strike. Where government is providing funding to employers in the health and education sectors, funding could be reduced so that employers would be forced to pursue reducing compensation in contract negotiations.

- The second approach is a cooperative one in which governments approach unions with the problem, share information, and attempt to resolve the issue. Unions might agree to wage concessions in return for job security provisions, or the parties might develop other options such as early retirement plans that save money.

- The third approach involves changing compensation and working conditions unilaterally through legislation. In the past, this has been done by passing legislation that imposes restrictions on compensation, or directly imposes the terms of a new agreement.

The collective bargaining approach is slow and uncertain; and in situations where interest arbitration is the final dispute resolution mechanism, it is not guaranteed that an arbitrator would award reduced compensation. The cooperative approach is no faster or surer. Accordingly, the legislative approach is attractive to governments. However, because the *Charter* now protects collective bargaining, governments will have to ensure that they do not substantially interfere with the collective bargaining process. Unless a government is willing to rely on the *Charter's* notwithstanding clause, this will impose a constraint on the use of legislation to resolve disputes.

In recent years, governments have relied more on legislation or the threat of legislation than the collective bargaining or cooperative approaches referred to above. From 1982 to 2012, back-to-work legislation that imposed contract settlements on the parties was utilized 8 times by the federal government and 42 times by eight of the ten provincial goverments.[16]

It is important to note that the governments that adopted the legislative approach were able to do so without political penalty. Gene Swimmer notes that although some governments that resorted to the legislative approach were not re-elected, there is little evidence that their handling of public sector labour relations was a factor in their defeat. In jurisdictions where governments were replaced, the successor government continued with the legislative approach.[17]

The details of developments in public sector labour relations in each province are beyond the scope of this text. Readers interested in the Nova Scotia, Ontario, Manitoba, Alberta, British Columbia, and federal jurisdictions should refer to *Public-Sector Labour Relations in an Era of Restraint and Restructuring* edited by Gene Swimmer. Swimmer concludes that public sector labour relations have been permanently changed. He notes that employers should consider the costs associated with rejecting the traditional collective bargaining model, including lost productivity. He submits that it is in government's self-interest to return to the collective bargaining model instead of relying on legislation. He challenges governments to think of employees as a source of value rather than a cost to be reduced. On the union side, Swimmer observes that unions will have to come to terms with the new environment. Taking a "no concessions" position will encourage the government to take unilateral action.

A 2002 survey found that public sector managers and labour leaders have different perceptions about the state of labour–management relations. Sixty-two percent of labour leaders, in contrast to only 28 percent of public sector managers, said labour–management relations were poor.[18] Given recent events in the public sector, and the prospects for the future, the pessimistic view held by labour leaders is not surprising.

Website with information regarding legislation ending strikes or lockouts: www.hrsdc.gc.ca/eng/labour/labour_law/ind_rel/index.shtml

PUBLIC SECTOR COMPENSATION

The effects of unionization will be considered in Chapter 12. However, one important question relating specifically to unions in the public sector will be addressed here. Has the unionization of public sector employees led to higher compensation in the public sector than in the private sector?

Some members of the public apparently perceive that public sector employees are overpaid. For example, in a news item entitled "Voters Could Change Collective Agreements" published November 21, 2009, Howard Levitt refers to "excessive wages and benefits of municipal employees."[19] He recommends that candidates for municipal office be asked to clarify if they would "gut agreements" and that public sector employers take strikes using replacement workers. "This eliminates the impact of a strike on the public, effectively breaking it and ultimately compelling workers to accept management's terms."

Are these perceptions of the public sector accurate? Thompson and Juliette have noted that wage surveys comparing jobs similar in terms of qualifications, tasks, and responsibilities have shown that public sector wages more often lag behind those in the private sector. Their research also examined wage increases in the public and private sectors between 1979 and 2007 in collective agreements covering more than 500 employees. It was found that the cumulative wage increases gained by private sector employees were higher than the increases gained by public sector employees. Thompson and Jalette conclude: "There is no support for the contention that unionized public sector wage settlements have outstripped those in the private sector since 1979; indeed the reverse appears true."[20] It appears that claims that public sector employees are being paid "excessive wages" deserve scrutiny.

Implications for Practice

1. Some observers are concerned with the state of labour relations in the public sector because of government reliance on legislation instead of negotiation. In the post-2008 recession era, it remains to be seen how political leaders at the federal and provincial levels approach the delicate balance between their direct and indirect roles as public sector employers versus their legislative authority to mandate solutions that preclude "union-management made" bargaining results.

2. In view of the willingness of some governments to legislate instead of negotiate outcomes, union leaders have been advised by some to rethink "no concessions" policies.

3. The proponents of the designated strike model contend that it meets public policy needs better than unrestricted strikes or interest arbitration. More governments may adopt the designated strike model in the future.

Key Terms

designated or controlled
  strike, p. 281

public sector, p. 275

replication principle, p. 280

Review Questions

1. Discuss the importance of the public sector in contemporary Canadian society.

2. Why were public sector employees not provided the right to unionize at the same time as employees in the private sector in most jurisdictions?

3. How are public sector employers different from private sector employers?

4. How are public sector employees and unions different from private sector employees and unions?

5. Why are there restrictions on the issues that can be the subject of contract negotiations in the public sector?

6. Outline the possible advantages and disadvantages of the three main methods of contract dispute resolution in the public sector.

Discussion Questions

1. Three key methods to resolve contract disputes in the public sector are interest arbitration, strike, and designated strike. Consider the following employees: clerical staff at Revenue Canada, air traffic controllers, and teachers. Which method of dispute resolution would be preferred by the union and by the employer?

2. Do you think that teachers should have the right to strike? Support your point of view using key concepts and discussions from this chapter.

3. Are there any reasons why labour relations would be more confrontational in the public sector as opposed to the private sector? Explain.

Web Research

1. Visit the website for the labour federation in your province. Locate and discuss information dealing with a current public sector union topic.

2. Visit the website for the Canadian Union of Public Employees (http://cupe.ca) and locate a topic that you believe is relevant to public sector unions today. Discuss.

CASE INCIDENT ROADWAY SERVICES

Roadway Services maintains highways in British Columbia pursuant to a contract with the Ministry of Transportation. In addition to clearing debris in the summer, and plowing snow in the winter, the company operates several ferries crossing waterways. Roadway employees are represented by a union. One of the ferries operated by Roadway crosses a river at Beautytown. Most of the municipality is located on the east side of the river, and the town's medical, police, and fire services are headquartered on the east side. The only gas stations and grocery store serving the community are also located on the east side. Approximately 500 residents of the town live on the west side of the river. There are two alternative routes to the ferry: residents can walk along trails and cross the river using a railway bridge near the centre of town, or they can drive one hour along the river one way to another ferry and then drive back along the other side. The relevant portions of the *Labour Relations Code* provide as follows:

Essential services

72 (1) If a dispute arises after collective bargaining has commenced, the chair may, on the chair's own motion or on application by either of the parties to the dispute,

   (a) investigate whether or not the dispute poses a threat to

   (i) the health, safety, or welfare of the residents of British Columbia,

   (b) report the results of the investigation to the minister.

   (2) If the minister

   (a) after receiving a report of the chair respecting a dispute, or

   (b) on the minister's own initiative

   considers that a dispute poses a threat to the health, safety or welfare of the residents of British Columbia, the minister may direct the board to designate as essential services those facilities, productions and services that the board considers necessary or essential to prevent immediate and serious danger to the health, safety or welfare of the residents of British Columbia.

   (3) When the minister makes a direction under subsection (2) the associate chair of the Mediation Division may appoint one or more mediators to assist the parties to reach an agreement on essential services designations.

   ...

   (8) If the board designates facilities, productions and services as essential services, the employer and the trade union must supply, provide or maintain in full measure those facilities, productions and services and must not restrict or limit a facility, production or service so designated.

   (9) A designation made under this section may be amended, varied or revoked and another made in its place.

Normally the ferry service operates 6:30 A.M. to 10:30 P.M. seven days a week. Prior to the expiry of the collective agreement, the company and the union entered into an essential services agreement in March 2010 that provided that if there was a strike the ferry would operate from 6:30 to 9:30 A.M. and from 2:30 to 5:30 P.M. weekdays, and in the event of an emergency an additional crossing would be arranged. A strike started on April 16, 2010, and the ferry operated pursuant to the essential services agreement until June. For three weeks in the month of June, the operation of the ferry was suspended because of high water. On June 28, at the end of the school year, the union filed an application with the Labour Relations Board to reduce the level of service provided by the ferry, claiming that during the summer school break the service should be reduced. In the school year, there are two large buses and three small buses using the ferry making round trips each day. In July and August, there would be only one school bus making a round trip each day. The union proposed that the hours of operation be reduced to 7:45 to 8:45 A.M. and 1 to 2 P.M. in July and August. The union's application also provided that the hours of operation be restored to those provided in the original essential services agreement when the new school year started.

The employer opposed the reduction in hours, and made a counterapplication requesting that the service hours be restored to normal hours of operation. The employer based its application on complaints it had received during the operation of the essential services agreement and a few specific incidents. Many residents on the west side were using the railway bridge and wheelbarrows to obtain groceries. At the end of the hours of operation provided in the essential services agreement, there were on average five cars lined up on each side. A pregnant woman who required medical attention had walked across the railway bridge. Several farmers on the west side who normally use the ferry to transport produce were concerned that they had been forced to take the alternative road route. There had also been an incident in which an ambulance was delayed crossing when the ferry was not operating because there was no cellular phone service in the area, and employees had to be tracked down to operate the ferry.

Questions

1. Outline the argument that the employer will make before the Labour Relations Board.

2. Outline the response the union would make to the employer's request for a return to normal hours of operation.

3. What powers does the British Columbia provincial minister responsible for labour relations have in this situation? How might this work stoppage be ended?

Chapter 12

Effects of Unionization and Employee Relations Programs

Chapter Objectives

1. Explain the effects of unionization on union and non-union employers
2. Outline the implications of unionization for employees
3. Identify the features of job control unionism
4. Identify alternative forms of employee involvement
5. Describe barriers to increased employee involvement
6. Outline factors affecting the future of unions
7. Identify the factors affecting a transition to more collaborative labour relations

Required Professional Capabilities (CCHRA)	HRPA Human Resources Professionals Competency Framework
30101, 50101, 50106, 50110, 50111, 50118, 50201, 50203, 50301, 50302	C030, C056, C057, C058, C079, C111, C112, C113, C114, C115, C118

In 1996, Human Resources Development Canada (HRDC) released the report *Investing in People*, which found that just over 40 percent of textiles companies surveyed said their employees lacked the essential skills to do their current jobs, and about 40 percent of production personnel did not have a high-school diploma. At the same time, HRDC also revealed that only 40 percent of Canadian textiles firms had any formal human resources plans in place, and only about 20 percent had a full-time HR person—or a joint employer–employee committee—to address training needs.

A corporate response to this reality took place in Woodstock, Ontario, when Firestone Textile in collaboration with the United Food and Commercial Workers Union (UFCW) created a partnership to provide resources and support to general literacy and academic programs for plant employees. The Woodstock plant established an Education and Development Centre offering courses covering everything from boosting productivity to improving safety. With teaching expertise from Fanshawe Community College in nearby London, Ontario, participants in the 20-week, on-site program attended two morning sessions per week, with the flexibility to match classroom sessions with their work schedules. Running classes in a 24/7 work environment was certainly a challenge, according to plant management. So having an education facility on-site was a significant means to success. At the end of the program, employees could write the Ministry of Education's General Education Development (GED) exam and obtain their high-school diploma.

Today, through its learning centre and the GED program, Firestone, which produces nylon tire cords for its parent company as well as industrial yarn and nylon resins, is planting the seeds of a learning culture. This is one example in a range of similar programs in the textiles sector aimed at overcoming numerous challenges, including increasingly stiff competition from low-wage countries. With the union–management initiative in place, employees who had emigrated to Canada without sufficient English-language skills or those forced to enter the labour force before finishing high school now had achieved not only a diploma but a sense of personal accomplishment.

A key catalyst to developing this type of collaboration was the Textiles Human Resources Council (THRC). Formed in 1994, this Ottawa-based, non-profit partnership, led by a board of six industry executives and six senior union representatives, receives funding from the federal government and from members in the textile industry. THRC employs 12 staff and has two standing committees made up of representatives from business, unions, industry groups, educational institutions, and government. The Council aims to build a solid training and education infrastructure for textiles manufacturers. Firestone's learning centre is one example of a transformational partnership between union and management to not only meet corporate goals in the marketplace, but also develop their own human capital in a very competitive market.

In this chapter, we will consider the overall effects of unionization, the possibility of increased employee and union partnerships in the workplace, and the question posed in Chapter 1 regarding confrontation versus collaboration.

EFFECTS OF UNIONIZATION

The unionization of approximately 30 percent of the Canadian workforce affects all employers and employees. Unions affect the level and structure of employee compensation, productivity, profitability, employment levels, and the distribution of income in society. Some of the effects of unions are contentious, and definitive conclusions cannot be drawn. For example, there is a debate about the effects of unions on productivity. Knowledge and thinking relating to the effects of unions have been dramatically affected by the work of Freeman and Medoff, who studied unions and produced *What Do Unions Do?*[1] Although that book was published in 1984, it has recently been described as "the most famous book in labor economics and industrial relations . . . a true classic . . . anyone interested in labor unions needs to read. . . ."[2] In 2004–05, the *Journal of Labor Research* published a series of 21 papers entitled "What Do Unions Do: A 20-Year Perspective." The papers reviewed the work of these authors and considered whether their findings still held up. The original work, the papers referred to in the series, and their reference material are recommended to readers who wish to explore the effect of unions in greater depth.

Freeman and Medoff made a distinction between two aspects or faces of unionism. Unions have a largely negative "monopoly face," associated with their power to raise wages above competitive levels, and a largely positive "voice face," associated with the representation of employees that could lead to improvements. Freeman and Medoff contended that both the monopoly face and the voice face might lead to improvements in productivity. Higher union wages might shock or force employers to adopt more efficient methods including better technology, although this may also reduce employment. Employers may be forced to establish more efficient job standards and increase management accountability because of higher labour costs. The voice effect could improve communication with employees and might lead to higher productivity by reducing turnover. Union firms have lower turnover, perhaps because dissatisfied workers stay and attempt to improve their situation through the union instead of quitting. Lower turnover is associated with reduced hiring and training costs, and less disruption of the workforce. Lower turnover might encourage investment in training. The voice of employees expressed through unions might lead to increases in efficiency and more effective compensation packages. The adoption of a compensation package that meets the needs of employees will provide more satisfaction per dollar.

The employment security provided to senior employees in unionized firms may reduce rivalry between employees and lead to more informal training and assistance. Perhaps the most interesting and contentious conclusion reached by Freeman and Medoff was that unions had a positive impact overall and labour policy in the United States should be changed to encourage an increase in union density. We will consider the effects of unions on compensation, productivity, profitability, investment, employment, and management practices.

Compensation

Union Wage Effect   Numerous studies have examined the question of how much unions increase the wages of unionized employees above the wages of non-union employees. The concept of union wage premium refers to the degree in which union wages exceed non-union member wages. It is argued that because union employers tend to pay higher wages, they are able to hire more skilled and experienced employees. Accordingly, it is difficult to determine the extent to which higher wages are being paid for additional skills and experience, and the extent to which higher wages are due to union representation. At one time the union wage impact was estimated to range from 10 to 25 percent.[3] In 2013 the unadjusted union wage premium was higher in the private sector (9 percent) compared to the public sector (3 percent). This disparity is explained in part due to the higher union density level in the public sector. The average hourly wage for unionized employees in the private sector was $23.90, compared with $21.85 for non-unionized employees. In the public sector, unionized employees earned an average of $30.52 per hour; non-unionized employees earned $29.52.[4] Studies in the United States have found that the union wage premium has declined from the 1970s to 2001.[5] It has been suggested that the decline in the union wage premium has been caused by increased competitive pressure that has forced employers to reduce compensation costs. A recent U.S. study found that over the past two decades, there has been a decline in the union wage premium in that country; however, it was not uniform. The decline was more significant in some industries and for women.[6]

The ability of the union to increase wages will depend upon the union's bargaining power and the employer's position in the market. The factors that would increase the union's bargaining power were referred to in Chapter 8. If the employer sells its product or service in a competitive market, there is less potential for the union to increase wages. In this situation, there is a limit on wage increases because the employer must remain competitive. When the employer has market power and can increase prices, its ability to pass along wage increases in the form of higher prices increases the possibility of the union increasing wages. If the employer has cost advantages over its competitors, the union's ability to obtain wage improvements increases because the wage improvements may come from the firm's cost savings instead of price increases.

The union wage impact varies according to a number of factors, including the industry, the gender, occupation, and skill level of employees, and the size of the firm. Female employees have gained more from unionization than males. There is a larger union premium for blue-collar employees than white-collar employees. Employees at lower skill levels gain more from unionization than higher-skilled employees, the overall result of which is a compression of the wage structure.

Union Effect on Benefits   Unions raise benefit levels more than they raise wages.[7] One explanation provided for this is that unions are a voice for the average worker. The average worker is more likely to be older and have a family, which makes benefits more attractive. It has also been suggested that benefits are a form of deferred compensation, and employers may see benefits as a way to encourage employee interest in the continued success of the firm.

Effect on Non-union Wages   The overall effect of unions on the wage level of non-union employees is not clear. Unions may lead to higher wages for some non-union employees

The **threat effect** is an upward pressure on non-union wages caused by the possibility that employees may unionize.

The **crowding effect** is a downward pressure on non-union wages caused by an increased supply of labour in the non-union sector.

because of a **threat effect**. Some non-union employers may increase wages to avoid unionization. Conversely, it is argued that there is a **crowding effect** that may reduce wages in the non-union sector. This refers to the fact that higher wages in the unionized sector lead to a reduction of employment in that sector, and a resulting increase in the supply of labour in the non-union sector. The increased supply of labour in the non-union sector might reduce the wages of non-union employees.

Variable Pay and Incentive Systems   Unions reduce the likelihood of variable pay plans, such as profit sharing, stock ownership plans, and merit pay. Unions are generally opposed to individual pay incentives; however, they are less opposed to group incentives based on measurable criteria.

Productivity

The effect of unions on productivity—the output per worker—has been the topic of a great deal of debate. The effect on productivity must be distinguished from the effect on profitability, discussed below. Freeman and Medoff found that, generally, unions increased productivity largely because of the voice effect referred to above. Subsequent studies examining various industries in the private sector have had mixed results. This situation has been described as follows: "To date, the empirical score is about even. For every study that finds a positive impact another finds a negative impact, and clear conclusions on the net impact are wanting."[8] Unions may reduce the productivity of each dollar spent on labour by artificially increasing the price of labour. They may reduce productivity by imposing work rules that reduce efficiency. If the application of seniority rules results in job vacancies being filled by employees who have less ability, productivity could be reduced. It has been argued that unions lead to inefficiencies because they cause employers to invest more than the optimum amount in capital. For example, if non-union wages are $12 per hour, a labour-saving capital investment might not be efficient; however, if a union causes wages to be increased to $15 per hour, the same investment may now have to be made. Some observers suggest that unions promote an adversarial relationship, which reduces productivity.

In the public sector, Gunderson has found that "[Regarding] the effect of public-sector unions on productivity, the evidence is too mixed to assign a clear grade."[9]

The labour–management climate or relationship is a major factor affecting the productivity issue. A poor relationship may well lead to reduced productivity and a positive relationship to increased productivity. At least one study has found that workplaces with more grievances, which suggest a poor union–management relationship, have lower productivity.[10] A Canadian study surveyed management and unions to determine the relationship between the labour–management climate and perceptions of organizational performance including productivity, product quality, and customer satisfaction. It was found that a positive labour–management climate was associated with perceptions of favourable organization performance.[11] Further research is needed to determine if a positive labour relations climate leads to improved financial results. A study in British workplaces found that management's response to worker voice practices was a critical factor affecting productivity.[12] It was found that the managerial responsiveness to worker voice affected the amount of the productivity improvement in non-union workplaces. This relationship was not found in unionized workplaces. Although the study referred to was qualitative (based on perceptions of productivity instead of quantitative data), it still points up the possibility that productivity gains could be obtained if management's response to employees was improved.

Profitability

On average, unionized firms have lower profitability.[13] Unions apparently shift some profits from shareholders to employees. Studies have found that unionization leads to a drop in share values. The effect of unions on profitability may be a factor in employer opposition to unions.

Investment

Although some employers may increase investment to substitute capital for labour, there is evidence that unions have an overall negative effect on investment by employers. One study, which considered investment in Canadian manufacturing, found that the effect of unionization on investment varied according to the union density in the industry.[14] When the union density was less than 50 percent, there was a negative effect on investment; when it increased to over 50 percent, there was a small positive effect. This may be due to the fact that employers would prefer to invest in non-union operations; however, once unions have organized most of the industry, unionization is no longer a deterrent to investment.

Employment

U.S. studies have found slower employment growth in unionized firms.[15] As of this writing, the U.S. Senate is considering the *Employee Free Choice Act (EFCA)*. This legislation would implement certification based on membership cards and first contract arbitration, changes that should lead to union growth. A U.S. consultant, Anne Layne-Farrar, has used Canadian data to argue that an increase in unionization following the passage of the *EFCA* would cause job losses. Numerous Canadian academics have criticized this report's methodology and results. The margin notes here reference the Layne-Farrar report and a series of papers by Canadian academics commenting on the advisability of the U.S. passing the *EFCA* and reviewing the effects of unionization in Canada on employment levels and other outcomes. The Canadian academics reach the conclusion that "in the Canadian case there is no consistent empirical evidence that Canada's more extensive unionization has affected employment or unemployment either way." At the level of the firm, employment is an issue some unions are able to negotiate. In the auto industry, unions have been able to avoid or at least delay some employment losses by bargaining for restrictions on plant closings and requiring additional employer investment to keep plants operating.

Website with Layne-Farrar's report, "An Empirical Assessment of the Employee Free Choice Act: The Economic Implications": http://papers.ssrn.com/sol3/papers.cfm?abstract_id=1353305

Website with comments on the Layne-Farrar reoport: www.justlabour.yorku.ca/index.php?page=toc&volume=15

Employer Recruiting and Selection Practices

Except for the limited case of a closed shop, unions do not play a direct role in hiring. However, unions may have an indirect effect on recruiting and selection. Because unions raise wages and reduce turnover, unionized employers may not have to engage in as much recruiting as non-union employers. It has also been suggested that because unions make it more difficult for employers to terminate poor performers, employers will be encouraged to engage in more extensive use of screening devices such as skill and aptitude tests. A U.S. study that contrasted the recruiting methods and selection procedures used by union and non-union firms found a link between the recruiting effort and selection methods used and unionization.[16] Unionized firms were found to use fewer recruiting sources, and they used newspaper ads and company recruiters less than non-union firms. Unionized employers are often required to post jobs internally. The reduced recruiting effort might mean cost savings for unionized firms. Unions also had an effect on the selection procedures; however, the results were not as definitive. More selection tools were used to select employees in unionized firms, and a higher percentage of unionized employees were hired using aptitude and skills testing in some of the data sets used in the study.

Employers should be aware that making a mistake in the selection process might have more important consequences in the unionized sector, where the arbitration procedure makes it more difficult for the employer to terminate an employee. Employers should take steps to reduce such errors, including training interviewers, and more extensive use of testing.

Training

Studies have found that spending on training is higher in unionized firms. One of the reasons for this may be the "shock" effect on management caused by increased compensation.[17] Training could also be an issue that is raised in contract negotiations, especially in the public sector where there could be collective agreement provisions relating to professional development.

Managerial Control and Decision Making

Previous chapters covering collective agreement terms and the administration of the agreement have outlined how unionization might affect management control of the workplace. Recall that management's ability to contract out, fill job vacancies, make workplace rules, lay off employees, introduce technological change, and terminate employees might all be constrained by provisions in the collective agreement.

OVERVIEW OF TRADITIONAL LABOUR RELATIONS

In order to understand the magnitude and significance of the possible changes referred to later in this chapter, let us review the features of the traditional labour relations system that developed after *Privy Council Order 1003* in 1944. The following description relies heavily on the work of Anil Verma and Richard Chaykowski in *Contract and Commitment: Employment Relations in the New Economy*.

The collective agreements negotiated after the 1940s contained rules regarding hours, overtime, contracting out, transfers, limits on management rights, and seniority provisions. They might be viewed as entrenching or codifying what are called **Tayloristic work principles**, after Frederick Taylor, the father of scientific management, whose work at the start of the 1900s emphasized increasing efficiency by finding the best ways to do work. One of Taylor's principles was that there should be a separation of management and employee roles. It was the responsibility of managers to plan the best methods of work, and it was the role of workers to follow management instructions. Jobs would be broken down into their simplest components with extensive repetition. Taylor also advocated an improved climate of cooperation between workers and managers, and higher wages for increased output. Collective agreements established job classifications reflecting the breakdown between jobs, and movements within and across job classifications were subject to seniority rules. These job classifications and rules established an internal labour market, which had only a few points of entry, and formal rules regarding advancement. In this market, the skills required were obtained on the job, which was satisfactory at a time when most jobs were narrowly defined, slow to change, and subject to close supervision. The collective agreements and approach of unions that developed on the basis of Tayloristic principles have been referred to as **job control unionism**. Job control unionism includes the features listed in Key Considerations 12-1.[18]

Tayloristic work principles include the separation of management and work activities, and increasing efficiency through specialization.

Job control unionism emphasizes protection of jobs by controlling management and entails an adversarial relationship.

Key Considerations 12-1

Features of Job Control Unionism

1. Narrow job definitions
2. A high number of job grades
3. Communication with management through the union
4. Emphasis on the grievance system as opposed to other forms of communication with management
5. A distrust of teams because they may involve peer pressure on workers and weaken the role of the union, especially in discipline situations
6. Seniority as the basis for allocation of jobs
7. Distrust of employee involvement
8. Standard wages across an industry that are not linked to firm performance
9. Pay tied to jobs as opposed to pay for knowledge
10. Unions protecting jobs by limiting management authority

The traditional system involved an adversarial relationship between the union and the employer, and ritualistic distributive bargaining, which frequently led to labour disputes. Both sides supported the division between labour and management that developed. In organizing campaigns, unions emphasized that employees have different interests from management, and in some campaigns unions portrayed employers as exploiting employees. Management appeared comfortable with developing distinctions by way of symbols such as separate parking, washrooms, and other status symbols. The system also involved a distinction between contract administration and contract negotiation. The administration of the contract limited any changes in the rules governing the workplace that might be required to adapt to a changing environment. The change or development process was left to contract negotiations, which typically occurred every two or three years.

Some have argued that the traditional system worked satisfactorily at a time when many markets were protected and the environment was stable. However, some of the features of this system are viewed as being a mismatch with the realities of a world with increasing environmental challenges. The traditional system has been criticized for the lack of union–management cooperation needed to respond to rapid change.

EMPLOYEE RELATIONS PROGRAMS

Advice and guidance to managers regarding effective employee relations strategies is a required professional capability for contemporary human resources professionals. Consultations with supervisors in building effective communication networks, staff recognition, employee involvement programs, progressive discipline and diversity management assist in strengthening relationships with company employees. Such improvements have been identified to improve productivity, ensure implementation of corporate strategies, reduce employment costs linked to absenteeism and turnover, and facilitate employee growth and development.[19]

Employee Communications

Organizations are made up of networks of individuals who come together to achieve a common purpose. Whether this outcome is aimed at profit, personal growth and well being or socially desired achievements, it is assumed that individuals in that organization must effectively communicate with one another. To not do so may lead to needless errors, poor performance, and the perceptions of unfairness or abandonment. Effective communication practices as seen in Key Considerations 12-2 offer a set of best practices that strengthen employee commitment.[20]

Such practices are important as a result of significant organizational transformation. While hierarchical management structures still exist, many companies have opted for flatter organizational paradigms. This shift was often caused by the need to cut costs to remaining competitive in a globalized marketplace. One of the spinoffs of such restructuring was the emphasis on more employees becoming directly involved in communicating with their peers, customers, and suppliers.

The rapid transformation of communication technologies has also set up an interesting dynamic regarding the expectations of the speed of sending and the immediacy of response time between communicators in the workplace. This is particularly true between a supervisor and his or her employees. Communicating "up and down," the organization may now be faster because of leaner corporate structures and the proliferation of technologies. Such communication patterns are still key ingredients in building successful employee relations in contemporary workplaces.

Communications patterns in today's workplaces include both formal and informal patterns to sharing information. Two main approaches involve upward and downward communication

Best Practices in Employee Communications

Practice	Benefit
1. Conduct a communications audit.	1. Such analysis reveals where communication gaps occur and assists in determining solutions.
2. Create well-designed outlets for employee to communicate suggestions and concerns to management.	2. Using a variety of systems creates a sense that employees are able to influence company decisions and practices which in turn helps drive motivation and innovation.
3. Have leaders interact with employees at all levels of the organization.	3. When employees have an opportunity to meet, talk with, and be empowered by organizational leaders, they feel more emotionally committed to the organization, engaged, and willing to work harder for the organization.

Source: Adapted from "Foster Positive Employee Relations Using Communication Best Practices," ERC: Where Great Workplaces Start, http://greatworkplace. wordpress.com/2010/08/17/foster-positive-employee-relations-using-communication-best-practices, accessed June 9, 2014.

networks. Downward or "top-down" communication is designed to inform or influence others in the organization. Such means for communicating also provides knowledge about "what is" in the company at a given point in time as well as informing employees regarding their work performance. An example that combines the desire of management to communicate their successes to others in the company with the immediacy brought about by technology is Eli Lilly, an international pharmaceutical firm that showcases employees who have made a special contribution by putting their pictures on video screens throughout the firm's Toronto corporate offices.[21]

"Bottom-up" communication allows employees to share their work experiences and perspectives on the business with those in a position of power—whether it be their supervisors or executives in the C-suite. Several common upward communication strategies have been outlined by Schwind, Das and Wagar.[22] One of the more intriguing forms of moving information "out and up" the organization is the 21st century's equivalent of the office "grapevine": the use of social media. Savvy employers have encouraged such upward communications by establishing various social media platforms within the company and integrating this employee communication strategy into their corporate culture. Not only do social media replace the more static communication vehicles to today's workplaces, such as newsletters, it also allows employees to directly distribute information and engage in conversations about workplace issues. The concept of employee relations is realized, particularly by millennials accustomed to social media, through social networks that provide greater connectedness in traditional corporate hierarchies and between organizational members who otherwise may not talk to one another because of distance, staffing level, or job design. In fact, it has been noted that millennials can force corporate leaders to adopt a culture oriented to internal customer service, treating employees in the same manner as their clients.[23]

Staff Recognition Programs

In 2012, *Forbes* reported on a study of employee recognition programs that showed companies spend between 1 and 2 percent of payroll in this human resources activity. The study also showed that 87 percent of such recognitions were based on employee tenure as opposed to job performance. This emphasis is due, in a historical context, to the union movement in North America. Contemporary thinking suggests that the purpose of recognition programs is to encourage greater levels of discretionary effort by employees. The *Forbes* research referenced companies such as Intuit and Deloitte that have linked their recognition rewards to corporate mission and goals. In such settings, what is "thanked" relates to behaviours tied to the company's strategy and witnessed in acts of customer service, innovation, and teamwork. Such "recognition-rich" business cultures have reported reductions of thirty-one percent in voluntary turnover.[24]

Unions and their supporting organizations are involved in the topic of employee recognition programs. The Professional Institute of the Public Service of Canada discussed this issue in 2013, noting five award categories at present. These included milestones and retirement, people's choice, instant recognition, awards of excellence, and external awards at unionized workplaces. A broader level of community recognition of union members was displayed between the United Way of London-Middlesex in Ontario and local trades and labour councils. Their Images of Hope award recognizes the effort of an extraordinary individual from the labour community who provided outstanding volunteer service to the local United Way and to the community. Although such recognition may move beyond the normal scope of awards sponsored by an employer, the company has an opportunity to showcase award winners to fellow employees, thus contributing to the individual's recognition by her peers as well as symbolizing important elements in corporate responsibility and values.[25]

Employee Involvement

As mentioned in Chapter 2, changes in the environment such as globalization, new technology, and increased competition are forcing employers to change methods of operation. Some have attempted to move toward a high-performance organization that includes employee involvement, flexible jobs, increased training, and variable pay. Employers may pursue these new approaches to utilize employee knowledge and expertise, increase motivation, reduce costs, and increase productivity and quality.

Some employers may adopt changes such as employee involvement in order to increase employee satisfaction, which will have a positive impact on retention and recruiting. Some may be forced to adopt employee participation because of a crisis caused by a loss of business or some other external shock. Others may have adopted it in order to copy what is viewed as the best practice of other employers. In some cases, employee participation has been adopted as part of a program to deal with a deteriorating labour–management relationship. Employee involvement may be adopted in conjunction with other workplace changes such as job sharing, employee attitude surveys, and job rotation.

Forms of Employee Involvement

Employee involvement, also called *worker participation*, *employee participation*, or *the high-commitment organization*, includes a range of possible measures to increase employee input into business operations: quality circles, employee problem-solving groups, joint employee–management committees, employee work teams, and co-determination. Co-determination, sometimes called *joint governance* or *strategic alliance*, raises special concerns regarding the role of the union, which are referred to below.

Quality circles are groups of employees who investigate problems relating to quality and make recommendations to management for improvements. **Problem-solving groups** are teams of employees who meet to deal with particular issues such as the installation of a new computer system. Problem-solving teams make recommendations to management; however, they do not have the authority to implement their recommendations. As the name indicates, **employee–management committees** include representatives of both management and employees charged with the responsibility of making recommendations to the employer. A health and safety committee is an example. **Self-directed teams or self-managing work teams**

Quality circles are groups of employees who investigate problems relating to quality and make recommendations to management for improvements.

Problem-solving groups are teams of employees that consider issues and make recommendations to management.

Employee–management committees are ongoing groups made up of management and employee representatives who advise management.

Self-directed teams or self-managing work teams are groups of employees that take on functions previously performed by management.

are distinctive because they have more autonomy and responsibility. Typically, they take on tasks formerly undertaken by management. For example, work teams may assume the tasks of tracking and distributing their own overtime.

Co-determination refers to a system in which management shares decision-making authority with the union, and the union plays a role in day-to-day business decisions. Co-determination is rare in Canada and the United States. Two brief examples will clarify this concept and its significance.

The Framework of Fairness Agreement (FFA) between Magna and the CAW (now Unifor) contains an element of co-determination. The FFA outlines a new role for the union through an Employee Relations Review Committee (ERRC). The ERRC consists of three company and three union representatives. The agreement provides that the committee "will discuss . . . top-level issues related to investment, production, employment, technology and the general state of labour relations." It lists a number of collaborative goals and projects for the committee including working jointly to promote new investment and production opportunities, and joint presentations to, and dialogue with, applicable government representatives on matters of importance to the Canadian automotive industry. Although it remains to be seen how much the union will actually be able to influence management decisions, the agreement sets out a new role for the union.

It has been suggested that there are two contrasting models of employee involvement. One is a joint team production model that includes worker empowerment and the use of self-managed teams. This model is typically developed and implemented with collaboration between unions and management. The second is a lean production model that is more management directed, using groups with a narrower focus, aimed at improving quality and productivity. It should be noted that employee involvement is not one-dimensional, and the term has been used (or misused), to cover a range of measures.

Implications of Employee Involvement

The various forms of employee involvement vary on a number of dimensions. Some initiatives involve changes in the organization of the workplace, and others work within the existing structure. Quality circles do not involve a change in workplace organization, but self-directed work teams do. Some employee involvement initiatives may be temporary, as in the case of a problem-solving group established for one particular task, and others may be permanent. There is also considerable variation regarding the amount of authority given to employees. The lean production model involves only consultation with employees, and management retains sole decision-making authority. The joint team production model involves the delegation of some decision-making authority to employee teams.

Employee Involvement Under the Collective Agreement

Employee and union involvement can be achieved either pursuant to provisions contained in the collective agreement or outside of the agreement. Collective agreements between Inco and the United Steelworkers of America have established committees regarding compensation, employment security, training, and the environment. These committees comprise equal numbers of management and union representatives. Generally, they are consultative bodies that make recommendations to management. The joint compensation wage study committee has a mandate to determine job descriptions and rates of pay. After reviewing the activities of these committees, Chaykowski found that their influence was considerable.[26]

Employee Involvement Outside of the Collective Agreement

Union Viewpoint   An employee involvement program undertaken outside of the collective agreement should take into account union concerns about such programs. Some unions have been more receptive to employee involvement programs than others. The reasons for unions' possible support or opposition are referred to in Key Considerations 12-2.

Many of the reasons for union support or opposition to employee involvement relate to a basic difference in approach to the relationship between unions and employers. Those who think there is a fundamental conflict between the interests of the employee and the employer is more likely to oppose such programs. Some union leaders view employee involvement as a management attempt to increase the pace of work so that more output can be obtained for the same wage. They view "working smarter" as a means to get employees to work harder. They allege that teams lead to peer pressure and short-staffing, which increase stress on employees.[27] A few union leaders believe that increases in efficiency and productivity will only benefit management. They allege that management will use employee involvement to have employees work themselves out of a job. Because employee involvement programs seek to have employees adopt company goals, union leaders fear that employees may develop a greater attachment to the employer's goals and objectives than those of the union. In other words, instead of empowerment, some union leaders view aspects of employee involvement as manipulation. Union observations of what has occurred in the United States may be a reason for this view. In the U.S., in companies that have adopted voluntary employee involvement programs without participation of the union, participants have tended to be individuals who are not supportive of the union. Also, it appears that participants have identified more closely with employer goals and some programs have been part of a strategy to eliminate the union. Some union leaders have questioned the scope of employee involvement programs, pointing out that employers do not allow unions or employees to become involved in strategic decision-making questions such as investment. They allege that employers turn to employee involvement programs only in a time of crisis, when their objective is to take something away from employees.

Some union leaders believe that if change is to be undertaken, they will be better off if they get involved so that they have an opportunity to protect employee interests. Some view increased efficiency and competitiveness that may flow from employee involvement as a way to improve job security. There is recognition that Tayloristic approaches to the workplace reduce output, which is not beneficial to employee interests. For example, at Weston Bakeries employees were trained and expected to solve workplace problems on their own as part of an employee involvement program. A union leader described the situation as follows: "Before, when a conveyor belt stopped, you waited for the foreman. Now, you are responsible, you're autonomous and you can make a decision."[28]

Employee involvement often involves training, which may benefit employees. Programs have included training in language skills and computers. This may have benefits for employees outside of the workplace. In one case, employees observed that training in English allowed them to talk to the friends of their children for the first time. In some cases, the increases in job skills can be the basis for higher job classifications and increases in wages. Some employees may benefit from a reduction in boring and mundane work, increasing job satisfaction.

Employer Freedom of Action and Union Reaction

Where the employer implements an employee involvement program without the involvement of the union, questions regarding the legality of such programs and union opposition may arise. There are two key points here. First, the union is the exclusive bargaining agent of employees. Second, unions cannot engage in a stoppage of work that would amount to an illegal strike. Employers are allowed to communicate with employees where the subject matter of the communication is an item that the collective agreement leaves to management's discretion. If the collective agreement does not refer to methods of operation, and most do not, the employer can obtain input directly from employees without violating the union's exclusive bargaining rights.

Conversely, an employee involvement program cannot relate to matters covered by the collective agreement. For example, a program that solicited employee views regarding compensation or working conditions might be in violation of labour relations legislation. Programs undertaken without union involvement have led to union complaints of unfair labour practices. In one case, the CBC developed an "Opportunities for Change" program without union involvement. The program solicited employee input on job categories and processes for complaint resolution. The union filed a complaint with the Canada Industrial Relations Board, which was upheld, and the employer was ordered to discontinue the program. It was found that the program violated the *Canadian Human Rights Act* because it "could only undermine the union in the eyes of its members and have an adverse effect both on the administration of the trade union and its representation as the exclusive bargaining agent of unionized employees."[29]

If the union encourages employees to boycott an employee involvement program, such action might be viewed as an illegal strike in violation of the collective agreement and labour relations legislation. In one case, a municipality established a continuous improvement program with employee participation but without union involvement. Teams of managers and employees studied ways to reduce costs and improve the quality of various services provided by the employer. Subsequently, the union directed employees to refuse to participate. The employer claimed that this refusal amounted to an illegal work stoppage, and filed a grievance. The arbitrator held that the call for a boycott by the union was an illegal strike in violation of the collective agreement.[30] An arbitrator in this situation might award damages to the employer. In the case referred to, the arbitrator did not award damages, because the employer's evidence on the issue was inadequate and a cease-and-desist order was granted. If a union directed employees to boycott an employer initiative, the employer might also pursue a remedy with the Labour Relations Board, because the boycott might be an illegal strike.

In summary, employers must ensure that an employee involvement program undertaken without union involvement does not violate the exclusive bargaining rights of the union, and unions must not prohibit employees from becoming involved in employer programs if the refusal amounts to an illegal strike.

Outcomes of Employee Involvement

Studies have examined the effects of employee involvement programs on productivity, employee satisfaction, and workplace conflict. Although it appears logical that employee involvement programs would improve productivity that has not always been confirmed by research. Most studies do show increased productivity, but there is significant variation in the outcomes and a few studies have found no improvement.[31] Studies indicate a small increase in employee satisfaction where employee involvement programs have been undertaken.[32] A study has confirmed that employee involvement programs reduce conflict in the workplace as measured by the grievance rate.[33] However, some critics have claimed that the reduction in grievances is a reflection of the union having been co-opted by management and the suppression of conflict. Illustrating the complexity of employee involvement, the type of employee involvement that led to reduced conflict varied by industrial sector; in the goods-producing sector, self-directed teams had the larger effect, whereas in the service sector problem-solving groups had a greater effect.

Website with study regarding employment involvement and productivity: www.iir.berkeley.edu

It appears that employee involvement programs are difficult to maintain over time. One study examined the survival of employee involvement work practices over a three-year period. It was found that the death rate for employee involvement practices was significant: 35.2 percent of problem-solving groups, 46.8 percent of joint employee–management programs, and 59.1 percent of quality circle programs did not survive for three years. The author concluded that high-involvement work practices are fragile and do not often last very long.[34]

We have seen that employee involvement programs do not guarantee improved performance and may not be suitable for all workplaces. Let us turn to the question of what might be done to improve their chances of success in unionized workplaces.

Implementing an Employee Involvement Program

Employer Perspective   Employers should think twice before adopting an employee involvement program without the union's participation. Although union participation may require a trade-off providing for job security, there can be advantages to union involvement. It might avert a legal challenge to the program or allegations of unfair labour practices referred to above. Also, if management attempts to avoid union participation, it runs the risk of union supporters not taking part. Some studies have indicated that the chances of productivity improving are increased if the union is involved.[35] The union's involvement may also protect employee interests so that success of the program is more likely—the union can perform a watchdog role.

The issue of job security has been a concern for the success of employee involvement programs. It has been suggested that employers would have to make formal guarantees of job security in order for a program to succeed. However, one study has found that workers' expectations about job security have changed and they no longer expect unconditional job security. Researchers found that employee involvement programs could succeed without strict formal job guarantees if workers perceived that management was doing their best to secure jobs.[36] In any event, the chances of success in an employee involvement program are increased when concerns over job security are reduced.

Union Perspective   Union concerns that employee involvement programs will cause employees to identify more closely with management objectives assume that employee loyalty is to either the union or the employer. However, a number of studies have found that employees have dual loyalty. Employees believe that they can be concerned for the employer's interests and union supporters at the same time.[37] If unions do not become involved in employee involvement programs, they run the risk that they will not have input into communications with employees, and they increase the chances that employers will use the program to influence employees against the union. A study that examined employee involvement programs in organizations where the union was a joint sponsor of the program found that this arrangement was likely to have positive outcomes for the union. Workers who were involved were more likely to get involved in union affairs and hold more favourable assessments of the union.[38]

Barriers to Employee Involvement

1. History and adversarial relationship between the parties	**3.** Attitudes and beliefs of unions and employers
2. Knowledge gap between union and employer leaders	**4.** Labour relations legislation

Website for Saskatchewan program regarding resolving workplace conflict and joint problem solving: http://gr.gov.sk.ca/work/collective-bargaining-and-mediation

Website for Labour–Management Partnerships Program: http://www.labour.gc.ca/eng/relations/

Barriers to Employee Involvement   Key Considerations 12-3 lists some barriers in the way of the adoption of employee involvement programs in unionized workplaces.

Relationship Between the Parties.   In many union–management relationships, there is a history of conflict, which has led to an adversarial relationship and a lack of trust. Although some of the simpler forms of involvement may not require complete mutual trust, meaningful involvement does. Prior to starting a program, the parties should make a special effort to clear up outstanding grievances. They might also take advantage of government programs aimed at helping them to improve their relationship, which are available in some jurisdictions. The websites in the margin describe some typical programs available in Saskatchewan and the federal jurisdiction. The ministry responsible for labour issues in other jurisdictions may have similar programs.

Knowledge Gap.   The *knowledge gap* refers to the fact that management representatives may be more familiar with the techniques and advantages of employee involvement than union leaders. The relationship issue and the knowledge gap might be addressed by having the parties engage in joint information and training sessions on employee involvement and by making use of a facilitator acceptable to both parties.

Leadership Attitudes.   Even if the parties improve their relationship, the attitudes and beliefs of leaders on both sides may still pose a problem. Union leaders will have to abandon the belief that employer and employee interests are inherently in conflict. Management will have to be willing to give up absolute control over operations in order for some forms of employee involvement to work.

Labour Relations Legislation.   Current labour relations legislation does not encourage continuous bargaining or collaboration between unions and employers. Management can make changes in operations without the union's involvement pursuant to the management rights article in the collective agreement. Management cannot be forced to negotiate during the term of the collective agreement. Where management does agree to negotiate changes during the term, the changes expire with the contract and must be renegotiated. Management can withdraw from any agreements relating to employee involvement concluded outside of the collective agreement. These difficulties might be addressed by amending labour relations legislation to require employers to consult with unions. A consultation requirement is not beyond the realm of possibility.

Progressive Discipline   In Chapter 9, an explanation of progressive discipline was referenced in the context of administering a collective agreement. Except in situations of misconduct which constitute "just cause," employers are expected to apply progressive discipline that sees the application of increasing penalties should employee misconduct continue to occur after an initial warning. See Key Considerations 12-4 for an example. The application of progressive discipline is based on the assumption that such action will correct undesired employee behaviours and maintain the employment relationship.

A Progressive Discipline Framework

1. Verbal warning to the employee by supervisor
2. Written warning to the employee with a copy placed in their file
3. Suspension(s) from job duties for a defined (unpaid) period
4. Termination for cause

From an employee relations perspective, the principles of progressive discipline seen in a unionized setting should also be applied to non-union staff. Not only does this provide a perception of procedural justice among employees, particularly when the work setting is comprised of union and non-union workers, but it also helps reinforce desired behaviours that support key aspects of organizational culture.

The collective agreement recognizes the management right to discipline bargaining unit members. The union then demonstrates its value as an advocate for the affected member by filing a grievance. The grievance process tests the principle of **due process** which assures an employee that proper rules and procedures are followed. More importantly, the concept provides the employee an opportunity to present their perspective on allegations made against them.

In instances of non-union-staff discipline, the human resources department is frequently called on to ensure due process is observed. This is accomplished through company policy and procedures regarding employee discipline which would clearly set out a progressive discipline framework. It is also assured by the human resources department providing advice and counsel to line management in dealing with disciplinary matters. In progressive organizations, the HR office may also construct an appeals system to non-union employees subject to discipline that parallels a union grievance procedure. In such instances, the human resources department facilitates a form of advocacy to assure the affected employee may appeal the disciplinary action within the management hierarchy and be assured of the opportunity to provide their viewpoint on the facts and subtleties that may be part of the circumstances related to the situation.[39]

Due process is a process related to employee discipline that follows a predetermined set of rules and allows the accused staff member to present their perspective on the alleged misconduct.

Diversity Management

In Chapter 2, diversity was described as a trend that will affect the Canadian labour market in the coming decades. Diversity in this context relates to demographic characteristics of managers and employees such as their age, ethnic origin, religious beliefs, sexual orientation and physical abilities. Progressive companies recognize that employee diversity offers a tremendous opportunity to advance corporate goals and objectives in today's globalized economy. The Royal Bank of Canada's diversity business council recognized several practical examples of how a diverse workforce could realize desired corporate objectives:[40]

- Women on a product development team give male team members perspective on how female customers may respond to new product ideas.

- Partnerships with Aboriginal people result in increased economic and business opportunity to the Aboriginal community and improved success for service providers.

- Employees who grew up in the Maritime provinces give the marketing team in central Canada some first-hand insights into regional tastes and expectations.

- Customers in a predominately Chinese neighbourhood are served by employees who speak the language and relate to the customers needs.
- Older and retired employees of the bank understand and serve the needs of the seniors' market.

A focus on diversity management in today's corporations is a reality for those involved in both employee and labour relations. The Human Resources Professional Association, in partnership with Knightsbridge Consulting, ran a four-part dinner series on generational diversity in the workplace. The presentations in that series focused on building the alignment and engagement of all employees, creating a work environment that provides flexibility and support for staff and explored how to address employees' needs as well as build leaders' capabilities to inspire and develop the their company's human resources in a climate of openness and collaboration.[41] At the 2014 convention of the Canadian Labour Congress the importance of attention to demographic diversity to the future of the labour movement in Canada was discussed. It was recognized that the demographic changes occurring across the country will need to be understood by, and reflected in, the labour movement. Convention delegates heard that by 2020, sixty-five percent of all job openings will be attributed to retirements. The CLC noted that such projected labour shortages will require the union movement to lobby governments and support innovative programming on behalf of key demographic groups that have the potential to replenish the projected tight labour market. Government funding, innovative outreach programming and advocacy on the part of the labour movement can facilitate social programming initiatives to assist with sourcing and developmental opportunities for women, Aboriginal persons, immigrants and persons with disabilities to replenish the talent gap in Canada that is projected in the coming decades.

CONFRONTATION OR COLLABORATION?

In Chapter 1, a framework for labour relations was provided, and the question of union–management confrontation versus collaboration was raised. Subsequent chapters considered the environmental factors affecting labour relations, and the processes the parties engage in. The possibility of increased collaboration through approaches such as interest-based bargaining and grievance mediation has been considered, and the Magna-Unifor Framework of Fairness Agreement that entails more collaboration has been referred to. Figure 12-1 contrasts traditional labour relations to the provisions of the Framework of Fairness Agreement. The FFA, including a requirement that the employer facilitate unionization and the union give up the right to strike, is a significant development. It should be noted that the agreement has critics among both employers and unions. Some union leaders have expressed concern about giving up the right to strike; and some employers have claimed that by encouraging unionization, management at Magna have abdicated their responsibility to educate employees about what they perceive as the negative aspects of union membership. Time will tell whether the agreement is the beginning of a fundamental shift in labour relations toward collaboration that will be widely adopted, or whether it will remain an exception to the traditional labour relations model.

It appears that environmental factors are a barrier to increased union–management collaboration. Although the increasingly competitive economic environment has been noted as a factor that might encourage the parties to move toward a more cooperative relationship, the economy might also be a cause of conflict. Employers will continue to be forced to do more with less, and this will lead to attempts to contract out, introduce technological

	Traditional Labour Relations	Framework of Fairness Agreement
Employer strategy before bargaining rights obtained	Employer attempts to prevent unionization through union avoidance.	Employer recommends unionization to employees.
How bargaining rights are obtained	Union applies to Labour Relations Board for certification, employer may challenge application.	Employer agrees to vote; recognizes union when union has majority support.
Contract negotiation	Distributive bargaining—strike or lockout in event of impasse.	No strike or lockout; interest arbitration in event of impasse.
Management of operations	Labour–management committees possible; however, in some cases employer manages and union reacts.	Employee Relations Review Committee provides union opportunity for input.
Contract administration	Grievance procedure and rights arbitration.	Dispute resolution procedure, including hotline and Fairness Committee.

Figure 12-1 Traditional Labour Relations vs. Framework of Fairness Agreement

change, and limit compensation, all of which will bring the employer into conflict with the union. It is important to note that unions are political and social organizations. It may be difficult for union leaders to cooperate with employers on a project in one area, such as grievance mediation, while the employer is eliminating jobs and increasing discontent.

The extent to which the legal environment is conducive to collaboration has been questioned. The Wagner model of labour relations involves the union–management relationship starting with a conflict over union certification. Subsequently much of contract negotiation can be viewed as an attempt by the union to limit management control of the workplace. The political environment does not seem to encourage collaboration, with some politicians trying to make political points by attacking both public and private sector unions.

The past has been marked by conflict and employer opposition to unions. Union leaders who wish to move toward collaboration may have to hope that union members have short memories. This is especially the case in the public sector, where governments have passed legislation eliminating commitments made in collective agreements.

The processes presently in use are often inherently adversarial. Grievance arbitration produces winners and losers. Traditional distributive bargaining appears to be a barrier to collaboration. Although there have been calls for the adoption of interest-based bargaining, the approach has not yet been widely adopted. This brings us to a key reason why collaboration, including interest-based bargaining, has not developed further: the beliefs and values of management and union leaders.

Collaboration requires a basic level of trust, and a consensus on the importance and role of employee involvement. Terry Wagar conducted a survey of union officials and employers from 1977 to 1998 and found that they had very different perceptions of labour relations issues.[42] One of the questions asked in the survey concerned the extent to which organizations valued people. Approximately 91 percent of employer respondents indicated some agreement with the statement that people were the organization's most important asset; however, only 40 percent of union officials thought that the employer valued employees. Fifty percent of union officials felt that management viewed cooperative programs as a way to reduce union power, and 48 percent of union officials expressed some level of agreement with the statement that the interests of the union and the employer are in conflict. With regard to innovation in the workplace, 77 percent of union officials disagreed with the statement that the organizations supported

Website for *Workplace Bulletin*: www.
hrsdc.gc.ca/eng/labour/labour_relations/
info_analysis/bulletin/archive.shtml

bargaining unit members who tried new things and took calculated risks. Overall, Wagar found that union leaders see only moderate support for cooperative programs on the part of supervisors and upper management. These findings suggest that the foundation of trust and consensus between the parties regarding the role of employees does not exist. Hopefully further research regarding methods to build the foundation required for union–management collaboration will be conducted. The *Workplace Bulletin* website provides information relating to developments in labour-management issues.

In Chapter 1, the importance of labour relations for all Canadians was noted. Let us end by expressing the hope that the three key actors in the labour relations system—government, employers, and unions—can find ways to improve labour relations processes and outcomes despite the environmental challenges that lie ahead.

Implications for Practice

1. The unionization of employees has significant consequences for employers. Typically, unionized employers will find that compensation costs are increased. Productivity may be reduced, maintained, or increased depending on the relationship between the employer and the union. Because the union–management relationship is critical, employers should take measures such as establishing a labour–management committee to deal with problems and issues as they arise.

2. Employee involvement has the potential to increase productivity, employee job satisfaction, the employer's ability to recruit and retain skilled employees, and employee commitment to the organization. Although employers can pursue employee involvement programs without union involvement where such programs do not impinge upon provisions of the collective agreement, it may be advisable to involve the union.

3. In order to deal with the challenges they face, some unions may have to improve their knowledge and administration. This would involve the adoption of long-range planning and human resources management practices such as performance appraisals.

4. Improving the union–management relationship is necessary to move toward more collaboration. Unions and employers might make use of programs available from the ministry responsible for labour issues to assist them in improving their relationship.

Key Terms

co-determination, p. 298

crowding effect, p. 292

due process, p. 303

employee–management committees, p. 297

job control unionism, p. 294

problem-solving groups, p. 297

quality circles, p. 297

self-directed (self-managing

work) teams, p. 297

Tayloristic work principles, p. 294

threat effect, p. 292

Review Questions

1. A union has just organized a company's employees. Describe the possible effects of unionization on human resources management.

2. Explain and give examples of the following: threat effect, crowding effect.

3. The overall union wage effect is expressed as a range. What are the factors that determine the size of the union wage effect?

4. Outline the barriers to increased employee involvement in unionized workplaces. Which of these barriers will be the most difficult to overcome?

Discussion Questions

1. There are alternative arguments that unions increase and reduce productivity. On the basis of your experience, observations, and what you have read in this text, what is your opinion regarding the effect of unions on productivity?

2. Assume you are a union leader. What concerns and hopes would you have if the employer introduced an employee involvement program?

3. Outline the challenges that unions will have to overcome if they are to increase membership.

4. Prior to reading this text, you may have had a positive or negative opinion towards unions. Referring specifically to what you have learned about seniority, the union's duty of fair representation, and the dismissal of unionized employees, has your opinion been changed or confirmed? Referring to any other issues discussed in this text, has your opinion regarding unions been changed or confirmed?

5. Reference has been made to labour relations being more or less confrontational or collaborative. Do you think that it is possible or desirable that unions and employers be more collaborative?

Web Research

1. Conduct a Web search to identify five common "best practices" in employee relations that human resources professionals might integrate into their program offerings in a work setting.

2. Observers have commented extensively on the possibilities for union renewal. What information can be found about this issue on the Web?

CASE INCIDENT   TROUT LAKE PRINTING COMPANY

The Trout Lake Printing Company, family-owned and in operation for 60 years, publishes a newspaper in a city with a population of 275 000 people. The newspaper has a circulation of 10 000 copies per day and is in competition with another newspaper in the same city. In addition to the newspaper, the company has a printing department that prepares material such as brochures, menus, and flyers for area businesses. The offices and printing facilities are in the same building.

The main departments in the newspaper are reporting, advertising, circulation, and administration, and each of these departments has a manager who reports to a general manager, who is also the newspaper's editor. The reporting staff consists of 10 full-time and part-time employees, and from time to time the newspaper uses freelance writers for special projects. Most reporters spend the majority of their time working on stories in one of the following areas: sports, local news, business, and family. In the printing area, one manager is responsible for the production of the newspaper and another for the outside printing work.

The company does not have a human resources manager, and department managers have been left to deal with human resources issues as they arise. The office manager has performed some human resources management activities such as record keeping and the administration of benefits. The company has tried to keep compensation costs down; wages are slightly lower than those of the competing newspaper and other printing businesses. The company pays the premiums for group life insurance and has a dental plan. The company has an annual incentive bonus plan that provides for payment of 1 to 3 percent of employees' salaries on the basis of performance. It is rumoured that a few members of the owner's family who work in the business always receive at least the maximum bonus allowed. The company provides the holidays required by employment standards legislation. The company's vacation policy is as follows: two weeks after one year, and three weeks for employees with more than five years of service. The company has experienced some problems with turnover, as employees who have gained experience have moved to other newspapers or competing printing businesses when the opportunity arose.

Because the company does not have a human resources manager, there are few formal established HR policies. The owner has considered hiring an HR manager when managers have complained about HR matters taking up too much of their time; however, there are no plans to hire one at this time. Managers have handled employee behaviour and performance problems on a case-by-case basis. In the printing area, the newspaper printing manager and the outside printing manager have handled the problem of absenteeism differently. The newspaper manager has tended to be more lenient and has issued numerous warnings before taking any further action, while the printing manager has usually issued fewer warnings and dismissed problem employees.

The company has filled job openings by referring to résumés submitted or putting advertisements in the help-wanted section of the newspaper, but this approach has recently caused several employee complaints. In the reporting department, selection decisions have been based upon interviews of candidates. One of the printing area employees had completed a journalism studies program as a part-time student, hoping to be hired as a writer. When a reporting position became available, the manager filled the position by reviewing résumés she had recently received and hiring someone who had not previously worked for the employer. The selection procedures used by the company have been simple, especially in the production area where the company appears to rely on the probationary period. Approximately 20 percent of candidates have not been hired as full-time employees.

Management of the company would appear to be paternalistic in some ways. Last year, one employee became pregnant, and it was suggested that she take a leave of absence even though she wanted to work for two more months.

The company operates from 8 A.M. to 5 P.M. except in the peak holiday season. In the holiday season, there is some additional printing work to be done, and hours have been extended and overtime used. Although some employees would rather not work additional hours, most want to earn extra income. In the past, managers have chosen employees for overtime work on a random basis, paying the overtime rate provided for in employment standards legislation. On a few exceptional occasions, when the printing area has fallen behind, office employees have been called in to help.

Employees at the company have never been represented by a union. There was some talk of a union organizing the printing employees several years ago; however, the employee leading the unionization drive left the company. Two recent situations have led to a union trying to organize the newspaper writers and printing employees. The manager responsible for reporters has dealt with the issue of employees working at home in an uneven manner. She has allowed some reporters to work at home, quietly providing financial assistance to upgrade home computers, while she has told other reporters they must work at the newspaper. A safety incident in the printing department appeared to trigger the organizing drive there. An employee was slightly injured when she was lifting a box of paper; but when the incident was raised at the health and safety committee, management representatives on the committee dismissed the matter, saying it was the employee's fault.

The newspaper faces an ongoing battle with the competing newspaper for circulation and advertisers. The company has not adopted computer and information technology as quickly as its competitors, who established websites to market their products and provide services online. It is expected that the company will have to adopt newer technology in the future, and this could result in a loss of some jobs.

Questions

1. If the union organizing the printing and reporting department employees is successful, what implications might a collective agreement have for the company?

Appendix A

Cases

COLPOY'S BAY NEWS

John Samuels worked two days per week as an independent contractor in the human resources department of the *Colpoy's Bay News*. Samuels's duties included safety and WHMIS training, and other HR tasks. Employees at the newspaper are represented by the Communications, Energy and Paperworkers Union of Canada. During a strike at the newspaper, Samuels crossed the union picket line and continued his non–bargaining unit work in the HR department. After the strike, Samuels was hired for a part-time position in the promotions department of the newspaper. The position was in the bargaining unit.

The collective agreement between the union and the employer provides that all employees in the bargaining unit must become union members. The agreement also provides that the union will admit all employees to membership subject to the provisions of the union's constitution. Samuels applied for union membership. Later he was advised that an objection had been made to his membership application, based on his crossing the picket line during a strike. The union constitution prohibited union members from crossing a picket line. Samuels was advised that he could attend a meeting of the union's executive board at a specified time, when the issue of his application for membership and the allegation that he had crossed the picket line would be dealt with. Samuels was provided with a copy of the union's constitution and bylaws. He was advised that he would be given an opportunity to be heard and to call witnesses, and could be asked questions.

At the meeting, Samuels made a submission and acknowledged crossing the picket line to do non–bargaining unit work. He stated that if he had not done so, his contract would have been terminated. It was noted that Samuels would be holding two positions, one in the bargaining unit and the other outside of the bargaining unit, and he was asked whether he would cross a picket line in the future. He responded that he might cross a picket line to report for his work in the HR department. Subsequently, Samuels was notified that the executive board had decided against granting him union membership and he could appeal this decision to a local council.

At the local council meeting, Samuels was asked again if he would cross a picket line in the future, in light of the fact that he would be holding two positions. Samuels replied that he would have to consider the situation at the time, and if he had to cross the line he would resign his union membership. He was later told that his membership application had been dismissed because of his position regarding the crossing of a picket line. Samuels was advised that he could present his case at an appeals committee at the annual congress of the local. The appeals committee consisted of individuals in the local who had no previous involvement in Samuels's application.

Prior to the appeals committee hearing, Samuels and the committee members were given an information sheet that referred to previous cases in which individuals had been denied union membership and the outcome of their appeals. One case involved an employee (Sneling) who was transferred from the United States to the *Hope Bay Herald* during a strike. Subsequently, Sneling had been hired by the *News* as a sports editor, and his application for union membership was rejected because he had crossed the picket line at the *Herald*. At his appeal, Sneling said he was ordered to cross the picket line at the *Hope Bay Herald*, and if he had refused to do so he would have been terminated. He also made an unconditional commitment at the appeal hearing that he would not cross a picket line in the future.

The members of the appeals committee were advised that they were to treat the proceedings as a new application for membership. Samuels was given an opportunity to speak to the committee. When he was asked if he would cross a picket line in the future, he responded that he might be forced to resign his union membership and cross a picket line. The appeals committee denied Samuel's application for membership.

QUESTIONS

1. What is your assessment of the fairness of the union procedure?

2. If you were on the appeals committee, what would your decision have been?

3. In some jurisdictions, labour relations legislation provides that a union cannot expel a member or suspend membership for any reason other than the failure to pay union dues. Are you in favour of such a provision?

HAY LAKE MANUFACTURING

The Hay Lake Manufacturing Co., located in Winnipeg, Manitoba, manufactures high-pressure cylinders for the storage of propane. The original company was established in 1990, and in 1995 the plant's production workers were organized by the United Steelworkers of America. There are 300 full-time production workers in the bargaining unit. The following is a summary of some of the terms of the current collective agreement between the company and the union:

> Article 2 Recognition: provides that the union is recognized as the bargaining agent for all employees of the company in Winnipeg, Manitoba, save and except quality control technicians, supervisors, persons above the rank of supervisor, office, clerical, and sales staff.
>
> Article 4 Bargaining Unit Work: provides that no work shall be performed by persons outside of the bargaining unit when qualified employees are available or on layoff.
>
> Article 20 Seniority: provides that in the event of a job vacancy, the employer shall promote or transfer employees based upon skill, ability, and job knowledge required, and when in the company's opinion skill, ability, and job knowledge are equal, seniority shall be the deciding factor.
>
> Article 21 Job Posting: provides that job openings shall be posted for three days and applications for open positions will be accepted for three additional days.

In 2005, Hay Lake purchased the company. After the purchase, there was an increase in business and the company needed additional warehouse space. In 2010, the company leased a warehouse in Winnipeg, 3 kilometres from the plant. Subsequently the company hired two new part-time employees, Singh and Olson, as warehouse coordinators. They work four hours per day, five days per week. The new warehouse includes a computerized system that allows the company to keep track of all materials and inventory. The inventory system at the plant is still based on a manual or paper system. The warehouse coordinators receive materials and parts, tag them, inspect for damage, enter items into the system, and move them into their designated area. Singh does most of the paperwork and computer entry, while Olson does most of the moving and unloading of materials, using a forklift truck. Olson takes day-to-day direction from Singh. The warehouse coordinator position is not listed in Schedule A of the collective agreement, which sets out the positions in the bargaining unit and their wage rates.

The union approached the company shortly after the jobs in the warehouse were filled and claimed that the jobs were in the bargaining unit and should have been posted. The employer disagreed and took the position that the jobs were not covered by the agreement. The union filed a grievance, which alleged that the warehouse coordinator position was bargaining unit work and the company was in breach of the collective agreement. At a grievance meeting, the plant manager noted that the collective agreement was signed prior to the time that Hay Lake owned the business; and furthermore, there was no warehouse at the time the collective agreement was signed. The employer denied that the two employees were performing bargaining unit work, and also claimed that at least one of the jobs was a management position.

QUESTIONS

1. If you were a union officer, how would you respond to the employer's position?

2. Assume that you are the arbitrator hearing this matter, and explain what your decision would be.

TIMBERWOLF FAMILY COUNSELLING

Timberwolf Family Counselling provides assistance to individuals with marital, financial, and other personal problems. Jennifer White started to work at the agency as a counsellor on April 1, 2010. The agency's counsellors are covered by a collective agreement that provides new counsellors are on probation for the first six months of their employment. The collective agreement also contains a management rights clause, which provides the following: "The union recognizes that the management of the operations and the direction of the employees are fixed exclusively in the employer and shall remain solely with the employer . . . and without restricting the generality of the foregoing, the union acknowledges that it is the exclusive function of the employer to hire, promote, demote, classify, transfer, direct, layoff, recall and to suspend discipline or discharge employees." The agreement also contains an article relating to probationary employees, which provides that "A probationary employee may be discharged at the sole discretion of and for any reason satisfactory to the employer." The collective agreement provided that employees were entitled to pregnancy and parental leave in accordance with employment standards legislation. In July, White gave her employer notice that she wished to start a pregnancy leave at the end of August. The agency was experiencing staffing problems, and White's manager asked her to defer the start of her maternity leave for one week. White declined this request, confirming that she wished to start her leave on the original date requested. After White had her baby, she advised the employer that due to complications with her child's health she wanted to work half-days for the first three months after her return. White returned to work, and four days later she did not yet have a reply to her scheduling request. At the end of her first week back, White was called to a meeting and advised that she was still on probation and that she was being terminated. When White asked if the termination was prompted by the fact that she had not agreed to defer the start of her pregnancy leave or her request to work half days, the employer representatives at the meeting did not respond. When White asked why she was being terminated, she was told that management had determined that she was not suitable for the job as she was not a "team player." White discussed her dismissal with a union steward who in turn reviewed the situation with management. The union steward raised two issues with the employer. First, the employer was in violation of the reprisal provisions in employment standards legislation which provided that "No employer or person acting on behalf of an employer shall intimidate, dismiss or otherwise penalize an employee or threaten to do so, because the employee asks the employer to comply with this Act and the regulations." Secondly, the employer was in violation of human rights legislation that provides: "Every person has a right to equal treatment with respect to employment without discrimination because of race, ancestry, place of origin, color, ethnic origin, citizenship, creed, sex, sexual orientation, age, record of offenses, marital status, same-sex partnership status, family status or disability." The agency's director of human resources indicated that it was the employer's position that (1) because the collective agreement did not contain any discrimination provision the matter was not arbitrable and (2) in any event, White was still on probation at the time of her termination.

QUESTIONS

1. How will any grievance filed in the situation be worded?

2. Assume that you are the arbitrator hearing this matter.
   a) If the employer responds to the grievance with an argument that the grievance is not arbitrable, explain what your decision on that issue will be.
   b) If you were required to make a decision on the merits of the grievance, explain what your decision would be.
   c) If you upheld the grievance, what remedies would you order?

EAT RITE LTD.

Eat Rite Ltd. operates a chain of grocery stores across the province including a store in Yourtown. The Yourtown store is the largest in the province, and it has a large deli department and bakery. The management team in the store is comprised of Max White, the store manager; Lucy Hightrees, the assistant store manager; Diane Parker, the bakery manager; and Drew Roberts, the deli manager. Prior to the appointment of White as store manager in January 2010, employee relations had been positive. When White was hired as the store manager, he was directed to improve the store's performance that had declined in the previous year, and he made changes that caused employee discontent. In order to reduce costs, White directed that overtime would not be approved except in emergencies. Also, he directed that the time allowed for breaks and lunches be strictly adhered to, and established a new formal policy relating to employees changing shifts that made a shift exchange more difficult. Some employees felt they were being pressured to work additional time without compensation.

Sandra Coulis was hired as a cashier in 2002 and promoted to the position of head cashier in 2005. The head cashier's responsibilities include training new cashiers, ensuring continuity of service during breaks, checking and verifying the accounting clerk's cash count at the end of the day, and locking up the store and setting the alarm system. Coulis was particularly upset and frustrated with the changes implemented by White. The situation was made worse by the fact that there was a personality conflict between Coulis and the new store manager. White was "all business" and spent little time discussing anything other than job responsibilities. Coulis on the other hand enjoyed joking with her colleagues and thought that the work day should involve some fun. When White insisted that the errors in the cash count at the end of each day be reduced, this led to the accounting clerk taking even more time to track down errors to reconcile the count. This led to tension with Coulis because she had to sign off on the cash report at the end of the day; and if the clerk was delayed in preparing the report, Coulis was required to stay until the report was finished.

In August 2010, Coulis was involved in an incident that subsequently led to her contacting the Retail Workers Union about the possibility of unionizing the store. Perhaps because of her increasing frustration and dissatisfaction, Coulis started to take extended coffee and lunch breaks. On one occasion, contrary to store policy, she left the building on a break. While she was absent, the store alarm went off; and because she was not there to reset it, the alarm went on for 45 minutes. This incident disturbed White so much that he wanted to fire Coulis. When he raised the possibility of terminating Coulis with the HR advisor at Eat Rite's head office, White was told that the alarm incident was not serious enough to justify terminating Coulis. White was further advised that unless there was more serious misconduct that amounted to just cause, Coulis could not be terminated without providing her reasonable notice. White was told that reasonable notice for Coulis would be at least six months, and he was advised to give her a formal letter of warning instead of dismissing her. Subsequently, a disciplinary letter was provided to Coulis; and she was told that if her performance and behaviour did not improve, further discipline would be imposed. Coulis was further upset when a friend of hers applied for a job at the store and was not hired. Coulis asked the assistant store manager why her friend had not been hired. The assistant store manager told Coulis her friend was not hired because she had previously worked in a unionized store. The assistant manager told Coulis she had been issued a set of interview questions to ask applicants and had been directed not to hire applicants who had worked for a unionized employer.

Coulis contacted the union and the union began an organizing campaign at the store on November 2, 2010. When management heard about the organizing campaign, there was a prompt response. Managers asked employees what issues and concerns had led to the union organizing attempt. White advised employees not to sign union cards until the employer had an opportunity to respond. One of the employees who knew that Coulis had initiated the union campaign told her that she had been called into the store manager's office for a meeting that included the regional manager. The employee reported that she was asked if she knew who had contacted the union, if she had signed a union card, and if she knew how many other employees had signed cards. Management also distributed a brochure that read as follows:

A Union? Think About It!

We do not believe that the union will advance the interests of employees. The union may take you on strike and we will have to hire and train new employees. Be careful when you talk to a union organizer and know what you are signing. Union organizers will tell you that everyone else is signing a union card when in fact that is not the case. Signing a union membership card is a serious step which cannot be undone. Some of our competitors are unionized and when employees in those stores unionized they started to pay on average over $600 a year for union dues. You will have to maintain your union membership no matter what the union says or does. If you do not maintain your membership the law requires us to terminate your employment. When a union gets into a workplace it is impossible to remove the union. The union may tell you that it will be able to obtain wage increases. No one can make such a guarantee in this economic climate.

On November 23, Coulis was involved in another incident. When she determined that there would be a delay in the cash count for the day, she left the store and went to a nearby bar to have a drink. She returned after one hour to complete the cash count for the day. When White heard that Coulis had left the store, he terminated her after checking with head office on November 25. On November 26, the deli manager, Roberts, told his employees that the company would not operate with a union and certification would lead to closure of the store. He referred to Coulis's dismissal as proof that the employer would not tolerate a union. After November 26, the union was not able to obtain any signatures on union membership cards. The relevant labour relations legislation provides as follows:

1(1) No employer or employers' organization and no person acting on behalf of an employer or employers' organization shall
  (a) participate in or interfere with
    (i) the formation or administration of a trade union, or
    (ii) the representation of employees by a trade union,

(2) An employer does not contravene subsection (1) by reason only that the employer expresses the employer's views so long as the employer does not use coercion, intimidation, threats, promises or undue influence.

2(1) No employer or employers' organization and no person acting on behalf of an employer or employers' organization shall

(a) refuse to employ or to continue to employ any person or discriminate against any person in regard to employment or any term or condition of employment because the person is a member of a trade union or an applicant for membership in a trade union,

(b) impose any condition in a contract of employment that restrains, or has the effect of restraining, an employee from exercising any right conferred on the employee by this Act;

(c) seek by intimidation, dismissal, threat of dismissal or any other kind of threat, by the imposition of a pecuniary or other penalty or by any other means, to compel an employee to refrain from becoming or to cease to be a member, officer or representative of a trade union;

3. Nothing in this Act detracts from or interferes with the right of an employer to suspend, transfer or lay off employees, or to discharge employees for proper and sufficient cause.

QUESTIONS

1. Assume that you are a national representative of the Retail Workers Union. Outline how you would proceed, including the details of any complaints that would be filed.

2. Assume that you are the HR manager responsible for the store, and outline the response that you would recommend to the employer to any union complaints.

RELIABLE AUTO PARTS

Reliable Auto Parts produces trim, mirrors, hubcaps, and other, related accessories for the auto industry. Employees at the company are represented by the Canadian Auto Workers union. The union was certified to represent production employees in 2002. The union and the company reached a first agreement in 2003, and subsequently there have been renewals of the collective agreement. The most recent collective agreement expired December 15, 2009. The union and the employer met prior to the expiry of the agreement knowing that the company was in financial trouble; however, it was anticipated that new investors and a recovery in the auto industry would put the company back on sound financial footing. On December 20, 2009, the union and employer bargaining teams reached a tentative agreement. However, when the agreement was referred to the bargaining unit for ratification, it was rejected by 88 percent of employees. Employees subsequently voted 85 percent in favour of a strike. After the rejection of the agreement, the bargaining teams resumed negotiations, and the employer made a revised offer to the union. By January 8, 2010, the union and the company had reached agreement on all but two issues: shift premium and wages. The parties were $.10 per hour apart on both issues. The employer bargaining team refused to make any further concessions and told the union that it had received the employer's last and final offer. The union bargaining team did not accept the employer's final offer.

On January 9, 2010, the union started a strike. In the first two weeks of the strike, the employer was able to resume operations by hiring replacement workers and using employees who crossed the picket line. Two weeks into the strike, the union bargaining team made calls to the employer's representatives to resume bargaining; however, the calls were not returned. The strike continued with several incidents of violence on the picket line but the employer was able to continue operations. Telephone calls from the union's lead negotiator to the employer were not answered. On March 23, the union held a meeting for bargaining unit employees. At the meeting, the bargaining unit agreed to accept the offer made by the employer on January 8. The union communicated the acceptance of the offer to the employer and inquired about a return to work under the terms of the new contract. The employer responded that there was no contract because the January 8 offer that the union had purported to accept had expired. The union claimed that the employer had not indicted that the January 8 offer would be "off the table" if there was a strike. The parties agreed to resume negotiations. At the first meeting of the negotiating teams, there was a confrontation between the union and employer lead negotiators. The union spokesperson demanded to know why the employer had failed to respond to requests to resume negotiations during the strike. The employer representative responded that he did not see any point in resuming the negotiations on the basis of discussions with employees on the picket line as he was entering the premises. Those employees told him that the union was not willing to change its position. The employer representative also said that the employer would not talk to the union while the violence on the picket line was ongoing.

On April 18, the employer sent a new offer to the union that included the following: a wage freeze, the removal of restrictions on supervisors doing bargaining unit work, a reduction in the number of days allowed for union leave, a reduction in the shift premium, a reduction in the overtime provisions to the minimum provided in employment standards legislation, changes in the dental plan decreasing benefits to coverage from every six months to nine months, and other concessions.

QUESTIONS

1. Assume you are a union official involved in the situation. Explain your position and supporting arguments. Include any complaints that would be filed with the Labour Relations Board.

2. Explain the decision that you think the Labour Relations Board would make in this situation. Include the remedies, if any, the Board should order.

BAYSVILLE SCHOOL BOARD

The Baysville School Board has a separate school for exceptional children who have cognitive difficulties and/or physical conditions that require special assistance. Teachers and educational assistants follow a program that is individually designed for each child. Patrice Jackson was hired as an educational assistant in August 2009. When employees are hired at the school, it stresses the importance of modelling good behaviour and the ability to interact with colleagues so that a positive environment is maintained for the students. On the evening of January 11, 2010, Jackson felt ill, and she followed school procedure and called her supervisor, Rhonda Fraser, to advise her that she would not be able to attend work the next day. The next morning Fraser forgot to advise the school secretary that Jackson would be absent. Following standard operating procedure, the school secretary phoned Jackson at home to find out if she was going to be attending work. On January 13, Jackson confronted Fraser in the staff lounge in the presence of several teachers and educational assistants and in a loud voice told her that she did not appreciate being called at home when she was sick. Fraser apologized for failing to advise the school secretary of Jackson's absence and attempted to explain that she had been called to an emergency situation on her way into the school on the morning in question. Jackson interrupted and said that the school could "shove" the call in procedure. On February 18, 2010, Fraser was in a private meeting with a teacher. Jackson interrupted the meeting and asked the teacher for her car keys, explaining that she had to go home because her bull had gotten out of its corral. Jackson took the teacher's car and the student she had been assigned to for the morning to her home and returned two hours later. On April 1, Jackson had a discussion with a national representative of the Provincial Teachers Union. She obtained union membership cards for her co-workers to sign. The national representative and Jackson planned to start an organizing campaign at the school after Jackson had spoken to a few other employees who she thought would also take part in an organizing drive. On April 6, Jackson spoke to two educational assistants about the possibility of joining a union to improve wages and working conditions. One of the individuals that Jackson spoke to reported the conversation to the school principal on the same day. At the end of the week, the principal was transferred to another school. On April 12, a staff meeting of teachers and educational assistants was held, and Jackson was vocal about several issues. Minutes for this meeting were prepared by Tim Parker, Rhonda Fraser's assistant. One week later when the minutes of the meeting were circulated, Jackson was offended because she was referred to so often in the minutes and she felt that some of the suggestions attribute to her were inaccurate. On April 20, Jackson was working in an open computer area with a small group of students. When Parker walked through the area, Jackson called him over to her and in a loud voice complained about the "God damn" minutes. When Parker suggested that they should talk about the issue at another time and place, Jackson replied that it did not matter because the students could not understand anyway. Jackson stated that she would be refusing to attend further staff meetings and the school could deduct her pay accordingly.

Fraser became concerned with Jackson's behaviour, and she spoke to a superintendent at the school board about the situation. The superintendent suggested that a meeting be held with Jackson to review her behaviour. Jackson was called to a meeting with Fraser and the school board superintendent on April 23. At the meeting, Fraser outlined the school's concerns regarding the absence call in incident, taking a student away from the school on February 18, and the confrontation with Parker regarding the staff meeting minutes. Fraser emphasized the importance of modelling good behaviour for students and positive relationships with co-workers and indicated that she hoped Jackson would change her behaviour. Jackson indicated that she had done nothing wrong, did not plan on changing her behaviour, and reiterated that she would not be attending staff meetings in the future. On the basis of Jackson's response at the meeting, Fraser and the superintendent decided that Jackson should be terminated, and she was provided a notice of termination on the next day.

QUESTIONS

1. Assume that you are the national union representative that Jackson has contacted. What action could you take to deal with Jackson's termination?

2. What does the employer have to do to justify Jackson's termination?

3. Will the employer be able to defend the dismissal? Explain.

GOODTIME FOOD PRODUCTS LTD.

Goodtime Food Products Ltd. produces processed foods, including pickles, relish, and canned vegetables. The production workers of Goodtime are covered by a collective agreement. One year ago, the company discharged Rano, one of the employees in the bargaining unit, after an incident in the plant. She had worked for the company for seven years without incident prior to the day of her dismissal.

Rano worked at a packing station monitoring a machine that filled pickle bottles with small cucumbers. Occasionally when there was not enough work, Rano had been moved to another job inspecting bottles. On the day of the incident, Ed Thomas, her supervisor, decided that another employee should be trained on Rano's regular job so that there would be a replacement available if Rano were absent. Because Rano spoke very little English, Thomas instructed another employee who spoke the same language as Rano, Lucy Battaglia, to tell her to report to the inspection area when she arrived for work.

When Rano arrived for work and Battaglia told her she was being taken off of her regular job, she became outraged and swore about Thomas. She then walked a short distance to another workstation where Thomas was speaking to another employee, and swore and gestured at Thomas with a pair of scissors that were at the workstation. A few minutes later, Rano spoke to the shop steward. The steward immediately prepared a grievance.

When Rano and the shop steward presented the grievance to Thomas in his office, he crumpled it up and threw it in a wastebasket. Thomas told Rano to get back to work. Fifteen minutes later, Thomas went to the inspection area where Rano was working. Rano became outraged. She swore at Thomas, picked up a knife that was on a workbench, and shouted and made slashing gestures about three feet from Thomas' lower body. Thomas left the area.

The company discharged Rano later the same day. The union filed a grievance challenging the dismissal. The matter has gone through the grievance process, and the arbitration hearing is next.

QUESTIONS

1. At the arbitration hearing, what arguments would be presented by the union?

2. At the arbitration hearing, what arguments would be presented by the employer?

3. If you were the arbitrator, what would your decision be? Provide reasons for your decision.

OTTAWA HOSPITAL

Rolf Smith was one of several hospital orderlies working in the orthopedics ward of Ottawa Hospital. The hospital serves a large number of francophone patients, some of whom are unilingual French-speaking. The job of nurses' aid in the dialysis unit of the hospital was posted. The position involves significant amounts of interaction with patients. There is one nurses' aid on duty who moves patients to and from beds, provides snacks, and answers call signals for assistance. He or she does not provide any medical treatment or nursing care, but may have to communicate patient problems to a nurse.

The collective agreement provided that "In matters of promotion, and staff transfer appointments shall be made of the senior applicant able to meet the normal requirements of the job." The collective agreement also prohibited discrimination on a number of grounds, including language.

Smith applied for the nurses' aid position. The hospital referred to a policy requiring nurses' aides in the dialysis unit to be bilingual, and awarded the position to an employee with less seniority who spoke French and English. Smith had managed to get by when communicating with francophone patients in the past, using his limited French and sign language. However, both times Smith had taken French proficiency tests provided by the hospital, he had received a failing grade. Smith filed a grievance claiming that he should have been awarded the job.

QUESTIONS

1. What arguments might the union make at the arbitration hearing?

2. What arguments might the employer make at the arbitration hearing?

3. Explain the decision you expect the arbitrator to make.

REGIONAL TRANSIT COMMISSION

The Regional Transit Commission operates buses in a city with a population of 250 000. Employees of the Commission are represented by the Canadian Auto Workers.

The Commission posted a job opening for an inspector. Inspectors act as lead hands and are not supervisors. They ensure that schedules are met and signs are correctly displayed, deal with complaints from the public, distribute monthly passes, approve the trading of shifts by drivers, and allocate authorized overtime. The job posting provided that the minimum requirements were as follows: Grade 12 education, three years' experience in the transit industry, the ability to make decisions, the ability to complete projects and meet deadlines, the ability to deal with the public, written communication skills, good health, and the ability to walk for extended periods of time.

The collective agreement provides that "Seniority shall always be given utmost consideration in making promotions, demotions and transfers, and when skill and ability are equal, seniority will prevail." The agreement also contained the following management rights clause: "The Commission has and shall retain the exclusive right and power to manage its business and direct its working forces including but without restricting the generality of the foregoing, the right to hire, suspend, discharge, promote, demote and discipline any employee for just cause."

Five individuals applied for the inspector job. As part of the selection process, the Commission gave all five employees a test they had first used for the inspector's job six months earlier. The applicants were tested when they were interviewed, and were not told about the test in advance. The test used was developed after input from current inspectors had been received and an analysis of the inspector's job had been completed. It included questions regarding terms of the collective agreement, mathematics, problem solving, and health and safety.

Jill Akers, who had been employed as a full-time driver for 10 years, was one of the applicants—her first application for an inspector's job. The position was awarded to Voakes, another applicant who had less seniority but a higher test score. It was later determined that Akers' score on the test had been 38 percent, while Voakes had scored 68 percent. It was also found that he had written the same test six months earlier as part of a previous application for an inspector's job. He had improved his score by 22 percent. Voakes had not been provided with a copy of the first test or been advised about the test results.

Akers filed a grievance claiming that she should have been awarded the job.

QUESTIONS

1. What arguments might the union make at the arbitration hearing?

2. What arguments might the employer make at the arbitration hearing?

3. Explain the decision you expect the arbitrator to make.

Appendix B

Grievance and Arbitration

NORTHERN TIMBER COMPANY

Northern Timber Company operates lumber cutting sites in remote areas of the province. Employees are flown in for 14 work days and then flown out for 14 days off. They live in trailers provided by the company. They are covered by a collective agreement between the company and the Timber Workers Union. The company hired Hank Bradford as a timber cutter in 2005. In the course of his work, Bradford operates a chain saw and other hazardous equipment. Prior to being hired, Bradford was advised that no drugs or alcohol were permitted on company property, including the residences occupied by employees. The company adopted this policy after it was determined that an employee who had been killed on the job had been consuming alcohol the night before an accident. In June 2010, there was an incident in which a timber cutter was severely injured. A subsequent investigation determined that the employee had been smoking marijuana in his trailer prior to the accident. The company and the union issued a joint announcement to employees as follows:

> The company and union are committed to the safety of employees. Individuals who have been drinking alcohol or using illegal drugs are a risk to themselves and others. Employees must be alert and safety conscious. There have been incidents in which employees have been found to be in possession of illegal drugs and/or alcohol on company property. It has been determined that some employees are using illegal drugs including marijuana on company property. The company and the union are concerned about the use and possession of drugs and alcohol. This is a reminder that illegal drugs and alcohol are not permitted on company property at any time. This includes an employee's residence. The company's policy is that the use or possession of illegal drugs or alcohol on company property is cause for immediate dismissal.

The company provided a copy of the announcement to each employee and required employees to sign an acknowledgement that they had received the statement. Bradford signed an acknowledgement that he had received the statement. On August 10, a security guard thought he smelled marijuana in the area of Bradford's trailer. The security guard reported this to the health and safety officer, and together they investigated. When they knocked on Bradford's door and he opened it, the smell of marijuana emanated from Bradford's trailer. Bradford allowed the security guard and health and safety officer to search his residence. They found a pipe, 2 grams of marijuana, and two company hand tools.

The next day Bradford was called to a meeting with the site manager, Bradford's supervisor, and the health and safety officer. At the meeting, Bradford admitted that the marijuana found in his residence was his and he had been smoking it. The health and safety officer asked Bradford how often he smoked marijuana. Bradford stated that he had been smoking marijuana for over 10 years and in fact he smoked two or three joints every day, including one in the morning before he went to work. The management representatives reminded Bradford about the company's employee assistance plan that was available to employees. The site manager suggested that Bradford had been stealing company tools to pay for marijuana. Bradford denied that he had stolen any company property and stated that he sometimes brought tools back to his residence at the end of the work day instead of returning them to a tool crib. When Bradford was reminded that company policy required all tools to be returned at the end of each work day, he did not reply.

After Bradford left the meeting, the management team reviewed the situation. It was found that Bradford had not been involved in any previous misconduct or health and safety violations; however, a decision was made to terminate his employment. Within a week of Bradford's termination, he sought treatment for his marijuana use and joined Narcotics Anonymous. The union reported to the employer that Bradford had abstained from marijuana use for the previous 10 days and requested the employer to reconsider his termination. In reply, the company indicated that because Bradford had violated the zero-tolerance policy, and the health and safety risk, the termination would stand.

Proceed as instructed or complete the following:

1. Assume that you are the manager responsible for this file. Prepare a notice of termination that would be provided to Bradford.

2. Assume that you are a union steward whom Bradford has contacted after receiving a termination notice. Outline how you would proceed, and provide any documentation involved.

3. Assume that you are the manager responsible for this file, and outline the argument that could be made to an arbitrator to uphold the termination.

4. Assume that you are the union officer responsible for this file, and outline the argument that could be made to an arbitrator to have Bradford reinstated.

5. Assume that you are the arbitrator in this situation. Outline your decision, providing reasons.

Appendix C

Contract Negotiation Simulation

DIAMOND CASINO

You will be provided with further information and instructions regarding an analysis and a possible renewal of the collective agreement provided below between the Provincial Lottery Corporation and the Gaming Employees Union. Assume that the casino operated by the corporation is located in the major urban centre of your province. The current agreement expires on the date specified by your instructor.

Background

The Provincial Lottery Corporation operates the Diamond Casino, located in a major urban centre of the province. The casino opened five years ago, and employees at the casino are represented by the Gaming Employees Union, which was certified four years ago. The parties negotiated their first collective agreement, which is expiring shortly. The casino operates 24 hours a day, running three eight-hour shifts employing 400 people. Three-hundred sixty casino staff belong to the union. The job classifications are shown in Schedule A of the collective agreement. The casino has three revenue-producing departments: slot machines, table games, and a restaurant/bar. Dealers may be trained and experienced in one or more table games, including blackjack, poker, roulette, and baccarat. Attendance and revenues have been declining over the term of the agreement. It appears that the novelty of the casino has worn off and new marketing efforts may be required. The value of the Canadian dollar and the opening of new casinos in the United States are both influencing the number of U.S. patrons.

Issues Arising Under the Current Agreement

A number of issues have arisen during the administration of the current three-year collective agreement.

Temporary Shift Supervisors   The agreement provides that employees in the bargaining unit may temporarily work as shift supervisors. The employer has interpreted this provision to mean that employees do not accumulate seniority or pay union dues while serving as a shift supervisor. In the last round of contract negotiations, the union put forward a demand that employees on temporary shift super assignments would accumulate seniority and have dues deducted from their pay. The union eventually withdrew the proposal.

Employee Appearance   As part of its dress code, the employer adopted a rule prohibiting male security guards from wearing earrings. The union filed a grievance, and an arbitrator found that the rule was unreasonable and ordered that it be deleted from the policy. On another occasion employees started to wear dime-sized union pins. When the employer directed employees to remove the pins, the union filed a grievance.

An arbitrator upheld the grievance, and some employees are now wearing the pins. Several managers strongly feel that the union pins are inappropriate when worn by employees while on duty.

Absenteeism and Turnover   Absenteeism has been a problem. The casino has found that absenteeism is 50 percent higher than normal on days before and after public holidays. Several employees have been disciplined for absenteeism. In one case, an employee who did not come to work because he was attending a friend's funeral was given a written warning. Subsequently, the same employee was absent because he was attending the funeral of a cousin. The casino suspended the employee for three days; however, the suspension was reduced after the union filed a grievance. Another employee was extremely upset when her mother died because she had to travel 2000 kilometres each way, and she was advised that the agreement provided her with only two days' leave. Many employees who have quit have given only a few days notice.

Work Done by Management   When the casino first opened, the employer scheduled more employees to work each shift than it currently does. Supervisors have been used by the employer to cover employee breaks and on occasions when employees leave early. The union is concerned that the employer is not scheduling a sufficient number of employees for some shifts and is using the supervisors to do bargaining unit work.

Meals   An employee is scheduled one unpaid meal break during their regular shift. Two paid breaks are also scheduled during the first half and last part of the employee's scheduled work period. However, neither party is pleased with the current contract provisions relating to meal allowances when an employee must work overtime. Some employees think that they should receive a voucher to cover the cost of a meal in the casino restaurant. The union is concerned because the $7 meal allowance when employees work overtime is not sufficient to cover the cost of a meal in the casino restaurant, and the allowance has not increased over the term of the agreement. The employer is not pleased with the overtime provision because there is no minimum number of overtime hours that must be worked. Some employees have worked only a few minutes of overtime and are still entitled to the meal allowance under the current practice.

Maternity Leave   Both parties are concerned with the current provisions relating to maternity leave. The union wants the leave to be increased. Some managers would like to see the contract provide that an employee could be required to commence a maternity leave when they think that a pregnancy interferes with the employee's work. The union alleges that such actions would be a breach of human rights legislation.

Future Developments

There has been informal discussions between the union and the employer relating to the work done by the maintenance and security departments. The employer is considering the possibility of contracting out some of the work done by employees in those departments.

OTHER NOTES

Schedule A seen at the end of this case contains the hourly wage rates for all classifications as of the last year of the expired contract. It should form part of the next contract between Diamond Casino and the Gaming Employees Union, Local 1.

Appendix 1 following this wage schedule indicates the number of full-time equivalents (FTE) for each job classification. It is included in this case study *not* as a formal part of the collective agreement between the parties but rather to assist in calculating wage proposals in negotiations between the parties.

Collective Agreement Between Provincial Lottery Corporation, and the Gaming Employees' Union, Local 1

ARTICLE 1—Recognition

1.01 The Employer recognizes the Gaming Employees' Union, Local 1 as the sole bargaining agent for all employees of the Diamond Casino in the City of _____, save and except Shift Supervisors and persons above the rank of Shift Supervisor.

1.02 With an employee's agreement, he or she may fill the role of Shift Supervisor on a temporary basis.

ARTICLE 2—Union Security

2.01 The employer shall deduct from the wages of each employee in the bargaining unit the amount of union dues as determined by the union, and remit the dues to the union in accordance with article 2.02.

2.02 The amounts deducted in accordance with article 2.01 shall be remitted to the union within a reasonable period of time after the deductions are made and shall be accompanied by a list of names of all employees from whom deductions have been made.

ARTICLE 3—Management Rights

3.01 The union recognizes the right of the employer to operate and manage its business in all respects, to maintain order and efficiency in its facilities, to determine the location of its facilities, the work to be performed, the methods and schedules of performance and equipment to be used. The union further acknowledges that the employer has the right to make, and alter from time to time, reasonable rules, regulations, and policies to be observed by employees. Such rules, regulations, and policies shall not be inconsistent with the provisions of this agreement. All changes in the posted rules and regulations and policies must be discussed with the union prior to being implemented. The Employer will provide the union with copies of all new policies and changes to existing policies prior to implementation. The union acknowledges is that it is the exclusive function of the employer to discipline or discharge probationary employees, provided such action is not motivated solely by bad faith and recognizes that such discipline or discharge is not subject to the grievance/arbitration procedure set out in this agreement, except where such bad faith can be established.

ARTICLE 4—Human Rights

4.01 The employer and the union shall neither discriminate nor harass any employee and agree to comply with provincial human rights legislation.

ARTICLE 5—Discipline

5.01 The employer shall have the right to discipline employees for just cause.

5.02 An employee who has a disciplinary record placed in their personnel file may request in writing the removal of the record if 36 months have passed since the disciplinary record was issued and no other subsequent disciplinary records have been issued.

ARTICLE 6—Union Business

6.01 The union shall elect a body of officers and stewards and will advise the employer in writing of the names of the individuals representing the union.

6.02 A union representative shall not suffer any loss of pay as a result of undertaking the following responsibilities during their regularly scheduled work hours: investigating a grievance, meeting with management to deal with a grievance, attending any other meeting called by management.

6.03 The union stewards may investigate and process grievances during regularly scheduled hours of work, provided that the operations of the employer are adequately maintained.

6.04 The stewards shall obtain permission from their manager before leaving their work area for the purposes of union business. Such permission shall not be unreasonably withheld, subject to the operational requirements of the employer being met.

6.05 An employee shall not suffer any loss of pay as a result of meeting with management to deal with a grievance during their regularly scheduled hours.

6.06 A leave of absence without pay and with accrual of seniority shall be granted:

(a) to employees representing the union at conferences, conventions, and seminars.

(b) to up to three representatives on the union's bargaining committee to carry out negotiations with the employer.

6.07 A leave of absence without pay and no accrual of seniority shall be granted:

(a) to employees elected to public office.

(b) to employees elected to the union's national executive.

6.08 The employer shall supply the union with a glass-enclosed locked bulletin board in each staff break room.

ARTICLE 7—Probationary Employees

7.01 New employees shall be on probation for three months from the start of their employment.

7.02 Upon successful completion of the probationary period, seniority shall be effective retroactive to the date of hire.

ARTICLE 8—Grievance Procedure

8.01 **Step I**—An employee who has a complaint shall, within five calendar days of the date he or she became aware of, or reasonably should have become aware of, the event prompting the complaint, first discuss the matter with his or her Department Manager and attempt to informally resolve the situation. In the event that it is not resolved, it may become a formal grievance at Step II, provided it is submitted in writing in accordance with the following provisions.

Step II—Within 14 calendar days of the meeting at Step I, a formal grievance shall be submitted in writing to the Operations Manager. At the request of either party, a meeting shall be held at this Step. The Operations Manager shall reply in writing within 14 days of receiving the grievance. If the grievance is not settled at this stage, it may be advanced to Step III.

Step III—Within 14 calendar days of receipt of the Step II response, the union shall submit the grievance in writing to the General Manager. At the request of either party, a meeting shall be held at this Step.

Step IV—If a settlement is not reached, the union or the employer, in the case of an employer grievance, may refer the grievance to an arbitration board by providing the other party notice in writing within 14 calendar days of receiving the written response at Step III. The notice shall contain a statement of the grievance and the name of the party's appointee to the arbitration board. The recipient of the notice shall within 14 calendar days inform the other party of the name of its appointee to the arbitration board. The two appointees shall within 14 calendar days of the appointment of the second of them, appoint a third person who shall be the chairperson.

8.02 The arbitration board shall hear the parties and shall issue an award in writing. The decision is final and binding upon the parties and upon the employee(s) affected by it. The decision of the majority of the board is the award of the arbitration board. When there is no majority decision, the decision of the chair shall be the decision of the arbitration board.

8.03 Each party shall bear the expense of its respective nominee to the arbitration board, and the parties shall each pay one-half of the expenses of the chairperson. The costs of related meeting location expenses shall be equally shared between the parties.

8.04 In the event that the time limits prescribed in this grievance procedure are not complied with, the grievance shall be deemed to be abandoned.

8.05 Either the union or the employer shall have the right to submit policy grievances arising from the interpretation and application of this agreement. Policy grievances shall commence with Step III and shall be filed within 14 days of the date a party became aware, or should reasonably have become aware, of the issue giving rise to the grievance.

8.06 The union may submit group grievances. A group grievance is an unresolved complaint involving more than one employee in the bargaining unit.

ARTICLE 9—Strikes or Lockouts

9.01 The parties agree that during the term of this agreement there shall be no strikes or lockouts.

ARTICLE 10—Seniority

10.01 Seniority is defined as the length of an employee's continuous employment.

10.02 Seniority rights and employment shall cease when an employee:

(a) resigns,

(b) retires,

(c) is dismissed for cause and is not reinstated,

(d) is laid off for a period in excess of 12 calendar months, or

(e) fails to respond to a call back from the employer within five days.

10.03 A seniority list will be prepared by the employer by January 31 of each year based on service to and including December 31 of the previous year. The list will be posted in all break rooms, and a copy will be provided to the union.

10.04 If two or more employees have the same start date, the order of their seniority shall be determined by their birth dates. The older employee shall be deemed to have the most seniority.

ARTICLE 11—Job Posting

11.01 All vacant or new positions in the bargaining unit shall be posted for six calendar days. The notice shall specify the knowledge, skill, and ability required for the position. A job description may be requested by interested employees.

11.02 Applications for posted positions shall be submitted to the employer within eight days of the job being posted.

11.03 If two or more employees are considered by the employer to be relatively equal in knowledge, skill, and ability required for a position, the employer shall refer to seniority as the determining factor.

11.04 An employee who accepts a new position shall be on a trial period of three months. Subject to satisfactory performance the position shall become permanent after the trial period of three months. In the event the employee proves unsatisfactory in the position during the trial period, or if the employee finds he or she is unable to perform the duties of the new position, he or she shall be returned to his or her former position, at his or her former salary. An employee found to be unsuitable may grieve the decision commencing at Step III of the grievance procedure. The decision at Step III is final for such grievances and is not arbitrable. Any other employee promoted or transferred because of the rearrangement of positions shall be returned to his or her former position at the former salary. A newly hired employee could be released.

ARTICLE 12—Layoff and Recall

12.01 Employees may be laid off by the employer.

12.02 The employer shall lay off employees in reverse order of seniority. The employer shall determine the employees to be laid off considering the seniority and ability of employees as provided in this article.

12.03 Employees who are laid off may retain employment by bumping junior employees, provided that they have the required knowledge, skill, and ability to do the job that they move to. Employees must indicate if they intend to exercise this right within two days of being notified of a layoff. Employees displaced may retain their employment by bumping junior employees, provided they have the necessary knowledge, skills, and ability to do the job they move to.

12.04 Employees who are laid off are entitled to two weeks' notice.

12.05 When employees are recalled, the recall shall be done on the basis of seniority within an employee's classification.

12.06 On a recall, the employer shall notify the employee by phone. It is the responsibility of the employee to provide the employer with a current phone number. Employees shall respond to a recall within five calendar days. Failure to respond to the recall within five days will result in the employee's name being removed from the recall list, and the termination of employment.

Article 13—Severance Pay

13.01 Upon termination of employment, employees may be entitled to severance pay as provided in provincial employment standards legislation.

Article 14—Uniforms

14.01 Employees are required to wear the uniform provided for in the employer's policies.

14.02 Employees are required to purchase required uniforms. The cost of the uniform to employees shall be equivalent to the cost incurred by the employer. Uniform purchases may be processed through payroll deductions.

14.03 Employees are responsible for the cleaning of their uniforms.

Article 15—Vacations

15.01 A vacation year is equivalent to the calendar year.

15.02 Employees are entitled to vacation leave and pay as follows:

(a) An employee who has completed less than one year of service at the conclusion of the vacation year is entitled to leave at the rate of 4 percent of regular hours worked in the concluding vacation year. The vacation leave is to be taken in the next vacation year. Employees are entitled to vacation pay when they take their vacation equal to 4 percent of their wages in the vacation year.

(b) An employee who has completed one to five years of service at the conclusion of the vacation year is entitled to two weeks' vacation leave. The vacation leave is to be taken in the next vacation year. Employees are entitled to vacation pay when they take their vacation equal to 4 percent of their wages in the vacation year.

(c) An employee who has completed six to nine years of service at the conclusion of the vacation year is entitled to three weeks' vacation leave. The vacation leave is to be taken in the next vacation year. Employees are entitled to vacation pay when they take their vacation equal to 6 percent of their wages in the vacation year.

(d) An employee who has completed ten or more years of service at the conclusion of the vacation year is entitled to four weeks' vacation leave. The vacation leave is to be taken in the next vacation year. Employees are entitled to vacation pay when they take their vacation equal to 8 percent of their wages in the vacation year.

15.03 Annual vacations shall be scheduled as follows:

(a) All employees shall submit their requests for vacation leave on or before January 1 of each year for vacation to be taken during the year. Requests submitted after January 1 may be granted subject to the operational requirements of the employer.

(b) Vacation requests submitted on or before January 1 shall be approved on the basis of classification seniority and the employer being able to meet its operational requirements.

15.04 Where a statutory holiday falls within the vacation period of an employee, an additional day's vacation may be added to the vacation with the agreement of the employee's immediate supervisor. Failing such agreement, the employee may take an additional day's vacation at a later date of the employee's choice.

Article 16—Statutory Holidays

16.01 The parties agree that the statutory holidays provided in provincial employment standards legislation shall be holidays for the purposes of this agreement. An employee who works on a holiday shall be paid double his or her regular rate of pay.

Article 17—Bereavement

17.01 Employees shall be entitled to two days' paid leave upon the death of a member of their immediate family. Immediate family means a spouse, common-law spouse, parent, child, brother, sister, father-in-law, mother-in-law, grandparent, and grandchild.

Article 18—Maternity and Parental Leave

18.01 Employees shall be entitled to maternity and parental leave as provided in provincial employment standards legislation.

Article 19—Sick Leave

19.01 Employees are entitled to paid sick leave when they are unable to work because of illness or injury as provided in this article.

19.02 Sick leave credits shall accumulate at the rate of three hours per 75 hours worked. The employee's sick leave credit shall be reduced by the number of hours paid by the employer when the employee is absent.

19.03 The employer may require the employee to provide a medical certificate from a qualified practitioner that the employee was unable to work as a result of illness or injury.

19.04 Employees who will be absent for any reason shall notify the designated employer representative at least three hours prior to the commencement of their shift.

Article 20—Personal Leave

20.01 Unpaid leaves of absence may be granted when it is deemed reasonable by the employer.

20.02 Personal leaves of absence are only available to employees who have completed one year of service.

Article 21—Special Leave

21.01 Each calendar year, an Employee shall be entitled to four special leave days without loss of pay, as either family leave or pressing necessity leave.

(i) Family Leave

Family leave is intended to provide employees with a way of attending to the health needs of members of their immediate family. It is for use when the employees' attendance is necessary and they are unable, through other means, to change the time when they need to be in attendance, or to arrange in advance time off work when needed through other means such as shift trades, time off in lieu, or vacation. Employees are required to provide the employer with notification of leave requirement as early as possible after determining the need.

(ii) Pressing Necessity Leave

A pressing necessity is a sudden or unusual circumstance that could not, by the exercise of reasonable judgement, have been foreseen by the employee and which requires the employee's immediate attention or makes the employee's attendance at work impossible. This may include sudden or unusual circumstances involving a need to attend to members of their immediate family.

Article 22—Incarceration Leave

22.01 An employee convicted of an Offence under the Criminal Code arising out of the operation of a motor vehicle and who is absent from work as a result of such conviction for a period not to exceed 12 consecutive months shall be treated as though he/she is on a leave of absence without pay or benefits.

22.01 Where an employee is incarcerated pending charges or arraignment and subsequently scheduled for work, the employer will not penalize the employee under the employer's attendance policy where the incarceration duration is confirmed to be a maximum of 10 calendar days. An employee incarcerated under this clause will be considered on an incarceration leave of absence for a period not to exceed 10 calendar days.

Article 23—Overtime

23.01 The employer may require employees to work overtime.

23.02 The overtime rate shall be 1-1/2 times the employee's regular rate of pay and shall be paid on hours worked in excess of eight hours per day, exclusive of any unpaid breaks, and on hours worked in excess of 44 hours per week, commencing on Sunday, exclusive of unpaid breaks.

23.03 The employer shall establish a voluntary overtime signup sheet for each day. Overtime shall be allocated to those employees on the list on the basis of their classification seniority, provided that the employee has the knowledge and skills required for the work available. If there are insufficient volunteers to work overtime, the employer may require employees to work overtime to meet operational requirements.

23.04 Employees who work overtime shall be allowed a meal allowance of $5.00.

Article 24—Hours of Work and Scheduling

24.01 Full-time employees shall work five eight-hour shifts per week. Each shift will have a half-hour unpaid meal break and two 15-minute breaks during their scheduled work day. Part-time employees may be scheduled to work less than eight-hour shifts; however, in no event will a shift be less than three hours.

24.02 The employer will post a 28-day schedule two weeks in advance for both full-time and part-time employees.

24.03 Part-time employees may be called in to fill in shifts. The call-ins will be offered to part-time employees in the job classification required on the basis of seniority.

24.04 Employees will be off at least 11 hours between shifts.

24.05 Employees may exchange shifts with the approval of their manager. The employer shall not incur any additional cost as a result of a shift exchange.

Article 25—Technological Change

25.01 For purposes of this article, technological change means the introduction of new equipment into the employer's operation, which affects the security of employment of a significant number of employees.

25.02 When the employer intends to introduce technological change, it will provide the union with 90 days' notice prior to the date the change is to be effective. The parties will meet to discuss the steps to be taken to assist the employees who could be affected.

Article 26—Health and Safety

26.01 The employer and the union recognize the importance of health and safety and agree to cooperate to prevent accidents and establish a healthy workplace.

26.02 A health and safety committee consisting of at least three union representatives and three employer representatives shall be established. The committee shall carry out the duties assigned to it by provincial health and safety legislation.

26.03 The employer shall provide all available information relating to accidents and occupational diseases that occur in the workplace.

26.04 Minutes of health and safety committee meetings shall be posted in staff break rooms.

Article 27—Contracting Out

27.01 When the employer proposes to contract out work and there will be a layoff of employees in the bargaining unit as a result, the employer will provide the union with 120 days' notice. The parties shall meet to discuss the reasons and possible alternatives to the proposed contracting out and shall attempt to avoid job losses through retraining and/or reassignment of employees.

Article 28—Performance Appraisal

28.01 Where a formal assessment of an employee's performance is made, the employee will be provided with an opportunity to read the assessment before the employee is required to sign the formal assessment indicating that he or she has read it. The employee shall have the right to place his or her comments on the performance and development form.

28.02 If the employee perceives the performance and development form is an inaccurate assessment, the employee may submit a written request to the general manager to initiate a review of the contents of the form, which are alleged to be unfair or inaccurate. The written request for review must be received within 10 days of the employee having been provided with a copy of the performance and development form and provide the details of the alleged inaccuracies. The general manager shall meet with the employee in an attempt to resolve their concern(s). A review under this process is non-grievable.

28.03 A copy of the employee's performance evaluation shall be placed in the employee's personnel file.

Article 29—Wages

29.01 The wages for the first year of the agreement are set out in Schedule A.

Article 30—Duration of Agreement

30.01 This agreement shall be effective for three years, from _____, 20xx to _____, 20xx.

Schedule A: Wages			
Classification	Year 1 Dec. 31, 20__	Year 2 Dec. 31, 20__	Year 3 Dec. 31, 20__
Slots			
Slot Technician	22.07	22.44	22.90
Slot Attendant	17.29	17.55	17.90
Change Attendant	13.75	13.96	14.24
Dealers			
Dealer 1 (one game)	14.19	14.41	14.70
Dealer 2 (two games)	14.68	14.90	15.20
Dealer 3 (three games)	15.16	15.39	15.70
Dealer 4 (four or + games)	15.64	15.88	16.20
Finance			
Count Attendant	16.60	16.85	17.19
Cashier	18.55	18.83	19.21
Auditor	26.22	26.62	27.16
Kitchen			
Chef	27.41	27.83	28.40
Cook 1	23.07	23.42	23.90
Cook 2	19.94	20.24	20.65
Aide	14.19	14.41	14.70

Classification	Year 1 Dec. 31, 20__	Year 2 Dec. 31, 20__	Year 3 Dec. 31, 20__
Restaurant			
Host	16.36	16.61	16.95
Bartender	14.65	14.87	15.17
Server	12.43	12.62	12.88
Guest Services			
Door Person	12.07	12.25	12.50
Coat Attendant	11.68	11.86	12.10
Maintenance			
Janitor	16.08	16.34	16.67
Lead Hand	17.30	17.56	17.92
Groundskeeper	16.36	16.61	16.95
Repair Person	16.51	16.76	17.10
Information Technology			
Computer Technician	20.80	21.12	21.55
Audio Visual Technician	22.00	22.33	22.80
Systems Analyst	26.30	26.64	27.18
Purchasing and Receiving			
Buyer	24.65	25.03	25.54
Purchasing Clerk	19.45	19.75	20.15
Stores Clerk	19.34	19.63	20.03
Office			
Receptionist	16.18	16.43	16.80
Mail Attendant	16.34	16.59	16.93
Scheduling Clerk	18.49	18.77	19.15
Marketing Clerk	11.68	11.86	20.10
Marketing Coordinator	26.53	26.93	27.48
Security			
Security Officer	18.68	18.96	19.35
Security Coordinator	20.51	20.82	21.25

Appendix 1 Full-Time Equivalent (FTE) as of December 31, 20__

Classification	# of FTE
Slots	
Slot Technician	12
Slot Attendant	13
Change Attendant	25
Dealers	
Dealer 1 (one game)	15
Dealer 2 (two games)	20
Dealer 3 (three games)	25
Dealer 4 (four or + games)	25

Finance

Count Attendant	10
Cashier	18
Auditor	2

Kitchen

Chef	3
Cook 1	6
Cook 2	8
Aide	12

Restaurant

Host	6
Bartender	10
Server	30

Guest Services

Door Person	6
Coat Attendant	12

Maintenance

Janitor	5
Lead Hand	3
Groundskeeper	5
Repair Person	7

Information Technology

Computer Technician	20
Audio Visual Technician	14
Systems Analyst	6

Purchasing and Receiving

Buyer	2
Purchasing Clerk	4
Stores Clerk	4

Office

Receptionist	2
Mail Attendant	4
Scheduling Clerk	4
Marketing Clerk	6
Marketing Coordinator	1

Security

Security Officer	12
Security Coordinator	3
Union total	**360**
Non-management staff	4
Management staff	36
Diamond Casino total FTE	**400**

Appendix D

Canadian Council of Human Resources Associations' Required Professional Capabilities

The Canadian Council of Human Resources Associations in 2014 revised its Required Professional Capabilities (RPCs) classification system. Nine functional areas are outlined in this system. Six hundred and fourteen knowledge and skill elements are identified within the nine categories. The RPC knowledge and skill elements that are supported in this text are seen in the following list.

10101   Economic, societal, technological, political, demographic trends and their impact, or potential impact, on business and human resources practice

10102   All important developments that are impacting and will impact the business environment and human resources practice

10211   Global and industry trends

10301   Business unit goals and objectives and strategic planning process

10303   Stakeholder groups and their needs and interests

10304   Conflict management principles

10310   Aligning human resources goals and objectives to business strategy

10405   Stakeholder groups and their needs and interests

10407   Conflict management principles

10503   Human resources strategies and objectives

10504   Business objectives and strategic priorities

10509   Creating a strategic human resources plan

20103   Hierarchy and organizational power dynamics

20105   Conflict management and dispute resolution techniques

20106   Negotiation techniques

20107   Decision-making processes

20110   Stakeholder groups and their needs and interests

20204   Conflict management and dispute resolution strategies

20206   Effective communication techniques

20211   Educating and informing managers

20301   Relevant and impending acts, legislation, regulations, regulatory bodies, and legal precedents

20302   How decisions get made and how they apply to the organizational decision-making environment

20307   Legal trends and precedents

20406   Relevant and impending acts, legislation, regulations, regulatory bodies, and legal precedents

20611	Make decisions about existing human resources policies and practices based on relevant evidence
30101	Theories and models of human motivation and engagement including the predictors of employee engagement
40403	Performance management programs, methods, and metrics
50101	Labour and employee relations principles
50102	Relevant and impending acts, legislation, regulations, regulatory bodies, and legal precedents
50103	Collective bargaining process
50104	Proactive relationship and conflict management practices
50106	Global and industry trends and issues in regards to labour and employee relations
50107	Collective bargaining principles and strategies
50108	Union charters, constitutions, and by-laws
50109	Maintaining a strategic perspective
50110	Building, influencing, and managing collaborative relationships
50111	Building and managing multi-stakeholder relationships
50112	Influencing and collaborating
50113	Resolving conflicts and disputes
50114	Negotiating collective agreement and remedies to disputes
50117	Using research skills needed to prepare and execute collective bargaining
50118	Using communication and relationship skills on remedies, decision making, and problem solving
50201	Labour and employee relations principles
50202	The union certification process
50203	The role of labour Ministries, Labour Relations boards, and other employment law tribunals
50204	Structure and interpretation of collective agreements
50205	Relevant and impending acts, legislation, regulations, regulatory bodies, and legal precedents
50206	Educating managers and supervisors about legal compliance and contract requirements
50301	Organizational and labour or employee relations strategies
50302	Labour and employee relations principles
50304	Relevant and impending acts, legislation, regulations, regulatory bodies, and legal precedents
50305	Arbitration process
50401	Organizational strategies and business conditions and objectives
50402	Relevant and impending acts, legislation, regulations, regulatory bodies, and legal precedents
50403	Global and industry economic and social trends
50404	Current labour disputes and settlements
50405	Circumstances requiring external expertise
50411	Negotiating collective agreements, related agreements such as Memoranda of settlements, Letters of Understanding, and solutions to disputes

HRPA Human Resources Professionals Competency Framework

The Human Resources Professionals Association in Ontario set out in 2014 its own competency framework. Nine competency functional areas are seen in the framework. Two hundred and thirteen competencies are identified within the nine areas. The underlying competencies in the HRPA Human Resources Professionals Competency Framework that are supported, at least in part, in this text are seen in the following list.

C001   Maintain awareness of broad economic, societal, technological, political, global, and demographic trends.

C002   Identify HR opportunities and risks inherent in changes in economic, societal, technological, political, and demographic forces.

C003   Formulate HR strategies within the organization that are informed by factors that are both internal and external to the organization.

C004   Execute HR strategies that enhance the value of the human resources within the organization.

C013   Direct HR activities towards the implementation of the business plan.

C014   Manage risk in the execution of HR activities.

C016   Apply sound business practices in carrying out the HR function.

C018   Direct the HR function towards realizing the organization's vision and goals.

C019   Adhere to the organization's values while carrying out its mission.

C021   Assess variances between current HR practices and those required to achieve the organization's strategic plan.

C022   Develop potential tactics to achieve desired HR practices.

C024   Establish a work plan that prioritizes the most effective steps to achieve the desired HR practices.

C028   Build productive relationships both inside and outside the organization.

C029   Adhere to accepted HR standards of practice.

C030   Balance the interests of all affected parties in carrying out HR activities.

C031   Act with integrity in all undertakings.

C032   Make decisions only after considering all accessible and relevant facts.

C035   Demonstrate understanding of the application of HR legal requirements in the workplace.

C036   Keep current on changes to the laws that govern HR practices.

C037   Adhere to legal requirements in carrying out all HR activities.

C038   Identify risks to the organization stemming from the need to adhere to legal requirements.

C048   Keep current on business information and trends.

C056   Maintain knowledge of literature on employee engagement.

C057   Advocate strategies to enhance employee engagement with senior management.

C058   Develop potential strategies to enhance employee engagement.

C079 Communicate with unions in a respectful manner that promotes understanding of the organization's challenges and developments.

C101 Oversee the organization's performance management system.

C111 Seek opportunities for collaboration between the employer and employees.

C112 Seek opportunities for collaboration between management and unions and other representative groups.

C113 Encourage open and clear dialogue between management and employees/unions.

C114 Focus collaboration between management and employees/unions on the end goal of a productive and engaged workforce.

C115 Champion respectful communication in all interactions between the employer and employees.

C116 Maintain knowledge of the details of collective agreements in place in the organization and in related organizations.

C117 Maintain knowledge of legislation that affects the HR practices at the organization.

C118 Treat employees in accordance with the principles of natural justice.

C119 Manage the risk of litigation and conflict in all interactions with employees.

C120 Evaluate the risks associated with alternative labour and employee relations strategies.

C121 Evaluate the costs associated with alternative labour and employee relations strategies.

C122 Evaluate the benefits associated with alternative labour and employee relations strategies.

C123 Formulate alternative labour and employee relations strategies to achieve business objectives.

C124 Analyze the overall strengths and weaknesses of alternative labour and employee relations strategies.

C125 Recommend optimal labour and employee relations strategies.

C126 Formulate negotiation strategies that take into consideration variables within and outside the organization.

C127 Negotiate to resolve labour and employee disputes.

C128 Participate in mediation processes in an effective and balanced manner.

C129 Participate effectively in or facilitate arbitration proceedings.

C130 Identify institutional structures or practices that may present barriers to some facet of diversity.

C131 Develop an effective program to remove institutional structures or practices that present barriers to some facet of diversity.

C132 Implement a program to remove institutional structures or practices that present barriers to some facet of diversity.

C133 Manage cases appearing before tribunals.

C134 Provide advice to individuals and organizations appearing before HR-related tribunals.

C136 Create equitable and effective rewards structures which include compensation, pensions, benefits, and perquisites.

C194 Align HR decisions with organizational strategy.

Endnotes

Chapter 1

1. Thomas Kochan and Harry Katz, *Collective Bargaining and Industrial Relations: From Theory to Policy and Practice*, 2nd ed. (Homewood, IL: Richard D. Irwin, 1988), p. 1.
2. Morley Gunderson and Daphne Taras, *Canadian Labour and Employment Relations*, 6th ed. (Toronto: Pearson–Addison Wesley, 2008).
3. Mark Thompson, Joseph B. Rose, and Anthony Smith, *Beyond the National Divide: Regional Dimensions of Industrial Relations* (Quebec: Canadian Industrial Relations Association, 2003).
4. Michael Lynk. Labour. "Law and The New Inequality," Just Labour, http://www.justlabour.yorku.ca/index.php?page=toc&volume=15, p. 125.
5. Morley Gunderson and Daphne Taras, *Canadian Labour and Employment Relations*, 6th ed. (Toronto, Pearson–Addison Wesley, 2008).
6. John Dunlop, *Industrial Relations Systems* (New York: Holt and Company, 1958), and *Industrial Relations Systems*, rev. ed. (Boston: Harvard Business School Press, 1993).
7. Thomas Kochan, Harry Katz, and Robert McKersie, *The Transformation of American Industrial Relations* (Ithaca, NY: ILR Press, 1994).
8. Alton Craig and Norman Solomon, *A System of Industrial Relations in Canada*, 5th ed. (Toronto: Prentice-Hall Canada, 1996).
9. Gary Svirsky, "The Division of Labour: An Examination of Certification Requirements," *Osgoode Hall Law Journal*, vol. 36 (1998), 567.
10. John Godard, *Industrial Relations, The Economy, and Society*, 3rd ed. (North York, ON: Captus Press, 2005).
11. Ibid., p. 67.
12. W. Craig Riddell, *Labour–Management Co-operation in Canada* (University of Toronto Press, 1986); Thomas Kochan and Paul Osterman, *The Mutual Gains Enterprise: Forging a Partnership Among Labor, Management, and Government* (Boston: Harvard Business School Press, 1994).
13. Donald Wells, "Are Strong Unions Compatible with the New Model of Human Resource Management?" *Relations Industrielles*, vol. 48 (1993), 56.
14. Anthony Smith, "Canadian Industrial Relations in Transition," *Relations Industrielles*, vol. 48 (1993), 641.

Chapter 2

1. New Bank of Canada, *Monetary Policy Report Summary*, April 2014, http://www.bankofcanada.ca/wp-content/uploads/2014/04/mpr-summary-2014-04-16.pdf, accessed June 12, 2014.
2. "Go West Call Angers MPs," *CBC News*, June 9, 2006.
3. "$500 Million Auto Investment Strategy Means Better Workers for Better Jobs in an Innovative Economy," *Ontario Newsroom*, April 14, 2004, http://news.ontario.ca/archive/en/2004/04/14/500-million-Auto-Investment-Strategy-means-better-workers-for-better-jobs-in-an-.html.
4. J. Brown, "Feds Invest in Saskatchewan Dairy Industry's Health," November 30, 2013, http://globalnews.ca/news/1000906/feds-invest-in-saskatchewan-dairy-industrys-health, accessed May 26, 2014.
5. Statistics Canada, "Manufacturing," *Canada's Yearbook 2011*, http://www.statcan.gc.ca/pub/11-402-x/2011000/chap/man-fab/man-fab-eng.htm, accessed May 26, 2014.
6. "Forestry Profits Triple," *Globe and Mail*, July 13, 2005.
7. Paul Marck, "Axe Hangs over Forestry Industry," *Edmonton Journal*, January 28, 2006.
8. David Foot, *Boom, Bust, and Echo 2000: How to Profit from the Coming Demographic Shift* (Toronto: MacFarlane, Walter and Ross, 1998).

9. D. Scwabel, "10 Ways Millennials Are Creating the Future of Work," December 13, 2013, http://www.forbes.com/sites/danschawbel/2013/12/16/10-ways-millennials-are-creating-the-future-of-work, accessed May 26, 2014.
10. Statistics Canada, http://www4.hrsdc.gc.ca/.3ndic.1t.4r@-eng.jsp?iid=13, accessed May 25, 2014.12.
11. T. Grant, "In Canada, the Fading Union Movement Is a Male Phenomenon," *Globe and Mail*, November 26, 2013, http://www.theglobeandmail.com/report-on-business/economy/economy-lab/in-canada-the-fading-union-movement-is-a-male-phenomenon/article15609673, accessed May 26, 2013.
12. Statistics Canada, http://www.statcan.gc.ca/tables-tableaux/sum-som/l01/cst01/labor12-eng.htm, accessed May 26, 2014.
13. K. Maher, "Two Unions Set Pact for US Airways–AMR Merger," May 14, 2013, http://online.wsj.com/news/articles/SB10001424127887324031404578483344114009384, accessed May 26, 2014.
14. Jeff Rubin, *Why Your World Is About to Get a Whole Lot Smaller: Oil and the End of Globalization* (Toronto: Random House Canada, 2009).
15. Eric Gagnon, *Free Trade in North America: The Impact on Industrial Relations and Human Resource Management in Canada* (Kingston, ON: IRC Press, Industrial Relations Centre, 1998).
16. R. Littlemore, "Do Unions Have a Future?" *Globe and Mail*, March 27, 2013, http://www.theglobeandmail.com/report-on-business/rob-magazine/do-unions-have-a-future/article10310754/?page=all.
17. John Godard, "Managerial Strategies, Labour and Employment Relations and the State," *British Journal of Industrial Relations*, vol. 35, 399.
18. Terry Wagar, "Consequences of Work Force Reduction: Some Employer and Union Evidence," *Journal of Labor Research*, vol. 22 (2001), 851.
19. Simon Tuck, "Ottawa May Allow Airlines to Use Fewer Flight Attendants," *Globe and Mail*, May 8, 2006.
20. Anil Verma, "From POTS to PANS: The Evolution of Employment Relations in Bell Canada Under Deregulation," *Contract and Commitment* (Kingston, ON: IRC Press, 1999).
21. "Now for the Reckoning: Corporate America's Legacy Costs," *The Economist*, October 15, 2005, p. 91.
22. "Legacy Costs of Public Sector Employees," Hamilton Chamber of Commerce, http://www.chamber.ca/cmslib/general/29-Legacy.pdf#search=%22Ontario%20%22legacy%20costs%20of%20public%20sector%20employees%22%22, accessed August 23, 2006.
23. "City to Track Employees by Computer," *CBC News*, April 25, 2006.
24. Gary Chaison, "Information Technology: The Threat to Unions," *Journal of Labor Research*, vol. 23 (2002), 249.
25. Ibid., p. 254.
26. "Canada's Unions Still Have Majority Support, Poll Finds," *The Huffington Post Canada*, December 20, 2013, http://www.huffingtonpost.ca/2013/12/20/unions-canada-poll_n_4479321.html, accessed May 26, 2014.
27. Seymour Martin Lipset and Noah M. Meltz, *The Paradox of American Unionism: Why Americans Like Unions More Than Canadians Do but Join Much Less* (Ithaca, NY: ILR Press, 2004).
28. Peter Bruce, "Political Parties and Labor Legislation in Canada and the U.S.," *Industrial Relations*, vol. 28 (1989), 115.
29. *British Columbia (Public Service Employee Relations Commission) v. B.C.G.S.E.U.* 176 D.L.R. (4th) 1.
30. *Vriend v. Alberta* [1998] 1 S.C.R. 493.
31. *Independent Electricity Market Operator v. Canadian Union of Skilled Workers*, http://www.canlii.org/en/on/onlrb/doc/2009/2009canlii66091/2009canlii66091.html.
32. *Reference Re Public Service Employee Relations Act (Alberta)* [1987] 1 S.C.R. 313.

33. *Lavigne v. Ontario Public Service Employees Union* [1991] 2 S.C.R. 211.

34. *Dunmore v. Ontario (Attorney General)* [2001] 3 S.C.R. 1016.

35. *Mounted Police Association of Ontario v. Canada (Attorney General)*, 2009 CanLII 15149 (ON S.C.), http://www.canlii.org/en/on/onsc/doc/2009/2009canlii15149/2009canlii15149.html.

36. *United Food and Commercial Workers, Local 1518 (U.F.C.W.) v. KMart Canada Ltd.* [1999] 2 S.C.R. 1083.

Chapter 3

1. Labour Program, Government of Canada, "Union Coverage in Canada, 2013," http://www.labour.gc.ca/eng/resources/info/publications/union_coverage/union_coverage.shtml, accessed May 29, 2014.

2. Bureau of Labour Statistics, United States Department of Labour, "Economic News Release: Union Member Summary," January 24, 2014, http://www.bls.gov/news.release/union2.nr0, accessed May 27, 2014.

3. Leo Troy, "U.S. and Canadian Industrial Relations: Convergent or Divergent?" *Industrial Relations*, vol. 39 (2000), 695.

4. Clive Gilson and Terry Wagar, "The U.S./Canada Convergence Thesis: Contrary Evidence from Nova Scotia," *Industrial Relations*, vol. 50 (1995), 66.

5. NLRB Election Results 2008 Totals, http://www.nlrb.gov/publications/reports/election_reports.aspx, accessed May 6, 2010.

6. Ian Bruce, "The Processing of Unfair Labour Practice Cases in the U.S. and Ontario," *Relations Industrielles*, vol. 45 (1990), 481.

7. Hoyt Wheeler, *The Future of the American Labour Movement* (Cambridge, UK: University Press, 2002), p. 3.

8. Joseph B. Rose and Gary Chaison, "Unionism in Canada and the United States in the 21st Century: The Prospects for Revival," *Relations Industrielles*, vol. 56 (2001), 34.

9. "Unionization," *Perspectives on Labour and Income*, Statistics Canada, August 2009, http://www.statcan.gc.ca/pub/75-001-x/75-001-x2009108-eng.pdf, accessed May 6, 2010.

10. Table Unionization rate, by region 2012 (percent of employees) http://www4.hrdsc.gc.ca/.3ndic.1t.4r@-eng.jsp?iid=17. Employment and Social Development Canada, 2014. Reproduced, adapted, revised and translated with the permission of the Minister of Employment and Social Development Canada, 2014.

11. Ibid.

12. Alex Bryson, Rafael Gomez, Morley Gunderson, and Noah Meltz, "Youth–Adult Differences in the Demand for Unionization: Are American, British, and Canadian Workers All That Different?" *Journal of Labor Research*, vol. 26 (2005), 155.

13. Statistics Canada, "Labour Force Survey Estimates (LFS), Employees by Union Status, Sex, Age Group and Education Level, Canada," Table 282-0221, CANSIM database, accessed May 17, 2014.

14. John Godard, "Beliefs About Unions and What They Should Do: A Survey of Employed Canadians," *Journal of Labor Research*, vol. 18 (1997), 621.

15. *Re Kingston General Hospital and CUPE Local 1974* (2004) 135 LAC (4th) 88.

16. Human Resources and Social Development Canada, "Union Membership in Canada-2012," http://www.labour.gc.ca/eng/resources/info/publications/union_coverage/unionmembership.pdf, accessed May 29, 2014.

17. British Columbia Federation of Labour, http://www.bcfed.com/featured, accessed May 29, 2014.

18. Human Resources and Social Development Canada, "Union Membership in Canada-2012," http://www.labour.gc.ca/eng/resources/info/publications/union_coverage/unionmembership.pdf, accessed May 29, 2014.

19. Human Resources and Social Development Canada, "Union Membership in Canada-2012," http://www.labour.gc.ca/eng/resources/info/publications/union_coverage/unionmembership.pdf, accessed May 29, 2014.

20. Clive Gilson and Terry Wagar, "The U.S./Canada Convergence Thesis: Contrary Evidence from Nova Scotia," *Industrial Relations*, vol. 50 (1995), 66.

21. Craig Heron, *The Canadian Labour Movement: A Short History*, 2nd ed. (Toronto: James Lorimer & Co., 1996).

22. Desmond Morton, *Working People: An Illustrated History of the Canadian Labour Movement*, 3rd ed. (Toronto: Summerhill Press, 1990).

23. "UFCW Canada Organizes Kingsville Mushroom Factory; Employees Working Under 'Appalling' Conditions," http://www.ufcw.ca/Default.aspx?SectionId=af80f8cf-ddd2-4b12-9f41-641ea94d4fa4&LanguageId=1&ItemId=0d8ba214-fdb6-4332-81a0-e928c8ba2168, accessed June 27, 2006.

24. Unifor Constitution, http://www.unifor.org/sites/default/files/attachments/unifor_constitution.pdf, accessed May 29, 2014.

25. Errol Black and Jim Silver, *Building a Better World: An Introduction to Trade Unionism in Canada* (Halifax: Fernwood Publishing, 2001).

26. K. Thorpe, "The State of the Unions in 2012 Inside Edge," *The Conference Board of Canada's E-Magazine*, February 7, 2012, http://www.conferenceboard.ca/insideedge/2012/feb2012/feb7-unions.aspx, accessed May 29, 2014.

27. Pradeep Kumar and Gregor Murray, "Innovation and Change in Labour Organizations in Canada: Results of the National 2000–2001 HRDC Survey," p. 6, http://www.hrsdc.gc.ca/asp/gateway.asp?hr=en/lp/wid/ics/01_innovation_change_2000–2001_survey_a.shtml&hs=wyi, accessed May 7, 2010.

28. Jon Peirce and Karen Joy Bentham, *Canadian Industrial Relations*, 3rd ed. (Toronto: Pearson Education Canada, 2007), p. 52.

29. Errol Black and Jim Silver, *Building a Better World: An Introduction to Trade Unionism in Canada* (Halifax: Fernwood Publishing, 2001), p. 143.

30. Alan Freeman, "Wages Post Lowest Quarterly Increase in 15 Years," *Globe and Mail*, May 19, 1993.

31. Parbudyal Singh, "NAFTA and Labour: A Canadian Perspective," *Journal of Labour Research*, vol. 23 (2002), 433.

32. Casey Mahood, "Maple Leaf Strikers Vote for Contract," *Globe and Mail*, March 7, 1998.

33. Graham Lowe, *Bank Unionization in Canada: A Preliminary Analysis* (Toronto: University of Toronto Centre for Industrial Relations, 1980).

34. Desmond Morton, *Working People: An Illustrated History of the Canadian Labour Movement* (Toronto: Summerhill Press, 1990), p. 154.

Chapter 4

1. Ian Ross, personal communication, December 11, 2013, discussion of management interactions with library employees in the context of non-union work environment.

2. Conference Board of Canada, "Labour Productivity Growth," March 2013, http://www.conferenceboard.ca/hcp/details/economy/measuring-productivity-canada.aspx.

3. Certified General Accountants Association of Canada, "Fading Productivity: Making Sense of Canada's Productivity Challenge," http://www.cga-canada.org/en-ca/ResearchAndAdvocacy/AreasofInterest/FadingProductivity/Pages/_ca_fading-productivity_index.aspx, accessed January 14, 2010.

4. Gary Chaison, "Airline Negotiations and the New Concessionary Bargaining," *Journal of Labor Research*, vol. 28 (2007), 642.

5. Anil Verma and Daphne Taras, "Managing the High-Involvement Workplace," *Union–Management Relations in Canada*, 5th ed. (Toronto: Pearson Education Canada, 2005).

6. Michael Porter, *Competitive Advantage* (New York: New York Free Press, 1985).

7. Mark Thompson, "The Management of Industrial Relations," *Union–Management Relations in Canada*, 4th ed. (Toronto: Pearson Education Canada, 2001).

8. Karen Bentham, "Employer Resistance to Union Certification: A Study of Eight Canadian Jurisdictions," *Industrial Relations*, vol. 57 (2002), 159.

9. John Godard, "Managerial Strategies, Labour and Employment Relations and the State: The Canadian Case and Beyond," *British Journal of Industrial Relations*, vol. 35 (1997), 399.

10. Richard Chaykowski, *Fostering Human Resources in the New Economy* (Kingston, ON: Industrial Relations Centre, Queens University, 1997).

11. Pradeep Kumar, *Unions and Workplace Change in Canada* (Kingston, ON: Industrial Relations Centre, Queens University, 1995).

12. Ibid., pp. 13–14; Anil Verma and Daphne Taras, "Managing the High-Involvement Workplace," *Union–Management Relations in Canada*, 5th ed. (Toronto: Pearson Education Canada, 2005); John Godard, "A Critical Assessment of the High-Performance Paradigm," *British Journal of Industrial Relations*, vol. 42 (2004), 349.

13. Anil Verma and Daphne Taras, "Managing the High-Involvement Workplace," *Union–Management Relations in Canada*, 6th ed. (Toronto: Pearson Education Canada, 2009).

14. Gordon Betcherman, "Workplace Change in Canada: The Broad Context," *Contract and Commitment: Employment Relations in the New Economy* (Kingston, ON: IRC Press, 1999), p. 28.

15. Anil Verma and Daphne Taras, "Managing the High-Involvement Workplace," *Union–Management Relations in Canada*, 6th ed. (Toronto: Pearson Education Canada, 2009).

16. John Godard, "A Critical Assessment of the High-Performance Paradigm," *British Journal of Industrial Relations*, vol. 42 (2004), 349.

17. "Research and Theory on High-Performance Work Systems: Progressing the High-Involvement Stream," *Human Resource Management Journal*, vol. 19, no. 1, 3–23. January, 2009.

18. Pradeep Kumar. *Rethinking High-Performance Work Systems* (Kingston, ON: IRC Press, 2000).

Chapter 5

1. Greg Keenan and Simon Tuck, "Liberals Shower Auto Industry with Aid," *Globe and Mail*, June 14, 2004.

2. "Protecting Retail Workers' Rights," Ontario Ministry of Labour bulletin, October 2013, http://www.labour.gov.on.ca/english/news/2013/bul_retail20131016.php.

Chapter 6

1. Larry Cohen and Richard W. Hurd, "Fear, Conflict, and Union Organizing," in *Organizing to Win: New Research on Union Strategies*, ed. Kate Brofenbrenner, Sheldon Frideman, Richard W. Hurd, Rudolph A. Oswald, and Ronald L. Seebar (Ithaca, NY: Cornell University, ILR Press).

2. Daphne Gottlieb Taras and Jason Copping, "The Transition from Formal Nonunion Representation to Unionization: A Contemporary Case," *Industrial and Labour Relations Review*, vol. 52, no. 1 (October 1998), 22.

3. David McPhillips and Geoffrey England, "Employment Legislation in Canada," in *Union–Management Relations in Canada*, 2nd ed., ed. John C. Anderson, Morley Gunderson, and Alan Ponak (Don Mills, ON: Addison-Wesley Publishers Ltd., 1989), p. 62.

4. B. Ruth Montgomery, "The Influence of Attitudes and Normative Pressures on Voting Decisions in a Union Certification Election," *Industrial and Labour Relations Review*, vol. 42, no. 2 (1989), 262.

5. Graham S. Lowe and Harvey Krahn, "Recent Trends in Public Support for Unions in Canada," *Journal of Labor Research*, vol. 10, no. 4 (1989), 407.

6. Charlotte Yates, "Expanding Labour's Horizons: Union Organizing and Strategic Change in Canada," *Just Labour*, vol. 1 (2002), 31.

7. *Lovatt v. Saskatchewan Government and General Employees Union*, http://www.canlii.org/en/sk/sklrb/doc/2006/2006canlii63021/2006canlii63021.pdf.

8. George Adams, *Canadian Labour Law*, 2nd ed. (Aurora, ON: Canada Law Book), paragraph 6.20.

9. Section 1(1), *British Columbia Labour Relations Code*.

10. *Journal Le Droit*. 11 C.L.R.B.R. (NS) 53; *The Citizen*. [1985] O.L.R.B. Rep 819; *Ajax/Pickering News Advertiser*. [1993] O.L.R.B. Rep 473.

11. "FTR Now. The Fraser Decision: The Supreme Court of Canada Revisits Scope of Charter-Protected Collective Bargaining," Hicks Morley Hamilton Stewart Storie LLP, May 3, 2011, http://www.hicksmorley.com/index.php?name=News&file=article&sid=941, accessed May 26, 2014.

12. *Island Medical Laboratories and H.S.A. of British Columbia*. 19 C.L.R.B.R. (2nd) 161 at 181.

13. *Strathroy Middlesex General Hospital and P.N.F.O.* 17 C.L.R.B.R. (2nd) 216.

14. Susan Johnson, "Card Check or Mandatory Representation Vote? How the Type of Union Recognition Procedure Affects Union Certification Success," *Economic Journal*, (2002), 344.

15. "Annual Information Form," Magna, March 26, 2014, http://www.magna.com/docs/default-source/ar-2013/aif-final.pdf?sfvrsn=2, accessed May 26, 2014.

16. Ibid.

17. *S.G.T. 2000 Inc. and Teamsters*. 99 C.L.L.C. 220–055.

18. *The Globe and Mail Division of Canadian Newspapers Co. Ltd.* [1982] 2 C.L.R.B.R. 73.

19. *Alliance Homes Inc.* [2001] O.L.R.B. Rep 1.

20. Canada, *Canada Labour Code*, s. 94(2)(c); Alberta, *Labour Relations Code*, s. 148(2)(c); British Columbia, Labour Relations Code, s. 8; Manitoba, *Labour Relations Act*, s. 32(1); New Brunswick, *Industrial Relations Act*, s. 3(5); Nova Scotia, *Trade Union Act*, s. 58(2); Ontario, *Labour Relations Act*, s. 70; Prince Edward Island, *Labour Act*, s. 9(8)(a).

21. *Re Michelin Tires (Canada) Ltd. and United Rubber, Cork, Linoleum & Plastic Workers of America*. 107 D.L.R. (3d) 661.

22. *C.U.P.E. and University of Toronto*. 18 C.L.R.B.R. (N.S.) 321.

23. *Manitoba Labour Relations Act*, Section 33(2); *Ontario Labour Relations Act*, Section 77.

24. *Atlas Specialty Steels*. [1991] O.L.R.B. Rep 728.

25. *Re Prichard, and CAW*. 98 C.L.L.C. 220–072.

26. Ontario Labour Relations Board, annual report, 2011–12.

27. British Columbia Labour Relations Board, annual report, 2012.

28. *Canada Labour Code*, ss. 44–46; *Alberta Labour Relations Code*, s. 46; *British Columbia Labour Relations Code*, s. 35; *Manitoba Labour Relations Act*, s. 56; *New Brunswick Industrial Relations Act*, s. 60; *Newfoundland and Labrador Labour Relations Act*, s. 93; *Nova Scotia Trade Union Act*, s. 31; *Ontario Labour Relations Act*, s. 69; *Quebec Labour Code*, ss. 45–46; *Saskatchewan Trade Union Act*, ss. 37–37.2.

29. Section 44(1), *Canada Labour Code*.

30. *Ajax (Town) v. C.A.W. Local 2221*. 185 D.L.R. (4th) 516.

Appendix to Chapter 6

1. *Manitoba Food & Commercial Workers, Local 832 and Kittson Investments Ltd. (Re)*, 90 C.L.L.C. 16,036 (Man. L.B.).

2. [1980] O.L.R.B. Rep. Mar. 304, at pp. 305–306.

3. [1982] O.L.R.B. Rep. Jan. 84 at p. 92.

4. *OPSEU and Grand River Conservation Authority (Re)* [1988] O.L.R.B. Rep. 298.

5. *Great Lakes Fishermen & Allied Workers' Union and F. Causarano Fishery Ltd. (Re)* [1988] O.L.R.B. Rep. 23.

Chapter 7

1. Donald Brown and David Beatty, *Canadian Labour Arbitration*, 3rd ed. (Aurora, ON: Canada Law Book, 2002).

2. *Parry Sound Social Services Administration Board v. Ontario Public Service Employees Union, Local 324*, [2003] 2 S.C.R. 157.

3. Canada, *Canada Labour Code*, s. 60(1.1); British Columbia, *Labour Relations Code*, s. 89(e); Manitoba, *Labour Relations Act*, s. 121(2)(e); New Brunswick, *Industrial Relations Act*, s. 73(3.1); Ontario, *Labour Relations Act*, s. 48(16); Saskatchewan, *Trade Union Act*, s. 25(2)(f).

4. "Collective Bargaining in Canada 2012", http://www.labour.gc.ca/eng/resources/info/publications/collective_bargaining/collective_bargaining.shtml Copyright © 2014 by the Employment and Social Development of Canada. Used by permission of the Employment and Social Development Canada.

5. Court of Appeal for Ontario, Judgments & Endorsements, *Canada Post Corporation v. Canadian Union of Postal Workers*, http://www.ontariocourts.on.ca/decisions_index/2001index.htm#11, accessed July 31, 2006.
6. *Newfoundland Association of Public Employees v. Newfoundland (Green Bay Health Care Centre)*, [1996] 2 S.C.R. 3.
7. *Ronald C. MacGillivray Guest Home Corp. and C.U.P.E., Loc. 1562* 128 L.A.C. (4th) 225.
8. *Toronto East General Hospital v. Ontario Nurses Association*, http://www.canlii.org/en/on/onla/doc/2009/2009canlii6022/2009canlii6022.pdf.
9. Krista G. Stringer and Travor C. Brown, "A Special Kind of Downsizing: An Assessment of Union Member Reaction to Bumping," *Relations Industrielles*, vol. 63 (2008), 648.
10. *Re Plax Inc. and United Rubber Workers, Local 143.* 17 LAC (4th) 44.

Chapter 8

1. Jon Peirce, *Canadian Industrial Relations*, 2nd ed. (Toronto: Prentice-Hall, 2003), p. 299.
2. Robert Rogow, "The Structure of Collective Bargaining," *Collective Bargaining in Canada*, ed. Amarjit Sehthi (Toronto: Nelson Canada, 1989), p. 132.
3. Ezio Tarantelli, "The Regulation of Inflation and Unemployment," *Industrial Relations*, vol. 25 (1986), 1.
4. Richard E. Walton and Robert B. McKersie, *A Behavioral Theory of Labor Relations: An Analysis of a Social Interaction System*, 2nd ed. (Ithaca, NY: ILR Press, Cornell University, 1991).
5. Mary P. Follett, "Constructive Conflict," in *Dynamic Administration: The Collected Papers of Mary Parker Follett*, ed. H. C. Metcalf and L. Urwick (New York: Harper, 1940).
6. Richard E. Walton and Robert B. McKersie, *A Behavioural Theory of Labour Relations: An Analysis of a Social Interaction System*, 2nd ed. (Ithaca, NY: ILR Press, Cornell University, 1991).
7. Bruce Dowbiggin, *Money Players: How Hockey's Greatest Stars Beat the NHL at Its Own Game* (Toronto: McClelland and Stewart Ltd., 2003).
8. Section 50, *Canada Labour Code*.
9. Canada, *Canada Labour Code*, s. 80; British Columbia, *Labour Relations Code*, s. 55; Manitoba, *Labour Relations Act*, s. 87; Newfoundland and Labrador, *Labour Relations Act*, s. 81; Ontario, *Labour Relations Act*, s. 43; Prince Edward Island, *Labour Act*, s. 22(2); Quebec, *Labour Code*, s. 93.1; Saskatchewan, *Trade Union Act*, s. 26.5.
10. Roy Lewicki, David Saunders, and John Minton, *Essentials of Negotiation* (Burr Ridge, IL: Richard D. Irwin, 1997), p. 45.
11. Ray Fells. "Labour–Management Negotiation: Some Insights into Strategy and Language," *Relations Industrielles*, vol. 55, no. 4 (2000), 583–605.
12. Roy J. Lewicki, David M. Saunders, and John Minton, *Essentials of Negotiation* (Burr Ridge, IL: Richard D. Irwin, 1997).
13. *St. Thomas More College v. St. Thomas More College Faculty Union*, 2008 CLLC 220–024.
14. Roger Fisher, William Ury, and Bruce Patton, *Getting to Yes: Negotiating Agreements Without Giving In*, 2nd ed. (New York, NY: Penguin Books, 1992).
15. David S. Weiss, *Beyond the Walls of Conflict: Mutual Gains Negotiating for Unions and Management* (Burr Ridge, IL: Irwin Professional Publishing, 1996).
16. Ibid.; Brenda L. Kennedy, *Interest-Based Collective Bargaining: A Success Story* (Kingston, ON: Industrial Relations Centre, Queens University, 1999).
17. Ira B. Lobel, "Realities of Interest-Based (Win-Win) Bargaining," *Labour Law Journal*, vol. 14 (December 1994), 771–777.
18. David S. Weiss, *In Search of the Eighteenth Camel: Discovering a Mutual Gains Oasis for Unions and Management* (Kingston, ON: IRC Press, 2003).
19. Joel Cutcher-Gershenfeld, Thomas Kochan, and John Wells, "In Whose Interest? A First Look at National Survey Data on Interest-Based Bargaining in Labor Relations," *Industrial Relations*, vol. 40, no.1 (2001), 1–21.

Chapter 9

1. *Weber v. Ontario Hydro*, http://scc.lexum.umontreal.ca/en/1995/1995scr2–929/1995scr2–929.html.
2. Sean C. Doyle, *The Grievance Procedure: Heart of the Collective Agreement* (Kingston, ON: IRC Press, 1999).
3. Richard B. Freeman and James L. Medoff, *What Do Unions Do?* (New York: Basic Books, 1984).
4. *Municipality of Metropolitan Toronto vs. CUPE Local 43.* 69 D.L.R (4th) 268.
5. Ali Dastmalchian and Ignace Ng, "Industrial Relations Climate and Grievance Outcomes," *Industrial Relations*, vol. 45 (1990), 311.
6. Sean C. Doyle, *The Grievance Procedure: Heart of the Collective Agreement* (Kingston, ON: IRC Press, 1999).
7. Marguerite Jackson, "Lost Overtime Opportunities: Cash or In Kind Remedies?" *Labour Arbitration Yearbook*, 1996–97 (Toronto: Lancaster House), p. 347.
8. *Labour Arbitration Cases* (Aurora, ON: Canada Law Book).
9. Donald Brown and David Beatty, *Canadian Labour Arbitration*, 4th ed. (Aurora, ON: Canada Law Book,).
10. Martin Mitchnick and Brian Etherington, *Leading Cases on Labour Arbitration* (Toronto: Lancaster House, 2002).
11. *Parry Sound (District) Social Services Administration Board v. Ontario Public Service Employees Union, Local 324.* [2003] 2 S.C.R. 157.
12. *Re Ontario Teachers Pension Plan Board and OPSEU.* 65 LAC (4th) 138.
13. *Toronto Transit Commission and A.T.U.*, 132 L.A.C. (4th) 225.
14. *Greater Toronto Airports Authority and P.S.A.C., Local 004*, 191 L.A.C.(4th) 277.
15. *Dunsmuir v. New Brunswick*, 2008 SCC 9, [2008] 1 S.C.R. 190, http://scc.lexum.umontreal.ca/en/2008/2008scc9/2008scc9.html.
16. *Canada (Citizenship and Immigration) v. Khosa*, 2009 SCC 12, [2009] 1 S.C.R. 339, http://scc.lexum.umontreal.ca/en/2009/2009scc12/2009scc12.html.
17. *KVP Co. Ltd.* 16 LAC 73.
18. *IKO Industries Ltd.* (2005), 140 L.A.C.(4th) 393.
19. *St. Peter's Health System and CUPE Local 778*, 106 L.A.C. (4th) 170.
20. *Re Grey Bruce.* 35 LAC (4th) 136.
21. *Re CN/CP Telecommunications and Canadian Telecommunication Union.* 4 LAC (3rd) 205.
22. *Metropolitan Separate School Board.* 31 LAC (4th) 35.
23. George W. Adams, *Grievance Arbitration of Discharge Cases* (Kingston, ON: Industrial Relations Center Centre, Queens University, 1978); Allen Ponak, "Discharge Arbitration and Reinstatement: An Industrial Relations Perspective," *Labour Arbitration Yearbook* (Toronto: Lancaster House, 1991).
24. *Loyalist College of Applied Arts and Technology and O.P.S.E.U., Local 324.* 122 LAC (4th) 155.
25. *Re United Steelworkers of America, Local 12998 and Liquid Carbonic Inc.* 135 DLR (4th) 493.
26. *AFG Industries Ltd.* 68 LAC (4th) 129.
27. *Re Sure-way Transport Ltd. and Canadian Union of Heavy Haulers and Maintenance Workers.* 45 LAC (4th) 193.
28. *Caressant Care Nursing Home and Service Employees Union Local 183.* 44 LAC (4th) 24.
29. *Ottawa (City) and CUPE Local 503.* 102 LAC (4th) 503.
30. *Re Mount Sinai Hospital and ONA.* 13 LAC (4th) 230.
31. *Re Battlefords and District Co-operative Ltd. and Retail Wholesale and Department Store Union Local 544.* [1998] 1 SCR 1118.
32. *Re Marimac Inc. and Amalgamated and Textile Workers Union Local 2343.* 15 LAC (3rd) 57.
33. *Re Metroland.* 4 LAC (4th) 307.
34. *Acadian Platers Company and USWA, Local 8059*, 68 L.A.C. (4th) 344.
35. Rick D. Hackett, Julie Pyper, and Joseph B. Rose, "Canadian Labour Arbitration Decisions Involving the Employment Interview," *Labour Arbitration Yearbook*, 2000–01 (Toronto: Lancaster House).
36. Donald J. Carter, *Canadian Labour Law at the Millennium: The Growing Influence of Human Rights Requirements* (Kingston, ON: Industrial Relations Centre, Queens University, 2000).

37. *OPSEU v. Ministry of Community and Social Services*. 96 CLLC 230–016.

38. *World's Biggest Bookstore and Retail Wholesale Canada, Local 41*. 83 LAC (4th) 1.

39. *Sun-Rype Products Ltd. and Teamsters Union Local 213*. 67 LAC (4th) 301.

40. Section 37, *Canada Labour Code*.

41. *Re Parsley and Kennedy*. 86 CLLC 16,018.

42. *Re John Daniele v. Teamsters*. 1987 OLRB (July) 990.

43. George W. Adams, *Canadian Labour Law*, 2nd ed. (Aurora, ON: Canada Law Book, 2006), paragraph 13.160.

44. Ibid., paragraph 4.900.

45. Stephen B. Goldberg, "Grievance Mediation: A Successful Alternative to Labour Arbitration," *Negotiation Journal*, vol. 5 (1989), no. 9, 9–15.

46. David Elliott and Joanne Gross, *Grievance Mediation: Why and How It Works* (Aurora, ON: Canada Law Book, 1994).

Chapter 10

1. Canadian Foundation for Labour Rights, "Restrictive labour laws in Canada: Summary of Legislation Restricting Collective Bargaining and Trade Union Rights in Canada 1982–2014," updated April 2014, http://labourrights.ca, accessed May 26, 2014.

2. I. Lee, "Striking Out: The New Normal in Canadian Labour Relations?" *Journal of Parliamentary and Political Law*, 2011 [5 J.P.P.L.], http-server.carleton.ca/~ianlee/pdf/Lee,%20JPPL,%20Striking%20out%20-%20the%20new%20normal%20in%20Cdn%20labour%20relations, accessed May 26, 2014.

3. *Canada Labour Code*, s. 3(1).

4. Chart no. 12 "Number of work stoppages and workers involved, by sector" found on page 9 of Collective bargaining in Canada 2012. http://www.labour.gc.ca/eng/resources/info/publications/collective_bargaining/collective_bargaining.pdf Copyright © 2014 by Employment and Social Development of Canada. Used by permission of Employment and Social Development of Canada.

5. Shafiq A. Alvi, "The Impact of Strikes on Canadian Trade Balance," *Applied Economics Letters*, vol. 8 (2001), 389.

6. Robert Hebdon and Robert Stern, "Tradeoffs Among Expressions of Industrial Conflict: Public Sector Strike Bans and Grievance Arbitrations," *Industrial and Labour Relations Review*, vol. 50 (1998), 204.

7. Peter Cramton, Morley Gunderson, and Joseph Tracy, "The Effect of Collective Bargaining Legislation on Strikes and Wages," *The Review of Economics and Statistics*, vol. 81 (1999), 475.

8. John Godard, "Strikes as Collective Voice: A Behavioral Analysis of Strike Activity," *Industrial and Labour Relations Review*, vol. 46 (1992), 161.

9. Edward Montgomery and Mary Ellen Benedict, "The Impact of Bargainer Experience on Teacher Strikes," *Industrial and Labour Relations Review*, vol. 42 (1989), 380.

10. Peter Cramton, Morley Gunderson, and Joseph Tracy, "The Effect of Collective Bargaining Legislation on Strikes and Wages," *The Review of Economics and Statistics*, vol. 81 (1999), 475.

11. Ibid.

12. John Godard, "Strikes as Collective Voice: A Behavioral Analysis of Strike Activity," *Industrial and Labour Relations Review*, vol. 46 (1992), 161.

13. Ibid.

14. Morley Gunderson, Allen Ponak, and Daphne Gottlieb Taras, *Union–Management Relations in Canada*, 4th ed. (Toronto: Pearson Education Canada, 2001), p. 329.

15. John Godard, *Industrial Relations, the Economy, and Society*, 3rd ed. (North York, ON: Captus Press, 2005).

16. Peter Cramton, Morley Gunderson, and Joseph Tracy, "The Effect of Collective Bargaining Legislation on Strikes and Wages," *The Review of Economics and Statistics*, vol. 81 (1999), 475.

17. *British Columbia Labour Code*, s. 72; *Alberta Labour Relations Code*, s. 112; *Canada Labour Code*, s. 87.

18. *R.W.D.S.U. Local 558 v. Pepsi-Cola Canada Beverages (West) Ltd*. 208 D.L.R. (4th) 385.

19. Canadian Foundation for Labour Rights, http://www.labourrights.ca/restrictive-labour-laws, accessed May 26, 2013.

20. Statistics Canada, "Strikes and Lockouts, Workers Involved and Workdays Not Worked, by Selected Countries," http://www40.statcan.gc.ca/l01/cst01/labor30a-eng.htm, accessed June 2, 2010.

Chapter 11

1. Statistics Canada, "Public Sector Employment (Employees)," Table 183-0002, CANSIM, May 30, 2012.

2. Statistics Canada, "Labour Force Survey Estimates, Employees by Union Coverage," Table 282-0078, CANSIM, http://www5.statcan.gc.ca/cansim/a05?lang=eng.id=2820078&pattern=2820078&search, accessed June 19, 2014.

3. Public Service Alliance of Canada, "Veterans Speak Out Against Loss of Front Line Services," February 5, 2014, http://psacunion.ca/help-our-veterans-stop-veterans-affairs-office-closures-0.

4. John Fryer, "Provincial Public Sector Labour Relations," *Public Sector Collective Bargaining in Canada*, ed. G. Swimmer and M. Thompson (Kingston, ON: IRC Press, 1995), p. 345.

5. Gene Swimmer, "Collective Bargaining in the Federal Public Service of Canada: The Last 20 Years," *Public Sector Collective Bargaining in Canada*, ed. G. Swimmer and M. Thompson (Kingston, ON: IRC Press, 1995), p. 371.

6. Morley Gunderson and Douglas Hyatt, "Canadian Public Sector Employment Relations in Transition," *Public Sector Employment in a Time of Transition* (Ithaca, NY: Cornell University Press for the Industrial Relations Research Association, 1996), p. 255.

7. Ibid.; Morley Gunderson, Robert Hebdon, and Douglas Hyatt, "Collective Bargaining in the Public Sector: Comment," *American Economic Review*, vol. 86 (1996), 315.

8. Jon Pierce, *Canadian Industrial Relations*, 2nd ed. (Toronto: Pearson Education Canada, 2003), p. 282.

9. Gene Swimmer and Sandra Bach, "Restructuring Federal Public Sector Human Resources," *Public-Sector Labour Relations in an Era of Restraint and Restructuring* (Canadian Policy Research Networks and Oxford Press, 2000), 178.

10. Bernard Adell, Michel Grant, and Allen Ponak, *Strikes in Essential Services* (Kingston, ON: IRC Press, 2001).

11. Robert Hebdon and Maurice Mazerolle, "Regulating Conflict in Public-Sector Labour Relations: The Ontario Experience (1984–1993)," *Relations Industrielles*, vol. 58, no. 4 (2003), 667.

12. Bernard Adell, Michel Grant, and Allen Ponak, *Strikes in Essential Services* (Kingston, ON: IRC Press, 2001), p. 202.

13. C. Lamman, "Your Share of Canada's Government Debt: $34,000+," *Huffington Post*, December 12, 2012, http://www.huffingtonpost.ca/charles-lammam/canada-government-debt_b_2303891.html, accessed May 26, 2014.

14. Thomas Walkom, "Recession's Next Victim Will Be Public-Sector," *Toronto Star*, November 7, 2009.

15. John Fryer, "Provincial Public Service Labour Relations," *Public Sector Collective Bargaining in Canada* (Kingston, ON: IRC Press, 1995), p. 341.

16. Canadian Foundation for Labour Rights, http://www.labourrights.ca/restrictive-labour-laws, accessed May 26, 2013.

17. Gene Swimmer, "Public Sector Labour Relations in an Era of Restraint and Restructuring: An Overview," *Public-Sector Labour Relations in an Era of Restraint and Restructuring* (Ottawa and Oxford, UK: Canadian Policy Research Networks and Oxford Press, 2000), 32.

18. Canadian Labour and Business Centre, "Viewpoints 2000: Labour Management Relations in Canada," http://www.clbc.ca/files/Reports/viewpoints02_labour_relations.pdf, accessed May 14, 2007.

19. Howard Levitt, "Voters Could Change Collective Agreements," *Telegraph Journal*, November 21, 2009.

20. Mark Thompson and Patrice Jalette, "Public-Sector Collective Bargaining," in *Canadian Labour and Employment Relations*, 6th ed. (Ontario: Pearson Education, 2009), p. 423.

21. Excerpt from "Part 6 — Essential Services" in Labour Relations Code [RSBC 1996] Chapter 244. Copyright © by the Queen's Printer. Used by permission of the Queen's Printer. "These materials contain information that has been derived from information originally made available by the Province of British Columbia at: http://www.bclaws.ca/ and this information is being used in accordance with the Queen's Printer License – British Columbia available at: http://www.bclaws.ca/ standards/2014/QP-License_1.0.html. They have not, however, been produced in affiliation with, or with the endorsement of, the Province of British Columbia and THESE MATERIALS ARE NOT AN OFFICIAL VERSION."

Chapter 12

1. Richard Freeman and James Medoff, *What Do Unions Do?* (New York: Basic Books, 1984).
2. David G. Blanchflower and Alex Bryson, "What Effect Do Unions Have on Wages Now and Would Freeman and Medoff Be Surprised?" *Journal of Labor Research*, vol. 25 (2004), 382.
3. Morley Gunderson and W. Craig Riddell, *Labour Market Economics*, 3rd ed. (Toronto: McGraw-Hill Ryerson, 1993).
4. K. Thorpe, "It Still Pays to Be in a Union—But for How Long?" *Globe and Mail*, February 5, 2014, http://www.theglobeandmail.com/ report-on-business/economy/economy-lab/it-still-pays-to-be-in-a-union-but-for-how-long/article16697608, accessed June 14, 2014.
5. David Blanchflower and Alex Bryson, "What Effect Do Unions Have on Wages Now and Would Freeman and Medoff Be Surprised?" *Journal of Labor Economics*, vol. 25 (2004), 381.
6. McKinley L. Blackburn, "Are Union Wage Differentials in the United States Falling?" *Industrial Relations*, vol. 47, no. 3 (2008), 390.
7. Morley Gunderson and Douglas Hyatt, "Union Impact on Compensation, Productivity, and Management of the Organization," *Union–Management Relations in Canada*, 5th ed. (Toronto: Pearson Education Canada, 2005), p. 403.
8. Brian Bemels, "How Unions Affect Productivity in Manufacturing Plants," *Industrial and Labor Relations Review*, vol. 40 (1989), 241.
9. Morley Gunderson, "Two Faces of Union Voice in the Public Sector," *Journal of Labor Research*, vol. 26 (2005), 393.
10. Casey Ichniowski, "The Effects of Grievance Activity on Productivity," *Industrial and Labor Relations Review*, vol. 40 (1986), 75.
11. Terry Wagar, "Is Labor–Management Climate Important? Some Canadian Evidence," *Journal of Labor Research*, vol. 28 (1997), 163.
12. Alex Bryson, Andy Charlwood, and John Forth. "Worker Voice, Managerial Response, and Labour Productivity: An Empirical Investigation," *Industrial Relations Journal*, vol. 37 (2006), 438.
13. Pasquale Laporta and Alexander Jenkins, "Unionization and Profitability in the Canadian Manufacturing Sector," *Relations Industrielles*, vol. 51 (1996), 756.
14. Cameron Odgers and Julian Betts, "Do Unions Reduce Investment? Evidence from Canada," *Industrial and Labor Relations Review*, vol. 51 (1997), 18.
15. Stephen Bronnars, Donald Deere, and Joseph Tracy, "The Effects of Unions on Firm Behavior: An Empirical Analysis Using the Firm Level Data," *Industrial Relations*, vol. 33 (1994), 426.
16. Mariane Koch and Greg Hundley, "The Effects of Unionism on Recruitment and Selection Methods," *Industrial Relations*, vol. 36 (1997), 349.
17. Anil Verma, "What Do Unions Do to the Workplace? Union Effects on Management and HRM Policies," *Journal of Labor Research*, vol. 26 (2005), 415.
18. John O'Grady, *Job Control Unionism vs. the New HRM Model* (Kingston, ON: IRC Press, 1995).
19. Canadian Council of Human Resources Associations, *Human Resources Professionals in Canada: Revised Body of Knowledge and Required Professional Capabilities (RPCs®): Principles of Employee Relations (PPC 94-11)*, 2008, http://c.ymcdn.com/sites/www.chrp.ca/resource/resmgr/pdf/body_of_knowledge_rpcs.pdf, accessed June 12, 2014.

20. "Foster Positive Employee Relations Using Communication Best Practices," ERC: Where Great Workplaces Start, http://greatworkplace.wordpress.com/2010/08/17/foster-positive-employee-relations-using-communication-best-practices, accessed June 9, 2014.
21. Canadian HR Reporter, "10 Tips for Communicating in Tough Times," November 13, 2008.
22. Hermann Schwind, Hari Das, and Terry Wagar, *Canadian Human Resources Management: A Strategic Approach*, 8th ed. (Toronto, McGraw-Hill Ryerson, New York: Basic Books, 2007).
23. Claire Raines, *Connecting Generations* (Rochester, NY: Axzo Press, 2003).
24. J. Berzin, "New Research Unlocks the Secret of Employee Recognition," *Forbes*, June 11, 2014, http://www.forbes.com/sites/ joshbersin/2012/06/13/new-research-unlocks-the-secret-of-employee-recognition.
25. United Way of London-Middlesex, "Labour Programs," http:// unitedwaylm.ca/labour-programs.html, accessed June 11, 2014.
26. Richard Chaykowsi, "Adaptation Within the Traditional Industrial Relations System: The Development of Labor Relations at Inco Ltd.," *Contract and Commitment: Employment Relations in the New Economy* (Kingston, ON: IRC Press, 1999), p. 76.
27. Buzz Hargrove, "Decision-Making in the Workplace: A Union Viewpoint," *Labour Arbitration Yearbook*, 1998 (Toronto: Lancaster House, 1998).
28. Human Resources Development Canada, *Labour–Management Innovation in Canada* (Ottawa: Minister of Supply and Services, 1994), p. 31.
29. *Canadian Broadcasting Corporation and C.U.P.E., Broadcasting Division. (1994)*, 27 C.L.R.B.R. (2nd) 110.
30. *Re City of Waterloo and Canadian Union of Public Employees, Local 1542*. 50 L.A.C. (4th) 197.
31. Anil Verma and Daphne Gottlieb Taras, "Employee Involvement in the Workplace," *Union–Management Relations in Canada*, 4th ed. (Toronto: Pearson Education Canada, 2001), p. 463.
32. Peter Berg, "The Effects of High Performance Work Practices on Job Satisfaction in the United States Steel Industry," *Relations Industrielles*, vol. 54 (1999), 111.
33. Alexander J. S. Colvin, "The Relationship Between Employee Involvement and Workplace Dispute Resolution," *Relations Industrielles*, vol. 59, no. 4 (2004), 681.
34. Terry Wagar, "Seemed Like a Good Idea, But . . . The Survival and Death of High Involvement Work Practices," *HRM Research Quarterly*, vol. 6, no. 1 (Spring 2002).
35. William Cooke, "Product Quality Improvement Through Employee Participation: The Effects of Unionization and Joint Union–Management Administration," *Industrial and Labor Relations Review*, vol. 46 (1992), 119; "Employee Participation Programs, Group-Based Incentives, and Company Performance: A Union–Nonunion Comparison," *Industrial and Labor Relations Review*, vol. 47 (1994), 594.
36. Gil A. Preuss and Brenda A. Lautsch, "The Effect of Formal Versus Informal Job Security on Employee Involvement Programs," *Relations Industrielles*, vol. 57, no. 3 (2002), 517.
37. Anil Verma, "Joint Participation Programs: Self-Help or Suicide for Labour?" *Industrial Relations*, vol. 28 (1989), 401.
38. Ibid., p. 405.
39. H. Schwind, H. Das, and T. Wagar, *Canadian Human Resources Management*, 9th ed. (Toronto: McGraw-Hill Ryerson, 2010).
40. Ibid.
41. Human Resources Professional Association, "Generational Diversity and Its Impact on Engagement and Effectiveness," Professional Development Dinner Series, http://www.hrpa.ca/ ProfessionalDevelopment/Pages/HRBroadcastKnightsbridgeDinnerSeries-4_GenerationalDiversityanditsImpactonEngagementandEffectiveness.aspx, accessed June 14, 2014.
42. Terry Wagar, "Considering Labour Management Relations Issues: Are the Views of Unions and Employers All That Different?" *Workplace Gazette*, vol. 4, no. 4, 56.

Index